THE MOTHMAN SPEAKS

THE MOTHMAN SPEAKS

CANDID CONVERSATIONS CONCERNING

COSMIC CONUNDRUMS – CRYPTIC CREATURES,

CHIMERAS, CONTACTEES AND THE CLEVERLY CODED

COINCIDENCES AND CORRESPONDENCES

OF THE COLLECTIVE UNCONSCIOUS

Andrew B. Colvin

METADISC BOOKS
THE SEATTLE CONCEPTUAL ART MUSEUM | SEATTLE

Books by Andy Colvin

The Mothman's Photographer: The Work of an Artist Touched by the Prophecies of the Infamous Mothman

The Mothman's Photographer II: Meetings With Remarkable Witnesses Touched by Paranormal Phenomena, UFOs, and the Prophecies of West Virginia's Infamous Mothman

The Mothman's Photographer III: Meetings With Remarkable West Coast Witnesses Touched By The Anomalous Activities Of Interdimensional Entities, Archetypal Avatars, And The Eerie Yet Enlightening Phenomenon Known Infamously As "Mothman"

The Mothman Speaks: Candid Conversations Concerning Cosmic Conundrums - Cryptic Creatures, Chimeras, Contactees and the Cleverly Coded Coincidences and Correspondences of the Collective Unconscious

The Mothman Speaks II: Continued Conversations Concerning Cosmic Conundrums - Cryptic Creatures, Chimeras, Contactees and the Cleverly Coded Coincidences and Correspondences of the Collective Unconscious

The Mothman Speaks

The Mothman Speaks: Candid Conversations Concerning Cosmic Conundrums - Cryptic Creatures, Chimeras, Contactees and the Cleverly Coded Coincidences and Correspondences of the Collective Unconscious

ISBN 978-1-4392-7486-6

First edition published 2010.
Second edition published 2011.

PUBLISHED BY: Metadisc Books and The Seattle Conceptual Art Museum

SERIES CONTACT/IMAGERY/PRODUCT: www.andycolvin.com

FRONT COVER: Scott Ward, "The One Who Can Will the Single Thing"

BACK COVER ILLUSTRATION: Ancient Hindu statue symbolizing the power of the Garuda to connect human nervous systems

CONTENTS

ACKNOWLEDGMENTS

To each and every "squib," may your spurts of fire not go unrecognized. It takes a lit torch to lead through darkness and to truth - provided the gathering mob chooses to chase the correct "monster."

Thanks to Keith Hansen, Farrah Karapetian and Joseph Miller for their help creating the many digital recordings, transcripts, and pages necessary to complete this project.

Thanks to the folks at Metadisc, the Seattle Conceptual Art Museum, the Cincinnati Gallery of Conceptual Art, Forteans West, and CreateSpace. May these wonderful things you have started continue on, into infinity.

Thanks to all the local and regional investigators, including Jeff Wamsley, John and Tim Frick, Donnie Sergent, Kurt McCoy, Steve Ward, Josh Bell, Bob Wilkinson, Phil Reynolds, Peter Massaro, Robert Denton, Jr., David Day, Dave Scott, Sandy Nichols, Eddie Middleton, William Ross, James Smith, Taunia Derenberger, Chris Robinson, Ted Torbich, Eric Otto, Randy Maugans, Eugenia Macer-Story, Bob Brightbill, Rosemary Guiley, Regan Lee, Stan Gordon, and the late Kenny Young. Your contributions have helped build a solid foundation for future researchers.

Thanks to my many camera assistants, each brilliant in their own right: Ben Camp, Fish Ofiesh, Ariane Moore, Tim Dempsey, Sharon Rogers, Lisa Neesvig, Chuck Atkins, Jen Bolten, Cheri Forrest, J. Frederick Edwards, Neal Mindrum, Scott Van Horn, Lillian Crist and anyone else who may have spent a day or two on the road with me.

Thanks to the late John Keel for being such an inspiration. I never met a man with a better sense of humor, nor one who was more honest and direct. He will be sorely missed.

Thanks to the town of Pt. Pleasant for embracing change, opportunity, and diverse points of view. Your openness touches the hearts of all who visit.

Thanks to the local Indians for keeping the history alive.

Thanks to the MIB for making it obvious that something secret was going on.

Thanks to Mothman for pointing to the most secret spots.

Thanks to all of the witnesses, researchers, and experts who corresponded with me during the first decade of the 21st Century. Without your thoughts, feelings, and theories, this book would not have been possible.

FOREWORD

Andy Colvin showed up in Los Angeles recently, so of course I had to ask him to be a guest on my show, *Radio Misterioso* (archived at radiomisterioso.com). Colvin is the author of three previous books on the Mothman phenomenon: *The Mothman's Photographer I, II and III,* a title referring to artistic talents Colvin feels he received as a result of his personal involvement in the notorious paranormal events that occurred 40 years ago in Point Pleasant, West Virginia. Colvin also directed a 36-hour documentary on people and events surrounding the phenomenon.

This volume assumes that the audience is somewhat familiar with the "standard" Mothman story. If the reader is not up to speed on the legend, please refer to John Keel's landmark book, *The Mothman Prophecies,* or to Colvin's *The Mothman's Photographer II,* which has several chapters of previously unpublished material from Keel, in addition to Colvin's own recap of the events.

Within these pages, Colvin delves into little-known strangeness connected with the history leading up to the collapse of the Silver Bridge across the Ohio River in December of 1967. He recalls his childhood in the area and the plethora of defense and chemical company employees in the communities surrounding Point Pleasant.

Letters from Mothman witnesses in this volume reveal deeply personal encounters with various creatures and craft, as well as some government intrigue looming in the shadows. There were many unusual encounters with Men in Black in those days – some baffling, some terrifying. As Gray Barker, author of *The Silver Bridge* used to say, the MIB were there to "hush up" UFO witnesses.

Were the MIB protecting the manufacture of secret flying saucers or atomic payloads? Colvin delves into this idea, as well as the theory that some of the MIB activity was aimed at suppressing organized labor at the nearby Union Carbide chemical facilities. Such Cold War secrecy and tension would have fed into the general paranoia, thus creating a rich local paranormal/ psychic stew.

Colvin muses about semi-famous contactee Woodrow Derenberger and his creepy spaceman friend, Indrid Cold. Colvin guesses that Cold may have been completely human and employed by industrial concerns to monitor labor unrest under a disguise of strangeness. Ironically, Colvin seems to feel that Gray Barker's story of Cold piloting a real flying saucer may be the most accurate of all, given that such saucers may actually have been technically possible at the time. But since people have been having strange UFO-type encounters for centuries, WWII "nuts-and-bolts" saucer inventions could have been easily folded into the pre-existing milieu. Earth lights, ball lightning, manmade craft, and electromagnetically induced hallucinations would become indiscernible from one another.

The text also describes a group of genius-level children in the local schools, a couple of whom may have connected with the Mothman entity and had prophetic, apocalyptic visions of not only major public events like 9/11, but also private ones that continue to come true in their lives. At the time, several children reported flying saucers, "intelligent" balls of light, and entities like Mothman and Bigfoot.

Colvin long ago dubbed himself "The Mothman's Photographer." Good photography involves both sides of the brain. It is both a technical and creative act, using apparent reality focused and filtered through the ostensibly neutral lens of a camera, but resulting in something more personal and powerful when placed in the hands of an artist. My favorite part of Colvin's outlook is that he doesn't "believe" everything he finds in his research; he simply remains fascinated by the synchronicities, connections, and implications (real, symbolic, or otherwise) of what he has found in the last several years.

Delving for a scientific and logical "answer" may only be part of the path to understanding the Mothman enigma as well as other paranormal events and mysteries. The arc of Colvin's story throughout his books appears to spring from a free-associative approach that borders on art or shamanic divination. Readers and reviewers who discount his efforts may be missing the point and using only one side of their brains. Andy Colvin could be at the threshold of some sort of breakthrough in how we perceive the mysterious.

Sound intriguing? Unbelievable? Paranoia-inducing? You have no idea. Enjoy the ride!

-Greg Bishop, Los Angeles, CA October 2010

Image of Colvin (top left) taken in 1973. Note reptilian bird face in lower left of window (inset). The face resembles not only the Thunderbird masks of the Wakashan tribe of the Pacific NW (below center), but the Garuda carvings of New Zealand's Maori tribe (lower right). Oddly, its eyes seem to stare like those of Samudranath (below left), a Buddhist monk who teaches that Thunderbird and Garuda are one. In his book "Cities of Lightning," Samudranath claims, shockingly, that he can turn into a Garuda. Upon seeing his face, Mothman witness Harriet Plumbrook revealed that Samudranath had been visiting her in dreams and visions.

INTRODUCTION

"In 1943, the Supreme Command of the Luftwaffe conducted a highly unusual study. The study consisted of a map, a map of lower Manhattan Island. On the map are concentric circles detailing the blast and heat damage radii of an atomic bomb detonation over New York City. The most unusual aspect of this 'study' is that it shows the detonation of an atom bomb in the 15-17 kiloton range, approximately the same yield as the Little Boy uranium bomb dropped on Hiroshima – an odd 'coincidence' in the series of 'odd coincidences' we have already encountered. The Luftwaffe's intentions were quite obvious and clear. The destruction of the financial and business center of New York City would have been a unparalleled military and psychological blow against America. Beyond this, given the fact that New York City was an important point of embarkation for American shipping and troops, as well as a naval base, and a transportation hub for the entire American northeast, the [effects of] such a blow would have been incalculable.

"In 1944 [the Nazis flew a] massive Junkers Ju390 transport plane from Bordeaux, France to within 12 miles of NYC, snapped a picture of the Manhattan skyline, and flew back – a nonstop flight of 32 hours. Within the context of the German SS atom bomb project, this flight was more than a mere feasibility study. Photo reconnaissance could only be for target identification... In 1945, the Luftwaffe completed construction of an enormous airfield near Oslo, Norway, capable of handling very large aircraft. In an article for the June 29, 1945 issue of *The Washington Post*, a report that originated from the 21st Army Group HQ outlines the frightening discovery that awaited Allied military personnel who came to occupy Norway after the German forces there surrendered:

> RAF officers said today that the Germans had nearly completed preparations for bombing New York from a 'colossal airfield' near Oslo when the war ended. "*Forty* giant bombers with a 7,000 mile range were found on this base – the largest Luftwaffe field I have ever seen," one officer said. "They were a new type bomber developed by Heinkel. They now are being dismantled for study." German ground crews said the planes were held in readiness for a mission to New York.

"The presence of such an airfield and its deliberate construction so late in the war strongly suggests a connection to the SS atom bomb program... At least two atoms bombs were built and possibly transported on the [captured Nazi U-boat] the U-234. The surrender of the U-boat to the

American authorities not only provided the Manhattan Project with much-needed stocks of enriched uranium, but quite possibly also with two fully functional atoms as well."

-Joseph Farrell, *Reich of the Black Sun: Nazi Secret Weapons and the Cold War Allied Legend*, pp. 90-95

The following interview took place in October of 2008 at the Lowe Hotel in Pt. Pleasant, West Virginia. RAI, the large European broadcasting corporation, was filming a special called "American Mysteries" for their big-budget paranormal show, Voyager, *which has an audience of 5 million viewers. Interestingly, the producers decided to focus on an unusual mix of American mysteries: the 9/11 conspiracy, Mothman, Marconi, and Marilyn Monroe. Popular conspiracy writer Jim Marrs was the main guest, along with mainstream ufologist Linda Moulton Howe. Marrs and Howe were interviewed on the balcony of a skyscraper in Manhattan, seemingly in an effort to recall the feelings of 9/11. The first segment, which was about 9/11, seemed to focus on various conspiracy theories that the U.S. media usually ignores. One historical conspiracy mentioned was the Nazi plan to bomb lower Manhattan during WWII; this can be seen as a precursor of sorts to 9/11, thus raising the question of whether or not former Nazis had anything to do with the 2001 WTC attack. Marconi's U.S. radio company was accused of being a spy operation just before it was seized and incorporated into RCA by the Rockefeller syndicate, which itself was secretly supporting the Nazis through financial conduits like Herbert Hoover and Ohio's Prescott Bush...*

In the Mothman segment, the focus eventually fell onto Mothman's foretelling of 9/11, which was first communicated to a childhood friend of mine in 1967. This precognition allowed the Mothman segment to dovetail nicely with the 9/11 segment. Before and after station breaks, "teaser" montages seemed to connect 9/11 with Mothman. In fact, there seemed to be an implied thread connecting all four seemingly disparate stories... In my interview with RAI, I was asked to paint a broad picture of my Mothman experience, one that would be easily understood by those unfamiliar with the story. The resulting discussion therefore serves as a good introduction to this book... Interestingly, the day I first edited this section, Feb. 26th, 2009, I received a synchronistic email from Austin, TX ufologist S. Miles Lewis, which referenced Marilyn Monroe. I hadn't received an email from Lewis in several years, so it got my attention. For some strange reason, he playfully chided me about the stage name I had used in the 1980s Austin music scene: "Merlin Monroe." At that time, my band was performing take-offs on pagan "occult" music, so I was sometimes depicted in posters as a wizard or reincarnated pharaoh. This turned out to be prophetic because, years later, I discovered that my family, the

Colvins, had married into the Montauk tribe, the purported descendants of the Egyptian pharaohs. Why Lewis chose to email me at that time about the Monroe persona remains unclear.

RAI: What is the strangest Mothman sighting you have heard about?

Andy Colvin (AC): Well, I can say that I have interviewed a few people who have seen Mothman in their homes and even in their bedrooms, floating above their beds. This is something that happened to *Mothman Prophecies* author John Keel and to the nephew of Gray Barker. Barker was a UFO investigator from West Virginia who first coined the term "Men in Black." He wrote the first book on Mothman, *The Silver Bridge*, which came out in 1970. Interestingly, most witnesses see Mothman in slightly different ways. Mothman will often look a little different to each person. In my case, it was a dark silhouette flying behind our car. Then, years later, I saw another silhouette seemingly coming out of a tree. I saw it on the property of a friend who had received a precognition of 9/11 from Mothman... Here in Point Pleasant, people were often chased in their car by Mothman. Some, like Marcella Bennett, had face-to-face encounters with the creature. Marcella described to me how she was pulled by some hypnotic force to be in the spot where she saw Mothman. Oddly, she said her brother was being hypnotized by a UFO at the same time. She seemed to think that the UFO was trying to keep him from meeting Mothman! It may sound hard to believe, but I have heard similar things from other witnesses about disagreements flaring up between UFOs and creature entities. As time went on, Marcella became more and more psychic, but not her brother.

RAI: So, the Mothman experience seems to open up people's minds...

AC: Yes, they can better access their own unconscious, as well as the collective unconscious. They can see what is going to happen next. I have found this to be true in my own life. I will get glimmers of things that are about to occur... As I mentioned, when I was a child, my friend saw a vision of 9/11 that he attributed to Mothman. He said, "If you go stand in this spot in my yard, *you* will see it, too." I was incredulous, of course. But, I did stand there and, sure enough, I *did* see brief images of exploding buildings in what Tommy said was "New York City in 2001 – the beginning of WWIII." At that time, I also received some type of "download." It happened very quickly. It was sort of like "seeing your life pass before you." I almost got killed by a rockslide once, so I *have* experienced seeing my life pass before me. The two experiences, seeing the future and seeing the past, are very much alike... When I got this download, I picked up pieces of information about my life to come. Even now, this process is still in effect. For instance, I just turned 49 today. Believe it or not, I got a message back when I was a kid that something important in my personal life would happen when I turned 49. I've already discovered what that was. It actually happened *today*; being on your show facilitated a reunion with someone important in my life… A similar thing happened when I was 47 as well. As my life goes on, the messages from that original download continue to play out, although I have the ability to influence them in certain ways. They seem to be possibilities from which I can choose. Tommy was also told things about his future life, such as working at NASA and so forth, which later came true…

RAI: Do you think it's a mental vision or projection? Where do they come from, these visions?

AC: I think it is the collective unconscious at work. We're telepathically plugged into each other, and to nature. At some level, all of our consciousnesses are linked. Reality is alive. We are in separate bodies, but we're also linked "nonlocally."

RAI: Very interesting point: the concept of global consciousness…

AC: If you look at the *core* of each of the major religions, there is this prevailing idea that consciousness is what creates the universe, not the other way around. Most of us, in the modern, "scientific" world, think that the physical world creates consciousness, but the older beliefs say the opposite. This consciousness underlying reality is what links us from the get-go. You have global – actually, "universal" – consciousness manifesting through each person. Each person is born and reveals a seemingly "separate" piece of that whole consciousness. In certain situations, you can plug back into the group consciousness and receive messages from other parts of it.

RAI: What is your explanation of the Mothman phenomenon?

AC: I don't know that there really *is* a tidy explanation for Mothman. It's a *process*, and it extends into subconscious realms. Reality is physically made up of electromagnetic frequencies and waves, which John Keel called "the superspectrum." Our brains process these waves as best they can. It is difficult because we sense only a sliver of the superspectrum. This disconnect, this inability to understand all of the signals, causes us to occasionally experience overloads and glitches. When this happens, our minds try to interpret the tangle of frequencies through a process of visualization. The visions that people see are an interesting blend of the "physical" and the "mental." They are partly hallucinatory and partly real, a temporary manifestation of something that can be identified as both physical *and* nonphysical. Certain places on Earth seem to manifest a higher number of sightings. The dynamics of how it works are not well understood, but it appears that these beings can become "real" during the short timeframe that the event is happening. They can leave physical traces; they can dent your car or give you a sunburn. Scratches have appeared mysteriously on witnesses' bodies upon waking up in the morning. Something "nonlocal" comes into our locality for a short time, and then it goes out. While it's here, it may or may not create a linkage with one's mind. In some folks, that linkage may become more solidified afterwards. A lot of the Mothman witnesses I've talked to feel that they've been linked to the creature ever since they saw it. They feel like he's always around the corner, quietly watching, standing guard. They feel that Mothman is a protector, not a demon. If you look at the symbologies of similar birdmen like the Thunderbird, Garuda, and Piasa, they all have positive aspects. They give us a "heads up" when and if something bad is about to happen.

RAI: There is one explanation that says Mothman is just a "big bird." Why is this an impossible explanation?

AC: It's not impossible; it just doesn't explain why people see Mothman as having humanoid characteristics. You have to realize that there are large religious and governmental organizations that don't like the idea of "unauthorized" angels or protector deities. If everyone started viewing Mothman, or any other unsanctioned entity, as a beneficial angel, it might cause problems. It might undermine the established organs of Church and State. The major religions have a *need* to spin interpretations of the paranormal. If unauthorized angels really *were* visiting us, it would be logical and necessary for such bureaucracies to write them off as "big birds" or something else. The interesting thing is that in the ancient world, large, "normal" birds were often thought to have supernatural qualities as well. Even today, in places like New Guinea, the aboriginals believe that human souls go into the bodies of birds upon death. In Egyptian lore, cranes could be "activated"; they could become temporarily supernatural. Like genies, supernatural cranes are said to emanate from caves and fly around the countryside. I grew up here in WV. You rarely see very large birds flying around here, other than chicken hawks and vultures. But, if someone *does* see a large bird, it could, according to the Egyptians, *still* be a supernatural event… Similarly, Mothman has a shapeshifting quality. Even though the moniker "Mothman" is a media creation, it shares etymological roots with the winged Egyptian goddess, Mut (pronounced "Mott"). "Mut" links to the word "mother," and to the symbologies of goddesses that came later, like Isis and Mary. "Muth" bears a relationship to the words "mouth" and "mound." The mound is a gateway, or mouth, to other dimensions. Our English word "mutt" refers to a mixture, a state where hybrid forms like Mothman exist… The earliest known UFO sightings were in Egypt, in 1500 B.C., and they occurred at a temple dedicated to Mut; even "random" arisings in the Mothman world have symbolic meaning.

The very act of having a "moniker" (a "mon" word) denotes a second identity, which is something necessary for hybrids. These creatures seem to be able to appear as female or male, wrathful or protective, aerial or earthbound, depending on the witness' state of mind.

AC: Horus and Seth were Egyptian birdmen who took on other forms; they were hybrids. Horus was an emanation of Osiris, just as Buddhism's Dorje Shugden, who rode aboard the Garuda, was an emanation of the archetypal Tibetan deity, Je Tsongkhapa. Horus was associated with downriver Egypt, while "Seth," whose name later developed into "Satan," was associated with upriver "Sudan." "Satan" thus became a word for the enemy, the "other." In Charleston, the Mothman had more of a dog face, like Seth. Downriver in Pt. Pleasant, he had more of a bird face, like Horus. In Asia, the dog and bird versions of the Garuda are called "Barong" and "Bonaspati," respectively. Basically, *any* river system with a lot of mounds is prone to these sightings. The Ohio and Kanawha valleys once had hundreds of mounds that were later torn down. Chemical plants were placed on top of those spots. There were a lot of mounds and Indian burial grounds here. Most people think that all mounds were built by the Indians, but most were not. The Natives claimed that they did not build them. The mounds may be naturally created energy nodes, sort of like pimples on the earth. They have energy running up into them. They store energy nicely because of their shape. They are very potent places for creatures to be seen. The word "monster" seems to be a combination of the words "mound" and "star." If you see an anomalous light around a mound, you may likely see one of these temporary monsters. In Point Pleasant, we have these munitions storage mounds. These domes are very similar to Indian mounds in shape and size. In Native lore, you could build a specific type of domed tent to call in monsters and spirits. Shamans would enter them and see into the future. Sparks were said to have flown out of the tents as the shamans accessed the psychic world. I myself have twice encountered strange creatures immediately after building a tent. Mounds and domes were said to have attracted dragons in the Middle Ages, and the same appears to be true today… In WV, people have seen invisible entities with glowing red eyes. Until the body comes into view, you don't know if it's Mothman or Bigfoot. As it passes into our physical dimension, it goes through somewhat predictable color shifts. These "chimera" are an ancient pattern. The very name "chimera" refers to "khem," the land of Egypt, as well as to "alchemy" and to "mer," the Moorish people who traveled north to the British Isles and then to America.

RAI: In 1966 and 1967, there were a lot of sightings of UFOs in the sky. Many people say these were connected to Mothman. Do you think that they are manifestations of the same thing?

AC: In some cases, yes. In *The Silver Bridge*, Gray Barker mentions a witness here in Point Pleasant who actually saw Mothman change into a ball of light. He also reported on a 1922 sighting in Nebraska where a UFO turned into a birdman. In the Buddhist lore, it is said that high lamas can shapeshift into balls of light *and* into birdmen; they travel around that way. People have seen them go from ball of light into birdman, and from birdman into ball of light. There is a lama named Samudranath who claims to shapeshift into a birdman; this is how he ministers to his "flock." There is a picture of him on the back of his book. One witness, whom I have known since childhood and trust, claims that Samudranath has visited her in dreams and visions. The picture of his face looks very much like a creature that my sister took a picture of in 1973. It was looking in our kitchen window. That was the same week I was chased by the dark silhouette that came out of a tree. The thing in the photo looks very much like a Garuda mask from New Zealand. It also looks very much like a Wakashan Thunderbird mask from the NW coast of America. "Wakashan" is very similar to "Wakinyan," the Lakota name for the Thunderbird. From his refuge "within earth and stone," the Natives' birdman, the Thunderbird, is still thought to influence life today. You see similar names for these entities across the world, across languages.

RAI: What do you remember about the Silver Bridge collapse?

AC: The collapse was very tragic. It was extremely cold that night. I was at home with my parents when the news came across. It was very shocking. A lot of people still haven't gotten over it. I suppose one "silver" lining is that the bridge collapse brought more attention to Mothman and to the mystical process that seems to be going on here. Mothman has helped revitalize the town to some degree, reversing the economic losses caused by the bridge collapse. The Mothman story is, frankly, one of the most important stories *ever*. You've got angels, UFOs, aliens, creature entities, prophecies, and top-secret conspiracies. Reality – our collective unconscious – seems to create situations to learn from. It creates an order to the universe at varying levels. No matter what sort of "evil," conspiratorial things might be hatched, an opposing message of "truth" will get out, via the psychic feedback loop. In a way, it is a self-regulating mechanism that allows society to right wrongs, balance energies, and heal wounds through the application of justice. Mothman can be viewed as a crime-fighting superhero or as a cosmic, metaphysical process – or anywhere in between. Ancient birdman symbols depict the nervous systems of human beings as being connected. The Garuda is an archetype that allows one to stabilize spiritual advances in one's life. These may be linked to jumps in creativity or intelligence. The Garuda keeps you from "backsliding" into ignorance and isolation. He keeps you linked with others.

RAI: Why did you start to paint the Mothman? I know you have some paintings…

AC: I don't necessarily paint the Mothman. But after I saw the Mothman, I suddenly had the ability *to* draw and paint. I also bought a camera and started taking photos. For many years, I did mostly drawings and paintings, but then I shifted more into photography. I've found that my work over the years seems to unwittingly symbolize aspects of the Mothman story. For instance, in the early 1980s, I traveled around the U.S. to different national monuments, taking pictures of myself as a flying man who came out of the earth. Even then, I wasn't consciously aware that it was connected to Mothman. Most of this process has occurred subconsciously… Before the 9/11 attacks occurred, I wasn't paying close attention to it. But after that event, I suddenly realized that "Mothman" *was* capable of sending messages from the future. Nowadays, all of this makes sense to me. I can do my art *and* recognize the surrounding percolation of symbols. They support each other. It's a vast topic… What I've said here today is just the tip of the iceberg.

RAI: Can we see some of your images?

AC [*gestures*]: This is a photo for an article I recently wrote in *Paranoia* magazine. In 1982, I went to New York for the Anti-Nuke Rally. It was the largest rally ever held in New York City. I helped carry this float that looks like a "big bird" or Mothman. We carried it past Rockefeller Center and into Central Park. I often get caught up in things that involve bird symbology. [*shows book*] This is my second book, *The Mothman Photographer II*, which talks a lot about synchronicities. One such synchronicity is that the Kanawha River, which the Mothman flew along between Pt. Pleasant and Mound, is called the "River of Death" by Native Americans. And Natives just happen to associate death with the Thunderbird. In fact, they place Thunderbird totems in their graveyards. [*points to photos*] This is the Space Needle in Seattle. It was once an Indian burial ground. It's quite haunted, in fact... The Christ symbol, the cross on a mound, is very similar to the Garuda symbologies in India. The Garuda is an emanation of energy; there seem to be male and female versions. Just as humans manifest as male and female, these entities also manifest as male and female. [*gestures*] Here is an ancient statue of Garuda carrying Vishnu. The Garuda provides support for the awakening process. One of the older Hindu statues shows the birdman connecting two cobras, each representing the human spinal column. The birdman symbolizes the spaces between – the background, the sky, the breeze upon which things fly... Here we have a Native American totem pole. The figure on the bottom is a female Bigfoot, and on top is the Thunderbird. Therefore we see, in ancient lore, an amazing connection drawn between Bigfoot and Mothman.

RAI [*points*]: Is this the photo for which you are famous?

AC: Yes, this is a high-resolution copy of the picture that was taken in 1973 by my sister. It was a random shot of me in the kitchen drinking from an upside down 7-Up glass. Uri Geller apparently once heard a voice coming from such a glass. The witness to Geller's experience, CIA scientist Andrija Puharich, was a follower of the British UFO cult "The Nine" and a possible agent of Standard Oil. The emblem on my shirt in the photo is "West Virginia Tech," which is close to where Union Carbide, a subsidiary of Standard Oil, has its famous Alloy plant. That plant has been polluting the air in the Kanawha Valley, at a level equal to the entire New York City metropolis, for decades. Over the years, a lot of conspiratorial things have happened in the Kanawha Valley. For instance, the family behind Jim Jones and Jonestown, the Laytons, were from Alloy. The family patriarch, Dr. Lawrence Layton, married the daughter of I.G. Farben's stockbroker and became head of U.S. Army Biowarfare between 1956 and 1963. Layton's son was one of the doctors at Jonestown. There were a lot of links between Standard, Carbide, and I.G. Farben. It is rumored that the Nazis' flying saucer program was real, and that it took place on I.G. Farben property. The saucer program may have been transferred to WV after the war, to a Carbide location, which would explain all of the UFOs in the TNT Area… Anyway, when my sister sent this kitchen picture to me, my 3-yr. old son pointed to the window and said "Garuda." Even though he didn't know what a Garuda was, he immediately recognized something in that face. If he had not said anything, no one would have ever noticed it. It looks like a reptilian bird. In the Mothman world, the clues come large and small… *[gestures]* Here is an interesting image… When we were doing the cover for the DVD, the designer made a mirror image and overlapped them. When she did, all of these bird faces appeared. One of them looks like a terrorist, actually. You can even see a skull face, the symbol of death. Mut, the aforementioned Egyptian goddess, is said to weigh the hearts of men after death. The Tibetans say you will meet a Heruka, or wrathful deity, after death. The Garuda is one of these Heruka. A person who sees the Thunderbird is considered to be a "Heyoka" by Native Americans. Again, the names are similar across great distances. There appears to have been a global religion and language at one time, most likely emanating from Tibet and Mongolia. The religion was first called "Mon," then "Bon." Today, remnants of it can be seen not only in Hinduism and Buddhism, but in Islam and Christianity. The imprints this early religion made on the human psyche still seem to resonate today.

"The following is an excerpt of a premonition involving the collapse of the World Trade Towers in NYC during the terrorist attacks of Sept. 11th, 2001. Physician Betsy MacGregor and her husband, Charles, were on a plane, flying to their home on an island in Puget Sound near Seattle after visiting friends in NYC. The date was Sept. 10, 2001. Dr. MacGregor writes:

> Spotting an empty row across the aisle, I decided to move there and stretch out. I expected to fall asleep promptly but something didn't feel right. [This] strange feeling started to come over me. It began with an awareness of how absolutely still my body was. I…felt a growing urge

to move but, to my surprise, my limbs did not respond... Something hard and unyielding surrounded my body, immobilizing it. I felt clearly that I was completely encased and held fast in concrete. The feeling of being imprisoned intensified [until it] was a sense of dread. I was hopelessly trapped and on the verge of claustrophobic terror. Then, the pain began. Faint at first, it rapidly grew stronger until if filled my whole body. The concrete was pressing in on me, tighter and tighter; squeezing me with unbearable force. My body was about to be crushed... It was perfectly clear; there was no escape. In another instant, my life would be over. I saw death before me... We headed home and tumbled gratefully into bed. Three thousand miles away, the World Trade Center was bursting into flames. As Charles and I slept, the [towers] crumbled into dust. Thousands of lives ended that morning in the crush of concrete.

"Here is a similar experience, reported a few weeks before the 9/11 terrorist attacks by a woman named Marie. This is just one story from a compilation of 14,000 cases of spontaneous psi experiences collected by the Rhine Research Center over many years:

My husband was driving. I was just trying to close my eyes to relax for a minute. Then he told me, 'When we come around the bend up ahead, you should get a good view of the Pentagon because our road goes right by it.' So I opened my eyes to look, and when I looked to the right, there was [the Pentagon]. But it had huge billows of thick, black smoke pouring out of it – like a bomb had gone off... I yelled out and slammed my hands on the dashboard. My poor husband didn't know what was happening. I truly felt we were in danger... I thought it was on fire. My husband said the Pentagon was *not* on fire. Then, I realized that, in fact, it was not.

"Many similar forebodings of 9/11 have surfaced... In Sept. 2000, I designed a suite of web-based games hosted by the Boundary Institute that allows users to test their psychic abilities online... As of late 2005, the database consisted of over 60 million individual trials contributed by almost a quarter of a million people... On Sept. 9, 2001, a user nicknamed 'Sean' wrote the following impression in a series of trials:

Airliner (seen from left-rear) against stormy cloud backdrop, flashes of streaky cloud… A dragonfly, then a log [or] branch suggestive of the Everglades, then a fast dynamic scene of falling between two tall buildings, past checkered patterns of window. Tall structure like an industrial chimney, then flashes of peacock-like headdress of American Indian, then volcanic ash plume…

"Sean's precognitive descriptions…provide a rather startling, impressionistic sense of the chaos associated with the events of 9/11 in NYC. The next day, Sept. 10, 2001, user *Shakey* wrote these words:

It is of something falling; it will be a chaotic scene…

"A half hour later, a different user, nicknamed 'Justatest,' wrote:

Intense… Too hot to handle; blasting; is the coast clear? They were checking the coast!

"The following morning, Tuesday, Sept. 11, 2001, about an hour before the first airplane crashed into the WTC, user 'Xixi' wrote:

White House; gone in the blink of an eye; scald; man's folly; band red; surging; palace; not easily conned; U.S. power base; flexing muscles; surprise…

"The ideas suggested by these words were unusual in the context of this online precognitive experiment, as most of the photos in the test are of benign landscapes, people, animals, and other pleasant scenes with neutral content. So, I devised a way to judge whether the words used in this test prior to 9/11 were, in fact, unusual… It illustrates a way that web-based experiments are beginning to offer new ways of studying *collective* psi effects… I first examined the data from all online precognition trials contributed from Sept. 2, 2000 through June 30, 2003. There were 428,000 trials contributed by about 25,000 people. I matched the words entered against a set of nine concepts that captured the chaotic context associated with 9/11: *airplane, falling, explode, fire, attack, terror, disaster, Pentagon,* and *smoke*… This analysis showed, to my surprise, that on 9/11 the curve dropped to its lowest point in 3 years of collecting data. Rather than increase, as might be predicted if lots of people were suddenly having spontaneous premonitions of disaster, the scores significantly *dropped* as 9/11 approached... The data did not indicate that premonitions intruded into people's thoughts just prior to 9/11. Rather it suggests that, on average, such thoughts were significantly *avoided*. One possibility is that in the day before 9/11, many people began to unconsciously sense trouble brewing. But [since] there was no context for those feelings, they were repressed...

"As it turns out, I was also examining data from another online test, a card-guessing test. From Aug. 2000 through June 2004, this online test collected 17 million trials. The results showed a huge drop in performance observed prior to 9/11. The odds against chance of seeing a drop that deep is 2,700 to 1. This means that the users were actively *avoiding* hitting the correct card just prior to 9/11. This outcome is consistent with the possible repression effect that we observed in the precognition test. Together they suggest that, days before 9/11, many people may have been unconsciously avoiding their psi impressions to suppress awareness of a looming disaster... The likelihood that two independent online tests would both display strong negative tendencies just prior to the same meaningful date is associated with odds against chance of 1.8 million to 1. That seems to offset the possibility that we're dealing with a mere coincidence."

-Dean Radin, *Entangled Minds: Extrasensory Experiences in a Quantum Reality*, pp. 25-33

CHAPTER 1

"The test of a first-rate intelligence is the ability to hold two
opposed ideas in the mind at the same time, and still retain
the ability to function."

-F. Scott Fitzgerald

"An accumulation of minute details, however silly it may
appear, is the only correct means to reach fundamental
truths."

-A.F. Bandolier

"For every complex problem, there is a solution that is simple,
neat...and wrong."

-H.L. Mencken

*I thought it would be of interest to readers to see some of the corre-
spondence that I received while working on my Mothman project,
which began just after the 9/11 attacks. During the first year, most
of this correspondence was between myself and Harriet Plumbrook,
my childhood friend who had seen Mothman in 1968. As time
went by, I posted occasional summaries to the Mothman discussion
list about what was happening to Harriet and other witnesses. In
some cases, these summaries were put on videotape and included in*
The Mothman's Photographer *DVD series... Harriet lived just
a couple of houses away from Tommy Burnham, who had also seen
Mothman and had, in 1967, been given visions of the 9/11 attacks.
As Harriet and I shared our accounts, it became clear that the
memories I had of odd childhood events were accurate. The valida-
tion that Harriet provided was a key impetus to continue researching the situation. As Harriet told her story, it became clear that the
phenomenon had deeply affected her. It had also given her "powers"
that seemed truly otherworldly.*

MOTHMAN DISCUSSION LIST – SELECTED LETTERS & POSTS – 2002

Andy, I have sat bolt upright in my bed – out of a deep sleep – many
times over the last 20 years whenever something wasn't right with you.
When I moved to Maryland in 1971, I missed you terribly. It was like a

part of me had died. I had had you around to play with, fight with, and compete with since we were two years old. Communicating with you now is unbelievable, but it is something I somehow *knew* would happen. I actually thought I saw you in 1999 in Tulum, Mexico. It was the most vivid vision I had had of you in years... In May of 2000, I was in Ephesus, Turkey when your doppelganger came to me again. I don't know why... I find it odd that you worked for UPS Air as a Loadmaster, just as I worked for FedEx Air for all that time as a loadmaster – a coincidence that is *too* strange... Another strange experience I had was regarding my father. I had come in from work about 2:30 a.m. one morning after handling a rough night of flights. I fell right to sleep. I woke up with serious chest pains at 4:30 a.m. My doorbell was ringing like crazy at 5:30 a.m. It was my mom's best friend. When I opened the door, I said, "I know why you're here. My dad died, didn't he?" I gave her quite a jolt. My father had been dying of a heart attack, in his sleep, at 4:30 a.m.

-Harriet 3/22/02

My family was visiting the Alley family in Pt. Pleasant a few days before the Silver Bridge collapse. I have verified this with my mother. The Alleys had moved from Woodward Drive to Pt. Pleasant when we were 7 years old. We spent an entire weekend down there. There was another neighborhood couple over there that weekend. One week later, they were dead, victims of the collapse. That event haunted me as a child... Mom made me stop watching the news. She took the newspaper away from me. I remember the adults talking about all of the strange things that were happening at the time. They would shut up every time I came in the room... Earlier that year, in late spring of 1967, the skies over Charleston were blood red. We had gone out to dinner at Joe Fazio's – a rare occasion that I remember vividly. After we ate, my father threw us in the car and headed up to that hideous mountaintop airport, convinced a plane had crashed. We soon saw all of these fires burning in straight lines. One of the emergency workers told us that the gas lines had exploded. The next morning, *The Charleston Gazette* made mention of several eyewitnesses who had seen a hovering object that was following the exploding gas lines. Again, the paper was taken away from me... The incident was never mentioned in front of me again... In July of 1968, we had the infamous chlorine gas leak at the FMC chemical plant, where we all had to evacuate the city. There were numerous reports that contradicted the plant's statements about what really happened. Again, there had been sightings of strange objects and flashing lights. We had to evacuate with our neighbors, as my dad was away at his job near Moyers, WV. Until I read *The Mothman Prophecies*, I never thought there could be a correlation between such events. I personally know most every place mentioned in the book. I share John Keel's viewpoint; I don't believe in "extraterrestrials." People see and experience the unexplained from whatever their point of reference may be. UFOs, apparitions, and other strange phenomenon are glimpses of another dimension that I *know* exists. There is a tremendous energy force accompanying it. I've seen too much to doubt this. Since the beginning of time, great works of literature, including the Bible, mention these sightings…

I have been blessed with great intuition since I was a child. I have been told several times in my life – each time by an Indian – that I have the hands of a healer and a "blue aura" surrounding me. I often tell people what they are going to say before they say it. I have strange waking premonitions. I screw up electrical systems sometimes. On several occasions, I have climbed into the cockpit of my small plane and all of the instruments have gone out, either shortly before takeoff *or* while in flight. I gave my flight instructor every gray hair on his head… I make clocks speed up, which is funny, as my gift seems to be predicting future events. Streetlights go out when I walk under them. My cousin, who is two years younger than me, remembers all the weird stuff going on. She also shares these strange visions about the future with me. Two and a half years ago, she told me that I would encounter someone from my past – whom I now know to be you – who would come to figure prominently in my life. She told me that I would encounter visions of this person in May of that year. The incident at Tulum, with your doppelganger, happened right on schedule… A similar thing happened in 1981. A friend went with me to see a spirit medium named "Medula." I was going to expose this "quack," Medula. But, before we arrived, I was told by my friend that a spirit had told him I would never be able to write the story; something would be channeled to me at that time, which would render me unable to write. I would become *part* of the story myself… And things happened exactly as predicted; news of your father came through Medula, leading me to contact you at the University of Cincinnati… Do you sleepwalk? I have been a sleepwalker since I was a small child. It increases during my periods of "intuition." I have said and done some extremely bizarre things to my parents, roommates, and husband at these times, and have absolutely no memory of ever doing it… My phones have been oddly ringing and buzzing since the Ohio State University alumni office left that message about you. It began *that* day. But this has happened to me all of my life, even at places of employment. It seems to happen in waves. Before reading that damned *Mothman Prophecies* book, I never would have correlated any of this stuff.

-Harriet 3/25/02

I probably spent more time with Tommy Burnham than you did. His mom and my mom knew each other from working at the phone company years before. They resumed a great friendship after the Burnham's house was built. My mom was shocked that it was they who had moved in. My dad was only home on weekends so, for years, my mom and Phyllis spent almost every day together. About the "alien" thing… Tommy would cry to me that no one believed him; he would always ask me if I did. I remember days when Tommy would tell me: "*They* have been here today." "They" would come to him in the wee hours of the morning. He would always look so exhausted at school… I remember the biting incidents when he became obsessed with vampires. He was put under the care of a child psychiatrist, which really carried a stigma in the 1960s. I remember a specific incident with Tommy on the day that I learned to ride a bike. I was six. It was in the fall of 1966. He showed me circular markings in the semi-wet ground – where the spaceship had been that morning. I remember it frightening me… Your story brings to light some memories. I had "waves" of intuition about you after we moved. I began having vivid waves in June 1972, which lasted for a couple of years. Could this be when you had your second sighting? That spot on the blacktopped lane, where you had your sighting, gave me a chill every time I walked by. Every day, on the way to the bus stop, I would *run* past that spot … I remember walking up the big hill to a beautiful place I had never found before. I saw what looked like a C130 plane approaching, but there was no sound. The best way to describe it is "cigar-shaped." I remember being frightened; I couldn't move. It passed, and I went down the hill. I was afraid to come out for a few days. When I did start combing the ridge again, I could not find that "place" ever again. I just found a reference to this sort of phenomenon in *The Mothman Prophecies*. There is so much that keeps flooding back to me… My obsession with flying started when I was 6 or 7. My flying dreams were so intense in 1989 that, in March of 1990, I started taking flying lessons. No one believed I was taking flying lessons. But I *had* to understand flight. I had to know what I had seen when I was a child. It led to a career of being around planes. I have now worked around C130s, so I know that that is *not* what glided above me that day. Since I proved to myself that I could fly, I scarcely pilot anymore.

I have always felt "different." I've always been a person who lives "outside the box." It's as if something deeply recessed in the confines of my subconscious is piloting me through the different courses I take in life. It's as if I've been searching for a missing link. I "boil" beneath the surface. No one knows how strange and disconnected I sometimes feel. I've always felt like I was hiding a part of me from everyone else. Something has followed me all of my life, like a shadow… I've been crying a lot lately. The tears are a relief. It's very hard to explain. I've never really felt like this before. Hell, I'm crying now… I've always felt like I was carrying some heavy burden around with me, one that I could never put my finger on. Funny how I was led to the paranormal… I was a rational, intelligent person who sought to "prove it as quackery" but somehow got sucked up in it. This feeling I carry around has shaped and molded me. It has clearly controlled me at times. Tommy always had large, dark circles under his eyes, and an anguished face… You have to ask yourself if things like schizophrenia and manic depression aren't really just brushes with "the other side." I feel that since my contact with you, I have become "enlightened," if you will. It feels like you have found, in this labyrinth that is "Mothman," what I have been searching for all these years.

-Harriet 3/26/02

There is an incident that is bothering me. On January 8, 1968, my father went down the steps of the hill where we lived to start his Grand Prix. It blew up – a car bomb. It was a black car that he loved like a child. Shortly after that, the "FBI" came to visit us. They linked the bombing to our mysterious next-door neighbor, Mr. Bruno, whom they said had "mob ties." We were just the innocent victims; the bombers got the wrong black car (Bruno had a black Lincoln Mark IV at the time). The agent stopped me and asked if I had seen any strangers around in "black cars…" Bruno was a very odd looking man. Some of his features resembled those of the Men in Black in *The Mothman Prophecies*. This 1/8/68 date is forever etched in my memory. The sound of the explosion, and the fire, is still with me. My dad was burned, but not seriously. Not long after this incident, some men, presumably FBI agents, came and carted Mr. Bruno off. He was incarcerated in a federal penitentiary in Harrisburg, PA. Years later, when I was in journalism school, I decided to look up his case, but could find no record of it. I would have never thought a thing about any of this until now. I'm now starting to question every strange thing that happened to me as a child. The events in Pt. Pleasant, particularly the Men in Black, could definitely be tied in with all the strange happenings in the Kanawha River Valley and on Woodward Drive. I'm becoming a true believer here.

-Harriet 4/1/02

I remember an article about Bruno in *The Charleston Gazette*. Mom let me see it at the time. By the way, she told me today that she was actually an FBI *informant*. It was she who got the whole thing rolling against Bruno. She had a contact agent by the name of "George K. Adams." I remember Adams as plain as day. He would call us frequently and ask if we had seen certain cars. He himself drove a VW bug. He would always park so that his license would face downhill, so no one could see it. I'm freaking out; this is so unreal... Mom said Bruno was hauled away on racketeering charges – an eleven-count indictment. J. Edgar Hoover was the one who made the announcement. I remember Bruno's creepy smile most of all. He used to shoot an elephant rifle. Mom was afraid he would hit me or my sister, which sparked the initial call to the FBI. Then, she found a case in the woods full of drugs! Adams came out and took it away. The car bombing occurred after the drugs were found. Instinctively, I do not buy the FBI's explanation of the bombing. Let's face it, Bruno could have killed us all if he wanted to... My mom never told anyone about Bruno. She had sworn to the FBI that she would keep quiet. Her family didn't know until years later. She said Bruno was into drugs, porno, and various other "fun" things. My mother was very young when all of this happened. I doubt that she realized the danger she was in. My dad was always *so* anxious and "on edge." He was an electrical engineer for Western Electric. He was constantly traveling to Washington, D.C when we were small. It wasn't until we moved that he seemed to calm down. After he retired in 1984, he became really laid back – a different person. Dad *never* talked about his job, ever... Perhaps it was only my father who really understood the significance of the bombing. I couldn't understand your paranoia at first, but now I get it. Holy cow... Is everyone else's childhood this freaking strange? What *was* this hellhole we lived in? It's a wonder we both got out of there alive...

-Harriet 4/2/02

I just got ahold of Tommy's mother. I asked if she thought Tommy would like to see us. She emphatically said, "Absolutely not." She was cordial enough to take me and my mom's phone numbers. This is what she would tell me about Tommy... She said Tommy was granted a full scholarship to Indiana University in Chinese, but turned it down. He is fluent; he could speak Chinese in high school. I could maybe understand that in San Francisco or Seattle, but in Cocoa Beach, FL? A blonde, blue-eyed kid obsessed with Chinese is pretty unusual. He attended Broward Community College and received a computer engineering degree. He attended Eckerd, but was a thesis short of a Masters in philosophy. He worked in the space industry for some time, which he predicted when he was young. He now does landscaping and floral design. He has never married. Phyllis is 66 and just got a huge promotion at work. She works for the Commander of the U.S. Alliance at the Space Administration. She said, "You sound all grown up." She wanted to know if you were married. She never asked if I was married, but asked about my kids. It was the oddest conversation I've had in a long time. Every answer I seek ends with more questions.

-Harriet 4/3/02

Like Mulder and Scully on *X-Files*, I thirst for knowledge; it is insatiable. I have to always learn. I need to read more of the UFO books. Much of what is said to be "alien" actually seems staged. I read a UFO article recently that mentions marks on the bodies of witnesses, which look like someone scooped the skin away. Oddly, I have two skin indentations at the base of my neck, which showed up when I was seven years old. It looks like someone just scooped the skin away. I sometimes have pain that shoots down from that point, It radiates to my right arm and fingers, making them numb. I remember my mother asking me where they came from.

-Harriet 4/4/02

Harriet, did you know that my sister, Loretta, has one of those scoop marks on her leg? She also saw a flying saucer land in our yard, and claims to have been visited by Mothman, Men in Black, and "little green men." Regarding your dad being employed as an electrical engineer by Western Electric... I've been re-reading *The Puzzle Palace* by James Bamford, which is a history of the NSA. Apparently Western Electric did all the engineering for the major NSA installations. One of them is near Sugar Grove, WV, which is just a few miles from where "Red" Brown's family used to vacation. I was playing basketball with Brown's sons on that fateful night in 1973 when I saw the tree entity on Woodward Lane. Steve Slack, whose family had moved into the Burnham's place, hosted the basketball games... Sugar Grove has been the NSA's main East Coast eavesdropping facility since it was completed in 1975. The purpose of the project was to build radio dishes that mimicked those operated by AT&T in nearby Etam, WV. The NSA can freely download all of the phone calls, data transfers, and satellite uplinks that travel through the AT&T system. A chief designer at AT&T at that time, William Baker, was also secretly an NSA man. He was a consultant to Congress when they drafted the privacy legislation. He made sure that there was a loophole allowing the government to eavesdrop on any and all communications. Your dad may have been working on some aspect of that project. The NSA has its headquarters near Baltimore, which is where you moved after leaving WV. They were extremely concerned about security leaks throughout the 1960s and early '70s. The NSA contacted the CIA and asked for help in checking out *everyone* who worked on eavesdropping projects or installations. According to Bamford, no holds were barred. The bombing of your dad's car indicates that he may have been targeted by one side or the other. While we may never know if the bombing was a result of your family already being under surveillance, we can safely assume that your family was put under surveillance *after* that. Perhaps the recurring "nightmare" that my sister and I have, of our whole family being in a trance, and under interrogation, is a *real* memory... Bamford's new book is *Body of Secrets*. The last chapter has some interesting stuff about recent NSA endeavors. Apparently, they are creating computer switches using organic material like e. coli bacteria. This will allow the NSA to further miniaturize their drives and push their processing power into the petaflop range, which is billions of calculations per second. Biochips will also allow them to push aggressively towards merging computers and the human body.

-Andy 4/7/02

Oh my God, Andy... My dad worked at Sugar Grove! I know this for a fact. I didn't know at the time that the place was actually a secret base. It doesn't surprise me, though. I worked in the aviation industry for a long time. I know of things being developed that the average person won't know of for decades. This stuff stretches beyond what most of us can believe. As I told you, Dad never talked about his work. He was always gone; he would only come home on the weekends. His mind was always someplace else. He always seemed distant from us. The only time Dad ever said anything related to his work was when I was in college. I was taking astronomy. I asked him if he knew about the big satellite dishes on the west end of the Ohio State campus. They are supposedly listening devices for outer space. His comment was: "I know all about that kind of technology. I had a hand in the installation of something just like it many years ago." My dad was over in the Pacific, at Okinawa and Guam, during WWII. When he was stateside, he was assigned to NORAD. He had some sort of security clearance. He was assigned to Western Electric when he got out of the service. He was supposedly a regular, union employee until we moved to Maryland. That was a huge promotion – perhaps a "thank you" – for him. He wasn't degreed, but he did go to Marshall University for a couple of years. He was a high-level Freemason, even though he didn't join until he was in his fifties... There was an installation just north of where we lived in Towson, MD called Aberdeen Proving Grounds. It belongs to the Navy. Jim Hatcher, who lived next door to us on Woodward Drive, was stationed there in the early 1960s. According to Mom, his wife was always concerned. He was never allowed to speak of his work. When he came back to Charleston, he worked for Pepsi.

I now have a clearer picture of where you are coming from on all this. So much of the paranormal appears *not* to be paranormal at all. I think

I need to learn more about mind control. I find the *MILABS: Military Mind Control and Alien Abductions* book by Lammer to be most interesting. I would have never thought to look for a conspiracy behind all of these sightings. I guess the government is counting on people just being frightened and not looking behind the curtain. Linda Scarberry, one of the chief Mothman witnesses, felt that "Big Bird" was meant as a distraction from something else. Considering the Garuda's many appearances throughout history, I tend to think the Mothman sightings may be real – not a government operation. There were many witnesses to Mothman. Do you suppose that the Charleston, Huntington, Pt. Pleasant triangle was chosen for experimentation due to poverty and lack of education? With all those chemical plants and reduced life expectancy, I don't doubt that the government was exploiting the situation.

-Harriet 4/7/02

What do you make of the make of the Men in Black? Other than George K. Adams and Jack Bruno, my only experience with the MIB was when I got the weird visits and phone calls after you released your video. I can't help but wonder about our old Woodward neighbor, Red Brown. I'm picking up vibes that he is not to be trusted. There is something rotten there. Do you think Woodward Drive was one big experiment? What do you make of your second Mothman sighting? What was Mothman trying to tell you in junior high? I still wonder if my dreams about you then didn't correlate with that sighting. I remember the dream. You were being chased in the dark, struggling to get away. I felt you to be in a life-or-death, dangerous situation. I saw you plain as day. In some sense, I was flying above you, telling you to run. Your theory of Tommy projecting back there is not so far-fetched. I go back there all the time in dreams and visions, so why not him? I can feel his vibration. It is incredibly strong, yet frighteningly unstable. He is psychic like us. I woke up screaming my head off when you were being chased. That dream bothered me for days. It still haunts me now. What the hell were you running from, and why would I feel it?

-Harriet 4/8/02

Here's a kooky theory that came to me last night regarding the "Oriental" MIBs. Since certain monks were drawn into CIA service as part of the operation to get the Dalai Lama out of Tibet, perhaps knowledge of some of the CIA's other, less humanitarian, tactics spread among the monasteries. Some monks may have decided to subvert the agency, either by remote viewing or by directing their reincarnations towards the U.S.

Perhaps they even tried to reincarnate into the bodies of children born to intelligence agency couples. This would explain why there were Oriental MIBs around, and why some MIBs were trying to photograph or abduct children. They were looking for the monks who had been reincarnated. Such reincarnations would explain the heightened IQs and talents of certain children in the area. As the "Godphone" case of SRI physicist Jack Sarfatti shows, the government was locating young recruits for future remote viewing experiments.

-Andy 4/8/02

Synthetic "alien abduction" seems to be a takeoff on the natural phenomenon of seeing fairies and the like. Alien abduction would be a great device for blocking real memories of interrogation, for it replaces the interrogation with a "screen memory." The belief in ETs has long been pumped into society from various angles, including religion. If followers of the major religions can be made to believe that aliens are real, then one-world government becomes more of a possibility... After WWII, there appears to have been a shift away from obvious human experimentation, such as in the Nazi camps, to *covert* experimentation. I don't think all of the UFO phenomenon is necessarily artificial. It's just that you can't be sure anymore. Since a mountain of evidence has come out about military abductions and mind control (where voices can be beamed into the cranium with microwaves), it calls into question every instance of someone "hearing voices" and then shooting up their school or workplace. We now need to rule out synthetic involvement before falling back on the old line that the shooter was simply a "loner" who "went postal." Sadly, we may never know which mass killings were manufactured and which were not. The paranormal and the manipulation of the paranormal are intertwined. Knowing that our minds can be easily manipulated should give us the ability to empathize with others whose lives have been harmed by mind control experimentation. The more we share that awareness, the better the outcome for all.

-Andy 4/9/02

My CIA aunt is a deeply religious conservative who lives and breathes the words of Rush Limbaugh. She has attended the McLean Presbyterian Church in Virginia for 40 years. It is full of CIA people. She had her 70th birthday party at the church. I flew in and surprised her. It was like a *Who's Who* of the intelligence community. When I showed up at her house, someone she used to work with became very uncomfortable that I was there... My father used to have knock-down-drag-out arguments with my aunt. They would "get into it" constantly. They did it in private, but you could hear their raised voices. Mom was never involved… Your dad used to spend a lot of time with my dad when he was home. They were a lot closer than I had realized. Dad probably talked to him more than any other male friend he had. I remember distinctly that when your sister's husband was killed, your dad came and talked to my dad for hours, way into the night. It wouldn't surprise me if they talked about electrical stuff, too. I didn't realize your father had gone back to school. Dad had tons of electrical books around. He became an instructor for Western Electric, and literally wrote most of their manuals. Dad accepted early on that I was cut from a different mold, unlike my mother, who always thought I should be gracing the country clubs. Dad didn't have that much of a problem with me being a journalist. He just didn't want me getting into "questionable" stories. In college, I was hauled in for questioning a couple of times for stories I was looking into. Dad used to say that "Big Brother" was watching me – that I had better watch myself. While returning from Sugar Grove, one Friday in Nov. 1966, my dad was involved in a very serious head-on collision. He was hospitalized for several days. Dad said that the guy came at him on purpose. I remember being with my dad one time, near the Carbide plant, when smoke started pouring out from the under the hood of the car. This was the summer following the Jan. 1968 car bombing… He told me to get ready to jump from the car. Luckily, it was just a broken radiator hose.

-Harriet 4/9/02

Life in the Ohio Civil Air Patrol was interesting, to say the least. I was the only woman ever to be in this squadron. The average age of the men was about 60. Although civilian, the CAP follows all Air Force rules and regulations. There is extensive training involved. Most of the members were ex-military. You have to submit fingerprints for entrance. You get a low-level security clearance. There were several weirdos in there. One of them went by the name of "Kitchen." He was a retired Air Force major. He used to ask me all kinds of weird questions, like how I got to have such a high IQ. I had never discussed my IQ with anyone there. I found that a bit odd. He asked repeatedly about my art talent, but he had never seen any of my art. He used to get about a foot from my face and stare into my eyes. He would tell me that he had never seen such an odd eye color. My squadron commander never put me on a plane with him, for which I was grateful.

-Harriet 4/15/02

Me and my mom, sister, and several neighbors saw a UFO in the summer of 1978. That fall, I wanted to do a story about Project Blue Book for *The Lantern* at Ohio State. My dad went ballistic. He told me I shouldn't go snooping around where my nose didn't belong – that I could get myself killed. He seemed to think I had a "death wish." At the time, I figured he was just being overprotective. He would panic whenever I'd start my sleepwalking episodes. I had several as a teenager and young adult. He was the most freaked out when he found out that I had been found wandering on the street one night in the summer of 1978. He and mom were away at Cape Cod at the time… I have had several sleepwalking events in my married life as well, which freak out my husband. I have absolutely no recollection of what takes place during those times. I can't help but feel we are working with two different phenomena here: one real, one man-made. I once had lunch with an expert on Indian lore, who told me that the Indians have been seeing UFOs for thousands of years. There was a wave of UFO sightings on Cape Cod in July 1975, around the time you got deathly sick in Haiti after trying to sneak into that voodoo ceremony. I was up there for a whole month that summer. Seems like a little too much of a coincidence. I had a dream about you then. You were on a table. I could see your eyes. You seemed to be in a daze, which makes sense because you said that you hallucinated for three days.

-Harriet 4/21/02

Please think positive thoughts for me, as a lot of little things are going haywire right now. I have ringing in my ears quite badly at times… The computer sometimes goes berserk when I am writing… The guys at the Volvo shop say that I am the cause of my car's electrical problems… Every time I try to copy something regarding Mothman or the Silver Bridge, there is a copier malfunction. The librarian asked me if I ever thought someone was trying to keep me from writing this story… My phone is acting up all of the time… The kids and I have a skin condition called pilaris. It is associated with allergies. We have rashes that flare-up for no apparent reason. We look like we are having a major allergic reaction to something. Nasal and chest congestion will accompany the rash. I have heard that pilaris flares up when there is high solar activity… A couple of weeks ago, I woke up in the kitchen with no idea how I got there. Actually, that happens a few times a year… Last year, I woke up in bed to find that my feet were wet, like I'd been walking on grass. The next morning, we found that the back door was unlocked. I had probably been outside. I have run the sweeper, done laundry, and carried on ridiculous conversations with my parents while asleep… My "waking visions" are continuous, so I usually dismiss many of them. I'm starting to pay more attention these days. I know that I "zone out" a lot when I drive. In fact, I drive to relax. When it's too cold or rainy and I can't walk or run, I will drive. I have 46,000 miles on a car that is a year and a half old. I've been hypnotized once. When the hypnotist snapped me out of it, she had the most horrified look on her face. I've always wondered about that… I still can't believe how much I am remembering about my childhood. The floodgates have opened.

-Harriet 4/22/02

I picked up Whitley Strieber's *Communion Letters*. On page 42, something leapt out at me. A man wrote him about the "underground UFO base at Hamilton Field, CA." My dad was stationed at only one place stateside while in the Air Force: Hamilton Field. Another thing mentioned in the book is the association between the scent of cinnamon and UFO abductions. This smell has been around all of my houses all of my life. I routinely smell it in the hallways, especially when I have to get up in the middle of the night… When I was 30 weeks pregnant with my son, I almost died. I went to the OSU hospital, where I remained for two weeks. I had a dream where someone was checking the baby with a probe. In the Strieber book, a woman claimed that the "visitors" started visiting her when her children were in the womb. Her kids and mine were all born 5 weeks early… Six weeks before my daughter was due, I started bleeding. I was rushed to OSU again. When they got the heart monitor on her, it all of a sudden died. They rushed me to surgery. She had completely abrupted. She was born dead…

But, they revived her! She was given only a 5% chance of survival. Amazingly, she pulled her ventilator out, all by herself, when she was 12 hours old, and started breathing on her own. I had had a "visitation" dream the previous night, one of many I have had in my life. Towards the end of giving birth to her, I started having out-of-body experiences, where I was floating above my body in the operating room. The panicked doctors were saying, "We're losing her!" But I was revived, too. It turns out that when I went back for my routine checkup and told them of my dream, they told me that they had revived me on the table. I had gone into cardiac arrest due to extreme loss of blood. While floating, I was told to "go back" – that my life wouldn't "begin" until after I was "40+ years old." A social worker came to visit me in the hospital, to ask if my husband had hit me or pushed me down the stairs. They were trying to explain the abruption, but there was no explanation… When I was in junior high, a hypnotist came to class. I was chosen to be the subject. He hypnotized me in no time flat. His comment was, "The last time I saw someone drop off like that, it was an abductee." I didn't know what he meant at the time.

-Harriet 4/25/02

In fifth grade, a film crew came to our school to film "exceptional" children in Appalachian schools. I remember what I was wearing that day. They got permission from my mother to film me. They gave me an encyclopedia and told me to study something in it, and then give a talk about it. I studied "Ethiopia" for a half-hour before they filmed me. Besides the person actually filming me, there were two people introduced to me with the title "Doctor." Mrs. High, our teacher, kept trying to comfort me. I distinctly remember an Air Force officer being present. I kept wondering what he was doing there. I recognized the uniform from my dad's pictures. I got up and drew a map of Ethiopia and talked about the ruler, Haile Selassie, without looking back at the book. The "doctors" were amazed. They kept saying, "She has total recall!" The guy in uniform took lots of notes. They asked me a bunch of questions before the filming took place. For some reason, they moved my hair and looked at the back of my neck, where I have those two weird puncture marks, like Scully on *X-Files*. Strangely, the doctors and the guy in uniform left after I was done, but the film crew stayed. They said we would eventually get copies of the movie, but we never did. When I was in high school, I did a report on Ethiopia again. It was one of the strangest déjà vu experiences I've ever had.

-Harriet 4/26/02

Today, Haile Selassie is worshipped as God incarnate among follow-ers of the Rastafari movement. He is the Messiah who will lead the peoples of the African diaspora to freedom. His lineage from Solomon and Sheba is perceived by Rastafarians as confirmation of the return of the Messiah in the prophetic Book of Revelation in the New Testament. He was called the "Conquering Lion of the Tribe of Judah." When Haile Selassie visited Jamaica on April 21st, 1966, one hundred thousand Rastafari from all over Jamaica descended on Palisadoes Airport in Kingston, having heard that the man whom they considered to be their Messiah was coming to visit them. That day, widely held by scholars to be a major turning point for the movement, is still commemorated by Rastafarians. Defying expectations of the Jamaican authorities, Selassie never rebuked the Rastafari for their belief in him as the returned Jesus. Instead, he presented the movement's faithful elders with gold medallions… Rita Marley, Bob Marley's wife, converted to the Rastafari faith after seeing Selassie on his Jamaican trip. In her book No Woman, No Cry, *she claimed that she saw a stigmata print on the palm of Selassie's hand that resembled the envisioned markings on Christ's hands after being nailed to the cross. After Rita converted her husband Bob, Rastafari became more well known throughout the world...*

According to conspiracy researchers such as Alex Constantine and John Judge, Marley was aided in contracting cancer by the son of CIA director William Colby. (The elder Colby was more or less "suicided" just before giving testimony regarding George Bush and the October Surprise; the part of Colby's brain that controls speech was "accidentally" removed.) Colby's son, who later happened to live next door to the murdered Nicole Brown Simpson, gave Marley a pair of boots with a strange wire in the toe area; after the wire pricked Marley's big toe, Marley contracted cancer in that toe. Neil Bush is also rumored to have also been involved in the boot affair... Selassie, too, was likely the victim of CIA intrigue. As a result of the 1973 oil crisis (falsely engineered by the oil companies), Ethiopia fell into an economic crisis. Food prices and unemployment spiked, and the military mutinied. In 1974, members of the Imperial family were imprisoned or executed without trial, including Selassie's grandson. These killings, known to Ethiopians as "Bloody Saturday," heralded the end of the Solomonic dynasty. In August 1975, state media officially reported that the "ex-monarch" Haile Selassie had died on August 27th of "respiratory failure" following complications from a prostate operation. His doctor, Asrat Woldeyes, denied that complications had occurred, and rejected the government version of his death. Many believed that the Emperor had in fact been assassinated, and this belief remains widely held. In 1992, the Emperor's bones were found under a concrete slab on the palace grounds, reportedly beneath a latrine.

I spent the night in Charleston yesterday. I slept with the TV on all night because I felt "they" might be coming for me. I've had these feelings off and on all my life. I don't remember half of the trip. They were in the midst of a flood. What a mess! The water was coming down the hills in sheets. I ventured up Woodward Drive. It was creepy. I didn't remember it being so narrow. It is haunting me. The place is so run-down. North Charleston looks like someone dropped a bomb on it. I cried hysterically when I came to the area below Tommy Burnham's house, where I always "land" in my flying dreams. There were flashes of light coming from the dash of the car. Then, a premonition came to me that I would be a healer. I get those flashes before I have premonitions… I am not just a bit psychic; I am profoundly so. I scare myself sometimes. It became clear to me this weekend that you are psychic as well, much more than you give yourself credit for. Let's just say that I am a lot clearer as to why this whole thing is going as it is. I no longer think I am crazy. *Something* happened to us. It is really no accident that we would find each other after all of these years. It was strange; I "had" to go down there. As a result, I was supplied with a "vision."

I also find it strange that I had a "feeling" when I passed by what turns out to have been your second house on Woodward, at the top of the hill. No one told me that you had moved to a second place… Another strange thing I wanted to tell you… About two and a half years ago, right before I left FedEx, I woke up one morning with deep scrapes on the inside of my right wrist. They took forever to heal. They were all the way up the forearm. I had to keep antibiotic ointment on them for weeks. I actually have a little scarring left. To this day, I have no idea how they got there. They weren't there when I went to bed. They hurt like hell. It looked like a sharp instrument was used. I now remember why I used to get so upset when Tommy would tell me that "they" were coming, or had been there: somehow, someway, I *knew* who "they" were. I have always had these feelings of panic whenever I think of UFOs. I try to shut the pictures I get out of my mind. I had a very strange reaction to *Close Encounters of the Third Kind* years ago. Since then, I avoid science fiction movies.

By the way, there are several accounts in Edith Fiore's book of people being probed with something very thin, with a bulb that "hooks" out at the end. It is small enough to maneuver the urethra and milk ducts in the breasts. I have recently seen this device on TV. It is now being used here at Ohio State to remove breast tumors. You have to wonder how we initially tested such "space age" inventions. I still say we are looking at two things here: one is paranormal, and the other capitalizes on the paranormal… Chapter 15 of Fiore's book was very scary to me. She goes through each of the symptoms of alien abduction. I have them all… I should also mention that I have this thing under the skin on my left hip; it's about an eighth of an inch long. It has been there probably four or five years. It is really strange; there is a lump, like something is under the skin there… There is another episode that troubles me. In January of this year, I woke up with "puncture" marks all over the inside of my right forearm and wrist. Yes, the same side as the scrapes… The puncture marks looked like "allergy tests." One could argue that they were chigger bites, but it was January. It gives me butterflies in my stomach… My deepest fear would be finding out that my children are involved, and that there is nothing I can do about it. My son has had two seizures of unknown origin. He saw "lights" the day before the seizures. It frightens me, I must admit.

Fiore specifically mentions waking up at a consistent time. I have done this hundreds of times in my life. Of course, I notice it more now that we have digital clocks. The times will repeat themselves. For instance, I'll wake up at 3:33 for months at a time. Then, the time will change, and the new time will repeat itself. The number that consistently keeps coming up throughout my life is 7:47. I always thought it was cool that I worked on a 747 airplane. I am obsessed with that plane. But it sends a chill down my spine whenever I hear a disc jockey says "it's 7:47," or I see it myself on a digital display. The other thing Fiore mentions is not being able to fall asleep naturally. This is my biggest problem and has been for as long as I can remember. I take Excedrin PM or breathe lavender oil every night just to fall asleep. And I sleep very lightly. I hear everything. I have slept with a fan on for years, to create "background" noise. What I am trying to drown out? Did you ever have the feeling that if you just kept your eyes closed, everything would be alright? I've been having that a lot lately, just like when I was young. I also keep having this dream of looking at the sky and saying "come and get me." And they do! Something else Fiore mentioned is this feeling that you should be doing "something else" with your life. I always feel like I should be doing something else, but I don't know what it is. Perhaps writing about all of this is what I am supposed to do. I haven't felt this energized in my entire life. You have really expanded my mind here, pal. Before this, I would never have thought anything about these incidents.

-Harriet 4/28/02

Allen Greenfield, who wrote the introduction to the first Mothman book, The Silver Bridge, *claims he never met the infamous Indrid Cold. However, he said that he had met someone who claimed to know Indrid very well. That person's name was "Terry R. Wriste." This name phonetically sounds like the phrase "tear your wrist" – a description of what happens to Harriet periodically (she mysteriously gets cuts on her wrist). I was told by an informant in 2009 that the "tearing of the wrist" is a Masonic phrase. Could Harriet's periodic episodes of sleepwalking and injury be the result of abductions by rogue or fringe Masons, perhaps even by Indrid Cold himself? Is this what made her father so uncomfortable about her missing time and sleepwalking incidents?*

According to Albert Budden's twelve year study, *UFOs and Psychic*

Close Encounters: The Electromagnetic Indictment, certain underground rock formations, mining pits, electromagnetic facilities (radio towers and substations) and pipelines can cause a variety of phenomena like earthlights, hallucinations of "aliens," marks in the earth, scratches on the body, scoop marks, rashes, erased tapes, etc. The earth holds charges from lightning storms and solar flares for some time. If these charges are released in a quick burst, it can affect humans quite strongly. WV and Ohio have a lot of lightning. Many of us on Woodward Drive lived just yards from a pipeline that ran along high, exposed ridges. Budden explains that typical childhood allergies are heightened by exposure to EM fields. They can be quite severe in extra sensitive "ES" persons. An ES person can even become allergic to specific EM frequencies if repeatedly exposed to those frequencies. In order to affect streetlights and so forth, the ES person has usually been repeatedly exposed to high EM fields… Apparently the phenomenon can "manipulate" both the psychic and material phases of the encounter. There does seem to be an intelligence behind the phenomenon, but that intelligence may simply be a result of the human consciousness observing it. It is a mixture of electromagnetism and the human mind. Apparently, if two ES people are physically together, they can cause hallucinogenic earthfields to develop all by themselves, whereas most people need a chance encounter with fields already in place. One wonders if these EM factors also cause precognitions and synchronicities to occur and, if so, how it is done. Our unconscious seems to find expression by interacting with nature. Or, perhaps our unconscious *is* nature itself.

Speaking of synchronicities, I recently walked into the library to return a book. I glanced at a bookshelf and noticed a book about a famous KGB defector named Alexander Orlov. The book was written by an ex-FBI agent out of Cleveland, Edward Gazur, who was the handler for Orlov. While most of the book is about interviews with Orlov, there are a couple of pages that discuss other cases Gazur worked on. One of them was the JFK assassination. Right after the assassination, Gazur was asked to do a background check on everyone who had been in an orphanage with Lee Harvey Oswald when he was a pre-teen. This is reminiscent of Charles Manson, who was also raised in an orphanage – a Catholic orphanage that happened to give ex-Nazis access to the boys. Gazur felt like the Oswald background checks were overkill – a waste of time. However, if one approaches it from the standpoint of the government *knowing* Oswald didn't pull the trigger, it makes more sense. They were probably trying to ascertain which of Oswald's old acquaintances might be able to pinpoint where, when, and how he was controlled. It has long been rumored that Oswald was mind-controlled in some fashion. Dozens of people who knew something about Oswald were killed in the aftermath of the assassination…

Another case that grabbed me was one that involved an engineer who worked at NASA's secret LPL Propulsion Lab near Cleveland. Gazur was asked to check the engineer's background after the engineer was found dead at home from a bomb blast in 1967. The bomb had been placed in a parcel delivered to the engineer's house. The FBI was concerned that the engineer, who had access to space secrets, might have been reporting to the KGB as a spy. In 1967, the Soviets were extremely interested in recruiting American engineers working on secret projects. They would go to great lengths to leverage key employees, especially if there was a weakness to exploit. To counter this, James Jesus Angleton of the CIA launched a major counterintelligence offensive to root out American engineers who might be collaborating with the Soviets. Gazur mentioned TRW as a company targeted by the Soviets, but one can imagine that other companies, like Carbide and Western Electric, were on the Soviets' list as well.

Gazur makes it clear that Ohio was a hotbed of spy activity in the late 1960s. It stands to reason that WV would have been under the same microscope… The Oriental MIBs in Pt. Pleasant may have been spies for the Soviets or the Chinese, both of whom had fallen under the sway of Rockefeller oil interests. Peter D. Beter wrote that the Rockefellers had already loaned these countries (and the American companies operating in them) lots of money by the early 1970s. The notes came due in the late 1980s, prompting the fall of the Berlin Wall and further investment in China by American corporations.

-Andy 4/29/02

The failure of Russia to make good on its treasury bonds in 1997 led to the failure of a major U.S. hedge fund, Long-Term Capital Management (LTCM). The gruff manner in which LTCM was allowed to fail later led to a feud that helped cause the failure of Bear-Stearns in 2008. Due to the importance of Bear-Stearns on "the street," a global financial meltdown ensued after it was snatched up for cheap by Chase Manhattan. In late 2008, the administration of Pres. Bush, whose family is longtime friends of the Rockefellers, created over $2 trillion dollars out of thin air and gave it to banks and insurance companies like AIG. When the American people found out about the swindle in March of 2009, citizens began picketing the homes of AIG executives, who had cashed huge bonuses paid for with the government bailout money. At the same time, it was revealed that AIG had been founded by the CIA following WWII. In fact, AIG *still occupies NYC offices that were once home to the CIA.*

I've been feeling tremendous pain around my thoughts of you. Not in the physical sense; it's that nagging little problem of never quite "fitting in" – the sense of disconnectedness I've talked about before. It is the longing for someone to understand the pain we feel in our souls. It's that desire to rise above and understand, the frustration we have with society in general, the "smallness" of what we must endure on a path to some form of "greatness." I repeatedly hear a woman's voice in my dreams. She says, "You'll remember when you want to." She is more an entity of light than a physical being. She is the one who spoke to me when I had that near-death experience during my daughter's birth…

I had thoughts of you one day while you were in the Grand Canyon. I was shivering like crazy, which is odd for me. You looked "wet." I saw you isolated from the others, but I saw tremendous growth from it… I find it odd that both of us have studied Eastern religion. I must admit I have had a strong distaste for conventional religion since I was a child. At the risk of sounding like a snob, I always knew it wasn't *the* truth, but just part of it. From the time I was four years old, I felt that religions were nothing more than an attempt to explain what we didn't understand. Where did I get such an idea at such a young age? I've always felt I had a higher consciousness than what organized religion could offer. I can't even force myself to go along with it.

When my dad died, he gave me something of his to keep. It is a Past Master's pin from the Masonic lodge. It is very, very old. It has weird symbols on it. I get a strange feeling when I hold it. In the center is something like the Man in the Moon on a starburst. There is an "eye" at the base that I take to mean the "third eye." I identify with this, as this is how I get my "readings." When I was a child, I remember my paternal grandmother had a locket in which she carried dirt that her grandmother had collected in Sweden. She claimed it had "powers." Way up north, in Lapland, they have some of the richest known magnetic fields. In fact, many inhabitants of that area today still wear medallions around their necks, which have a round space in the them where the dirt is carried. In conjunction with the magnetism, supposedly the dirt gives them greater psychic and healing ability.

-Harriet 5/20/02

Harriet, I managed to practice a little animal hypnosis on my Grand Canyon trip. No one took me seriously until I telepathed to a bird that kept flying alongside our raft, telling it to land on our raft. It landed on the front of the raft for a couple of minutes. I took a picture of it. No other birds landed on any of the rafts the entire trip. When we were fishing, I looked at the choices of bait we could use and instinctively "knew" which one would work. After choosing that one, we started catching large fish. As this animal communication was going on, I thought of Tommy Burnham and how adept he was with animals. Amazingly, the exact time you saw me and started shivering was the *exact* time I was attempting to send you an astral projection of myself. I was fully immersed in the freezing water of the Colorado for well over a half hour, longer than is said to be necessary to cause hypothermia. I had a fit of shivering a few minutes after I got out…

Early the next morning, I got up to go to the bathroom and saw three headlamps walking through some bushes in the morning mist. Since I was groggy, I didn't really compute the fact that no one else in our group was up yet. As we were leaving, the guide told a story about that campsite, saying that once upon a time many years ago, three government surveyors had gotten separated from their group and killed by Indians. Since they were working at the behest of mining concerns, they were probably wearing headlamps. Had I seen their ghosts? Also, a friend of mine from Seattle saw two UFOs following each other. One looked like it was maybe a satellite, but the other followed haphazardly. A Japanese lady saw a different UFO making zigzag movements. Her husband was a rocket scientist who had worked at Sandia Labs and other such facilities. The husband's friend was there. He had seen three UFOs while flying for Northwest Airlines. They all live on a private airstrip in Silverdale, WA. Another guy on the trip does "energy audits" for the government. He flies around in a little experimental craft that is half helicopter, half airplane. He probably causes a lot of UFO sightings all by himself.

-Andy 5/20/02

I'm not surprised that you have a thing with animals. I had an encounter with a group of deer last Feb. or March. I looked out the bedroom window one night and they were all staring at me from the lawn. It sends chills up and down my spine when I think of how that entire group was just looking at me. The master bedroom phone had been going crazy for a couple of days before that. It rings three short rings on just that one particular phone. There will be no one there. What *will* be there is a high-pitched tone or major static. It always acts up before I have strange dreams, experience bizarre activity, or have sleepwalking episodes. It happens mostly when I'm the only one around, although my husband has heard it himself on a couple of occasions.

I tried some animal telepathy at the zoo today. I kid you not, I had amazing success. First I tried it with a white Bengal tiger. What a beautiful animal. It was lying in the corner, far away from all of us. I talked to him through the Plexiglas barrier and asked him to come to me. I told him how handsome he was. He got up, glided right to me, and stood directly in front of me. He held my gaze. There were probably 20 people there with me, and they were stunned. It was the most incredible thing that has happened in a long time. I thanked him and wished him well. Then, I tried it with some gorillas. I communicated with a female who was nursing her baby. I got her to come to a corner away from everyone else. It was incredible. I was chaperoning four little girls, and they were going nuts over it.

-Harriet 5/20/02

My psychic cousin has been asking me to "read" her son. She says that he is "obsessed" with aliens and talks about traveling on spaceships. He has some outrageously advanced knowledge for a 5-yr. old. He also experiences frequent nosebleeds, and has bled from the rectum on a couple of occasions. She knows nothing about the UFO phenomenon. She asked me to see if it was autism; it wasn't. She took him to a regular psychologist who, frankly, didn't know what to do with him. Personally, I think he has had encounters. This kid would really remind you of Tommy Burnham.

-Harriet 5/28/02

I saw Andee Boothe for my first hypnotic regression. She motioned some bad energies to leave the room at the beginning, due to the fact that there was "some green" in my aura. I told her about our Mothman experiences, and she immediately turned off the electrical equipment in the room. She said a patient's energy once burned out $5,000 worth of equipment. She thanked me for giving her advance notice. She then described a "hole" in my aura, which was connected to "something that was taken from me" at age 8. She marshaled some protectors and had me revisit the night I spent with Tommy – when Mothman came. She laughed when I told her that I had said "no" to the experience – that I had called my mom to take me home. She felt as if there was an energy in me that wanted to avenge my dad's death. Her take on it was that the malevolence of the region – the way Carbide did not "step up" after my dad's death – created a hole that was naturally filled with negative energy. She tried to help me integrate that. She said that whatever is behind all of this is very big – that the energy was, and still is, overwhelming. She thinks it is good that we are doing our research away from the Kanawha Valley… Today, I went to the local Buddhist shop to ask if they had found any Garuda amulets for me. I had left some pictures of examples there a week ago. The lady at the counter was amazed. She said, "Oh my God! You must be psychic. I just thought of you and those amulets." It seems like others can pick up the energy behind all of this. I told her that maybe it was not just me that was psychic.

-Andy 5/30/02

I asked my sister, Spring, about her black panther sighting. She recalls seeing it twice. She put it at about 50 lbs. She then told me about a "dream" she had once. She was dozing on the couch some time after my dad had died, when these globes of light came in through the window. They circled her, and then became larger. She remembers feeling paralyzed. She said that there were "four moons" in the sky during this, which is interesting because I once had a dream – apparently while sleepwalking – where balls of light were flying around. There was a heavy, glowing mist in the air. The balls of lights moved around, like sparklers. I heard a loud "crack" as I went out the door to sleepwalk and mingle with them. All in all, it was a pleasant dream. Spring, however, had a second dream that she described as troubling. In that dream, which again occurred while she was dozing on the couch, she saw dad standing outside the kitchen window, facing away towards the hill. You could see that window from the couch. That is the window where I often dreamed of seeing Bigfoot. When dad turned to look at Spring, those little globes of lights began encircling his head, like electrons around an atom. They went faster and faster until she got scared and woke up.

-Andy 6/8/02

Spring's seeing the four moons is kind of weird. That is mentioned in one of the Budd Hopkins books. Spacecraft can appear as "moons…" Last Friday, I was speaking with Mom about my cousin who is in the NSA. He is around 50 years old and has four kids. He is on assignment, so no one knows where he is. I asked about his father, who deserted him when he was young. I had not mentioned the father in years. Unbelievably, it turns out that the father had just died *that* very day! I do pick up on things happening on "the other side." And so does my daughter… Today, we were in the kitchen getting her ready for the dance recital. She was facing the foyer. She said, "Mom, that same man I always see just walked down the stairs and into the living room." She described him as "strange looking" and about 20 to 30 years old. She said she has seen him at school before, too. He always smiles at her. She says that she can see "a bit more of him" than she does of her grandpa, who died on Dec. 15th, the same date as the Silver Bridge collapse. She went on to tell me that her grandpa "floats" through the window all the time. He talks to her until she goes to sleep. She said his face looks "windy." She doesn't always see his whole body. "Pop" first came to visit her when she was only two and half – right after he died… She describes this other man as having brown eyes, brown hair, a black and brown checkered shirt, and black pants. I'll send you a picture of what she drew. What do you make of this? She knows nothing of this phenomenon. Last Sunday night, she said a man wearing a black *mask* walked through the wall of her bedroom. It was the first one to really make her afraid. Like mother, like daughter, I suppose… She is definitely *not* prone to lying or storytelling. I told her she has a "gift" and to not be afraid of it. I told her to challenge these spirits. I'm totally freaked out at this point.

-Harriet 6/10/02

In the following letter, after having dreams about a muse with dark hair and blue eyes, Harriet amazingly predicts the coming of the "Kitchen Mothman" photo, where something similar to a Thunderbird or Garuda was captured on film looking into our kitchen window; it had apparently followed me home after I had seen it coming out of a tree. My sister Spring, who has dark hair and blue eyes, took the photo. It was taken in the summer of 1973, around the time Harriet dreamed of me running from an entity. A year or two after Harriet's prediction below, the photo was randomly found. The Garuda was first identified by my young son. The window in which the entity appears is the same window Spring had dreams about – where she saw Dad's head surrounded by swirling balls of light. Our dad had died just a few months before the photograph was taken. Questions thus arise… Had my deceased father somehow engineered the taking of the photograph? Had he merged with the entity in some fashion? Was it his *spirit that had come out of the tree when I was alone on the lane?*

You know that woman whose voice I feel I should know? She has been visiting me in my dreams again. She has blue eyes and dark hair. I just get bits and pieces, but it is about WV. I wonder who she is. She has visited me three times since January. It is obvious she "knows" me. I have also dreamed about you "catching" something on film in WV. It is something paranormal that has *already* been shot. It is the feeling I wake up with in the pit of my stomach that makes me think this is *really* real.

Last night I slept in the guest bedroom, where all of the weird stuff happens. I kept seeing flashes of "sparkler-like" light. Then I began to see, all around me, figures with a bluish cast. I was completely awake. This wasn't a dream. I didn't feel anything menacing about it. Perhaps they were my "protectors." My friend – who took me to that séance where your dad said you had a "protector" – told me that I have a "Tibetan" protector. So you aren't the first person to tell me about glowing balls of light in Tibet. Speaking of which, the thing I saw in 1968, which morphed into the "Virgin Mary" and then into an "Indian guide," originally appeared to be over 7' tall, with huge eyes. Its eyes were huge, deep, and dark, without eyelids. The head was large and the neck thin. There was no mouth to speak of. There appeared to be almost a "coffee stain" on the face. The base color of the face was like a dingy, beige caulk or putty. The skin was porous and seemed to have a texture, like someone who had had serious acne. It gave off a strong odor. It was musty and mossy, unlike anything I had ever smelled before. The odor itself was "hypnotizing."

It was dressed in a dark brown cloak, cinched at the waist with a high collar. I couldn't see its feet, and it never touched the ground. It glided most of the time, at treetop level. I never saw it "walk." It dropped down to study me more. It spoke to me telepathically. The "voice" was strong and commanding, directing me to urgently "leave at once" with it. I was paralyzed... I couldn't move. My feet were glued to the blacktop lane. Frankly, I'm unclear whether or not I left with the being. For all we know, this could be the same entity appearing differently to us in different situations. I have the creeps writing about it, but not the terror that used to grip me before... It is really hitting home now about the "illusion" that the ego is the true self. I understand now that this feeling I've had of being "out there on my own" is simply ego-based. There really is *nothing* outside of me. This "oneness" I seek is already there. You tried to get this concept across to me early on, but it is only now coming to my consciousness. It's such a wonderful concept. It is a great feeling of peacefulness to finally understand that the "connectedness" I so desired was already there.

-Harriet 6/12/02

We apparently have a ghost that keeps jiggling the doorknob to the garage. Our dog goes crazy when it happens. It seems to do it either when I am about to fall asleep, or just as I am getting up. I heard a bang this time instead of a jiggle. And now, the doorknob is noticeably bent, like someone hit it with a hammer. I have told the ghost to please move along... By the way, today happens to be the 20th anniversary of the Anti-Nuke Rally in NYC, which I attended with Neal Mindrum. He and I helped carry a large white bird float from Soho to Central Park. We went right past Rockefeller Center – the "valley of the shadow of death." I saved Neal's life at one point that day. He was about to step in front of a speeding truck down in Soho when I grabbed him. Interestingly, the night before, we had encountered some kind of invisible entity, maybe a Bigfoot, while camping on Bear Mountain. It came after us after we got our tent pitched. The foliage was clearly parting and moving, and we could hear twigs snapping with each footstep. But we could see nothing where the body should have been. The hair stood up on my body as I watched it moving. I quickly pulled the tent out of the ground – stakes and all – and threw it in the trunk. Then we got the hell out of there, shotgun in hand. I am now wondering if this wasn't "protector activity," in the sense that this Invisible Bigfoot, or whatever it was, put my nervous system on high alert, which allowed me to quickly notice that Neal was in trouble the following day, and to successfully react. We got a heads up prior to a tragedy. It makes me wonder if we didn't encounter an invisible Mothman. Maybe Mothman and Bigfoot are related species. Bigfoot and Thunderbird do appear together on Native totems.

-Andy 6/12/02

You'll love this. While I was out, my husband got a call from our old neighbor, Red Brown, from Woodward Drive. Red is in Columbus visiting his cousin, who lives not more than a mile from me. His cousin's daughter is graduating from OSU. President Bush is speaking at the commencement. Too bad you aren't here to pick Red's brain.

-Harriet 6/14/02

Red Brown stopped by for about an hour on his way back to Charleston. He was very nice but came "armed" with lots of pictures. I heard lots of stories about old man Bishara, the industrialist who employed a lot of people on Woodward Drive. He described Bishara as a "paranoiac" (sic). He was telling me all about our old Woodward drive playmate David Turner. Evidently Turner lives in Jackson Hole, WY. Red visits him frequently. Red just kept staring at me creepily. Yuck… I took him outside on the screened porch, because I didn't want him surveying my house… Now, for the strange part… I started asking him about the last time he saw Mothman witness Tommy Burnham. Get this… He hasn't seen Tommy since the last time *we* saw Tommy in 1969! As many times as Red was in Florida to see Tommy's mom, Phyllis – whom he was dating – he never saw Tommy. Ever! I find that very strange. Could Tommy be in an institution somewhere? Last night, right before I was dropping off to sleep, I had the most detailed and clear vision of the "being" that came out of the woods at me on Woodward Lane. I saw its face in detail… The skin was reptilian, with a coarseness to it. The eyes were deep, dark, and inky. The skin was the color of putty. There was a slight nose. I don't recall seeing any ears. I jumped about ten feet out of bed when I saw it, which scared the hell out of my husband. There was also a little discoloration of the skin toward the chin area, as if someone had spilled coffee on its face. More and more of this stuff is coming back to conscious memory. Lots of memories are flooding back. I'm still trying to deal with it…

-Harriet 6/17/02

Here's a coincidence of note… In Loren Coleman's Mothman book, on page 77 where he talks about Thunderbirds, he mentions a sighting in Brookfield, WI on Sept. 21st, 1988. A man was looking out the windows of Brookfield's Elmbrook Memorial Hospital when he saw something that could be interpreted as Mothman. My sister-in-law and her family live at the base of the hill beneath that hospital. I suppose it wouldn't do me any good to ask them if they saw or heard of this creature. Given their Catholicism, they would have seen it as an apparition of the Blessed Virgin… Speaking of which, do you remember the religious neighbor I told you about? My daughter was just down there. The neighbor was reading scripture to her about "sorcery," telling her that Harry Potter was against the Bible. I could spit nails. I know where she is going with this. She is mad because I'm going to make a life for myself by practicing hypnotherapy. She already told me yesterday that what I am doing is "evil" and against the Bible. I asked her if there was an 11th commandment: "Thou shalt not practice hypnotherapy or herbology." That was the end of that conversation… What she is angry about is her own life. She's stuck at home with a moody law enforcement officer who doesn't want her to go out into the world. So, she's using scripture to attack me. I'm not even going to dignify this B.S. with a response. If I react, she could get the church to attack me somehow when I go into business.

-Harriet 6/24/02

I've had a chance to read up on the famous mind control victim, Kathleen Sullivan. Sullivan claimed that she was at a programming base at Cockeysville, MD. Guess who lived there? That's right: me. Before my dad was transferred to Columbus, I lived for one year in Towson and six months in Cockeysville, which is a suburb of Baltimore. Many conscious memories are coming back to me. None seem similar to Sullivan's, thankfully. One must admit that it's a little strange that I lived in the same place… By the way, on the 20th of last month, there was definitely "someone" unseen here.

My dog was going crazy, and I kept hearing thuds and footsteps. While I have had this happen before, it is by no means a common occurrence in this house. I have a feeling that my dad was here today. My cousin saw a psychic, Gayle Pelz, recently. My dad came through to tell her about her own father having heart problems. Less than a week later, I got the three short rings on the bedroom phone followed by constant static and loss of phone service. It is *way* too weird… On a lighter note, my family reunion in WV was a stitch. My uncle's farm was the perfect place for it. You should have seen the row of tents. My NSA cousin wasn't there. Supposedly he is on assignment at Ft. Bragg, but no one really knows. I tried to get my CIA aunt to reveal something about the Mothman events on Woodward Drive and Pt. Pleasant. When I started asking questions, it was like someone flipped a switch. After what you told me about the brainwashing agents go through, I would have to say that this is exactly what I was witnessing in her. She told me absolutely nothing, but talked endlessly. I'm not overly paranoid, but I could see that I was being given a song-and-dance routine.

-Harriet 7/1/0

Here we go again… Yesterday morning at about 4:45 a.m., my daughter came into my bedroom and woke me up. She told me that the men with the "bug-eyes" were back. I told her it was just a dream. She disagreed… I heard three short rings on the bedroom phone at about 7 p.m. Then, last night, she got up and told me there were sirens all over the place. I didn't hear them because I had my fan on full blast and the TV blaring. It turns out our neighbor's house was on fire. My daughter said that she had dreamed about it the night before. God… This is just what I need: more Mothman prophecies. This one was minor but, still, it's unsettling. I only talk about this stuff with her when she wants to. I try not to make an issue of it. Kids are cruel and would make fun of her if they knew. I know how it feels to grow up "knowing" what is going to happen next.

-Harriet 7/9/02

I'm coming into a period of high paranormal activity. I can always tell because the dream activity picks up. I see "flashes." Strange things happen with me and electronics… I'm getting a little nervous about facing the lane and the house where I used to live. But I have to… And since you had a sighting there, you probably need to do it as much as I do. The dream of that house on the hill, and talking to that blue-eyed man (who advises us to move forward with our research) is back. I've probably had this dream ten times now. I've never had a dream this many times.

-Harriet 7/10/02

I have ordered a galvanic skin response (GSR) meter for my trip back to WV. Psychics often have no GSR, meaning they do not naturally impede signals. The meter gives a general reading of a person's electrical field. One of the women they recently investigated on *Ghosthunters* had a GSR of 0, yet had high EM readings in her house. There was a paranormal incident where she got deep scratches on her leg in the shower. It reminded me of the scratches you said you got on your arm while in the shower. When the *Ghosthunters* lady started the water running, she suddenly got the smell of putrid earth. Then she hallucinated that she had been transported to some location outside, like a grave. Her husband pulled her out of the shower, and she had deep scratches....

-Andy 7/13/02

I've had a couple of strange experiences this past week. The first one took place in the guest bedroom. I opened the closet door, and a very strong rush of cold air passed through me. It blew my hair back like a gust of wind and nearly pushed me over. The next day, I was walking through the hardware store and felt the most inexplicable feeling of heat engulf my lower back and radiate around my abdomen. It felt like this presence had taken hold of me. I've never had anything happen like that before. My daughter says spirits always come through her bedroom windows... After reading what you said about those scratches, I'm really curious. I have smelled several strange odors; one is "earthy" like dirt; another is definitely cinnamon, which is linked to paranormal activity. Another smell that I have gotten up to check on at night has been the smell of natural gas – like the burners on the stove were left on. And twice within the last year, I have smelled something like a match that has just been blown out. I smelled that once after I awoke to find myself outside the house. As for Bigfoot, I recently talked to a dance dad who, for a long time, didn't believe in what he calls "paranormal shit." Now, however, he believes he saw Bigfoot about a year ago near Jackson, OH, on one of the major trails.

I've been having another memory of an incident by the Copen's old house, which was the last one on our lane. I used to hike beyond it and up to the top of the hill, where you could see Casdorph Rd. and Sissonville Rd. Something happened there, something I'm blocking out. I remember Mom saying I had been gone "for hours." I had no idea what she meant. I was about 8 or 9 at the time. I know it was the weekend, because my dad was home, and it was warm and sunny... Today is Mom's 65th birthday. She is leaving to go to Las Vegas tomorrow to meet her sister, who was Civilian Commander at China Lake Naval Base.

-Harriet 7/14/02

Harriet, this is pretty interesting and "coincidental…" You, Sharon, and I saw the energy field and wispy beings on Woodward Drive on July 19th, 2002. This was *exactly* fifty years, to the day, from the first of two famous UFO incidents over Washington, D.C. The first occurred on July 19th, 1952. The second occurred a week later, on July 26th, 1952. A week after our energy field event, you and I visited the Sugar Grove Naval facility in eastern WV. We hurriedly drove back on July 26th, 2002 to Charleston, to attend the first night of our high school reunion – exactly 50 years after the *second* D.C. UFO sighting. You predicted we would meet an "Army doctor" at the reunion, which we did. He lived on the same block as my wife's uncle in El Paso. Bizarrely, there was yet *another* UFO incident in D.C. on the night of our high school reunion! The blog *Xymphora* had this to say about this most recent UFO incident:

> It has been reported that two F-16 jets from Andrews Air Force Base were scrambled early on July 26 after radar detected an unknown aircraft in Washington, D. C. airspace. Local residents reported seeing a "bright blue or orange ball moving very fast, being chased by jets." There had been a UFO incident in Washington, D. C. involving Andrews Air Force Base exactly 50 years before (the first of the two sightings was on July 19, 1952 and the second was on July 26, 1952). *The Washington Post* had reminded everyone of it with an article published on July 21, 2002. Therefore, those inclined to see such things were well primed to see all manner of suspicious lights in the early morning of July 26, 2002. Note that the article was published two days *after* the fiftieth anniversary of the first 1952 sighting, but five days *before* the fiftieth anniversary of the *second* sighting. This is starting to look like the set-up of a false UFO incident. After the article was published, people would be looking to the sky on July 26. [It's not much of a stretch to think] that the military has some odd [experimental craft that is] capable of displaying colored lights and flying around like a UFO. It could have been sent up on July 26 with the F-16's in hot pursuit, all being viewed by people looking for such things because of the July 21 *Washington Post* article. Nothing was ever found, because "whatever it was disappeared." Why would the military do this? I quote from the July 27 article:
>
>> "It was a routine launch," said Lt. Col. Steve Chase, a senior officer with the [113th] Wing, which keeps pilots and armed jets on 24-hour alert at Andrews, to respond

to incidents as part of an air defense system protecting Washington after the Sept. 11 terrorist attacks."

Note that the article states "as part of an air defense system protecting Washington after the Sept. 11 terrorist attacks." This little UFO incident, at one fell swoop: 1) proved that Washington was safely protected from harm by the jets at Andrews Air Force Base; and 2) emphasized that Andrews Air Force Base was not in a position to provide such protection prior to September 11, thus "explaining" why no planes were scrambled from there on the morning of September 11 to intercept Flight 77's attack on the Pentagon. There has been much speculation about why no intercepting jets were sent from Andrews, as it was only 10 miles from the Pentagon. The site *The Emperor's New Clothes* has written a lot on this issue, and in particular how the original websites for The District of Columbia Air National Guard and the 113th Wing had been oddly altered so as to remove references to how ready they were to respond in the event of an emergency. We can now see that they *are* ready to respond, having I guess "learned" something from the events of September 11. This would not be the first time that a fake UFO flap was used by the military to accomplish propaganda goals.

It is interesting that Mothman, or whatever it was, would decide to manifest to you, me and Sharon on that anniversary. What exactly was Mothman trying to say? At it most basic, it seems to be saying that there is some connection between major military UFO psyops and the things that happened on Woodward Drive. And certainly, one can say that UFO-related genres like NASA, satellite technology, atomic energy, and military intelligence were all represented in our 'hood. The work of local petrochemicals like Carbide was crucial in developing wiring and armaments for aircraft of all kinds.

-Andy 8/2/02

Remember, you and I both "saw" UFOs on the night of the 26th. We both intuited them. Yours was green and glowing, while mine was "underwater." That in itself is noteworthy, given my premonitions that night.

-Harriet 8/2/02

I just visited my book designer, Joseph Miller. He told me that he used hypnotherapy as a "transitional technology," as a way to move past obstacles and into a new time of his life. He also knows a hell of a lot about the UFO phenomenon. Joseph has had a few run-ins with a haunted spot on Guemes Island, in Washington State, which sound similar to our experiences on Woodward Drive. He feels that the woods *themselves* are haunted – or *were*, since they have since been cut down. He understood perfectly when I described what it was like to face a morphing energy field... I am currently reading *Entering the Circle*, which is about Russian indigenous shamanism. One of the ideas in the book is that in order to find our true calling, each of us must work hard to find out which of these seven "spirit twins" resides in our internal "spirit lake": healer, magus, teacher, messenger, protector, warrior, or executor (doer). I actually feel like my experiences in 1967 with Mothman were designed to help me with this decision, but I couldn't remember any of it until the "cloud" was removed during a recent energy treatment.

-Andy 8/5/02

My niece, Sharon Moore, got a treatment from Andee Boothe recently. It was amazing how fast she got right to Sharon's issues with her mother. Boothe bypasses the conscious mind (and maybe even the subconscious) and asks the *body* what is going on, resulting in a very fast treatment – what might take 2 to 4 hypnotherapy sessions. She then simply has the patient repeat back positive suggestions. She even has the patient repeat back reflexive suggestions – for instance, that they forgive themselves for ever having felt forced to use defense mechanisms. It is an elegant twist that is powerful and efficient. Andee and I are attending a class next week based on aboriginal medicine. One "taps" the body in order to reprogram it.

-Andy 9/11/02

I dreamed of Tommy as if we were children again. It was the re-telling of an actual event that took place. It was the day he came to me crying, asking me if I believed that a flying saucer had landed in his yard – that these aliens were visiting. It was the day I learned to ride a bike. He showed me the marks where they had landed. There were three of them in the grass, and they went down into the clay mud. In the dream, I relived feeling baffled. The marks were clearly there, including some burnt grass, which I feel that he could *not* have done himself. I felt he couldn't have done it then, and I *know* it now. I saw the dark circles under his bloodshot eyes in the dream. It all seemed so real. I flew off and landed down on Woodward Drive. I haven't had that happen in a while. A couple of days before that, I had a dream with your voice in it. I never physically saw you, so it was weird. But I recognized the place… It was the area that had the rocks jutting out of the hillside on the way to Romney, WV – the place I had dreamed of *before* we actually saw it on our trip. I woke up from that dream extremely troubled. I don't know why. Sometimes after a dream, you're left with more of a "feeling" than anything else.

-Harriet 9/24/02

In the following letter, Harriet amazingly predicts that my long term marriage will implode after the birth of my first child. She only gave her opinion after I had asked her outright if she thought we should go ahead and have a second child… As it turned out, during the course of my Mothman investigation it became clear that most, if not all, of the paranormal events I was experiencing (e.g., poltergeists, synchronicities, etc.) were caused not by something in my own personal Mothman history, but were the result of my wife's situation. It seems that the phenomenon was trying to warn me about the impending breakup. It wasn't until two or three years into The Mothman's Photographer *project that I began to suspect that the paranormal events in my life were being triggered by my wife, whose personality had radically changed. The changes had begun during a period when I was harangued by various "skeptical" disin-formationists on the Mothman discussion list. Some of the provoca-teurs seemed very interested in witchcraft and the occult. Due to the parallel timing of events, I naturally wondered if occultists on the list had attempted to influence my relationship with my wife…*

Interestingly, the properties owned by my wife's family (in the towns of Corrales and Cuba, NM, and on Indian School Road in Albuquerque) are all located in old Indian settlements. In fact, Corrales and Cuba have had their share of Navajo witchcraft incidents, including witch burnings. In Clyde Kluckholn's impor-tant anthropological work, Navajo Witchcraft, *he cites Corrales and Cuba as villages rife with Frenzy Witchcraft, which most often involves enchanting women with magic – making them fall in love against their will… This type of witchcraft is not present in other nearby tribes and so is thought to have been a European form brought in either by Pueblo Indians (who were feared by the Navajo for their ability to manipulate reality through supernatural means) or by tribes from California who had prior Spanish/Moorish contacts… Interestingly, the Navajo also perform something called "Eagle Pit" witchcraft, which involves casting a spell on someone using the mightiest of predatory birds. First, the witch must catch*

*an eagle and place it in a ceremonial pit. After giving the eagle a
piece of meat, the witch tells the eagle the name of the victim and
gives it instructions. Once the eagle is released back to the wild, the
curse is enacted. Eagle Pit witchcraft is thought to be among the
most potent and effective forms of Navajo witchcraft. The victim
often wastes away and dies.*

Remember when I picked up on the gender of your child when you told
me that your wife was pregnant? Recently, more pieces of the puzzle came
together for me. I think your "Dr. Jekyll and Mr. Hyde" subpersonalities are a
reflection of what you live with and are pounded with. The "dark side" of you
is mostly environmental; I am absolutely sure of this. You absorb negativity
and then reflect it. You don't see it as "negative" because you have been conditioned to believe it is all so wonderful and good. For this I am deeply sorry.
That is *not* the inner you. This is what I have been trying to tell you all along.
You are on this constant path to enlightenment because you are being driven
to it by a negative vibration. But if that's what it takes, then so be it. You will
only benefit. There is much more that I have read concerning you, vibra-
tionally, which I have kept to myself. I don't think you could handle what I
"see," and I don't like the idea of ever "hurting" you. When the things I had
previously "read" were confirmed in front of me during my meeting with your
wife, it couldn't be denied... You are in a period of extreme and profound
growth. With that will come disenchantment, but it is part of the process. You
already know, subconsciously, what I am talking about... You will continue
to grow because – and you'll just have to trust me on this – you will *not* have
a choice. If I told you what I see is about to happen, you wouldn't believe
me anyway. I'll just let it happen, and let you experience it. It was eating me
alive when we all met in California, but I couldn't say anything. My heart
was aching on your behalf. That "ominous" feeling was evident when I met
her, just as it was when you remote-viewed Tommy and realized that he *knew*
you were viewing him. Always remember that you are *not* a nameless, faceless
being who exists only to cater to the whims of someone else's insecurity, no
matter how much they try to mask it. You are an incredible, highly evolved
human being who can teach us all a lesson. You've been following the path,
now stay with it. You will *have* to...

-Harriet 9/25/02

*The same day as Harriet's email, I happened to get a treatment at a
small healing conference I was attending. The master who was treating me seemed to think that I had picked up an "entity" somewhere*

*along the way, which needed to be removed. Incredibly, some of
the same things Harriet had mentioned showed up in the session,
including the words "ominous" and "disenchantment." It seems as
if the master had also seen, psychically, that my marriage was about
to end, but did not feel comfortable telling me. This reluctance may
have been because my wife's mother was also attending the conference… When I privately asked the master if the entity, called a
"secondary matrix," had come from my wife, the master stated that
it had not. It was some sort of archetypal feminine force, perhaps
from a past life. Remarkably, over the next few years, several other
psychics would make similar comments regarding this force around
me.*

Harriet, I just had an energy session in front of a class here in Seattle.
According to the teacher, who is a Qi Gong master, my "body" indicated
that I needed work on my 8th chakra, which is outside of the body – above
the head. This is where we see the Garuda "wings" in the chakra charts. In
drawings of the caduceus, the wings emanate from the head itself, which
is called the "medula" – the same name as the psychic you visited, who
told you about my dad and the "protector." The 8th chakra is the portal
through which we access other dimensions, and where things we have
carried from the past – even from past lives – reside. It holds knowledge
of the future as well. Issues with "women" and "humility" came up for
me, seemingly from the past. It got really weird when the master said that
I had a "secondary matrix" in my pituitary gland. This is akin to having
another energetic being, or subpersonality, in one's "third eye." It appeared
to be controlling my adrenal glands. My body indicated that this link
needed to be severed, so the master severed it, by initiating a "clockwise
turn" within my third eye. As this was done, I felt as if I was traveling
through a time tunnel. I felt a huge expansion of consciousness. I felt
heat going out through my sacrum. The master whispered something
about me being a "freak of nature." It is apparently rare for this issue to
come up… The master described the secondary matrix as "ominous."
Naturally this worried me, so I asked more about it. However, the master
seemed to hold back, for fear of telling me something I couldn't handle…
I heard gasps in the crowd as the "secondary matrix" left the room. One
frightened woman asked if it had entered someone else in the room; the
reply was that it had not. After the session, I truly felt different, as if a
confusing cloud had been taken away. Everything felt "clear." My mother-
in-law said that I looked completely different, as did a couple of other
people I saw later, who didn't even know about my session. Interestingly,
I immediately started remembering more about the events with Tommy
on Woodward Drive. Perhaps the ritual I did with him on Woodward

Drive – where we shared a blood-brother pact to get back together in 2001 and trade back our plastic shrunken heads – was responsible for the clouding of my third eye. If that link was severed, it might explain why you immediately dreamed of Tommy.

-Andy 9/25/02

Later in the series, psychics Mina Bast and Eugenia Macer-Story both saw that a female archetype had "entered" me when I was a child (see The Mothman's Photographer III, *Chapters 20 and 25). Bast even specified that I was about 8 years old at the time, corresponding roughly to my experiences at Tommy's house during Mothman. Ironically, Andee Boothe felt that I had also "lost something" at the time of the encounters. Had I lost some measure of freedom? Had I been sent on some sort of cosmic mission? In addition to viewing all of this as the workings of my own mind or the collective unconscious, one could also interpret the troublesome entity as any of the following: Mut, Isis, Lilith, Kali, Nekhbet, Sekhmet, Bast, Amaunet, Hathor, Minerva, Kuanyin, Tara, Maya, or the Virgin Mary, whom Harriet feels she may have seen at Tommy's house in 1968…*

I should tell you about something strange… The night before last, at 4 a.m., I woke up outside in the backyard in my pajamas and bare feet. I noticed my predicament because it was cold and the grass was dewy. My feet were freezing. I didn't panic… I calmly walked back to the house and upstairs to bed. The back sliding door was open. Later, I had a hard time believing it was real, but there was grass on the floor and in the bed. Beats me…

-Harriet 10/6/02

I just got a frantic call from my daughter's teacher. A parent had jumped all over her for allowing me to lead an anti-anxiety "visualization" yesterday in class. The parent said it was "un-Christian" and that we were "worshipping the devil." The teacher was trying to explain the whole hypnotherapy thing to the parent. I told her that she didn't have to; I told her to have the parent call me. But I didn't attempt to explain it to her, either. *She* is the one assessing this as "evil"; I won't defend something that isn't… You run into this crap here in Ohio. And this parent is a high school teacher! She and her husband are both "ministers." Whatever… It is interesting to be on the forefront of something, watching a new consciousness unfold. Two steps forward, one step back… My mantra is: "Don't react." When she called me, I complimented her on what a fine son she had raised. He came to her about something he didn't feel comfortable with, rather than go along with it. She told me that I sounded like a Christian. So, I told her that I *was* one.

-Harriet 10/8/02

On Monday, Oct. 14th, 2002, Ann Marlowe (age 62, of Los Angeles), Noreen Borino (age 52, of Elko, NV), and I we were returning from a day trip to Mendocino, CA. At just after 7 p.m., while traveling south on U.S. Highway 101, just north of San Rafael, CA, we witnessed a most unusual event. I was the first to notice an unusually bright object streaking in a southeast to northwesterly direction. I remarked that it must be a shooting star. Then I realized it wasn't dying out, but becoming more intense. The object emitted a bright white, bluish "spray" contrail, unlike those of familiar jets. The spray looked like a common firework – a "sparkler." It was flying too fast to be an F-18 fighter jet. I estimate its speed at 1500-1700 mph. The object took a sharp due west, almost in a hook shape. I pulled over so we could all watch. The object was huge, larger than anything I've ever seen flying in the sky. It appeared to be cylindrical in shape, but not quite what one would think of as a missile. It was more cigar-shaped.

Then, in an instant, a beam of light came from overhead, and the object disintegrated. All of us were horrified. We sat speechless for a moment, not knowing what we had just witnessed. Having just finished a conversation about UFOs, we were very shaken. I offered the only other possible explanation, which was that it was a launch from Vandenburg AFB south of the Bay Area. I had a hard time rationalizing why there would be such a display over a populated area. It was still rush hour in the Bay Area, and the Giants and St. Louis Cardinals were still playing a game at Pac Bell Park. Usually such launches are done in the middle of the night, and sent directly out to sea. All we were sure of was that thousands of other people must have seen it. Fifteen minutes later, we ran into Pierre Ropel of (age 52, of Los Angeles) and Eddie Scott (age 38, of Charleston, SC). They had also witnessed the event. Ropel and Scott saw the beam of light intercept the object, and the resulting explosion. Scott pointed out that he had put his fingers in his ears to muffle the sound of a sonic boom that never came. This means that the object must have been larger and higher up than we initially thought. There was a resulting "glow" in the sky that lasted for over an hour. The "glow" was like nothing ever seen by any of us.

That evening, all three major networks reported that they had been inundated with calls about the object. Three stations actually had footage of the event. The "story" appeared to be a "prepared" statement. The reports from the various stations didn't deviate at all. The reports stated that a Minuteman II missile had been launched from Vandenburg and then intercepted by a missile launched from the Marshall Islands. This was a "routine exercise" according to the report. The resulting "glow" in the sky was attributed to "atmospheric conditions." But those who witnessed this event feel it was anything but routine. After those 11 o'clock news reports, the event was never to be heard of again. This is odd since everyone was still talking about the event days later. All five of us did not feel well the next day. We all were suffering from headaches and nausea.

-Harriet 10/21/02

My psychic ability has been increasing lately. I picked up a couple more clients this week. It is really amazing to go through this process with patients, watching them gain new understanding of their life. I was able to track the visualizations of my most recent client right along with them. I actually see it in my third eye. I explained to them how I am able to tap into their visions. They couldn't believe that I was describing things as they were thinking them. I explained to them that I wasn't just "reading" their mind, but was seeing into them. I guess I didn't freak them out too badly, since they are coming back.

-Harriet 10/27/02

I *still* don't feel well, two weeks after viewing that missile explosion. Everyone I've spoken to about the incident seems to lean toward the side of "UFO," which I find odd. I think it was a missile shot down by a laser.

-Harriet 10/28/02

My dreams have been about you lately. They started with you as a little boy, and continued for six straight nights, ending with you at your present age. I saw you on the hillside on Woodward at about age 9. You were hanging out with your favorite tree. I really felt some pain you were feeling at the time. I think you were mad at your dad. These dreams progressed to when you lost your father. I felt all the feelings associated with that. Then I had one about when you were in high school. The most devastating dream was when your mother remarried. I felt *all* of your feelings of abandonment. All of these dreams were intense. I woke up crying each night. That just doesn't happen to me normally. I would rather hold off discussing the last dream. I can say that I saw purple light streaming up from your root chakra and out of your third eye. The light entered *my* third eye. This dream may have something to do with my being extremely psychic lately. My whole life is about to change for the better. The first step in eliminating issues of abandonment is letting them come to the surface.

-Harriet 10/29/02

Regarding that mosque around the corner from my house, which the D.C. Sniper attended... There were always guys hanging around there. It had a grocery store and pool hall attached to it. I went in there a couple of times. A local architect wanted me to take some photos. He needed them for the city application to turn the building into a historical landmark... I actually got a kick out of it when they would blast their Islamic music out over the neighborhood. A couple of times, after having a few beers, I turned on competing music. I had a 300-watt public address system left over from my Austin band days. I would play Tibetan chants at the Muslims. It was all in fun. This was back in the mid-1990s when things were pretty crazy in the neighborhood. Crack was still readily available. There were many shootings with both semi-automatic *and* fully automatic weapons. Several people were killed on our block and surrounding blocks, including our next-door neighbor. It was not a place for the timid.

-Andy 10/30/02

Last night's dream tells me that I need to pay attention to the number "4" in association with you and Tommy. I dreamed of four stick bundles. They were thin and straight. I interpret my dream of the four stick bundles as relating to the Woodward Drive mystery. They stood out as being the only "real" things in a dream otherwise cluttered with "conscious chatter." The bundles seemed to be beyond ordinary consciousness. They reside in a "nonlocal" psychic space. At this "location," I am able to dip into universal consciousness – a non-dual dimension. I have dreamed of it many times before. Sometimes it is an open "book" that has all the secrets of knowledge. Other times, it is an object, or even an entity like Bigfoot. When I was kid, I had some kind of subconscious relationship with a Bigfoot. He seemed to "telepath" to me at night. I dreamed of him repeatedly for years and years. He was always outside the kitchen window. Each time I dreamed of him, my fear of him subsided just a bit. Eventually, when I was probably in my 30's, he turned into a dog. I never saw him again in the dream. I have dreamed of the kitchen window since, but he is not in the dream... By the way, I tried to call Tommy Burnham today. The ring sounded normal, but there was no answer.

-Andy 10/31/02

Are you really calling Tommy? I wish I had the guts. Andy, he scares me. I don't like what I see. He is not stable. I have seen the same vision all along: him going "nuts" when you tell him who you are. Just hearing the sound of your voice may trigger all that may not be "right" in him. Just make sure you ground yourself before *and* after you talk to him. Be very conscious of anything he may trigger in you. I think I'm more interested in what he triggers in you than your actual conversation. Bathe yourself in a protective light before you talk. Perhaps this will all turn out better than either one of us could ever predict… Interesting about your dream… I constantly dream about a stream, possibly the Elk River, holding "secrets." This has been a recurrent dream for me since childhood… In July, you dreamed about a spaceship underwater. Your dream happened the night you had the vision about the transient who lived in my house and wound up dead in the river. Then, a couple of days later, after you spent the evening with your brother, you saw them looking for a body at the mouth of the Elk. That was indeed strange. It threw me for a loop. The strangest thing was the intensity of your vision about the murder associated with my house. It haunts me… Water does seem to hold information… By the way, Ian, the hypnotherapist from England, who saw the famous Portsmouth UFO, was really impressed that you visualized the face of the D.C. Sniper prior to his being caught. All of this psychic stuff is a little too much for Ian, but he is interested. He asked me if you had "special powers." I told him "yes."

-Harriet 10/31/02

Yesterday, I consciously remembered a recurring "alternate" landscape within my dreams. This place has special healing powers. I have been dreaming about it for years, but never remembered it while awake. I remembered the entire landscape by tracking one specific dream that I had earlier this week. In that dream, I was making audio recordings using *water* as the medium – not audio or videotape. When I poured the water out of a container, the recording played back. Another dream I had involved Red Brown's house on Woodward Drive… As I was approaching his house, I looked toward where it should have been, but saw nothing but a "void." When I got past it, I looked back again. It was still behind some sort of black veil. But, when I chose to rise up and float like Mothman, the house came into view. Instead of it being their usual house, it was an enormous white mansion, as big as the White House. It was covered with symbols, sort of like a Christmas tree… I also dreamed of a wonderful "alternate" landscape that lies somewhere between Charleston, WV and Columbus, OH. There were sand dunes and snow-capped mountains with shimmering glaciers. The dream had a profound healing effect on me… FYI, I have decided to quit trying to call Tommy. I will send him a certified letter to coincide with the upcoming Leonid meteor shower. This is supposed to be the best showing of them for the next 100 years.

-Andy 11/4/02

I am in a period of profound psychic activity. It all started three weeks ago, with that missile sighting in CA... I see the "Big Bird" appearing close to you in the Pacific Northwest. This time, it is in association with a one-shot catastrophe. Now, for you... After three nights of dreaming the same vision about you, I feel I must tell you what I am dreaming about. I have awakened the last three nights to see you sitting in a straight-backed wood chair, painted white. You are sitting in an empty room. All four walls of the room are painted in a different color. The walls begin to move in on you. You curl up into a little ball in the chair. What troubles me about this vision is the look on your face. It is a look that says, "I don't believe this is happening to me." I pick up so much in the course of a day. Much of it I feel you wouldn't want me to relay, but this recent one bothered me... I've really enjoyed all the stuff you sent on the D.C. Sniper. Did you see *Alias* last night? It was about programming children for future spy work. It *really* bothered me... A couple of people have asked me about you, as if they are concerned about your interest in conspiracies. I have to laugh. They just don't know you. They see the "serious" side of you and freak out. Little do they know the goofball who lurks underneath. You can take us out of West Virginia, but you can't take the West Virginia out of us...

-Harriet 11/4/02

I had a bizarre dream with you in it last night. I dreamt that there were news crews in the driveway across the street. They were interviewing a little boy about strange "blue lights" that he had been seeing for 10 straight nights, in which *hieroglyphics* had somehow been written on the driveway. When we went up to the little boy, he told us to turn to the west and look at the sky. In the black of the sky, there was an intense area of blue sky. We both smiled at him like we "knew." I sat bolt upright in bed. I looked outside and there was a blue glow to the night sky. It totally wigged me out. I haven't stopped shaking since.

-Harriet 11/6/02

Dropping the "I" is really the only way to reach out to others. At that point, one no longer has a "me" to be defensive about and protect. Balance comes when the grip on the "I" is released. This doesn't necessarily mean that you give into peer pressure, however. All one can do is be who one is. Sometimes you may feel like being happy and "centered" despite the corruption around you. On the other hand, those who believe that *everything* is currently "okay" are seriously mistaken. Those who refuse to see the corruption right before their eyes are deluding themselves. The treadmill of class, money, and hierarchy will – for all but the top 1% of the population – end in a big crash. Many who typically follow the rules will no longer do so, once they realize that they have been screwed. The reptile in us all will grow, resulting in increased toxicity. As Stephen Dobyns said, "What is virtue but the lack of strong temptation? Better to leave us with our lie of being good…"

-Andy 11/13/02

Something major shifted in me last night. What you wrote back to me is exactly what I was trying to get across to you. You have been the one male who has not tried to bash me for trying to expand spiritually. Women generally aren't "allowed" to do these kinds of things. We have to "take care" of all the men on the planet, to free them up to do whatever they want… I have been working on my shadow traits – sort of "cleaning house." I realized last night, while pondering over my disagreements with you, that you rarely received attention growing up… You had to deal with issues of self earlier; you had a head start. And you are right, the best place to seek acceptance is not outside, but from within. You are absolutely right about my "fears" about psychic ability. I'm not afraid of the ability in and of itself, but in sharing it. It's not that I don't have confidence in what I see. It's just that it often serves little purpose to share it. I go through extreme vacillations regarding whether to share my intuitive knowledge of others' medical problems. It is something I have struggled with since I was a child.

-Harriet 11/15/02

I have read numerous times that Edgar Allan Poe was thought to have been an abductee. He was tortured most of his life by "memories" of such… One of the women I saw the "missile" with had a strange childhood. She grew up in Wyoming on an isolated farm. She told me of the light globes that would appear for consecutive nights on her farm. Family members and neighbors would gather to watch them when they would appear. She said that the globes would just "hang" about and then dart away. It was during one of those times that she saw a "hand" appear through her door. It was not a human hand. This began her lifelong fear of the dark. Amazingly, after her session with our hypnotherapy teacher, she has been just fine. She also spent a great deal explaining Mormon doctrine to me. It is basically a "paleo-seti" theory. I was stunned, for "paleo-seti" is the term that got us kicked out of Sunday school that one time. She said that most of the inner circle know that Mormonism is based on a belief in ancient "aliens." This is why the Latter Day Saints are so drawn to Mayan culture. There is no doubt in my mind that she has had some form of "contact."

-Harriet 11/18/02

There was an article two weeks after the missile shootdown, verifying that the Army had successfully shot down a missile with a ground-based "laser cannon." It sounds like the media is trying to confuse everyone. Me and about 100,000 other people saw how it was destroyed from above. Perhaps we are being acclimated to war, without any mention of how extensively satellites would be involved in laser attacks, either directly or from drones.

-Harriet 11/22/02

This morning, I was watching *The Today Show*. They had this kid on who was the gunman in a school shooting in Paducah, KY about five years ago. He was 14 at the time of the shootings, and is now rotting away in the KY state reformatory. He killed three people who were praying at the time. He seriously wounded five, and left one in a wheelchair for life. He is speaking for the first time about why he did this. He started with the usual "I was bullied," but then admitted that he has a "mental problem." It got really interesting when he started to describe why he became so paranoid in the first place. Get this... He claimed that he would receive visitations from "monsters" in his room. They would wake him up. They would tap his legs or feet. He would see their eerie hands touch him. He would go numb. They would take him from his bed. These visitations started when he was very young and plagued him up until the time of the shootings.

-Harriet 11/26/02

My WTO documentary, *Verbatim: The Real Battle in Seattle,* is being shown around by the hip-hop artist who starred in it, DJ Novocaine. He has organized some viewings in San Francisco, Santa Fe, Taos, and Portland. A tie-in between Mothman and WTO is that something looking very much like Mothman was drawn on the door at the spot where protestors repeatedly clashed with Seattle Police. This spot just happens to be in front of the haunted building, 905 E. Pine, which Harriet remote-viewed for me as a test. Amazingly, she accurately saw that there had been a murder there... Strangely, her initials, "H.P.," were carved in the sidewalk, along with some Iberian markings similar to those

Kewaunee Lapseritis claims mean "place of protection." Also, Harriet's dad's favorite saying, "Big Brother is Watching You," was pasted on the telephone pole there. Following WTO, I was sick in bed for five weeks, after being gassed with white phosphorus in front of 905 E. Pine. An old Oddfellows ballroom is right next door.

-Andy 12/2/02

Conspiracy research *can* be a good adjunct to the spiritual path. I recently discovered that my theory about Tibetan lamas being reborn in America – perhaps under CIA auspices – was echoed in the work of the late T. Lobsang Rampa, who claimed he had formerly been a Tibetan lama. That lama, who was dying, had an important mission to complete, so his soul supposedly took over the body of a younger Englishman. Regardless of whether or not that is true, Rampa repeatedly stated that his difficult, painful mission – being sent to the West by Tibetan leaders, to die in America, the "Land of the Red Man" – was just the first in a long line of such missions. In a chapter concerning teleportation and its role in the spread of Buddhism, he states that "others will follow me" – that his mission was to "make it easier for them." One senses that the Tibetans focused their teleportation and reincarnation efforts on West Virginia and Ohio because these were recognized sacred areas. This sacred history might explain why Tibetan monks are said to have visited Pt. Pleasant prior to the filming of *The Mothman Prophecies*. When I dream of this beautiful alternate landscape between Charleston and Columbus, I may be seeing a visualization of this sacred area, some kind of Shambhala.

-Andy 12/22/02

So what *would* Jesus drive? I think he would drive a big, gas-guzzling pickup truck or Suburban because, after all, he *was* a carpenter. He would have to carry around his tools and materials… Did you see any of the show *Taken*? My son is still freaking out over the fact that the couple in the series went to visit a hypnotherapist in Seattle whose name was "Harriet." She was shot in the back by the government because of what she knew… A little freaky, but he will get over it… I am inclined to agree with you that conspiracy research could indeed be a good adjunct to the spiritual path. I wouldn't have thought that a year ago but, now, I've seen *too* much. I just read the article about scientists being murdered at Sugar Grove. The description in the article, about how Sugar Grove is laid out, matches exactly what I saw: steps going down, large rooms, and large screens where craft were being tracked in the world's oceans. God, it freaked me out. What I saw inside the mountain near George Washington's mansion, in Romney, also fits this mold. You have to realize that I have never read anything describing these installations before. So, this is validating my remote viewing skills, which is comforting. By the way, you may be right about Chinese involvement. There is an Asian look to what I have been spontaneously viewing lately in these installations. I find that odd. I'll bet Tommy could read such screens.

-Harriet 12/22/02

Recently you sent me an article about an experimental, Cold War-era "single-use" plane with clear plastic wings and fuselage, which could be completely filled with fuel before ditching in the ocean… There has been "lore" around since the 1950s about UFOs entering Lake Erie north of Cleveland. Richard Sauder mentions it in his *Underwater and Underground Bases* book. It's the first time I've seen anyone give it print. I remind you that what sits at the foot of the runway of Cleveland's Hopkins Airport is a top-secret NASA installation. A bunch of passengers were taken off of planes on 9/11 and sequestered there. Security is tighter than a drum. These UFOs entering Lake Erie are probably just our own craft, either entering an underwater base or being ditched.

-Harriet 12/24/02

One of the best things you ever did was have your "cord cutting" ceremony with Andee Boothe, where you "let go" of dysfunctional friends and family. As for "forgiving" them, forgiveness is an overstated Christian concept that bears very little resemblance to what actually happens in reality. The only thing that needs to be forgiven here is that you tried, tried, and tried. Forgiveness was meant for the self, not for the benefit of others. But modern Christianity has warped the original concept. You can do nothing for lost causes. Don't let them darken your psyche for a moment. You, a Buddhist, aren't closed off in your thinking; you actually entertain Christian concepts in your thinking. But Christians, like most people, think that Buddhism is a competing religion, which it is not. And since it is not *their* religion, it must be wrong. Behind those facades lie intelligent people to whom you used to be close – who listened to you. But they are gone. Let them go. Enjoy the beauty of that little miracle that is probably crying in the next room. He deserves your attention; they do not. If I have to, I will remind you of this for the rest of your life…

-Harriet 12/28/02

The Caduceus, Magic Wand of Mercury, Messenger of the Gods, is an ancient symbol of electromagnetic flight and cosmic energy.

According to Clendenon, the Caduceus is a simplified diagram of a Mercury Vortex Engine:
A. Air is the flight propellant/propeller/wings
B. Expansion of vortex coils/cooling
C. Compression of vortex coils/heating

1. Liquid metal mercury, the bearer of electro-magnetic energy.
2. Mercury boiler
3. Antenna/starter/core
4. Closed circuit serpentine heat exchanger/condenser coils
6. Poisonous mercury vapor reservoir

Within hours of the author's 2010 Mothman Festival talk on NASA's possible use of Nazi flying saucers in the 1960s, an English woman took a purported photo of Mothman flying over Nuremberg, Germany (top left) - provocative, even if a hoax. The swastika, an ancient symbol co-opted by the Nazis, appears on the meditation apron (top right) of Geshe Kelsang Gyatso, one of the author's teachers. The four-petaled flower symbol in the center can be seen as a top-view of a spinning caduceus. The caduceus (lower right) relates not only to enlightenment, but to physical flight via the element mercury. The "caduceus spaceship" design is hinted at in this remote aerial vehicle (top center) used by the USAF - very similar to what landed on Woodward Drive. The morphing gender of the creature seen at the Woodward landing site is reflected in Masonic symbols linking the Goddess with the caduceus and the Garuda (lower left).

CHAPTER 2

"One of our carefully phrased, key questions is: 'Did you ever dream there was a stranger in the house in the middle of the night?' When we directed this question to Mrs. Doris Lilly, who lived in the south end of Pt. Pleasant, she told how she woke up one night and saw a large figure towering over her bed:

> It was a big man. I couldn't see his face very well, but I could see that he was grinning at me. He walked around the bed and stood right over me. I screamed and hid under the covers. When I looked up again, he was gone.

"She thought that he was wearing a 'checkered shirt.' Occult literature is filled with references to ghosts wearing a 'checkered shirt,' but the occultists tend to skip over this seemingly irrelevant detail. During a hurricane in 1963, the 'man in the checkered shirt' visited Mr. and Mrs. George Clines of Pensacola, FL. As it took a step backward [the man] disappeared… From Cape Cod to Florida, we have heard of unidentified prowlers roaming the countryside at night. In Pt. Pleasant, strange unearthly faces peered into the windows of homes – windows too high for ordinary men to reach… In the Spring of 1966, an Air Force [officer] returned to her apartment and found her window open. A pair of very pale hands with extraordinarily long fingers was resting on the windowsill, as if a man were about to climb in. She screamed and the hands withdrew… We asked her if she had ever seen any monklike figures, and she recounted an incredible incident.

"Several years before, she had been staying in a hotel in Mexico when she woke up one night to find a giant cowled figure standing over her bed in a monk's robe. It extended one arm above her, and she reached out to touch it. The second her fingers touched the arm, the whole powdery thing crumbled and disappeared. What have 'powdery ghosts' got to do with flying saucers? In several cases [flying saucers] themselves have reportedly disintegrated into powder. On August 18, 1966, a disk-shaped object discharged some pieces of flaming metal. The witnesses retrieved some of this substance. Although they stored it carefully in a jewel box, it rapidly disintegrated, shrinking to the size of a pea. Since a thorough analysis can cost thousands of dollars, the metal has never been tested...

"Large, broad-shouldered men wearing capes and hoods have been seen all over the world, usually walking along desolate roads in thinly populated areas. They have an uncanny habit of disappearing without a trace. In October 1967, three men were driving along Route 2 in West Virginia when they saw a large, caped man walking beside the road. They stopped and looked back, but he was gone. There were open fields on both sides of the road... In July 1968 three schoolboys were camping out when they saw a bright UFO-type light bobbing and weaving over the barren hills of Cumberland Fells. One of the lads, Owen Moran, had a camera and snapped some pictures. When the film was developed, everyone was amazed to find that the object appeared as a pale light resembling the head of a woman in profile, wearing a bonnet tied under her chin! Are ghosts really UFOs (and UFO entities), or are UFOs ghosts? Take your choice..."

-John Keel, *Strange Mutants: From Demon Dogs to Phantom Cats*

Here we continue the series of interviews begun in early 2006 with conspiracy talk show host Keith Hansen, aka "Vyz," whose show was originally called "From the Grassy Knoll." In 2008, Hansen took his show off of AM radio in Tampa and began broadcasting it on the Internet under the revised name, "Beyond the Grassy Knoll." After a year or so of broadcasting under that name, Hansen took a sabbatical due to frequent, tiring attacks from disinformationists within the Patriot and 9/11 Truth movements, who do not seem to appreciate his adherence to reporting the truth. In 2009, the show re-emerged with renewed vigor under the name "Think or Be Eaten." Over the years, Hansen has interviewed many interesting guests whose collective research has added greatly to our overall understanding of the parapolitical world.

COLVIN, ANDREW – GRASSY KNOLL RADIO INTERVIEW 25 – MARCH 2008

"Vyz" at *Beyond the Grassy Knoll* (GK): Today we have Andy Colvin back with us... Before we talk to Andy, however, I would like for Jim Gilreath of Illinois, our webmaster, to share with us what he found out there along the Mississippi. Jim believes that this might be some kind of extension of the Garuda reality.

Jim Gilreath (JG): Hi, I have listened to all your shows with Andy. I remember Andy saying something about how people merely chuckle [when they] hear stories about Bigfoot. However, they attack you when you mention a [creature] that flies. I was thinking about this Piasa bird [legend in and around Alton, Illinois]. When I was a little kid, the Native Americans would come down from Wisconsin and northern Illinois, and they would paint that bird every couple of years. My dad took me up there one day; they were hanging off the side of the cliff painting it. There was an old man there running the show. When I asked him how many people that this bird had supposedly killed, he got mad. He told me that that was a lie [made up] by the Catholics. He said that that bird was a protector for the Indians. I got to reading [and found] that the ["bad" Piasa] story was handed down from Pierre Marquette, who was a Jesuit priest. Originally there were two different stone carvings there, and two paintings. They blew up the stone carvings of the bird when they widened the highway back in the '60s. A few years back, they quit painting the bird [as they had done before. Then] they moved it about a mile south. [Then] they just made one out of aluminum and hung it on the side of the bluff. The people in the area raised so much hell that they took it down and repainted it. But when they put it up there again, they turned it around and had the head facing the other way. It's the only time you'll ever see it facing the opposite direction. If you go online and type in "Piasa," you'll see a million different pictures of it [facing in the other direction].

Andy Colvin (AC): I've been following Jim's story. I remember him saying that the Oddfellows Lodge had gotten involved in taking the Piasas over. There was a cave that ran from one of the carvings to the top of the bluff.

JG: Yes... I know that this sounds like a fairy tale, but as soon as you get on River Road, you'll look over and see the Piasa Bird where it is now. If you go almost exactly one mile past that, you'll see two gas pipes that stick up out of the ground – the only ones on the highway – up against the edge of the cliffs. They're white pipes. If you look directly between them, you'll see the cave, way up on the side of the bluff; there is a waterfall coming out above it. If you climb up there and go behind that waterfall, it will come up right in this Oddfellow's backyard. When I was a kid, I used to climb around up there. There is a huge pool up on the top of the bluffs. There are two huge stone towers, or "chairs," carved into the bluffs that look like they were built in the medieval days; everybody calls them the "King's chairs." We used to go up there and jump off the cliff into the pool.

AC: By the way, it's a scientific fact that due to the increased generation of negative ions, waterfalls increase psychic phenomena. Same with salt deposits. The Kanawha Valley has lots of salt mines and, at one time, had lots of waterfalls. The Mississippi Valley had salt mines that were manned by slaves as early as the 1700s. Everyone was fighting the Indians for the salt. The Church has really made an effort to cover the birdman lore up, due to its importance to the Natives. The Jesuits and secret societies are always trying to spin the facts – science be damned – so that none of the earlier pagan or Native beliefs continue on in any pure form.

Natives used divination and other occult forms to secure and protect salt. Waterfalls and former salt mines are therefore perfect places for people to experience psychic phenomena and to see creature entities… Iron Mountain Corporation, a notorious name in the conspiracy world, has converted several former salt mines into data storage facilities. Bill Gates purchased a salt mine for storing his photo collection in Butler County, PA, where The Mothman Prophecies *was filmed. Gates has also purchased a large chunk of land outside of Columbus, Ohio, near Battelle's West Jefferson facility. After years of developing dangerous bioweapons and keeping tabs on UFO witnesses and researchers, Battelle is now one of the leaders in secretive "backdoor" data mining.*

GK: Chica Bruce did a show with me. She was talking about the Fatima sightings of the Virgin Mary, etc. She didn't think they were just beatific visions; there was very regular, punctual UFO activity. A Jesuit priest "spun" them so that they would seem to be associated with something spiritual. But these things were UFOs. The Church went ahead and changed the story. That doesn't sound so astounding, does it?

AC: No, and it gets more bewildering. These "Marian" visions of a woman in flowing white garb – sometimes thought to be a "bride" – occur all over the world. And they often occur right alongside darker imagery. People will see weird creatures and/or Men in Black at the same time, and in the same area.

GK: Understand that I never prompted Chica to say anything about the Jesuits… The French priests were mostly Jesuits. They put a spin on what might be happening with the Piasa bird.

AC: Marian visions are the bedrock of the Catholic faith. These are visions from the earth. They arise from earth energies. People see these different beings, both good and bad. But then simplify it down to: "Well, it was just Mary, Christ's mother." By the way, there's an etymological link between Mary, a "mar" word, and "mer," "men," "mor," "mon," and "man" words. These names often involve hilltops and mounds, where visions of "mon-stars" (monsters) occur. "Mar" is pronounced "ma" in Portuguese. It means "water" or "sea," and its *pronunciation* indirectly associates it with Egypt and the Moors. Many of our place names in America come from northern Africa.

GK: Thanks Jim… Andy, let's pick up where we left off at the end of show 24…

AC: Well, we last spoke on Oct. 19th, 2007, which was almost five months ago. I'm going to try to do the impossible here and cover that whole 5-month period. What I did in preparation was to look at each week in the last five months and note what I thought were the "problems" for the elites. This would be stuff that *has* to be reported in the news – which needs to be mitigated somehow. When I say the "elites" you can envision whatever group you want. It could be the Rockefellers, Rothschilds, Bilderbergers, or Bushes – they're all related.

GK: Yes, they are…

AC: And you know the Jesuits and the Brits are always involved, as well as the Masonic orders and the military. They've got a longterm plan. They have centralized media. They have a way to get things done. What I do is I just look at Yahoo! News, or maybe the Associated Press or Reuters. I don't try to get fancy with it. I stick to whatever it is that they're trying to make the average person believe. In the past, you and I have talked about the seeming fact that whenever Bush is losing on some issue, he strikes back in indirect ways, doing certain things that terrorize us. What I'm going to do is name the problems that might antagonize the rich, and then specify which media stories were thrown in to distract from the "problems." This distraction technique is necessary because many of these problems are purposely not ever going to be solved. So, looking back to the last week of October, what I wrote down for the "problem" was "Blackwater crisis/Iraq." Now, if you think this doesn't have anything to do with the supernatural, you're wrong. If they have a problem in Iraq or anywhere else, one of the cheapest ways to get a lot of people to *not* think about it is to have a big, well-publicized UFO sighting. Or, you have some heartfelt NASA story, or a story about dinosaurs or global warming… It just keeps everybody off track. So, in that week where we had the Blackwater crisis, we also had the Bhutto situation brewing in Pakistan. They were bringing our attention to Bhutto. Of course, she would be assassinated within a few weeks… It seems to me that they had a plan even then to raise oil prices. Some things happened in that week to get it going. The dollar was dropping, and the subprime crisis was just hitting the news. Since then, it's really been a terribly active five months. Just a real strange mix of things… Elites had certain stories they wanted buried in the second half of October… So… What media stories were brought in to distract from the bad situations in Iraq, Pakistan, Afghanistan, and Iran? Well, on the 19th, the day that I talked to you last, we had an image of Pope John Paul II supposedly seen in the flames of a bonfire. That was reported by Matt Lauer.

GK: Matt "Liar," the Ohio University graduate!

AC: Oddly, on Oct. 19th, a witness I had quoted in my first book, Emil Hach, who saw Mothman in his bedroom in 2005, experienced a "missing time" incident. It was the day after I had asked him to join my discussion list. Emil lives east of Akron. His sister saw Mothman many years ago. He studied at a mining institute in Russia, then married a Russian woman. In December of 2007, he experienced an unusual precognition. In a dream, he saw the death of someone in his work crew. The next day, one of his co-workers fell to his death. Emil had seen the fall through the victim's eyes… By the way, Oct. 20th was the 40-yr. anniversary of the Patterson Bigfoot film anniversary… On that same day, there was a big article about how the dinosaurs survived the polar climate. We're now hearing a lot of stories about the Ice Age, because that ties into the global warming campaign. There was an article on that day about "rising seas" threatening coastal cities as well. The UFO hacker, McKinnon, in England, who hacked into our military database looking for UFO data, claimed that he saw a "non-terrestrial officer list" in the database. This would be the same as an "alien officer" list – "greys" working for the government. It seems like an attempt to provoke ET believers into believing more… On the 21st, there was an article about how the debris from Halley's comet was going to hit the earth. Turkey began seriously invading Iraq at that time, and the movie Hitman came out. In the movie, the star is a genetically modified, mind-controlled agent called "Number 47." He has a barcode tattooed onto the back of his neck.

In May of 2008, as I was editing this section, an article came out in Natural History *magazine about how humans have only 46 chromosomes. The article claimed that we used to have 48 chromosomes, just like the monkeys and apes, but that two of them fused into one for some unknown reason. The article never adequately addressed the fact that this means we should have 47 chromosomes today, not 46. Lamely, they suggested that there is "a tendency for them to settle into even numbers." Nor did the article address the fact that gene fusing, or splicing, usually requires a synthetic application – the use of a high-speed "gene gun" that can pierce the cell wall fast enough to allow introduction of the new gene without harming the cell. Apparently whenever a human has 47 chromosomes, it usually means that the child will have Down's syndrome. Both biologically and symbolically, there seems to be something significant about the number 47. It seems to represent a mysterious, unusual state. This was echoed in the number of Silver Bridge victims: 46. Although there are rumors of a missing 47th victim, no one seems to know that victim's identity.*

AC: On the 21st, I saw the last Jason Bourne spy film. In the film, they revealed the address of a "mind-controlled assassin" training center in NYC. I looked up that address just for kicks. In real life, it is the address of the Frick Collection. "Frick" is a name that comes up in my Mothman story. Researcher John Frick and I seem to have all of these synchronicities happening to us at the same time – weird phone calls, doppelgangers, name games, etc. On the 22nd, they announced a new Bin Laden tape… A counter-terrorism chief, an Admiral, resigned because he critiqued the Bush job in Iraq… There was a viral "superbug" that closed schools in Knoxville… There were wildfires in California… A Carbide-Dow pipeline blew up in Port Arthur, TX. This was the point at which they started to jack up the price of oil. The dollar had been dropping against the Euro all through October… There was saber rattling towards Iran on the 24th. There was a lot of talking about the "S-chip" kids' healthcare bill, about whether poor kids should have healthcare… Bill Clinton was verbally attacked at speaking engagements by "9/11-Truthers" loyal to Alex Jones.

GK: With Bush and the Clintons, they're supposedly cats and dogs – opposites. But they are anything but that. With Hillary and Obama, we're looking at a horse race that is very well scripted. That Hillary is on the ropes is interesting. My point has always been that they brought her out of nowhere, reinvented her, and got her to be a

Senator in NY. This is what Robby Kennedy did, and that ain't for nothing. I don't know where it is going, but it makes for good drama.

AC: The whole Obama/Hillary thing does seem scripted and divisive. It also has a magical feeling to it, too. People are really believing in him. I suppose that is fine. At the same time, until we get the process cleaned up, you just can't trust most of what is happening.

GK: Well, it will never be cleaned up. I know that may [sound defeatist] but it's true.

AC: I just don't see enough real activism out there for Obama to make a change. Things aren't the way they were prior to Reagan. I felt a glimpse of activism when I was kid. They were having serious strikes and turmoil. People were talking back to power. That's *not* what we have now. We have a lot more "manufactured consent" now.

GK: I go back to being in college. I entered college in September 1969. The stuff we saw in those first two years… I look back on it and think, "How did I ever get through that?" It was far more chaotic than it is now. They may be getting back to that in the near future, however.

AC: The blog *Xymphora* is always saying that it's all about the Israeli lobby and how they influence our decision-making. They are supposedly the reason why Cheney is so obstinate and mean-spirited about this war, and why Pelosi isn't going to do anything to stop it. According to *Xymphora*, once you understand the Israeli lobby, a lot of the weird behavior makes sense… Okay, on Oct. 25th, they have another story designed to scare us: "The Earth is Reaching the Point of No Return," according to a UN environmental report. And there was a fake FEMA news conference, where proven intelligence agents were pretending to be reporters. Also on that day, my wife saw an aura around me, which she's never done. She's always been a non-believer in all of this stuff… On the 26th, a "problem" arose with the big Countrywide Mortgage debacle; they lost $1.2 billion. Everything was starting to implode in late August. Rumsfeld fled France, fearing arrest, and there were Iraq war protests in twelve cities in the U.S. Despite this, AP radio was throwing out old Kecksburg UFO crash stories. This might have helped cover up the fact that the government was forced to release the U.S.S. Cole bombing "mastermind" on the 28th. Plus, it was revealed then that Litvinenko, the "Russian," was actually a *British* agent.

GK: You mean the one who got dosed with radiation?

AC: Yes… There was also a U.S. surge against the Taliban in Afghanistan that day, and it was the second anniversary of a Mothman sighting near Midland, PA… By the way, the hometown of Indrid Cold, Midway, WV, is right next to the old Indian site, Ft. Ancient, along the Kanawha River (not to be confused with the Ft. Ancient in Ohio). Allen Greenfield has confirmed that Midway, which is near the Winfield Locks and Dam, was the location of Indrid's home. It would have been the perfect place for Indrid to have been located, especially if he was an agent of some kind. Midway is on Rt. 62, along the Kanawha River, right between the major industrial centers of Charleston, Point Pleasant, and Huntington. It was twenty minutes to any of those – a perfect place for him to carry out mind control or other operations. Interestingly, he liked to meet his contactees on Rt. 681 in Joppa, Ohio, which is near Reedsville and the Belleville Locks and Dam. Perhaps Indrid was a defense intelligence agent who, like Fred Crisman, helped provide "security" at energy sites and defense manufacturing plants… On the 29th, we had the terror alerts for U.S. and British embassies, and the new O.J. Simpson case was in the news. Those, along with the job promotion of the guy who set up the fake FEMA news conference, would distract from Iraq and the recession. They would also distract from the admission that, since 1990, a total of $2.9 trillion has gone missing from the Pentagon budget. That story originally came out the day before the 9/11 attacks. No one knows where the money went… Oil hit a new high on the 30th, and the dollar hit a new low vs. the euro. Gold hit a new high… The State Department gave Blackwater immunity… They sure slip things in all at once, don't they?

GK [sarcastically]: What a surprise…

AC: On the 31st, Paris Hilton was in Russia. Bill O'Reilly ambushed Rosie O'Donnell regarding 9/11. O'Reilly's attacks are a really good way to keep people's minds off of the issues. These jumbles of stories start to make sense when you begin classifying them as either 1) a problem for the administration, or 2) something that's helping to "fix" the problem.

GK: I was walking by the TV set this morning and they had good old "Shrub" Bush on. He's going, "We can't pull out of Iraq now because that would create chaos and killing," and I'm thinking, "Well, what were you giving them before that? And what are they going through now? It is, and has been, chaos and killing. So, what's the difference?" Secondly, he came on later trying to tell people, "Help is on the way" – the old FDR "prosperity is just around the corner" shtick. Bush was saying that we're going to get substantial tax rebate checks in May. But is $1200 bucks for a family substantial? That's a mortgage or rental payment at best. And who's paying for that, but us? I just had to laugh… OK, an email just came in… This is probably not foreign to you, but I've got a message saying there that is an "anti-Mothman" book coming out next month. The author is, guess who, Mr. Loren Coleman.

AC: This begs the question: "How can one write an 'anti-Mothman' book and claim to be a neutral, fact-driven scientist at the same time?" You know, Cal State just did a great experiment. They were testing wine preferences. You could use other products for such a test, of course. They discovered that how much something *costs* affects your taste of it, including your subjective experience with flavors. This must be an outgrowth of the class system. Concerns about class make people afraid to do anything that even hints at being less than perfect, less than spendy. The system has ingrained in us values that say you are worthless without money. Classism and exclusivity are so embedded that people can't even trust their own senses anymore. They can't even figure out whether or not they truly like something. Our appreciation of beauty is affected by this ranking of price and cost. I think it may work that way with parapolitical research, too. The public would do better to look at what any "scientist" *does* rather than at his academic pedigree. That way, they might catch some obvious contradictions. In the case of Mothman, "death curses" and "demons" don't really mix with sober, scientific study.

GK: Shall we try to cover the first week of November 2007?

AC: Yes. The "problems" then were that stocks plunged and there was a Pakistani intel crisis. We were controlling their intelligence, but we had to keep that fact under wraps, for fear it might get connected to 9/11 and a host of other ops. The Pakistanis are the best bomb makers in the world, apparently… Also, NSA and AT&T linkages were coming out in the news. Those two share in the Echelon eavesdropping that happens in WV. The British probably control Echelon, since it primarily covers their former colonies. Plus, the dollar was still dropping. So… What diversions did they create to keep us occupied? As far as our conspiracy subculture goes, Alex Jones' *Endgame* video came out, with its tales of future concentration camps in "Amerika…" The FBI inserted itself back into the O.J. Simpson saga. They are setting up O.J. These G-men (the

"G" is said to be an allusion to Masonry) are traditionally pretty racist… There was a story about a chupacabras in Texas that turned out to be a coyote… On the 3rd, it came out in *The Washington Post* that Donald Rumsfeld led our military psy-ops programs… King Tut's face was revealed on the 4th… Dennis Kucinich began saying: "Impeach Cheney!" Hollywood writers went on strike… Citibank posted huge losses… We had the largest drug bust in Mexican history on the 5th… Bush pretended to tell Pakistani General Musharraf to stop beating up on lawyers… The *Bounty Hunter* star, "Dog," used the "N-word" on the 7th. There is often this odd mix of racial inflammation, bad economic news, bad military news, the supernatural, dinosaurs, and NASA stories… On the 8th, Mark Klein of AT&T said that they had given the NSA all of their data early on in the Bush administration… Merck agreed to a $5 billion dollar settlement regarding Vioxx… The King of Spain told Chavez to "shut up" on the 10th… Glenn Beck called 9/11-Truthers dangerous "anarchists and terrorists," and the Homeland Security Sub-Committee started a hearing on "terror and the Internet." The first thing they did was go after the 9/11 Truthers…

GK: A quick comment from somebody: "The world is coming to an end, but you can still get *one* more DVD from Alex Jones. Buy, baby, buy!"

AC: Week Two's problems… We had more Blackwater scandal, bad industrial numbers, and Iraq War money issues. They needed to downplay the fact that the U.S. government was going to give the insurance companies a bailout. So, up pops the Parma, Ohio "blue orb at the gas station" story. Remember? People were supposedly seeing a blue orb at a gas station. There are a lot of gas station stories in the paranormal world. This may be because oil companies sometimes find it convenient to use their own properties to create misdirection. Keel talked about it for years. Parma is near Cleveland, which is not surprising. In fact, the long-running Cleveland UFO group meets just a couple of blocks away from the gas station in question, which is a Marathon Station.

GK: J.D. Rockefeller…

AC: Yes, Marathon was once a Standard Oil subsidiary. The station is on Pleasant Valley Road, reminiscent of "Point Pleasant" and "Pleasant Dell" in Mound… On the 12th, New York City cops gunned down a teen holding a hairbrush… Following Glenn Beck's lead, a House sub-committee equated 9/11-Truthers with terrorism… Hitler's desk globe fetched a hundred thousand dollars on the 13th... On the 14th, there was an earthquake in Chile, and a pancake with the face of Jesus on it was found in Florida... The Blackwater killings, where they fatally shot 17 innocent Iraqis, were ruled "unjustified..." O.J. went on trial, Musharraf backed off, and Mukasey was sworn in as the new Attorney General... There were a lot of important stories that week... On the 15th, ten people died of the common cold... Industrial production was down... A comet "bigger than the sun" was found... In south Texas, there was a "birdzilla" sighting... On the 16th, the Senate temporarily blocked Iraq war funds... Barry Bonds was indicted that day... Oh, and they went ahead and extended that "terror bailout" to insurance companies. The companies don't have to pay if something is caused by terrorism.

GK: The insurance companies rule. That's all there is to it...

AC: It seems like the media is alternating each week right now. They'll lump all the disappointing corporate and military stuff, which they want to cover up, together with a bunch of crazy, distracting stories. Then, the next week – when they *could* go back to revisit any of the important stories – they move on to *replacement* distraction stories that are controlled from the start, like bogus "terrorism" plots. If no replacement stories are available, they will simply claim that nothing newsworthy is going on. It doesn't matter how many of us want to hear an important follow-up story. They aren't going to give it to us. They'll give us a placebo.

GK: Honestly, this *is* the news business. They'll pound you into the dirt, give you no hope and, then, the next week, they will give you something to hang onto.

AC: I don't even know if they give you anything to hang onto anymore; they just lay off of you for awhile. It's like a torture chamber; they torture you until they feel like taking a break to eat lunch... In week three of November, there weren't many issues other than the Obama "threat" (i.e., that Obama is a somehow a threat to the oil companies). The oil bosses know that he will play ball. But, to make sure he does, they add a little media pressure. Behind the scenes, low-level oil employees are sending around alarmist emails calling Obama a crazy, terroristic Muslim. Someone sent me a couple of these emails. By the way, *that* was the week that oil really shot up, to a hundred bucks a barrel. To distract from that, journalist Robert Novak started attacking Obama. I don't remember exactly what he said, but he started in on Obama.

GK *[sarcastically]*: That's okay. *He* doesn't remember, either.

AC: Oh, here's something they probably didn't want us to think about on the 19th: There are 50,000 ancient Iraqi manuscripts, which had been "found" by U.S. troops in 2003, that are still missing. So, on that day, Sybil Edmonds started talking again about her important Iraqi "intelligence."

GK: Or lack thereof…

AC: And Scott McClellan stated that Bush was involved in the Valerie Plame scandal… Now, in the fourth week of November, the "problem" was the testimony of witnesses to Blackwater atrocities. So, they got us off of the Blackwater story by talking about how the Internet will be "full" in two years. Then, Cheney came up with an irregular heartbeat. We've talked about this before: the convenient timing of his heart problems.

GK: I'm surprised he has one.

AC: A "superbug" virus in Seattle grabbed some headlines… Bush held his own "peace" summit! Every time there is a real summit somewhere, he and Condi host their *own*; they cannot bear to operate in the same universe as the rest of us. Also, it was announced that "taser drones" are coming out. These are flying drone craft that zap people with tasers.

GK *[sarcastically]*: I'm alright with *that*… OK, here's a caller…

Q: Andy, I always appreciate your insights. You really taught me to expand my perception of what's going on. I appreciate how you perceive reality in an open-ended way. I learned a lot from listening to you and Vyz in all of those shows. During one of your freethinking moments, you talked about Puharich and how he could reproduce certain visual patterns via RF frequencies transmitted into the brain. It's a freaky concept. I [have personally] experienced the patterns you described at various times in my life… I wondered if you have heard of the mathematical principle of "E8," which I connect to this particular pattern Puharich talked about. There was a big hullabaloo about an English scientist and this concept of E8. It is sort of a visual perception of a mathematical principle, which supposedly would explain the universe. If you search on E8 in Google images, you'll see the pattern that I'm talking about. It is exactly the pattern that I saw. Normally I would see [this pattern when] waking out of a deep sleep, in a very calm state. The E8 pattern exactly replicates what I saw; only when I saw it, it was in motion.

AC *[looking at E8 image on computer]*: Yes, the E-8 image looks just like what I saw. I have seen it only a handful of times, always while at rest… By the way, I did a little experiment recently where I was staring at the sun with my eyes closed. I propose that there is something in our binary brains that tends to make one point of light split into two. I think that may be what's happening when people are seeing these two glowing eyes in the forest. They may be standing in front of a single emanation of light or energy, but their brain is turning it into two… Coincidentally, I was reading a story about new cloaking devices being developed. They stack discs that look like little flying saucers, forming a kind of cylinder. Then, as the cylinder spins, it reflects, or diverts, electromagnetic waves (such as light) around it. You end up seeing nothing. Now, in order for any person inside such a cloaking device to see out, there would have to be eyeholes. Those eyeholes would not be cloakable. An outside percipient would be able to see those holes. It could be that the Bigfoots or Mothmen have a similar problem with whatever cloaking mechanisms they are using. We're able to see their red eyes through holes that can't be cloaked.

Q: The other thing that resonated with me was that a certain teacher at Columbine had one of these radiowave mind control devices. Puharich talked a lot about RF inducing certain patterns.

GK: That's a pretty hot topic. Bill Zabel did some good work on that.

AC: Beyond the single E8 pattern, there are double and quadruple E8 patterns formed whenever the psi-plasma coalesces and begins replicating itself. I would guess that each spin forms an upside down, conical spiral. The Holy Grail is a conical vessel representing the feminine source of life. You find this "four" thing happening all over, from the Native Americans to DNA research, where there are four widely accepted coding mechanisms for DNA language. By the way, at the Pacific Science Center in Seattle, they once had an exhibit showing what the code for a human genome pattern would look like if printed out on paper. It was a stack of books 30 feet high, with each book containing thousands of pages. That's how many dots and dashes and so forth are in that code. The codes tend to be palindromes, which read the same backwards and forwards. Our DNA is therefore an expression of duality. It's an underlying duality that plays out in the brain. It could explain why my brain sees two sources of light when I close my eyes and look at the sun. Visions such as Ezekiel's Wheel may be caused by this mechanism as well.

In his entertaining and informative book Shockingly Close To The Truth: Confessions of a Grave-Robbing Ufologist, *Jim Moseley states that his personal outlook on the phenomenon is best summed up by the interdimensional thesis – what used to be called the "4-D" theory of ufology. While most UFO sightings have common explanations, a small percentage of them seem to be based on unexplained electromagnetic phenomena that cause people to see quasi-hallucinatory objects passing through our normal 3-D sensory bandwidth.*

AC: I was reading a Buddhist book about thought patterns and how you can practice controlling them. It sort of ties into the symbology of the cross. One way of thinking of the cross is to imagine it as the dividing line between four regions of space. These four regions may each contain spinning vortices, each replicated from one single, original spin, along the lines of Puharich's basic psi-plasma diagram. The cross is the *symbological* compliment, if you will, to Ezekiel's Wheel (a "4-wheel" vision) – a reverse way of thinking of Puharich's diagram. Now, each of these vortices can allegorically be envisioned in the bodymind complex – called biophysical "winds" in Buddhism. These winds "cause" thoughts and emotions. Assume for a moment that your consciousness is at the center of the cross. This may be the deeper symbolism of Jesus Christ, by the way... He represents the human being, formed by the four Earth elements *plus* a fifth element, consciousness; the vessel for a larger, more cosmic "God."

In her scholarly work on Christ in Egypt, Acharya S. provides many historical linkages between the Horus myth and the story of Christ, indicating that the tale of Horus was used to build the details of Christ's supposed earthly existence. Christ and Horus both share similarities with Krishna and Garuda. According to Acharya S., one can also find many obvious parallels between Isis, mother of Horus, and Mary, mother of Jesus. By triangulating these various myths, one gets a clearer picture of why birdmen and the "Virgin Mary" are seen so often in the same locales. As the energy gets interpreted by the human mind, it begins to appear to have gender. Mary and what we call "Mothman" have been appearing in the same places for centuries. The name "Mothman" actually implies dual gender by combining "mother" and "man." Acharya S. mentions the Egyptian name "Mery Mut" as meaning "Beloved Mother" or "Mother Mary." She cites evidence that the concept of

*a "Virgin Mery" existed long prior to the Christian era… In some
creature sighting cases, both male and female birdpeople are seen.
In the early 1950's in Brazil, a couple reported seeing what they
thought at first were two large "birds." After the "birds" landed
nearby, the couple were able to ascertain that they were actually
seeing people with wings, both male and female. After realizing
they were not alone, the birdpeople attempted to conceal themselves.
When this failed, they flew away.*

AC: So your mind is pulling energy up from the earth. The thoughts
come up from the earth. The Buddhists feel it is an illusion to believe
that thoughts are your own, since they are just sort of popping into
your brain. Responsibility comes in *after* the thought has arrived.
What do you do with the thought that has popped in? Allowing it to
dissolve back into its own essence is often the best response. It simply
travels through you. You let it out where it can meld back into the
psi-plasma. It's like a solar wind coming from the sun… There has
been a lot of solar activity in recent years, which has translated into
higher temperatures and auroral activity. If you look at the shapes of
solar winds and auroras, they're very similar to DNA strands and to
the caduceus, the birdman-inspired symbol for health and protection. Synchronistically, I just talked to Bruce Bickford about his dad,
who actually experienced standing inside a "tent UFO." What Mr.
Bickford called an "aurora" came down and spread out around him,
like he was inside of a circus tent. These ribbons of energy actually
"touched down" around him in certain spots… Interestingly, the
recent Stephenville, TX UFO sightings had this quality. Bruce calls
them "jellyfish UFOs." They are morphing globs of electromagnetism that reach out with tentacles… Speaking of reversals, here's a
little synchronicity about "Apol," the entity that Keel was talking to
on the phone during Mothman. A vowel reversal of that name gives
you "opal." Curiously, synthetic versions of opals, called "reversed
opals," are used to make cellphones. According to an article in
the Seattle papers a couple of months ago, many of the cellphone
companies were set up by AT&T from the get-go. The cellphone
industry has essentially been fueled by the Rockefellers. Back in the
late 1960s, certain elites already had cellphones; the CEO of United
Fruit casually took his to the Indian Hill Country Club pool in
Cincinnati. By the way, NBC was formed by a group of companies
that included United Fruit, RCA, and Western Union – whose
equipment, according to Keel, was seen inside of flying saucers by
contactees. There seem to be more and more clues that Rockefeller
agents were trying to manipulate Keel. If they had cellphones back

then, it would have been easier for them to pull off some of the weird things they did to Keel. Keel's use of the name "Apol" may have been his way of telling us that it was AT&T that was monitoring him. Another weird thing… I was looking at old pictures of the Bohemian Grove Great Stone Owl. There is a crescent moon on its torso, which refers to a Muslim or Moorish underpinning. I'm starting to see these crescent moon symbols at Catholic shrines. There is one at the oldest church in Nevada, the Order of Alhambra, in Silver City. A plaque there looks like it came straight out of Baghdad. There was a similar crescent at the Catholic Church in Boomer, WV, where the Carbide plant is located. There, the Catholic Knights of Columbus lodge is located right on plant property.

GK: The director of the library where I worked went to Catholic University. One of the buildings of Catholic University is ringed by Stars of David. Now tell me what *that's* about.

AC: In the Mothman story, you'll often have hoaxes that actually end up having significance as "correspondences." In my second book, I mentioned John Kerry being photographed with Anton LaVey. A book reviewer said, "Well, that was a hoax, Andy." But it turns out that the hoax is still quite interesting. They used a shot of LaVey taken when he was *actually* posing with Marilyn Manson, whose name is derived from "Marilyn Monroe" and "Charlie Manson," both of whom connect to the Kennedy assassinations. RFK was the man responsible for funding my elementary school, which was located on Sara Jane Moore's old homestead. The shot of Kerry was lifted from a handshake pose he did with Rami Salami, a clown performer. Coincidentally, a Mothman experiencer I know, who is a counselor, told me recently that she had counseled someone whose relative was a member of a "clown assassin team." They dress as clowns to escape detection… Another hoax correspondence is the name "Mothman" itself, which the cryptozoologists love to point out. Of course, we *should* be calling it the Garuda or Thunderbird. But the "hoax" name ties in, too, because "Mut" is an Egyptian winged goddess with similar symbologies to Mothman. She is a Virgin Maryish figure. Hatshepsut, the only female Pharaoh of Egypt, built a temple featuring Mut. This was the temple where some terrorists shot a bunch of tourists a few years ago… The Crowleyites at the O.T.O worshipped a deity named "Ma'at." They named the latter part of the 20th Century the "Era of Ma'at." Now, they are saying that we are in the Era of "Ma-ion," which seems like a drawn out "mon" word. Crowleyites use birdman imagery all the time, such as on the covers of their Enochian publications. In India, "math" means "place of learning." There are a lot of name games. The name "Moore" comes up a lot. William Moore is a teacher from Minnesota who wrote books on the Philadelphia Experiment and Roswell. Moore was involved in MJ-12. Another guy involved in MJ-12 was C.B. Scott Jones, head of the Human Potential Foundation and a former Navy Intel officer. William Dean Ross, whom I've mentioned before, lives near Midway, WV, where Indrid Cold lived. Ross lives east of Liberty, WV, where the NSA and NASA have supposedly been studying vortexes. Ross says that when he was at the Cayce Center in Virginia Beach, he overheard discussions about a meeting in Sweden in 1989 with a Dr. Walter Uphoff. The meeting involved CIA and KGB agents who were calling up the ghost of Albert Einstein on a TV. Before you laugh, this "electronic necromancy" process is actually something that Keel experimented with and found to be feasible. Keel wasn't talking about Einstein per se, but he talked about how easy it is to get what *seem* like specific spirits to show up on TVs. You use infrared lights and cameras, plus a mirror or two. Ross said that the men attending that Swedish meeting were C.B. Scott Jones and John Alexander, the famous remote-viewing military officer. Also, there was a telekinesis expert there from West Virginia University, Oleg Jefiminco. So, there are West Virginia links to MJ-12 and "The Aviary." The Aviary is this secret group supposedly directing MJ-12 and the whole Roswell "coverup." Here we're seeing names that connect the 20th century's biggest UFO story, MJ-12, to Mothman. The largest American UFO flap ever recorded paralleled the Mothman sightings. The largest concentrations of UFOs were in the Ohio Valley. However, the flap was left out of the Rockefeller Foundation's "definitive" study of UFOs, perhaps because those were real sightings of early "drone" aircraft.

At the website of the Paradigm Research Group, there is a section outlining "The Rockefeller Initiative, 1993-1996." C.B. Scott Jones is listed as a major player in this scenario, which ostensibly was about leveraging the Clintons towards becoming ET "believers." One researcher listed was Bob Teets, author of the book West Virginia UFOs: Close Encounters in the Mountain State. *On Headline's website, Teets is listed as having been managing editor for Jones' "Human Potential Foundation" (HPF) in the early 1990s, as well as being a trained hypnotherapist and "Spirit Releasement Therapy" practitioner. Amazingly, Teets is listed as having interviewed more than 2,500 percipients of paranormal phenomena, an incredible number. Teets' most recent book,* UFOs and Mental Health, Book One: A Briefing on the Phenomenon, *contains highlights of an "analytical briefing presented to President Clinton by Human Potential Foundation benefactor Laurance S. Rockefeller." According to Jim Keith in* Mass Control: Engineering Human Consciousness, *the first seminar on Human Potential at Esalen was led by Willis Harmon of SRI, who was anything but a hippie. Charles Manson and his Family Jam played a concert at Esalen three days before the Helter Skelter murders in 1969. Physicist Jack Sarfatti reported that "many of the regulars" at Esalen had received training from fugitive Nazi occultists in Chile. Also, the Soviets played a role at Esalen. They reportedly interfaced with John Mack, the Rockefeller-funded professor who almost single-handedly legitimized alien abduction in the 1990s...*

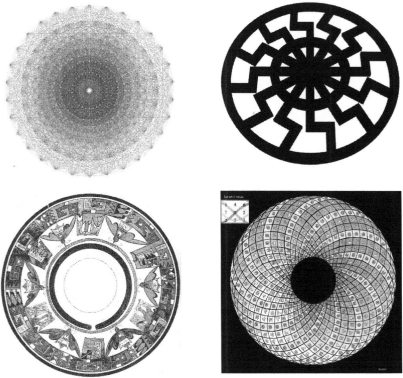

The E8 mathematical shape (top left) represents the interactions of the 248 known subatomic particles, and is based on the torus (lower right). Certain Mothman experiencers, such as the author, have seen the E8 while resting with their eyes closed. The E8, which is akin to "Indra's Net" in Hindu lore, is suggested in an Anasazi pot found at the Pottery Mound complex near Albuquerque, NM (lower left). Prof. Gary A. David feels that the Mothlike entities depicted on the pots and walls of the complex may represent Mothman. A version of the Nazi's "Black Sun" symbol (top right), representing the Void and its "dark" energy, suggests a spinning disc and may be the basis for early Nazi saucer designs.

CHAPTER 3

"Pour yourself a strong one while I tell you one more CIA-type tale… It involves Jennings H. Frederick, a young Air Force veteran (in his early thirties) who lives about thirty miles from me. Previous to his entering the service he encountered a weird UFO-related creature, which I call 'The Vegetable Man,' because of its green, stalklike appearance. The thing grabbed him and induced a state of paralysis while it drew a blood sample from his arm. At another time his mother was terrified by a devilish creature, which emerged from a UFO parked in a pasture above her home… Frederick's clear and precise language, like the letters he sent me, hardly gave a hint of his rural upbringing. He never employed the localisms and brogue that often crept into my own speech. He was an amateur rocket expert. Frankly, he impressed me. I knew he wasn't a kook or a candidate for the nut house. Although… Beneath the surface of his calm demeanor, I could sense something else, maybe a note of controlled urgency, or maybe pangs of suppressed terror. I also sensed this wasn't due to the frightening creature encounter, but to something else – something that had happened more recently, after his honorable discharge from the Air Force…

"Near the end of his enlistment, he was assigned to temporary duty with NASA and given a security clearance. While working for NASA, he encountered evidence of some secret project dealing with UFOs. He hinted that there had been a lapse in security at NASA and that 'several people had been sacked' as a result. I got the impression he had seen plans or models of secret aircraft. He questioned me at length about what I knew of the history of the AVRO saucer, an early jet-powered airfoil taken over from the Canadian government by the U.S. [It had been] highly touted in publicity releases by the Air Force [and] is now on display at Wright-Patterson AFB. About 4 months after his discharge, Frederick had a run-in with the Men in Black:

> I was living with my parents and slept on a cot near a window. One night between 1:00 and 4:00 a.m., I was awakened by a red flash. I thought the gas furnace had

caught fire, so I raised up in bed and looked into the living room where my younger brother, Bill, was sleeping, and saw a small canister come bouncing across the living room floor. It was giving off a red-colored vapor. I instinctively reached for my .38 pistol, which I always kept loaded under my pillow when living in the country, but a hand stopped me. I felt the prick of a needle in my left arm. I saw three men dressed in black turtleneck sweaters and ski masks entering through the window. The fourth one gave me the needle. One of them said, 'The dogs have been darted and everybody gassed!' Another one asked, 'What about this one? Will he remember?' The other replied, 'He's going out soon; he's half asleep already! Don't worry, the needle will only make his arm sore for a day or two, that's all!' Just as the red gas was beginning to reach me, the men put gas masks over the ski masks they had on. The last thing I remember seeing was one man opening a suitcase with a tape recorder in it, and another grabbing the canister and stuffing it into his pocket. Then they stuck something over my face and began to ask me questions, mainly about my UFO sightings and what I thought the UFOs actually were. Their other questions sounded very stupid, such as: 'What do you know about time?' [They also asked] questions about the future.

"Next morning, nobody else in the household reported anything strange about the previous night. Frederick assumed the red vapor from the canister had knocked them out… When we analyze Frederick's account, we are struck immediately by the ideas that the MIB acted and sounded very much like terrestrial visitors, with their talk of 'gassing' and 'darting the dogs.' It does not require an immense stretch of the imagination to connect the visit with his inadvertent contact with classified information while with NASA. The injections suggest some form of narco-hypnotic drug or 'truth serum.' Whoever the visitors were, they didn't seem to be indoctrinating him with ideas. And unlike other MIB, they didn't threaten him or warn him to stop talking about his experiences. From what he could remember of their questions before he lost consciousness, his testimony suggests the men were merely trying to find out what he knew – possibly how much classified information he had retained from the NASA [assignment].

"Of course, I probably couldn't convince UFO expert John Keel that these were human intelligence operatives. If you've read his books, you'll remember his many references to UFO occupants who, in their contacts with Earth residents, often seem to be confused about time – [like] Frederick's visitors. There are always little doubts that creep into the MIB cases that leave us without decent, ironclad explanations. Any writer expressing pat explanations has just never studied occult tradition, in which the MIB are firmly established. Military 'secret weapon' theories can never explain [all] UFOs, which have been seen from the dawn of recorded history. [Likewise] the CIA could not be responsible for [all of] the MIB who have, down through the centuries, meddled in our affairs."

-Gray Barker, *MIB: The Secret Terror Among Us*, pp. 142-145

In The Mothman's Photographer II, *I introduced my sister, Loretta, who saw Mothman not long before the 9/11 tragedy. Loretta has lived in and around Mound, WV her entire life. She has experienced several genres of paranormal activity, including flying saucers, "little green men," black panthers, shapeshifting balls of light, and ghosts. Loretta took me hunting for Mothman during the original 1966-67 flap, thus providing me with the initial impetus to study the creature. I checked in with her during my 2007 trip to West Virginia, and found that she had just purchased a locally famous haunted house, where an entire family was once murdered. While most people would be terrified at such a proposition, Loretta – probably because of her long history with the Mothman phenomenon – casually shrugged it off. She seemed to welcome the ghosts and poltergeists at the new location… Strangely, we heard an unusual, high-pitched squeaking in the trees around the house during my visit. Loretta said that she had never heard that sound before (nor has she heard it since). According to a local plant specialist, the property yields a curious overabundance of poisonous plants.*

The road that Loretta lives on is called Coal River Road, and it is extremely narrow, foggy, and winding. Pieces of the road are prone to collapsing, and deer often stand in the middle of the curves at night. Loretta explained that she has rushed to help so many car accident victims that county paramedics were persuaded to supply her with blankets, bandages, and other first-aid gear. In April of 2010, 29 coal miners were killed just a few miles down the road, at the Big Branch Mine. It was the nation's worst coal mine disaster in decades. The Coal River has a long history. It was the first commercially viable river for exploiting the southern coalfields of WV. Prior to the discovery of crude oil, the first industrial oils were made from coal mined in WV. The raw material was shipped down the Coal River to its confluence with the Kanawha River at St. Albans, WV. The Nitro/St. Albans/Institute area thus became a major center for industry, eventually attracting Union Carbide, who built key plants at the mouth of the Coal starting in the early 1900s. The Institute plant made synthetic rubber for Standard Oil and I.G. Farben during WWII. However the plant may also have had a hand in the manufacture of flying saucers (like the AVRO) following the war, because its sister plant in Germany (Dora) reportedly developed the first Nazi saucers.

Loretta was holding her black cat as we talked next to a crackling fire. She spoke of the many strange ghosts seen on the property. I peered into the shadows, wondering when and if I would see one. At some point, she casually mentioned that a Man in Black had come into her bedroom "looking for something" in the early 1950s. I hadn't heard this one before, and so my ears perked up. As she told it, I began to realize that our family had been watched for a long time – probably since 1943, when my father had been stationed at Norfolk Naval Yard, the location of the Philadelphia Experiment. At that time, Dad was also training at the National Bureau of Standards, which today houses Harry Diamond Labs (HDL), a leader in satellite laser technology, semiconductors, electromagnetic pulse weaponry, micro-electronics, telemetry, and mind control devices – all of the things rumored about during Mothman. In 1966, HDL was already proficient in the above disciplines, and was actively recruiting in national magazines. Loretta worked for the local Bell Telephone subsidiary in those days. John Keel experienced a series of bizarre incidents with Bell, eventually concluding that the company was aiding and abetting the harassment of UFO researchers. Interestingly, the mothers of Mothman witnesses Harriet Plumbrook and Tommy Burnham also worked for the phone company in years immediately preceding Mothman.

COLVIN, LORETTA – MOTHCHASER – TORNADO, WV 2007

Andy Colvin (AC): I had almost forgotten about this… You drove me around in the car to find Mothman in the late 1960s. Tell us about that…

Loretta Colvin (LC): The 11:00 news came on. I was there alone with my younger siblings… They said that Mothman had been spotted flying around the dome of the state capitol building. So I gathered up the kids out of bed, grabbed some blankets, and went searching for Mothman. But I never could find him.

AC: I remember going to the capitol building. Weren't we in the Volkswagen?

LC: Yes…

AC: I was hunched up in the back saying, "Where is he? We've got to find him!" Truthfully, however, I was a little nervous about that prospect.

LC: And you probably *should* have been. There were other occasions when we drove around looking for Mothman, too.

AC: If you hadn't done that, I probably wouldn't be a Mothman researcher today.

LC: Behind Stonewall Jackson High School, where people used to park and make out, there was a big opening where you could see down over the city. We would go up there. I figured that would be the best place to spot him.

Loretta was referring to the Swarthmore Drive neighborhood, which is above the confluence of the Elk and Kanawha rivers, a place Harriet Plumbrook flies to in dreams. The owners of the rubber company that employed many Woodward Drive men lived right next to the overlook. I spent many nights there hanging out with the owner's son. He was with me when I saw something – a "monster," as it came to be known – while camping near the Green Bank Observatory in eastern West Virginia… The Elk-Kanawha confluence was the location of a tragic bridge collapse on Dec. 15th, 1904.

LC: Mothman was always on the news, so I watched the news each night. If they had seen it somewhere, into the car we would go. It finally came to see me at my house in 2001. You've already got that story…

AC: Since I last talked to you, you had something happen with your daughter involving the telephone. Anything related to telephones is of interest; there is a rich history of phone shenanigans in the Mothman story. Tell us about that call.

LC: To start with, on several occasions, I have picked up the phone to make a call, only to find that Sharon is on the other end. The phone has not yet rung. I will go, "What do you want?" And she will say, "I haven't dialed yet."

AC: You just happen to pick up at the exact same time?

LC: Yes, it is very common for us. But this time, I picked up the phone and heard: "Mom, help!" And that was it; *that* was the message. Later, we found out that, at the same time I got that message over the phone, she was in the middle of a flooded creek, in a car that was being swept away…

AC: Where was that creek?

LC: Near Beckley, WV. Everything turned out okay. She got across the creek.

AC: Have you had any strange experiences recently in your new place here in Tornado? It has a history of multiple ghost sightings. And didn't someone murder his whole family here?

LC: Yes, a man murdered his wife and two kids here, in the house.

AC: You have no problem with that?

LC: No.

AC: It seems like you're almost immune to this stuff nowadays. Most people couldn't handle it.

LC: It doesn't bother me.

AC: Aren't there several neighbors who will *not* come onto your property?

LC: Yes. Some of them have seen ghosts coming out of the pond – in a group, like they are marching in a procession. A couple of them happened to drive their car *through* a ghost – a "woman in white" who likes to stand in the bend of the road here. That's why they are afraid.

AC: Earlier, you mentioned sleeping under trees during rainstorms. Did you do that a lot when you were young?

LC: When I was a kid, I had this fascination with the woods. I would always go off and hide for hours and hours. It would get dark and my parents couldn't find me, because I was in the woods asleep or something. Since I have moved to this new property, I'm starting to have the same feelings I did as a child. I spend a lot of time in the woods. It's like I'm back to my roots of being a child again. That's why I enjoy it so much here.

AC: It sounds like you occasionally experience "missing time."

LC: It's a good feeling. I lose myself for hours out there, just like I did when I was a kid – stalking.

AC: Have you had any other paranormal things happen in your life lately? You've had some things fly across the room, haven't you?

LC: Yes I have. Last night, some objects moved downstairs. Then today, my makeup bottles moved around by themselves.

AC: I remember when I was probably 5 or 6, which would have been right before Mothman, you said that "little green men" had been going through your dresser drawers. You were upset about sleeping in the corner room, where you saw the flying saucer land.

LC: The one I remember the most was when we lived out on Grapevine. I must have been 4 or 5 years old. This would have been in the early 1950s. One night, a man wearing a dark trenchcoat and hat came into my room through the window. He looked through all my dresser drawers and things. He obviously seemed to be looking for something. I acted like I was asleep. He didn't pay much attention to me. When he was finished looking, he went back out the window.

"Possibly the very first area witness of Mothman, the manager of an important civic-commercial organization in Pt. Pleasant, told us of a frightening phenomenon she and her father witnessed in 1961. In the summer of that year, she took her father out for a drive on Route 2. She braked the car when they saw what appeared to be a very tall man, in gray clothing, standing, facing them in the middle of the highway. When they approached to within 100 yards of it, the figure suddenly spread a set of huge wings, filling the entire width of the road. The man, creature, or whatever it was, then zoomed straight upward. Both were greatly frightened by the incident. Her father wanted to report it to the police, but they finally decided to keep it to themselves, fearing ridicule if they let the story get out…

"Prior to the sighting, odd thumpings on the outside and roof of her house, occurring at three different times, had frightened her. At one time during the thumpings, she looked out the window and saw a shadowy shape suggesting a winged creature. She heard high-pitched beeping sounds, 'somewhere between the cries of a bird and electronic noises,' which seemed to emanate from all around her – similar to the experiences of the Mallettes who, for several weeks after their encounter with Mothman, were awakened at night by loud bangings and beeping sounds. Her house was on a backroad, and she was often there alone… Because of the incidents, she moved into Pt. Pleasant…

"Another housewife was driving home from an evening church service with her daughter when a huge creature, much larger than a man, flew across the road in front of them. It had a wingspan of more than ten feet. Its body was white, and they saw long white hair streaming from the thing's head. The family belonged to a small fundamentalist religious sect and was very devout. They believed the creature was supernatural in nature and was either Jesus Christ or one of his angels. They, too, reported puzzling events associated with the experience. Their telephone often rang, with nobody on the line, and sometimes did not function for brief periods. Their television set developed interference, while neighbors' sets worked alright. In one instance, they reported that 'a Communist program' had been received on an otherwise unoccupied channel. They had also seen lighted objects land in a gravel pit about a mile from their house."

-Gray Barker, *The Silver Bridge*, p. 111

CHAPTER 4

"I joined the U.S. Navy and was stationed on a submarine. On a transit from Seattle to Pearl Harbor in 1966, I saw a UFO. It was the typical saucer shape. It was metal; it was a machine. It did not glow. It was not covered with lights. It was broad daylight. And it did something incredible. It came up from beneath the Pacific Ocean, rose into the air, tumbled on its axis, and flew into the clouds. Here I am standing on a submarine; I know what it takes to go under the water. I had served in the Strategic Air Command of the U.S. Air Force, so I knew what it took to fly in the air. And I knew that those two things were not compatible in any way, shape, or form with the technology that we possessed at that time. I was shocked and astounded. It has made an indelible impression upon everything I have done since then... We were not allowed to leave the vessel when we reached Pearl Harbor. Five of us actually witnessed this [scenario] repeat itself over and over again – either the same craft or ones exactly like it – entering and leaving the water. I was made to sign documents that I would never talk about this [event]. Before the debriefing was over, I was forced to say that I had not seen [anything]. If I had not seen it, why did I have to sign an oath to not talk about what I had 'not seen?' I never did talk about it... This may be one reason why I was eventually chosen to be attached to the Office of Naval Intelligence [with] NEC job description 9545: internal security specialist.

"I served in Vietnam as a patrol boat captain – one of the few enlisted men who has ever [done that] during wartime. I am very proud to say that during my tour in Vietnam, I did not lose one single member of my crew [even though] we engaged in heavy combat near the DMZ... While I was there, I learned that there was extensive UFO activity in the Vietnam theater. Because it was considered to be classified and highly sensitive information, we used codewords when we talked about it. The codephrase we used [for UFOs] was 'enemy helicopter activity.' I can guarantee you that the North Vietnamese did *not* have helicopters. That [codephrase] *always* refers to UFOs... I saw documents that stated unequivocally that there was a secret government guiding our country and a secret government guiding the world government – what they would later call the New World Order (a one-world, totalitarian, socialist state). The intelligence community does not work for the U.S. but for the United Nations... I saw State Dept. documents that outlined plans to disarm all peoples and armies of the world and combine them into a United Nations police force. The precedent for this was established by the war in Iraq.

"This country was founded as an experiment by members of secret societies. They go by many different names and occupations. Sometimes they appear to be opposed to each other. At the very highest levels, they are playing a game of chess that you and I may find it difficult to understand. But we are the pawns. Our forefathers belonged to this secret society, the Order of the Quest. This order was the last in a long line of societies that began before the mystery schools. They have been guiding nations since its inception. These men have been withholding math, technology, and physics – the secrets of the universe – from us for hundreds of years. They have been developing this technology to manipulate us... It is not a conspiracy; they are doing it right in front of our noses. This Order of the Quest was founded in 1110 A.D. in Jerusalem. Add the numbers '1110' and '666' and you get '1776.' This nation was founded to bring to pass the prophecies in the Book of Revelations; *that* is the purpose of the United States. Why *did* the U.S. government name the first project to investigate UFOs 'Project SIGN?' Because the prophecy given to the children at Fatima said that if Russia is not consecrated into the Sacred Heart, God will punish mankind. When God has determined that he is going to punish mankind, he will cause a sign – a light in heaven – that will be seen in every nation on Earth. The only sign or 'light' that has *ever* been seen in the heavens by all people, in all nations, is the UFO. This is a spiritual thing. It is not a joke. There are no benevolent space brothers coming to rescue you. You are engaged in the vital battle between good and evil. It is time to quit playing and wake up. This is for keeps..."

-William Cooper, author of *Behold a Pale Horse*

"Vyz" at *Beyond the Grassy Knoll* (GK): Here we are on the Grassy Knoll, and we have Andy Colvin with us. He was with us last month. Let's pick up where we left off…

Andy Colvin (AC): While you were doing the intro there, my screensaver popped on and showed an image of the Monster of Ravenna. He was a human being born with winglike appendages in the 1600s. In this depiction, there is an inverted crescent moon drawn onto the torso of the "monster," with a triangle pointing down to the crescent. The crescent is on his left breast. I found a similar configuration on the Bohemian Grove Stone Owl in a photo from the late 1800s. It's the Moorish/Egyptian/Freemasonic influence.

GK: Egyptian sun-god worship covered the Sahara. Interestingly, John Seurat, who was implicated in the plot to kill Lincoln, fled and went into the Vatican guard. He was supposed to be extradited back to the U.S., but an escape was arranged for him. He wound up going to, of all places, Alexandria, Egypt, where he eventually was caught and brought back. About the Monster of Ravenna… It is almost a depiction of Nosferatu, with the pointy ears and veinous wings… My wife and I ride around on our bicycles. We passed by a house recently that had four black, winged gargoyles outside. Excuse me, but why in the heck would you have *four* gargoyles? Is this something *Better Homes & Gardens* is recommending?

AC: The last time I was in Albuquerque, I saw a gargoyle statue sporting a Santa hat… By the way, it was reported on the news that the daughter of Albuquerque's Fire Chief had a premonition of 9/11 before it happened… As you know, the big player in Albuquerque is Sandia Labs. Interestingly, Sandia does disaster research for the coal mining industry. They study cave-ins and so forth. You and I have talked about the different mining and oil disasters – how their timing seems to distract from other events that are more politically explosive. Plus, these disasters may be a way to get rid of trouble-makers in the unions.

GK: Yes…

AC: Sandia has a Thunderbird as their logo; their supercomputer is called the "Thunderbird." They're involved in nuclear technology, too, which is the province of the Rockefellers. The Rockies must have great influence at the DOE. Sandia builds satellite lasers, too

– another area where the Rockefellers are already nicely situated. Harriet saw a laser weapon in action; it shot down a missile in San Francisco. The Rockefellers can use the satellites as weapons, or as cash cows for their phone and computer companies – to send raw "chatter" off to the NSA. Sandia is sort of a West Coast extension of Carbide… By the way, the model number of that RCA device reportedly used at Montauk was FRR-24. It was some kind of special vacuum tube used to generate unusual electromagnetism, supposedly leading to "time travel" situations… Hundreds of skeletons were reportedly found at Montauk, which is reminiscent of the skeletons found in Point Pleasant in the mid-1970s.

According to Loren Coleman, prolific serial killer Henry Lee Lucas confessed to the killing of Sheila Wears Pierce, whose father saved several people from drowning in the icy waters of the Ohio following the Silver Bridge collapse. Could Lucas have been in league with David Ferrie or Fred Crisman in the quest to terrorize the town? Exactly who was on the "turtleneck team" that was jabbing NASA and Carbide employees with needles? Oddly, Lucas and his killing partner, Ottis Toole, were granted unusual leniency from George W. Bush during their prison terms. Rumors swirled in the conspiracy press that both Lucas and Bush had connections to an "occult ranch" near Brownsville, TX, where 17 ritually murdered bodies were once found. Other rumors had Lucas delivering psychotropic drugs to Larry Layton at the Jonestown compound in Guyana. Decades ago, Mae Brussell claimed that the drugs for Jonestown came from a doctor in Westchester County, NY, which is very close to Carbide's Tuxedo Park plant, as well as to Iron Mountain, West Point, and to the homes of Andrija Puharich, the Rockefellers, and the cult that spawned the Son of Sam. In fact, David Berkowitz is rumored to have been programmed at Jonestown.

AC: A man-beast was seen at Montauk in the 1980s. It was a Bigfoot type creature that supposedly got loose and ravaged some of the buildings, ending the active use of the base. There is a photo of it in one of Peter Moon's books. It supposedly was photographed while in the act of wrecking the base… There was an article in *The Washington Post* last month about *Paranoia* magazine, the "paranormal conspiracy" journal. One of the stories the Post utilized to make fun of conspiracy theories was when David Icke called the Rockefellers "reptilian shapeshifters." Not only is it interesting that Icke made such ridiculous claims, but it is interesting that the Post chose to highlight that fact. Both transmit the subtextual message that any time you hear something negative about the Rockefellers, it *must* be an exaggeration. They go way out of their way trying to convince us that accusations against the Rockefellers must be bunk. It is a very creative form of disinformation.

GK: That's what we said about *The X-Files*. They'll tell you the truth, and then they'll tie it into something ludicrous. Then everybody goes, "Oh, this subject matter is stupid," and walk away. By the way, I kind of got "the willies" when you sent me the Indian Head Test Pattern… When you look at the configurations in it, they look like those ancient crosses: the Maltese cross, the Templar cross, the Ku Klux Klan cross, the German iron cross… Wasn't the Test Pattern found in an RCA garbage can in Harrison, NJ?

AC: Yes, they found the original drawing of the Indian Head Test Pattern in an RCA dumpster. In addition to supplying Montauk, RCA built most of the early TV equipment.

GK: I hung out in Harrison in the early 1970s; Western Electric and Otis Elevator were there. At that time, Harrison was a very ethnic place – Polish. When I was going to Jersey City State, I passed it every day…

AC: Well, RCA and Western Electric *are* basically the same company.

GK: They *are*, aren't they?

AC: Western Electric is the company that employed Harriet's dad when he was in WV. I don't know if there are still any Western Electric offices in Charleston or not. Which reminds me… Remember that guy I mentioned last time, William Dean Ross, who claims NASA is cooking up an Ezekiel's Wheel holographic "end of the world" scenario? In his article "Catch a Falling Star," he claims that his wife was attacked with EM radiation while at work in downtown Charleston.. Someone was pointing a device at her building from afar. He thinks it was coming from the Federal Building, because her window faced it. In the next paragraph, he talks about the book *Kundalini Tales* by Richard Sauder, who also wrote the interesting book *Underground Bases and Tunnels*. These huge, underground tunneling machines do exist, and some of them are *nuclear* powered. Sauder describes kundalini-based visions he had, which sound similar to the ones I had in 2002. On page 16 of *Kundalini Tales*, there is a picture of the NASA doctor Ross worked for at WV State College: John Sutton. Sutton was leading a project studying vortexes in and around Institute, WV. Sutton and another doctor, named Spaniol, were working with psychics who claimed to be able to "talk" to UFOs. It sounds like a branch of the remote viewing program at SRI, which went all over the country doing these experiments. Ross claims that the key players were Masons with huge influence at NASA. He also called them "Luciferians."

GK: Sounds like a good read…

AC: Ross claims that the perpetrators have a mobile white van that they use for pointing these devices at people. They've pointed them at him on occasion. In one instance, he got pissed because this was going on while he was at church. He rushed out and caught them in the act. He claims that there is some link to a group in Mount Shasta, led by a Barbara Max Hubbard, which is ultimately connected to Michael Aquino. He says that the group, "The U.S. Army First Earth Battalion," is connected to Aquino's Church of Set.

GK: There's something going on with Mt. Shasta … Matthew Tartaglias, the EMT worker out of southeast Pennsylvania who went to WTC Ground Zero, was talking about underground tunnels in the northeast. He said that there is a portal to these tunnels at 130 Midland Ave., Paramus, NJ. I know that building very well. I've never been inside it, but it's the only building on this little short block that leads to Route 17. It's an onramp, an outpost for the Bergen County Sheriff's Department. It's got smoky black glass. The whole building is black.

AC: People should check out Richard Sauder's work. It's sad to think that tunnels are now necessary for the human race to survive. I'm not sure I'd want to be in one of those tunnels if everything was destroyed. Many devotees in Tantric Buddhist sects believe that we destroy ourselves every few thousand years; we advance and decline. This may be why so many of the old legends say that we came out of the Earth. We came out because we had probably destroyed ourselves in a previous age; a few of the strong managed to survive. Of course, that would dumb us down pretty good. In order to advance again, we would have to live a subsistence lifestyle for a time, and then relearn everything from the symbols available to us.

GK: I think we can agree that a lot of what is going on today is in preparation for what is most likely a third world war. Some of these cats want to sit it out underneath. I doubt that they will be bereft of the accoutrements and trappings of home.

AC: Tesla warned about this kind of destruction. He was particularly concerned about setting the sky on fire. Experiments such as his may explain certain fireball phenomena we have seen, which get swept under the rug by the media. They just report it and move on. They try to get us to "move along," as if things like that cannot be explained. Synthetically induced sky phenomena would tie right into Biblical prophecies – some of the horrible things that we will supposedly have to undergo during the last days.

GK: Tribulation…

AC: Yes, and it makes me think of the Chicago Fire. Vincent Gaddis, in his book *Mysterious Fires and Lights*, talks about how it didn't really start in any particular place on the ground. The "cow tipping over a lantern" was a cover story. It was a wave of heat that came through the sky and set everything on fire.

GK: Where was this juxtaposed in time to whatever took place out in Siberia?

AC: The Tunguska event happened in 1908, thirty-seven years after the Chicago fire. Either one of those events could have been caused by Tesla. I am amused by the theory that – because of the differing trajectories of objects seen at Tunguska – "intelligent" globes of earth energy must have come to the rescue and intercepted a comet before it hit… While fanciful, it does imply that energy was sent to the region. The only person who could do that then was Tesla. The HAARP facility is based on a Tesla design. They are charging up chemtrails with electromagnetism from there, which seems dangerous. It could lead to what Tesla was talking about – the sky catching on fire. Then we might see some of the scenarios that Mothman witnesses have been having unusual dreams about. Interestingly, Tesla built transmission towers at Sayville and Shoreham on Long Island, very close to Montauk and to Brookhaven Labs. There was a huge Nazi contingent in that area, based around Yaphank. The nation's foremost atomic research lab, Brookhaven, was dropped right into a major Nazi stronghold. Tesla was funded by J.P. Morgan, so it is safe to assume that RCA and the Rockefellers also got in on the action. Brookhaven and Montauk were devilish extensions of Tesla's work.

GK: Laser weaponry could also cause the sky to burn. Look at what they did with just conventional means. They dropped so much ordinance on Dresden that it actually became a wildfire out of control. They couldn't do anything to stop it, except let the thing burn itself out. That was as bad as, if not worse than, what took place in Japan.

Apparently Dresden was an artsy-craftsy place, full of Bohemians who were not behind the war…

AC: It figures that they would bomb the dissidents… A couple more notes… Here is another "mon" word: "man-ta ray." A lot of people, particularly the ones having indoor Mothman encounters, have described the entity as looking like a "manta ray." The manta ray navigates by vibration. Beams of light that make vibrating sounds are called "rays." "Ray" comes from "Re" or "Ra," referring to the sun. The Garuda and Thunderbird are symbolically associated with both vibration (thunder) and rays of light (lightning). Chris Knowles is always talking about the "inseminating beam" or ray from Heaven. Many science fiction stories and ancient myths feature the concept of interstellar travel and "seeding" of Earth. A possible form of interstellar communication might be the neutrino ray. First detected in 1953, neutrinos pass easily through most matter, making it possible for a signal to pass through space without being blocked by planets and stars. Neutrinos are also not subject to the "noise" of light and radiowaves in space. The very name, "neutrino," alludes to "Nut," the Egyptian goddess of night, plus "Re," the sun, indicating a beam that works both day and night, around the clock. The Egyptians were trying to make goddesses manifest inside the Great Pyramid, from starlight coming from outer space. which is a form of insemination – an occult conjuration… Another "mon" word is the name of the Indians who lived on the east side of the Appalachians, called the "Monacan" or "Manahoac" Indians. They still have pow-wows around Amherst, VA… Here's an item I mentioned in my article for *Paranoia #47*. In his book, *Men in Black: The Secret Terror Among Us*, Gray Barker investigated the case of a military man who was assigned to the AVRO flying saucer program at NASA. His name was Jennings Frederick. He lived a few miles outside of Charleston. It may sound weird to hear that space vehicles were made in that area, but the trend continues today. Engines for the space shuttles are made in Ohio and WV. By the way, I just heard them talking about the new Airbus contract on the radio. That contract didn't go to Boeing, but to the Europeans. Apparently this wasn't such a big deal for us, because Airbus engines are still made in Ohio. General Electric makes the Airbus engines for the European planes! We're almost being used as a slave state for some of these other countries. I think that may have been the plan all along.

GK: You know, you're exactly right. The other day, I was thinking to myself that one fine day, the means of production and manufacture will come back to the United States. Why? Because we have now been colonialized again – reduced to what is going to be a very captive working force. It's "free trade" for the corporations, but it's not going to be too free for the workers… Remember the Italian magazine that had those very interesting ads about refrigerators made by GE in 2000? One of them was showcased as the "New York, New York" model, with a plane bearing down on the Twin Towers. Is that just coincidence, or did GE know something?

AC: I don't know, but appliance salesmen like Woody Derenberger and Tad Jones played roles in Mothman events. By the way, Derenberger mentions in his book that he toured the TNT Area and was told by an off-duty officer that the columns of dust and/or smoke shooting up from the TNT were just "dirt devils" or "twisters." But dirt devils are rare in WV, so that sounds weak. The AVRO saucer would be a somewhat better explanation, given the circumstances, as it would probably pull up a bunch of dust when it took off vertically. Jennings Frederick could have lived 30 miles from Barker and still commuted to the TNT Area every day… Speaking of GE, I have an old friend from the Art Academy of Cincinnati whose father was once head of the GE medical department. He recently sent me an email about Pyramid Hill, which is near Hamilton, Ohio. The guy who owns it is a wealthy Mason named Wilkes. The entrance to the Wilkes house is a pyramid similar to the one at the Louvre, as featured in *The DaVinci Code*. There is a publicly subsidized sculpture park next to the Wilkes house. One of the artists in the park, Walter Driesbach, taught sculpture at the Art Academy of Cincinnati. My friend and I both studied with him. The sculptures I did in Driesbach's class had Mothy symbolisms, but are now buried on Woodward Drive. My friend actually helped me bury the sculptures. He recalled Walter always using Masonic acronyms in class like, "As above, so below." Mount Adams, where our school was located, has long been a key place in the Masonic world. It has underground tunnels once used by German Jesuits and wealthy Masons. According to several sources, the Knights of the Golden Circle (KGC) fomented the Civil War from there. The wealthy Indian Hill section of town was once covered in Indian mounds.

GK: Cincinnati was a hotbed of manipulation and intrigue in the 19th century. The KGC morphed into the KKK later on. They were instrumental in instigating a warlike attitude, in order to get everyone prepared for what would become the Civil War. They call Cincinnati the "Queen City" because the KGC came out of England.

AC: It was very popular with blacks, too. Historians will say that this was because the slaves used Cincinnati as a gateway to the north, which is true. However, it may also obscure a deeper truth, which is that the blacks were there, all along, in Ohio… Speaking of Ohio, Columbus was just named the "fastest growing tech city" in the U.S. The media is attributing this mostly to Battelle, which has nabbed several new government contracts recently. One last point about Jennings Frederick, the NASA employee who worked around the AVRO saucer… Basically, a SWAT team, wearing turtlenecks, gassed his house and injected the family with some kind of truth serum. Jennings happened to see the gas canister rolling into the house. With Frederick, we have an example of another family being treated the same way as mine. These teams were evidently going around, breaking in, and interrogating anyone with a family member working on a secret project. They were probably checking for security leaks. There were a lot of foreign spies in the area. It was so bad that our different government agencies were spying on *each other* – having these tremendous turf wars.

GK: There is some similarity between your story and the storyline about Fox Mulder and his sister on *X-Files*. When you're young like that, you can't be sure what in the world's going on, but *something* happened.

AC: Some of this "hypnosis" can happen by natural means. Those natural means were studied over the course of centuries. They were mimicked, modified, and applied to the citizenry, thus insuring elite dominance. Military doctors today know how to use hypnotic confusion techniques. If you ask a nonsensical question during hypnosis, the patient goes deeper into trance. The whole abduction thing is a great cover. They can try stuff out on their human guinea pigs and then blame it on "the aliens." Here's a new page of notes… There is a Jesuit university in Wheeling, WV that is now training prison guards to be able to quell "large-scale riots." We have Jesuits involved in things you'd never think they would want to be openly involved in. It seems they have decided to train people in decidedly non-spiritual matters – a real throwback…

GK: That's the deal, though; they are *not* a spiritual order. That's only what they're supposed to be *perceived* as. That's why they call the head man the "Jesuit General." This training facility is somewhat close to the infamous prison at Moundsville. Doesn't the Mounds-ville "mound" look like a pyramid? It looks kind of pointy to me.

AC: There could have been a pyramid over it at one time. By the way, the East Coast Indians didn't live in tee-pees. Their homes looked African – domed. I think the Indians were originally Moorish or from Northern Africa. It could be that the very name "Indian" means that they came from India, via Egypt, Morocco, or other countries.

GK: That's right.

AC: This *is* the story told of the Scots. They were originally from India, but came through Egypt before going to Scotland. Maybe a few went to America, too.

GK: Our "vanilla history" textbooks claim they are called "Indians" because they came from the "Indies," but they *didn't* come from the Indies… I was sent pages of a 1916 book about the Rosicrucians' 68th Conclave… They talk about the fact that Mexico "must be brought back into the United States" before the capstone can be set upon the truncated pyramid, because Mexico was part of Egypt long ago. There is something going on with the similarities between pyramids in the Yucatan and the pyramids in Egypt – actually everywhere around the world. The whole Midwest is laced with them. They're not as majestic in the Midwest, and they seem to be earthen, but were they not a part of this network as well?

AC: Some of the biggest ones were in China… But to me, not only do these East Coast Indian homes look like African round huts, but they also look like mounds. They were round, like igloos. And their boats looked like cigars.

GK: They were dugouts. Down here in the Southeast, the huts were round. The tent thing was only with the Plains Indians, who were nomadic and followed the buffalo.

AC: Moving on… West Virginia is allowing their highway cameras to be used for spying any time they have an "alert." It is very *1984*-ish… Did I mention that I may have found out who Charles Manson's dad was? Manson kept referring to being raised by "the Nuremberg judge," which initially made me consider Judge Robert Jackson. However, that was before I found out about the *other* judge at Nuremberg, Francis Biddle, who bears a great resemblance to Manson. He was the federal judge for western Pennsylvania, which is very close to where Manson's grandparents lived.

GK: Wasn't Manson supposedly a "Maddox?"

AC: Right... The Maddox's lived in Wheeling, right across the border from Pennsylvania. Manson's promiscuous mom may have run into Mr. Biddle there.

GK: Are you saying that they hooked up?

AC: Well, if they did, that *would* explain why Manson looks so much like Biddle.

GK: That is so ironic, because "Biddle" is one of those Mayflower families. The one Biddle who gained notoriety was the "Mayflower Madam" in the 1980s, who was running a prostitution ring.

AC: Oddly, Manson changed his middle name from "Milles" to "Willis" in 1967. He had a connection to John Phillips of the Mamas & the Papas. Manson hung out with Phillips' bandmate, Mama Cass, at the Spiral Staircase house. I was told years ago that Phillips once lived in Madeira, an area of Cincinnati that once had mounds. It is near Indian Hill. I went to art school with a guy whose dad was mayor of Madeira. They supposedly lived around the corner from Phillips. Roman Polanski was walking John Phillips' dog in Hollywood when the dog got loose and ran down to the old Barrymore mansion – this is when Polanski was living on Cielo Drive. Inside the Barrymore mansion lived a member of the Process Church, which was connected to Manson. Polanski almost got ripped apart by these dogs owned by the cult. The Process member who was living there worked for Joey Bishop. Remember, Sirhan Sirhan has been linked to the Process, too. Sirhan can therefore be potentially linked to Manson. The Process may have been the Brits' way of helping to destroy the Peace Movement. The Process Church disappeared right after the RFK hit. One of them worked in the Ambassador Hotel kitchen, where RFK was shot – where Sirhan had visited the day before. A few months ago, some photos surfaced showing three CIA officials at the assassination. They probably knew that Sirhan had been programmed. He and Manson both disappeared during the summer of 1967.

In May 2008, attorney William Pepper, of MLK fame, came forth to say that he was going to represent Sirhan and try to get a new trial. He spoke on CNN of shots coming from two directions, and how Sirhan – to this day – doesn't remember any of the events of that evening. Pepper stated that Sirhan still seems to be mind-controlled, all of these years later.

GK: Maybe they hired Tavistock to turn Sirhan into a Manchurian

Candidate...

AC: We have to ask where Manson was during all this, because he was loose then. He was out of prison. He had family in KY. Sirhan had Kentucky connections from being a horse trainer and jockey. Sirhan also saw the famous CIA hypnotist, William Joseph Bryan, Jr. in L.A. Bryan consulted on psychological horror movies like Francis Ford Coppola's *Dementia 13*.

Bryan is famous for inducing Albert DeSalvo's confession to multiple homicides while under hypnosis. He ran the American Institute of Hypnosis, edited his own journal, and created the Bryan Method of hypnoanalysis. William Turner and Jonn Christian hypothesized in The Assassination of Robert F. Kennedy *that Bryan was responsible for inducing Sirhan to fire blanks at Robert F. Kennedy with posthypnotic suggestion. Bryan died before he could sue for libel. He was found dead in a Las Vegas hotel room in 1978.*

GK: Yes, this was before the whole Tate thing in '69. They were all out there. They were still at Spahn Ranch. Dennis Wilson died a strange death. And what the hell happened with Mama Cass? Many of these deaths were choking deaths or in bed, like Hendrix, Mama Cass, Jim Morrison, etc.

AC: My point is that during the Mothman craze of 1967, Manson was loose, with family in the area. Robed occultists, like the ones in California, were seen in the TNT Area. There have been persistent rumors of a Manson Family cell in the area. Manson's uncle was brutally murdered near Kenova, WV in the summer of 1967. Maybe Manson and Sirhan got some of their programming in the TNT Area – only a half-hour drive from Kenova.

GK: I was in 7th grade when JFK was popped. Then, that weekend, I watched Ruby pop Oswald. My father and I looked at each other and went, "Is this theater?" My junior year in high school, MLK was shot, and then RFK. I don't know how I dismissed all of that stuff. I must have been chasing skirts and playing baseball. I look back at it now and say, "Why didn't some flags get raised?" I'm starting to wonder if [Manson and Sirhan] weren't used by the government – double-crossed.

AC: Absolutely. In fact, James Earl Ray's brother now says that James was working for DISC, Defense Industrial Security Command, which is out of Columbus. According to the Torbitt Document, DISC was one of the agencies involved in JFK. That's one of the older theories, and probably fairly accurate except for the fact that it may have included disinformation from the CIA, MI6, or the Jesuits. All were apparently trying to put more emphasis on the FBI's role.

GK: Hell yes! And by the way, they never *really* implicated Manson in killing anybody. He might have said, "Go and do what you have to do," but that doesn't normally put you up for Murder One.

"William Torbitt" is the pseudonym for the author of Nomenclature of an Assassination Cabal *(1970) – also called "The Torbitt Document." Jim Marrs, who interviewed Torbitt, claims that Torbitt was actually David Copeland, a lawyer from Waco. During WWII, Copeland served in the Navy. After completing a law degree from the Univ. of Texas, Copeland claims that he represented people involved in the "financial dealings of organized crime in Texas." The Torbitt Document argues that a Swiss Corporation, Permindex, engineered the assassination. Also reportedly involved were Defense Industrial Security Command (DISC), NASA Security, and the American Council of Christian Churches. Torbitt claims the following were DISC agents: Clay Shaw, Guy Banister, David Ferrie, Lee Harvey Oswald, and Jack Ruby, with Louis M. Bloomfield of Montreal in charge. Torbitt also argues that J. Edgar Hoover and Bloomfield planned the execution of MLK and RFK, utilizing the help of Albert Osborne (John Howard Bowen). Maury Island's Fred Crisman is thought to have been a DISC agent. The notorious Indrid Cold may have been one as well…*

AC: Manson was not a DISC agent, although he may have been a low-level Jesuit stooge of some kind. Oswald probably *was* DISC; James Earl Ray probably was, too… By the way, the name of Oswald's CIA controller, George DeMohrenschildt, contains a "mohr" ("moor") syllable. According to Bruce Adamson, LBJ's personal secretary was Olga Fehmer. Olga's mother was very close to DeMohrenschildt. We can now see that LBJ – who designed the triple overpass in Dealey Plaza as an architect in his younger days – *could* have been directly apprised of Oswald's movements… Speaking of setups, did I mention Sean Hannity's show about miracles? He does this show on Fox that is designed to make the Catholic Church look *really* good. Every Sunday, he'll do this thing called "Beyond Belief" – a paranormal segment. Usually, they'll start with a pagan or Protestant paranormal miracle, which Hannity will pooh-pooh. Then they'll have a Catholic version, which Hannity will claim is obviously genuine – the only one to be believed. One night, he talked about a vial of blood kept at a Catholic shrine near Naples. They bring it out once a year and let the people look at it. If the miraculous happens – if it momentarily turns back into real, fresh blood – then everything will be fine the coming year. If the blood stays old and crusty, they will probably have an earthquake or some terrible event. Have you heard of this?

GK: No, but apparently it must have turned back to fresh blood the last several times.

AC: Yes, rarely does it not. But when it doesn't, they apparently *do* have an earthquake or some tragedy. Once I heard this, something clicked. Remember that Keel found that most paranormal events happen when the magnetic field of the earth is *low*, not high. It's the opposite of what you might think. Also, remember that Puharich found that when one cohesive field has low magnetism, a nearby field develops high magnetism. It's sort of the like the goop in a lava lamp; it undulates back and forth. A human receiver who is lounging, relaxed, or sleeping will pick up the ESP of someone in trouble, who has adrenalin flowing. Charged signals undulate out, to a less pressurized region. So, when the earth's magnetism goes down, the psi-plasma/magnetism of individual beings on the surface expands out; the Earth pauses for a moment, so that your psychic power can expand. A decrease on one side means an increase on the other. My theory is that when the earth's energy is high – when that earthquake is about to happen in Naples – it interferes with our psychic ability to make that vial turn back to real blood. Our conscious and unconscious belief systems can't operate as strongly, due to the magnetic interference.

GK: HAARP could flood the atmosphere with signals designed to keep everybody from accessing their own innate intuition.

AC: Now *that's* a scary thought… One more item… According to John Keel, the date of the Silver Bridge collapse was predicted by some of the contactees. Coincidentally, the bridge collapse occurred on the same day that the Saturn Five moon rocket engine began being used at NASA. The Saturn Fives were tested at Redstone Arsenal in Huntsville, Alabama, which is also home to Marshall Space Flight Center and the main office of NASA Security.

On Feb. 22ⁿᵈ, 2008, a massive explosion occurred at Redstone, which sounded like an "atomic bomb," according to a witness who wrote to Linda Moulton Howe's "Earthfiles" website. The explosion was covered in newspapers, but odd excuses were given… In May 2008, in Decatur, AL, just 20 miles west of Huntsville, a "white sphere" about 3 feet in diameter was seen being placed in an ambulance by men in white hazard suits. Writers to Earthfiles also described seeing the spheres in Arizona, Florida, and Los Angeles. Images of the "alien" spheres were found on Google satellite images. After looking at shots of the spheres, I realized that I had seen one outside my plane window while flying out of Burbank Airport on May 8, 2007. Since that was the same day as the Griffith Park Observatory wildfire, I am guessing that these orbs are most likely drone craft used for monitoring fires, traffic, and criminal activity. Occasionally, large metropolitan police departments will announce the purchase of such craft.

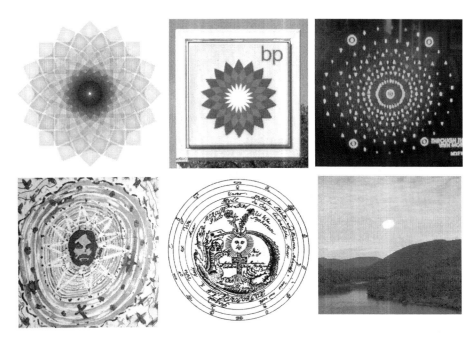

Variations of the E8 exist, such as one that resembles a flower (top left). Also called the "violet flame" or "burning lotus," it appears to meditators as they reach deeper subconscious levels. The author experienced a vision of the burning lotus in late 2001, in Mazunte, Mexico, after it was induced by a shaman during a sweatlodge. Certain transnational corporations, like British Petroleum (top center), have adopted logos suggestive of the E8 lotus. Morgan Freeman's TV show, Through the Wormhole, *depicted the four mysterious E8 particles believed to cause gravity as an "X" (top right), with each particle looking like the "all-seeing eye" logo of CBS - a Masonic reference. An ancient Rosicrucian symbol (bottom center) uses an E8-like layout in depicting the importance of the element mercury. Even WV's famed criminal, Charles Manson, depicted himself within the E8 in one of his self-portraits (lower left). Certain UFOs, like the one captured on film by Tim Frick just prior to the 2010 Mothman Festival (lower right), seem to take the shape of a torus, as that shape may result in less aerodynamic "drag."*

CHAPTER 5

"Let me tell you something about meditation. At the absolute center is the vortex we are spun from like clay – a shaping hand which is neither Godlike nor peaceful as you imagine."

-Forrest Gander, *The Violence Of The Egg*

"I thought that in order to remain a human being – in order to simply survive – shooting President Ford was the only option I had… Looking back [at myself then is like] looking at a different person. One gets tired of being looked at as a kook, monster, or alien. I don't know what was going through my mind [as I aimed the gun]. It started out as culture shock. I had no idea of the poverty in this country. I couldn't believe [the state of the poor] in San Francisco. I wasn't prepared for it. It was so alien to me – to what I thought the world was, or [should be]. It was a time that people [prefer not to] remember. We had a war both *within* this country and in Vietnam. I became immersed in it. The "radical left" in San Francisco was our world. [My age and profile only seemed out of place because] a 20-yr. old was more used to the ways of this [new] world. When I became involved in it, at age 45, I really wanted to understand. In trying to understand, I put on blinders and only listened to what was feeding in from one side. I still think that if I hadn't [shot at] President Ford, someone else *would* have. That was the tenor of the time. There was more talk about [assassinating Ford] than people realize. This sounds a little strange, but I *really* thought it would trigger a new revolution. The country needed to change. I genuinely thought that the only way it was going to change was through violent revolution.

"I hated solitary confinement, but it allowed me to stop and get acquainted with myself – to try and figure out who I was, and what had *not* happened as a result of what I had done. I gradually began to realize that I had let myself be used. I let myself believe things perhaps more deeply than others. I think what I did was wrong, but *understandably* wrong. I was misled. I was mistaken. I made a serious error. Prison destroys people – both staff and prisoners. To survive, you have to shut down your heart. You meet people, you like people, and then they grab them up and they're gone. *You're* grabbed up and taken off. Life goes on… You can't let yourself care because, as they say, 'a heart broken too often turns to stone.' And I saw that happen to both staff and prisoners. So, I shut down part of my heart and part of my thinking. After I got out, I gradually [began to feel again]. I remember the first day that someone actually hugged me. I said [to myself]: 'Welcome [back] to the human race…' People are kind. [To those who think that attempted assassins should] never see the light of day, I [defer] to Pres. Obama. We have a Constitution and we have laws. They apply to everybody. I broke the law. They put me in prison. Regardless of who you are, there are conditions to be met for parole, and I met those conditions. So, they let me out. If people object to that, they can write their Congressman and ask for the law to be changed. And it *has* changed, to a certain extent. There is [effectively] no more parole for people who are given a life sentence. I hope that they change the law again, so that those [inmates] will have a chance for freedom."

-Sara Jane Moore, interview with Matt Lauer on *The Today Show* 5/28/09

MOTHMAN DISCUSSION LIST – SELECTED LETTERS AND POSTS – 2003

Last night, we were up late watching the national championship game. At approximately 8:00 a.m. this morning, my son came in where I was sleeping and shook me violently. He was in absolute hysterics. As you know, he is usually very laid back. He said he had felt a really cold chill go up and down his spine. He couldn't move; he was completely "stuck." Someone was pulling on his toe, while lifting the covers up from the bottom of his bed. Someone else was whispering in his ear, "Come with us, now." He said that he felt a weird tingling all over his body. In his mind, he told them to "go away." He does *not* believe this was any kind of dream. He *insists* that he was awake.

[Eventually] the feeling went away. He tried falling back asleep, but the exact same sequence started over again. I have never, ever, seen this kid so terrified of anything in my life. I tried to tell him that it *could* have been something positive, like a spirit guide. But he wouldn't have of that. He insists that it was "up to no good." He is normally so mild mannered. To see him so shaken up was a sight. It got freakier moments later, when Ann Marlowe, the older African American lady who was with me when we witnessed the infamous "missile" incident in CA, left a message on my cellphone. She said, "Something odd happened in your house this morning, didn't it?" It turns out that her sister, who is a professional psychic, had picked up on it. I haven't had anything this odd happen in quite a while. My intuition and psychic ability have been running freakishly high... What do you make of all this?

-Harriet 1/5/03

Harriet, it is possible that the high energy of the championship game, which *was* a classic battle, brought the energy level up in your house to the point where "inorganic" beings manifested. And, as you say, your own psychic energy level *has* been running high. In Carlos Castaneda's final book, *The Active Side of Infinity*, he spoke of how his aunt's high level of intensity made ghosts, elementals, and poltergeists appear. According to don Juan, Castaneda's mentor, you can control this type of phenomenon by emptying your mind. He called it "keeping the inner silence." Elementals, who feed off of our auras, are not attracted to such minds. Just be as peaceful, soothing, and egoless as you can be. Jay has been given an opportunity. Perhaps this is a bit of an "initiation" for him. Initiations usually involve fear, but that is just part of the deal. Perhaps this signals a psychological change in your relationship with him. He *is* moving into a new phase with college. It was probably appropriate that he told them to go away. It mirrors the psychological independence he will need to become comfortable living on his own.

-Andy 1/5/03

I had breakfast with Ann and her sister Ruth Macklin, who is a spiritualist medium and a very lovely lady. She is very spiritual. You would love her. I asked Ruth about this thing with my son. Her take was *exactly* the same as yours. She said that the energy attracted this. She said to bathe him in a "Christ light" and put a cup of water in his bedroom to absorb the entity. The 12th chakra, which is below the feet – about 12 inches below the ground – is the point from which these entities rise. The pulling of the toe and the whispering into the ear are common. She said that my energy could indeed be drawing it in. She could feel it. What you called "keeping the inner silence" is just what she was describing. She said that I should go into his room and visualize green, blue, and purple light bathing his room. She advised me to have no fear, as fear might attract more of this kind of thing.

By the way, Ruth saw *you*. I asked her nothing about you. I wasn't thinking of you at all when she described you. She asked me was who the tall, dark man, who "appears to be a Buddhist and lives in the northwest." I just listened, without comment. She said that you were "dissatisfied," and working through "issues of the past." My job was to be your support. She said that your "chanting" will lead you to what you already know in your spirit. You will be making changes that no one around can believe, nor that you yourself felt possible. She said that I must meditate to give you the strength to chant more. She said that chanting is what will truly set you free. I don't know what that means, but she said that I never need to know. She visualized you chanting, either sitting or lying down. I said nothing. She told me that I am a "natural" channeler. She gave me a very practical technique for "clearing" my mind. She said I will grow stronger and stronger in my "non-absorption." She saw your son, and felt your joy with him. She could feel your energy. She kept coming back to you – your quiet reflection… She said that you will break totally free of whatever is holding you, and achieve an "incredible" spiritual level. This woman had a love and presence about her that could *not* be denied.

-Harriet 1/6/03

In Feb. of 2010, J.C. Johnson of the Four Corners Crypto group released a video interview with a Navajo girl who had been visited at night by Men in Black since childhood. The Navajo MIB dress exactly like the ones seen in WV, with hat and trenchcoat. They tend to behave the same way – looking into the doors and windows of target homes. Amazingly, J.C. was able to set up a night camera and catch an image of the creature, which appeared to materialize from a black goo or vapor rising out of the earth. This "elemental" sounds very similar to what Harriet saw in her office in 2004, and to what I saw in the early 1970s. It may also be the type of entity that could pull on the toes of Harriet's son. I was reminded of the Buddhist monk, Samudranath, who made it clear that the job of Garudas and Thunderbirds is to "subdue planetary spirits." Therefore, one can posit that the Mothman visitations of Pt. Pleasant might have been triggered by an increase of planetary spirits in the area, which may have been conjured up by occultists either working at, or visiting, the TNT Area.

I dreamed last night that you and I, and some others, were looking for

Tommy. We were flying around in a "helicopter" visiting sites in an "alternate" Woodward Drive – an alternate reality. I have dreamed of this alternate Woodward many times before. There is one long, woodsy slope from which I typically take off and land (like you do). There was a white, cinder-block "classroom" where I interviewed Tommy's aunt, uncle, and grandfather. They all looked Middle-Eastern. I think these may be the same three I dreamed of just before I read the non-fiction book *Entering the Circle* by Olga Kharitidi. Amazingly, that book featured three shamans (two men and a woman) who visit people around the world, via the dreamstate, and heal them. Olga actually met them in real life... It seemed that a key question in my dream was whether or not Tommy had been asked if he wanted to come along to "their world" – whether or not permission had been sought. I myself felt that I had turned down the offer. I did however, at one time or another, dream of visiting some planet in a spaceship. Anyway, this recent dream seemed important; I rarely dream about Tommy...

Tibetans say that all spirit guides are really just your own "oversoul" communicating with you. The guides are *not* distinctly "outside" of us. In *Voices of Our Ancestors*, Dhyani Ywahoo states – in connection with the electromagnetic grid that covers Earth – that the Thunderbird is "the conveyor of aspirations toward enlightened action." Apparently, in 1987, we entered the "sixth phase of existence" in the Cherokee calendar, where it becomes easier to become enlightened. There is increased "purification" happening in this phase. Ironically, this is when the Strieber book *Communion* came out and everyone started believing in the ETs again. There is a lot of overlap between Cherokee and Tibetan beliefs. Ywahoo talks again and again about Tibet. Alexandra David-Neel, who lived in Tibet in the old days (disguised as a man), referred to the Tibetan "protectors" many times. There are six basic vehicles to enlightenment in the Tibetan system. Some involve meditating on "form," some involve meditating on the formless. The "form" modes are more intellectual, the "formless" more emotional.

-Andy 1/23/03

Well... Last night, *I* dreamed of seeing hundreds of lights in formation in the sky. I watched them land. They were pursuing me. You were with me. We had little to say as we climbed on top of the ridges of Woodward Lane. We were trying not to lose sight of where the lights were... I have dreams all the time – what seem like memories – of a very tall, blonde "teacher" with a pointer. He works with me in a white, cinder-block classroom. At first I am traveling, watching stars out of the window of some vehicle or craft. I always end up in this classroom, with this guy teaching me things that are way over my head. He talks about my "gifts." It is always in this same white, cinder-block building. It seems very odd that you would dream of a white, cinder-block building as well.

-Harriet 1/23/03

On Friday night, I had a dream – at least I think it was a dream – of my tall, blonde teacher in the cinder-block classroom. This time, I was *not* a child; I was the present-day me. He told me that we, as a society, are going to experience catastrophes until we learn to work "against" gravity. We need to move "sideways" through it. The next morning, I was listening to the TV when I heard about the Columbia Space Shuttle catastrophe. I was dumbfounded. I *knew* that this is what he was talking about. Out of the blue, I then had a migraine. Remember when I told you a while back about a "plane" crash that was coming? The shuttle was it!

-Harriet 2/2/03

Coincidentally, I had a migraine the day before the shuttle catastrophe. I also had a second migraine on the day of the shuttle catastrophe. Having two like that is very unusual for me. This doesn't relate to the tragedy but, today, the day after the catastrophe, I randomly cracked open a book. There, it said that there are seven types of people. The seventh type is the "transformer," who follows the "violet flame" and "wears the amethyst." As you may recall, it was the "violet flame" meditation that Ormond McGill led us through in hypnotherapy school. Also, the violet flame is what I visualized after that shamanic sweatlodge in Mazunte, Mexico, right after the 9/11 catastrophe. There may be some connection between the two tragedies, 9/11 and Columbia.

-Andy 2/2/03

Do you recall me telling you how I became obsessed with flying? I had to learn to fly in order to understand my childhood UFO sighting. My obsession started in 1987. I was at home with a new baby, but I couldn't stop studying flight. At that time, these flying dreams were occurring every night... Anyway, I was just listening to a tape about success. The underlying message was that a sense of *purpose* is the key to true success, not goal-setting. It is "mind vs. mind" in all that we do... Why *does* consciousness choose to show itself through form? I think it is to remind us "concretely" that it is there. Most souls go through life never questioning this. It chooses form in order to show us that we indeed create our own reality – with every waking moment – in the mind. What is in the individual mind starts with what is in the universal mind, which literally brings to fruition – in the physical state – thoughts and concepts. I truly believe that the subconscious is mind dwelling within all of us… We are a society of "drifters." We rarely tap into this great potential. I must admit that I previously couldn't quite grasp what you were talking about, with "divisions" simply being "apparent" – not ultimately real. Now, I get it. We *really* are all part of one big source, not at all separate. There really is no such thing as "I." None of us have any more intrinsic talent or skill than the next. It is all in what we can grasp from the collective source around us. That is why these "attributes" are called "God-given" by some.

-Harriet 2/10/03

I keep having a dream – a persistent little sucker – about an air disaster in Seattle. It would be on an inbound flight. I see residential tragedy involved here. This dream is extremely vivid, very logical, and sequential. I have no choice but to believe it may be prophetic. I hope I'm wrong. The catch with this dream is that the craft is "blown" from the sky. Speaking of terror, the kids in school here are scared to death by these proficiency exams instituted by Pres. Bush. Fear isn't a good motivator for most people. It is downright paralyzing, especially to young kids. I am trying to get the principal to listen, which he seems to be. The teachers are also rated in this process. I'm sick to death of their "Chicken Little" behaviors filtering down to the kids. Bush is definitely "over the edge" and looking more like an idiot every day. My CIA aunt sends me these damned emails about praying for him. I blasted her last week. I asked her that if she were such a devout Christian, how could she support this war in the Middle East? I'm the black sheep in the family this week, which is a familiar place for me… Our biggest fear should be destabilization in the Middle East, not test scores. My aunt thinks it is "righteous" to invade. If you think you have freaks in your family, take a number…

-Harriet 2/14/03

One can't reach personal enlightenment by compassion alone. If compassion is your sole vehicle, it may never be more than a form of pity. A complete understanding of the Void must be added – ying and yang together. A lot of people have a misunderstanding of what compassion is. The western form of "compassion" doesn't always include empathy. Psychics generally have a greater capacity for compassion; they receive strong, empathic body responses through the sternum, the secret chakra. Emotion has a role, but one must remember that emotion can sometimes get in the way. A therapist needs to lead the client *through* emotions from a position of neutrality. American therapists have to constantly overcome the many abuses of emotion around their clients: violence in the media, titillation, and bogus sentimentality. The Void is really just understanding that what you see before you is an illusion. It is, in varying degrees, temporary. The Void can range from seeing your parent dead, in the coffin, to achieving some great goal and realizing that even *that* isn't enough to make you happy. It is about perceiving the moment directly, without "concepts."

The Void is the emptiness that underlies all phenomena. All form arises out of emptiness. This is why they say that everything is an illusion. All things return to the Void sooner or later. The "body of visions" is a visualization that Tantric Buddhists practice. When they come back from experiencing emptiness in some way, such as through deep meditation, extreme loss, intense love, or total exhilaration, Tantric practitioners have a method for not letting material forms, those misleading "reference points" of reality, draw them back into the illusion. The illustration of a shuttle re-entering the atmosphere is given in the *Body of Visions* book. The tiles on the shuttle suck up the heat, so that the astronauts are not burned. In the same way, the "body of visions" sucks up the "heat," or desire for, the reference points of consensus reality. Such visualizations set up the conditions for the practitioner to have a good chance at reaching enlightenment. Right after the moment of death, the practitioner needs to be able to take on a separate "astral body" in order to escape rebirth. The illustration inside the front cover of the book is of a Garuda... This is echoed in the work of Castaneda, where we find the "Eagle" being the first entity that one meets upon death. In Huichol philosophy, it is the Eagle that takes your life-force and recycles it into a new, reincarnated body on Earth. The task of the "warrior" is to create a separate "double" body and present that to the Eagle. While the Eagle is occupied with the doppelganger, the "real" body or soul of the warrior slips past and escapes rebirth. This is another example of the striking similarity between Native American and Buddhist traditions.

-Andy 2/17/03

I experience the "Void" all the time. I experience a complete void each time I receive my psychic messages. That's the *only* time I receive, and the only *way* I receive. It's just that I never recognized it as such until now. I sometimes can't put my experience into words. It's probably because I never try to analyze it. I just take it as it is. It is a continuous "movie" in my head. I keep it to myself unless I can help someone avoid potential disaster. I am becoming much better at separating myself from what I see. My life goes at such a hectic pace. It is only during those down times, those relaxed moments, that the "antennae" are up. I have some of my best "viewings" on Wednesday evenings. I have become quite good at emptying my head before each session with a client. If I empty out before a session, the right thing always comes to me, without fail. I just go into a trance and let it flow. About the only time I use a standard script with a client is for a first visit for weight loss or smoking. If I try to split hairs and analyze something, it causes too much "noise" for me.

I have a quiet knowing about what I do. I would have to say that I spend a good deal of my day in "emptiness." My life has a greater calm and knowingness from this… I was on the phone last night, for over two hours, with a psychic friend of mine. A baby owl landed on her porch Saturday night. Then, the same owl ended up on her *mother's* porch last night. They live more than 7 miles apart. The Indians believe owls are messengers. My friend had a son that died 13 years ago. I think he is trying to contact her. One night, I got a clear visual of him standing over her shoulder. Her dead stepmother was over the other shoulder. It floored me. This all started when I began to seriously view "auras." I hope this owl doesn't have bad news for them. My feeling is that it doesn't. It is just her son trying to get her to "move on." He is trying to show her that we don't really die – that he is with her all of the time.

-Harriet 2/18/03

At first, me and my brother were watching the movie *The Mothman Prophecies*. After that, we were fascinated by Mothman and started researching it. We started to try to think of a way to lure it to our city, Red Oak, Texas. We tried to replicate what others had done before they saw the creature. [Since one witness claimed to have] yelled out, "If there are any demons out there, then come and get me," I was made to say it, too. Minutes later, the night grew red. It was amazing. We had never seen anything like it. The whole sky was red, like the sun was going to come up. Later that night, I woke up because my friend had taken all the covers. I was freezing. I looked around the room, and everything was glowing red again for some reason. It was like someone was shining red headlights into the room… I started to hear a light tapping noise on the back door window. The tapping slowly progressed to a beating sound, then a banging sound. It was as if someone was saying: "I know you are in there, and I'm here for you." I was afraid. I acted as if I was still asleep. I started to hear a hissing sound. I stayed under the covers. My friend awoke. He went to the window and looked out. He could see the outline of an 8-ft. tall creature looking upward to the sky. He was half asleep, but he couldn't help but keep staring. After a while, he noticed that he couldn't see it anymore. There was just a big black blotch that he couldn't see past. So, he went back to bed.

Soon we started seeing things standing at the foot of our beds, just staring at us – studying us. We started to feel like we were being watched. There were many things that happened. I broke my arm for no apparent reason, as did my friend. A slight paper cut bled all over the place. Then, after a couple of days, the space shuttle exploded over Red Oak. [At first we thought that] Mothman was here for the shuttle – that we just caught him at the right time. But now [I wonder if] maybe we *caused* it to explode by luring Mothman. [Not long after that] we saw a guy ride up on a motorcycle… The guy kept following us, so we hid in some tall grass. We watched the guy load his cycle into a black truck with a green strip along the side. [Later] the same truck stopped in front of my house. I was frozen with fear. After a few minutes, it slowly rode down to my friend's house and did the same thing. A day later, there were no screens left on my friend's house… I don't think Mothman has left. You can feel it when he comes to visit. It's been about 3 months, but the memory won't go away. [Luckily] we are still around to tell our story. We will find out what it is. Nothing will stop us.

-A. Wolf 7/1/03

My research so far indicates that there is a relationship between all of these "unrelated" phenomenon. John Keel's books do a good job of explaining the mechanics of interdimensional beings. It's an easy concept to grasp when we realize that we live in a holographic universe. In this month's issue of *Scientific American*, they point out that there are several dimensions. They even go so far as to describe the nature of them… I stumbled onto the seeming connection between Mothman and Bigfoot only by accident. First, I happened to see Mothman when I was a kid. Second, I had several dreams, over several years, about Bigfoot. Intuitively, I came to realize there *is* a connection. However, proving it is another matter. But for grins, let's assume that these beings are interdimensional. Shooting at them will only frighten them away or make them attack you. When shot at, they seem to have the ability to always make it back to their own dimension, where they recover from any "wounds." No bodies will ever be found. Another point… Do not shoot at Men in Black. There is one case where it is rumored that someone shot at an MIB, only to find that they had been delusional and had actually shot their best friend. What they thought was a black Cadillac was actually their friend's car… If you see Mothman, Bigfoot, or the MIB, try to remember that you are probably in an altered state. Back up, take a breath, and regain your senses before proceeding.

-Andy 8/7/03

The Kanawha Valley appears to be a node in this phenomenon. There are plausible, scientific, electromagnetic "reasons" for much of the paranormal activity. It has a propensity to exist in certain places. Particular combinations of water, metal, rock, magnetism, and electricity increase the likelihood of seeing a supernatural creature. The Thunderbird and Garuda are both associated with lightning, and Bigfoot is often seen in conjunction with strange lights. Such sources of energy suggestively impinge on the human brain, causing us to experience unusual phenomenon. Mothman experiencers across the country see roughly the same thing. I know what witnesses are talking about when they describe the "man with the hat and coat." I even wrote about him in a song. Putting these fellows into your art seems to help dissolve their influence. By the way, our family farm was just south of Ripley, on the very route that Woody Derenberger and Indrid Cold used to drive. In Bob Teets' book on West Virginia UFOs, he calls Ripley "UFO Central."

-Andy 8/28/03

Something incredibly strange happened today… I called a friend of mine, Judy, who lives in *Apollo*, PA, to ask her if she could make it to the Pennsylvania Bigfoot Conference in Jeannette, PA tomorrow. Judy has had a lot of peculiar things happen to her in the past. Unfortunately, she can't make it to the conference. During the course of our conversation, she told me that a guy she took to be a police officer came to her door about an hour before I called. He was wearing a black uniform with some sort of star badge. He was driving an old style (1950s or '60s) gray car. She said he was very pale and had the straightest nose she had ever seen in her life. Strangely, he laughed [for no reason] when they first starting talking. He asked her if she knew anything about this family that lived in the neighborhood named "Magerran," or something like that. She told him that she had never heard that name before. She got the impression that the police were investigating this family [yet] this guy never identified himself as a policeman or FBI. She assumed he was [FBI, though] because of the way he was dressed. She said there was another person waiting for him in the car. As she was telling me all this, I was blown away… I had just read an email from Harriet less than thirty minutes before, about [her dad being car-bombed, then getting visits from MIBs and, possibly, fake FBI men]! I had not mentioned Harriet, or her story, to Judy at all. I've talked to Judy about MIB before, but she didn't know much about them. I don't think there was any chance of her making any of this up. She had no idea that I had just heard a similar story from Harriet. [Oddly] there was a UFO sighting in the suburb right next to Harriet's on Monday. It took place on the approach to the Columbus, Ohio airport. That location makes sense, because Barbara from Youngstown has seen three different strange lights in the last 6 weeks.

-John Frick 9/26/03

Ed Oundee, who posted about his Mothman sighting in Georgia in 2001, was at the Mothman festival last September. Ed and his mother drove from Virginia to find out more about what they had seen. I interviewed them for well over an hour. My niece, Sharon Moore, was also present at the interview. She saw Mothman in her home in 2001. It was interesting for us to share our sightings. Eddie and his mom were still visibly shaken by their sighting. I spent a lot of time assuring them that they were *not* crazy, and that they will continue integrating the experience. Eddie's life story somewhat parallels that of my friend, Tommy Burnham, with whom I built the shrine that seemingly prompted our experiences with Mothman… It seems that encounters with Mothman while in a car are more socially acceptable than seeing him in the bedroom. There still seems to be a stigma attached to these very close encounters, similar to the stigma facing Betty and Barney Hill when their encounter was first published in the 1960s. People were willing to believe that UFOs were flying around, but skeptical of the idea that these UFOs might land or unload occupants on the ground. Such delays ended up providing cover for the MIBs for two or three decades.

While this stigma seems to have lessened for those encountering aliens today, I think it still applies to modern day witnesses who have extremely close Mothman experiences. Even though such witnesses, like my sister and niece, are not claiming to be "contactees," there is a danger that they will be treated with the same condescending "wink and nod" reserved for the contactees of the 1950s. This is unfortunate, for it marginalizes those who need help and support the most, while allowing the MIBs to do their dirty work. It also keeps us from knowing some of Mothman's secrets, as those who are ostracized are often those to whom Mothman is revealing himself most fully. Until people realize that this creature is continuing to manifest, in very close and personal ways, he will remain an enigma and the MIB will win. If Mothman can, as Ed claims, fly *without* flapping its wings – beyond the laws of known physics – it is quite probable that it can materialize in your bedroom, or even read your mind. He might even help you fight off the MIB.

-Andy 10/7/03

I am writing you exactly one year after my sighting of a "missile" that supposedly shot down another "missile" launched from the Marshall

Islands. On page 17 of *Life With a Cosmos Clearance*, there is the testimony of Col. Ross Dedrickson from Sept. 2000:

> For example, a Minuteman missile was destroyed after launch from Vandenburg AFB. That is now a matter of public record. In this incident, they actually photographed a "UFO" following a missile as it climbed into space and, shining a beam on it, neutralized the missile...

That is pretty much what I saw, in a nutshell. I said it then, and I'll say it now: why in the world would a missile be launched at 7 p.m., over a heavily populated area, flying over a baseball game with thousands of witnesses, only to be "intercepted" by another missile shot from the Marshall Islands. The most likely scenario in my mind then, as it is now, is that we launched that missile, possibly with a nuclear warhead, in order to take down something else. And, then, it was shot down from above. That is what I saw. The question is, "Who shot it down?" It could have been "us" or it could have been "them." But the beam came from above. I saw it with my own eyes. Of course, it was passed off as a "test" on the evening news, and forgotten about. But I will never forget what I saw.

-Harriet 10/14/03

I liked the recent discussion on how interdimensional entities rely on mimicry. Mimicry can occur on very subtle levels. People go through life mimicking what they think looks the best. They observe this process from the place of ego, called "Platform A." The Buddhists actually have a meditation where they observe Platform A as a sphere with an "A" inside. The key is to realize that there is also a platform B, the equivalent of the superego, where they can observe the mental processes of Platform A. Consciousness is not just the bodymind complex. Consciousness can take on new forms, like a change of clothes. Few of us realize that there are more subtle platforms, so we haven't taken advantage of them effectively. From any particular platform, we can dissolve thoughts arising at another platform.

Two weeks before the festival last Sept., the "balloon eye" crop circle formed across the road from the Serpent Mound in Ohio. I made a point of going to the Serpent Mound prior to the festival, in order to do some filming. I had a very clear sense that I needed to go there. One of my theories is that the Serpent Mound was built to honor the Thunderbird. I wanted to go there and commit the theory to film. I did a little Native ritual there. As we were walking to the car, Harriet's spirit guide told her to drink the water there, so we found a fountain and drank the water. Two days later, there was a large triangular UFO seen within five miles or so of the Serpent Mound. It was seen very close to the community of "Harriett," Ohio. The "name game" thus came into play. Also, Berryville, the closest town to Harriett, features the name of a key family of experiencers on Woodward Lane. As we drove away, Harriet and I saw something that looked like a crop circle in a soybean field. It looked pretty insignificant from the road, but we took a quick look anyway and, sure enough, it was the now-famous "balloon eye" or "Eye of Horus" circle. So, we got to experience real crop circle energy, something I had been wanting to do for years.

We then went to Columbus, OH, to film a bit about the Bush family having once lived there. We wondered whether or not the Mothman had anything to do with the Bohemian Grove Stone Owl that the Republicans seem to worship. Five days later, a huge UFO was seen in Gahanna, which is very close to where we were filming. On the way to Columbus, we were talking about how the D.C. Sniper got active just when the vote to go to war in Iraq was being decided. Then we got to talking about the West Virginia sniper. Harriet did a psychic reading. She predicted that he would stop, but then start up again. Sure enough, the WV shootings stopped, only to re-emerge again later in Columbus, where Harriet lives. She also predicted the next big terrorism attack would be directed at "a bridge."

If there is any truth to the rumor that the I-35 Bridge collapse in Minneapolis was sabotaged (in order to increase spending for bridges along the proposed NAFTA Superhighway), one could argue that Harriet's prediction came true when that bridge collapsed. Mothman was supposedly seen nearby, just a couple of weeks before the collapse. Mainstream paranormal shows are now starting to agree that Mothman activity may still be happening. However, they don't want to go so far as to really look at what sort of creature might cross state lines and float into people's bedrooms. In the Mothman episode of the History Channel show Monsterhunters, *aired in early 2010, all that was really acknowledged is that the creature looks the same in Wisconsin, California, and West Virginia. Along the way, unfortunately, it was implied that Mothman kills animals, which may not be true at all. He is most likely a "first responder," not a perpetrator... Producers for the show apparently told UFO Digest's Regan Lee that her metaphysical ideas about Mothman being an beneficial archetype were not wanted, even though they ended up stating much the same. Their show made several references to how Mothman warns people of tragedy.*

One senses that it is not necessarily the "archetypal angel" idea that these shows dislike, but the idea that Mothman can be linked to revelations about specific conspiracies. Corporate and governmental conspiracies are large in scale and often tragic for those lacking political clout. Sometimes, the conspiracies result in many needless deaths. Such a fact needs to be avoided on TV, in order to keep advertising revenue flowing. To try and tackle conspiracies would be folly for media insiders, because any Mothman-inspired "conspiracy" revelation might potentially hurt their bottom line... But it's not just big conspiracies that seem to concern Mothman. Any issue that means a lot to us, on a personal level, can trigger the pineal gland; this, in turn, can subtly trigger the surrounding physical environment to respond. Mothman responds readily to emotional upheavals of the romantic variety, since those are among the highest stressors, especially if children are involved. According to Keel, falling in love can trigger a paranormal sighting. Conversely, a paranormal encounter can trigger the hormones necessary to fall in love. This was proven in an experiment done on Vancouver Island in 2009, where subjects were found to desire sex more if the immediate environment contained an element of fear. This is not a new idea, of course. Sociology studies of the 1960s indicated that the fear involved with riding on a motorcycle markedly increased the likelihood of a sexual encounter, making biker gangs a focal point for both criminals and police.

According to the UFO reporting website, *Filer's Files*, a "cigar" UFO was seen in Harriet's part of Columbus just a few weeks after I was there, in Dec. 2003. She has seen UFOs in Columbus several times. Her childhood sighting on Woodward Dr. was of a cigar-shaped UFO. In the fall of 2003, Harriet saw a man materialize and then de-materialize in her living room. He said nothing. Her dog barked wildly. She described him to me. She told me that he looked like he had "liver failure." It turns out this was probably a deceased friend of mine, Aryadaka, who was a Buddhist priest here in Seattle. Aryadaka had died just one day before, of a failed liver transplant. He and I had some personal issues that were never quite resolved. The message Harriet got from him was that "everything is fine between Andy and me."

Another witness in the series, Bill Bryant, recently called with a story. He was driving through Utah, when he saw the same car *and* driver pass by *twice*. This sent him into a trancelike state, where he was shown a vision of the Earth's energy matrix. He said that he saw the grid in its entirety. There is a grid at ground level, and there are other grids going up into space. He saw "nodes" where the grid came together, high in the atmosphere, at the edge where it meets outer space. He was told that these nodes were guarded by beings "who make sure that life on earth is protected." John Keel, in his interview with me, expressed disappointment that we are not very good stewards of Earth, so maybe these protector beings are a necessity.

An aficionado of "phantom cats" met with me on the island of Maui recently. We went looking for a big cat that was sighted near the village of Olinda, where Mark Twain once lived. We found that the volcanic areas above Olinda, where the cat has been seen, are highly magnetic. In fact, the main crater is called "Magnetic Peak." It has so much magnetism that it will deflect a compass. This same cat researcher called me recently to report his first UFO sighting. He left a message saying: "It is one o'clock in the afternoon on a bright, sunny day. Look up in the sky. There are five extremely large, bright stars shining above Seattle." Unfortunately, I wasn't home at the time and didn't get to see them.

Another witness interviewed in the series, Ken Alton, feels that he may have been abducted by aliens while on a recent camping trip. His girlfriend, Mercedes, corroborated his story. One night during the trip, Kenny dreamed he was being instructed on how to kill certain robots. These robots were sent by aliens to control us. Then, his dream shifted. He felt he was being pulled from his tent by grey aliens. Both he and Mercedes stated that they were in a "trance" all the next day. She left her purse on top of the car when they drove off. Kenny said that he shut his eyes and simply "knew" where on the highway the purse had fallen. Sure enough, that is where they found the purse. I saw them immediately after they returned to Seattle, and both seemed shaken by the experience.

-Andy 12/22/03

This is really interesting. You are probably right about the Serpent Mound being connected with the Thunderbird. I wish I had [gone] with you when you went out there. I've recently realized that the events in Point Pleasant in 1966-67 are somehow tied in with the Indian mounds all over that area. I do not want to go public with all the details yet, because I still have a lot of research to do… In *The Mothman Prophecies*, Keel said that UFOs commonly appear in areas where there are Indian mounds… I'm curious if you think Thunderbird and Mothman are *exactly* the same thing. I think I remember you telling me that they are. I suspect this may be true, but all I know for sure [now] is that they are connected in some way… I've recently realized that these beings are likely using magnetic energy to help them materialize. In other words, they can't appear out of nothing; they need something that is already there: magnetism. I think they are also using human thought-energy to manifest. I believe our thoughts are also a form of energy. This is deep stuff...

-John Frick 12/22/03

We can't be sure that Mothman and Thunderbird are *exactly* the same thing, but the relationship seems strong. Acknowledging that relationship is an important step. Take Western medicine... It uses a Cartesian model, which is basically about isolating individual "symptoms" or "causes," and then treating said causes with a pill or other temporary relief technique. Western medicine is good for many things, like sewing your hand back on after an accident, but it's not very good for preventing or repairing complex disease patterns. It's the same with this phenomenon. You can't just isolate one thing and find the total solution. All the different routes and crossroads matter. One can't accurately "diagnose" if one comes in with a specific agenda. While there are certain predictable patterns and commonalities of treatment, the practitioner should always be open to unique solutions. But even that unique, one-in-a-million solution will still involve a series of relationships. Those relationships are revealed via the human innate system. The human innate can access anything within the body. It has a tremendous range outside the body as well. It can tap into the collective unconscious and pull out information. Magnetism may amplify or hinder this ability, depending on the situation.

Regarding electromagnetism, the Albert Budden book explains it well. Not only do more "abductions" occur around strong EM fields, but also their qualities are more varied. The *Secrets in the Fields* book does a good job of explaining the way in which an EM current can form between underground water sources and points high up in the ionosphere. There is a lot of underground water in eastern Ohio and western WV. This is a physical mechanism believed by some to be behind the formation of crop circles. There are also EM connections between the surface of the Earth and points even higher up, *outside* the ionosphere. I say this because whenever lightning comes down to strike the ground, there is a corresponding flash (much smaller) that goes *up*. It can be measured and photographed. No one can figure out what is attracting these upward flashes, since these storm systems are already extremely high up. The "vacuum" of space appears to be a conductor of electricity...

-Andy 12/23/03

Did anyone notice this? Not long after the recent reports of kids being sent home early from school due to chemtrail plumes, we had the big "flu epidemic," which led to the cost of vaccines going up tenfold. This has lead the public health industry to speculate that they may be forced to use genetically altered "monkey serum" for incubation, instead of eggs. Excuse me, but wasn't bad monkey serum long ago pinpointed, by several sources, as being the probable cause of AIDS?

-Andy 12/24/03

I have kept up somewhat with the False Memory Syndrome (FMS) debate, simply because it comes up a lot in regards to mind control. An academic proponent of FMS was a professor here at UW in Seattle. The FMS debate appears to have been devised because revelations about government mind control were resurfacing with renewed vigor in the 1980s, and a direction was needed in which to funnel that interest. Maury Terry's *The Ultimate Evil*, which laid out credible evidence that a national "satanic" group was sacrificing animals and humans, had recently been published. According to Terry, Son of Sam, Wayne Williams, and Charles Manson are all considered to have been part of this national network. Each time investigators got close to identifying the upper echelon, they were called off because of "national security." The NYC cult controlling Berkowitz – whose work was apparently filmed by a crew producing "snuff films" – was found to be headed by a rich film producer, Roy Radin. Radin had a mansion on Long Island, like the one in *Eyes Wide Shut*. Radin was murdered in L.A. right before he was scheduled to testify in court. Jim Keith implied that this national satanic group had some sort of Freemasonic leadership. He cited connections to the UFO community and implied that "magical workings" were being performed in order to manipulate UFO events. Keel has alluded to these, indirectly, as well. The gist of it is that certain groups appear to be in the habit of brainwashing innocent civilians. They apparently have "orphanages" for these abducted people, who are later turned into assassins, drug mules, spies, and so forth. The beauty is that these victim/killers are programmed to forget. And, if they *do* remember, there is always "false memory" to debunk them.

-Andy 12/26/03

CHAPTER 6

"Grey Walter and his associates decided, in 1946, to try imposing new brain patterns through the senses. They began by flashing a light, at regular intervals, into the subject's eyes and found that this flicker produced new, strange patterns... At certain frequencies, the flicker produced violent reactions in a large number of otherwise normal people... A feedback circuit, in which the flashing light was actually fired by the brain signals themselves, produced immediate epileptic seizures in more than half the people tested. In [one] case, a man found that every time he went to the cinema, he would suddenly find that he was consumed by an overwhelming desire to strangle the person sitting next to him. On one occasion, he came to his senses to find that he had his hands clutched around his neighbor's throat. It was found that he developed violent limb jerking when the flicker was set at 24 cycles per second, which is exactly the [rate at which] film is recorded. The implications of this discovery are enormous. Every day, we are exposed to flicker in some way, and run the risk of illness or fatal fits. Infrasounds can affect us in the same way as flickering lights [and] are responsible for the way in which some drivers wander across the [median] of roads, quite oblivious to the danger of oncoming traffic. [Engine] vibrations may account for a large number of otherwise inexplicable accidents.

"An engineer in Marseilles, named Gavraud, almost gave up his post [before] he discovered that a very low frequency air-conditioning [motor] across the street was making him ill. Fascinated by the phenomenon, Gavraud decided to build machines to produce infrasound... In casting around for likely designs, he discovered that the pea whistle of French gendarmes produced a whole range of low-frequency sounds. So, he built a police whistle six feet long, and powered it with compressed air. The technician who gave the whistle its first trial blast fell down dead on the spot. The next test, more carefully done, broke the windows of every building within half a mile of the test site. [It was eventually] discovered that two generators, focused on a particular point miles away, produce a resonance that can knock a building down as effectively as a major earthquake. These machines can be built very cheaply; plans for them are available [at] the patent office… A fascinating postscript [is that] a million-dollar project [attempted] to X-ray the pyramid of Chephren. The recorders ran 24 hours a day for more than a year, until early 1969… The scientists had to admit defeat: the pyramid made no sense at all. Tapes recorded with the same equipment, from the same point and on successive days, showed totally different cosmic-ray patterns. The leader of the project, Amr Gohed, said, 'This is scientifically impossible. Call it what you will – occultism, the curse of the pharaohs, sorcery, or magic. There is some force that defies the laws of science at work in the pyramid.'"

-Lyall Watson, *Supernature*, pp. 90-100

COLVIN, ANDY – GRASSY KNOLL RADIO INTERVIEW 27 – APRIL 2008

Andy Colvin (AC): Say Vyz, do you remember those airship sightings back in 1897? Most of them were in Texas and California, but one or two were in WV. A series of letters were supposedly written by the inhabitants of the airships. The letters were written in blue and red ink which – wouldn't you know it? – is very similar to the VARO edition of Morris Jessup's *Case for the UFO*. Many studying the Philadelphia Experiment were entranced by the fact that the VARO edition had supposedly "alien" writings in the margins, in blue and red ink. Actually, what happened was that they simply regurgitated an old idea from 1897! This happens all the time in the UFO business. Similarly, they rehash themes when fomenting wars and revolutions. The VARO Corporation, the company that reprinted Jessup's book – in order to highlight the ink colors – was a Navy contractor. They were the developers of night vision goggles used by snipers. These tentacles always seem to come back to assassinations, lasers, and satellites. Were all of those "lightning strike victims" Keel spoke of actually killed by lightning, or by hitmen? Lots of people were disappearing in WV in those days. Why is it that a famous UFO case is connected to a defense contractor making sniper rifles? It seems kind of odd. What else have we got here… 47 boxes were found in the 1990 murder investigation of Rabbi Kahane in NYC. It's that number 47 thing again… The Kahane hit connects to Ali Mohammed, who supposedly trained the 9/11 hijackers.

"Vyz" at *Beyond the Grassy Knoll* (GK): I remember the day that happened. I was listening to WCBS. I think Kahane was on the entrance to some bridge when he got popped. That investigation went away real quick. Interesting...

AC: Yes, because it leads to this whole "Al Qaeda" network involved in the '93 Trade Center bombing... By the way, the right-wing media outlet, McClatchy, has a logo that looks just like the Iron Mountain logo – the winged triangle.

GK: Holy mackerel... Isn't that the name of the woman who came up with the photograph of the supposed Shanksville smoke plume during 9/11?

AC: Yes. McClatchy's slogan is "Truth Speaks Power." They are the third largest newspaper in the U.S.

GK: WING-TV met with the woman, named McClatchy, who took the photo. She was – excuse my French – a raging bitch. She is supposedly a realtor in Shanksville. She supposedly heard the rumble, ran outside, and took the famous photo of a smoke plume from the crashed Flight 93. But it can't be *that*, because it's a freaking ordnance mushroom. When a plane hits the ground, you don't get a mushroom-shaped cloud. A mushroom cloud means ordnance, not a plane. The whole thing is bogus. WING-TV went out and talked to her, and she was nasty. The timing – how she could hear it and then make it outside just in time – was suspicious. You know the photo: a black mushroom beyond the red barn. It wouldn't surprise me if they handpicked her to pull this stinker off.

AC: I can tell you that the McClatchy logo looks a *lot* like Iron Mountain's. They are almost identical, except that McClatchy's has an extra little pyramid in it.

GK: That's funny, because what was Iron Mountain originally developed for? Mushroom harvesting... After the mushroom business went belly up, they turned it into a document depository. You can't make this stuff up...

AC: By the way, a new company that is shuttling valuables around, Iron Mountain-style, is called "Garda." I'm seeing their trucks in Seattle now. Around the same time I started noticing them, there was a death on the set of a new James Bond movie being filmed on Lake "Garda" in Italy. Just add a "u" to "Garda," and you have "Garuda!" Add a couple more letters, and you have "guardian," the protector deity.

GK: I went to the McClatchy website and, you're right, that logo is very close to Iron Mountain's. Apparently that branch of the family has holdings in Pennsylvania and out west, by you.

AC: The father of Tom Slick, the famous CIA cryptozoologist, was from Clarion, Pennsylvania. He went to West Virginia in 1899, at age 16. Later, father and son worked together in the oil fields. Dad made $75 million, which was passed to junior when he was 14 years old. That's how junior became the "jetsetter," flying to Tibet to find the Yeti. Not surprisingly, he was also in Navy Intel. Having made their money in oil at such a critical time, the Slicks must have had associations with the Rockefellers... There is a "Tom Slick Avenue" in San Antonio, which runs through the Southwest Research facility. Southwest is notorious for having a huge array of monkeys that are used for gruesome experimentation. Onward... According to the testimony of a Red Cross volunteer named Atmo Kabir, there were bomb squads at the Freshkills sorting area following 9/11.

GK: That would make sense if they were looking to sniff out bombs that may not have been detonated.

AC: Switching to the famous Dr. Steven Greer, who is a major pusher of the ET thesis... It's hard to sort out fact from fantasy when it comes to Dr. Greer. He now claims that he has lost two friends, and almost his own life, to "cancer attack." My source on this is Steve Calkins, a "former NSA employee" on my Mothman discussion list. Greer claims to be the only one who survived the "cancer attack," which was mounted after he and former astronaut Ed Mitchell facilitated a "secret" Congressional hearing on the UFO question in 1997... One wonders if this is an agency attempt to muddy the waters regarding cancer attacks. No one in the agency goes after ET proponents, as most of them are dupes or are paid by the agency. After a few months of these created "false alarms," no one will ever believe that cancer attacks are real... Okay... The Akron, Ohio airdock... This is an enormous hangar that Goodyear and the Rockefellers built for dirigibles. It was so big that *clouds* formed inside of it. Goodyear was more or less a Rockefeller company at one time. I like the theory that the Hindenburg disaster was a Big Oil plot to make sure that alternatives to automobiles were not available. Goodyear technicians were involved in the development of the Hindenburg, whose destruction must have helped Standard Oil.

GK: It got singed in Southern New Jersey...

AC: There are many links between Goodyear and the Germans. The

Rockefellers were originally a German family. I recently was reading about cattle mutilations, and found a case where somebody got a good, close look at one of these "silent helicopters" thought to be frying the cattle. Behind the glare of the lights shining out, the witness could see some sort of *dirigible* on top. Dirigibles are very quiet. This is one more possibility for the cattle mutilations: they are camouflaging blimps to make them look like something else – helicopters or UFOs. This way, they can more easily perform the animal muscle testing necessary to find out where the underground mineral deposits are... The Crawfordsville Sky Monster... In 1891, there was a squirming, weaving man-bird seen in Crawfordsville, Indiana. Crawfordsville comes up in my own personal story, because I dated a woman from there. While I was dating her, I owned the Linda Blair car, which spontaneously caught on fire the day after I sold it. Come to think of it, those 1897 airship sightings occurred mostly in Texas and *Indiana*.

GK: Were those older airships dirigibles?

AC: That would be the best guess, barring some sort of mass hallucination. They looked like all sorts of different things, from Spanish galleons to steam boilers. The inventors probably wanted to hide the shape of any underlying balloons.

GK: I wanted to ask you about the dirigibles, because that is what my wife and I *thought* we saw in Jersey once. At first, we thought it was landing in Peterborough, which is where they moored dirigibles like those used to shoot Monday Night Football at Giant Stadium. So, in a way, we thought that was kind of normal, except that when it went behind a bank of clouds, it never reappeared. Now you're talking about using them for what might be stealthy, undetected involvement in cattle mutilations. What we saw was cigar-shaped, like a dirigible.

AC: For centuries, reputable people have seen all sorts of things in the sky. It would be hard to ferret out whether that was paranormal, or just a manmade craft... Did we talk about the Clintons' visit to the Rockefeller ranch? Hillary was photographed with Cheney and Laurance Rockefeller at his JY Ranch in the Grand Tetons a few years back. This is where they held those "healthcare reform" meetings with the insurance companies, which ended in *zero* progress towards healthcare.

GK: They are all peas in the same pod.

AC: Another sighting note: *thirty three* days (note Masonic number) before the Minneapolis I-35 bridge collapse, on June 27, 2007, in Stewartville, Minnesota, there was supposedly a Mothman sighting. June 27th is a date that usually sees a lot of paranormal activity. However, there could be a Masonic element at work here, in that a Mothman sighting was hoaxed in order to provide adequate "revelation of the method." Elites want the "little people," the average Masons out there, to know that the bridge collapse was necessary to build the NAFTA superhighway, which will fulfill the Masonic dream of bringing Mexico back into the British Empire.

GK: Again, we have those good old "workers on the bridge" before the thing goes down… Now I'm starting to wonder what happened with that I-40 overpass in Arkansas.

AC: Speaking of felling bridges, that "black box" that witnesses were seeing in Pt. Pleasant and Mound could have been a Tesla coil, which causes vibrations capable of bringing any structure down. Tesla claimed he could fracture the entire earth with it, were he able to set one up big enough… If mankind ever reached a technological height at some point in the distant past, one wonders what brought it all crashing down. Was it Mother Nature, or was it a Tesla-type device? By the way, there were four possible types of black boxes in WV during Mothman. The first would be the Tesla type. The second would be the mind control type. Keel saw someone holding a black box at the Tad Jones sighting spot, which looked like something out of the playbook of Persinger or Puharich, who both tinkered with devices that could alter brainwaves. The third type of black box was the early cellphone, which was initially very large and came in a black case. The fourth was the handheld laser or EM device, which was used by the MIBs that were terrorizing UFO researchers. They sometimes drove a blue VW bug with WV license plates. Their vehicles sometimes had a "lightning bolt" symbol painted on them, as if it were a Nazi or Freemasonic secret society. This may be a clue regarding the allegiances of Indrid Cold… Michael Persinger's box reportedly made people "hallucinate aliens," by the way.

GK: What color was Pandora's box? Can we ever know?

AC: Another note… This Pioneer spacecraft we have deployed is now drifting back towards the sun. Some force is hindering the craft – a subtle field of energy. It is probably a magnetic ring, like those that cause "natural" UFOs – balls of light that circle vortices at a distance of approximately 30 kilometers. These balls of light mimic what happens at the atomic level, where electrons tend to prefer circling around a central node. This reputed node, or vortex, at Liberty, WV may have been responsible for whatever "natural" UFO waves occurred in Charleston and Pt. Pleasant. Both cities are approximately 30 km from Liberty, which is very close to where Indrid Cold lived… Whether or not these balls of light can be interpreted by the human mind as solid, metal craft is another question. But clearly, some of the UFOs in WV definitely seemed synthetic and manufactured… I received an email from a witness not too long ago, John Cain, who saw Mothman on Rt. 62 between Charleston and Pt. Pleasant. He saw it in 2006, fairly close to Liberty and the Ft. Ancient Indian site. Another note… I found a reference to an Army bioweapons director being from the Merck Corp. Then, I saw a video on YouTube featuring a whistleblower, Dr. Hilleman, who had worked for Merck way back when. Hilleman claims that Merck came up with the cancer-causing "SV-40" virus. SV-40 was in the original polio vaccines and, perhaps, in David Ferrie's needles. It is interesting to consider that Oswald may have been investigating Ferrie on behalf of Naval Intelligence. Dr. Hilleman is also blaming *AIDS* on Merck, and for similar reasons: bad vaccines…

Two scenarios in which Ferrie – or perhaps Ferrie's "ghost" – may have played a role in UFO events are mentioned in Tim Beckley's The UFO Silencers. *One is the Johnny Sands case, where a hairless "spaceman" (seemingly with Vegas mafia affiliations) hypnotized Sands. Sands was then drugged and abducted by what was later discovered to be a fake TV crew. Hours later, he woke up with hazy memories of being filmed cavorting with "small Bigfoots" and "aliens" in the desert… The other scenario is the famous case of Dr. Herbert Hopkins, a UFO enthusiast who, on the date of Sept. 11th, 1976, (note Masonic, bicentennial date) met with an MIB who seemed to make a coin "disappear" from his hand. The reason for the visit seemed to be to hypnotize Hopkins into destroying all of his UFO materials – which he did. The MIB specifically asked about Hopkins' interest in Betty and Barney Hill, a case that looks to have been a demonstration of military mind control. Barney Hill initially remembered meeting a man in Nazi uniform, not an ET. Hill was actually programmed to forget what he had seen by an Army hypnotist, thus pointing towards a coverup.*

David Ferrie was an avowed racist with Nazi leanings, who probably would have enjoyed interfering in an interracial marriage such as the Hills. Interestingly, Hopkins' MIB bore similarities to Ferrie: no facial hair, eyebrows, or eyelashes of any kind, very white skin, thin lips with a hint of lipstick, and a receding chin. The MIB wore a nicely tailored suit and dark shirt, like a mobster (which Ferrie was), and spoke in a monotone voice that put Hopkins into a trancelike state. Ferrie, of course, was a uniquely gifted hypnotist... The Hopkins MIB had to leave abruptly; he said his energy was "running low," much like the "Jell-O MIB" in Pt. Pleasant, who happened to drive the same model car as both James Earl Ray and his CIA handler, "Raoul." Hopkins observed the MIB walking very slowly and unsteadily, grabbing the handrail, and taking one step at a time. Ferrie, of course, was rumored to have cancer and various other ailments. Oddly, the MIB did not move his head much, as if his skin was tight or sore, and his nose was described as "small." If Ferrie's death, which occurred just as he was about to be deposed by Jim Garrison, was faked, it might have been necessary for him to undergo plastic surgery. Such things are not uncommon for "retired" CIA assets.

AC: A friend of mine is dating a woman whose father-in-law was once stationed at Fort Carson. She comes from a "Romany gypsy" family in Germany. They were brought over because of their psychic talents. At least, that is the story... This is a friend I've known for years. He is one of my Mothman research supporters. He is a hunter with a side focus on Bigfoot. He hunts deer, elk, and bear mostly. He recently started dating this gypsy woman, who is a bartender. She claims that she has had both a Bigfoot sighting *and* a UFO sighting. Her uncle is some famous euroterrorist. Her mother had psychic talents that drew attention. Her father was stationed at Fort Carson, which is where Carlos Allende, the Philadelphia Experiment witness, spent his last days. It is also where Intel assets from Tibet and other high-elevation countries were sent, as it is easier on their bodies.

GK: That sounds similar to what Hitler did. He brought the Buddhists into the bunker so that they could perform their mojo.

AC: It was way worse for them in Berlin than in Colorado. If you took a Tibetan and stuck him in a basement in Berlin, he wouldn't last very long.

GK: That's true because, when the Russians broke through, there were about 50 of them dead.

AC: Did you know that "Donner and Blitzen" means "thunder and lightning?" That's sort of a Thunderbird-Garuda linkage to the date of Dec. 25th, as well as to Christ and to Santa, whose Norwegian backstory involves the ritual ingestion of hallucinogens that lead to beneficial visions. There is an article about Donner and Blitzen, by Alex Tomlinson, called "The Nazis Hijack of Christmas," in the Nov. 2007 *Fate* magazine... In an unrelated matter, Bush Sr. has given several speeches to groups supporting Rev. Moon.

GK: Moon has financial ties to many American televangelists. An ex-Moonie told me that a "white van" always followed him around while he was a member. He was well aware that he was being surveilled. One day, his wife went out for her daily walk but didn't come home. He found her with her brain fried. She was in some hospital, having been raped... He never got back to me. The next thing I knew, he was nowhere to be found; his website had gone down. What's interesting is that the guy who did the graphics on his website *also* did the website for Jeff Rense. His last name is Neff.

AC: Since there are a lot of Renses and Neffs in Cleveland, it makes you wonder if there isn't some connection between the Moonies and the "Bushefellers." Speaking of which, the company that John Paul II worked for at Auschwitz, Solvay, was a division of I.G. Farben. Guess where Solvay has another big plant: in Ashland, KY! Charles Manson, who claimed Moon harassed him when he tried to collect royalties on Manson Family songs recorded by the Beach Boys, lived in Ashland for a time, as did Lynndie England, the Abu Ghraib chick who took the "stacked terrorist" photos. Eastern KY was also the location of Carl Stanley, the Universal Life Church minister who brought David Ferrie into the Wandering Bishops. Fred Crisman, the CIA operative and Wandering Bishop involved in the Maury Island UFO case, was a Universal Life minister. Richard Branson of Virgin Air just became a ULC minister, too.

GK: Do you remember Cott Soda when we were growing up? It has disappeared since.

AC: My first Little League team was sponsored by Cott Soda.

GK: Branson bought Cott around 1990. The story was that he was going to use that beverage on his Virgin Airlines – that it was really going to do well financially. So I threw a grand down and bought some stock in Cott. Branson then went flying around the world in a damned balloon, and the stock tanked. But the dismantling of I.G. Farben begat BASF, Aventis, Hoechst, and Bayer, whose logo is the iron cross.

AC: If you connect the four corners of the "X" inside the circle of the iron cross, creating an "X box" inside a circle, you have what's called "the diamond wheel." The Indians use a variation of it to depict the four directions. If you repeatedly envision this wheel spinning in your spinal column, it can cause kundalini. That shape is *also* supposedly what you would see if you flew above the "giant crystal" at Montauk and looked down upon it. If you stripped the earth away from Montauk, so that you could see down into the underground levels, you would supposedly see this huge crystal that is diamond shaped. It is essentially two pyramids joined, one pointing up and one pointing down. This is just like the pyramid in Egypt, which has an underground part that is the same size as the top part. The Montauk mind control doctors supposedly used this crystal to amplify signals to and from psychics' minds.

GK: The inversion of that would give you the Star of David. If you interlocked the two with point up, point down, you get a six-pointed star.

AC: Yes... Switching gears... I've talked about the kingfisher being the bird most associated with the Garuda in Southeast Asia. Well, it turns out that the Natives here in the Pacific Northwest *also* use the kingfisher in Thunderbird imagery. You have the same bird being used, all around the Pacific Rim.

GK: Kingfishers are excellent predators, because they will stay in one place and just sit there. They eye their quarry, hunker down, and never miss.

AC: Random tidbits... Alex Jones now claims that in a dream he had before 9/11, he saw "a plane flying into buildings." This would be a precognition of 9/11. The source on that is S. Miles Lewis, the Austin UFO researcher... According to John Keel, Zoroaster was looking into cattle mutilations 2500 years ago. Zoroaster was speaking to an entity, Mazda.

GK: Why not?

AC: The updated *Loose Change* movie was released on the Masonic holy day, November 11th. There was a hoax involving Bhutto of Pakistan after she was killed. *India Times* floated a story that she was killed by a laserbeam. Ultimately, it seems like a story designed to make us believe that laser weapons do *not* exist.

GK: In *Conspirator's Hierarchy*, Dr. John Coleman talked about the assassination of Bhutto's father. There was a hoax story that some beam or pulse crashed *his* plane, too.

AC: I just saw an article last week that a company has developed a $1 million dollar item that you can stick on the bottom of any commercial plane. It senses any missiles coming at it. It sends out an electronic beam that kills the missile's guidance system…

GK: They will say it is too expensive…

AC: Which will allow for further terrorism at strategic moments… Next… There was a guy named "George Clark" who logged all of the different fake calls that John Keel was getting. Clark is mentioned in the Derenberger correspondence. Apparently, someone already had synthetic voice replication back then. Mysterious hoaxers impersonating John Keel, Jim Moseley, and Gray Barker were calling around. There were several calls where it obviously could not have been them – calls that could not have been Barker hoaxes. Due to the sheer number of overlapping calls, Clark proved that it would have taken a *group* of people, or machines, to do it. It couldn't have been done by one single person. It had to be a conspiracy… Interestingly, Clark's name is the same as an old military hero around the Pt. Pleasant area, George Rogers Clark, who helped subdue the Indians. It turns out that "George Clark" was also the alias of the CIA agent who was manipulating famous psychic Ted Owens during the Mothman days. Owens was from southeastern Indiana. He was part of the SRI-style psychic testing going on in WV and OH at the time. Also, the FBI agent investigating Harriet's neighbor was named "George K. Adams," which is sort of in the ballpark.

GK: Will we ever know what technology was in place at that time?

AC: We know they had cellphones, lasers, infrasound, and EM weapons. I imagine that they had synthetic voice, too.

GK: That explains why, on 9/11, you could have people supposedly talking to their loved ones when, in fact, they may *not* have been talking to their loved ones. The NSA has access to our phone calls and thus our voiceprints. It would not be a stretch.

AC: Onward… Northgate Mall in Seattle, where I did some interviewing, turns out to have been the first mall in the United States. It took everyone away from "Main Street" to huge parking lots. Now, paranormal stuff tends to happen there.

GK: Don't you think that malls are excellent places for observation and testing?

AC: I now wonder exactly who was behind the mall concept… Around the time of the first mall opening, you had all these crucial world events involving the Rockefellers. The Korean War started and with it, a continued "internationalist" Pacific Rim program. Charles Willoughby was chief of Navy Intel in the Pacific. Do you know who worked under him? Future players like Nixon, Gerald Ford, Joseph McCarthy, LBJ, and Robert Morris, who I think later worked with Reverend Moon and the China lobby. JFK was in that group, too. Mae Brussell fingered Willoughby for the JFK hit.

GK: The Naval Intelligence office in New Orleans was where Oswald was hanging out. They always say, "There's no intelligence but Naval Intelligence." They are the masters.

AC: They would be the ones running the West Virginia eavesdropping station.

GK: The host of *Coast to Coast,* George Noory, is also "former" Navy Intel.

AC: The sinister thing about Willoughby is that he was very tight with the Nazis. He went by the alias of "Kurt Weidenbach." He gave the Japanese doctors the go-ahead to experiment on Americans. The Japanese were more brutal than the Nazis in that regard. The U.S. brought a bunch of the Japanese doctors over after the war. It was a slightly different "paperclip" operation, all organized by Willoughby.

GK: The CIA was built on a framework that came from the Nazis and the Vatican. We won't go into all that now, but there is definitely a correlation between the cardinals in the U.S. and a global intelligence network run by the Knights of Malta.

AC: Apparently it was Council of Foreign Relations (CFR) agents that gave up the Dora rocket facility to the Russians.

GK: Who started the CFR? The Rockefellers… And how many blocks away are they from St. Patrick's Cathedral?

AC: By the way, in 2007, around the time I found out about this whole Ashland-Solvay-Manson thing, I was contacted by a gallery in Ashland, the Ann Davis Gallery, to do a show. Also, at the same time, there was a UFO sighting at Morehead State University (note "Moor" name), which is near Ashland. Someone filmed a craft going across the full moon. There was an eclipse that night. Everyone was out looking at the moon, and this guy supposedly filmed this craft. It is unusually creepy footage. Wouldn't you know it, there is a

NASA research center at Morehead State… On Dec. 5th, we had the Nebraska mall shooting. Another mall incident…

GK: The original reports out of Omaha were that they had found a person dressed in camouflage, hiding under a bus kiosk bench. They thought they had their guy, but that did not explain what else was going on inside the mall. Do we have two shooters? There were also descriptions of two different types of men who were doing the shooting. They said that the original weapon was a Russian automatic rifle, which you have to manually reload. It was not the usual AR-15, where you can just pull out a clip and put another clip in. They called it a "Kalashnikov" first, and then they had it as an "AK47." It's a stinky situation.

AC: And Bush was in Omaha that day!

GK: That's right. Shit happens when he comes around…

AC: Omaha is where Bush went on 9/11.

GK: That is where he finally landed – where Warren Buffett was throwing the soirée. A "survivor" of the towers, the head of Goldman Sachs, was in Omaha bending the elbow with martinis. Omaha was also home of the Franklin cover-up, where the Republican committee there got away with some kind of pedophilia involving Boystown, which Manson once attended.

AC: Is it just a coincidence that that shooting happened the day after the Guantanamo torture cases came before the Supreme Court? Those cases would definitely be a "problem" that elites would want to misdirect us from. Also, the new "Intelligence Estimate on Iran" was released that very day, effectively saying that Iran was *not* up to anything – a problem for the warhawks… It's also the day that Morgan Spurlock, the WV filmmaker, came out and said, "I'm doing a new movie about Osama bin Laden. And, by the way, I *found* him." The name of the movie at that point was *Finding Osama*. But, it's already facing a lot of behind-the-scenes pressure, because nobody in power wants that kind of movie to come out, showing that Osama is simply hanging out in Crawfordville, Texas or wherever.

GK: Or, he's deader than a doorbell, man. That's the best bogeyman you can have…

AC: Also on Dec. 5th, there were estimates that the U.S. housing market would drop by 30%… The Russian navy went on a surge. They started putting their subs back out.

GK: What were they looking for, Santa Claus?

AC: Funny you should say that, because Dec. 5th is a Dutch holiday called "Sinter Klaas." It's the day before the beginning of Hanukah; you've got a small occult window there for strange stuff to happen. Then immediately, the next day, they have weird stories like this: "CIA Torture Tapes Accidentally Erased." Oops…

Sinter Klaas is like our Santa Claus. The story goes that sometime in the middle of November, Sinter Klaas, who is from Spain, comes into the different ports where boats are docked. He arrives with a boat full of presents for all the children of Holland. Children and their parents go to the ports to meet Sinter Klaas. He brings his white horse with him, and his partner, Zwarte Peiten, or "Black Pete." The white horse is a symbol of "time" linked to the Egyptian birdman, Horus. The Black Pete and Spanish sailing angles point to a history linking Scandinavia with the Moors. Add the Yeti, the magical elves, and the flying reindeer to the equation, and one begins to sense the supernatural underpinnings of our major "Christian" holidays… An interesting point of fact is that the reindeer of Scandinavia are known to eat hallucinogenic mushrooms. For centuries, the reindeer's hallucinogenic urine provided shamans – who could not ingest the strong mushrooms unless diluted in such a manner – with a means to divine where game could be found. Such divination might have been essential for providing "gifts" that helped a family get through the long winters. Interestingly, the Sami shamans of Scandinavia build tents that look almost exactly like Native American teepees, possibly indicating a common origin.

AC: The Blackwater probe was back in the news in December. They were forced to start reporting on that again, which meant a misdirection was also required. So, the FBI jumped in and said, "Oh, by the way, there are *terrorists* in our malls." Simultaneously, in the UFO world, they started saying, "Oh, by the way, *aliens* have been visiting our malls and infiltrating them." There appears to be some coordination there. One could almost say that the words "alien," "Nazi," and "terrorist" are somewhat interchangeable since, if you look under the rug; the "aliens" simply seem to be ex-Nazi mind control doctors dabbling in terrorism-for-profit.

GK: Forget the quality of our atmosphere; how can the aliens tolerate spending all that time in malls? *[laughter]*

AC: It gets pretty ridiculous sometimes... Now, there was a pattern change in February, around Washington's birthday. I noticed that they changed from having misdirection events early in the week to doing them later in the week. Plus, they started using weekends to do *additional* misdirection stories. In the past, they generally avoided weekends.

GK: They now have temps come in on the weekends.

AC: Recently, we've been seeing stories that relate to older mind control ops from the 1960s. Manson was in the news last week... Sara Jane Moore got out of prison at the end of December... Sara Jane *Olsen* was recaptured... Sirhan Sirhan has a new lawyer. They found new acoustical evidence for a second shooter in the RFK case... Lynndie England was back in the news with her Abu Ghraib story, and so on...

GK: They give Manson just enough leash to reinforce in everyone's minds that he is crazy. They let him blow smoke. They publicize the most inflammatory sections of whatever he's saying. It keeps him behind bars and promotes fear.

AC: They have also resurrected the idea of contacting aliens by remote viewing. They are throwing this old meme out all the time now, citing DoD experiments at SRI and the like. However, according to Keel, they were remote viewing way back in the 1950s. L. Ron Hubbard was doing it. Remote viewing the aliens is a scam, and a stale one at that.

GK: Who knows what was unleashed and allowed to proliferate after WWII. I think civilization took a really bad turn...

AC: A lot of things came together after the war. The Dead Sea Scrolls were found in 1947. Edgar Cayce more or less predicted that they would be found. There are theories about the sudden increase in UFOs at that point. The stories attributing them to Aleister Crowley's communication with the alien "Lam" may be a way to misdirect from other possibilities. While the synchronicities around Crowley are tantalizing, it could be that the controllers simply realized that the Scrolls might undermine the story of Christianity – the validity of the Bible. Maybe they felt it was time to get the "alien" cover story out and solidified, in order to have an option if religious myths collapsed. They're trying to convince us that remote viewing is a solid method so that they can then say, "Hey, because we're using this solid method to contact aliens, it must mean that aliens are real." But the method isn't solid; while it does work on occasion, it cannot be relied upon, especially when you go beyond viewing real objects in physical space. If you set the human mind to finding an actual place in 3-D space, it can often do it. The trouble is, if you set the mind to contacting an imaginary spirit, it can do *that*, too. The only results that can really be measured or defined, unfortunately, are the ones regarding physical objects. The process becomes subjective with anything else. Even if you could come up with a way to measure the results of entity contacts – assuming there really are such things as real spirits – the entities would probably skew the results by mirroring whatever is happening in the minds of those observing them. The mind can do lots of interesting things, and results are always dependent on the structure of the tasks given... Speaking of imaginary spirits, if you look into the whole MJ-12 scam, you find that the insiders, those with knowledge of our supposed alien-government partnership, have bird names! The group itself is called "the Aviary." The top guy is called "Falcon." Since the Egyptians were so into birdpeople, one can make an educated guess that the Aviary has Masonic or Jesuit underpinnings. They want us to escape reality by believing in their alien drama.

In 2010, the author encountered a vulture resting on top of an obelisk (right) in Washington Courthouse, OH, reportedly the place where George Washington convinced the Indians to capitulate. Many of the Virginia soldiers fighting for Washington were later given land in central Ohio. The vulture and obelisk are a potent Masonic duo dating back to ancient Egypt. The "Spirit of Washington" sculpture (left) in Seattle is located in an old Masonic neighborhood, Columbia City. Washington's obelisk is depicted as a whale fin, typically associated with the Thunderbird in Native lore. The sculpture has an entity carved into it that looks very much like popular depictions of the Flatwoods Monster. However, according to Harriet Plumbrook, it also looks exactly like the entity she saw on Woodward Dr., which changed from male to female, and then back to male.

CHAPTER 7

"Numerous Indian tribes in the western U.S. and Canada
have legends about 'little men' who come to specific lakes
and rivers for water, year after year; these places have been
avoided by the Indians and regarded as sacred. In Mexico,
there are extensive legends about the 'Wachoqs,' little people
who visited Mexican streams and lakes in the distant past,
walking underwater in glittering 'diving suits.' The Irish have
always told us of little men in tight-fitting green or brown
costumes who frequent lakes and rivers on the old sod. While
most of us tend to dismiss the Leprechaun lore of Ireland
as folk tales and myth, there are a number of impressive
and well-documented books relating the numerous appearances of tiny, elusive beings. In many of these accounts, the
witnesses allegedly encountered Leprechauns on the banks
of a stream or lake where they were filling a receptacle with
water. Like most of our ufonauts, the Leprechaun is supposed
to be skittish and flees from human beings. And, also like our
ufonauts and monsters, the Leprechauns are supposed to be
capable of leaping great distances and disappearing into thin
air. In Sweden and Denmark we hear about trolls – gnome-
like beings who live in the earth and who are physically
deformed. The Leprechauns are supposed to live underground, too. Woe to anyone who tries to find their hiding
places. From time to time, they are said to kidnap children
and whisk them away forever.

"In UFO lore, we have the 'Deros' (detrimental robots) who
are supposed to live underground in secret caves, or even
in the hollowed-out center of the earth. Variations on this
underground-dweller theme can be found in ancient Oriental
legends going back thousands of years. Not all of the 'little
people' mythology is baseless. Archaeological evidence of a
sort does exist. The ruins of ancient cities in South America
have been found honeycombed with tiny tunnels, staircases,
and passageways so small that normal men have to traverse
them on their hands and knees. Who built these things, and
why? Even in the United States, in New Salem, NH (not far
from Exeter, site of a UFO flap in 1965), there is an ancient
construction of tunnels and tiny chambers built long before
the Indians arrived. They say that the 'little men' constructed

the place. Another elaborate system of tiny tunnels lies outside of Cusco, Peru, home of many intense saucer flaps. A large number of people reported seeing two luminous dwarfs get out of a disk near Cusco on August 20, 1965. The Lt. Governor of Santa Barbara, Peru, solemnly declared that he encountered two tiny humanoids, walking in the snow, near Lake Ceulacocha on September 12, 1965. They disappeared, he said, in the midst of a 'deafening noise.'"

-John Keel, from *The Complete Guide to Mysterious Beings*, pgs. 163-164.

DAUGHERTY, SHARON – PAST LIVES IN THE QUEEN CITY – OCT. 2008

Andy Colvin (AC) *[to camera]*: Here we are at the site of the Beverly Hills Supper Club Fire. This is in Southgate, which is right next to Fort Thomas, Kentucky. Fort Thomas is right up the hill. We have our local expert here, Sharon Daugherty, who attended art school at the Univ. of Cincinnati. She now works for a large graphic design firm here in town. I myself studied at U.C. for a year, which is how I originally got to know her. Sharon, can you tell us anything about the fire? You went to the club during high school, did you not?

Sharon Daugherty (SD): We had most of our junior and senior proms here. *[points]* This drive here went up to the Supper Club. It sat on top of the hill. I was working at McDonalds in Crescent Springs when we heard the news that the Beverly Hills was on fire. The fire was so huge that we could see it from the other county. 165 people died here. And nothing has been built here since. It's been 30 years.

AC: Didn't they reopen the investigation recently?

SD: Yes, just this year… A man who had worked there as a busboy remembered seeing some workers up in the ceiling in the Zebra Room, where the fire began. He asked them what they were working on, and they told him that they were working on the air conditioning. He later remembered that there was no air conditioning in that room. He got suspicious, and he's been suspicious all these years.

AC: Ft. Thomas is where they have an Army Engineering and Research Division. That division is said to have been responsible for bringing in Nazi scientists during Operation Paperclip, some via the Vatican "ratline." You lived in Ft. Thomas for a while, didn't you?

SD: I lived here for six years.

AC: Is this area around Fort Thomas traditionally an Italian mob area?

SD: Yes, Southgate is a mob area.

AC: Earlier, you mentioned that Jeff Ruby, a local mobster, might be a relative of JFK conspirator Jack Ruby, who once owned a casino here with Meyer Lansky.

SD: Jeff Ruby owns a lot of upscale steakhouses in the area. His restaurant in Newport was closed because of some dispute he had with the landlord. That one, the Tropicana, was on the levee. He also owns The Precinct, which is in an old police station on the east side of town. He owns a restaurant at Belterra Casino, and there is a restaurant downtown called Jeff Ruby's.

AC: Could you verify the story about your basement, where some girls saw an entity that was able to burn crosses off of their necks? You were there, right?

SD: Yes.

AC: Can you tell us what happened?

SD: I had a slumber party. It was my birthday. I had probably five to eight girls spending the night. We would always do séances because, when you are thirteen or fourteen, that is the thing to do. We had all been to band camp that summer. Some of the girls in one of the dorms claimed that they had seen a ghost. We decided to try to beckon the ghost from band camp during the séance. We were in my basement, all in a circle. I had received a cross pendant for my birthday. One of the girls said, "You'd better take that cross off." I don't know why she said that, but I took it off and set it down. We did the séance. In the corner, we could see this entity. We all started to scream. *Everybody* saw it. We turned the lights back on. My cross was sitting on the table, and it was broken. Nobody was around it. It was placed off to the side.

AC: Could this have saved you, by sending the energy towards the cross instead of you?

SD: Maybe.

AC: Did anything else odd happen there?

SD: Years later, you came to visit. You intuited that some guys were coming to break in.

AC: Yes, they broke the bulbs in the sidewalk lamp outside your house. I watched them do it. Right before they did it, something told me to look outside. After disabling the light, they came to your basement door. I freaked out and started yelling, which thwarted them. I got a weird, scary feeling down there.

SD: My sisters and I now have kids. When Mom and dad babysit, *none* of the kids want to go down there.

AC: Still?

SD: Still… They don't like it down there. Mom even redecorated, hoping that people would want to gather down there for family gatherings. But nobody wants to go down there. Everybody likes to stay upstairs.

AC: It says here that they used Fort Thomas as a holding place for the bodies burned in the supper club fire. *[points]* Interestingly, if you look over there, you see the "Moore" name on that sign. As I said on the drive over here, the Moore name tends to show up in paranormal areas… There is a V.A. hospital here in Fort Thomas. I suppose this makes it a candidate for mind control, due to all the Nazi doctors coming through. This is the place written about by Shelby Downard in his book *Carnivals of Life and Death*. Fort Thomas was apparently a Masonic control center. It is built on a promontory above the Ohio River. It may have had some mounds on it at one time. The Army likes putting forts on sacred spots… Most of the stately old homes on the base are now uninhabited. Strange… As a witness, would you say that your experiences have increased your psychic abilities? Earlier you said that you "followed your gut" on a lot of things. Plus, you were talking about the differences between dreams…

SD: There are different types of dreams for me. One type is where my spirit guides are trying to convey a message that I can embrace in my subconscious, usually while I'm sleeping. Another type is where a past-life memory comes into my mind, in order to help me with something I'm dealing with now, in this life. Sometimes, they just come up for no apparent reason. For instance, I've had this past-life dream in which I was a seamstress in Paris. I lived above this café. It is very vivid – in color. I know the people I'm with. Recently, I spoke with Rhonda Homan, a past-life regression therapist in Texas. She described this life in Paris *exactly* as I had seen it in my dream. She is awesome. She helped me figure out the purpose of that life – what I was there to learn. And she has described other past lives to me, which I already had a lot of detail about. When I met my second husband, I *knew* that I had known him before. It turned out that there was a "karmic debt" there. Once the marriage ended, the debt was paid, and I could move on.

AC *[to camera]*: By the way, viewers, whenever you pick up your Tide, Cheer, Downy, or Bounce products, remember that Sharon is the one who's responsible for their package design. She is yet another creative person with a paranormal history. Would you say that those experiences have helped your creativity in any way?

SD: Yes. One night I was lying in bed by myself, except for the cat. I looked over towards the door and I saw a figure standing there. The cat saw it at the same time. It freaked out and ran into the other room. Rhonda told me that it was an angel. She said that it was a good entity. She said, "Pay attention. If you let yourself, you're going to start seeing more entities." I fully expect that this is what will happen, and that it will somehow help.

The scabbard of an 18th century Balinese kriss knife (left) reveals the face of Bonaspati, the spirit said to reside within the Garuda. Such knives are still used today by shamans wanting to tap into the precognitive powers of the Garuda.
Strangely, the hairstyle of Bonaspati is reminiscent of George Washington's, and his face is very similar to the entity photographed in my kitchen window in 1973 (see opposite page 1). Bonaspati's face is also similar to the face of Geshe Kelsang Gyatso (right), head of the Kadampa Tibetan Buddhist lineage. Kelsang wears a pointed hat similar to the crown of the Garuda on the back of this book. In Asia, the Garuda is also called "Avarta," referring to his status as a key "avatar."

CHAPTER 8

"Unusual aerial phenomena have been reported throughout history and prehistory, from flying saucers in cave paintings in Hunan, 47,000 B.C. [to] southern France in 20,000 B.C. On September 24, 1235, General Kujo Yoritsune and his army observed unidentified globes of light flying in erratic patterns in the night sky near Kyoto, Japan. The general's advisers told him not to worry, as it was merely the wind causing the stars to sway. On April 14, 1561 the skies over Nuremberg, Germany were reportedly filled with a multitude of objects seemingly engaged in an aerial battle. Small spheres and discs were said to emerge from large cylinders. Whatever their actual cause, such sightings were usually treated as supernatural portents, angels, and other religious omens. Some contemporary investigators believe them to be the ancient equivalent of modern UFO reports. Art historian Daniela Giordano cites many Medieval-era paintings, frescoes, tapestries and other items that depict unusual aerial objects. She admits many of these paintings are difficult to interpret, but cites some that depict airborne, domed, saucer shapes that are strikingly similar to UFO reports from later centuries.

"Before the terms 'flying saucer' and 'UFO' were coined in the late 1940s, there were a number of reports of strange, unidentified aerial phenomena. These reports date from the mid-nineteenth to early twentieth century. In July 1868, the first modern documented sighting happened in Copiapo City, Chile... On January 25, 1878, *The Denison Daily News* wrote that local farmer John Martin had reported seeing a large, dark, circular object resembling a balloon, flying at wonderful speed. He compared its size when overhead to that of a 'large saucer...' Reports of 'mystery airships' appeared in American newspapers in 1887 and 1896-7, and another wave of sightings occurred in 1909-12, in New England, Europe, and New Zealand... On February 28, 1904, there was a sighting by three crew members on the U.S.S. Supply 300 miles west of San Francisco, reported by Lt. Frank Schofield, later to become Commander-in-Chief of the Pacific Battle Fleet. Schofield wrote of three red, egg-shaped objects flying in echelon formation that approached beneath the cloud layer, then changed course and soared above the clouds, departing directly away from Earth after 2 to 3 minutes. The largest had an apparent size of about 'six suns…' Reports of unusual aerial phenomena date back to ancient times, but reports of UFO sightings started becoming more common after the first widely publicized U.S. sightings in 1947. Many tens of thousands of UFO reports have since been made worldwide. Many sightings may remain unreported, due to fear of public ridicule. [There is] a social stigma surrounding the subject of UFOs."

-Michael Diesman, review of Gray Barker's *They Knew Too Much About Flying Saucers*

COLVIN, ANDY – GRASSY KNOLL RADIO INTERVIEW 28 – APRIL 2008

Andy Colvin (AC): Vyz, you said something off-mic that reminded me of something Thom Hartmann, the progressive talk show host out of Oregon, said the other day. He was offering the suggestion that ADD may be viewed as an impairment of the decision-making process. For instance, somebody who has ADD will make choices based on desire over necessity. They may say to themselves, "I really need to clean out this sewer line, but I'd rather go chase butterflies." So, they go chase butterflies. Such people are labeled as being "attention deficit." A drug is prescribed that will help them "focus." Once we have them "focusing," the issue of *what* to have them focus on comes into play. For the controllers, this is an important question. For business purposes, workers should be "helped" to do those things that they normally wouldn't want to do, such as performing repetitive tasks over and over for less and less wages. Antidepressants are great for the globalists of the New World Order.

"Vyz" at *Beyond the Grassy Knoll* (GK): In the 1970s, I had a friend whose daughter was thought to have ADD. One of the things they suggested was Ritalin. When he saw what Ritalin did to his daughter, he said, "I can't do it." She was like some kind of limp puppet without a puppeteer, sitting in the corner. He was really proactive and sought people who could give him advice about how to control it. That's how I started to learn about what artificial preservatives and processed foods do to people. They really demonized Ritalin throughout the 1970s, so I was shocked when it came roaring back in the '90s. If it was a no-good thing in the '70s, why is it a good thing now? Because it is part of the plan for a Brave New World…

On May 30th, 2008, during Adam Gorightly's interview with Vyz on "Untamed Dimensions," the subject of employee control came up. Apparently, some corporations are now putting computer chips in all vehicles driven by employees – even their private cars – and having the information downloaded into a central computer. Year-end bonuses are being tied to whether or not an employee goes along with this "voluntary" surveillance program. Simultaneously, there is serious lobbying now to put implants into all military personnel… Coincidentally, on the same show, guests spoke about the Laurel Canyon research of Dave MacGowan, indicating that many key players in the counterculture movement, such as Frank Zappa, John Phillips, and Jim Morrison came from elite military families… On that same day, the recently catholicized Tony Blair launched his Faith Foundation effort, designed to "bring the world together through religion." The day before, a priest in Chicago, who was visiting Barack Obama's church, seemingly tried to sabotage Obama's campaign by painting opponent Hillary Clinton as a racist. While some news pundits wisely noted that electoral campaigns need to back away from religion – asserting separation of Church and State – the Catholic Church merely said that priests shouldn't be "partisan," subtextually implying that priests need to be part of political debates.

AC: Getting back to our recap of 2007, the second week of Dec. was important as far as mass control goes. Scooter Libby dropped his appeal on the 9th. You could sense that that week was the last hurrah before all the agents went on vacation… The "problems" that week for elites would have been the Blackwater, Iranian Intel, and Libby embarrassments, and the CIA torture tapes that were found to have been erased. Perhaps as a response to those problems, the shooting at disgraced minister Ted Haggard's New Life Church in Colorado Springs occurred, along with a second shooting at the "Youth With a Mission" facility further south in CO. Other problems consequently swept aside were the Princess Diana probe in England and the increasingly bogus Sears Tower terrorism trial… There were some oddities in the New Life shooting. A female guard kind of went into a trance and killed the shooter. Yet somebody else got hit with a shotgun blast from the wrong direction, which points to additional shooters. They interviewed the man hit with the secondary blast on TV, but I don't know if his testimony ever made it into the official story. On that same day, the 9th, the cannibalistic pig farmer in

Vancouver was found "guilty." He was picking up prostitutes and feeding them to his pigs. It was one of those cases where the authorities simply didn't care enough about the victims to stop it sooner... Evel Knievel had his funeral that day, which got some airplay... The next day, on the 10th, a university study (rightly) blamed the sun for global warming. This would be something that elites might have an issue with, because certain companies profit handsomely from the fear and guilt that *manmade* global warming brings. Al Gore comes to mind with his involvement in the burgeoning "pollution credit" industry... Qaddafi was in France buying arms that day, which brings a little terror into the mix... There was a big WaMu layoff... Conrad Black got six years in jail – a real embarrassment to the right-wingers... On the next day, the 11th, the Algerian U.N. offices were bombed. Al Qaeda was blamed... In Las Vegas, six students were shot getting off the bus... On the 12th, there was testimony that Princess Diana's driver was *not* drunk, which points at conspiracy.

GK: They continually ignore the fact that the tunnel they were in had video cameras. Yet for some strange reason, on that night, they suddenly didn't work! They never say a thing about why there isn't any footage. They *have* to monitor that tunnel, because it is so extensive. You need to see what's going on, especially if there is some kind of wreck or disabled vehicle...

AC: Even at the time it happened, there was some pretty obvious, damning evidence that it was murder. There were many witnesses, some of whom seem to have disappeared since.

GK: The driver was not drunk. He went into that tunnel. The perpetrators positioned a car in front of him. Camera flashes were used to blind him. They may have had automatic control of his vehicle, too; Di's Mercedes had been sent off earlier in the week to have electronic work done on it.

AC: There is a strong British influence on a lot of what happens in the U.S., including in Mothman country. The British originally owned the coal mines and a lot of the oil rights, and they fashioned our legal system. They still own over half of our real estate. Our influential families, like the Bushes, are often related to British royalty. A certain percentage of the Oscar awards always have to go to British actors, directors, and producers. News that happens in England is now seen as "our" news. It is drilled into our heads that somehow Britain's trends matter to us – that their problems are also our problems. A significant event in either country influences both of them, politically and legislatively. You were alluding to that bond before the show, about the globalness of 9/11 – how it really was a global operation. It was not meant to benefit U.S. security and defense companies only.

GK: In Leon Trotsky's *Terrorism and Communism*, terrorism was the last card that was going to be played. The greatest boogeyman in the world is terrorism, because it can be anywhere in the world, anytime. You can freak people out about the fact that it *might* happen. In a sense, that is just as good as it happening. It's going to be used by those who wish for a world government. It will rein in the freedoms of *all* nations, wherever they are. Once they're all constrained, it becomes an easier job of amalgamating them all. You can't be a globalist and a 9/11 Truther at the same time. There is a connection between terrorism and globalism.

AC: I was interviewing a skeptic friend of mine, Britt Wilson, who is more or less the star of my upcoming "slacker" reality series. We were debating a *Reader's Digest* book compilation. When I first saw the compilation I thought, "These particular four books seem to be related." The first book was written by one of the Layton sisters involved in Jonestown. Their father was from Boomer, WV. The second book was called *Rocket Boys*, a true story about boys doing rocket science in WV. The third book was on J.D. Rockefeller, called *Titan*. The fourth book was about Princess Di. *Reader's Digest* must have lumped these together for a reason. There must be some links between these, particularly regarding petrochemicals in WV.

GK: Most would say that mass consumption dictates which topics are worthy of inclusion. But, as it always is, there is a wink and a nod behind the curtain as to which choices are made.

AC: Continuing on with Dec. 12th... After that Di article about her driver *not* being drunk, Korea gave us a story about the cloning of a "glow-in-the-dark" cat. That story seemed to be floated to counter another story that came out earlier that day, which was about Merck – how it had allowed there to be a shortage of kids' vaccines. The cat cloning story sort of glorifies bioengineering, implying that we're always moving forward with cutting edge technology. The geneticists always tell us not to worry, as they would *never* go "too far" and clone humans. Yet, they go and clone every animal under the sun and spend billions of dollars on mapping all of the genomes. The 12th was also the day that Bush vetoed healthcare for poor kids for the *second* time.

GK [*sarcastically*]: But he's all for the kids!

AC: All of those lumped together do tend to make your stomach turn... Nothing really happened the rest of that week, other than the Sears Tower trial collapsing, and Bush threatening judges about the CIA tapes. He basically said, "Don't ask me for the CIA tapes..." On the 16th, The New York Times said, "Bush wanted AT&T to spy on Americans two weeks into his administration." The popular perception that eavesdropping only came into play after 9/11 is bogus. They started right away, probably in order to get the machinery rolling for 9/11.

GK: Their "asking" to do surveillance now is a mere formality...

AC: Yes, they're doing it anyway... On the 17th, the House passed a $516 billion spending bill. Bush Sr. went back to the Skull & Bones headquarters at Yale... On the 18th, Turkey bombed Iraq, and Diana's letter about Prince Charles threatening to kill her with a car wreck was released! It was read in court. Is there any more damning evidence than that? There is a paper trail on this murder...

GK [*sarcastically*]: That was just the "paranoid" delusion of an unhappy woman...

AC: So, what do we have the next day? A fire at the White House! It was a small fire, but that is all you need to protect British royalty. The Navy "saved" a 14-year-old girl that day, too. Navy good, British good... On the 20th, there were protests in New Orleans about housing after the Katrina flood. Certain Coke ads in Russia were labeled "Satanic" on that day. The media claimed: "Bush may face CIA hearings on the torture tapes." Not that this would ever happen, but what exactly is a "CIA hearing?" It sounds like an oxymoron... Homeland Security's spy satellites were turned on that day, just to remind us that multiple agencies have us covered... The Seattle airport began "profiling" fliers. They're sending people around the airport simply to watch people and ask them questions. The program is called SPOT... On the 24th, Christmas Eve, which was a full moon, there was no terror whatsoever.

GK: What do you know? Funny how that goes...

AC: But then, on the 26th, a tiger killed a teenager at the San Francisco Zoo. Somebody sent me an article by a scientist named Pandolfi. It links Hughes Electric to a surveillance program sponsored by the Defense Intelligence Agency. The program somehow uses tigers to spy on people... On the 27th, Pakistan's Bhutto was assassinated. Muslims were blamed. Then, six people were found dead in Carnation, Washington, which is near Seattle… A "mall shooter" story from two years before was trotted out. They brought up the Hawkins shooting and talked about how he "wasn't on his meds." This was significant because, up until that point, the media generally tried to play down the fact that these shooters were on meds. Rather than deal with it head on and start monitoring psychiatric doctors and the quality of the drugs, the media simply started suggesting that these shooters are killing people because they are *not* taking their meds as prescribed.

GK: Right. There is definitely yardage to be gained there. The other thing that struck me was the girlfriend saying that he normally wasn't like that. She was crying. I believe her. I'm now wondering if he wasn't a Manchurian Candidate.

AC: That was the week that home sales really starting plunging – a big, bad story that needed to go away. "Shoot to kill" orders were given in Pakistan to deal with protesters. A lot of stuff for one day… On the 28th, we were told that a new Bin Laden tape was about to be released. They were really hitting us hard after Christmas.

GK: What was the backdrop "Bin Laden" used for that one? Coney Island? What a cheap-ass production… It's so ridiculous.

AC: We had a Pope story on the 28th. The Pope has set up "exorcism squads" for each diocese. Also Newsweek blamed the Teresa Duncan "suicide," which was probably a murder, on "the Internet"… Also on the 28th, there was a ghost in my house. I heard the door open and slam shut. We've had this happen before. We've heard slammings and poltergeists. One time, the doorknob was completely bent out of shape. I have begun correlating this stuff to things that are happening with my wife, not necessarily with me.

GK: You're thinking it is geared to familial events…

AC: Yes, but I do happen to live next to a spot that is very similar to where we saw the entities in WV: an old schoolhouse. Abandoned schoolhouses often have paranormal activity. A lot of schools were add-ons to churches, which were already built on sacred spots. My Seattle neighborhood used to be an Indian village. It's par for the course that we would get some supernatural occurrences here… On the 29th, the new "Bin Laden tape" warned against "unity government in Iraq," and Robert Novak claimed the CIA was undermining Bush.

GK: We would *hope* so… That's what the CIA is *supposed* to do.

AC: Yes, an undermining CIA sounds more realistic than one that holds open hearings. Let's try to cover what happened in late January 2008… In the third week, what were the "problems?" It came out that the White House had taped over email archives detailing the situation in our overseas torture camps. They're still covering that up… Obama "caught up" with Hillary in the Democratic race. Problems with Bush's fiscal policies were exposed. An embarrassing study was done on him. So, to steer us away from these problems, they started covering the writer's strike in Hollywood – how it might affect the Oscars. That was a good diversion; it got some mileage. Then we had the Stephenville, Texas UFO story on the 14th, which got even more mileage… The FDA approved "cloned meat" on the 15th. Another cloning story…

GK: There was also the story about a California meat processor shipping tainted beef out, which somehow got sent to New Jersey schools.

AC: Exactly… That was a big story. On the 16th, the New York Stock Exchange acquired the American Stock Exchange. Hillary and Obama were suddenly in a "dead heat." Stocks took a big dive… On the 17th, Bush announced his fiscal policy, and chicken abuse was discovered at Tyson.

GK: They're dead! How can they be abused? *[laughter]*

AC: There was a crackdown in Kenya, and a big stock drop on the 21st, which was MLK's birthday… The wall between Gaza and Egypt was breached on the 22nd, sending thousands of people flooding over to buy stuff in Egypt. The U.S. deficit was announced: $250 billion, which sounds low to me… On the 23rd, it was announced that Bush had lied literally 1000 times regarding his Iraq policies… There was a UFO sighting on the 26th in Anaheim, which is a place we went to film… There wasn't much else that month… Okay… In February, in the first week, what were the problems? The Princess Di trial was still going on. Obama was surging, which the right-wing whites hated. Exxon was fighting Venezuela on some things. There were some stock drops. Waterboarding, a form of torture, was starting to be exposed, and the eavesdropping issue was still in play. Bush wanted retroactive immunity for the phone companies; elites want to keep eavesdropping at all costs… So, to divert from these… On the 2nd, we had a mall shooting in Tinsley Park, Chicago. That's a good tactic to get people's minds off of embarrassing revelations. Also on that day, the underwater Internet cables supplying

Lebanon and Palestine were mysteriously cut. Probably the only people capable of quickly doing that are Navy Seals. Turkey then bombed Kurdish Iraq. Willie Nelson said 9/11 was an "inside job." An Angelina Jolie movie glorifying assassins was advertised... On the 4th, we heard that the proposed Bush budget was $3 trillion. He asked for cuts to Medicare. More "global warming" stories came out... On the 5th, Aetna dropped anesthesia from its coverage, and we had the Hillary vs. Obama "Super Tuesday." Kenya and Chad had riots. Tornadoes killed 47 in Tennessee. There's that number 47 again... The U.S. admitted to waterboarding. Stocks dropped. And, amazingly, an article came out saying that John McCain was *never* tortured... On the 6th, The History Channel mentioned that a particular cattle mutilation "UFO" actually looked like a blimp. And the 9/11 reporter, McWethey, died in a ski accident.

GK: John McWethey is dead? Holy [expletive].

AC: Also on the 6th, Exxon froze millions of Venezuelan dollars. So how does a corporation freeze the assets of a country? Unbelievable... On the 7th, there was a sugar refinery explosion in Georgia, a New Zealand plane hijacking where a woman stabbed the pilots, and a City Council shooting in Missouri that left six dead... In the second week of February, what were the elites' problems? The Guantanamo Bay torture trial began. There were problems with East Timor, and Obama was surging. There was a recall at Bayer, and the fight to allow eavesdropping continued... So, what were our diversions? Iran's possession of nuclear technology (that we originally gave them) was brought forth. On the 8th, Infraguard, a private company, was given "shoot to kill" authority from the FBI in cases of "national emergency." On the 9th, or right around that time, retroactive immunity was very quietly given to phone companies by the Senate. On the 10th, a possible Yahoo-Microsoft merger was hyped... There was a Swiss art robbery on the 11th. Chavez threatened an oil embargo. It was announced that West Virginia will use inter-state cameras to spy on people whenever they want. Bush pressed Congress for eavesdropping immunity again. Bloomberg, the NYC billionaire mayor, compared global warming to terrorism; this is exactly what we've been saying all along, except for different reasons. I say it fills a need for the billionaires, because it makes us all think expensive gasoline is normal and necessary. The whole situation seems designed to make us feel anxious – to make us think of oil as a guilty pleasure that may someday be unavailable.

GK: Yes, I would agree. The whole thing is for the freakout value.

AC: On the 13th, we had the Iran uranium-processing story. They eventually want to make nuclear bombs, supposedly. A big diversion from "problems" would be the Northern Illinois University shooting on the 14th. Six students were shot. The shooter was staying at a Travelodge, which is odd. What's a student doing at a Travelodge?

GK: Being controlled?

AC: There was an embarrassing recall of Trasilol, which is a Bayer drug. Since 2006, 22,000 people are estimated to have died from taking it. I imagine the numbers are really higher.

GK: You hear these ghoulish, ridiculous caveats at the end of pharmaceutical commercials: "May cause high blood pressure, stroke, or death…"

AC: Yes, some of them literally say, "Death may result." What started as an attempt to inform the public has turned into a program to desensitize us to the risks. We don't really know what the longterm risks are and, pretty soon, we won't care. These commercials seem to be revisiting the 1960s and '70s "sex and death" subliminal advertising tactics… On the 18th, we had that 143 million pound beef recall you mentioned earlier. That was the same day that the Ruby-Oswald tape surfaced at the Frank Crowley Building in Dallas. That was probably just a diversionary story; it didn't really go anywhere. That was also the day that we announced we were going to shoot down a spy satellite from a Navy ship. The satellite, which may have been nuclear powered, was failing, which is a problem for elites wanting to keep the many risks from satellites secret. Bush apparently made the decision to shoot it down himself.

GK: That can't be… Bush making a decision himself is impossible!

AC: That was also the day of a big refinery explosion at Alon USA, in Big Spring, TX, which is near Dallas. That well-timed event helped raise gas prices. Dallas oilmen helped kill JFK, so one doubts they would have many qualms about taking out a few workers. On the 19th, a Wal-Mart checkout person offended a Muslim woman, who was veiled, by calling her a "terrorist." Obama grabbed the lead from Clinton, and Willie Nelson was blackballed over his comments about 9/11 being an inside job.

GK: He's *always* being blackballed.

AC: Oil went up to $100 a barrel. There was a lunar eclipse on the next night, Feb. 20th. They probably figure an eclipse is a good time to increase the occult power of their mass control ops. For instance, there was a lockdown at a Kentucky school that day… Al-Sadr threatened to break the ceasefire in Iraq; such tensions help the war profiteers. An aborted Superbowl terrorism plot conveniently arose. M-16, the Brits' version of the CIA, denied in court that they had anything to do with Diana's death. That's like Hannibal Lecter saying that he is a vegetarian… The Supreme Court limited suits against problematic medical devices – a big giveaway to the pharma-chems. Then, the Serbs attacked the U.S. Embassy! On the next day, the 21st, Gitmo prosecutors said that the trial of terrorist Khalid Sheik Mohammed was rigged. A study came out, from Tufts University, stating that 9/11 had a deep psychological impact on people… On the 22nd, there was a noticeable stand-down of the Secret Service at an Obama rally. The media is always implying that he might be assassinated, which probably makes wealthy racists feel a little better; they can always *imagine*, which lessens the sting of having to bow to blacks angered by all the crap Bush pulled.

In May of 2008, Republican presidential candidate Mike Huckabee made a joke at an NRA convention about a noise backstage, saying that it was Obama "ducking to avoid getting shot." Also that month, Hillary Clinton alluded to a similar thing by saying that her refusal to cede the nomination to Obama was necessary because "you never know what might happen. RFK was shot right before the Democratic convention."

AC: On Feb. 23rd, it was reported that Obama and Hillary were "at each other's throats." Nader jumped into the presidential race on the 24th… On the 25th, the trial began for the NYC cops who shot a black groom (Sean Bell) exactly one year after they had shot *another* black guy (Diallo)… There was a power outage in southern Florida on the 26th, supposedly related to a nuclear plant. There was an earthquake in the U.K. Jay Rockefeller wrote a letter, along with some other senators, criticizing Pres. Bush about eavesdropping. I imagine that there *was* some disagreement between the Senators, since one of them, Jay, owns the company that is doing the eaves-dropping! It was implied that they agreed in spirit, however nothing specific was proposed. They just *said* that they didn't like what Bush was doing. It seemed like an empty political ploy by the Dems. Obviously they're not *really* going to do anything, due to the fact that the "Bushefeller" syndicate is benefiting.

GK: It just looks good to the public…

AC: Yes. On the 27th, a 9/11 hijacker was found to have been booked on future flights – flights that came after 9/11. You know, a lot of those hijackers are still alive. Most were victims of identity theft. Someone should call Lifelock! *[laughter]* Jobless claims went up on the 27th. Oil hit $123 a barrel. Bush again lobbied Congress directly, calling for retroactive immunity for the eavesdroppers… On the 28th, an Illinois shopping center bomb exploded. A U.S. warship was sent to Lebanon. There was an anti-Muslim photo flap involving Obama; the media often plays the race card… A poisonous chemical, ricin, was found at a Las Vegas motel. The execution of "Chemical Ali" was approved. Prince Harry of England was taken off of the front lines in Afghanistan. There was a "mystery force" reported to be affecting the spacecrafts Pioneer 10 and Pioneer 11. The only thing missing was a dinosaur story… They usually like to mix items from the future and past – stories about outer space, cloning, and archaeological finds. It gives us the false sense that we have a dependable historical timeline. These genres get consumers out of the present moment, so that their minds are free to travel to pre-designated, noncontroversial points of intellectual interest. It doesn't necessarily have to be all that soothing, either, because anger and frustration have been proven to make shoppers want to buy more.

GK: There is definitely some kind of conditioning factor in this; they are creating a bogus anthropological continuum.

CHAPTER 9

"When we watch a television wrestler gouge, foul, and snarl at his opponent, we are quite ready to see that he is merely playing at being the 'heavy,' and that in another match he may be given the other role, that of clean-cut wrestler, and perform this with equal verve and proficiency. We seem less ready to see, however, that while such details as the number and character of the falls may be fixed beforehand, the expressions and movements used do not come from a script but from command of an idiom, a command that is exercised from moment to moment with little calculation or forethought... In reading [the behavior of] persons in the West Indies who become the 'horse,' or one possessed of a voodoo spirit, it is enlightening to learn that the person possessed will be able to provide a correct portrayal of the god that has entered him because of the knowledge and memories accumulated in a life spent visiting congregations of the cult; that the person possessed will be in just the right social relation to those who are watching; that possession occurs at just the right moment in the ceremonial undertakings, the possessed one carrying out his ritual obligations to the point of participating in a kind of skit with persons possessed at the time with other spirits. But in learning this, it is important to see that this contextual structuring of the horse's role still allows participants in the cult to believe that possession is a real thing and that persons are possessed at random by gods whom they cannot select.

"It is commonplace to say that different social groupings express in different ways such attributes as age, sex, territory, and class status, and that in each case these bare attributes are elaborated by means of a distinctive, complex cultural configuration of proper ways of conducting oneself. To *be* a given kind of person, then, is not merely to possess the required attributes, but also to sustain the standards of conduct and appearance that one's social grouping attaches thereto. The unthinking ease with which performers consistently carry out such standard-maintaining routines does not deny that a performance has occurred, merely that the participants have been aware of it. A status, a position, a social place is not a material thing, to be possessed and then displayed; it is a pattern of appropriate conduct, coherent, embellished, and well articulated. Performed with ease or clumsiness, awareness or not, guile or good faith, it is nonetheless something that must be enacted and portrayed, something that must be realized. Sartre, here, provides a good illustration:

> Let us consider the waiter in the café… All his behavior seems to us a game. He applies himself to chaining his movements as if they were mechanisms. He is playing at being a waiter in a café – his condition – in order to *realize* it. This obligation is not different from that which is imposed on all tradesmen. There is the dance of the grocer, of the tailor, of the auctioneer, by which they endeavor to persuade their clientele that they are nothing but a grocer, an auctioneer, a tailor. A grocer who dreams is offensive to the buyer, because such a grocer is not wholly a grocer. Society demands that he limit himself to his function as a grocer… There are indeed many precautions to imprison a man in what he is, as if we lived in perpetual fear that he might escape from it – that he might break away and suddenly elude his condition.

"When the individual moves into a new position in society and obtains a new part to perform, he is not likely to be told in full detail how to conduct himself. Ordinarily, he will be given only a few cues and hints, and it will be assumed that he already has in his repertoire a large number of bits and pieces of performances that will be required in the new setting. The individual will already have a fair idea of what modesty, deference, or righteous indignation looks like, and can make a pass at playing those bits when necessary. He may even be able to play out the part of a hypnotic subject or commit a 'compulsive' crime on the basis of models for these activities that he is already familiar with."

-Erving Goffman, *The Presentation of Self in Everyday Life*, pp. 74-76

DAY, DAVID & ANDY COLVIN – NIGHTSEARCH UFO RADIO – DEC. 2008

Nightsearch UFO host Eddie Middleton (EM): We're here with the

Mothman's Photographer, Andy Colvin, who many of you are familiar with, as well as our old friend, Penn State psychology professor, David Day. David, you used to live in the area of Point Pleasant, right?

Prof. David Day (DD): I was born in Elkins, West Virginia, and I went to school in Morgantown. I lived in Wheeling. After I went to college, my [parents] lived in Charleston and Huntington. My father was a wholesale food district manager. I had to work the vacation [period] in the summertime. I went across the Silver Bridge between Pt. Pleasant, WV and Gallipolis, OH probably eight to ten times a month. It was a very scary bridge. It had only two lanes, and looked like [it was made of] bicycle chain. It would sway in the wind. It was a long drop to the river. One pin came out and sent it down.

EM: Didn't you talk to some people who had sightings of Mothman?

DD: Yes... I've reported them. Mothman is very big there; it's not urban legend... As you investigate these things, you [find that the witnesses] are very credible people; there was even a state trooper [among them]. The kinds of people reporting these things are very levelheaded folks.

EM: Tell us your ideas of what the Mothman phenomenon is all about.

DD: Everytime I hear, or sit in on, a [mainstream] discussion regarding the Mothman, there seems to be a [misguided] consensus among researchers that it's very malevolent – causing harm. But when you actually question them and ask what happened – who they talked to, what report they relied on, or what records they checked – all [that can be said] is that the Mothman scares the crap out of people. Big deal... If fear *itself* were evil, the Old Testament would have to be classified as being from the gates of Hell. Religion is *full* of fear. [And our society generally seems to think] there is nothing wrong with fear. Boiled down, the Mothman only scares people. When witnesses have an encounter with this entity, it's almost always a warning of very serious, life-threatening events, some of which can be altered. Mothman portends catastrophic events further down the path; but both the agent (Mothman) *and* the subject (the witness) can take action to avoid them. Very supernatural, scary things ensue. Fear itself is not malevolence, however. To cut a long line short, the Mothman is not malevolent. There is no harm intended. It's all very scary but, after it boils down, people start having Mothman festivals. [They do this because] there is no evidence that the Mothman has abducted anyone or caused any injuries. The last [witness] we talked to thought it was psychological, a [growth response no different than] Abraham's life being changed when God scared the crap out of him.

EM: Andy, do you think Mothman is an archetype, or an actual creature?

Andy Colvin (AC): I think there is a continuum to how he is seen. You can see the entity at different points in its transmogrification process. It can, therefore, look different to different people. I saw a shadowy being come out of a tree, similar to what recent witnesses in Cincinnati saw. At that same spot, my friend saw a solid-looking Mothman, a flying saucer, and some aliens. Another friend saw something there that looked like the Flatwoods Monster. It morphed into the "Virgin Mary" and, then, into an "Indian guide." She also saw a cigar-shaped UFO. So, you can have all of these archetypes appearing in the same exact spot over a period of time. It appears to be the same energy manifesting in different forms.

EM: That sounds like a pretty heavy-duty vortex.

AC: Yes… It's also where a school burned down and killed some kids. There may be some connection between the sightings and the deaths.

EM: You interviewed the Cincinnati family who saw the shadowy "Four Mothmen." How were they affected by their experience?

AC: They've had ghostly phenomena going on for years. It didn't seem like it was freaking them out too much. To some degree, I think they were already desensitized to it.

EM: We know of Mothman's reputation for heralding catastrophe… What about this family? Did anything tragic happen after their August 2008 sighting?

AC: No, it had happened *before*, not afterwards. Three people had recently died in the neighborhood. It is suspected that the shadowy beings were emanations of those dead people. Interestingly, there were three smaller "Mothmen" and one big one. Perhaps the three smaller ones were spirits of the three dead people being shepherded around by Mothman in the afterlife… It's not necessarily catastrophe that brings these entities, however. Jung did studies on synchronicity. He found that patients were having more synchronicities as they reached a personal crisis or had a breakthrough. Right before they would experience a jump in understanding, the synchronicities would increase. You can see these entities before any spike in mental energy, positive *or* negative.

DD: [Mothman presents] a community or an individual [with a coded puzzle]. If you don't figure it out, the result could be dangerous or harmful. [The national media] twists interpretations of Mothman. Mothman is not bad; it just intervenes to stop bad things.

AC: People tend to "see" based on their societal beliefs and preferences.

DD: That's right.

AC: In Buddhism and Hinduism, adepts approach the birdman as a stabilizer of the many phases of Enlightenment. Each time you make a jump in understanding, the birdman is there to help you preserve that new state. It is a very positive role.

DD: I see what you mean. It is kind of like Freemasonry, with the stages and degrees.

EM: Andy, can you comment on the Flatwoods Monster that transformed into the Virgin Mary? The original Flatwoods Monster was in West Virginia also, right?

AC: Yes, the original one was seen in 1952. Since it coincided with the CIA deciding to use the subject of UFOs as a psychological weapon, I am thinking that the original Flatwoods Monster may have been some kind of synthetic event. They had a National Guard Intelligence Unit watching everything from the woods. Some industrial oil was found at the scene; they probably had a mechanical contraption out there that would mimic a creature from outer space. The "monster" looked suspiciously similar to one of the classified military drones that had already been developed. Most could only fly remotely, but a few could carry passengers. One of them apparently landed in my friend's yard. A couple of us saw the landing marks in the ground... This new, ever-expanding Flatwoods theory put forth by Stanton Friedman and Frank Feschino is that there were multiple "landings" on different hilltops around Charleston – not just Flatwoods. Feschino pointed out that "balls of light" were seen landing. Perhaps spotlights were shining out from the drones, advertising their presence. This would create a media "buzz," from which the public's reaction could be gauged. Oddly, the landing spots mapped by Feschino are places where Mothman was later seen. It could be that Mothman was trying to expose any nuts-and-bolts USAF saucer operations by mimicking the Flatwoods landing patterns. Or, it could be that some of the Flatwoods entities were *also* sightings of Mothman. "Gurudas," human gurus who can change into Garudas, are said to travel as balls of light. Once they arrive at their destination, they change into the birdman. It could be that the gurus were trying to alert us to the fact that the monster seen in Flatwoods was a government creation – a drone, or some kind of set-up. The Garuda has a reputation for exposing crimes and conspiracies. If UFO abductees were being experimented on, that might be a case where the Garuda would want to step in and let people know. Many witnesses were harassed by frightening Men in Black; they deserved sympathy. One wonders if the Four Mothmen were flying around in 1952 during Flatwoods, creating those multiple landing sites. There have been some other sightings of the Four Mothmen. I got an email from a lady who saw the three-plus-one Mothman configuration in a hotel room in Spain last year. More recently, on the *Paranormal State* show, they were speculating about the Four Mothmen being this same 3+1 configuration. The awareness of this configuration continues to grow…

DD: Andy, you have been associated with odd Mothman encounters involving the manipulation of time… This isn't scholastic philosophy like you and I are familiar with but, in West Virginia, there is this idea that God chooses [to let certain tragedies happen]. Two cars collide [yet] God chooses to do nothing about it. Not that Mothman is God, mind you, but Mothman has this [quality that is beyond time and space]. Physicists say that time is an illusion. Mathematicians say that time is only happening in the now. Mothman seems to move in this "now" by predicting the future. Maybe he is our insight into a higher intelligence – a way to understand time, or how we can deal with time. You are finding [birdman] archetypes within Hinduism, the oldest religion in the world. The oldest writings known to man are the Upanishads from 5000 B.C. Anything coming out of there is certainly going to be archetypal. I wouldn't be surprised to find that Andy is correct about the close similarities between Jungian archetypes, the Mothman, and [the Garuda] in the East. That's all very consistent.

EM: Very intriguing, as always…

"During 2008, there were numerous reports of UFO sightings and other strange incidents reported from across the Keystone state…There has been a history in Pennsylvania and [neighboring] states of sightings of giant birds with enormous wingspans, commonly referred to as 'thunderbirds.' In recent years, the reports of these huge flying creatures have increased. Rick Fisher of the Paranormal Society of Pennsylvania received a report that occurred in February at a rural location outside of Harrisburg. The driver of a vehicle, who was also an active hunter, saw a huge birdlike creature drop from the trees and approach his vehicle. The man stopped and got out to take a better look at the creature, which seemed to soar or glide without flapping its wings. He hesitantly told Rick that what he saw looked 'almost prehistoric.' Researcher Jim Brown investigated an incident that occurred on the afternoon of May 20, on a major roadway in Washington County. Motorists reportedly pulled off the road to watch as a huge, dark flying creature (that looked more like a giant bat than a bird) circled low and passed over some cars. One witness noticed that the wingspan extended beyond the edges of the two-lane highway. One man was seen taking pictures of the giant flying creature. That person has never come forward…

"While there was a lot of UFO activity reported from the eastern portions of the state, many UFO sightings were reported in western Pennsylvania and elsewhere. While spherical and disc shaped objects were reported, as well as formations of luminous objects, there were numerous triangular shaped objects sighted as well… It was during the early morning hours of October 4 that two hunters in Elk County encountered something unusual. As they moved into a wooded area, they first noticed two baseball-sized glowing lights about 15 feet above the ground. Soon they noticed multiple beams of light, which seemed to originate from about 10 feet from above the ground, and projected parallel with the ground. Their attention, however, was drawn to a glowing, humanlike form, which was estimated to be about 3 feet tall. The color was described as a light green, lime color, and it had arms that hung straight down and were longer than that of a human. The movement of the being gave the impression that it was gliding. On that same date in nearby Tioga County, witnesses observed a silent, solid cigar-shaped object approaching from the north. It suddenly faded out and vanished as it moved overhead."

-Stan Gordon, Jan. 2009

CHAPTER 10

"On Halloween, 1979, at the Jerome Bar in Aspen, Colorado, I met a man who was a master at 'remote viewing.' When he asked about my life, I told him about my adventures promoting my book on [mind control]. Most people, in those days, responded to my information about mind control with either disbelief or horror. He was most matter of fact, and his response surprised me:

> A friend dared me to remote view the inside of the NORAD site within Cheyenne Mountain outside Colorado Springs. I've never been there in my body. What I do is 'astral projection' or 'out of body travel.' It's apparently different from what Price or Swan did in that government-supported remote viewing experiment at Stanford Research Institute. I went out of my body and, suddenly, I was inside the NORAD tunnel inside the mountain. A bell went off, and I was frozen, trapped by some ray. All I thought was 'I'm dead! I'll never get back to my body!' I was aware of a lot of activity – warning lights blinking, sirens blaring, security guards running around with weapons cocked. Then, this one security chief comes up to me and aims some kind of device at me up where I'm trapped, near the ceiling of this tunnel. He reads the feedback and says, 'Okay. You can let him go. It's just another one of those sleepwalkers.' And suddenly I was back inside my body. After that, I thought about what I'd seen in one room off this tunnel. I'd seen large half-orbs stacked on top of each other, like bicycle bells diminishing in size. I realized that these were being used in an experiment designed to influence a local election somewhere in Florida. Later, I saw a picture of a Tesla generator. It looked just like those stacked-up bells. I think our secret government has some really [space-age] technologies to control us.

"I thought it would be clever to put a number of remote-viewers to work *for* the Bill of Rights for a change – against the cryptocracy. So, I called Ingo Swann, the famous remote-viewer who had participated in the SRI project. I asked him to repeat the view inside Cheyenne Mountain. I could hear the tremble in his voice when Ingo said, 'They're not all bad. The CIA people are not all bad people.'"

-Walter Bowart, *Operation Mind Control: The Cryptocracy's Plan to Psychocivilize You* (Revised 1994 edition)

COLVIN, ANDY – GRASSY KNOLL RADIO INTERVIEW 29 – APRIL 2008

Andy Colvin (AC): So, what *were* the elites' media problems in the first week of March 2008, you ask? They were, in a nutshell, the recession, Bush's support of "waterboarding" torture, and the fallout from the meat recall of the previous week, which is still in the news as we speak. People are pissed that tainted meat is being fed to our kids at school.

"Vyz" at *Beyond the Grassy Knoll* (GK): That's right…

AC: The fact that they're going to have to withdraw troops is also a problem. They just can't keep up the same levels. So, what did we have to distract us from those issues? We started off the week, on the 3rd, with the "eco-terror" fires in Woodinville, Washington, a suburb of Seattle. Judging from the poor state of the housing market, one would imagine that the burning of these huge eco-McMansions was probably an "inside job." The evidence for it being an "eco-terror" group was really flimsy. A single "protest" sign was left; anybody could have left it. It was just one or two phrases scribbled on a piece of board. But that was all that was needed to blame it on "the terrorists." But, in reality, they weren't going to be able to sell those megahouses; they cost too much now. So, they went for the insurance claim instead…

GK: Construction "lightning." Yes…

AC: On the 4th, Venezuelan troops moved to the Columbian border. There was the Iraq puppy throwing case on YouTube, where a soldier looked to be throwing a puppy to its death. It turned out to be a hoax. Hillary Clinton won Texas and Ohio. Those really seemed rigged… There was a nuclear plot in Colombia featuring a laptop. Salmonella was found in Aunt Jemima syrup. The Grand Canyon was purposely flooded. The media tried to make the flooding seem like a good thing but, let me tell you, it's not. Excessive dam runoff destroys the eco-system. It washes all the beaches away.

GK: They spun it like there was a reason for it, but it wasn't making a lot of sense to me.

AC: Also on the 5th, there was a building collapse in NYC. Anytime something in NYC collapses, it brings back memories of 9/11 and feeds the "terror" machine... Fox TV ran an article claiming that "public shaming" is good. They showed examples of people making their kids stand outside for hours, in public places, with signs that read things like, "I did such-and-such and I apologize to society." Have you heard of this?

GK: Yes, we had one down here in Florida.

AC: On the 6th, a military recruiting station in NYC was bombed by some mystery terrorist on a bike. Home foreclosures were rising. Two thousand troops left Iraq. A Pittsburgh home exploded due to a "gas leak." There was "chaos" at the Sean Bell wrongful death trial in NYC. Bell was shot by the cops on his wedding day for no reason... There was a California moth spraying debate. The Longshoremen decided that they will strike in May. There was a shooting in Jerusalem, at a seminary, which killed 8. And a golfer was charged with killing a hawk.

GK: Yes, that happened down here. The hawk was just doing what hawks do. It was probably calling for its mate or whatever and the guy got teed off. He took an iron at the thing, hit it in the head, and killed it.

AC: A ton of stuff got thrown at us that week, probably to cover up the various vote fraud allegations in the Hillary victories. On Friday, March 7th, the Univ. of California at Davis had a bomb scare. Bogus attempts were made to connect the Times Square bomb to "Hollywood" and to "Canada." The UNC student body president was shot to death. Recession was in the news. Countrywide was caught defrauding people. In Iraq, bad water was being given to the soldiers... On the 8th, we had tornadoes in Lafayette, Tennessee. The Lafayette name comes up a lot with tornadoes. According to Jim Brandon, people living in trailers, in towns named Lafayette, are the most likely to get hit by a tornado... The meat worker who was shipping the tainted meat said he was just "following orders." An article came out saying that husbands will get more sex if they "do more housework." It makes you wonder if that meat worker was sleeping with the boss. *[laughter]* The Buckingham Palace Masonic Lodge opened. Bush vetoed the anti-torture bill. Lastly, it was reported that there are pharmaceutical drugs in our water supply.

GK: Isn't that supposedly the result of people throwing their meds in the toilet?

AC: Supposedly, yes… City water officials here in Seattle said that they simply don't filter for drugs. They could, but it would mean reengineering the system. Right now they only test for things like heavy metals and solvents. Seattle is not a good example, probably, because we have some of the best water in the country. It comes straight down from the snowpack in the Cascades. The reservoirs are fairly wild and protected.

GK: And aren't they fluoridating the water supply? Fluoride is an aluminum manufacturing waste product. It's never been good. They made money off of it by promoting it as being good for teeth when, in reality, it is not.

AC: Same thing with gasoline. It is a waste product of the chemical separation of crude oil. Originally it was marketed as a household cleanser.

GK: We need a carburetor that can run on fluoride…

AC: Tesla invented an engine that runs on water, but they will never market such a sensible alternative… In the second week of March 2008, the elite problems consisted of: keeping the lid on the entrapment aspects of Elliott Spitzer's sex scandal, the continuing fallout from the pharmaceuticals in the water, the collapsing dollar, and the "Winter Soldier" protests scheduled for D.C. To get us off of those issues, we got a story that the honeybees will all be dead by 2018… Then on the 11th, 200 people were killed in Pakistan by a bomb… On the 12th, Geraldine Ferraro made a few anti-Obama statements. Gold hit $1000 an ounce… On the 13th, Congress had their first closed session in 25 years to discuss – guess what? – the "eavesdropping is OK" bill. Will these telecommunications eavesdroppers be prosecuted, or will we snore while we wait for Jay Rockefeller to investigate the spying that has been going on under his nose for decades? It doesn't really matter, because an actress from Gilligan's Island was caught with marijuana! This got our minds off of the fact that Congress has to have secret sessions about our being spied upon… On Friday the 14th, when the Winter Soldier protests kicked off in D.C., they also decided to put the D.C. "gun ban" case in front of the Supreme Court – an interesting coincidence. Also, Obama denounced his pastor for questioning the official 9/11 story. That pastor story has gone on for a month now. Columbus, OH was announced the "high-tech city of the year." Battelle brought in a lot of that money, not just with their data mining, but also with their developments in "capturing natural gas in liquid form." They are especially busy perfecting ways in which everyone's personal data will be collated in times of "national crisis."

GK: They are *always* perfecting ways to collate our personal data...

AC: On March 15th, the Pentagon's main computer was supposedly hacked. Tibetan protests started in Lhasa. Bush warned about "overcorrecting" the economy. A Russian rocket carrying a U.S. satellite failed. Did you catch that detail? We've contracted our satellite work out to *Russia*!

GK: Listeners, I *truly* wish we were making this stuff up.

AC: The 15th is the day that a construction crane fell in NYC, and an F-16 crashed in AZ... On Sunday the 16th, the body of a "human sacrifice," 5500 years old, was found in the Sudan... The Ides of March was particularly interesting this year... The fifth anniversary of the Iraq War came during the third week of March. Cheney and McCain went to Iraq. There were major war protests in D.C. on the 20th, with a bunch of arrests. According to the AP, some journalists were arrested in Iraq by the U.S. Army on that day. To counter any potential focus on the extremely unpopular Iraq occupation, the U.S. media focused instead on the continuing protests in Tibet against the China Olympics. Then, the Supreme Court said, "Let's look at those gun rights." There was a deluge of distracting stories at this time. For example, they started talking about Lynndie England again, the Abu Ghraib "torture chick," who is from WV. They announced that the U.K.'s 7/7 terror inquest would be held in secret. To top it off – and this is not a joke – they apparently fixed the space shuttle with *duct tape*! You'll often see a pastiche of "past" and "future" type stories. Controlling both the past and future is an important Masonic tenet.

GK: Yes. There you go!

AC: On the 20th, President Bush's popularity hit a new low, Osama bin Laden came out with a new videotape, and the Pope was accused of attacking Islam. Can you believe that the Pope was accused of attacking Islam?

GK [*sarcastically*]: The Pope would never attack Islam! Seriously though... He already said, in July, that if you're not Catholic, you're not *Christian*. So what does that say about Protestants, Jews, and the rest?

AC: On the next day, the 21st, the day *after* the 5th anniversary of the Iraq invasion, there is nothing at all of consequence, except for Sara Jane

Olsen, the old terrorist, getting mistakenly released. She has a name similar to Sara Jane Moore's. I think it actually gets confused in people's minds.

GK: Yes, it does...

AC: By releasing and then recapturing Olsen, it sort of created a screen memory for Moore's surprising release. They "accidentally released" Olsen *eight* years before her parole date. Then they said, "Oh, that was a mistake," and grabbed her again. Before anyone could start getting down to really analyzing Moore's odd release, they substituted Olsen's. Re-arresting Olsen was almost a post-hypnotic suggestion to forget all about Moore. The door of awareness was slamming shut.

GK: Isn't that great? It was an occult holiday, too. It was the vernal equinox. Do you have anything more on the Pope "attacking" Islam?

AC: Just that it was an AP radio story; it was the AP that used the word "attack."

GK: In late March or early April, they made the statement that Muslims now outnumber Catholics globally. Now, what does that do in everybody's psyche? They start thinking, "Oh my god, here comes the Islamic hordes! The Ottomans are going to rise again!" They're always going to play this religious card whenever they need to inflame the situation. They're eventually going to ignite something. It goes right back to the crap that was pulled during the Crusades in the 1100s. They're going to keep that thing going until they finally set off the powder keg.

AC: After all of that, on the 22nd, they announced that two new "Manson" graves had been found in the desert. They brought Manson directly into the mix, in order to make sure that the subconscious linkage between Moore and Olsen was cemented. Bringing Lynndie England and Manson together with Olsen was genius, because the mix made us subconsciously want to forget about Iraqi torture, too. Still, there was no mention of the link between Manson and Moore. So far, your show is the only radio venue to have publicized this amazing fact.

GK: Are they now going to ask Charlie where the *other* bodies are? It's ridiculous...

AC *[laughs]*: They would simply get a long rant from Manson on how he was framed.

GK: Good luck with that, guys! Speaking of occult crime, I ask people to go to hillaryclinton.com and click on "states," then click on "New Hampshire," and take a look at the six photos of flags embedded with occult symbolisms.

AC: Do you think she's got Satano-Power behind her?

GK: I think they all do… But the thing is, why are the flags altered in that manner?

AC: We've been talking about her prayer group on "The Mothman's Photographer" discussion list on Yahoo.

GK: You know, these little synchronicities of ours are starting to scare me.

AC: According to Alex Constantine's site, it is a long-established prayer group that got its start helping the Nazis. He says that there is a book coming out in May called *The Family: The Secret Fundamentalism at the Heart of American Power*, by Jeff Charlotte. Constantine says, "A story has broken about the type of church Hillary chooses to attend, an organization cultivated in an open quest for power and undemocratic modus operandi." He quotes Barbara Ehrenreich:

> Hillary seeks spiritual guidance from The Family, a collection of powerful right-wing politicos that has included Sam Brownback, Ed Meese, John Ashcroft, James Inhofe, and Rick Santorum. During the 1940s, this organization reached out to former and not-so-former Nazis, and its fascination with Hitler has continued… The Family avoids the word "Christian," but worships Jesus – although *not* the Jesus who promised the Earth to the meek. They believe that in mass societies, it's only the elites who matter – the political leaders who can build God's dominion on Earth. Insofar as The Family has a consistent philosophy, it's all about power: cultivating it, building it, and networking it into ever stronger units or cells. "We work with power where we can," the family's leader, Doug Coe, has said. "And we build new power where we can't."

GK: You know, to call these people "Christians" is completely erroneous. These people masquerade as being Christian; it even goes to Pat Robertson and Billy Graham, I'm sorry to say… These "end-timers" want to hasten the Lord's coming, but it can't be done. This Family brouhaha sounds like another opportunity for an author to weave an intriguing story, like Levenda did with the Wandering Bishops; it must all be blamed on something *other* than the Jesuits. I don't know what the heck they're praying to, but I'm going to take a guess that it isn't Jehovah. People, take a look at this… Government is not of God; it is of the Pit; it is never good for the "little people" for too long… If you go to nancypelosi.com, and click on the photos of her and her interns, you'll see that she's got three Masonic occult grips: the extended index finger, the master grip, and the "maha bone" grip. I don't think I'm being wacky about this. Go take a look for yourselves. They all know the handshake… By the way, I just received a photo of "Joey Ratz," the Pope, with his creepy new Jesuit General.

AC: Will Bush visit with Joey Ratz prior to his trip here on April 19th?

GK: Whenever Bush or Blair are over there, they usually stop by the Vatican.

AC: By the way, Ratzinger was elected successor to Pope John Paul II on April 19th of 2005.

GK: Hitler's birthday?

AC: Yes, and it was also the anniversary of the OKC bombing, Waco, and many others. Perhaps the Vatican doesn't mind the subliminal connection to Hitler?

GK: You really *cannot* make this stuff up.

The notorious MIB "Indrid Cold," whose moniker alludes to the "free energy" motors supposedly built into WWII Nazi saucers, is said to have frequented the Midway Tavern in Midway, WV. Each dual set of windows in the tavern contains 32 panes - a key Masonic number.

CHAPTER 11

"Between March 30th and April 6th 1967, John Keel visited Pt. Pleasant again to do more research [with] Mary Hyre. In this period they saw several strange red lights and other UFOs over the town and river – including one that 'transformed' into an aircraft in front of their eyes. Keel, Roger Scarberry, and Steve Mallette also came upon a black Cadillac parked in the shadows of the TNT site. They approached a man who was sitting inside and seemed to be monitoring the situation, dictating notes into a microphone. He refused to answer any questions and just grunted… Throughout the summer, more witnesses suffered odd experiences. Cars and trucks parked for hours outside their homes in remote spots as if 'on surveillance.' Several reported how an 'Indian' or 'Hawaiian' complexioned man in a dark suit stopped them on the street, sometimes taking surprise photographs and running off. After a UFO sighting in June, a woman named Jane was told she had been selected for contact. She was then followed by a black Cadillac that drew up alongside her, out of which stepped a very suntanned man wearing a dark suit and sunglasses. He told her his name was 'Apol.' Apol turned up at her house on June 12th and requested water 'to take some pills;' then he gave Jane three of these capsules, one of which was for her to 'to have analyzed to assure her it was safe.' Surprisingly, she obliged and swallowed one, as if under some kind of spell. This gave her a blinding headache. When later tested by Keel, the drug was [found to be] a sulphur compound.

"Another witness, Jaye Paro, claimed she was abducted by a man in a black Cadillac that drew up alongside her in the street. There were flashing lights on the dashboard that seemed to hypnotize her. The inside of the shiny vehicle smelled like a hospital. At one point a pungent smelling bottle was held under Jaye's nose and she was asked all sorts of questions which washed over her and made no sense. Finally, she was dropped off at the point where she was picked up. Soon afterwards, Apol [began] making predictions about the political turmoil in the Middle East. When the events began to happen, Keel rushed to Pt. Pleasant to hypnotize the woman and attempt to get her to describe the mystery man in more detail. To his surprise, he found himself talking directly to Apol, who claimed to be in his Cadillac nearby using Jane's vocal cords to communicate with the ufologist. He warned Keel that Robert Kennedy was in grave danger and predicted a plane crash, which Keel says happened soon after. By October, Keel had received countless calls from Apol, many of which he tape recorded. The being said that he was trapped in time, forced to jump about from past to future because of the difference between linear time and the time he faced in his own 'dimension.' This was how 'predictions' were possible. On Dec. 15th, at 5:45 p.m., Keel was sitting in his Manhattan apartment, watching President Johnson switch on the Christmas tree lights at the White House. Apol had inferred that the 'visitors' would prove themselves by making [a] prophesied 'blackout' start as the switch was thrown. Nothing happened... It seemed that Apol had lied yet again. Then, a news flash came on the TV. The Silver Bridge at Pt. Pleasant had collapsed. More than 40 people died that night, including several of the witnesses to UFOs, Mothman, and the Men in Black."

-Jenny Randles, *The Truth Behind Men in Black: Government Agents – or Visitors From Beyond*, pp. 101-104

Announcer: Prepare yourself, Earthlings... *[eerie theme music plays]* Greetings, my friends. We are all interested in the future; that is where you and I are going to spend the rest of our lives. You are interested in the unknown, the mysterious, and the unexplainable. That is why you are here. Now, for the first time, we are bringing you the full story. We are giving you all the evidence, based on the secret testimony of the miserable souls who survived this terrifying ordeal. The incident, my friends, we cannot keep a secret any longer. Let us punish the guilty and reward the innocent. My friends, can your heart stand the shocking facts about *Untamed Dimensions*?!

GREENFIELD, ALLEN & ANDY COLVIN – MOTHMAN EXTRAVAGANZA – OCT. 2007

Adam Gorightly of *Untamed Dimensions* (UD): Good morning, afternoon, and evening to all of you listening out there, from the great

American heartland to the pyramidal structures on Mars. You are listening to another spine-tingling edition of *Untamed Dimensions* with me, your host, Adam Gorightly. Our guests tonight are Andy Colvin, aka "the Mothman's Photographer," who is fresh from a speaking engagement at the Mothman Festival in Pt. Pleasant, WV, and Allen Greenfield, the noted ufologist and ritual magician. I've summoned them forth tonight to speak on the strange subject of the Mothman.

T. Allen Greenfield, author of *Secret Cipher of the Ufonauts* (TG): I'm arcane, I'm weird, and I'm here… Hi, Andy! Andy and I have actually corresponded. I almost went to the festival.

UD: Yes, I wanted to ask Andy how that went.

AC: There were lots of strange things going on. We had doppelgangers and electrical anomalies. I heard about a mysterious murder in Mound, WV that was somehow connected to a church in the nearby Carbide "company town" of Boomer. We looked at Charlie Manson's newly abandoned house in Mound, and talked to someone who knew his guardian. Sara Jane Moore's house was up for sale, too, so we looked at that.

UD: What did you speak about at the festival?

AC: About the pattern of events happening this year – strange political machinations melding with both real and hoaxed supernatural events. One of my basic theories is that there is almost a corporate calendar to "terror" events. The "terrorists" seem to take vacations just when the rest of us take *our* vacations. You'd think the terrorists would want to attack us when we were all on vacation, but it's generally the other way around. A lot of "supernatural" events are reported at the same time as "terror" events. I like to keep a calendar of news coverage. I focus on what mainstream outlets like the Associated Press and Yahoo choose to report. I think that's where the bulk of the mass mind control occurs.

UD: Allen, you were slated for the Mothman Festival, but didn't make it. What were you going to talk about?

TG: I was principally going to talk about Gray Barker. I thought it would be a great opportunity to talk about the native West Virginian folklorist who had, so early on, gotten involved in UFOs and monsters. Gray did so much documenting and elaborating. I thought that it would be a fitting thing to do. I only had one previous opportunity [to do that, and that was] on the occasion of giving out the first annual Gray Barker "Lifetime Achievement in Ufology

Award," which went to Jim Moseley. I wanted to have the opportunity to talk about Gray in West Virginia, but they sort of pulled a surprise on me. This wasn't the reason I didn't go, mind you. I would have gone to speak about Gray regardless, but they said, "Try and stay away from the topic of the Silver Bridge. It's still a sensitive issue around here." While I can certainly understand that 46 people were lost on it, I thought it was a very unusual request. *Of course* the issue should be handled with a certain amount of sensitivity. Things like that don't go away for the people involved. But it *has* been a long time, and it *is* historical.

UD: The collapse of that bridge is a central part of the Mothman story.

TG: It perhaps is the core. While Mothman has appeared all over the world recently, the WV cases reached their peak just before the Silver Bridge collapse, and more or less [dropped in number] immediately thereafter. Other phenomena I tend to associate [with Mothman] have continued in other locations. There was a Mothman sighting in St. Paul, Minnesota just days before the recent I-35 Bridge tragedy in Minneapolis. Not being able to talk about the Silver Bridge disaster is sort of like talking about half of history without talking about the other half. But I respect those locals there who still have fresh wounds.

UD: Sure... The town is trying to bring in some revenue and make it a happy, fun event, like the Roswell UFO Festival. They probably don't want to get into some of the more dark, underlying aspects of the Mothman.

TG: I did not consider it censorship or anything.

AC: A point about bridge collapses... Mothman doesn't seem to be producing these tragedies. He seems to be saying something symbolic about the tragedies – what might be underlying them. There is usually some malfeasance involved... Let's assume for a moment that this creature is a Garuda... The Garuda's usual activity is trying to right some wrong, fight some crime, or expose something that needs to be exposed for the greater good. It's possible that certain elites were looking for a disaster in Minnesota, in order to create this NAFTA Superhighway from Mexico to Canada. Minnesotans are liberals and somewhat less prone to voting against their own interests. A tailor-made event might convince Minnesotans to pump money into turning I-35 into a superhighway. Anthropologist Jim Brandon apparently posted a map of that highway right after the collapse. It seems that he felt the collapse might have been purposeful.

TG: By definition, the collapse of a major bridge involves some malfeasance on the part of the government. No bridge should be allowed to go for years [without maintenance]. There were many inspection reports indicating that the I-35 Bridge needed to be replaced. And this was *certainly* true of the Silver Bridge. Without getting too political, the infrastructure of this country has been on the wane. I'm surprised that there haven't been more disasters. By the way, if you convert the name of the I-35 Bridge into a numerical cipher, it has the same cipher value as both the Silver Bridge and Mothman. Just a few days before the I-35 collapse, there was a birdlike creature seen by two people in St. Paul, which had the appearance of a UFO through binoculars. An enormous, birdlike creature was seen very clearly. I feel it was predictive of the collapse, not a cause of the collapse. I would compare it to the two birds of Odin in Norse mythology, whose names, Hugin and Munin, mean roughly "knowledge" and "wisdom." They are supposed to fly around the world, every day, and report back to Odin on the state of affairs. I think of Mothman in those terms. It is a watcher rather than a participant. It is a surveyor of events. If you saw an unmanned Predator aircraft, you could say that there was a war going on, but you couldn't blame the war on the aircraft.

UD: Andy, you mentioned that you sort of see Mothman as a crusader of sorts – a guardian angel that has touched your life since you were very young. Is that correct?

AC: Yes. The Buddhist point of view is one that I often draw on to explain this. There is an extensive Buddhist tome called *Cities of Lightning*, written by a monk, Samudranath, in upstate New York. Using poetic verse, Samudranath talks at length about all the different Thunderbeings, of which the Garuda is probably the main one. Samudranath looks at all the different ways you can think of the symbolisms involved. Amazingly, Buddhists feel that certain living masters can turn into the Garuda and fly around. This would be akin to the Navajo skinwalkers, but in reverse – for a positive affect… In fact, Samudranath himself claims to have done this. He also claims to have dispatched other "Thunderbeings" to do good works. Amazingly, I've found evidence that he might be telling the truth. When I saw his picture on the back of the book I thought, "Wow, he kind of looks like the thing that was photographed in our window in 1973!" That picture is in my books and on my website. I showed the Samudranath photo to my Mothman witness friend,

Harriet Plumbrook, and asked her if she thought his face resembled the bird thing looking in my window. Stunningly, she said, "*That's the guy who's been visiting me!*" She has seen an image of him in her house. I was absolutely floored by this synchronicity. What are the chances that the only known American monk claiming to be a Garuda would 1) also look like this 1973 creature and 2) be visiting Harriet in dreams and visions?

UD: Aren't these the type of synchronicities that had happened to you *throughout* researching this Mothman odyssey?

AC: Yes, and that's more or less why I had to write the book trilogy. It was synchronicity after synchronicity, leading to further break-throughs... One more thing about Harriet... I photographed a doppelganger of her prior to this last Mothman Festival. Unbelievably, we had *two* sets of doppelganger occurrences during the festival. In Point Pleasant, John Frick, one of the organizers, was in the TNT area on Friday night with some people. Yet back at the haunted Lowe Hotel, some other people saw his doppelganger. There are multiple witnesses in both doppelganger cases.

UD: These stories don't surprise me one bit. I myself have had experiences along these lines.

TG: As have I... One of them involved you, Adam. I heard a story that someone appearing to be you was at a convention, talking to people and being recognized, yet you weren't there.

UD: Yes, exactly. And you hear about these doppelganger sightings in relation to the Mothman.

TG: In the early days of ufology, the Garuda was discussed extensively as one of the types of beings associated with UFOs. The whole mythos of the great, protective, fierce-looking bird creature is a worldwide phenomenon. You find it known among the Southwestern Amer-Indian people as the "Thunderbird" and, of course, in Asia in various forms. I'm looking at one of them right now, carved in wood from Bali. The Garuda is classically regarded as both a protective and *projective* [medium between us and the creator].

UD: Mediumship seems to turn up time and again in UFO and Mothman sightings, as if there were some type of ritual being performed. There are definitely some "entities" here; whether they are from another planet is another question. Andy's whole Mothman experience started with a UFO experience. Wasn't there an event, early in your life, with alien greys and a UFO?

AC: After we built a Mothman shrine at the home of my friend, Tommy Burnham, he claimed he was getting regular visitations. He claimed a flying saucer was landing in his yard. One night, when I staying over at his house, he said, "They're coming tonight." I was skeptical. I can't say what really happened, for I was asleep. It seemed like there was activity in the room, however. Tommy woke me up, screaming. I remember dreaming about little green men. They were not "greys," but furry little Bigfoot creatures. I could not attest to anything definite like a physical encounter.

UD: Didn't this happen prior to your Mothman experiences?

AC: Well, I thought I saw something flying behind our car around that time, too. Five years later, I again saw something at Tommy's house. I saw something in the woods coming at me. It was coming out of a tree. It was an "elemental" – some sort of shadow being. My sister apparently photographed it after it followed me home. We had several other people seeing things in that same spot. Those events were the "hook" that kept me coming back, in order to figure out what was going on there. Across from the Mothman shrine house is an old Methodist church, and what was once an old school. The school actually burned down and some kids died. Energetically, something was going on there. Men in Black, like the one photographed by Allen in the late 1960s, were seen there, as well as cigar-shaped craft and dancing balls of light that seemed to communicate. Harriet Plumbrook saw something morph from the "Flatwoods Monster" into the "Virgin Mary" there.

UD: Now you're speaking Allen's language!

AC: In 2002, my team went back there one night. We all saw this energy field with three wispy beings. I recorded the events as best as I could. I looked over the transcript and realized that we may have encountered some kind of cosmic mirror. It was like an invisible curtain placed in front of us. The three beings we saw may have been aspects of ourselves – reflections or potentialities. There was a fourth creature, too, which may have been Mothman, observing our reactions to the mirror. The fourth entity did not glow; it was dark. The whole situation could have been Mothman's doing. The Garuda symbolizes *space* and our psychological growth through that space. The creation of a cosmic mirror fits its known function. In *Cities of Lightning*, Samudranath is adamant that the Garuda-Thunderbird leads us to enlightenment. The description he gives of a Garuda encounter is exactly what we saw. There is a fine mist that glows faintly, followed by a strong electrical charge running through you. This charge seems to trigger kundalini. I experienced kundalini after our encounter, and the others experienced a strong electrical charge. I picked up a premonition, which later came true, regarding a drowning at Magic Island, at the confluence of the Elk and Kanawha Rivers. This phenomenon is more real than people realize.

UD: Allen, you've investigated a lot of UFO cases, as well as paranormal cases. What do you make of Andy's experiences?

TG: He didn't use the word "conjuration," but it was an equivalent term, about something "morphing" into what could be considered positive religious imagery. In a certain sense, I think we get what we ask for. I see the universe as plastic. In everyday, consensus reality, if one invokes a positive energy, one will tend to get manifestations of a positive nature. By "invoke," I don't mean all of the paraphernalia of, and ritual of, occultism and magic; I mean according to one's particular discipline, whether that be kundalini yoga, or ceremonial magic, or high church mass, or whatever. One is going to invoke the great ectoplasmic glue out of which concrete reality is formed, and get what one expects. Like the monster in *Forbidden Planet*, the id produces [one] thing and our higher consciousness [another. But] they're not necessarily totally separate. What they *are* are differing manifestations. There can be the protective angelic being, described in a loose sense as the Virgin Mary, or the more fierce version, which would probably be described as a Garuda or Mothman – still very positive. You're talking about the same underlying phenomenon [shapeshifting or morphing] according to the individuals involved. That, in a sense, was Gray Barker's point; and it certainly is mine as well. Experiencing these things from a ceremonial magick point of view, one is always aware that it can be shaped. The key is to realize that most people, whether they're doing it intentionally or not, are shaping their reality continuously, according to their predispositions. [The paranormal] depends, in large part, on what we are and who we are. A monk who is filled with compassion, and who wants compassion for the entire world, is perhaps going to invoke something quite different from what a black magician would want to invoke. Human emotions, given the right circumstances, can invoke the foreshadowing of a disaster. There are strong energies involved in something like the TNT Area. It is an area associated with war, as well as with the heavy erotic energies of [being a local] lover's lane. One would expect latent energies to be there, waiting to form themselves according to the wishes of a Woodrow Derenberger or a Buddhist monk. These are classical "haunted" locales…

UD: Those released haunted energies [must have] played a part in Andy's hotspot. Children died when the school burned down.

TG: Right, the phenomena seem to be associated with these strong energy centers or nodes. I look for the common denominators in them. The classical ley lines in Europe are very much like the acupuncture meridians on the human body. I find that nodes, oddly enough, are associated with two things: religion and sexuality. I don't think that [those two] things are as different as we in Judeo-Christian civilization think. Those places seem to be far more prone to the whole range of phenomena, from apparitions to UFOs. They're also really good places to work magick and do healings. Gray Barker may have been the first ufologist to [see] that there is a definite relationship between sexually charged situations and the appearance of various apparitions. As I said, what you see is what you get. I don't mean that they are hallucinatory or not real; I mean that they tend to be somewhat plastic in nature, and will manifest according to the percipient.

UD: These energies seem attracted to the energy that is released during sex *and* death.

TG: That goes back to Freud… "Orgasm," in French, is le petit mort, "the small death." Both sex and death are forms of energy release. I'm sure Wilhelm Reich would have said that that is the essence of how orgone energy is usefully manifested. The different jargons from different disciplines amount to the same thing. I find that there are more people willing to accept that now than there were 20 years ago.

AC: From what I've seen, the phenomena can cause people to fall in love *or* break up. It can also be the other way around: breaking up or falling in love can cause paranormal phenomena… But this power spot in Mound is at the intersection of old Indian tracks where there were once mounds. People disagree about the origins of the mounds. Some say that Indians built the mounds, but the Indians deny this. There is also a theory that the mounds are *natural* formations. Such earth "warts" would probably emanate energies. Perhaps those energies animate various entities. Perhaps they connect to the processes of human origination and/or reincarnation, as with the Masons' "Adam Kadmon" or the Christians' "Adam" in the Garden of Eden.

Around the time of this interview, I happened to drive by the

"Cadman" company, a big supplier of sand, gravel, and concrete in Seattle. Cadman is nestled in alongside Lakeside Industries, a major road construction firm owned by Seattle's Lee family, who are wealthy Catholics. The Lees own an estate within the Rockefellers' gated community on Hawaii's Big Island. Their Seattle compound, on Hunt's Point, is very close to the home of Craig McCaw, who hosts George Bush and Rudy Guiliani when they are in town. Cadman is also located next to a major UPS hub in Redmond, WA, near the Microsoft campus. I once worked for UPS, where I heard a rumor that they have cheated the state of Washington out of millions of dollars in taxes by mislabeling the planes they buy from Boeing as "used." According to a Boeing test pilot I spoke with, such planes are quietly flown to Europe prior to actual sale, thus making them "used." On their maiden flights, they often carry items banned in parts of the E.U., like Pampers diapers. Many of my UPS bosses were Vietnam veterans who had been involved in Phoenix-type missions. One admitted to me that he and his platoon had seen UFOs. According to the book UFOs From Behind the Iron Curtain, *in Nov. 1968, a UFO was witnessed by hundreds of people in Kent, WA, a suburb of Seattle. It was seen floating above Boeing's Space Research Lab for close to 3 weeks. Photographs taken of the object showed that it looked exactly like an object seen that year in Romania, a country that has just recently entered into a closer relationship with the U.S. intelligence apparatus. On Feb. 5th, 2010, it was announced that Romania had agreed to host a new U.S. "missile shield" in its territory. The shield is aimed at protecting Western interests from the "emerging threat" of Iranian ballistic missiles.*

AC: Interestingly, our Mothman vortex spot is in an area called "Pleasant Dell," which has a name correspondence to Point Pleasant. Regarding Indrid Cold, it's hard to tell, at first glance, whether Indrid was a government agent, ultraterrestrial, Thunderbeing, or hoaxer. As I stated in the summer of 2005, the name "Indrid Cold" may have to do with the Hindu God, "Indra." Indra and the Garuda are closely linked in both Hindu and Buddhist mythology. The Garuda subsumes the heat energy of Indra. Indra in his cold form might actually *be* a Garuda. By using the name "Indrid Cold," someone knowledgeable in the occult may have been referencing the mythology of the Garuda. There is some evidence that Indrid Cold was a hypnotist. For instance, in 1968, a young man in Parkersburg, WV, Steven Law, said that Indrid tried to get him to "come away to

Lanulos for 8 years" because he was "unattached" to anyone. Indrid may have been looking for good mind control subjects to use in covert operations. He probably was friends with the Apol character who was messing with John Keel. Apol liked to use hypnosis on local witnesses, too.

UD: Are there hot chicks on Lanulos?

AC: I don't know, but Woody Derenberger described it as being in the jungle. One of the speakers at the Mothman festival, Susan Sheppard, mentioned that Woody disappeared for six months. Maybe he was taken to South America, to one of these Naziesque mind control camps in the jungle, such as Colonia Dignidad. I was told by Derenberger's daughter, Taunia, that Indrid Cold eventually moved to Cleveland. If he's moving to Cleveland, he's probably not from another planet.

TG: Indrid Cold described some things to Woody Derenberger that corresponded closely to the descriptions of the Icelandic medium, Indridi Indridason, who lived a very short life, from 1883 to 1912... Indridi produced out-of-body experiences, poltergeist phenomena, clairvoyance, dematerializations, and materializations. Some of them were extremely dramatic, and performed under comparatively controlled conditions. Indridason was known for his ability to appear and disappear. I find the name similarity between Indrid and Indridi to be very suggestive. The folklore of Iceland includes the aforementioned great birds, Hugin and Munin, which fit the classical Mothman description... What we *know* about Indrid is that he was still living in West Virginia in the early 1980s. He has since moved, mind you. He is not there anymore. I can say it now. In the past, I've talked around it. Terry R. Wriste [indicated to me] that Indrid's home was on WV Route 62 in Midway, WV. But I don't want Midway to be inundated with hundreds of amateur ufologists poking around, looking for Indrid Cold. Some poor local might wind up getting lynched or something. With all the recent [media coverage] I would say that that sort of thing *could* still happen. But Indrid moved away from Midway. He was using pretty advanced techniques in terms of mind control. It is likely that "Cold" is not his real name. It doesn't sound like a real name. It sounds like a name meant to alert people to look deeper into it. It has something to do with what he was there for, as opposed to who he is. Indrid Cold is a very clever name, real or otherwise. It contains useful information if one deciphers it properly... The name "Lanulos" is something I've been going over for years. "Land you lost" may be the deciphered [meaning]. It's a complex story.

UD: Andy's theory, which is that government agents were involved, may [have some validity]. Andy went to a special school where there seemed to be government tampering going on. And [there are active, secret] military installations there. As Andy has looked into this deeper over the years, a lot of military intelligence connections have reared their ugly heads. Isn't that correct, Andy?

AC: Yes. But I'm not saying that Derenberger was necessarily an agent. He may have been a *whistleblower* of sorts. I was referring to Cold possibly being an agent. Cold told Steven Law that he had been "shot in Arkansas." The pellets had been removed by a doctor there. At that time, Winthrop Rockefeller was the governor of Arkansas.

Interestingly, when we went to Midway with the "Ghost Box," which answers questions using words randomly grabbed from local AM/FM radio, the box told us that Indrid Cold's real name was "Johnny Morgan." When I googled that name, I found that Johnny Morgan was the nickname for J.P. Morgan, whose company eventually merged with the Rockefellers to form J.P. Morgan-Chase. Morgan controlled the natural gas industry in WV. According to the box, Indrid may have been associated with Columbia Gas or one of the many other energy concerns near Midway, such as the Amos Power Plant or the Winfield locks/hydroelectric dam. The historical importance of the area cannot be underestimated. The technologies that led to oil and gas drilling were pioneered in the Kanawha Valley, in the early saltmines. The abundance of salt in the area fomented several battles prior to, and during, the Civil War. George Washington and his troops were given much of the land by British generals, who had stolen it from the Indians through the skillful use of commercial contracts and religious missionaries.

UD: Also, it could be that disinformation agents picked up on the Indrid Cold legend and ran with it.

TG: There's another possibility, too, which reconciles both ideas: there is the government, and there is the [shadow] government. The late Kerry Thornley, who was a great friend of mine, and a fellow mischief-maker…

UD [*stunned*]: *Thornley* was a good friend of yours? Have you read my book on him?

TG: No, I have not.

UD: Well, I'll get you one. I'm kind of amazed here… Tell me what you were going to say about Kerry.

TG: Well, Kerry's story is one of "interference" in his life, from very early on. He even thought that he was the product of…

UD: …a military mind-control experiment?

TG: More than that… He thought he was the product of a genetics experiment, from conception on. He was a most interesting, colorful, and imaginative person, and one that I tended to trust. He died under somewhat mysterious circumstances, and certainly prematurely. For folks in Atlanta, Kerry was a fixture on the high-weirdness scene. I knew him for many, many years. Kerry felt that there was an invisible government that had nothing whatever to do with the elected government – a worldwide body hidden inside the Bilderbergers, the Trilateral Commission, and secret societies like Skull and Bones. I find that credible. Are we talking about something that is purely human, or an *X-Files* crossover? It is a tough nut to crack, and probably the most dangerous area to go into… But when we are talking about "the government," are we not talking about the [Big Oil] guys from Texas – the men in the shadows [who met often with] Nixon? Aren't *they* really in charge? They propose and dispose according to [their whims]. I don't tend to have a paranoid view of history, but the fact that the last Presidential election consisted of a choice between Skull and Bones and Skull and Bones *does* suggest that there is something to the notion that the world really operates [by conspiracy].

UD: To quote Charles Manson, "Paranoia is a higher form of awareness."

TG: Chuck is right.

AC: Allen, do you know Manson?

TG: I'm more likely to know Marilyn Manson than Charles Manson. During my period as the Prison Ministry Coordinator for a great occult body [dating back to] antiquity – which I am no longer associated with – I did not have occasion to be in contact with that former alleged member of the O.T.O.'s Solar Lodge.

AC: He lived in Mound for at least a couple of years during WWII.

UD: Another strange coincidence…

TG: That's just like Kerry Thornley being in the Marine Corps with Lee Harvey Oswald. This means something…

AC: Unbelievably, one of the witnesses I interviewed, has long suspected his father of being one of the Oswald doubles. His father was an USAF pilot who flew often to Japan during the time Oswald was there.

An eagle statue in the Blennerhassett Hotel (top left) takes on a Garuda pose. The idea of flight is reflected in Masonry's "compass and square" (lower left). In addition to symbolizing the balancing of male and female energies, it implies a flapping motion like the wings of a bird, and contains the letters "XX" - a possible allusion to the secret of gravity. The Moorish name "Og" is also seen, referencing the blue-blooded "Amazon queens" of Atlantis. This particular compass/square can be found on the lodge in Worthington, OH, the oldest lodge west of the Appalachians. Two Masonic aprons worn by Joseph Smith, the founder of Mormonism - who apparently became a Mason in nearby Cincinnati when he was 11 - are on display there. The Knights of Columbus lodge in Alloy, WV (right) sits at the entrance to one of Union Carbide's oldest plants. The family behind Jonestown, the Laytons, lived here until one of them married into a German family with major holdings in I.G. Farben.

CHAPTER 12

"The beginning of this report might be said to start on the battlefields of Korea, for it was while one of my informants, George Smyth, was fighting in that land that he became interested in UFOs. He and two other soldiers saw two saucers sweep over them, and reported the incident to their commanding officer. They were requested to report to intelligence. When they did so, they were then told that they were suffering from 'battle fatigue.' However they were *not* relieved of their frontline duty. When he returned to civilian life, he proceeded to study UFOs from his home in Elizabeth, NJ. On Oct. 10, 1966, two teenage boys in Elizabeth reported observing a very tall green being with beady red eyes in the woods. The creature had no nose, ears, nor hair. As Smyth was questioning the lads, two heavy-set men [driving] a large black car joined and questioned the boys, too. Two weeks after the incident, Smyth received a mysterious phone call telling him to give up UFO investigation. Then, on Thanksgiving 1967, a swarthy man with hypnotic eyes got out of a black car while Smyth was walking his dog in front of his house. The dog arched its back and began to howl like a wolf. The man told Smyth he wanted all of [his] UFO material. After Smyth refused, the man said, 'You'll be sorry!' As he returned to his car, the door, which had no handle, opened without his touching it. The license plate bore the number 'U 1496.' The next day, a car almost ran Smyth down in a deliberate manner. [Smyth began being] followed to work. About the same time [other witnesses] reported to me that [they were being harassed] by men in the same kind of car, which had red upholstery and an insignia on the door [that looked like a lightning bolt. The car apparently] had some kind of electrical equipment set up in the rear seat. The equipment, with extensive dials, illuminated in a bright, bluish light.

"During the first week of May, 1968, a car pulled up across the street from Smyth's home. Three men stepped out. He quickly identified them [as] John Keel, Gray Barker, and James W. Moseley – or so he thought. Smyth ran down the stairs to greet them, only to see their blue Volkswagen speeding away. It bore no license plate. Feeling there had been something strange about the men, he telephoned Moseley and Barker, who told him they had not been away from home all day. He checked a picture he had of them published in *Saucer News*. Although the men [in the VW] bore facial characteristics identical to the men in the picture, including Keel's then-copious beard, Smyth knew there had been something "wrong" with what he now believed to be an impersonation. Whoever the impersonators had been, they had goofed. The heights [of the three, in relation to one another, were wrong]. A week later, three men stepped out of a black Plymouth that bore West Virginia license plates. [The plates] were strangely distorted. The 'West Virginia' was printed at the top instead of properly at the bottom [and] the numerals, '1436,' have since been determined not to exist on such plates without some other type of prefix or designation. They displayed membership cards as if they were members of Gray Barker's organization, and accosted [Smyth with UFO questions]. Later, when Smyth spoke to Gray Barker by telephone, he learned that neither Barker nor any of his staff [knew the men]. On May 18th [after he and several others had seen] James Moseley's doppelganger, Smyth was preparing to leave [his house when] his dog began howling out the window. On the other side of the street was a large black car with two people in the rear attending electronic equipment. One wore earphones while the other raised a contraption that he described as a 'crystalline wheel' with a 2-3 foot rod extending from it. The wheel began to glow with a yellow light. Then, the light suddenly concentrated into a yellow beam, which shot out, striking Smyth in the forehead. He felt a blast of heat. Before he blacked out, he was able to note the license plate. It resembled a U.S. Government plate and bore the identification 'U 1436.' The car quickly left after the ray stuck Smyth. When he recovered consciousness, he was suffering from a splitting headache. The headache persisted throughout the day, and two more 'blackouts' occurred…"

-John J. Robinson, from *The UFO Silencers* by Tim Beckley

"Vyz" at *Beyond the Grassy Knoll* (GK): I'm interested in what will be happening tomorrow, on May 1st in Seattle, the high occult day of Beltane. Somebody in Seattle sent me information on the scheduled "terror" drills there. We talked about the source of this, and she showed me some emails. Everybody is now aware of how 9/11 *and* the London 7/7 attacks both coincided with nearby terror drills. Speaking of which, you sent me a personal story about a premonition or "wink from beyond." Do you want to talk about that?

Andy Colvin (AC): Sure. First of all, there were at least four or five terror drills on 9/11, not just two. And there have been other drills since… There was the Top-Off drill a few months ago. Some alarms were set off in Portland, at the Doubletree Hotel, where Chertoff was staying that day. There has been some speculation that terrorists were going after him, but this is probably just more fear mongering… This week, we've got this drill going on in Seattle, where the viaduct will be "attacked." They have to come up with scenarios for these drills. The viaduct is an old concrete, double-decker roadway that runs along the waterfront of Seattle. It's something that the developers want to get rid of, so that they can build luxury condos. It's prime land with views of the water and the Olympics. However, the viaduct is loved by the citizens of Seattle, because you get to drive along the coast, right past downtown, and see the beautiful views for free. With the viaduct gone, the average citizen will lose not only the views, but will lose one of only two routes allowing them to quickly cruise through downtown. It's a great way to avoid the traffic in Seattle, which sometimes gets voted "worst in the country." I use the viaduct all the time. Once it is gone, we lose, and the developers win. Seattle is one of the most corrupt towns around. At least one famous book has been written about Seattle corruption: William Chambliss' *On the Take*. It is used in university criminology courses. They are always finagling things in Seattle. Chambliss fingered the big contractors, jewelers, bankers, lawyers, and the city council, among others. Strangely, every time they are about to tear down some structure, they do a few million dollars of repair work on it first. This happened with the Kingdome and with Key Arena, which the Sonics are now leaving. Howard Schultz of Starbucks, the owner of the Sonics, knew the team was leaving. A bone had to be thrown to the big contractors beforehand. They knew they were going to tear down the Kingdome, too, so they did about $100 million in repairs on it just a couple of years before it was destroyed. It was imploded by the same firm that cleaned up the WTC and OKC sites, Controlled Demolition.

GK: Yes, I think their home base is out of Maryland.

AC: By the way, unless they've come up with a new method, somebody had to physically plant all of those charges into the Twin Towers. There had to have been hundreds of them. Many witnesses have come forward about advance explosions in the buildings, yet they're still lying about it in the media. The History Channel had one the other day called "The Rise and Fall of an American Icon." It was filled with garbage. They just passed over the fact that for weeks, cleanup crews had to be on a constant lookout for molten steel as they were cleaning. One cannot blame that on jet fuel with any shred of scientific credibility, yet The History Channel did just that.

GK: We're not necessarily fingering Controlled Demolition as being the ones who laid in the WTC explosives. They're just the company that's always called in to clean up these very large crime scenes.

AC: Right. And they would probably be the ones that would implode the Seattle viaduct if that ever happens. The people with money want it to come down, and it will, be it by earthquake or some other scenario; I've speculated about that for a long time. The vision that my friend Tommy had in 1967, about 9/11, which I got a brief glimpse of, included a round-topped building being destroyed. There is such a building in the Trade Center complex; it did not get destroyed. There is also a similar dome in downtown Seattle. Every-time I drive on the viaduct, I look over and wonder if the Seattle dome will ever blow. In 2004, during the filming of the reality series, my camera assistant and I were parked almost under the viaduct. He ran in to get something. I looked up at the viaduct thinking, "If that thing fell, would it fall on me?" At that exact moment, I looked at a train that was going by under the viaduct. Graffitied onto the train, I kid you not, were the words, "Andy, get out from under there!" There was an exclamation point at the end of it. I took a picture of it with the video camera; it's on the DVD. What a synchronicity *that* was; I'd have to rate that one in the top three. As I pondered its meaning, I was taken back to an experience with one of my Buddhist teachers. He and I were almost hit by a rockslide. We both jumped out of the way at the same time. I now wonder if that train graffiti was an echo of that rockslide event, or perhaps a prediction of something similar in the future. Or, maybe it had to do with my marriage… Once you get into this arena, you often don't know where things are coming from. The stone drops into the water, and vibrations go in every direction, into the past and into the future. Mothman witnesses seem to pick up on these radiative waves. Speaking of which, the word "Lanulos" backwards is "solunal," which refers to radiative shockwaves. Maybe the Silver Bridge was brought down by terror instigated by Indrid Cold. I've often wondered if there is going to be some serious terror in Seattle. Occasionally there are hints, like the guy getting caught at the border supposedly wanting to bomb LAX and the Space Needle right after the WTO protests in late 1999. We didn't have our citywide "Y2K party" because of that guy. It seemed pretty obvious that it was a bogus terror scare designed to punish those of us who had caused "trouble" at the WTO.

Eventually, terrorist Khalid Sheikh Mohammed would claim credit for planning the Space Needle debacle. Within a few years, after he had been waterboarded a few dozen times, Mohammed claimed responsibility for a slew of incidents, including the following: the 1993 WTC bombing, the 9/11 attacks, the murder of Daniel Pearl, the Richard Reid shoe-bombing incident, the Sears Tower plot, the Big Ben plot, the Empire State Building plot, and assassination plots against Jimmy Carter, Bill Clinton, and the Pope. People will say just about anything while under torture, thus proving its lack of effectiveness as an intelligence tool. Still, the media often referred to Mohammed's long list with a straight face – as if it might be true – thus proving that the "lone nut" scenario is still alive and well. If the population can be dumbed down enough, it may be possible to make a single patsy responsible for a whole series of incredibly elaborate, expensive state-planned attacks. A big money saver, and very handy politically…

GK: Nothing will probably take place in Seattle during these upcoming drills, because it's too obvious. In fact, one of our sources for the "parallel terror" rumor is "Captain May," who is *not* an accurate source. It seems to be one of these things where they can claim, "Because I warned everybody, nothing happened." Don't forget about the Minneapolis bridge collapse. There wasn't a drill, but there *were* workers on the bridge before the collapse, which was very reminiscent of the Silver Bridge collapse. There always seems to be somebody doing something on these bridges before it happens.

AC: Isn't it interesting that we just had a big NAFTA summit last week – with Bush in attendance – in New Orleans? We heard it was happening, but saw no updates. One would guess that that Minneapolis bridge collapse has helped move the NAFTA agenda along. It raised fears about some of these older bridges along the NAFTA "corridor" route. The architects of NAFTA need to build new bridges along that route running between Canada and Mexico, through Minneapolis and on down to Texas.

GK: That does bear watching, because that's the way they do things. Not to get too far afield with the situation, but we had a guest, an architectural photographer, who said he was privy to discussions that the Trade Towers were weakening because of flux from winds. They may have needed to be dismantled. If that information is legit, and they really had to do something about the situation, why not implode? The Rockefellers didn't necessarily want to deconstruct the towers and go through all that crap. Why not just demolish them? That may sound wild, but it doesn't sound so wild when you hear an architect talk about it. Here's another situation... We know that the infrastructure in the U.S. is crumbling. We know that the bridges and interstate systems are hurting. They could all use a revamp. What I find interesting is that there is still a Universal National Service Act floating around on Capitol Hill. It's still just a [House] resolution, but it calls for compulsory national service for two years. It's been modified two times since its original appearance in 2003. It calls for those 18 to 42 years of age to be involved. There's a military component in that, too. They can just let all this stuff go to the rats, because the working poor will come out and join the military when we have a serious financial meltdown or World War. Out will come a new WPA or CCC, and all of us will be out there repairing everything that needs to be done. We're heading back to 1935. Americorps is a clearinghouse for volunteering but, in the future, you're going to be "volunteered" whether you like it or not. That's what I see happening. When the shit finally hits the fan, this old bohemian will be out there sweeping streets. Everybody will have to do something for the Fatherland... Here's a question from a listener... It says, "Why is the government privatizing the road infrastructure, claiming that there's no money, when the federal government is reaping the largest gas tax revenues in the country's history? And why is no one making any mention of this?"

AC: Well, there is that old equation, which is "public subsidy for private profit." Whenever a service or project is going to make money, it gets privatized; whenever it's going to lose money, it gets put back into the public sector.

GK: You see a trend right now of more and more states talking about bankruptcy. New Jersey is moaning and groaning. They don't know what to do. They can't drain anything more out of property taxes, so now they're going to privatize. They are not being privatized by

U.S. companies, either, which is really questionable. For instance, a Spanish company has taken over a section of I-80 in Indiana. It has always been a toll road, but now it's *their* toll road. In Florida, they're not far away from doing this. Private companies are coming in to "help" us... They'll grab the water. They'll grab the energy. And then all of a sudden, you're seeing a Communist-style system with no competition.

AC: Our system is already communistic or "state capitalist," as Chomsky calls it. It increasingly operates for the benefit of corporations as opposed to individuals. The Germans own a lot of the water in WV now. It is all simply "structural adjustment," as written about in the book, *The Economic Hitman*. You sell off the public resources of a country to foreign companies.

GK: This is where you finally find the last face of the corporations. That listener also asked, "Did you see that Turkey is considering privatizing that county's lakes and rivers?" Well, the water is going to be the last – and worst – one that they go for. It'll be, "Guess what, folks? There's just not enough water." I don't know if it's made an impact out by you... You might have heard of Zephyr Hill Spring Water. It has been gobbled up a couple of times and now is under Nestlé. I mean if this isn't monopolization, then what is? The robber barons always get what they want. It all goes back to J.D. Rockefeller and Standard Oil, etc. They never lose... How did that article by Herb Meyer, where he speaks of the coming wars being about religion, hit you?

AC: I noticed that he summed it up by saying that we have to somehow preserve Judeo-Christian culture. It sounds like something a closet Jesuit might say.

GK: Supposedly, we've got two enemies to be on the lookout for: bad old China and bad old Islam. I thought he blatantly promoted some kind of racial/religious/ethnic agenda.

AC: It's the old east/west battle between the Christians and the Muslims. It's more complex than it looks on the surface, however. People constantly get confused when they think of China, because the media *wants* them to be confused. We end up thinking of China as a separate country. It's better to forget about geographic boundaries and think of it in terms of class. You've got to remember that it has been under partial control of American corporatists, like the Rockefellers and Bushes, for a long time. So, if China goes rampaging around the world, one has to ask, "Who's really rampaging? Is it them, or is it *us*?" Ultimately, it might come down to the internal politics of China. Are there nationalistic players in China who might suddenly switch gears and work against the Rockefellers and Bushes? It all gets very difficult to predict. Along the way, though, one must always remember that when it comes to business, what the media calls "them" may really be "us."

GK *[sings Beatles tune]*: Cuckoo-ka-choo, cuckoo-ka-choo… Such articles get everybody believing that the next war is inevitable. It goes back to the Crusades. There was a book written in 1908, called *Lord of the World*, by Robert Hugh Benson. You can download it from our website. In 1907, this Catholic priest, whose brother was a Jesuit, was talking about the way things would be in the 21st century. He envisioned, like Orwell did later on, that there would be three powers: the Eastern empire (China, Japan, SE Asia, and Russia), Europe, and America. This also goes along with what Sir Halford Mackinder wrote in 1904, about the battle for the "jewel of Eurasia" in the next century. MacKinder called the landmass between Lisbon and Vladivostok the "World Island." Our military is aware of this. There must be a mindset to fight for the "last empire." The problem is that you're on *their* chessboard. This is brinkmanship. I don't think it's all about the oil. Oil is just the pretense… Do you think we are looking towards an inescapable, final conflagration?

AC: Well, according to the Mothman prophecy from 1967, relayed by Tommy Burnham, we may have already seen the start of WWIII. I doubt if that's the "final" conflagration, but it *is* a move to usurp the Middle East and make it into an industrial area. They want to build factories there, and perhaps make Dubai into the new Babylon.

GK: Well, if they succeed in depopulating as they want, the vast expanses of Russia and China still have resources that have gone largely untapped. There'll be more resources than ever, and a lot less people to tap them – very acceptable to the global elite. *That's* what I think they want. Nobody really wants to think about things in these terms, of course. With the rise in oil prices translating into inflation and shortages of food, this is turning out to be a very rapid acceleration of events. Some might accuse me of being "doom and gloom." Do you think we'll be okay, or are we on the threshold of a time untold?

AC: Many industrialized countries have aging populations. For example, there aren't going to be enough young people to support the old folks here and in Russia. So the oil companies and others are taking advantage of the current bubble by milking as much of our excess cash as they can. Pretty soon, however, citizens won't be able to pay at those levels. They'll have to lower prices at some point.

GK: Brzezinski identified the whole geopolitical game in his book, *The Grand Chessboard*. If the U.S. were to encroach upon Iran, it would agitate an axis that would consist of China, Iran, and Russia. But Russia has fallen, and it's only a matter of time before all the Chinese and Japanese want to go westward. There are just too many arrows pointing in this direction. It is going to happen eventually.

AC: It would depend on who's running the show in those countries, and if war profiteers like the Rockefellers and Rothschilds can repeatedly influence or trigger events there.

GK: Right. To me, that's always been *the* question. Harry and I went back and forth about this time and time again. Rockefeller set up his oil combine in China as far back as the 1920s and '30s. Even though China seems to be "rogue," they still play their part for Big Oil. I do wonder if somehow, some way, China might think that they can "bust a move" and run the table. Asians have always been a bit separate from the rest of the world, geographically and conceptually. It doesn't make it good or bad, it just makes it different. They may be thinking, "We'll just play along to a certain point, and then go ahead and write our own script." I'll just ask you your feelings on that. You might have a little bit more insight on that than other Americans.

AC: I married into a Chinese family, so I do hear things. My wife's opinion is that there *would* be players in China that would try to "bust a move." Let's face it, there are always regional blocs vying for power. The real powerbrokers keep tabs on those who could potentially succeed in such endeavors. Elites make moves on the behind-the-scenes chessboard to control the game. It's complicated... An important question, though, always is: "Who is controlling the media?" As far as China goes, the Bushes have a hand in their satellite industry, which indirectly leverages their media. Media content in China is heavily controlled. Any rogue or nationalistic movement can be stopped that way. If not, they can always roll out the tanks again.

GK: The book *The Manisis Chronicles* came out of a Rosicrucian facility in Quakertown, PA. It foretells the U.S. being invaded by what they call the "Old World." The invasion is abrogated by tumultuous events; there are great geological upheavals around the world. They all just decide not to fight anymore. I think that possibly could happen. I also think that something might get out of control. We're looking at a period of tribulation. I don't know if we can avoid it…

AC: I definitely think the middle class is going to face hardships in America. But there has *always* been suffering going on here. Our system is set up so that a certain amount of the population is living in comfort while the rest are not. Our armies, corporate and otherwise, are going around the world causing misery in other places. This supports our comfort in the form of cheaper products and investments. Back when I was a budding young Buddhist priest, I tried to get that concept through to other Buddhists, who are often very naïve. Many were raised with financial comforts. They've never really thought too much about poverty or why it exists. At a subconscious level, they think that such events happen "out there" somewhere – that it doesn't link back to them. But it's exactly the opposite *Everything* we have is built on the misery of the poor here and in other countries. People ask, "What do you do about it?" Well, you can realize what the reality is, and let *that* inform your actions. Others will pick up on what you are saying and doing. If enough people do this, then some kind of paradigm shift has the possibility of occurring.

GK: *Something* is going to happen, and it's *not* going to be pretty. As Orwell laid out in his treatise on Patriotism and Nationalism, people will – as happened in Nazi Germany – become more myopic, not understanding why others hate them so. Americans will think, "We're just good guys. We're successful, and they just hate us for our success," not realizing that the hate is because we are occupying someone's country. In time, we could be looking at something akin to the Mongol hordes charging westward against Byzantine Europe. What is old becomes new again… By the way, Wayne from Austin sent me something called *Evidence of Revision*. It is old black and white footage of all the networks covering the JFK assassination – stuff you never see again after the first airing.

AC: Last weekend, I had a little synchronicity involving the number "911." My Buddhist teacher, Aryadaka, and I used to walk a lot in Seward Park in Seattle, which is this island that the Indians held sacred. He always talked about a "council spot" hidden in the woods there somewhere. He never took me there; he said I would have to find it myself. Another spiritual seeker I interviewed in the series, Ken Alton, hinted that he knew where it was. He once had something extremely large follow him through the park – what he thought might be a Garuda – flying high up in the trees. It had his dog quite spooked. Anyway, I found the council spot last weekend, on my own.

GK: So, you passed the test.

AC: I suppose so… It's a powerful spot. If somebody were to take you there before you're ready for it, it could negatively affect you. Some spiritual mentors don't necessarily want that kind of karmic responsibility. When I was there, I had this certain feeling that I get before synchronicities happen; it's a feeling of "universal clarity." I can feel the energy of the universe going through me. It feels like my body expands out to encompass the universe – the spontaneous eruption of a Buddhist practice I was once taught. In that practice, you imagine that everything is happening inside of you instead of "out there." That feeling was very strong when I arrived at the park. I *knew* something was going to happen. I rounded this corner and something said, "You need to go off into this area." There was just a hint of an old trail there, and lots of fallen trees to climb over. Eventually, I arrived at this cliff that overlooks the bay on the west side of the island. That bay is the gentlest part of Lake Washington. It's the only part of the lake where the public can freely anchor boats for the night. This would also have been the place where Indians came to moor *their* boats, too. To make a long story short, while I was there meditating, a client who owed me money decided to pay me half of what he owed me, or $911. An intermediary called me just as I was leaving the park and told me this… Later I found out that in the old days, the Indians believed that supernatural monsters called the Ya-hos lived just south of Seward. Coincidentally, I do most of my media research today using "Yahoo" news. The "Yahoo" was originally the name of the Bigfoot in Australia, before the crypto-zoologists changed it to "Yowie," thus confusing the situation… Another item is that in China, the Bigfoot is called "Bekk-bok," while in the Northwest Indian culture it is called "Bak-was." This is one more example of similar creature names in both the Northwest and in Asia. Another name relationship is "Moth" and "Mother." I've talked about Mut (pronounced "mott"), the female winged deity from Egypt who "weighs the hearts of men" in the afterlife. Mut morphed into Isis and Mary. Then we have the double entendre, "Mother Mary." We see visions of Mother Mary at the same places we see Mothman… By the way, one of my witnesses had another sighting last month. Sharon Moore, who I've talked about before, saw a "wire entity." This was an entity that looked like a thick wire. This type of thing could have given rise to some of the serpent legends; those seeing this wire figure might interpret it as a serpent. There is much Fortean lore devoted to wires, strings, and ropes falling from the sky. One of our Mothman list correspondents, the "Jesus Toast" lady, claimed to have seen a string fall from the sky in Youngstown, OH. Keel researched and found that a lot of these serpentine materials falling from the sky had things attached to them. Sometimes churches would be built where these things had fallen. Coincidentally, the same day I talked to Sharon about her wire sighting, I watched an old *Jonny Quest* cartoon, whose intro features a Hindu boy, Hadji, charming a rope by playing a flute. Not only can you charm a snake, but you can also charm a string or rope. Then there's the Indian rope trick, which involves a rope supposedly falling from the sky, which one can climb. The rope can be thought of as coming from a "magic carpet" flying above. The connection between rope and unidentified flying carpet was depicted in the episode of Jonny Quest I watched that day. The magic carpet is like a UFO of sorts. It unravels and sends down a magical, serpentine cord to tempt us. This is symbolic of the entire paranormal experience – the fact that one must take care with it. The serpent reaching towards the sky is an analogy for the kundalini experience which, when not performed correctly, sends people to the loony bin.

GK: I don't know how many people remember this, but there was a good show in the late 1950s, early '60s, called *One Step Beyond*. They did a show about those streamers coming down from the sky. I wish they would bring that show back on TV. Anyway, a listener wants to know, "Andy, do you have any opinion on Lloyd Pye?"

At the time, I wasn't familiar with Pye, but I did a little research and found that he describes himself as "the caretaker of the Starchild Skull," which he hints is the skull of an alien. Pye was an Army intelligence officer, like so many on the UFO circuit. These intel officers often claim, as Pye does, that they sell tens of thousands of books. They also mysteriously gain access to mainstream news programs such as FOX-TV. Pye hails from Houma, Louisiana, which at one time was a training area for occultist David Ferrie and his CIA pals, the Cuban exiles. There are munitions bunkers there just like at the TNT Area. After explosives were stolen from Schlumberger's Houma bunkers, Ferrie's operation came under the scrutiny of Jim Garrison. At that point, the CIA paramilitarists may have decided to move upriver to Pt. Pleasant's TNT bunkers, which helps explain the sightings there of both occultists and paramilitarists during Mothman.

AC: At Fatima, some of those streamers were seen. The main contactee, Lucia, had a premonition of the Pope being killed. Certain Mothman witnesses also had premonitions of high-profile assassinations. The Mothman flap *must* have been of interest to the Jesuits.

GK: Chica Bruce came on and said that those were basically UFO sightings at Fatima. But a Jesuit told Lucia, "No, that was Mother Mary you saw." The rest is history...

AC: Unbelievably, Mothman himself seems to have been seen at Fatima! I can read it to you from page 204 of Keel's book *Strange Creatures From Time and Space*. He says:

> [A] winged man – a headless angel – [was seen by] four young shepherdesses playing along a ridge near Cobeco, Portugal in the summer of 1915. They reportedly saw a figure like a statue made of snow, which the rays of the sun had turned somewhat transparent, hovering in the air.

AC: During Mothman, a few witnesses saw a white creature such as that flying around. The Ohio Valley has a history of sightings of translucent figures in the sky. Keel reported some other interesting Mothman sightings. One was from 1922, in Nebraska, and involved a birdman quoting Biblical texts to a pastor! It seemed to be reading the pastor's mind. It may have temporarily become an extension of his mind... Another 1922 Nebraska witness saw a UFO turn into a birdman! It is not all that uncommon for people see a craft turn into a flying humanoid. The psychiatric literature has many examples. Keel also said that there were birdman sightings in 1946 alongside the sightings of "ghost rockets" and "foo fighters." He noted that the birdmen angles were inexplicably dropped from any and all media stories about the ghost rockets. They only wanted to focus on the ghost rockets, probably because the Church doesn't want any birdmen to get too much press.

Soon after 9/11, a purported photo of Mothman (top) flying over the collapsed Twin Towers was posted to the web. A random crossfade of Harriet Plumbrook's eyes (lower right) from The Mothman's Photographer *video shows what looks like one of the towers falling amid smoke - just as our friend Tommy Burnham had seen it in his 1967 vision. Harriet and I were together during another tragedy, the JFK assassination, which we found out about while at her mother's beauty parlor on Woodward Drive (lower left), located across the road from Sara Jane Moore's house.*

CHAPTER 13

"In legend after legend, from every part of the world, we are told that early man was primitive and stagnant until the appearance of the god-kings. These mysterious beings introduced writing, laws, agriculture, and perhaps even the rudiments of stone building and medicine. The early peoples were so impressed and so grateful that they dedicated much of their time and effort to preserving images of the god-kings in great statues, temples, and monuments. In fact, many cultures left nothing behind except religious artifacts and carvings lovingly detailing their encounters with the gods. In all these legends there is another persistent theme: that the god-kings mated with mortal women, impregnated them, and thus started a royal lineage. Tradition claims that the 'bluebloods' of royalty actually had blue blood in their veins in early history, perhaps as a result of this crossbreeding. Even today, some royal families suffer from hemophilia. Their blood lacks the ability to coagulate, and even a small cut becomes a serious wound. The mating of ordinary women with supernatural beings is an integral part of all religious lore. It is emphasized in the Bible.

"Some modern rulers, such as the Emperor of Japan, still claim their family can be traced all the way back to a god-like ancestor. The pharaoh system in Egypt could have begun in this fashion, with the parahuman leader of the early Egyptians turning his rule over to a human offspring. By 1000 B.C., most of the god-kings had withdrawn, presumably going off to their legendary mountain hideaways. Their followers assumed, however, that their human descendants were equally wise and possessed of magical powers. Being human, these fallible kings often exploited the fears and beliefs of their people. The later pharaohs successfully masqueraded as gods for centuries. The earth had been divided up by the god-kings, each ruling – even owning – a specific area. This ownership was passed on to the human heirs and, for thousands of years, a few dozen families literally owned the planet. They intermarried and managed to keep the system going until modern times. Although the king system degenerated slowly, it did not really collapse until 1848. Early kings and dictators purportedly consulted with angels and supernatural beings that appeared frequently to advise them. Historical records assert that everyone from Julius Caesar to Napoleon had meetings with mysterious parahumans who materialized and dematerialized mysteriously. The Sacred Crown of St. Stephen is supposed to have been delivered by an angel to a Pope, who permitted Stephen to be crowned King of Hungary with it in 1001."

-John Keel, *Our Haunted Planet*

"I'm here in Seattle for 'Opera Night' at the Blue Moon Tavern which, incidentally, is scheduled so that it coincides with 'Monday Night Football' at the Blue Moon Tavern – a somewhat challenging overlap that the casual patron might fail to fully appreciate. I'm here for the flying saucers that made their first public appearance near Mount Rainier. And I am here for the mushrooms, which broadcast on transcendental frequencies."

-Tom Robbins, "I'm Here for the Weather," *Pacific Magazine*

MOTHMAN DISCUSSION LIST – SELECTED LETTERS AND POSTS – 2004

I happen to own a house about a block from the Seattle mosque that John Muhammad, the D.C. Sniper, attended. I visited the mosque a couple of times. I was taking pictures for an architect who was spearheading a drive to make the turn-of-century complex into a historic landmark. Following the sniper attacks, the building was conveniently "condemned" after a minor earthquake. Having lived at this location since 1990, and being within earshot of the many "calls to prayer" in its first years, it is my opinion that any impact the mosque made on the community had already waned by the time Muhammad got there. Muhammad and Malvo also went to our local YMCA, about two blocks from the mosque. There are some interesting local theories about the case. One of the most consistent theories is as follows: Muhammad was set up as a patsy. He most likely had an Army intelligence "handler" who talked him into infiltrating certain Islamic sects. If the sect wasn't all that important or active – like the one in Seattle – that was even better, as Muhammad wouldn't be mucking up any *truly* important sting operations. Muhammad's change to a Muslim name was fairly recent. According to his cousin, Muhammad was told his mission was to "locate stolen plastics explosives" within terrorist cells.

Around this same time, Muhammad began engaging in a practice common in the spy world: forging and selling fake documents, ostensibly to help immigrants aspiring to come to America. He also had previously trained at Monterey, CA, where a language school for training spies is located. The case of his Bushmaster rifle is an interesting one. There is no evidence that Muhammad or Malvo ever owned the gun. In fact, the gun appears to have made it straight from the Bushmaster factory in Maine (owned by a major campaigner for George W. Bush) to the shelves of a Tacoma shop (where it was supposedly "stolen" by Malvo) without any paperwork being generated. Reports of how the gun was found, when it was found, and what the serial numbers were vary quite a bit. It seems highly improbable that a black male teenager could walk into a gun store in the Seattle-Tacoma area and walk off with such a large and expensive rifle. Such armor-piercing weapons are always kept locked in the main display case. I have been to some of these stores. The employees are incredibly vigilant when showing guns to people.

The theory continues that, at some point, either prior to or during this operation, Muhammad was programmed by doctors to carry out a secret "sub-mission." Muhammad might have been asked by his handlers to "prove his worth" by programming Malvo in certain ways. There are many people in the U.S. and Canada who claim that their "agency" parents or guardians gave them "trauma-based" programming. Muhammad and Malvo may have been programmed to forget the details of the mission and to let themselves be caught upon hearing a certain pre-programmed phrase. Malvo's main defense was that Muhammad was brainwashing him. Whether or not the two actually shot anyone remains unclear. Humans can be programmed to admit to crimes that they did not commit. The phone tip to police from one of Muhammad's "friends" in Tacoma, and the ransom note for $10 million, are both fishy. They came at a time when law enforcement needed an excuse for how they finally tracked down the shooter.

At the time of the arrest, the vote to go to war in Iraq had finally been secured, but only after the shootings had, for weeks, terrorized those voting on the war. Basically, the reason for the shootings – the mission directive – had evaporated. A plausible reason was needed for ending it. Law enforcement dragged their heels just long enough for the war vote to go through. Once that was accomplished, Lt. Moose, who apparently served in the Oregon National Guard with Muhammad, came forth to utter the pre-programmed phrase "we know you need to hear this: the duck is in the noose." This refers to an old story about how an innocent party, the "duck," gets the crime pinned on them. After this announcement, Muhammad and Malvo decided to go to sleep in a public rest area where their license plate would be seen. Neat and tidy… According to this theory, the white vans everyone saw were actually being driven by the secret teams shooting the victims and monitoring the movements of Muhammad and Malvo, who foolishly thought they were on a real mission to locate plastic explosives for the CIA.

-Andy 1/21/04

I find it interesting that investigators describing the recent "flying humanoid" sightings in the Guadalupe section of Mexico City are comparing them to the Flatwoods Monster. Note the similarity of "Guadalupe" to a combination of "Garuda" and "loup," – i.e., to the name of the fabled were-creature of France, "Loup Garou." One witness, officer Leonardo Samaniego, saw a flying female monster that attacked his police cruiser:

> It was a woman with big black eyes; everything was black, no eyelids. Her skin was dark brown and her expression was horrible. She was furiously trying to get me with her claws while I was running away, in reverse, calling desperately for backup assistance to any units around. When I finally hit the end of the street, I was so shocked that I covered my eyes and then fainted.

When I was in Oaxaca in late 2001, I went to the Church of Our Lady of Guadalupe. I got a warm reception there, which seemed strange. After being yelled at for photographing at other churches, I was welcomed with open arms and given a special tour. Later that trip, I spent a week with a shaman and saw a vision of a flaming lotus, apparently induced by the shaman… When I was a teenager, I saw a creature in the same place where Harriet saw the Flatwoods Monster/Virgin Mary entity. What I saw quite closely matches the description of the Aurora, Indiana entity seen on Jan. 24 of this year. The Aurora entity was a shadowy, double-jointed figure that seemed to consist of "light-absorbing material." The entity I saw seemed to absorb light as well. It either came out of a tree, or was masquerading as a tree. I sensed that it may have had wings that were folded back. It was thin and spindly with flexible joints that stuck out like the Aurora entity. It did not seem to be a hallucination, because the leaves rustled when it moved… Recently, I found a story about a person who saw one of these shadow beings materialize completely from vapor. It materialized and then de-materialized.

-Andy 1/27/04

Personally, I don't think the government or any of its branches would waste time messing with us. They have enough to worry about without having to worry about citizens who are studying the paranormal. One of my friends who is interested in the paranormal said the government is probably oblivious to what is going on in the paranormal world. Whether that is true or not, the government is surely being toyed with in much the same way we are being toyed with. Back in the 1960s, the ultraterrestrials had a penchant for playing games with people's phones. Now, they seem to enjoy playing with computers. I know of one case where someone's doppelganger was seen on the Internet. The current rash of weirdness all started on December 22, which was the day I started digging on the Internet for information on the elusive "Thunderbird" photo. In post 6503 of Mothmanlives, John Behr said the following: "I am not sure how I got an invite to join your group but, nonetheless, I am glad to be a member." I asked him what he meant, but he did not respond.

A few weeks later, after more weirdness, I emailed him again. He got back to me and told me what he meant. He told me that he had been surfing at the mothmanlives.com website. A little while later, he got an email message to join this group. He had not given out his email address, and that puzzled him. I asked Donnie Sergent, owner of mothmanlives.com, if this is possible. He said that it is possible, but that he has never used software that would infringe on other people's privacy – that another site must have picked up his email address. I then put the pieces together. Behr was invited to join Mothmanlives the same day I started my Thunderbird photo search on the Internet. I emailed Behr to ask him if he knew anything about the Thunderbird photo. He said that he didn't, but that he was really into the Thunderbird and even had a Thunderbird tattoo. This is just not the kind of thing our government would care about, bothering to mysteriously invite some guy, who just happened to have a Thunderbird tattoo, to our group on the same day that the owner started looking seriously into the Thunderbird photo mystery. But this *is* the kind of game our extra-dimensional friends, the ultraterrestrials, like to play.

Another weird event happened when, in post 6589, someone named Cody said the following:

> How do you do that with my [computer]? I keep getting sent back to your site at random. I do not mind. Would love to know how you did it...

I tried to get him to elaborate further, but he never would. He eventually left the group altogether. Maybe he thought it was too weird, or that I was nuts or something. I really don't think the current problems are linked to the government anymore than the Men in Black phenomena is linked to the government. Whatever is doing this may want us to believe that, though, just to sow confusion. It seems that whatever they are, they have been sowing confusion among us for thousands of years. Sadly, it seems that the number one method to do this is religious separation and intolerance. Ironically, most Virgin Mary apparitions teach religious tolerance, which is highly indicative of there being both good *and* evil ultraterrestrials. If everyone in this world were tolerant of other religions, it would be a much better place in which to live.

-John Frick 1/27/04

There really isn't a huge mystery to the metaphysics of this phenomenon. The *physics* part of it is more difficult, of course. The symbolic part of it is, almost as if by design, the easiest. The ease comes from the generality of the symbols. They are broad enough to penetrate the consciousness of individuals living in different ages, who bring timeliness and specificity to the equation. When the individual's specificity is mirrored in the broader reality, say, through synchronicities, the person has connected to their source in some fashion. Symbols therefore act as a necessary proxy "source." This is mirrored in Garuda sculptures, which show one part of consciousness piggybacking on another, sharing a psychic experience. These are deific subpersonalities, or archetypes… Just about every culture has birdmen in their cosmology. In New Guinea, different birds represent different states of consciousness. We wonder why it is that people have lost so much of the ancient knowledge. John Frick suggested it was because of religious dogma… Name games, synchronicities, and sightings are not too difficult to explain once these ancient symbologies are apprehended. The birdmen are the bridges between sky and the earth, between void and physical manifestation, between this dimension and the next, between consciousness and the body.

-Andy 1/28/04

Salt, in combination with "special" water and a candle, is the traditional mix needed to fend off sorcery attacks. Today, I was reading Eugenia Macer-Story's *Doing Business In the Adirondacks: Bizarre Tales of the Supernatural.* She talks a lot about the synchronicities she and others have had once they began researching the identities of the ultraterrestrials. She mixes emails, group messages, and assorted random bits along with the narrative. She feels that psychic attacks are very common in this field. The question is: who, or what, is doing the attacking? Some of it seems like artificial intelligence. Some seems to come from non-human sources. Some of it seems like "remote viewing." Some seems like sorcery from witches interested in exploiting the situation. The possibilities seem endless... I remember getting an email from someone who claimed that remote viewing was being used to spy on Mothman discussion list members. Unexpected things can happen when one opens up the doors of perception. One way to protect yourself is by remembering that the seeker treads the path for the enlightenment of all beings. If selfish motives remain, then brushes with the other side will be turbulent. Psychological states may arise that are difficult to overcome. It is always prudent to think about the subconscious course of extended conversations – the shifting focus of attention and awareness, the timing of certain displays within a group. These things can be, and usually are, subtly manipulated. It pays to be attentive to the little things people say and do. It never hurts to be as clear as you can be. Sometimes undo speculation or "wooly thinking" works out but, most often, it does not.

-Andy 1/31/04

In a recent post about photographs of "orbs," I talked about feeling marginalized in art school for stating that my work was about locating and photographing "portals" to other dimensions – for saying that I was using them as visualization devices and linkage points with the collective unconscious... Looking back, I suppose my idea may have sounded a bit hokey, but so did a lot of the other projects students were working on. Today, I ran across the following in Eugenia Macer-Story's *Doing Business In the Adirondacks: Bizarre Tales of the Supernatural*. She describes an artist in NYC who does the same thing I was doing, but with paintings:

> Boston artist Paul Laffoley, well known in avant-garde circles for his paintings of visual "portals" into interdimensional space, regards these artworks as literal, talismanic gates to expanded awareness, asserting that these systems of mind/matter manipulation are actual hyperspace portals, and not simply science fiction.

Macer-Story goes on to describe how Laffoley was almost killed when he fell from a ladder at a gallery, apparently due to a "hex" put on him by someone interested in stopping his upcoming book release at the Yale Club. Macer-Story asserts that cloak-and-dagger resistance is almost always brought to bear whenever someone tries to discuss the involvement of elite secret societies in the occult. Elites do not want grassroots folk to access other realms or to know that they are doing so themselves. ESP is a threat to elites because it inverts status – reverses the flow of power. It equalizes the playing field for the poor. Macer-Story traced the aforementioned hexing evidence back to Yale University, which has the largest collection of rare books on both the occult and espionage. The founder of the Yale spy library, who recently died, was *the* key organizer of the CIA back in the 1940s. A story came out recently connecting the Skull & Bones crowd – the Bushes and other CIA folk – with an illegal slush fund being run through the Yale library system.

At the Univ. of Texas Austin, I had issues with a tenured professor who had a grand military record and two art degrees from Yale. I hobnobbed with him at the home of the director of the university art museum. I had a work-study job at the museum. James Michener was a huge supporter of this museum. The professor in question was rumored to be cheating on his wife. I witnessed him being cruel to her at a party. To make a long story short, this professor later tried to give me a terrible grade in a seminar class in which I had promoted the photographic study of the American poor and working class. After an intense discussion with me, he changed the grade to something closer to what I deserved. Interestingly, most of his paintings were realistic depictions of an imagined mass terror event: the blowing up of the U.T. football stadium. To me at the time, it seemed lazy, because the football stadium was right next to the art building. I figured he was just painting whatever was outside of his office window, adding some terrorism to it, and then passing it off as high art. Today, however, I wonder why so much of his art was about future terror. Did he know something about the national security situation that the rest of us did not?

I can think of a couple of U.T. professors who seemed to have occult leanings. One had an interest in Native American power medicine. He visited various pueblos photographing sacred items and structures. When I told him that I was part Native, he scoffed, as if I was some sort of pretender. He told me that I should go to school at some other university. Later, he almost lost his job for burning the body of a dog in one of the university pottery kilns. He is now a nationally recognized leader in photographic education circles. Recently, he headed up a conference that took place close to Yale, and which included Yale professors… Another U.T. professor that gave me trouble was from Yale. He was an expert on Hindu art. He specialized in the art of the many strange sex cults that once existed in India. He did tours there every year, where he took students to visit the temples of these cults. There was a rumor that he sometimes slept with male students on these trips. He was very "bitchy" and gave me crap the whole semester. One of my best friends was killed during finals week in a somewhat mysterious accident. I had to turn in my term paper a couple of hours late, just following the funeral. Even though I was grieving terribly, he – with an evil grin – rejected the paper and gave me a low grade. For a graduate teaching assistant, this was the kiss of death. He told me that if I said anything he would "fight it all the way up the ladder." He made no bones that this was just politics as usual – that the truth was irrelevant. I was devastated. I could not understand this behavior. I continued taking courses at the university for awhile, but eventually left, after some of my work was censored.

As Macer-Story notes, "we should expect to find the most clever, covert sorcerers and magicians among the contingent of designated 'skeptics' and protocol-particular academics." She quotes Anton LaVey, who said that the *real* witches at the Salem witch trials were those cheering from the sidelines – who were about to take over the belongings and properties of those being put to death. There is also the issue of "sliming by association," something practiced by agent provocateurs infiltrating a particular field of endeavor. They play along for a certain period of time, only to later make ridiculous claims that end up besmirching the field. This has happened many times in paranormal and conspiracy groups. The placing together of two seemingly unrelated objects, stories, photographs, or ideas has the effect of blending them in the mind. This is why it was so effective for authorities to wait a couple of days before reporting the Heaven's Gate suicides, in order to coincide with the King family's press conference (where family members stated that they felt it was the government, not James Earl Ray, who murdered MLK). The suicides, as if induced on command, tainted one of the biggest stories of the century. In the same way, I wonder about this supposed photograph of Mothman at the World Trade Center… It seems to be either a hoax, or just some mundane piece of debris. Perhaps both… Based on the "slime by association" technique, the result of this photograph could be that, in the future, discussions about Mothman's 9/11 prophecy will be easier for people to dismiss. The idea that you could have a real photo of Mothman might also be discredited.

-Andy 2/1/04

I think [this all] has more to do with reality replicating itself then it does with conspiracies. John Keel often talks about how the ultraterrestrial phenomenon is imitative. Reality itself seems to be imitative, which explains name coincidences popping up all the time, even in non-paranormal events.

-John Frick 2/7/04

Conspiracies tend to replicate themselves, too, as they are also a part of the greater psychological reality. In fact, some of today's best minds are now framing reality as being so "conspiratorial" that almost nothing of major importance gets accomplished without conspiracy. Even minor decisions are often conspiratorial. Most decisions are made in our society from the top down, with an individual or very small group, such as a board, making decisions. Total secrecy is becoming more and more acceptable. The right to vote, once our sacred cow, has now been almost completely discredited due to the various "votescam" scandals. Personally, I don't like the phrase "conspiracy theory," because that word has too much baggage connected to it. "Institutional theory" is a better phrase.

Institutional theory tends to shed more light on how and why it is that people are programmed to toss out good, solid ideas whenever they go against the needs of the plutocracy. For instance, the media has gone to great lengths to hide the truth about the JFK assassination, a conspiracy of gargantuan proportions. The media has *not* tried to keep the UFO "reality" from the public; they have actually promoted it. Other conspiracies like RFK, MLK, OKC/McVeigh, Muhammad/Malvo, and 9/11 are just as gargantuan, but remain hidden partly because investigative disciplines that might bring them to light (studies of twilight language, name games, Masonic symbology, occult techniques, mind control, etc.) are actively discouraged or obscured. Social pressure is constantly being brought to bear on those who try to bring transparency to daily endeavors. We see it every single day in the ways we do business.

The same happens with really good UFO research. Keel's *Eighth Tower*, probably his best book, has been blacklisted because it explains, among other things, the elaborate "conspiracy" behind the molding of the Christ story. It also discusses how what we see before us is a complete delusion – the ultimate "conspiracy." Keel himself told me that he feels there is probably one anonymous man in "a room somewhere" who "runs everything." Keel has often quoted Charles Fort, who felt that the human race was being "farmed" by a hidden, conspiratorial intelligence. But I would describe Keel as an institutional theorist who also leaves room for larger, more cosmic questions. For those who can stay the course and not get distracted, this phenomenon can be a gateway to understanding. What often leads us to that gateway are synchronicities, those miraculous glimmerings of the universal anti-conspiracy.

-Andy 2/7/04

I agree that conspiracies replicate themselves, too, and that [many] deaths were likely conspiracies. I know that Kennedy's was, but I'm not sure about Lincoln's. Regardless, details such as the [similar] names of their secretaries have got to be just happy coincidences. I doubt if the person who hired [Kennedy's] secretary did so because of her name, at least not on a conscious level. Even if they did hire her because of her name, I doubt if the person who hired her was in on the conspiracy. That's too conspiratorial for me. The way reality likes to replicate numbers, names, and events over and over again is a much better explanation.

-John Frick 2/7/04

It's not always a choice between a "human" conspiracy or one enacted by "reality," because the two often intertwine. In Kennedy's murder, there was a ton of money involved with such things as the oil depletion allowance and Vietnam War spending. The coincidences and multi-layered "cover stories," which today still tantalize conspiracy theorists were, in a practical sense, necessary and understandable. Even the hundreds of JFK witnesses who died violent deaths (many prior to testifying) are somewhat understandable from a Machiavellian point of view. What is creepy is that someone planned the details of the murders to match up with Masonic lore; there was an element of ritual sacrifice to it all. The assassination occurred at a "trinity" site, the triple overpass designed by LBJ when he was an architect. It took place at the geographic 33rd parallel, echoing the highest level of Masonic hierarchy. Various other details had to do with the Masonic "Killing of the King." Check out the writings of James Shelby Downard for a complete rundown of these Masonic "coincidences." The recent *Discovery Channel* documentary, by the Turner brothers, has some good things in it. There is testimony from an Army sniper who was asked to kill JFK's autopsy doctor at Bethesda Hospital. The doctor had the *real* autopsy photos, not the fake ones that showed the body of Officer Tippit, who was used as a stand-in for JFK… The sniper refused on moral grounds, but the doctor was killed anyway, right in his office at the hospital. I guess in some ways, it depends on which flavor one likes best. Is one creeped out more by a faceless "reality" conspiring against us, or by military/Masonic types just doing their patriotic "duty?"

-Andy 2/8/04

The blog *Xymphora* takes a critical look at the news. The author spends time comparing different pieces of news coverage, looking for the truth among the smoke and mirrors. There has been some decent analysis in the past, especially of 9/11 and related matters. On 2/23, there was this strange entry regarding Dick Cheney and his acquisition of Dresser Industries while he was heading up Halliburton. Dresser, Halliburton's only real competition at the time of the buyout, makes oil and gas equipment. Dresser also supposedly fostered the "use of cryptozoology as a cover for spying." Cheney is one of those rumored to worship the giant stone "owl," Moloch, at Bohemian Grove, CA. In "one of the biggest bone-head moves in American corporate history," Cheney managed to acquire liability-laden Dresser:

> The Cheney-Halliburton connection has to be the largest and most blatant example of corruption in modern American history. Cheney is the effective President of the U.S., and is clearly behind the awarding of massive contracts to a corporation that continues to pay him. If this were happening in another country, we'd sneer at the corruption. Spiro Agnew had to resign over allegations that he received payoffs from engineers seeking contracts when he was Baltimore county executive and governor of Maryland. Spiro had nothing on Cheney. The amounts of money Spiro stole would be chump change for Cheney. The best part of all this is that Cheney is going to get away with it.

> Dresser is one of the great corporations in American conspiracy theory, and it is the first place where George Bush worked. It is also connected to Tom Slick and, through him, to the use of cryptozoology as a cover for spying. Dresser is also reportedly connected to the JFK assassination, though the details are sketchy.

It is not unknown for cryptozoologists to be involved in the occult or to hype creature sightings that draw attention away from military operations. Cryptozoologists like to keep the dialogue on Bigfoot and Mothman focused at the very beginning of the process – whether or not anyone actually saw anything. Their fallback question seems to be "if they did see something, was it an unknown species, or a known species?" This pre-limiting of the scope of debate has the effect of keeping us from going into the subject in any depth. They will trot out the same witnesses for decades, as long as the witnesses do not stray too far from a purely physical, sensate description of the original sighting. They don't cover the subjective aspects, the individual journeys of the witnesses. Keel, for instance, told me that his reasons for studying the birdman were essentially personal. He did not endlessly market himself like many of the cryptozoologists. Like Jackson Pollock – who never found out that the CIA was funding his work from behind the scenes – cryptozoologists may not be as popular as they think they are.

-Andy 3/4/04

I am intrigued that you have had precognitions and Bigfoot experiences. Precognition is likely something that happens to certain people who can pick up "vibes" – who are more sensitive to things happening around them. I have always been good at reading people and situations. While I have not had any Bigfoot experiences, I have had several problems with possible MIBs and ultraterrestrials lately. Many of the incidents were preceded by an "energy rush" of fear. In fact, on 99% of the occasions, the hair on my arms will stand straight up. I feel as if I had walked into an electrically charged area… Several years ago, I was outside around sunset. There was a conjunction of planets, and I was looking to see if it was clear enough to take out my telescope. I was looking west. I had the oddest feeling, as if something was around me, but I couldn't see it. My attention was drawn to an object I saw in the sky, around 50 degrees above the horizon. It was a very large, black, bird-shaped object, with a very elongated body. The wings were flapping very slowly. It looked as if it was as long as a man. I thought I could see leglike appendages hanging from it. It was not an Ultralight plane. We have a lot of these fly over in the summer. They land in some fields a few miles from here. It didn't appear to be a bird; it was just too big.

-Barbara 6/9/04

I just had an interesting dream about Mothman. In the dream, I was flying above a beautiful Phoenix. We were both flying together on the lane I grew up on in North Charleston. The Phoenix looked like a gleaming superhero at the start of the dream. Suddenly, it changed into the Mothman, flew ahead very fast, and then started coming back straight toward me. As it came toward me, I felt every fear I have ever had, magnified many times over. I realized I was about to be engulfed, so I managed to make my body become transparent. The Mothman passed through me; I was not harmed. Later, I found references to the "clear body of light" in certain Buddhist texts. This clear light body is apparently a real phenomenon that occurs when one gets close to enlightenment. It may explain some of the orbs, flying figures, and shimmery veils that are seen in "window areas." There are some very old Hindu and Buddhist teachings that lean heavily on flying avatars like the Garuda. These texts are only beginning to be understood in the West, which means we have very little idea what may have been happening, on a spiritual level, during the Mothman era. The African shaman and educator, Malidoma Some, whom I recently did a workshop with, claims he was chosen by his tribe to come to America and help heal us. By sending Malidoma, the African elders feel that they are helping to prevent the destruction of the Earth by capitalists. Malidoma is a Messianic figure of sorts. Perhaps these flying beings are helpers coming from other parts of the world, like the Orient. Perhaps those of us who experienced these helpers are also meant to try and heal the ills of our capitalistic society. In a sense we, too, were chosen.

-Andy 6/11/04

SARA, a southern California defense contractor, and Dr. James Corum, were investigating an exotic propulsion concept involving rectification of the vacuum and the "heaviside force." Dr. Corum soon left SARA for the Institute for Software Research, later re-christened the Institute for Scientific Research, or ISR. The electromagnetic stress propulsion research and Dr. Corum's involvement were prominently displayed on the original ISR web-pages in the year 2000. Shortly after, ISR pulled the Corum promotional material, without comment. In their original web pages ISR pronounced:

> The addition of Dr. Corum signals the start of a new phase in the growth of our Institute, called a "national treasure" by the Office of the Secretary of Defense. Corum is known worldwide as an expert on antennas, radar, radiowave propagation, applied electromagnetics, radiofrequency engineering, and satellite communications...

Interestingly, Dr. Jack Sarfatti claimed that SARA Corporation had been collaborating on research into rectification of the vacuum of space for an exotic space propulsion system. Papers written by Sarfatti relating ideas in nano-scale technology to Corum's "heaviside force" ideas appear to confirm the connection. A NASA Breakthrough Propulsion Physics Summary notes that "if genuine, this effect may enable thrusting directly against spacetime without propellant..." ISR presented an overview of their concepts in a paper titled "The Electromagnetic Stress-Tensor as a Possible Space Drive Propulsion Concept," AIAA-2001-3654. Any genuine breakthrough in physics presents realworld risks to American predominance in the military technology game. NASA's BPPP Risk Management was lurking in the shadows. [They quickly] reduced [the visibility of the information, blaming] the "risk of credibility damage from non-rigorous research methods and reporting; the risk of national preeminence damage by missing a relevant breakthrough; and the risk to the national security from premature disclosure."

-Gary S. Bekkum 7/8/04

Dr. Corum attended Ohio State University and studied radio astronomy for his master's and Ph.D. In 1965, Corum joined

*the National Security Agency, working on classified projects as
an electronic engineer. He then took a faculty position teaching
electronics, physics, and mathematics at the Ohio Institute of
Technology in 1970. Corum moved to Morgantown, WV in 1974
and has since considered it his "base of operations." He was on
the faculty of the Electrical Engineering Department at WVU for
13 years. In 1994, at the Tesla Symposium at Colorado Springs,
Corum, along with his brother K.L. Corum, Ph.D. and J.F. Daum,
Ph.D., presented a paper titled "Tesla's Egg of Columbus, Radar
Stealth, The Torsion Tensor, and the Philadelphia Experiment"
detailing how they were able to replicate radar invisibility with
something called the "Egg of Columbus" apparatus. In the paper, the
scientists lend credence to the idea that the Philadelphia Experiment
was a real experiment having to do with radar stealth on ships with
electric drives.*

Of the vast array of characters surrounding the assassination of President
Kennedy, few are more mysterious and enigmatic than David William
Ferrie of New Orleans. Before and after the assassination, Ferrie's life
was full of mystery, strange activity, and puzzling behavior. Cuban exiles
christened him the "master of intrigue." Jim Garrison, New Orleans
D.A. during the 1960s, called him a key figure in the assassination of
the president and "one of history's most important individuals..." At the
time of the assassination, Ferrie was a 45-year old New Orleans resident
who was acquainted with some of the most notorious names linked to
the assassination: Lee Oswald, Clay Shaw, Guy Banister, Jack Ruby, and
Carlos Marcello. He possessed assorted talents and eccentricities. He was
a pilot and, at one time, a senior pilot with Eastern Airlines, until he
was fired for homosexual activity on the job. He was also a hypnotist, a
serious researcher of the origins of cancer, an amateur psychologist, and
a victim of a strange disease, alopecia, which made all of his body void of
hair. Anti-Castro, anti-Kennedy, and anti-Communist, Ferrie was also a
bishop of the Orthodox Old Catholic Church of North America. His odd
lifestyle was embellished with an equally bizarre appearance featuring a
red toupee and false eyebrows. Investigator and author Harrison Living-
stone met Ferrie and remembered him as "an intense, sinister, cynical,
disgusting, disheveled individual who was excited at the prospect of
preying upon the vulnerable, the helpless, and the innocent."

Ferrie wasn't always anti-Castro. In the fifties, he flew guns to Castro's
rebel forces as they fought Batista's army in the Sierra Maestra. In
1961, he flew bombing missions over Cuba and sometimes made

daring landings to retrieve anti-Castro resistance fighters. When Castro announced his intentions to become a Communist, and aligned his political philosophy with Khrushchev's Soviet Union, Ferrie turned against him. Communism in Cuba, and Kennedy's seemingly inability to do anything about it, drove Ferrie to become vociferous in his speech against the president. He turned against Kennedy during the Bay of Pigs debacle. At this time, Ferrie became a member of the anti-Castro Cuban Revolutionary Front, financed by New Orleans mafia boss, Carlos Marcello. In March 1962, Ferrie began work as a private investigator for G. Wray Gill, Marcello's New Orleans attorney. This arrangement continued through 1963. Eventually Ferrie worked extensively for Marcello and a New Orleans private investigator, Guy Banister. Mr. Banister was an ex-FBI agent and anti-Communist who kept an office at 544 Camp Street in New Orleans, a location known as a hotbed of sinister activities surrounding right-wing and anti-Castro organizations. [Ferrie] worked with Banister at the same time he was employed with Gill. It was at 544 Camp Street that Lee Oswald kept company with Banister and Ferrie.

During his public war on organized crime, documented in his book *The Enemy Within*, Robert Kennedy, as Attorney General, deported crime boss Carlos Marcello. Kennedy branded Marcello as an undesirable character who had no positive use for American society. On April 6, 1961, Marcello was whisked away in a plane and dumped on a Guatemalan beach. Two months later, Marcello found his way back into the country, possibly with the help of David Ferrie's pilot experience. Marcello privately vowed to get even... In September of 1962, private investigator Ed Becker met with Ferrie's boss, Carlos "The Little Man" Marcello. He hoped to obtain funds from Marcello for an oil venture. During a whiskey-laced conversation at Marcello's country estate in Louisiana, Becker mentioned Marcello's deportation. Marcello angrily announced that Robert Kennedy "would be taken care of." But, he hinted that it would be done in a roundabout manner. He declared that to kill a dog, you "don't cut off the tail, but the head." The head would be the president, and the plan would include finding a nut to take the blame, "the way they do it in Sicily." Marcello employed Oswald's uncle, Charles Murret, as a bookmaker in the New Orleans gambling world. In the 1970's, the FBI wiretapped many of Marcello's phone conversations. However, the FBI has refused to release 161 reels of tape containing these conversations. An FBI informant, Joe Hauser, who claimed he made several of these recordings, told author John H. Davis that Marcello spoke of involvement in the assassination and that he personally knew Oswald.

Though Ferrie officially denied knowing Oswald, it is widely believed that Ferrie met Oswald far before their alleged liaison at 544 Camp Street. In 1955, both Ferrie and Oswald were members of the Louisiana Civil Air Patrol. Ferrie was asked to leave the Air Patrol just before Oswald joined, but apparently still remained close to the members of the organization. Though Ferrie denied any relationship with Oswald, a former schoolmate claimed that he, Oswald, and Ferrie all worked in the Civil Air Patrol. Several other members of the organization said that Oswald and Ferrie were in the Civil Air Patrol at the same time. On the day Oswald handed out pro-Castro leaflets in New Orleans, Ferrie was leading an anti-Castro demonstration a few blocks away. Guy Banister's secretary Delphine Roberts told author Anthony Summers that, at least once, Oswald and Ferrie went together to a Cuban exile training camp near New Orleans for rifle practice... In 1954, Oswald joined the Civil Air Patrol. In an interview with *Look* magazine in 1967, Oswald's brother, Robert, told a reporter:

> According to Lee's own later statement, 1954 was the year
> when he first became interested in communism... I can't
> help wondering whether it might have been Ferrie who intro-
> duced Lee to Communist ideas. I realize that I have nothing
> solid on which to base such a speculation, except the timing.

House Select Committee on Assassinations records released in 1993 revealed a flight plan (HSCA RG 233) dated April 8, 1963. The flight plan details a pilot named "Ferrie" flying three passengers, "Hidell, Lambert, and Diaz," from New Orleans to Garland, Texas. It is well known that Oswald used the alias of "A.J. Hidell." More recently, there is evidence that Clay Shaw, the subject of Jim Garrison's New Orleans investigation into the assassination, used aliases of "Clay Bertrand" and "Lambert." An affidavit accompanying the HSCA RG 233 document claims that Georgian Edward J. Grinus stated in 1967 that one of Clay Shaw's aliases was Lambert. Several witnesses have maintained that Shaw and Ferrie were seen together at the New Orleans airport; speaking to each other in a limousine; together in Clinton, Louisiana; and at private parties and New Orleans bars.

In September 1963, Perry Russo, a New Orleans insurance agent, attended a party at Ferrie's apartment. According to Russo, after the party broke up, a group of anti-Castro Cubans began talking of the possibilities of assassinating Fidel Castro. Ferrie introduced Russo to a tall, distinguished-looking, white-haired man named "Clem Bertrand," whom Garrison believed was Clay Shaw. Whether Russo really encountered Shaw has been the subject of acute controversy. Ferrie also introduced

Russo to a man named "Leon Oswald." The conversation eventually drifted to the subject of Kennedy's inability to control the communists in Cuba. Ferrie dramatically took the floor and discussed the possibility of killing Castro and illustrated his points by showing the audience a map of Cuba – where the assassination team could land, and the routes to and from Havana. Russo claimed that he and Ferrie became friends and had several meetings. Russo said Ferrie at one time spoke of killing Kennedy and blaming it on Castro. This would give anti-Castro activists an excuse to invade Cuba – getting rid of two of Ferrie's enemies, Castro and Kennedy, and opening Cuba to free enterprise. He said Kennedy could be killed by a "triangulation" of rifle fire. Ferrie elaborated on his plan of triangulation, saying that two shooters would create "diversionary shots" [while] the third shooter would make the kill. There would be one shooter who would take the blame.

On the day of the assassination, Ferrie was in a courtroom with Carlos Marcello. Marcello was found innocent of all charges brought against him by Robert Kennedy. Only hours after the shooting, Marcello attorney, C. Wray Gill, visited Ferrie's home with unwanted news. Gill was telephoned by an unknown source in Dallas saying that Oswald's wallet contained a library card with Ferrie's name on it. Oswald's former landlady in New Orleans was paid a visit by a visibly agitated Ferrie, who wondered if she knew anything about the card. Ferrie then rushed to an ex-neighbor of Oswald's and again asked for any information about the card, but was again frustrated. Immediately after searching for information about his library card and finding none, Ferrie made a phone call to Houston to reserve a room at the Alamotel, a motel Carlos Marcello owned.

When asked why he took the trip to Houston, Ferrie told federal authorities that he and two male companions drove all night on November 22, 1963, 350 miles through a fierce thunderstorm, to Houston (to go goose hunting). He also claimed that the trip was designed to gather information on how to run an ice skating rink... On the 23rd of November, Ferrie visited the Winterland Skating Rink, managed by Chuck Rolland. Rolland told authorities that he never spoke to Ferrie about the skating rink business. All Ferrie did, said Rolland, was make and receive phone calls for hours at a pay phone... On the afternoon of Nov. 23rd, Ferrie called his roommate, Layton Martens, who told Ferrie that he was being accused of involvement in the assassination. Ferrie returned to New Orleans to find that the FBI and Secret Service had just learned about his library card being found in Oswald's wallet. An FBI teletype from the New Orleans office to FBI headquarters notified Director Hoover that Gill had notified Ferrie about the library card. Though someone at the

Dallas Police Dept. had tipped off Gill about the card, and information about it was teletyped to Hoover, an inventory of Oswald's personal property by the Dallas P.D. shows no record of a library card. On the evening of November 23rd, Ferrie drove to Galveston, stayed the night and returned to New Orleans the next day. There is no record explaining why Ferrie went to Galveston.

Garrison, a friend of C. Wray Gill, checked the records of office calls made from Gill's office during November 1963. He found that the records were missing, and that Ferrie had access to the records. Gill told Garrison that Ferrie had made numerous long distance phone calls from Gill's office in 1962 and '63... Minutes after the assassination, a search of the Dal-Tex Building, overlooking Dealey Plaza, yielded a man named Eugene Brading. Brading had recently had his name changed to "Jim Braden." An elevator man had noticed a suspicious person using the freight elevator and had called the police. The police detained Braden, who said he had taken the elevator to the third floor to find a telephone. The police released him, not knowing his real identity: Eugene Brading, a convicted felon. "Braden" had stayed at the now infamous Cabana Motel in Dallas the night before.

The Cabana was owned by the Campisi brothers, who had close relationships with Jack Ruby and Carlos Marcello. Ruby had visited the Cabana's Egyptian Lounge the night before the shooting, had met with a man named Lawrence Meyers, and made several phone calls, some as late as 2:30 a.m. on the day of the assassination. Early on the day of the assassination, Braden had checked in with parole officers at a Dallas federal courthouse. He gave his New Orleans address as the same building and floor where David Ferrie kept an office... Sometime in September 1963, Ferrie made a phone call to an apartment building that housed Jean West. Ms. West was the companion of Lawrence Meyers while they stayed at the Cabana Motel the night of the assassination. Records of Jack Ruby's phone calls in November of 1963 showed that he had also called Jean West's number. Ferrie was known to use an alias of "Farris" on occasions. Though there is no known physical link between Ferrie and Ruby, Jim Garrison claimed that Jack Ruby's address book contained the name of "Farris."

After the assassination, the Secret Service put Marina Oswald under protective custody, and so she remained for over three months. According to researcher Harold Weisberg in his book *Oswald in New Orleans*, on November 24, 1963, the day that Oswald was shot by Ruby, Secret Service agents asked Oswald's wife Marina whether she knew a Mr. David Ferrie. She said she did not... On November 26, 1963 a Georgian businessman,

Gene Summer, told the FBI that he was sure he saw Oswald accept money from a man he believed was the owner of the Town and Country restaurant in Louisiana. Hoover eventually ordered an investigation of the matter. The Town and Country restaurant was owned by Carlos Marcello...

Other FBI investigations at this time focused on New Orleans. The more agents investigated Ferrie's life, the more links they found between Oswald and Ferrie. The relationship surely caused some suspicion in the FBI, since they knew Ferrie had a verifiable relationship with Carlos Marcello, the well-known New Orleans underworld figure and hater of Robert Kennedy. Just when the investigation was yielding clearer links between all of these individuals, Director Hoover abruptly closed the investigation of Ferrie on December 6, 1963, only two weeks after the assassination. None of the information the FBI collected concerning Ferrie was ever presented to the Warren Commission. David Belin, a former Warren Commission counsel, wrote a book in 1988, *Final Disclosure*, in which he defended the Warren Commission's findings that Oswald was the sole gunman. In his book, Belin never mentions David Ferrie.

On February 13, 1964, Canadian Richard Giesbrecht unwittingly overheard a conversation between two men in the Winnipeg International Airport. Giesbrecht noticed that one of the men had "the oddest hair and eyebrows I'd ever seen." He later told the FBI that he was certain the man was David Ferrie. Giesbrecht heard Ferrie tell his companion that he was concerned about how much Oswald had told his wife about the plot to kill Kennedy. They spoke of the Warren Commission investigation and discussed a man called "Isaacs," his relationship with Oswald, and wondered why he had gotten involved with someone so "psycho" as Oswald. One of the men lamented the fact that Isaacs had been caught on television during the Dallas motorcade. Ferrie said that "they" had more money than ever. Giesbrecht caught a snippet of a conversation relating to a meeting that was to take place in March in Missouri, since there had been no meeting since Nov. of 1963. Giesbrecht immediately contacted the FBI through his attorney. He gave details of the conversation and, after seeing a picture of Ferrie, asserted that he was the man he had seen and heard at the Winnipeg airport. After questioning Giesbrecht and telling him that his information was important and "the break we've been waiting for," the FBI contacted him several months later and told him to forget about the matter. It was "too serious" and, since he was a Canadian, there would be nothing the FBI could do for him if he needed protection. In a 1969 interview, Giesbrecht told writer Paris Flammonde that he was 100 per cent certain that the man he saw at the Winnipeg Airport was David Ferrie.

In February of 1967, Jim Garrison announced that he was reopening the investigation into the president's assassination. Garrison's announcement came the day after John Roselli, a mafia figure with ties to various mafioso bosses throughout the country, told Chief Earl Warren that he had been involved in several CIA attempts to assassinate Fidel Castro. To retaliate, Roselli claimed that Castro's agents, in conjunction with mafia figures, planned the murder of the president. Garrison announced that one of his chief suspects was David Ferrie. He placed Ferrie in protective custody, accompanied by a bodyguard in a New Orleans hotel. Ferrie publicly scoffed at Garrison's allegations, telling journalists that "I have been pegged as the getaway pilot in an elaborate plot to kill Kennedy" and that it was "fruitless to look for an accomplice of Oswald's." On February 21, Ferrie was inexplicably released from protective custody before he had completely testified.

Ferrie was found dead in his apartment on February 22, 1967. He had left two typed notes that suggested suicide. The first began "To leave this life, to me, is a sweet prospect." For several paragraphs, he rambled on about crime in America and the incompetence of the American government [and court system]. The second note was brief and declared that "when you read this, I will be quite dead and no answer will be possible." New Orleans Metro Crime Commission director, Aaron Kohn, believed that Ferrie was murdered. The New Orleans coroner officially reported that the cause of death was natural: a cerebral hemorrhage. The day before Ferrie's death, Eladio del Valle was murdered in Miami with hatchet and bullet by unknown assailants. Del Valle was an ex-city councilman from Havana during the Batista regime. He was associated with Florida mafia boss Santos Trafficante. Del Valle and Ferrie were members of the Cuban Democratic Revolutionary Front, an organization devoted to overthrowing Castro. New Orleans D.A. Jim Garrison believed that del Valle paid Ferrie for bombing missions over Cuba. In 1961, del Valle boasted that he had assembled over 8,000 men in Cuba ready to overthrow Castro. In 1963, he was also a leader of the Committee to Free Cuba.

During his investigation, Garrison found that before the assassination, Ferrie had deposited over seven thousand dollars in his bank account. After the assassination, someone purchased Ferrie a gasoline-station franchise. Ferrie also secured a job with an air cargo service firm that he kept for several years. It is believed that all of these windfalls were the result of Carlos Marcello repaying Ferrie. Marcello testified that he paid Ferrie $7000 for Ferrie's paralegal work in November of 1963. Though Ferrie had several interesting connections to the assassination,

Garrison never linked any of Ferrie's activities to Marcello. Garrison never publicly recognized any mafia presence in New Orleans. Authors John H. Davis, Philip Melanson, Frank Ragano, Victor Marchetti, and many investigators believe that Garrison's investigation was designed to protect Carlos Marcello from being linked to the assassination. Though Ferrie's relationship with Marcello was obvious and a matter that Marcello publicly acknowledged, there is no mention of Marcello in Garrison's 1970 book on the assassination, *A Heritage of Stone*; nor is there any mention of Marcello in the Warren Commission Report. Executive Assistant to the Deputy Director of the CIA, Victor Marchetti, was told by a CIA colleague that "Ferrie had been a contract agent to the Agency in the early 1960s and had been involved in some of the Cuban activities." Marchetti was convinced that Ferrie was a CIA contract officer and involved in various criminal activities. Marchetti told author Anthony Summers that "he observed consternation on the part of CIA Director Richard Helms and other senior officials when Ferrie's name was first publicly linked with the assassination in 1967."

Raymond Broshears, an ex-roommate of Ferrie, said that Ferrie had told him that he went to Houston the day after the assassination to await a call from a man, allegedly one of the gunmen. This person was to fly from Dallas to Houston in a twin-engine plane that would take them to Central America and eventually to South Africa, where the U.S. government had no extradition treaty. South Africa, at the time, was the home of Permindex, an organization with a sinister and cloudy past that had reportedly been ousted from Europe for nefarious activities [such as] assassinations. Ferrie was to function as a co-pilot for the gunmen. The men had code names. The only code name Broshears could remember was "Garcia." Ferrie said that he never received the phone call. Ferrie told Broshears that the assassins panicked and tried to fly nonstop to Mexico, but they crashed off the coast of Corpus Christi and perished.

Broshears believes Ferrie was murdered. Ferrie told him "no matter what happens to me, I won't commit suicide." Ferrie had often boasted that he knew of ways of killing people that could be mistaken for suicide. Ferrie told Broshears that he knew Oswald, and that he felt Oswald did not shoot the president. Ferrie believed that Oswald thought he was working for Castro but, in reality, he was a pawn in an anti-Castro conspiracy. The plotters wanted to make the assassination look like it was a communist conspiracy. In 1963, Ferrie told Broshears that four people would shoot from different angles. Later in 1964, he said one was fired from a sewer opening, another from the grassy knoll, and one from behind the motorcade. Funding for the plot came from Marcello, Ferrie told Broshears, adding that Clay Shaw knew of many of the plot's details but did not engineer it.

On March 4, 1967, three days after Clay Shaw was arrested for complicity in the assassination of JFK, an Italian newspaper with strong communist ties, *Il Paese Sera*, reported that Clay Shaw was one of the directors of the Rome World Trade Centre, an organization that was run by the CIA to undermine communism. The CIA had admitted that Shaw was a contact for the agency's Domestic Contact Service during the 1950's. *Il Paese Sera* had strong links to Italian Fascists and Permindex. The article also claimed that Permindex was expelled from Switzerland because of criminal activities, and that Permindex was a financial benefactor to the OAS of France… A few days later, the same paper published the names of men involved in anti-communist activities through Permindex. Other communist newspapers, Italy's *L'Unita* and Moscow's *Pravda*, began to add to the fantastic conspiracy theories about Permindex. Eventually, many researchers began seeing the Permindex connection as a disinformation campaign orchestrated by the CIA or, more likely, communist organizations in Europe. The history of Permindex is complicated and mysterious. Though it was never ousted from Switzerland by the Swiss government, as *Il Paese Sera* reported, it did move to Rome and then South Africa. The Rome World Trade Centre and Permindex have a shadowy past, but that darkness may be nothing more than shadows cast by communist political organizations intentionally clouding "conspiracy" with disinformation.

CIA contract agent Robert Morrow claimed that while working at Permindex in the early 1960s, he received a call from David Ferrie from Switzerland. Ferrie had been instructed by CIA contacts to tell Morrow to go to Paris and pick up a packet of papers from an American couple that had recently been traveling in the Soviet Union. They had been given the packet of papers by a CIA agent, a "Harvey of Minsk." Since Oswald was living in Minsk during this time, Morrow firmly believes it was Oswald who was providing information for the CIA. Morrow also recounts a story about Ferrie's associate Eladio del Valle. Del Valle had called Morrow in the early autumn of 1963 and requested four low-frequency "walkie-talkies" that could not be traced. Morrow knew that del Valle had connections with the mafia and various anti-Castro groups. Morrow provided the equipment and believes that one of the radios he furnished can be seen in pictures taken of Dealey Plaza on November 22, 1963, hanging out of a man's back pocket.

In January of 1992, a former attorney for mob boss Santos Trafficante and Teamster leader Jimmy Hoffa, Frank Ragano, spoke of a meeting he had with Hoffa in early 1963. According to Ragano, Hoffa asked the attorney to tell Trafficante and Marcello that he wanted the president killed. Ragano didn't take the threat seriously, but passed the word on anyway.

He was shocked to see their reactions; it appeared to Ragano that they had already considered the thought. On November 22, 1963, Ragano said Hoffa called him and asked him if he had heard the good news. That night, Ragano says, he had dinner with Trafficante. Trafficante made a toast to the actions of the day, declaring that their problems "were over" and that access to Cuba would be a reality. Ragano said that Hoffa owed Marcello, and that Hoffa recognized that fact… Transcripts of Ferrie's FBI interview have been buried in the National Archives. They were not turned over to the Warren Commission. Author John H. Davis, who is on the Board of Advisors of the Assassination Archives and Research Center in Washington, D.C., has reported that a 30-page FBI report on Ferrie is missing from the National Archives.

-John S. Craig, 7/16/04

When I was 18, in Maryland, I was walking home from my girlfriend's house at about 12:45 a.m. I had walked this way home many nights and had never had any problems before. I walked through a field of chest-high grass and then out across a highway next to my house. Instead of going the long way around to my house, I decided to take a shortcut through a side street that was tightly lined with cedar trees. I got almost to the end of the street when I started to feel strange. I looked up, and about 20 feet in front of me, 15 feet above the ground, I saw this big black thing hovering in the air. It was about 8 feet tall. It had a body like a prehistoric bird, but it looked completely black. I couldn't make out its shape except for its outline. It had ears that were like spikes; they came straight up, kind of like the ones on Batman's suit. Its eyes glowed… I could hear this prolonged pulse sound in my head, like a vibration. When I saw it, I put my hand over my face and crouched to the ground in fear. It had wings, but they were only moving slow, like a jellyfish would move. It was there for about five seconds. Then, it turned its head to the side to look at a tree that was right next to it. When it did this, I saw the outline of its face. It looked like a *dog's* face! It let out a shriek, like a woman's scream mixed with an animal's scream. Then, like a Mack truck, it flew *into* the tree and vanished. I ran home and had trouble sleeping that night. I went to the cedar tree the next day with my little brother, and the side of it was destroyed. I've had many experiences with things like this, and so have a lot of the women in my family. Sometimes I wake up in the middle of the night and that pulse is in my head, accompanied by fear and disorientation.

-Derik 7/04

Derik's report sounds very much like what I saw in Mound, except that my entity came out of a tree instead of going into it. This coming and going from trees is random and bizarre imagery, not easily made up by someone just wanting attention. Perhaps the mystery will only be understood when trees are brought into the equation – when we begin to question how these sightings can bend the laws of physics... A study of the "immaterial" is essential. Unfortunately, a clear understanding of our own subjectivity – our subconscious mental construction – is generally lacking. The unconscious remains "classified" and out of reach to most people in the West. In the East, people may have a slightly better grip on the subjective side of the equation... While I didn't hear any pounding in my head like Derik's at the time of my sighting, I did have dreams where I would hear "binaural" sounds, which consist of different sounds in each ear simultaneously. In the dreams, I would be accosted by MIBs or aliens after hearing the sounds. Regarding the damage done to Derik's tree, it is debatable as to whether or not Mothman caused the damage. I have a theory that these forms may manifest *after* damage is done to a tree or other living organism. Similarly, the dead animals found in creature entity sighting areas may not necessarily be killed by the creatures. Their presence may be the result of ritual sacrifice by humans. Regarding creature screams, it is interesting that on the Apollo 11 flight, mysterious birdlike screams were heard. On transmission tapes now posted to YouTube, you can hear the astronauts commenting on the screams.

-Andy 8/4/04

While gauss meters, radios, and tape machines are old staples of the researcher's trade, may I suggest psychic techniques along the lines of Joseph DeLouise, author of *Psychic Mission: The Story of the Man Who Foresaw and Foretold The Identification of Charles Manson and His 'Family,' The Tragedy at Chappaquiddick, The Collapse of The Silver Bridge in West Virginia, The Indianapolis Plane Disaster, and The Manteno Train Crash.* In the title of his book alone, there are two seemingly unrelated items, Manson and the Silver Bridge, which seem to connect to my Mothman experiences in North Charleston. As I began to read the book, I found some more odd coincidences, one of which is that DeLouise's parents are from the same area of Italy as my grandmother. This area is known for its psychics. DeLouise gives many interesting examples of how psychic miracles manifested in his early life there. One of DeLouise's techniques is to visualize a "violet screen," upon which a "lotus" opens. Once the lotus opens, the psychic images begin to manifest. I experienced this phenomenon at the beginning of my Mothman investigation in 2001. I went to Mexico for a vacation. I almost broke my back when my hammock collapsed in Mazunte. I was healed by the shaman who ran the campground there, next to the graveyard on the cliff. Following a sweatlodge with the shaman, I saw a vision of the burning lotus. Later, Harriet and I went to California, where we happened to undergo the "violet flame" initiation under the tutelage of Ormond McGill, one of the fathers of modern hypnotherapy. Ormond was the first stage hypnotist to become famous on *The Tonight Show*.

Last night I could not sleep, so I lay in bed practicing some of DeLouise's techniques. As I went into the violet screen, I saw images of dust-covered debris on the day of 9/11. Then, I saw two sets of eyes, very close up. The owners of these eyes appeared to be aware that I was looking at them. I don't know if these men were co-conspirators in the crime, but they seemed to be guarding the secret of who was behind it. The most disturbing image was that of a military man at a desk. I got the impression that he was located in Florida. He, too, seemed to be aware that I was viewing him. I got a strong "occult" feeling from him. He definitely seemed to be connected to the disaster in some way. I then received images of the area where I grew up, which sent chills up my spine. I wondered if my friend Tommy had somehow made his 1967 vision of 9/11 come true – if he had been involved in the planning somehow. At this point, I lost the images... DeLouise goes into detail on several "ghostbusting" jobs that he and his partner completed. DeLouise's partner would often go into a trance and literally become "possessed" for a while, long enough for DeLouise to query him and find out what was going on "the other side." DeLouise mentions certain entities that can drain you and send you on a "bad trip" worse than LSD. Yogis report confronting these entities as they approach higher states of consciousness. It's like a test that one has to endure, in order to get to the next higher plane. DeLouise also discusses birds and their connection to the dead, something that comes up in the work of Univ. of New Mexico anthropology director Steven Feld, a former teacher of mine, who studied "bird tribes" in New Guinea.

-Andy 8/11/04

Someone asked if odd things happened to anyone on this list last night. There was nothing last night but, in recent days, my wife has heard "me" doing deep-throated Buddhist chants as I go up or down the stairs. The only problem is that I haven't been doing any chanting... I wonder if this isn't my recently deceased Buddhist friend, Aryadaka, letting me know everything is alright... Another thing I should mention are the "sharpened sticks" I recently found around my house. Not too long ago,

I read about these sharpened sticks being a witchcraft technique; witches somehow attack you with them. Synchronistically, as soon as I read this, one of these sticks showed up in my yard. I brought it in and examined it, then put it back outside until I got around to photographing it. It then disappeared. It looked like the kind of stake you would drive into a vampire. It had obviously been sharpened, and it had a "burnt" end. It looked very old, as if the sharpening had taken a place a long time ago… Then, another stick showed up. This one was long and skinny, with an "S" curve. It reminded me of a tree on our Woodward Drive property… I'm keeping a close eye on it to see what effect it may have. I hid it outside, just off of the property. Interestingly, there are two black lesbians in the neighborhood with obvious talismanic items in their windows; these dolls and things hint at Santeria, hoodoo, or some other occult variant. These women, who live in different houses on either side of us, are openly hostile. I assume one of them is leaving the stakes, but it is difficult to know for sure.

-Andy 8/17/04

Interestingly, it seemed as if my marriage really started to fall apart around the time of the above post. Not long ago, in 2009, my wife stated that she felt the break occurred in 2004. This seems to have been around the time we first got into a boundary dispute with one of the aforementioned lesbian voodoo practitioners. One wonders if the two sticks left on our property were talismans representing my wife and I. Both of the women seemed to have issues with my wife, who is Asian and somewhat outspoken. Even though I have tried to tell myself that "witchcraft attack" is a preposterous notion, there is no denying that the sticks were placed on or around the high occult day of Aug. 12th. The following year, on the 4th of July, one of the women had a party where a guest, a gang member, openly joked in my direction that he would like to see "that white man dead." In 2006, the other woman, who worked for Microsoft in their minority outreach program, made a false report to the police about me, hoping that they would allow her to tear down the properly placed fence separating our properties (she desired more of the unimproved alley than the law allowed). Later, she tried to get the court to issue a restraining order keeping me from using my backyard. At the hearings, in an otherwise empty courtroom, she wore all black and sat directly behind me and my attorney, muttering incantations. After trying to berate two or three judges into giving her extra land, she was eventually excluded from the proceedings, and the case was thrown out.

The owl is quite commonly used as a screen memory. I've even considered the possibility that the MIB themselves could be some kind of bizarre screen memory.

-John Frick 9/3/04

Yes, it is hard to know if the MIB are screen memories, ultraterrestrials (UTs), or actual human beings. If the MIB are screens, it raises the question as to what they would be screening. If aliens and UTs are real, they probably wouldn't mind it if MIB were the screens. However, it is more likely that certain MIB were screens for *other* MIB – military-industrial types involved in developing or covering up secret technology. Betty and Barney Hill initially remembered men in Nazi uniforms, which somehow changed to aliens and other MIB after they were hypnotized by an Army doctor.

There is a group of Buddhist teachings revolving around the idea of natural balance, or proper tension. A stringed instrument is often used as an example. For the instrument to sound the best and fulfill its role, the strings must not be too loose or too tight. The same is true with the mind and body. The bodymind complex differs from a simple instrument in that it is self-regulating; it can tighten or loosen its own strings. In fact, the bodymind is constantly trying to maintain this proper tension. When faced with an extremely confusing or highly complex situation, the mind will attempt to regain balance by interpolating the event in a more simplistic way. It will shut down a bit, and render the events with a broader palette. It may even make up "facts" that will make the meaning more manageable, such as after a terrorist event or untimely death in the family. Jim Keith talks about this in *Saucers of the Illuminati*. He says that abductees seem to remember the simplest set of characters that can possibly make up a face, which turns out to be the "grey alien" face. Tests with drugs and hypnosis have shown the alien face to be an archetypal image, one that people often see. Keith puts forward the idea that these abductions and UFO encounters may somehow be our way of psycho-logically coming to grips with future space travel. We may be testing out future realities before they happen; our minds may be pre-molding physical manifestation.

Conversely, when the mind is faced with a lack of stimulation, such as with amnesia or missing time, it may create details that are not there. It has been shown that people under hypnosis can make up lots of incredible details when they are mislead by "leading questions." Similarly, if someone is idly daydreaming, walking along with an empty mind (like I was when I saw the shadowy entity in 1973), they may be coming face-to-face with the voidness of their own subconscious. The sages say that the human mind can only begin to comprehend the Void after long practice on the path, as in the case of a Buddha or enlightened being. However, as one gets closer to death, the veil between Void and Manifestation gets thinner.

When my father was on his deathbed, he may have been seeing glimpses of the Void. Since he had not been preparing for death in the way a monk might, Dad's mind may have preferred to see an "MIB" instead of the Void. There could have been psychic "bleedthrough" that caused us kids to see the MIB as well... Certainly, there was such bleedthrough when my mother died. She was in Florida. I got down there a few days before she died. While she was at the hospital, an enormous owl kept hanging around her house. She always had owls around her, especially when she lived on the Poca River in West Virginia. They would visit her almost every night. I have a photo of the Florida owl. I *knew* when I saw that owl coming around that she was not going to make it. The last night, I woke up feeling like I was having a heart attack right at the time she was having cardiac failure. At the instant she died, I saw a shadow pass through her house. In less than a minute, the phone rang. I told my brother that it would be the doctor with the bad news. And it *was* the doctor...

-Andy 9/20/04

My brother, an Auxiliary Deputy Sheriff, has never been scared of anything. About three weeks before Hurricane Ivan hit us in Pensacola, FL, my brother called me. He sounded frantic. I raced over [because it sounded like a dire] emergency. He would not go into his house. He said that he had seen a figure in his home. Strangely, the circuit breaker to the lights in the rear of the house was tripped. I got the lights back on and asked him what was up. He was shaking and clutching his pistol, a .40 cal. Police issue, so tightly that his knuckles were white – as was his face. After he became coherent, he explained that he had seen a figure nearly 9 feet tall, the height of his ceiling. He described it as nude and black in color, with leathery, plastic-like skin and no sign of genitals. The "thing" resembled a person: bald, no wings, red eyes, and many short, sharp teeth with a foul odor... After talking a while, I got a picture from the Internet of the creature from the movie *Split Second*, which [also happens to look] like Mothman. My brother said that that was close to what it looked like. Does this sound like Mothman to you? Because three weeks later, our town, and four counties around, were leveled by Hurricane Ivan. Any suggestions [on how to help my brother]? I am open to anything at this point. My brother, a grown man with a family, is suffering from severe nightmares since this ordeal. It is affecting his job as a public official. I cannot offer any further details except for what I wrote. I hate to ask him anymore about it, because he has already been traumatized enough.

-Walter Esar 9/26/04

Not to beat a dead horse, but this recent Pensacola monster also sounds similar to what came out of a tree at the site of our Mothman shrine. I have described this being as an "elemental" or "shadow being" in the past. I want to clarify that this was not like the shadow beings that various list members apparently see darting around on the periphery of their vision. The being that I saw made the leaves rattle as it moved. It seemed to have mass and density, and it came right for me instead of trying to hide in the periphery. It, too, was black, nude, and seemed to lack genitals. It seemed to absorb light, like a black hole. There was something strange about its movements. It seemed as if its joints had the capability to bend slightly outward. I didn't stick around long enough to see if it had teeth, nor did I see red eyes glowing... Harriet saw something at the same spot in 1968 that she describes as having "plastic" skin and a foul odor, although hers was hooded and basically looked like a monk and/or nun. My niece, Sharon Moore, saw something very similar to this Pensacola beast in her bedroom, in Mound, prior to 9/11. She called it an "oily black man" with a bull's head – a satyr, more or less. It had pointy teeth. It just stood there in her apartment, staring at her menacingly. She saw it about a week before she saw Mothman in her bedroom. She told me that she success-fully "willed it away," so maybe that is the way to go. Tell it to go away.

-Andy 9/26/04

Dreams are "objectively" pointless; I usually do not write about them for that reason. The main benefit of dreams is that they contain symbolic messages that can be studied for insight into one's own subconscious. Trying to decide which dreams are "real" or "unreal," or from God or not, is even more problematic because it gets into relativistic, philosophical areas where each person's belief about God is different. I do know that people can, at times, share dreams. I have documented this. In these situa-tions, one can make a case that God, or something like God, is speaking to both dreamers. My own view of God is that it speaks to us at all times, in both waking and dreaming states. Whether or not we are picking up on that fact is another matter. The primary test of this life seems to be the fact that we are placed in a "physical" situation where it is very easy to delude ourselves into believing that "we" are only comprised of our bodies and our conscious minds, and that we are separate from others. One message of the Mothman phenomenon, I feel, is to remind us that physical shapes are not solid, and that our minds can reach beyond time and space – beyond concepts. In fact, if the universe is really a universal mind as the sages say, then we are simply God incarnate, made in the "image" of God. Therefore, one could almost say that any thought you have is from God. Looking at it more technically, quantum particles appear to be able to communicate much faster than the speed of light. They can communicate across galaxies in an instant. Our thoughts are made up of electrical charges that would have the same capabilities for long-range, instantaneous travel. Today, *The New York Times* described the Internet as the "ultimate meme," or fast-moving virus, but I would argue and say that, according to current science, the mind is a much greater meme.

I recently had a dream of an "alternate Pt. Pleasant." I saw a raucous "beer festival," which seemed to me to represent the takeover of the area by white settlers. The dream had an early "pioneer" feel to it, although there were modern elements as well. I was with my niece in the dream. We stayed at something resembling the Lowe Hotel. We met a middle-aged woman there, a local who was studying nursing or something medical. She seemed to be the key to solving the next phase of the Mothman riddle. I interpreted her presence as meaning that someone with medical knowledge, or access to records, will need to dig up necessary information. This information could be regarding chemical pollutants, illnesses visited upon the public, or something else… I don't know. There was also a tall, falling statue that I saw, but I'm not sure what that meant. Something like God told me that this woman's mission needs to be honored – that she needs to be given her space. He kept showing me a slice of bread being covered with some substance on both sides. The overall message had something to do with the old saying about "buttering both sides of the bread."

-Andy 10/26/04

I live in the South Charleston, WV area. Behind my home is a steep hill; there is a cave with a lot of Indian writing. When I was a girl, we found remains of humans in the cave. I assume they were remains of the Natives that lived in the South Charleston area. This cave is on my land and would not be known to the public. Not a lot is known about the Indians in this area, but I do know that this whole area was once a sacred burial ground for them. They called the Kanawha River the "River of Death."

-Hazel 11/15/04

Since my last post a few days ago, there is new information that points to NASA as being yet another arm of the CIA. In *The NY Times* printed version for Sunday, Dec. 12, in the article "New Spy Plan Said to Involve Satellite System," we find that a new genre of "undetectable" satellites are being built by the National Reconnaissance Office. The NRO is essentially the Navy's intelligence arm, similar to the NSA, but even more secretive. They also mention something called the "National Geospatial-Intelligence Agency." The article states that Gov. Rockefeller, the highest-ranking democrat on the Senate Intelligence Committee – appropriately so, since his state is so vital to the intel network – is somewhat against the program. This could be a faux contestation for the media, or it could be because the new satellites may need to be monitored elsewhere, out of WV, meaning a loss of revenue for the state or for Rockefeller's cellphone companies. One sentence in the article reveals the extent to which NASA is involved in spying:

> The existence of the first stealth satellite, launched under a program known as "Misty," was first reported by Jeffrey T. Richelson in his 2001 book *The Wizards of Langley*. Mr. Richelson said the first such satellite was launched from the space shuttle Atlantis in March 1990.

This puts a whole new spin on the shuttle disasters, as well as every intelligence failure that should have been prevented by these all-seeing satellites. The NRO was responsible for the building of the eavesdropping system that my dad's best friend was working on during the 1960s in Sugar Grove, WV. A new generation of satellites, to be monitored from Sugar Grove, were being deployed and tested at exactly the same time as the Mothman sightings in 1967. No doubt the costs for this project were astronomical. These costs could have been hidden within the huge NASA "moon landing" budget championed by JFK. A tremendous amount of spy activity was no doubt occurring alongside the building of the eaves-dropping base.

By the way, NASA's chief resigned today. It was noted on CNN that he is going back to Baton Rouge to be president of the college there. I recently read a book called *Barry and the Boys* about a famous spy from Baton Rouge, Barry Seal. One of America's most prolific drug runners, Seal was gunned down there in the mid-1980s by an 8-man hit squad of Latinos. It was merely a week after Seal was overheard yelling at George Bush, Sr. over the phone. Seal had reportedly set up a "sting" prior to that, which involved filming Jeb and Dubya picking up some cocaine at the Miami airport. Seal kept these and other tapes with him at all times as "insurance." However, the tapes disappeared from the crime scene. Two of Seal's murderers were simply deported, and never tried in court.

The mention of a National "Geospatial Intelligence" Agency got me thinking about another random clue that crossed my path while in Texas this year. I happened to stay with an old college friend who was housesitting at his uncle's mansion outside of Austin. The uncle is a former executive of Mobil and a U.T. Austin graduate. Some of Barry Seal's pilot buddies went to U.T. Austin. Oil companies are excellent covers for spies, and U.T. feeds that system with its famous petroleum engineering program. I was lounging in the library of the Mobil uncle when I randomly pulled a book off the shelf. It was the uncle's master's thesis. It had to do with "geospatial" issues, such as measuring the variations in low frequency EMF pulses (like those apparently monitored at Sugar Grove) as they are sent around the world. Obviously this could have an oil explorative value, but it could also have an intelligence or reconnaissance value. The uncle had a hundred-foot high shortwave tower and a separate building filled with communications equipment… I also stumbled across his wife's MFA thesis from U.T. Even though she was a "dance" major, her thesis was intriguingly entitled "Agitative Factors in the Speeches of Stokely Carmichael." One wonders why a dance major at a predominately white school would be interested in dissecting the work of radical black activists.

-Andy 12/14/04

I have posted a picture of myself in our kitchen, which my sister just sent me. She has had this picture since it was taken in 1973. When I got the photo out to look at it today, I was with my wife, my 2-yr. old son, and an out-of-town visitor. I looked at it and was reminded that the kitchen was the room I always had nightmares about – where Bigfoot or the MIBs were trying to get in. My son was in my arms as I held the photo up to look at it. He immediately pointed to the window and said "Ga-ru-da." I thought this strange, since I could not remember mentioning the Garuda to him. I looked at the photo more closely and noticed a face in the lower part of the window. It looks very similar to Garuda and Thunderbird masks. Could this be Mothman looking in from another dimension? Strange things have been going on here lately… We've had a deep, low frequency vibration going through the house. It is so strong that it makes it hard to sleep. There was a guy taking pictures on the street recently, who seemed strange enough that I took down his license. Yesterday, the TV changed settings by itself. The door to the garage opened by itself, and the recliner inexplicably went from the reclining position to the up position. My wife, normally a skeptic, was a bit unnerved by these events as they happened mostly to her, not me… I did have a strange moment today, however. A friend and her daughter came over for a visit. The daughter is considered to be "fey" or psychic. I glanced at the daughter and perceived that she was wearing braces. I looked them over and asked her when she had gotten her braces put on. She said, "Well, I'm actually getting them put on next week." I looked at her teeth again, and was amazed to see that she actually did *not* have any braces on yet. We had not talked for months, and I had no idea she was going to get braces. My wife was again spooked... Anyway, my advice to Mothman witnesses is to keep digging into their own family stories. Look closely at everything. Think about symbolism, and develop insight. You don't necessarily need an outside "expert" helping you decide what you have seen.

-Andy 12/19/04

Interestingly, all of the events in the above post happened immediately after my wife returned from her first trip home since giving birth. Unbeknownst to me, while away in New Mexico, she had rekindled a relationship with someone her father had kept her from seeing in high school. As that emotional energy grew, it began manifesting outwards in the form of strange synchronicities and poltergeists... Albuquerque's Sandia Labs, where my father-in-law worked, has links to Union Carbide and to satellite technology. As Ira Einhorn stated in 2002, Sandia is controlled by Bell Labs which, along with the Rockefellers' AT&T, controlled the early development of satellites, the Internet, electronic eavesdropping, facial recognition, and telemetric mind control. Einhorn, who claims to have been set up for the murder of oil heiress Holly Maddux by the CIA, got help for his defense from the Bronfman family. The Bronfmans' lead attorney was accused in the Torbitt Document of playing a managerial role in the assassination of JFK. Various JFK/UFO figures were involved with Bell Labs, such as Einhorn, Jacques Vallee, Alvis Maddox, Gen. Walter Dornberger, Michael Paine, and possibly David Ferrie. Was Mothman trying to clue us into the existence of shadowy forces bent on enslaving us with wall-to-wall, high-tech surveillance?

"Earth Day in Philadelphia was conceived as a necessary partnership between business, academic, political, and activist interests. Environmental protection requires a conscious restructuring of all we do. I did not give up my participation in opposition to the war in Vietnam, my work with black organizations, my campaigning for a sensible drug policy, my spreading of information about CIA involvement in the heroin trade, my investigative work on the assassination of JFK, my study of various techniques for changing consciousness, or my work in futurism, but rather shifted my focus and added a new arrow to my quiver... I felt that the entire planet needed the kind of shock that Arthur C. Clarke provides at the conclusion of *Childhood's End*, plus a new kind of technology that would allow us to live without destroying the delicate balance that supports us. I later realized that we also needed a comprehensive metaphysic that would subsume science and fold it into a more inclusive, value-laden structure... My study of Brecht, Artaud, and Gurdjieff taught me much about shock and its effects. [While] my study of UFOs quickly made me aware that the coverup of such information, irrespective of its meaning and explanation, was a 'Cosmic Watergate,' the elusive pattern of the recurring flaps made me aware that the phenomenon was beyond immediate use. [Still] I sensed that its attendant psychic phenomena were of great possible use.

"The opportunity arose in 1971 to work on the Uri Geller project with Andrija Puharich, as a result of my convincing my editor/friend Bill Whitehead to republish two of Andrija's earlier books (I wrote the introduction for *Beyond Telepathy*). I quickly combined my newly developed corporate contacts, Andrija's networks, and those past 'movement' friends able to deal with 'magic' into my 'Network,' called by some 'the Internet before the Internet existed.' The Network was originally set up under Bell of Pennsylvania, then the local telephone company, with approval of then president Bill Cashel (who later became vice-chairman of AT&T), in order to service the information needs of those people linked with Andrija and I in the Geller Project. At that time, AT&T was the largest corporation in the world. [Our] Network grew during the 1970s to over 300 key people, in a multitude of human disciplines, in 26 countries on *both* sides of the Iron Curtain. Each piece of information was circulated separately to those people in the Network that I thought would be interested in the information. Bell maintained a card file of names and addresses and did all the duplicating and mailing. No money ever changed hands. It was a barter arrangement between myself and the world's largest corporate entity. The information circulated on the Network soon grew to encompass emerging information in a large number of fields. The AT&T 'far watchers' – those paid to eliminate surprises – soon came to talk to me at regular intervals, host me at AT&T headquarters, and take me to Bell Labs, for I was circulating both articles and books that they *should* have known about but didn't.

"Unfortunately, all new technology can be used as weaponry as well as for human benefit. So, I was soon up to my ears in a multi-pronged intelligence game that is still waiting to be unraveled. A small subset of the Network soon found itself monitoring the 'Russian Woodpecker' signal emanating from Soviet territory, which appeared to have mind control properties. According to Eldon Byrd, the creator of a mind control device for the Navy, the CIA admitted as much in 1986. Gathering together information from many sources, I published the first article on the issue in *Co-Evolution Quarterly* in 1975. I was then inundated with mail from all over the world. One of my correspondents was Philip K. Dick, probably our best science fiction writer, whose work is slowly bleeding into popular consciousness through the movies. [*Blade Runner* and] others are based upon his prescient work. Dick wrote me a series of letters about mind control, which I circulated to a small group. [I] then poured out 500,000 words about the issues we discussed. I also began receiving translated reports from all over the Soviet Union of psychotronic/mind-control weaponry; weaponry so chilling that I only shared some of the content, not the actual reports, with two people: Arthur Koestler and Stafford Beer. I also circulated a general letter to the entire Network about mind control issues. I spoke to Arthur and Stafford about the issue only after I was warned by Tony Judge and others that they felt my life was under threat. At the time of my arrest, I had received over 200 reports, mailed from all over the world but obviously originating from behind the Iron Curtain… At the time, I was also involved in two major futures studies: one involving the future of communication for the Canadian Telephone Company, under the auspices of Jacques Vallee, using his newly developed computer conferencing technique; the other study I conducted myself, for a small multinational corporation. In addition [I was] beginning to lecture on the principles behind Networking for major corporations.

"To substantiate the reports about the mind control proper-ties of the 'Russian Woodpecker,' Andrija Puharich built a smaller version of the technology and tested it on some of our core group, in private and in a number of public spaces – indicating a devastating ability to modulate human behavior. [I wanted to] organize a conference on the suppressed aspects of Tesla's work in mind control and free energy. [I] found a way to directly demonstrate mind control to those who came to the conference. In the Fall of 1978, I was Fellow in Residence at the Institute of Politics within the Kennedy School at Harvard. I lectured in every conceivable venue at Harvard, conducted a number of public symposiums, brought a number of the members of my Network to Harvard to lecture, ate dinner with a host of well known political figures, and made an inordinate amount of noise about mind control technology to, among others, then CIA head Stansfield Turner... In 1979, I received a small private foundation grant to study free energy devices... The objective was to develop and bring one device to the marketplace. In late winter of 1979, I went to Yugoslavia, as a guest of the Yugoslavian government, to further my Tesla project... I had a number of official meetings, the outcome of which was that the government agreed to fly, from the Tesla Museum in Belgrade to the U.S., whatever I needed of Tesla material, at their expense. I was also encouraged to return to Yugoslavia during the summer and see more of the country at their expense.

"Reports of my success reached both Bogdon Maglich and the president of Pennsylvania Bell, Bill Mowbraaten, before I got back to the U.S. Mowbraaten had a message waiting for me as I returned. At breakfast the next morning, he told me that he wanted to take me to the next meeting of the Conference Board, representing all the major American corporations. American business was looking for a way into Yugoslavia, and I had made a breakthrough. I was much too busy to think about how Bill had gotten information so quickly about my Yugoslav meetings. I was immediately off to England again for a week with the Prince of Iran... There was intense interest among some of my Bell people, who fed me stuff that I now think was a way of trying to elicit response. Remember, Bell ran Sandia Labs and, at that time, was unequaled as a research lab: transistors, lasers, etc. I had access to everyone in the Bell system. I was up to my ears in projects [before I was arrested]. I was in the middle of doing an interview with

Omni magazine; I was about to conduct a book length interview with Arthur Koestler; I was in negotiation about acting in a play and in a TV series. [But] all was not to be. I was busted for a murder I did not commit, and all of my work on mind control and free energy became history."

-Ira Einhorn, web post, Sept. 2002

In 1963, Steve Underwood (top left), a former USAF technician, saw what may have been Mothman in S. Charleston, WV, directly across the river from Mound. Years later, in Mt. Vernon, OH, Underwood saw an orange orb in the sky. Could this have been an "intelligent light" pointing us in the direction of George Washington, the area's ranking military officer at the time of Chief Cornstalk's murder? In 2007, Mark Wilson (lower left) saw Mothman flying above the bridge (top right) between Belpre, OH and Parkersburg, WV. At one end of the bridge is the Oil and Gas Museum; at the other end is a BP station and an Adena Indian mound (lower right) overlooking Blennerhassett Island. Islands like Blaine and Blennerhassett are typically outside state jurisdiction, leading them to become havens for steel, chemical, and nuclear plants, as well as spies like Aaron Burr.

CHAPTER 14

"Scientists [with military intelligence backgrounds are always making claims about free energy] – that mass may be an electromagnetic phenomenon and thus, in principle, subject to modification, with possible technological implications for propulsion. A multiyear NASA-funded study at the Lockheed Martin Advanced Technology Center developed this concept... As a Ph.D. physicist, I know that none of the information on free energy and antigravity that Ira Einhorn had access to in the 1970s was real. It was all bogus pseudo-physics. Ira was no physicist. [He was] a 'useful idiot,' used to spread disinformation and misinformation for covert, Cold War psyops on both sides of the Iron Curtain. The same game is going on today with UFO Disclosure, only some of the players have changed... Hal Puthoff was a U.S. Naval Officer before [he went to the] NSA. He had very high security clearances, as high as those of Kit Green of the CIA and National Security Council. Kit was the psychiatrist/bioweapons expert in *Remote Viewers: The Secret History of America's Psychic Spies* by Jim Schnabel.

"The people we worked with at the SARA Corporation not only think that the 1943 Philadelphia Experiment was significant and real, but also [apparently] have evidence that the Nazis really may have stumbled onto something important in regard to propellantless propulsion – Hal Puthoff's obsessive dream for more than 25 years. At the NSA [Puthoff worked alongside] microwave-engineering genius Ken Shoulders, who had to tell Hal to shut up about the flying saucers, at least until after lunch. I cannot evaluate their beliefs, really... What is important is that the former SARA Chief Scientist, James Corum, went to the Institute of Software Research in Fairmont, West Virginia to work on electromagnetic stress propulsion. ISR is a pet project of Senator Robert Byrd. The latest ISR webpage has been completely changed, hiding the photo of Dr. Corum and his EM Stress Propulsion Project, which was on the original [site]. Dr. Corum is also an expert on Nicola Tesla and Gabriel Kron, and has had access to the complete Tesla Archive in Belgrade, even under the former Serbian government that committed war crimes. Corum has published on the Philadelphia Experiment, and thinks Jacques

Vallee is way off base in his article on that incident in *The Journal of Scientific Exploration.*"

-Dr. Jack Sarfatti, web post, Sept. 2002

COLVIN, ANDY – GRASSY KNOLL RADIO INTERVIEW 31 – JUNE 2008

"Vyz" at *Beyond the Grassy Knoll* (GK): We are back for another live show here on *The Grassy Knoll.* We have with us today, Andrew Colvin. We're going to pick up with the month of May. Welcome aboard… One thing I wanted to ask Andy about… Adam Gorightly is going to come out with a book on James Shelby Downard. Chris Knowles and I were going back and forth with that. I was thinking about what Downard dealt with, which was mostly synchronicity. I think we do the same thing; a *lot* of what we deal with has to do with synchronicities.

Andy Colvin (AC): Yes, it really seems to have turned into research about synchronicity.

GK: Not to say that some of it isn't orchestrated but, no matter what, synchronicity *is* out there. All of this just *can't* be coincidence.

AC: A synchronicity is a seemingly *acausal* relationship; there is no noticeable causation. By studying Mothman, I've come to sense that there is some force, probably coming from the collective unconscious of humankind, which is trying to balance the scales between right and wrong. One of the proponents of this idea has been Eugenia Macer-Story. She has been doing synchronicity work for decades, generally talking about the positive aspects of it. There are different kinds of quantum spirit entities. They have to be dealt with differently. One has to develop a language to recognize "what is what," or else one is going to be confused, and ripe for exploitation… By the way, I "partied" with Courtney Love at "Lollapalooza" one time. I'm just throwing that out because, before we came on, you were talking about your "Knollapalooza" marathon. You had Love's dad on your show yesterday. Coincidentally, I have a friend who worked for Love and Cobain. He now believes that there was something fishy going on. He feels that Kurt may have been murdered for the insurance money. The record company was able to collect on Cobain's death. According to Richard Lee, the top "Courtney killed Kurt" conspiracy researcher, the insurance was designed to pay off even if Cobain killed himself.

GK: That was the first time I ever spoke to Hank on-air… I was a bit taken aback by his pointing the finger at culprits… My head was spinning. Pretty heavy stuff…

AC: Not long after Kurt's death, Hank explicitly stated on TV that he felt Courtney was capable of killing Kurt… Speaking of Hollywood, shall we talk about Laurel Canyon?

GK: Yes, but let me mention what just popped up today regarding the precarious financial state of all nations… At this point in time, you should at least *try* to give yourself a stash of cash. Buy some storable foodstuffs. They are going to start cutting the horsemen loose on us in the not-so-distant future… If you've got all your eggs in other baskets, they're not in *your* basket. The Bank of Scotland came out with a warning today about a global financial crisis…. Your dollar is going to devalue.

AC: I would be suspicious of the media coverage. They may want to create a crisis here. Maybe they want to milk the treasury some more; maybe they want to put the crash off until after the election in November. That way, the Republicans can blame all of Bush's mistakes on the Democrats. Notice that in June of this year, we had very few covert ops, supernatural hoaxes, and disinformation campaigns. Usually, whenever Bush lost on an issue, there were some shootings and such. But that's not happening now, probably because he has become a lame duck president. Remember, June is usually very active. Last year, June was *extremely* active.

GK: They are usually distracting us by giving us a suitable point of focus.

AC: After Bush lost on Guantanamo, we didn't have a school shooting or any of the usual ops, except for a Manson story – Susan Atkins' brain tumor… We *did* have an increase in media reminding us of 9/11. There were references to terror, but no actual ops. I am wondering if this is the washout before the tsunami. On a beach, the tide goes out before the wave comes in.

It turned out that I was right. A concocted financial crisis in the fall of 2008 resulted in banks getting hundreds of billions of free bailout money. As shown in Michael Moore's Capitalism: A Love Story, *the bailout legislation was rammed through in the middle of the night during closed session, accompanied by a lot of hysterical rhetoric. By the end of 2009, over $141 billion had gone out to banks, mostly for executive bonuses at Goldman Sachs. Bush and his cronies were likely planning this manufactured crisis in June of 2008, just prior to leaving for vacation in July and August. According to Thom Hartmann, in the months leading up to the crisis, the Bush* *administration actively blocked attempts by all fifty State governors to regulate the mortgage industry, whose unbridled loans and credit default swaps caused the crisis.*

GK: Exactly… But how many people are really paying attention? How many people are still going to put money in their 401Ks and retirement accounts? I don't think anybody's going to move their money out. They don't believe it. Nobody pays attention, and life goes on. But… Let's talk about Laurel Canyon. You've got some connections there, too, don't you?

AC: Well, this artist-savant I'm working with, Bruce Bickford, spent some time there in the 1970s while doing animation for Frank Zappa. Bruce often has synchronicities relating to Mothman. He is a bit of a cipher. Zappa wanted to put him up in the famous Log Cabin in Laurel Canyon. Bruce remembers many of the players there. He used to eat at a restaurant run by a cult called "The Source," which was overseen by Father Yod, a former martial arts trainer for the U.S. Marines… Laurel Canyon is somewhat like Woodward Drive in certain respects. Hollywood was built on oil, just as West Virginia was. The first salt mines and natural gas wells were drilled in Charleston, just a couple of blocks from Magic Island and Luna Park. The technology for oil drilling was developed there, about a mile from where Manson, Moore, and I lived… At the top of Laurel Canyon, a secret CIA movie studio was built right after WWII. By the 1960s, all of these military intelligence families had moved into the canyon. These families ended up being the ones who jump-started the "peace" movement in L.A. Jim Morrison, who appeared to be deeply into the occult, was from one of these families. His dad was the captain of the U.S.S. Maddox, the ship involved in starting the Vietnam War. John McCain's grandmother was the main benefactress of that ship. The name "Maddox" ties into the Manson and Mothman stories. And Manson had connections to Laurel Canyon. There were lots of murders there, which Dave McGowan has researched. Neil Young wrote a song about Manson. In the song, Manson trolls Laurel Canyon, looking for victims.

GK: By the way, what is your take on the Stanford Research Institute?

AC: Andrija Puharich was involved with SRI. He probably built the mind control device that was being pointed at UFO researchers and witnesses. Many of the scientists at SRI were CIA and connected to MK-Ultra. They got some of their techniques, like remote viewing, from Scientology. A lot of the SRI researchers were not only

Scientologists, but also were into the Council of Nine, which dates back to the late 1800s in England and India, where industrial-age westerners were first starting to draw from Eastern philosophy. This East-West spiritual clash, or difference in philosophy, is almost *the* story of civilization. The Christ story seems infused with Eastern ideas. There are similarities between Western gods, like Mithras and Manitou, and Asian archetypes like Garuda and Krishna. And, in between, are Middle-Eastern avatars like Horus and Enki… Chris Knowles has been doing some good research in New York regarding such similarities. Birdman archetypes are all over NYC, especially around Rockefeller buildings. The winged Mithras holds a serpent like the Garuda does. AT&T, Western Electric, and Verizon have all used Mithras in their logos. They are very open about their worship – if you want to call it that – of these birdmen.

GK: There's a lot there. Chris is going to come on and deal with some of the toponomy and onomatology of the origins of the U.S. He would be quick to say that synchronicity factors into all this, and has for quite some time.

AC: The "powers that be" are spiritual, too, in a sense. They have their beliefs. They understand that these avatars are bearers of synchronicity, and that "synchronicities sink ships." Any average person out there can potentially get an important clue and foil the best-laid conspiracy. Elites want to maintain control of that process.

GK: Synchronicity is most interesting. By no means is it something we can dismiss… Do you think there might have been some kind of exotic weaponry used during Mothman?

AC: There are little hints of that – different stories about a "black box." Puharich had a black box. The Tesla coil comes in a black box. Major Downing, the Mothman "deep throat," talked about "rays" being used in Pt. Pleasant. Focused radio or sound waves could bring a bridge down. A Tesla coil can implode just about any structure… That might explain why guys were climbing around on the Silver Bridge a few days before the 1967 collapse. Those guys were dressed just like the MLK assassins, by the way, with checkered wool jackets and street shoes. Keel talked about the nightly intrusions of the "checkered shirt" MIBs into area bedrooms… There was the MIB with a white Mustang, the getaway car in the MLK assassination. He and the other MIB used similar fake names all over the country. Mothman witnesses were getting precognitions of the MLK and RFK assassinations… Some witnesses, by the way, had unusual sightings of vibrating objects. Craig Knebel (see *The Mothman's Photographer III*) saw vibrating "eyes" – two red dots in his room. He blacked out after he saw the eyes and felt his bed shake. He and his girlfriend couldn't remember what happened the next day. Synchronistically, I was listening to Jeff Ritzmann, a UFO researcher, the other day. He had the same exact thing happen to him. One wonders if these were paranormal experiences involving a natural energy source, or if they were caused by hardware. The authorities tested a "nonlethal" sound weapon on protesters not too long ago. They were using it in New York City while Alex Jones was bullhorning a 9/11 anniversary event. They apparently also have a microwave weapon that will burn your skin and make you want to run.

GK *[jokingly]*: There was something *more* repulsive than Jones and a bullhorn?

AC *[laughs]*: I suppose there were *two* sonic weapons in NYC, weren't there! But seriously… A Buddhist I meditate with, Pieter Drummond, told me an interesting story about a retreat he went to last week. He claims that he saw the "shadow" of a Thunderbird on the wall while they were meditating. He thinks it might be related to a recently deceased woman he knew, who had come to him in a vision. She had said to him, "Let me show you what it's like to drown." He then experienced her drowning! This is almost exactly like what I experienced in 2002, when we went back to that spot in Mound where we'd seen Mothman: I had a vision of someone drowning. It can be creepy when these synchronicities start to come together… By the way, they found the body of Mia Zapata, the murdered singer/activist, less than a block from a Thunderbird totem.

GK: Speaking of depressing stories, let's take a look at some of the events of the day. You keep a media calendar. Are you seeing any patterns?

AC: Patterns do emerge. There appear to be basic genres of stories, which are mixed together. One technique is to mix future, past, and present stories, in order to not only give us a sense of where we are in time, but also to feel superior in that regard. That's why we have so many stories about dinosaur/archaeological finds right alongside NASA/high-tech stories. Another basic technique is to combine stories that are geographically local with those that come from far away, in order to provide us with a sense of where we are in space. The U.S. is, of course, painted as a superior space, even though it is increasingly akin to a Third World country. You also have an action/reaction dynamic, at a subtextual level, within current events. Anytime a movement within the system challenges the hierarchy of the system, you'll see stories reflecting negative consequences. Thus, all of us have come to understand that those who complain about, say, safety issues at work will be retaliated against. Over the years, this negative reinforcement becomes engrained in us. That's why you have these knee-jerk reactions not only regarding workplace safety, but also regarding conspiracy theories and the paranormal. Everyone in the U.S. has been programmed to *not* question certain topics... There are also the misdirection stories. Recently, journalist Tim Russert died. Somebody wrote into my list and talked about how his death coincided with the Kandahar jailbreak. After a big jailbreak in Afghanistan where something like a thousand prisoners escaped, suddenly Russert died. His death completely swamped the jailbreak story. The media hyped the Russert story as much as possible.

GK: Tim Russert played the game as much as anyone else. He was Jesuit educated, and was NBC's man at the Vatican for quite some time. He seemed like a great guy; you'd buy him a beer if you saw him in a bar. But shows like his are scripted; the guests know what's going on. Tim did not have any special magic. Since he did what he was supposed to do, there was no reason to whack him. He was a good, useful tool for the networks, for the government, and for the powers that be. He wasn't killed. Was he a CFR member? I don't know. The big anchors, Brokaw, Jennings, and Rather, were all CFR, which says something about the Rockefellers' power.

AC: We had the earthquake in China recently. There was some speculation about concrete found around the perimeter of the site, as if an explosion had occurred. Somebody saw some kind of mushroom cloud. Russia has big oil reserves, yet their population is declining; China's population is going up fast. Eventually, the Chinese may stream through that earthquake area, in order to encroach on Russian oil fields. One way to control future paths of movement might be to cause nuclear devastation in certain regions beforehand. The Rockefellers were, of course, key players in our nuclear buildup during the Cold War. You have to wonder if they might use nukes again, perhaps under the cover of "accidents." There's this longstanding myth about Mothman being seen at Chernobyl. They say the same thing about Mothman being at Ground Zero on 9/11. In both cases, the real story may be that Mothman was giving people precognitions about the events years in advance. The sighting hoaxes tend to obscure the precognitions. Conversely, the myths and hoaxes often shed light on something else. The fact that everyone keeps talking about a Chernobyl-Mothman connection is no accident. People can feel the nuclear underpinnings to the story, just as they can feel the connections between UFOs, Nazis, and assassinations. In an airport in Winnipeg, Canada, David Ferrie was overheard talking about Mercury, NV (i.e., Area 51) and the monies being made from the transportation of uranium. The CIA was reportedly skimming off plutonium for the state of Israel, so that they could develop their own bomb. Maybe Mothman, or the collective unconscious, wants us to know this. Maybe Israel will be the first to use a nuclear device again…

GK: You know, one of the things about which speculation gets heavier and heavier is "weather modification." A lot of people harbor suspicions about it. Now we have this Mississippi river flood out in the Midwest, which they're calling a "500-year event." Nobody has seen this kind of destruction since before the white man came. Of course, suspicions abound. There was speculation about Hurricane Katrina and about the Aceh tsunami in the oil fields. Orwell alluded to weather control. Global warming is a big mess. It can almost make you crazy, which can be more of a danger than the weather itself.

AC: Employees who have worked on weather modification programs have come forth, talking about how much money is spent on them. Weather modification was in the U.S. budget decades ago, before large segments of it went "black." I think they toy around with whatever they can. Weather modification would be another thing to try. The tech personnel probably aren't even aware that some of the things they are ordered to do affect the weather. They may just get a message to beam a certain HAARP frequency at such and such a time. They just follow orders, not knowing exactly what effects are being generated.

GK: There was once an early weather modification white paper on the Internet, called "Owning the Weather by 2020." It has been since modified. But before they changed it, it mentioned aerosol spraying or "chemtrails." Of course, this is what we now have today. We know that something is going on. It's supposed to be weather modification, but there may be something else afoot. I don't necessarily think that it is for depopulation. They simply don't care if we are collateral damage. The nonlethal weaponry, the rays and EMPs, can get really lethal if you overdo it. They've been testing it on people. I feel badly for people like Eleanor White, who has been saying, "Look, this electromagnetic mind control stuff is going on." Unless you're one of the people they happen to target, it all sounds crazy. One can only imagine the torture these victims go through.

AC: I've known Eleanor for a long time. I don't know her personally, but we used to be on a couple of mind control discussion lists in the 1990s, back before Yahoo got started.

GK: I tell you what… She went through a lot. She took a lot of abuse. She got booted off of GCN. They just cut her off. Poor Eleanor was out there wondering, "Why did that happen?" But that's what they're about; the major "alternative" networks are phonies.

AC: Eleanor has a great work ethic. She was always putting stuff up about mind control. She helped me understand the weird world of electromagnetic harassment. The agencies have microwave devices that can target protesters in their own homes. Eleanor has been talking about this type of thing for at least two decades.

GK: When GCN dropped her, I had her come back on. Someone who is listening right now called in during that show. That listener is a very intelligent and reasonable human being, who also gave her testimony. We also had the testimony of two Sacramento sisters, who are now in law school, who were targeted by their neighbors. Even though they may be very credible, it is easy for skeptics to simply accuse them of being nuts.

AC: Eleanor is one of the few famous mind control victims who has *not* written a book making outrageous claims.

GK: Good point… Let me just throw this in. Someone with a sense of humor just emailed this:

> Recently, there was an article about Russia doing weather control. They got busted because they dropped a bag of cement on some lady's house… They were using [cement particles] to prevent poor weather on a holiday. They claimed that they did it "often." If they do it [openly] just for the sake of convenience, think of what they might use it for covertly [if it really mattered].

GK: I appreciate that. Will Thomas was on *Coast to Coast* last night. I listened for about 20 minutes. Will is a pretty straight shooter. One of the things they talked about is the fact that Beijing absolutely *guaranteed* that there would be no bad weather during the Olympics. I just wish I knew what is going on with chemtrails. It can make you paranoid… By the way, Tim Russert was *not* on the CFR list…

AC: You were talking about nonlethal weapons, which reminded me of the West Nile Virus. Some of these viruses can be considered weapons… I recently found out that the ex-father-in-law of an old girlfriend of mine got a grant from the Rockefeller Foundation to do West Nile mosquito research back in the late 1950s. The Rockefellers have been involved in virus research for decades.

The Rockefellers reportedly helped fund Richard Nixon's Special Cancer Virus biowarfare lab, a facility that could have served as a source for any radioactive materials used on rebellious Carbide employees. Such labs serve different branches of the military; each branch is probably able to pull from the virus inventory independently for their various ops. Conversely, such a facility might instigate the wearing of multiple insignia from different branches. The MIBs in Mound, like those mentioned by John Keel in his 1989 lecture (see The Mothman's Photographer II, *p.198), wore mixed Air Force/Navy insignia.*

AC: When the Rockefellers went down and opened up the oil wells in the Amazon, they also started studying the various flora and fauna as well. Some of that research may have found its way into the development of various viruses and diseases, such as AIDs and West Nile. By the way, this old girlfriend of mine, who is Norwegian/Italian, lives close to Dublin, Ohio. Her ex-husband is a professor at a Catholic school in Columbus. For added synchronicity, she once worked for Chase Bank.

Columbus is mentioned in a story related by Mary Hyre, the newspaper woman who made Mothman famous. Immediately following the Silver Bridge collapse, Hyre was approached by a classic Man in Black with Oriental features. He did not ask her about Mothman witnesses, but badgered her for the names of people who had seen mystery lights traveling down Camp Conley Road in the TNT Area. After she told him to leave her office, he went around to various homes asking questions, posing as a reporter from Cambridge, Ohio, a town that today has a high number of Bigfoot sightings. Since Cambridge is due east of Columbus, someone asked the MIB about Columbus, but he didn't seem to know where it was. All one can gather from this incident is that there was something about those mystery lights that someone wanted to keep hidden. Could these lights have been reconnaissance craft – "Nazi UFOs" – being manufactured in the area, where miles of secret, underground tunnels are said to exist? Were the finished craft then flown to Long Island to be inspected by ex-Nazi commanders, thus fueling John Keel's investigations there?

AC: Next item… A poster to my list, Emil Hach, saw Mothman in his bedroom 3 years ago. His son is now seeing orbs in that same bedroom… Speaking of orbs, I talked about how I had seen an orb flying out of Burbank last year, when they were having the big fire at Griffith Park. I was told by a friend in the security field that these orbs are probably drone craft. They are turning up on various Google satellite images. They look exactly like what I saw. The big ufology names, like Linda Moulton Howe, are trying to imply that these are "extraterrestrial" UFOs, but there is a perfectly Earthly explanation. A couple of other things… We had the "live alien" video, which came out on May 30, 2008. They're always throwing these things out in the UFO world. They usually coincide with key geopolitical events that are in the news. UFO researchers will come out of nowhere with questionable video footage. These videos often get huge media play, even though the researchers are complete unknowns. In this case, Stan Romanek supposedly shot footage of a "grey" alien looking through a window. There is a still shot of it on the web that looks similar to the photo that my sister took in 1973. This is the second example of a hoaxed photo reminiscent of my sister's photo. Colorado ufologist Jeff Peckman marketed the Romanek video. The two were on the Larry King Show making a case for the reality of the ETs. Once you've seen about twenty of these clips come and go, you can't take them seriously anymore… The last item… West Virginian Bob Teets was at the 2003 Mothman Festival. Teets turns out to be press director for the Human Potential Foundation (HPF). HPF is led by C.B. Scott Jones, who some imply was behind the whole MJ-12 scam. William Dean Ross fingered Jones as being involved in the NSA shenanigans around Liberty, WV's "interdimensional vortex." Interestingly, the HPF started at Esalen back in the 1960s. Charles Manson was reportedly at Esalen the weekend prior to the Tate-LaBianca murders… Bob Teets is a hypnotherapist who has written a book on West Virginia UFOs. He has now written a book about the psychology of UFO abductees. He claims to have examined *2500* different abductees, which seems like an enormous amount. Teets signed books next to John Keel in 2003. He kept a low profile. It was so low that it was noticeable. I mentioned it to Harriet at the time, and she concurred… I recently found a website about the "Rockefeller Initiative," a group that was flooding the media with UFO messages in the early 1990s. The Rockefellers were, of course, funding it. *This* is why we had all of those TV shows about UFOs in the early 1990s, playing off of the popularity of the Whitley Strieber and Budd Hopkins books. Teets was apparently in the thick of that activity. The Rockefeller Initiative was an effort, supposedly, to alert the Clinton administration to the UFO threat. That was the cover story. It was *really* about giving money to media outlets to make UFO programs asserting an ET presence. It was yet another well-funded attempt to push the ET thesis and obscure the reality of terrestrial saucers.

A collage drawing of the Silver Bridge site by the author's son (left) alludes to occult activity in connection with the collapse - a theory also put forth by UFO researcher Allen Greenfield. A scroll found in the Buddhist caves of Dunhuang, China (right), written in an unknown, undecipherable language, features Garuda-like imagery. While in Dunhuang, the author was shown a secret cave decorated with two thousand-year old erotic paintings, all done in a modern style similar to Picasso.

CHAPTER 15

"In my early teens, I found that I could sometimes sense what other people were thinking. I assumed that everyone had this ability. Now and then, I encounter someone whose mind is actually vulnerable to my own. I not only sense what they are thinking, but I can project my own thoughts into their mind; they accept these thoughts as their own. In short, I can control that person's mind on a modest scale. There are people who have this power to a very developed degree. They can control others, even from a great distance. It is probable that some world leaders, especially the evil ones like Hitler, possessed and exercised this ability. One famous [Russian] psychic could hand a railroad conductor a blank sheet of paper. The [conductor] would punch it, thinking it was a ticket..."

-John Keel, *The Eighth Tower*

"For many years now, I have been quietly interviewing warlocks, trying to develop a book based on the actual experiences of natural witches and warlocks – people who are born with the ability to perceive and control the elementals. They seem to be several steps beyond mediums. Mediums are *used* by the phenomenon. Warlocks, on the other hand, are able to use these forces. Unfortunately, most of them seem to come to a tragic end – suicides, murders, and bizarre deaths. But it is apparent that thousands of people in each generation suffer from this uneasy talent. I think I had it when I was an adolescent, but I diverted my attention by studying physics, chemistry, etc., and lost it by the time I was 18. At 18, I woke up one night in a furnished room near Times Square and had what can only be described as an illuminating experience. For a few brief moments, I suddenly understood *everything*. I was really one with the cosmos. The next morning, I could remember very little of it, but I'm sure it was all entered into my subconscious."

-John Keel, letter to author Colin Wilson

The following interview with John Keel was excerpted from The New UFO Sightings *by Glenn McWane & David Graham, written in 1974. The material can now be found online as well... While Keel flatly declares that most sensational UFO sightings are completely hallucinatory, he also states that certain UFO lights do seem real and natural. The idea that mind control might be involved is discussed, as well as the fact that Keel personally knew of several cases where young, bright West Virginia children were being tracked for future government service – the same thing that happened at my elementary school in Mound. Interestingly, the land on which my elementary school sits was once owned by the family of Sara Jane Moore.*

Q: John A. Keel is probably one of the most well-informed of all the UFO researchers. John, how do you feel about UFOs getting some national publicity after a rather long hiatus?

John Keel (JK): It is very interesting. Tonight on *NBC News*, they reported some of these sightings. They mentioned that a woman somewhere in the South not only saw a UFO, but that, on the side of this object, the letters "UFO" were painted. It was an amusing anecdote for the newscast, but I expect this was true – an ultimate joke. We may get more reports like this. A few years ago, I talked with two young men who had seen an object in a field that exactly resembled one of our space modules, and had "US Air Force" printed on the sides. But, of course, one of our space modules isn't going to be hovering over a field in New Jersey. I never wrote it up, because even the UFO buffs wouldn't believe it...

Q: Why do you think all of this UFO activity is taking place now?

JK: I keep trying to outguess the phenomenon but it is hard, because it is always one step ahead of you. On a number of occasions, when I was most active in my research, I would go to an obscure farm, on an obscure backroad, to research a story that had never been publicized. As soon as I would walk into the house, the phone would start to go crazy. But no one would be on the other end of the line. The farmer would be amazed, because this had never happened before. This occurred several times, in several different places. Someone was trying to get through to me that they knew every move I was making; they finally convinced me...

Q: It appears that a mysterious, unidentified "someone" is keeping an eye on things...

JK: A lot of people with [paranormal] claims get in touch with me, because they think I am going to believe their story, become enthusiastic about it, and write a glowing article about it. It is very difficult for me to tell them that I feel sorry for them; that I have heard it all before, and that I see them going down the "road to ruin" just as several others have done in the past. I believe that a lot of people who have written strange letters to me have really been mediumistic channels, and that the letters were produced by automatic writing. There was a case a few years ago in which I interviewed some witnesses on Long Island. It was a family that had seen some rather remarkable things. I taped the interview in their living room with three or four people. A year or two later, I went back and dropped in on them, to see how they had been doing and if anything new was happening. They didn't know me. They were amazed. I started telling them about their UFO experiences, and they thought I was crazy. They had no memory of all the things they had told me a year ago. They were not acting as if they were hiding anything or putting me on. They were nearly at a point of shock… There are several areas to this whole weird business. On the one hand, we have had real UFO phenomena – strange lights passing over the earth – probably since time began. The "UFO intelligences" are aware that we are going to see these lights occasionally when conditions are just right, so they have to give us an explanation. Different generations have been given different explanations. These intelligences have staged whole events, over a long period of time, to support those explanations. We have the fairy faith in Middle Europe; we have the vampire and various other kinds of legends. We have the mysterious airships in 1897. Now, we have spaceships. But all of these things are nothing but a cover for the real phenomenon – whatever it is… On the ground, as well as in the air, there are real things happening that they don't want us to know about. So they give us lots of cover stories. The Men in Black support the cover stories in many of these instances. What they are trying to hide may be frightening, even incomprehensible to us, but it does seem that they are using us in some fashion. It may be more than a rumor that young people are being collected from college campuses after their friends' and family's minds have been altered so that they will not remember the existence of these children. As farfetched as this sounds, there may be more truth to it than to some of the other theories we are kicking around. We are being used in some fashion, and the UFO intelligences don't want us to discover how they are using us. So, all this other stuff is camouflage. I keep trying to peel away the layers of this camouflage. I keep trying to come up with something real and substantial. Perhaps if we could find out what they are doing to us, we could stop them. But once we found out what it was, they might stop of their own volition, or do something else for a change. It may be the end of the game once we figure out what they are doing to us. When we have a new UFO flap, such as the one going on at the moment, I ask myself, "What is really going on? What are they covering up this time? What kind of manipulation is taking place that we don't know about?" This is a very big flap, because there is a lot of heavy news right now from the Middle East. It should have smothered the UFO reports, but it didn't. There must be a lot more UFO activity than the media have mentioned... Two nights ago, a TV cameraman in a town near here spotted an object in the sky. He had a camera and took pictures of it. He is a specialized cameraman but, when he developed the film, nothing came out on it. I have heard all of this before... Were the objects really there, or were the witnesses just thinking they saw them? Or was the film manipulated in some way? Both possibilities are possible.

Q: You seem to feel that the UFO phenomenon is some kind of delusion that is being perpetrated upon mankind by some unknown source.

JK: In an earlier time, when someone would undergo such experiences, people would say that he was "enchanted." Today, people are still being enchanted, even though we don't use that terminology anymore. More and more people are accepting these incidents as real experiences, when they probably aren't. What we have had in the last twenty-five years or so is a large propaganda movement designed to create a whole frame of reference for these manifestations – a frame of reference that could be used to conceal and cover up what is really going on. If it hadn't been for a relatively small handful of extraterrestrial enthusiasts, the concept of UFOs from outer space wouldn't have caught on; the UFO intelligences would have had to find something else. But the outer space propaganda *did* catch on, and we now have millions of people who accept "extraterrestrial visitors" as the explanation for the lights they are seeing in the sky. These UFO lights are appearing simultaneously in thousands of places all over the country. If it were really an invasion from outer space, it would be enormous!

Q: Have you observed any new variations to the UFO sightings?

JK: This summer we had a great increase in "phantom helicopters," which appeared in some twenty states. These are unmarked helicopters of a very large size – military helicopters. They are seen hovering over farm fields; when farmers see them, they think they are cattle rustlers… There is one other thing to keep on the alert for. I have come across six different cases, in six different parts of the country, in which exceptionally bright children, from fairly poor families, were given tests in school that determined these children were the brightest in their schools. These were children who also claim that their family has a great deal of psychic ability. These children were approached by someone claiming to represent the U.S. government. These representatives made an offer that the government would finance the kids' college education *if* the children would sign an agreement to go into government service when they got out of college. Not military service, but government service… This seems to me to be a rather extraordinary program. The government does have programs to finance exceptional children with the agreement that students repay after they get out of college, but I am aware of no deal wherein the students would have to go into the government when they get out of college. When I [worked] in Washington, I decided to get to the bottom of this… I was with the Department of Health, Education, and Welfare. I nosed around. No one had ever heard of such a thing. I've tried to keep in touch with these six contacted families, but now I have lost communications with all of them. I would like to find out what has happened to them – what will happen to them when their kids are out of school. This doesn't sound like something the CIA would go in for. They are interested in a certain psychological aspect of people, not intelligence. All of these kids have psychic ability. There are a lot of kids with high IQs who have not been approached, so psychic ability must be a credential… Essentially the phenomenon can be divided into two parts. The meandering nocturnal lights are the *real* mystery, and still remain unexplained by astronomy. The objects and apparitions seen on the ground, or close to it, comprise the second part. These range from complex hallucinations to elaborate transmogrifications, often accompanied by incredible distortions of reality and manipulations of time and space. Such manifestations have been known, and recorded, throughout history, and their true nature was recognized and defined thousands of years ago. Collectively, American ufologists are ill-informed and poorly educated in history, philosophy, and the behavioral sciences. So, they have failed to recognize what is actually happening. Ufology is essentially a new system of belief, not a new system of scientific fact. As such, it is no more substantive than the study of angels and the medieval cataloging of chimeras. Indeed, the deeper one penetrates into the ufological problems, the more one finds himself rediscovering Heraclitus.

According to Keel in Flying Saucer Review, *Vol. 17, No. 3, a reliable witness said that she had observed a silver disc hovering above a Point Pleasant, WV school in 1966. A male figure in tight-fitting silver coveralls was standing – floating – in midair, outside the open door of the object, gazing intently into the school playground. He had "pointy" features, silver coveralls, and shoulder-length hair, similar to descriptions of Indrid Cold. The same object later landed in the woman's yard and was witnessed by her children. A similar being was seen on that occasion as well. What exactly did these entities, whether supernatural or governmental, want from these children? Was this some form of mind control experiment, or just a nifty form of distraction? Just how important are UFOs for mass mind control? In the following lecture given in 1992, Keel discusses some of the ways UFOs are used for control and distraction.*

KEEL, JOHN – MOTHMAN PROPHECIES– 1992 LECTURE EXCERPT

In October of 1973, we suddenly had a major UFO wave. For two weeks, the newspapers didn't carry anything but UFO news. It was all very exciting to the UFO buffs and to the Forteans who were following the UFO stuff. Then, the Arabs attacked Israel... [Earlier] in 1973, Israel had shot down an Arab airliner filled with over 100 civilians. The Arabs said, "This is the last straw; we're going to get rid of Israel." And so, on Yom Kippur, they attacked Israel, which was a big mistake on their part. It was called the Six Day War. [As I mentioned before] the newspapers and news media here in the U.S. were all zeroed in on UFOs. NBC had teams running around the country interviewing the UFO witnesses. The war started and, suddenly, they had to divert all of their media to the war. The news on the UFOs stopped cold and, instead, we were reading about the war in Israel. But the UFO sightings continued. Most of the UFO buffs still erroneously say that 1973 was the big year for UFOs. It wasn't; 1975 was the big year. The UFO sightings and other Fortean things continued to build up in '74. Then in '75, we had them everywhere. We had everything. We had Bigfoot sightings. We had sea serpent sightings. We had all kinds of UFO sightings and landings and abductions. 1973 was just the start of it – a major pivotal year.

The animal mutilations began in the 1960s. In 1973, the animal mutilations got a lot of publicity in Puerto Rico. In fact, the newspapers there were headlining stories saying there were vampires loose in Puerto Rico. They were finding all of these animals with the blood drained out of them. Then the animal mutilations continued to spread around the United States. I followed it on a map, state by state. In '75, we had a national wave of animal mutilations that we don't have a real explanation for, to this day. By 1975, when we had all these Fortean things going on, a lot of people had dropped out of the UFO and Fortean scenes. With the big wave of the 1960s, literally millions of people took an interest in UFOs. We had networks all over the country and the world, watching the UFO sightings and other events. But, by 1975, there were only a handful of people who were still interested, still watching. The news media was also rather disinterested. It's only in recent years that all this stuff has trickled [back] in.

Now, from what I've told you so far, what happens when a global disaster is about to happen? Why, we have a UFO wave! So, maybe in '94 or '95, we will have another major UFO wave. It'll be very interesting if this comes to pass. As I say, in the 1980s, I was able to predict it all. Before Russia collapsed, they had a major UFO wave there. The Russians had ignored UFOs up until the 1980s. Then, suddenly, the UFOs were everywhere. The things happening in Russia were very similar, if not identical to, things that happened in the U.S. in the 1950s: the landings, the contacts, the strange monsters getting out of UFOs, the marks on the ground. All of this stuff that had happened in the U.S. in the 1950s – just prior to our involvement in Vietnam – was happening in Russia just prior to the collapse of their whole system. There are a lot of magazines in Russia now that are devoted to UFOs – UFOs that were laughed at in the 1940s and 1950s. UFOs are suddenly becoming a significant cultural factor all over the world. If you've read Dr. Vallee's books, you know about the [rash of mindbending sightings] in S. America.

For example in the 1960s, Ivan Sanderson and I talked to a family in New Jersey who had seen a UFO that was about a mile in diameter. They had a good description of it. It had windows in it. It looked like a gigantic flying saucer right out of the movies. This was in an area of NJ where if one family had seen this, then hundreds of other people should have seen it. Ivan put articles in the NJ newspapers, asking if somebody else had seen something unusual on that day. We got a number of UFO reports, but nobody had seen anything a mile in diameter. We were able to judge the size of it because the witnesses saw it low between two mountains. The family was attracted to it by the barking of their dog, which is common in a lot of UFO reports. The husband in the family was the president of a fairly large company in New Jersey – a pretty reliable person. They were not about to make up flying saucer stories just to entertain Ivan Sanderson and John Keel.

Now, what was our conclusion from that? Why didn't 3000 other people see this same thing? It had to be some kind of hallucination if only this one family saw it. The family down the road didn't see anything; the families in the next town didn't see anything. And certainly, if something a mile in diameter flew over New Jersey at an altitude of a couple of thousand feet, a lot of people would have seen it. So this is one of the many cases that convinced me that there is a hallucinatory process involved in this. No matter how reliable the witness is, what they see can be questioned. The same is true in many of our Bigfoot cases and strange monster cases; the people see some image that's *planted* in their mind. The creature itself probably doesn't exist at all – at least, not as what the witnesses "see." The thing may have six arms, instead of eight arms... I know that when I was in India, I was impressed at the number of people who were seeing the multi-armed gods of India. Whatever your belief is, these manifestations are going to assume that form.

Q: Do you think that all UFO sightings are hallucinatory?

No, I've seen a lot of these things myself. [Most] UFOs seem to be a form of energy rather than a mechanical object. That's why we have all of these injuries – people burned by them. The UFOs are putting out energy. I decided this years ago, after having some pretty cool sightings of my own. They seem to be masses of energy that have an intelligence of their own. A lot of witnesses also remark on that. They say, "You know, I think that thing was *alive*." I've heard that phrase over and over again from witnesses.

Q: Do you think that they're from Earth's energy field?

[They are] from this planet and this energy field, yes. I also think that if we lived on some other planet, we would be seeing UFOs, too, and wondering about them. I think they're definitely related to the human race. If we didn't exist, the UFOs wouldn't exist.

Q: Do you see a one-world government coming?

No. Maybe in the long run, 500 years down the road... I don't think we would ever be able to pull that off [today]. There are just too many differences in races and cultures...

Q: In your books, you mention "the great phonograph in the sky" – how it's stuck in this groove, giving prophecies of apocalypse. We're seeing spates of these prophecies again as the millennium approaches. Do you think the great phonograph is playing again?

Yes. In 1841, everyone went and sat on a hilltop, waiting for the end of the world. They did that in the 1950s, too, and they did it just recently again. We're going to hear that over and over again, because people who are tuned into the cosmic intelligence always get a garbled message; and it's always that the world is about to end next week. And it never ends… We'll just get more garbled messages next week.

KEEL, JOHN – MEMORIES AND UFOS – 1993 LECTURE EXCERPT

In my travels, I was always looking for people who had actually seen a flying saucer. I have interviewed thousands of people over the years. If I didn't interview them, I at least talked to them. Very few of these people ever saw a disc-shaped object. They'd seen all kinds of other crazy objects – objects shaped like question marks and so on – but very few had seen a disc. I remember two discs in particular that impressed me. One was in West Virginia. A fellow had been near an abandoned mine. He said he heard something like a buzzsaw first. And there, in the air over the entrance to the mine, were two very small discs. They seemed to be spinning rapidly like a buzzsaw would spin. They scared the hell out of him. They were just hovering over this little area. I talked to him at great length because I was so intrigued by this. I even went out and looked at the mine. You could only get a few feet into it. It had collapsed over the years.

All over the world, we've had reports of flying cylinders. If you are familiar with any of the literature, you know about some of these cases. About five years ago, a Delta airliner was flying at 30,000 feet and saw one of these flying cylinders coming straight for it. The pilot became very concerned because it looked like they were going to collide. Instead, at the last minute, the cylinder moved over to the side. This story got universal publicity in all the newspapers and news shows, and many of you probably remember it. These cylinders roughly look like a torpedo, except that they don't have any fins or motors at the back. There is no indication of propulsion. They are just metal cylinders – if it's metal at all. It could be plastic, it could be Styrofoam; we don't know. Around that same time, a Spanish reconnaissance plane took some photographs of one of these cylinders. The photographs were widely published. The pilot of the plane gave a long testimony on what had happened. He had flown up to the cylinder. He had circled the cylinder. Then, while he was still circling the cylinder, it disappeared. It didn't fly away. It just simply vanished from view, like a magician's trick. This is something that we hear about a lot in flying saucer reports.

When I was in Scandinavia a few years ago, I heard stories from people who had been walking along beaches and seen these cylinders. Usually, the cylinders would be five or ten feet off of the ground, just sort of floating by. They didn't make any sound, and they were all roughly the same size, which is about ten feet long and three or four feet in diameter. Again, they look like torpedoes, flying along without any sign of propulsion – no fire coming out of the back, no noises, no propellers spinning. They weren't flying [as much as] they were levitating. These cylinders are an old story. Back in the 1960s, when we had a massive UFO wave all over the world, there was one case that got a lot of notoriety. A teenage boy was behind a police station in London, Ontario when he saw one of these cylinders. It was just hovering a couple feet off the ground. The boy went up and touched it. He got a bad burn from it, and photographs of the boy's burn became famous. They were printed in papers around the world: "Boy Burned by Mystery Object." And this was right behind a police station! What the hell was this thing doing behind a police station? After the boy touched it, of course, it just soared off.

A lot of these cylinders are related with water; ships see them at sea. They're seen coming out of the water or going into the water. In the 1960s, we had a series of sightings at the Wanaque Reservoir in New Jersey, which is about 40 miles outside of New York City. These things were going into the reservoir, which led a lot of people to give up drinking the water. Mobs of people went out to the Wanaque Reservoir hoping to see these things. One of the local policemen had some very bizarre experiences. When he saw one of these things, he went deaf for three days. It was emitting some kind of sound frequency that deafened him. There was another policeman there that began to get strange, mysterious phone calls. Most policemen, as you know, have unlisted phone numbers. He didn't know how they got his phone number. We had some Men in Black incidents at the Wanaque Reservoir, too. Sightings of MIBs at reservoirs are common... All over the world, we have these cylinder sightings. In Sweden and Norway, they have many lakes. These things have been coming down into the lakes and causing great consternation. The local UFO buffs are always trying to plumb the bottom of lakes and get to whatever is down there. Of course, they never find anything. In 1905, off the coast of Africa, there was a ship that saw something come up out of the water and fly away. It seemed like a very large cylinder – a submarine shaped thing. The [trouble] is that, in 1905, there weren't many submarines around. Submarines were just being developed in that period. This was one of our first sightings of something coming out of the water and flying away.

I want to mention one more thing here, just to boggle your mind a little bit. There is a fellow who has lived in Russia most of his life [but who] now lives in California. He is able to read and translate Russian. He puts out a newsletter called *UFO Encounters*. He has a piece called "The Soviet Underwater Mystery." There was one case in particular that happened in the summer of 1982. He gives the names of these people, but I can't pronounce them. He said that the Russian frogmen working for the military – naval frogmen – were training at a lake called the Icic Kul lake in Turkistan. They were diving into this lake, practicing whatever frogmen practice. Suddenly they encountered a group of mysterious swimmers underwater. They said that these swimmers were dressed in silvery, skintight outfits. They were human-shaped, but they were about 9 feet tall and wore a spherelike helmet on their heads. They didn't seem to have oxygen tanks or any of the usual equipment with them. They swam around these frogmen, scared the hell out of them and, to make a very long story short, the frogmen surfaced too fast in their fear. They got "the bends" and three of them died. The fourth one has been an invalid ever since. The editor gives all of the names and dates in his newsletter. It probably took him months to get it all together and translate it…

But we've been hearing stories about phantom frogmen since the 1960s. If we looked into the right sources, we would probably find them going further back. I remember up near Ithaca, New York, there was a big UFO wave in the 1960s. Some people there reported driving by what was not much more than a pond when, suddenly, two or three frogmen came out of the pond! They were dressed in the full gear of frogmen. The frogmen got into a car and drove away. This seemed very peculiar, because it was late at night. If you go diving then, you're not going to be able to see a damn thing underwater. And why would they be there anyway? We've had a number of these frogmen reports from different parts of the country; it is a mystery. Who are these frogmen, and what are they doing in our ponds?

Q: John, what is your opinion of the studies in California, by Alvin Mossing, on the contactee phenomenon?

He did the same kind of studies that I did some years ago. He took people who had never had a UFO experience and hypnotized them. He told them, "You have just had an experience with a flying saucer; now tell us about it." That's all you need to do. The hypnotized person will go into elaborate detail about the "flying saucer" experience. It would be identical to many of the published reports, although this person actually had never had any experience; it was just suggested to them. I got into it in the 1960s because they had done it on CBS. They hypnotized a man on television and told him, "CBS is plotting to take over the world. You have attended one of the meetings of the conspirators. We want you to tell us what it was all about." And he went off into this big story. He described the meeting room, everybody in the meeting room – the whole [thing]. It all sounded very logical that CBS was out to take over the world... Ha! Actually, now that I think about it, it *is* true that CBS wants to take over the world! *[laughter]*

[You have to be careful] in ufology. There was a young investigator in Massachusetts who was seeing alligators all the time. The alligators were chasing him. He'd go into the bathroom and there would be an alligator in the bathroom. He'd get into his car and there'd be an alligator in his car. He was hallucinating *alligators*. A friend of mine, Dr. Berthold Schwarz, who is a psychiatrist and one of our better-known UFO investigators, went up there to investigate. Schwarz found this poor young man sitting in his apartment with a shotgun on his lap. He'd been seeing the Men in Black, too. But because he'd been seeing the alligators, we couldn't take his Men in Black story very seriously... We had another case up in Maine where a young UFO investigator had seen some UFOs... He started being followed by Cadillacs with mysterious Men in Black in them. He decided he was going to bag one of these Men in Black. So, he got a shotgun. He was driving around one night, looking for UFOs, when this Cadillac appeared. He got out of his car and fired at the Cadillac, trying to shoot the driver. It turned out that the driver was one of his best friends, and the Cadillac wasn't a Cadillac at all: it was his friend's old, beat-up Ford. This man's mind was so geared up that he was seeing things. He was seeing a black Cadillac with a Man in Black in it. And he damn near killed one of his friends.

KEEL, JOHN – ANCHORS – FROM *UFOS: OPERATION TROJAN HORSE* (PP. 171-174)

The following story is from the pages of the *Houston Daily Post* (April 28, 1897):

> Merkel, Texas, April 26 – Some parties returning from
> church last night noticed a heavy object dragging along with
> a rope attached. They followed it until it caught on a rail
> crossing the railroad. On looking up, they saw what they

supposed was the airship. It was not near enough to get an idea of the dimensions. A light could be seen protruding from several windows; one bright light was in front, like the headlight of a locomotive. After some ten minutes, a man was seen descending the rope. He came near enough to be plainly seen. He wore a light-blue sailor suit, small in size. He stopped when he discovered parties at the anchor. He cut the rope below him and sailed off in a northeast direction. The anchor is now on exhibition at the blacksmith shop of Elliot and Miller, and is attracting the attention of hundreds of people.

A small man in a blue sailor suit climbing down a rope from the sky… Rather silly, isn't it? Sillier still, researchers have discovered two identical stories in very obscure historical texts. An ancient Irish manuscript, the *Speculum Regali*, gives us this account from A.D. 956:

A marvel happened in the borough of Cloera, one Sunday while people were at mass. In this town, there is a church to the memory of St. Kinarus. It befell that a metal anchor was dropped from the sky, with a rope attached to it, and one of the sharp flukes caught in the wooden arch above the church door. The people rushed out of the church and saw, in the sky, a ship with men on board, floating at the end of the anchor cable. They saw a man leap overboard and pull himself down the cable to the anchor, as if to unhook it. He appeared as if he were swimming in water. The folk rushed up and tried to seize him, but the bishop forbade the people to hold the man, for fear it might kill him. The man was freed and hurried up the cable to the ship, where the crew cut the rope and the ship rose and sailed away out of sight. The anchor is in the church as a testimony to this singular occurrence.

For many years, a church in Bristol, England, is said to have had a very unique grille on its doors: a grille made from *another* anchor that allegedly came from the sky. Around A.D. 1200, during the observance of a feast day, the anchor came plummeting out of the sky trailing a rope. It got caught in a mound of stones, according to the story. As a mob of church-goers gathered around to watch, a "sailor" came down the rope, hand over hand, to free it. This crowd succeeded in grabbing him. They pushed him back and forth until, according to the Gervase of Tilbury's account in the rare manuscript *Otia Imperialia*, "He suffocated by the mist of our moist atmosphere, and expired." His unseen comrades overhead wisely cut the rope and took off. The anchor remained behind, as in the other stories, and was installed on the church doors… Researcher Lucius Farish remarked:

> Reviewing the similarities of these reports, one is almost tempted to speculate that someone merely updated the ancient accounts. Yet, a citizen of Merkel, Texas, possessing a copy of [a rare manuscript like] the *Speculum Regali* in 1897 would be fully as fantastic as the reports themselves.

A farmer fifteen miles north of Sioux City, Iowa, Robert Hibbard, claimed a distressing experience with an anchor-dragging UFO early in April, 1897. A dispatch that appeared in the April 5th edition of Michigan's *Saginaw Evening News* stated that "Hibbard's reputation for truth has never been bad, and the general opinion is that either he 'had them' or dreamed his remarkable experience." The article continues:

> On the night in question, he says he was tramping about his farm in the moonlight when suddenly, a dark body, lighted on each side, with a row of what looked like incandescent lamps, loomed up some distance to the south of him, at a height of perhaps a mile from the ground. He watched it intently until it was directly over his head.

At this point, the skipp evidently decided to turn around. In accomplishing this maneuver, the machine sank considerably. Hibbard did not notice a drag rope with a grapnel attached, which dangled from the rear of the [object]. Suddenly, as the machine rose again from the ground, it hooked itself firmly in his trousers and shot away again to the south. Had it risen to any considerable height, the result, Hibbard thinks, would have been disastrous. Either his weight was sufficient to keep it near terra firma, or the operator did not care to ascend to a higher level.

> On the bank of the dry run, where the farmer finally made his escape, grows a small sapling. Hibbard passed near this obstruction in his flight and, as a last resort, grabbed it with both hands. Instantly there was a sound of tearing cloth, and the machine went on with a section of Hibbard's unmentionables. Hibbard himself fell precipitately into the run. He related his experience to neighbors and, despite their grins of incredulity, firmly maintains the truth of the story.

We have only two choices: We can either dismiss all four of these stories as being somehow derivative of one another and pure poppycock; or, we can assume that mysterious airships, all dragging anchors, appeared in

956, 1200, and 1897. There are, in fact, a number of other reports in which UFOs were said to be dragging something along the ground. That still doesn't prove that anchors are standard equipment on some of the objects. If they were using anchors, what could the purpose have been? Could some of the early UFOs have been so primitive that the only way they could hover was by being anchored to the ground? Would spaceships from another world require anchors?

In 2003, a post was made to the local Mothman discussion list from a lady named "Barbara," who reported seeing a rope fall from the sky near her home in Youngstown, OH. Mothman researcher John Frick went to Barb's neighborhood a couple of times to check it out. On the first visit, he encountered a miracle at a church near her house – what appeared to be a real, bonafide "bleeding statue" of the Virgin Mary. However, he did not actually meet Barb on that trip; he met her on his second trip, which was in Nov. 2006. Following that meeting, Frick and his brother, Tim, were seemingly followed by Men in Black in a white van bearing the government license plate "11-1L," which they were able to photograph. Later, they got a call – possibly from the MIBs themselves – that led to the address 1111 Independence Ave. in Akron, where one finds heavy Masonic symbolisms. From the sky, the two original buildings at 1111 Independence Ave. look like a Masonic "11." Amazingly, in 2009, Mothman was seen only a mile or two away from 1111 Independence Ave., just days before I visited the area.

Barbara described herself as an amateur astronomer. She said she was married to a NASA employee with a serious heart condition, who worked on "classified" projects at the NASA facility next to Cleveland's Hopkins Airport. This facility is not far from where UFOs have been seen coming in and out of Lake Erie... Barb held an eBay auction in 2005 for a slice of toast she had made, which had the image of Jesus Christ's face on it. I checked the photo and, amazingly, it did look like Jesus. However, Barb seemed embarrassed that her auction had been revealed, and soon withdrew from the discussion list... Prior to that, Barb posted many times about a wide variety of supposed phenomena in her life, the timing of which often seemed highly coincidental to events in the lives of others on the list. The events were so coincidental that some list members began to openly wonder if she was making some of the stories up.

A couple of years after Frick's harrowing encounter with the MIB, some additional buildings were built at 1111 Independence Avenue. Amazingly, they formed "11-1L" when viewed from the sky — just as presaged by the MIBs' license plate! Oddly, a highly publicized UFO was seen over O'Hare Airport the same week Frick saw the MIB van in 2006. Around that time, Frick, Harriet Plumbrook, and myself were receiving phone calls from the number "000-000-0000." The following year, in 2007, doppelgangers of both Frick and Plumbrook were seen in the vicinity of the Mothman Festival in Pt. Pleasant... As I mentioned, Barb disappeared soon after her auction for the Jesus Toast. However, other women quickly showed up to pound out more fantastic new tales that, just as before, included practically the entire paranormal pantheon. These tales, many of which are obscure enough to require extensive research, continue to this day... Some of Barb's early posts were classics, leading Frick to declare her the "most interesting poster" ever on the list. Here is Barbara's rope story, dated 11/05/03:

No one will probably believe this... I took Jack outside around 12:10. My husband was up watching TV in the living room; everyone else was asleep. The neighborhood was mostly dark; no one else had lights on. Jack wanted to go across the street, into the field at the bottom of the school parking lot. We climbed up the hill a bit and he smelled around. The skies had a faint band of clouds over them. I could see the moon and Mars clearly, and most of the brighter stars. Just as we crossed the street and were heading up the hill, something fell out of the sky in front of me, about ten feet away; it seemed to almost snap. It looked like a rope or a cable or something. It was dark. I couldn't get a really good look at it, but it resembled a cable or a thin rope. I stopped short. Jack didn't notice this thing, or wasn't worried about it, because he tried to drag me in that direction. I wouldn't move. I kept staring up into the air, looking for something. All I could see was that this thing, whatever it was, kept going up. It was dark, and I lost it in the air. There was *nothing* over my head — no dark craft or anything. I could see stars. I grabbed Jack and moved back to the curb, revving up my inner engine in case this thing moved towards me. I got to the curb and stepped out in the street. Whatever this was whipped up, like a snapped rope, and vanished. I ran across the street to the porch. Jack was annoyed because I made him [urinate] off the porch into the bushes. We then cautiously went to the side of the house, where he went some more. But I wasn't about to go out in the yard. I kept looking up, but there was nothing above me – no dark shape, and nothing but sky.

After Barb left the list, a second woman named Barbara, with a new last name yet similar writing style, began posting. She wrote this message on 5/27/08, nearly five years after the first Barb's rope story:

This was a dream about a fatal car crash. I didn't know it, though, at the time. I just knew it was a psychic dream… In my dream, I was driving along a certain road, in a certain location I knew of, when something light as a feather touched the back of my shoulder and drew a line across my back – to the other shoulder – beneath my neck. It alerted me to an [unearthly] feeling. The dream stayed with me. I knew in the dream that when that 'something' touched the back of my shoulders, it meant something inevitable was going to happen. I just *knew* this. I couldn't control whatever it was. It was like walking into fate. Many things unfolded, telling me that the dream had come true… A woman who worked for me had to leave my employ this past week. We had decided to be friends the first day she applied for the job. She had only worked for me for a few months. We seemed to be getting closer and closer. We were planning to go places and do things together. She kept saying that she thought she had met me for a reason. She was interested in spiritual things and the paranormal, as I am. We had just decided that we would begin our friendship [as equals after she quit]. When I got back from my vacation in June, we would go to church. I wanted her to experience a healing ceremony. We said that we would keep in touch by phone until after my vacation. This Wednesday night (May 21, at 9:00) was the last time I spoke to her. On the next day, the day of the week she normally worked for me, she was killed in a car crash. It was a gruesome accident. Her car hit a flatbed tow truck, which had fishtailed out of control. The driver was speeding, hit his breaks and lost control. The truck peeled off the top of my friend's car. She was pronounced dead on the scene… The truck driver had an emotional meltdown, there at the scene, and was taken to the hospital. [One] gal who saw everything said that she will never forget it. She was terribly upset, saying that if the truck had come over the line a second later, it would have been her in that fatal crash. She said that my friend had been decapitated. I will never forget my friend, Bonnie.

Coincidentally on 5/19/08, a couple of days before the new Barbara's friend was killed, I got the following email from my niece's new husband, Jordan Rogers. The email concerns a "wire" entity seen by my niece that, in retrospect, seems somewhat similar to what the first Barbara saw in 2003. The combination of ropes and/or wires, along with decapitation, makes for potent symbolism. Falling ropes allude to the magic carpet – the mobile "lover's lane" of the Orient – found in the Arabian Nights. Regardless of whether or not either Barbara ever made up certain stories, there is still the question of whether or not hoaxes have symbolic power. Many hoaxes in the paranormal pantheon do often seem to have a strange sort of relevance. This is one of the reasons we are widely taught as children not to "cry wolf" or practice unnecessary deception. Because of the psi-plasma's ability to transfer thought energy between individuals, great care must be taken. Sensitive individuals, like my niece, Sharon, seem to be bellwethers for messages carried on the psi-plasma. Both the Thunderbird and Garuda are archetypal symbols of the psi-plasma or Void, the medium that carries the messages. Sharon's husband, Jordan, describes Sharon's shocking encounter with a creature from another dimension:

Sharon saw it. She was trying to nap on the couch, but was twice brought back to full awareness with the feeling that someone was in the room. When she looked over, it was this wire creature. It wasn't a rope or wire in the sense of being a household tool; it was a creature, in and of itself. It had no face, eyes, or distinguishable parts other than its wire-body. Both times when it was seen, it began retreating slowly around the door frame into the kitchen. Sharon somehow managed to doze off again after seeing it the first time. However, she was again awakened, this time with the creature much closer to her (five feet). Again, it slowly backed away and around the door frame. Someone online told us that they used to see these things all the time; the wire creatures want to remain hidden, but are terrible at it. They were under the impression that these beings are like "muses," in that they will attach themselves to an unsuspecting host and bring him or her some insight. This also sounds like the "ally" in the Carlos Castaneda books. The allies are inorganic beings that can be caught and used by sorcerers. Allies will whisper things to the sorcerer that the sorcerer might have trouble learning on his or her own.

In 2005, there was a crossover period, prior to the Jesus Toast debacle, when both Barbaras were on the discussion list at the same time. At the end of June, they got into a discussion together over a recent group event, which was about watching the skies for UFOs on a particular night. It turned out that both of them had seen the same thing, even though one of them was living in Youngstown, and the other outside Cincinnati. First, the original Barbara wrote:

The tally tonight is: one shadow person, one unusual light in sky, and one bright gold orb… I actually had my best sighting Thursday night, but it falls outside the timeline [of our group watch]. I was looking northeast, when I noticed a plane's lights blinking. Above the plane, at about the distance of two full moons, was an unblinking, round, white light. I thought it was some kind of weird plane, but then I thought that if it were that low, I should be able to hear it. I ran in and got the 10x70 binoculars, and went out to look at it. The blinking lights were definitely from a plane, but the white light above was a round blob of light with no discernable features. Suddenly, the white light veered away in the opposite direction and flew off fast. It was so fast that I couldn't keep track of it in the binoculars. The plane continued on its way. I have no idea what the white light was… On Friday night, between10:00 and 12:00, a *mist* rolled off the roof of the house, dipped towards my 8-year old daughter, changed direction, and then flew over the neighbor's house. [We then saw another] shadow person, possibly the same one from the night before… Anyone else see anything? Visibility was rather poor last night. It is hot and humid here and the dewpoint is high. There is a lot of light pollution around us. On nights like this, it reflects off the haze.

Even though visibility was very poor, the second Barbara seemed to chime in with the original Barbara, concluding that they must have seen the same thing:

We seem to have similar experiences… I saw the same thing on June 23rd. It was a white light, looked like a star, but it was very low on the horizon (unlike the other stars), plus it was brighter. I watched for a half hour, thinking it looked like one of the UFO's I had seen recently, but decided it had to be just a star. It hovered there for a half hour as I watched (it had been there when I came outside). I decided nothing was going on and went to look in another direction in another field. Something silent that looked like a triangle came cruising at tree-top level in this other field of mine. Although it was low in the sky and silent, I am not certain about it being anything other than a plane. I went back to the other field to watch the star again, and it was gone! Evidently it wasn't a star. All of the (other) stars were still in the sky...

Following the release of The Mothman Prophecies *film in 2002, waves of paranormal activity would sweep through the lives of discussion list members. Often, a particular type of paranormal activity would start with one person and then, within a day or two, move on to two or three more people. The synchronicities would get really spooky, and people would get emotional. We will never know how many of the reports were real and how many were the result of hoaxes, psychological contagion, or mimicry. I think it is safe to say that at least some of them were real. According to Frick, who is very vigilant about hoaxers, most everyone was telling the truth. He thinks the Jesus Toast and other miracles reported by Barbara are genuine, having seen at least one of them himself. Knowing his tenacity for rooting out falsehoods, I temporarily filed the cases away as genuinely "unexplained." As an investigator, being patient – not revealing one's suspicions – sometimes pays off. By March of 2010, the second Barbara had convinced several others on the list that "calling UFOs" was possible, and that she had been doing it herself. Better than that, they could do it, too! This trend led to the following post from one of the ladies learning how to call UFOs:*

It got clear in our area yesterday. I went out at 10:00 at night to try to call UFOs. Nothing happened. I went back inside, and then realized that perhaps it wasn't a good time to call for them since I had just watched the movie *Signs*. I hadn't seen that movie in years. I forgot how it creeped me out. My daughter was watching it with me. She had never seen it before. In the part where they show the alien video for the first time, she actually screamed.... I decided to go back out around midnight, but didn't see anything. I did feel horribly creeped out, but I put that down to a reaction from seeing the movie. I went back inside. My daughter was waiting for me. She was waiting for me to come in so that she could go to bed. After seeing that movie, she wasn't going to go to bed until she was sure I came back inside safely. Around 3 minutes after I came inside, all the power went off in our house. It wasn't a blown fuse or anything; the power just went off. My daughter and I were standing by the living room drapes. We pulled the drapes back and, to our surprise, all the other houses on our street were lit! This freaked my daughter out a bit. My son had come downstairs with a flashlight. He calmly said he'd call the electric company. He left the room to go find the phone book in the kitchen drawer. My daughter and I were standing by the window. Suddenly, we saw a bright flash of light through the drapes, and our lights went back on. I ran into the driveway and looked up, but I didn't see anything. I went right back in because my daughter was really scared. She was afraid that something else would happen. We reset all the electric clocks, then we all went to bed. I don't know what happened; I don't think anyone could turn off the power to a house as a prank. The power was only off for around two minutes. Anyone have any ideas? Does anyone know of a way a prankster could have done this?

This elicited the following response from Phil Reynolds, the editor at Invisible College Press. Regardless of whether or not paranormal events are "caused" by the simple investigation of them, or are triggered by fantasy, hoax, or obsession, it is always wise to be conservative when dealing with the phenomenon:

A prankster could do it by removing your meter, or by throwing your main breaker, which is usually inside… If they pulled your meter, the seal will be broken – usually a metal wire looped through the latch and held together by a plastic or metal tag. It's made to show tampering. You might also have an external disconnect, which would be in a metal box near where the line comes into your house. It seems unlikely that a prankster would do it, unless they knew about your UFO activity and wanted to "gaslight" you, but check those things out. If any tampering has been done, report it to the power company. You might want to reconsider "calling" UFOs, given how upset your daughter is…

"The host of the paranormal podcast *The Paracast*, David

Biedny, recently discussed a mysterious UFO photo that he seems to think is real. Biedny presents himself as an 'image analysis expert' who once professored at Yale. He claims that the 'real' UFO photo also has some artificial elements added to it. It is his opinion that the photo was distributed as a sort of entrapment, set out for anyone willing to put their name on the line by supporting its validity. The photo came from an anonymous Internet handle known only as '0000000.' I couldn't help but notice the connection between this and the "000-0000" phone number that you spoke of and interviewed the Frick brothers about... Like most people, I have had my share of sporadic, weird events throughout my life. However, I experienced a huge onslaught of synchronicities and weirdness [in the run-up to 9/11] between November 1999 and October 2001. Like the encounters with that phone number, many aspects of the accounts detailed in your [second] book ring true with my own experiences, including the fact that there seems to be a very natural and [yet] sometimes 'synthetic' nature to the experiences. I have often wondered where these boundaries begin, end, and overlap."

-Joshua Bell 3/09/08

 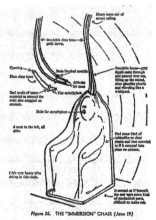 

Artist Jim Woodring, a friend of the author, drew a precognitive "9/11 drawing" the day before the tragedy in 2001. Woodring's drawing of a "tree mouth" (left) is reminiscent of Colvin's 1973 encounter with what may have been Mothman coming out of a tree - and perhaps wanting to communicate. Contactee Betty Andreasson, who saw the legendary Phoenix in a vision, reported being telepathically interrogated by "aliens" while in a clear plastic chair enclosure (center). The scarred husk of a possible Garuda statue in New Mexico's Bandelier National Monument (right) seems to mimic the seating position required not only by Andreasson's aliens, but also by the reputed mind-control doctors of Montauk.

CHAPTER 16

"Reports that say that something hasn't happened are interesting to me because, as we know, there are known knowns; there are things we *know* we know. We also know there are known unknowns; that is to say, we know there are some things we do *not* know. But, there are also unknown unknowns – the ones we *don't* know we don't know."

-Donald Rumsfeld, former U.S. Defense Secretary

"Corrupted by wealth and power, your government is like a restaurant with only one dish. They've got a set of Republican waiters on one side and a set of Democratic waiters on the other side. But no matter which set of waiters brings you the dish, the legislative grub is all prepared in the same Wall Street kitchen."

-Huey Long

"As soon as the relations of exploitation and the violence that underlies them are no longer concealed by the mystical veil, there is a breakthrough – a moment of clarity. The struggle against alienation is suddenly revealed as a ruthless hand-to-hand fight against naked power – power exposed in its brute force and weakness – a vulnerable giant. [It is a] sublime moment when the complexity of the world becomes tangible and transparent – within everyone's grasp…"

-Raoul Vaneigem, *Situationist International Anthology*

COLVIN, ANDY – GRASSY KNOLL RADIO INTERVIEW 32 – JULY 2008

"Vyz" at *Beyond the Grassy Knoll* (GK): This is *Beyond the Grassy Knoll,* and our interview series with Andrew Colvin continues. When we last spoke with Andrew at Knollapalooza, there was a weird technical glitch. I got dropped. Everybody was kidding around with me in the chatroom about how I must have been snoozing, but I wasn't; Andrew soldiered on. If anyone can take a dead-air situation and fill it, it would be him. Thanks a lot for coming back on.

Andy Colvin (AC): Thanks for having me. That chatroom was fun.

GK: It *was*, wasn't it?

AC: You must have slept for days after that. It was very close to a real 24-hr. marathon. I just want to give you "props" for doing it. It's not easy to do that many interviews in a row.

GK: The idea was to do them well, then sleep after it was over. We got into the really good stuff with you, Phillip Coppins from the U.K., Angie Reidel, Ellen Lacter, and Dave McGowan. We talked about some serious subjects that are very real – mind control and such. A few of the shows were pre-records. For the live shows, I chose you guys, because I know all of you.

AC: The technical glitch happened when I was talking about a crucial period in April, 2008. The Pope was in the U.S. It was an extremely active month. I was reeling off this stuff. Then, there was the glitch. *[jokingly]* I still think it was the NSA that glitched it. We should probably touch on a few of those points again, because something in there obviously hit a nerve.

GK: Your timeline/calendar is a living, breathing thing. You are staying with it. You and I have done the most interviews I've ever done with anybody. How do you look at all this? What's really going on?

AC: I think it's a great, grand adventure. But, then again, I am not a normal person. I have a very unusual personal history. I do things differently, sometimes even completely backwards. By going the "wrong" way, you can often find the right way, or at least reveal the pressures that are being applied to control your behavior. If we censor ourselves, then things get out of balance. There is an old Russian saying: "If everyone pulled together, the world would topple over." So I follow my heart. People sometimes have difficulty wrapping their heads around what I do and say, especially when it comes to art. But doing projects unconventionally, using multiple methods (e.g., video, print, photography, music, language) has allowed me to encompass the entire matrix. It reveals the map I can see in my head, so that other people can look at it. As far as Mothman goes, there are different players in the paranormal and conspiracy worlds that seem excited about the map I am seeing. Somebody wrote yesterday and said, "If you were doing this project to help someone, you've done it." They were happy and felt a connection… There are a lot of people out there who are in crisis. They have experienced strange, synchronistic events but do not have a context for them. Perhaps they are not used to seeing reality as conscious, alive, and plastic. Informing or reminding them that they are fully connected to that living reality can sometimes help. To aid someone, even if it is a stranger, makes me very happy. It's usually not something you can make a living at, but it is always fulfilling on a personal level.

GK: It was really interesting… I'd press you a little bit more each time on the Rockefeller–West Virginia connection. In the beginning, you were a little tentative, which was fine. But eventually, we found some kind of kindredness. We were okay with what we were doing. Then, we went on and on and on, and trust grew between us. We are okay with other views. Listeners were initially drawn in by the weirdness, but there is a serious element to it, too. There are multiple things going on. You can't plan this kind of thing; neither you nor I were the architect of where this went. We just let it go, and that's the best thing you can do. I don't know that it would have happened with anybody else. Where it's going to go I don't know, but I'm happy for it. I never thought we would be here, but here we are. I'm not interested in cutting this thing short anytime soon…

AC: These are really important times to chronicle. We may be sliding into a more openly fascist state; it's important to have some documentation of just how it was done. We need to keep constant tabs on this ever-evolving field of mass mind control. The elites seem to keep track of how to best control events, and so should we.

GK: It's funny… I remember being 7 years old and being very, very sad. I had measles on top of chicken pox – multiple diseases. My parents had saved newspapers from WWII. I read them, and my eyeballs just popped. I discovered what was going on… In this day and age, the printed word is sliding. But you and I have done something else: a digital recording. You've got to wonder if somebody someday, like your grandchild, will take a look at this CD – this crude form of recording – and play it, and ask, as H.G. Wells did, "Was there *really* a time like this?"

AC: I'm sure that that will happen with my son, because he is interested in this stuff. You and I talked about the Beatles and Tavistock – that they may have programmed the hippie movement. My son and I have been watching some of the old Beatles cartoons. He refers to John Lennon as the "strong one." He asked me the other day, "What happened to the Strong One?" Somewhere along the way, he had heard that the Strong One wasn't alive anymore… I said, "The

Strong One is dead now." He was upset by that news. It *is* weird how the Beatles burrow into our psyches. Right now, I'm trying to avoid giving my son the details of Lennon's death (i.e., murder by mind-controlled agent). Some day, when he realizes what really happened to Lennon, maybe he will do some research on him. Mark David Chapman, the shooter, links to World Vision, Jonestown, the CIA, the Bushes, the Rockefellers, and so on. Chapman went missing right before the murder. The Lennon story probably connects up with the Mothman events in some circuitous fashion... Anyway, maybe some good *will* come out of our doing this series.

GK: Without a doubt...

AC: We've got to keep the flame of intellectual freedom alive.

GK: Some child will take this arcane, old-fashioned thing, a CD, and throw it on the future's equivalent of a 70-rpm turntable and go, "Holy mackerel, check this out!" This series could be a hoot of a time capsule. Speaking of which, let's talk about April 2008 and see where that may lead.

AC: Okay... There was so much stuff in April that's it frightening. The highlight of the month was the Pope's visit. When the Pope came into the country, Bush broke protocol. Rather than stay at the White House, Bush went down to the tarmac to welcome the pontiff personally, which no president had ever done before. The stories in the media were alive with incantation. They were trying to tamp down popular rage resulting from the many recent pedophilia lawsuits against the Catholic Church. So, they found a polygamist cult in Texas that looked *worse* than the Catholic Church! Texas state officials went after the cult and took the kids away, resulting in a potent media distraction. When we got to April 19th, the eve of Hitler's birthday, the stories in the media started having an intriguing two-sidedness to them. They all had a weird "twist." One suspects that this was a deliberate attempt to induce confusion in the mass mind. For instance, in hypnotherapy, confusion is used to *deepen* hypnosis, not lessen it. The conscious mind is occupied by confusion at the moment any intended programming is sent into the subconscious.

GK: Shakespeare understood how dangerous were the Ides of March. And April has been very interesting in modern times, featuring everything from Hitler's birthday, to Waco, to the Oklahoma City bombing. I'm forgetting a whole lot more of them, too. It makes you wonder... All of a sudden, this has become some kind of target date where things are going to get weird.

AC: Leading up to the Ides of April, we had some bad economic news. We had a big bank bailout for WaMu and lots of housing foreclosures. It feels like a run-up to a new invasion. Ultimately, it will result in the gutting of the middle class in America. They will raise the oil prices to a crisis point, milking as much as they can before the entire thing collapses. If it does collapse and they don't get their bailouts, there might be terrorism and resulting crackdowns. It's all about squeezing the excess cash out of the population – a hidden type of economic reform. The World Bank and IMF often do it in Third World countries using power projects, so that energy companies can get resources more cheaply. They're doing that here now. Foreigners will own a lot more of our utilities. Homeland Security is about making sure that the population here stays under control as the overall standard of living is lowered. So… On the 11th, GE had a huge profit drop, the G7 finance ministers met, and E. coli bacteria was found in the water system in Clarksburg, WV. This was the week before the Pope got here. We had some scares to get people primed. The elites had some problems that they wanted us to ignore. We found out that Cheney had indeed "okayed" torture. Fears of a nuclear Iran were creeping in. As always, they threw in some paranormal stuff. It creates this odd mix in the mind. The paranormal stuff allows people to breathe for a second. People really do believe in the supernatural. So, they will throw in a Bermuda Triangle story, which is what we saw on the 12th. The word "Bermuda" makes you think of going on vacation, which is now almost a thing of the past due to the high price of oil.

GK: It gives people a distraction they can most happily hang onto…

AC: Yes, and when it gets to those key dates, there will be stories with confusion built into them. It's not just about one story conflicting with another; it's also about stories that have internal confusion built *into* them. This causes the conscious mind to get confused, occupied, and prepped for other programming. So if you're a hypnotherapist, you count the person down into relaxation *incorrectly*. You say, "Okay, I'm going to count backwards from one hundred." And, as you go, you get the numbers wrong, which confuses the patient. Then, at the moment of confusion, your very next verbal suggestion goes immediately into the subconscious. You usually instruct them to go deeper into the hypnosis at that point but, once they are deeply under hypnosis, you could introduce another form of confusion followed by instructions to carry out some national security task

– anything you want. Confusion is a standard technique. I suspect that they are doing it with media stories, too.

GK: Confusion in the media becomes a big element from this time forward. I think we mentioned this during Knollapalooza. It was pretty poignant. Chris Knowles has been agonizing over the fact that, for those of us who see clearly, sometimes there is a price to pay. I imagine you know that as well. He was trying to dance around some stuff; he just didn't want to come out with it.

AC: He's human; he doesn't want himself or his family to suffer negative consequences... The controllers use confusion selectively; that is the best way to do it. They don't do it all the time because, then, the confusion becomes normalized. People's minds are so facile that they will get used to anything in due time. You can only use confusion sporadically. Ordinary people use this technique everyday in their personal lives. They will often dissemble when you are on track to hold them accountable. People instinctively know that confusion may work to get them out of a jam. Groups try to structure in confusion using various means. Because of our penchant for class hierarchy, we usually give elites more latitude to sow confusion. These tendencies will only increase as society becomes more narcissistic. The drawbacks of being a "loser" are now so great that no one can take responsibility for screwing up.

GK: The stimulus needs to be inconsistent. If you *don't* always feed the animal afterwards, there will be better reinforcement.

AC: Yes. It's the uncertainty principle; consciousness needs variation... Leading up to the Pope's visit, food riots started on April 13th. The Dalai Lama was in Seattle that weekend, which was pretty odd. Why was the Dalai Lama here right before the Pope came? Maybe he works the West Coast, while the Pope handles the East Coast? The Dalai Lama has been on TV before, of course, helping people work through their feelings about 9/11. As you might expect, the media alluded to 9/11 in various ways that week. You had Bush talking about a "new 9/11" possibly being planned. On the 14th, my wife got a call from the 000-0000 (all zero) telephone number. On that same day, oddly, a big oil field was discovered in Brazil. You and I were talking earlier about those Brazilian UFOs that shot people with rays – how they are probably oil company reconnaissance craft looking for underground deposits. While some of these laserbeam strikes may have been accidental, some may have targeted recalcitrant natives who were "in the way." Blaming the deaths on ETs was kind of brilliant, when you think about it. Interestingly, there was a UFO case in West Virginia, which Keel investigated, where two little orbs were hovering outside an abandoned mine. Massey Coal, or perhaps some competitor of theirs, is probably keeping tabs on these old mines using remote vehicles.

GK: In one of the early James Bond movies, a chimera was created by the bad guys to scare the natives, so that scamming could be done on the side. Could we be looking at a realization – entangled within the UFO mystery – of what Bond author Ian Fleming wrote about ten years before?

AC: The evidence points that way. By the way, Fleming was a member of the British spy group called "XX." Those double X's are among the oldest occult symbols. They later morphed into the Masonic compass and square.

In 2010, Morgan Freeman's show, Through the Wormhole, *discussed what is believed to be the secret to magnetism and gravity: four types of particles within the 248 "dimensions" making up the E8 mathematical shape, which is based on the torus – itself the basis of the ancient Hebrew alphabet. The four particles were shown in a "X" shape, making one wonder if the "XX" symbol doesn't refer to gravity and antigravity, respectively. How the ancients might have discovered this secret is anyone's guess, but it may have played a role in the building of stone monuments like the Great Pyramid, whose construction remains a mystery.*

AC: In the 1960s, Jacques Cousteau discovered a tribe of small, hairless, bug-eyed natives in New Guinea who lived in caves. Peter Moon thinks such natives might have been used to fly Nazi-designed UFOs, such as the one that may have crashed at Roswell. Around the time of Mothman, the Rockefellers had already outfitted a plane that shot radar sideways to look for underground oil and mineral deposits. By the late 1970s, they may have had smaller ones flying around. There *did* seem to be a cover-up around these UFO deaths, particularly in Brazil. A doctor from the U.S. went down there, trying to help the natives. Her life was more or less threatened. She was forced to back off, and the files were confiscated by the military. Brazil has always had its share of weird ops. Puharich was down there studying psychic healers. There is a mining region there, Minas Gerais, where a lot of UFOs have been seen.

In Nov. 2008, I was in Charleston, WV visiting my sister, when I discovered that a doctor of hers, Alex DeSousa, was from Minas

Gerais. The colorful DeSousa, who uniquely combines shamanic and western methods in his practice, described cash-strapped Minas Gerais as the "West Virginia of Brazil." Could the mining companies in both places, and perhaps even the UFOs, be owned by the same people?

AC: Not long after the Bhopal, India incident, Carbide sent their leftover supplies of that deadly Bhopal gas to *Brazil*. The only other locations where that gas was made were Institute, WV and Texas City, TX. Keep in mind that Mothman was seen primarily in WV, TX, and Brazil in the 1960s and '70s. The Rockefellers have a lot of power in all of those places... But the Pope finally came to D.C. on the 16th. On that day, the media revisited the Virginia Tech shooting story, perhaps to remind us of terror and how Catholicism is at least better than terrorism. There was a WWII story from the Netherlands, where an ex-Nazi was indicted. This reminded us that Catholicism is better than Nazism, too, even though the two were closely intertwined. The media threw in some racial Islamic fear on that day, too, with the story of a wayward Minneapolis schoolteacher who was educating kids about the meaning of Islam... Benjamin Netanyahu made some controversial 9/11 comments, saying it was good for Israel that 9/11 happened. The Pope started apologizing about Catholic pedophilia just as the polygamist sect in Texas hit the news. This fundamentalist Mormon group was engaged in something that could be *misconstrued* as pedophilia, only because some of the wives were rather young. This subtextually indoctrinated us with the idea that the Catholic Church's pedophilia isn't as bad as other forms of religious pedophilia.

About a month after the aforementioned polygamist raid at "Yearning For Zion" Ranch, a large contingent of those children taken into custody by the State of Texas were ordered returned to their parents. It turned out that the original phone calls claiming abuse at the ranch were a "hoax" perpetrated by a woman named Rozita Swinton, who has a long history of such hoaxes. The fact that Swinton continues to get away with such antics could mean that she is a "protected" spy or provocateur, whose activities are condoned by officialdom.

AC: Mormonism seems to be a hybrid religion combining earth energies with angelic ETs. They have huge underground vaults containing compendious lineage charts. The word "Mormon," interestingly, contains the two words that I've been talking about so much: "moor" and "mon." Joseph Smith found those crucial tablets under the ground. He later claimed to have received inspired messages from the angel "Moroni." While it all sounds a bit concocted, I suppose it *is* possible that Smith had some real paranormal experience. Mormonism seems to draw on beliefs that already existed in America before the Europeans got here. The Spaniards who came "first," the Conquistadors, reportedly used the knowledge of the Moors who had come earlier. Some of the sailors on the Spanish ships were Moors. The term "moorage" comes from the fact that the Moors were known as great sailors. There are ancient reliefs at Monte Alban, above Oaxaca in Mexico, which clearly depict blacks and whites fighting the Olmecs many centuries ago. It seems that Joseph Smith and his Masonic buddies took some of the earlier symbols, mishmashed them up into a religion, and called it "Mormonism." It developed in the same area of New York where the Rockefellers got their start. Someone wrote to me that Rockefeller started off stealing horses in a little town in NY. This town, Owego, is where the Iroquois Federation was founded. The tenets of the Iroquois were supposedly influential in forming our Constitution. Women had equality in Iroquois society… But this spot where John D. Rockefeller grew up was sacred. He probably understood how important these spots were. It may have led to his oil and chemical companies taking over so many of these sacred spots. Today, this little town in the middle of nowhere, Owego, has strange things going. Owego is near Islamberg, where "Al Qaeda" supposedly trains terrorists. Owego is also very close to Apalachin, NY, where the Italian NYC mob was busted in 1957. One wonders if the Rockefellers took over and consolidated the mob at that time. Doug Valentine thinks that the FBI, CIA, Navy, and mob became integrated soon after that. In the 1960s, everybody fell in line against the hippies and war protesters.

GK: In my drifting days, up in South Royalton, Vermont, I visited the birthplace of Joseph Smith. Smith found the tablets and made his trek across the Midwest, through Illinois and, finally, to Utah. I'm sorry if I'm stepping on toes here, but there is a *very* close resemblance between the symbols of Freemasonry and Mormonism.

AC: Also, in that town of Owego, NY, you have Lockheed-Martin, which is the main operator in Denver near Columbine. You also have a company called Ensco in Owego. I'm not accusing them of anything, but Ensco does all of these different things that would have been utilized on 9/11. They do satellite tracking, defense transportation, robotics, underground facilities support, weather support for United Airlines, and NASA computer models involving the Space Shuttle. They do global positioning, also known as GPS. They work on the Presidential helicopter program, interfacing with Lockheed. They work with Boeing. They make "location devices" for use at emergency sites. If you have a steel building that has crumbled against all the known laws of physics, they can send in little robots to find survivors.

GK: My buddy, Pilot Pete, will never step foot in a helicopter. There's a reason why Presidents are usually in a plane and not a helicopter.

AC: According to Len Horowitz, right before 9/11, Bayer was on the ropes financially. After the anthrax attacks following 9/11, Cipro sales went way up, which literally saved Bayer. They made a half-billion dollars off of Cipro sales.

GK: Bayer was one of the companies birthed by the disassembling of I.G. Farben. The Bayer symbol on its aspirins is akin to the German iron cross, which goes back to the KKK and the Knight Templars.

AC: By the way, Dow and Bayer are now running the former Carbide plant in S. Charleston, WV... Did you know that prior to 9/11, the U.S. Army had an enormous wargame called the "Millennium Challenge?" John Judge spoke about this in 1989, when it was in its initial planning stages. No one knows exactly how much was spent on this full-scale exercise, which began in 2000. Some of it was done with computers. The virtual aspects of the exercise were designed to take place in Iraq. It is obvious that they were planning the invasion *before* Bush got selected to be President. The book *Blink*, by Malcolm Gladwell, describes how common sense, intuition, and "old school" physical methods eventually won the day during the Millennium Challenge... Back to our timeline... Once the Pope was here, the media stories started getting weirder and more contradictory. On the 18th, we had China and CNN involved in some fracas. We had the Homeland Security chief, Chertoff, saying that fingerprints aren't "personal" data anymore – an obvious contradiction... A lot of these stories are essentially koans that loop back onto themselves. Iran's president, Ahmadinejad, made a few "9/11 was an inside job" comments, which sounded purposely bungled. We already suspect that he thinks it was an inside job, so why did it come across so badly? Then, we had Morgan Spurlock, who made the *Finding Osama* movie, changing his tune. Instead of saying what he had said before, which is that he had actually *found* Osama, he changed the story, saying that it was "impossible" to find Osama... Then an Oklahoma "prison sex slave" story came out, just as a hero of the Oklahoma City bombing died in jail. There was a story about the Pope wearing "ruby red shoes," which seems like an allusion to *The Wizard of Oz*... On that same day, the 18ᵗʰ, Citigroup posted a five billion dollar loss. By throwing the Rockefellers' big loss in with some really odd stories that seemed contradictory, it made the Rockefellers loss seem like an aberration, even though they have a long history of dumping such losses onto U.S. taxpayers, via bailouts and other devices... On the 19ᵗʰ, there was an earthquake in the Midwest, which was kind of odd... The plans for the Freedom Tower, the new World Trade Center building in NYC, were found in a trashcan... The Pope visited a synagogue for the first time... Both Obama and Hillary were in West Virginia, talking about coal issues, acting like they care. Amazingly, a 9/11 "black box" was supposedly found; we didn't actually get to hear what was on it, of course... There were a bunch of shootings in Chicago. They always seem to have some killings in these mixes, just to consecrate the occultness of the whole deal... We had the NAFTA conference in New Orleans the following week. That's a key issue. NAFTA is one of the things that has destroyed our economy, at least for the working man. They needed to distract us away from any important details about NAFTA. *[sarcastically]* No sense giving the American people, the enemy, any undo assistance.

GK: The Epstein brothers were on the show. They just went to Ground Zero with their camcorder. They're telling me that WTC7 has been rebuilt. Apparently, there is some kind of electronic billboard down there that is running poetry and other testimonies from 9/11. There was a very occult reference to the white goddess, the Queen of Heaven, "Colombia," or "Isis." And also to "Laurel..."

AC: "Laurel" sounds Moorish. As with the cherry tree and the crescent moon, the Moors are symbolized by the wreath... The week following the 19th, we had some things that kept us on edge, like references to Columbine, the mysterious "Phoenix lights" UFOs, and two women "raped by a ghost" in Seattle. Jimmy Carter was called a "bigot" by the Israeli UN ambassador. The Virginia Tech massacre was brought in again; the gun dealer that sold the gun to the shooter visited the campus. The cops who shot Sean Bell in NYC were cleared, and China met with the Dalai Lama's envoy. David Rockefeller donated a hundred million dollars to Harvard. Some warning shots were fired in the Persian Gulf, off of Iran. There were earthquakes in Reno, and a bunch of stories about global warming and tax rebates. Global warming is a way to charge us more for "green" products, in the same way that avoiding pesticides is the excuse for charging us more for organic food. Supposedly, those small tax rebates are going to boost the economy. They are *still* playing that fiddle.

GK: My rebate check went to a rent payment. Whoopee!

AC: Interestingly, the amount of the check seems to equal the *extra* money we were forced to pay for gasoline this year; it is essentially a subsidy to Big Oil. It's also equal to the amount that corporations usually throw to union members during contract negotiations. Even though the contract itself may cut their wages and benefits, our dumbed-down workforce will fall for the quick $500 payoff every time... On the 29th of April, Houston police gunned down Roland Carnaby, a CIA contractor involved with Jack Abramoff... David Blaine held his breath for 17 minutes on the Oprah Winfrey show on the 30th. There's that number 17 again, which Chris Knowles is always talking about. By the way, the original WTC7 had 47 floors. 47 is another number to watch... On the 30th, the Rockefellers, being the hypocrites they are, chastised their own company, Exxon, for not being ecological enough. Subtextually, the story implies that the Rockefellers are separate from, and more moral than, Exxon. Pretty cagey... On the 4th, we had the "D.C. Madame" suicide. She had a "little black book" with lots of names in it... The Senate Intelligence Committee banned private contractors from CIA interrogations... Jay Rockefeller stepped forward to make it seem like he is against torture, even though he always votes for it. He's probably the one who pressured Obama to flip-flop on FISA – to allow broader eavesdropping. The Rockefellers do not want to get sued for all the spying they've allowed through their phone companies. Don't forget, AT&T was spying on people just two weeks into Bush's reign. Bush went to AT&T right away and got permission to start spying on us freely... On May 1st, that pagan holiday, the Rockefellers were involved in three major stories. One was on CNN, where Jay seemingly blasted the oil companies about high gasoline prices in WV. He was trying to distance himself from his companies, who are gouging people mercilessly. The hypocrisy is almost beyond belief.

GK: Are the people of WV buying this?

AC: I don't think so, because I saw billboards there blaming him for the gas prices. The people of WV are savvier about politics than most would ever imagine. However, when the media goes into West Virginia to interview somebody, they always pick the most toothless person they can find. There are some incredibly intelligent people there, who are very liberal, but they don't get any press.

GK: They probably have to bribe people with a hundred bucks to play to the cameras. In rural areas, people are not dumb. In fact, they've got great common sense. They understand the way things go, and they have traditions. Within extended families, there are remembrances of the way things used to be.

AC: Plus, they have a history in WV of fighting for labor rights, featuring figures like Mother Jones. Also, WV did *not* side with the South in the Civil War.

GK: That's right…

AC: Virginia is actually more racist and backwards than WV. WV is more like Ohio and the Midwest; there is a little more consciousness about such matters.

GK: WV, KY, and Maryland were *not* southern states. We think of them as being more southern than northern, but that was not the case. Regarding toponomy, they named it "Mary-land."

AC: The white goddess…

GK: The land of Queen Mary… They named Virginia after the Virgin, and put between them the ovum called the District of "Columbia." Not a coincidence…

AC: Just to follow up about May 1st, Walpurgisnacht… The day after that, the "smiley-face murders" crept into the news. The serial killer thing is another staple that they use. They've created these horrific killers, who are always out there waiting. The numbers of missing people in the world is very high today. I just read an article about it. It's an enormous number. Also on that day, May 2nd, they started the Haq trial in Seattle. This is the guy who shot up the Jewish center back when the Saudi royal family was here. At that time, I was talking about all the weird, senseless murders that were occurring in Seattle. I actually predicted something akin to the Haq murders. I said, "There's going to be another one." I could sense the momentum. Then he shot up the Jewish center. But it turns out that he's *not* Muslim. He is a Christian, baptized only a couple of years before the incident.

GK: Jeez…

AC: He was from the Tri-Cities, which hosts the Hanford Nuclear

Reservation. Battelle, Westinghouse, and various defense contractors operate there. They even have a NASA facility there, where they supposedly test lunar rovers for Mars. No one could find anything Haq ever said that was racist. So, the killings really don't make any sense. He was an electronics student, which makes you wonder. Electrical engineers are sometimes "used" because they can be plausibly approached to work on secret installations... The day after that, Ann Coulter compared Obama to Hitler. Bush was in front of the Knesset, making references to how terrible it was that the Nazi tanks rolled into Poland. He forgot to mention that his grandfather helped build those Nazi tanks!

GK: He has absolutely disintegrated...

AC: Bush is thought to be dyslexic. He's got some serious psychological traumas from childhood. His sister died, yet no one in the family really acknowledged her death. The book, *Bush on the Couch*, claims that he can only articulate when he is angry. I have an interview with Walter Bowart *in The Mothman's Photographer III*, where he reminds us that Bush had a large box strapped to him during speeches. There were several pictures of it on the Internet.

GK: Yes, there was this bulge in the back of his suit.

AC: They were pumping the words he should say into him. They probably were doing hypnosis on him, too, in order to get him to a point where he could talk properly. Now that he's a lame duck, they're probably not paying as much attention to him. He may be sliding back into old habits.

GK: I don't throw bricks at him more than anyone else... He's not being shown in a favorable light. Like this whole thing about the airlines... If they wanted you to fly, they would show you all kinds of great things about flying. But, now, they're showing single females getting jacked and monkeys being stomped on. What is this telling you? It's telling you, "Don't fly." But with Bush, it's freaking embarrassing. The soundbites are more horrendous by the day. It's like they woke him up from a nap and said, "Can you talk to us about nuclear physics?" And he's like, "Uhhh...." I switch the channel because I'm embarrassed for him. Anyway, before we go any further, for those who have never heard you before, tell folks exactly what this is all about.

AC: The interviews in the books and DVDs chronicle my early experiences in WV. I had this friend who got a message from Mothman,

back in 1967, about the WTC attacks. After 9/11, I started researching it more intently. I eventually found evidence that Mothman
is not a demon, but a Garuda. He works on different levels. You
can get personal messages that will help you, or more impersonal
messages about how to stop something bad from happening. A
witness who sees Mothman might start to have visions about an
assassination; this apparently happened before the hits on Martin
Luther King and Robert Kennedy. The media just focuses on the
fact that somebody saw a monster. They don't get much into the
ancient stories describing these creatures as prophetic messengers
– messianic figures coming from the collective unconscious, trying
to help us. You find these name similarities… A "heyoka" in the
Native American world is a person who sees the Thunderbird. In the
Buddhist world, the Garuda is considered to be a "Heruka," which
is a category of wrathful deities that scare the heck out of people
in order to get them to change. Some people need that sort of
prodding. It's like your grandpa telling you scary tales to make sure
you don't stick your hand into a sawblade.

GK: When I was in college in 1969, I did not understand the world. I
only understood that important things were going on. I listened to
protest speeches, but I couldn't handle it. The one place I fled to was
the ballfield, this little postage stamp of greenery in the New York
metropolitan sprawl. I would lie in center field, even though I was a
catcher. I would just lie there and watch the clouds roll by; I would
basically "detox." I know that you played baseball, too. I think you
understand it, even to the extent that I did. You know that there was
a release there, a hiding place.

AC: My first ballfield was on the banks of the Kanawha, directly across
from Carbide's Blaine Island plant. Sometimes the smell would
almost knock you down. My Geiger counter still goes off when I
visit there. Manson's old house is about a block away from the field.

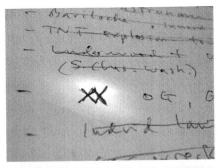 

In 2009, a mysterious man called "Mike the Cleaner" attended a party at the author's house sporting a tattoo (top right) featuring: the Masonic "XX" symbol, a Nazi-style lightning bolt, an Egyptian "anch," and a pentagram. Allen Greenfield took this photo of a dreaded "turtle-necked" MIB (lower right) during the 1969 UFO convention in Charleston, WV. This MIB was also active on Woodward Drive, and seemed to be in cahoots with either Indrid Cold or mobster Jack Bruno. Following the 2010 Mothman Festival, while doing a Grassy Knoll show that involved a discussion of the "XX" symbol, the author looked down to find a rainbow light illuminating the "XX" he had written in his notes (top left). The circular light, which was seen by other another witness, was half green and half blue, and exactly bisected the two X's at a 33 degree angle. The shape of the light was eerily similar to the UFO Tim Frick photographed only a couple of weeks earlier at a dam in Pennsylvania (see page 102). The "X" motif can also be seen in this Bella Coola tribal mask (lower left), depicting a ghostly entity from the land of the dead - not unlike our traditional Western conception of a Man in Black. The face in the mask resembles the Garuda-like face that my sister photographed looking in our kitchen window (opposite p.1). It also looks like the faces of "Indrid Cold" (p.376) and Samudranath (opposite p.1), who claimed that orb lights were vehicles for gurus, medicine men, and Thunderbeings - half-human, half-Thunderbird creatures along the lines of the Garuda.

CHAPTER 17

"The highest ambition of the integrated spectacle is to turn secret agents into revolutionaries, and revolutionaries into secret agents."

-Guy Debord, 1988

"A few years back, a man high up in the CIA named Ray Cline was asked if the CIA, by its surveillance of protest organizations in the U.S., was violating the free speech provision of the First Amendment. He smiled and said: 'It's *only* an amendment.'"

-Howard Zinn

"On Oct. 18, 1971, President Nixon announced that the Army's Biowarfare laboratories at Ft. Detrick, MD, would be converted to cancer research. As part of Nixon's 'war on cancer,' the military biowarfare unit was retitled the 'Frederick Cancer Research Center,' and Litton Bionetics was named as the military's prime contractor for this project. According to [their] 1971 annual report, the primary task of the center was the 'large scale production of oncogenic (cancer-causing) viruses to meet research needs on a continuing basis.' Special attention was given to primate viruses (the alleged African source of HIV) and 'the successful propagation of significant amounts of human candidate viruses.' Candidate viruses were animal or human viruses that might cause human cancers. For these cancer experiments, a steady supply of research animals was necessary... Primates were shipped in from West Africa and Asia for experimentation; and virus-infected animals were shipped out to various labs worldwide.

"By 1971, a total of 2,274 primates had been inoculated at Bionetics Research Laboratories, under contract to Ft. Detrick. Over a thousand of these monkeys died or had been transferred to other primate centers. Some animals were eventually released back into the wild. By the early 1970s, experimenters had transferred cancer-causing viruses into several species of monkey, and had also isolated a monkey virus (Herpesvirus saimiri) that would have a close genetic relationship to the new 'Kaposi's sarcoma' herpes virus that

produced the 'gay cancer' of AIDS in 1979… Researchers at
Bionetics injected human and animal cancer material into
various species of monkeys to determine the cancer effect.
Newborn and irradiated monkeys were injected with blood
taken from various forms of human leukemia. In other
studies, tissue cultures infected with various animal viruses
were inoculated into primates. How many 'new' and 'emerging' viruses were created and adapted to human tissue and
to various primates is not known… Some primates were
released back into the wild carrying lab viruses with them.
The possible spread of these lab viruses to other [animals]
in the wild has been ignored by scientists searching for the
origin of HIV…"

-Alan Cantwell, M.D., "Blaming Gays, Blacks, and Chimps
for AIDS," *Paranoia* magazine, Fall 2001

MOTHMAN DISCUSSION LIST – SELECTED LETTERS AND POSTS
– 2005

I dreamed of the tsunami two days before it struck. I couldn't figure it out
at all. I told my husband about it. I thought it strange to dream of a wall
of water and utter devastation. I passed it off to the horrific ice storms
happening here. We were out of power for days and days. I sent the kids
to my mom's. This place looks like a war zone – trees and limbs down
everywhere, roads closed, etc. Supposedly this tsunami hit at breakfast
time in the South Pacific on Sunday morning. We are about twelve
hours behind. I began pacing like an idiot Saturday night – like a caged
animal, which is unlike me. I was picking up on the earthquake as it was
happening… My daughter is seeing lots of spirits lately. Her grandfather
is gravely ill. "They" are coming to her and telling her it won't be long.
They are giving her other tidbits of information as well… It has been a
very odd but wonderful year for me in the spiritual arena. I have been
doing shamanic journeying; it seems very beneficial. I feel I have successfully integrated my fears now. There is a "pattern" as to what is revealed to
me, and when; there probably always has been, but I just didn't connect
the dots.

-Harriet 1/1/05

When my youngest son was [a toddler] I found him crying in our basement in the middle of the night. Andy, he wouldn't have gone there by himself… He was afraid of the basement during the day, let alone in the pitch dark of night. When I questioned him, he said a "monker" had carried him, and that the monker was "Darth Vader." He had just watched *Star Wars* with his dad. [I imagine that] if he had watched Batman, he might have used "Batman" for the description. I myself have vivid memories of being taken as a child, in the middle of the night, by "Batman" to the "Bat Cave." I also have dreams of being nude and chained to a stone altar. When my grandmother passed away a few years ago, my mother found a story my grandmother had written about a young girl and several creatures with wings. The [creatures] had a leader she called "the Beast." The setting of the story was identical to where she grew up, so [the story must be about her]. I have a hard time talking with others about all of this. One reason is the fear of being thought of as a total nut. It's hard to explain something that I don't understand myself. My soon to be ex-husband used my experiences and beliefs against me. He would threaten to take our son away from me on the grounds that I wasn't stable. When I was young, my mom would tell me to shut up or else someone would "lock me up and throw away the key." Then, there's my dad and his side of the family, who are devout Christians. They look down on my positive spiritual experiences. They see it as being all in my head…

So, you see, I've been programmed to be leery of others' reactions to my experiences. From what I've learned in the past few years, this has been passed down from at least as far back as my great-grandmother. My mother has since changed her views on [paranormal] things, since she has been through hell herself. She is one of a very few that I speak to about such matters. [While] growing up, I lived just about everywhere in the "Chemical Valley" (the Kanawha Valley), but mainly I'm from Poca. I lived most of my childhood in Bancroft. God knows there are times I've had to walk away just to keep my sanity. Even the people one would think would be open to this [phenomenon] are not; you have to accept that. You can't change anyone's mind if they don't want it changed, especially if they are stuck in a certain way of thinking. It was hard for me to accept certain things. To do that, I had to question my own sanity many times along the way. I also have many of the same beliefs as you about our so-called government. I have been shocked and sickened by the truths I have learned.

-Tara 1/2/05

How familiar am I with the paranormal? I guess that depends on what you think of as paranormal. I saw a UFO when I was about 12. After that, I read every book I could find about UFOs. After awhile, they were all the same: the same exact stories, same interviews, everything... So, I quit reading about UFOs and came to the conclusion that no one knew what a UFO was. But I've always been interested in this sort of thing. Science "teaches" us that we have everything figured out. We try to pretend there are no mysteries anymore. We even have "laws" of physics. I don't believe we know a fraction of what we think we know. There are so many things that are simply beyond our comprehension; *that's* the kind of thing I think of as "paranormal." I'm not psychic or anything, but I've always had strong feelings when I am around old battlefields. I've always been interested in ghosts. For the past few years, I've been helping my sister investigate her house, which we think is haunted. Some really amazing things have happened there. There is something new all the time... I've always been interested in Bigfoot and other rare creatures. When I was living in Colorado, I had a friend who was also keenly interested in Bigfoot. We were so into it that we considered taking a couple of years off to roam the woods in search of evidence. We never did but, a couple of years later, someone near Maysville, KY reportedly saw Bigfoot. I traveled down to the area to interview people and find out as much as I could. I wrote a report about it, and used it as one of my term papers at the Art Academy of Cincinnati.

-Dave Scott 1/2/05

I was going over some posts last night and saw where you mentioned living in Cross Lanes. I believe Cross Lanes is either a vortex or on a ley line. I went through pure paranormal hell living there for seventeen years. It was sort of a relief when I lost my house. The nightly visitations for me and my daughter stopped when we moved out of Cross Lanes. There is a lot of UFO activity there. There is also a lot of military air traffic, too... So, go figure... I saw a plane appear out of a "chem cloud" and then disappear, right after I took a picture of it. There is also a UFO in that picture. They look like orbs. I've seen them a lot in the pictures I've taken of chemtrails... As far as wacky conspiracy theories, I have several of my own, developed from trying to find answers over the past several years. Before that, it was all just something I lived with and never talked about. My grandfather, for instance, was admitted to Lakin State Hospital on more than one occasion. I truly believe that there were government experiments taking place there. My grandfather was an alcoholic, but most of his problems were due to the chemicals he worked in at Monsanto. The doctors said he drank to cover up what was really going on with him... I have enough personal and family experiences with the paranormal to fill a book. As a matter of fact, my mother and I are going to give it a shot. If you would have told me 10 years ago that my mother would be willing to write a book on this stuff, let alone talk about it at all, then I would have called you a liar. The only problem I have with it is what it would/could do to my children as far as being ridiculed. I suffered enough as a child. I can't imagine the backlash for writing a book of this nature. I remember one incident where a boy in my class was teasing me, saying that my grandpa had been "digging up graves" the night before in the cemetery. As you know, everyone knows everyone here in Chemical Valley, so [things like that can be very hurtful and destructive].

-Tara 1/3/05

The first night I slept at the new house here in Beckley, WV, I woke up feeling as if I were on fire. I could feel the heat on my skin and inside me. I ran into the hallway screaming. I finally fought it off and went back to bed... But I awoke again, a little later, and saw a man leaning across me over my bed! I jumped out and into the hallway *again* and said, "Enough of this!" So, I slept with all the lights on... The next day, I performed a purification and cleansing of the house. Now, everything is fine. I'm right across the street from a graveyard. I must have been picking up on some vibes from the dead people over there.

-Sharon Moore 1/8/05

The sighting I am writing to you about is a fantastic one, although there have been some other pretty incredible sightings [here in] Bethel, Ohio. Today, I was walking my cat down to our garage to put her in when, all of a sudden to the left, I saw 7 spherical UFOs flying through the sky. They were pale white, filmy sort of objects with a little dark dot in the center. I was treated to a dancing display of lights, which left me dumbfounded. During the dance, two smaller white spheres dropped out of the two larger UFOs and began to zip around in the sky, darting every which way. The two smaller discs then joined back up with the larger UFO's, almost as if they were being absorbed into these larger objects. The smaller discs were white and filmy too, but with no dot in the center of them. It was as if they were smaller scout ships or something. They looked like orbs of light. I quickly ran to my husband's shop to get my cameras. I ran back with my cameras in-hand and said, "Please come over so I can take your picture." Just as I said that, a UFO started to travel over. I was excited, but I [became afraid and] started to run back to my house. I just couldn't stop myself. The UFO kept coming, and I kept running. Just as I was approaching the house, a white flash went off with the sound of a click. I kept running… As I came to my house, I took another look. The object was ablaze in white, with a fiery motion to it. I saw the object stand stationary in the sky, about 30 feet in the air. It wasn't circular anymore, but looked to be sort of crescent-shaped. It kept rotating. Then, all of a sudden, a slender, milky white arm slinked down. It was about 15 feet long, translucent and gossamer-like, with a curly-cue tail on the end of it. The very last look I got before I dashed into the house was of a milky white sphere that had somehow appeared on the bottom of the arm. The attached sphere was see-through, similar to the arm. This UFO seemed to be in the material world, but the arm and sphere seemed to be in another dimension. This was like a science fiction movie. I couldn't believe it! I felt like I was being scanned by this sphere. My only thought was: "I feel so primitive." I ran into the house and didn't look out the windows the rest of the evening.

-Barbara 3/2/05

I have real concerns about Pope Benedict XVI. As you know, he is the former head of Opus Dei, and was a proponent of the Crisio movement, which is the "charismatic reborn" sect of Catholicism. Anytime you go to extreme measures, as the Vatican did to insure the secrecy of the papal election process, one has to wonder. I'm sure you heard of the soundproofing and security measures that were put in place in the Sistine Chapel; seems kind of funny for a centuries-old tradition. You have to wonder, what *was* the process, and *why* him? He is 78; in all likelihood, he will not serve that long… What is it that he is supposed to accomplish in such a short time? German Catholics are extreme fundamentalists. I see this Pope being even stricter. Most American Catholics fear his "iron hand" – his unrelenting stance on women, birth control, and gays in the church. He also wanted to bury the issue of molestation in America. He sort of has the "we've looked the other way for centuries and we will continue to do so" mentality. He probably wonders why people are standing in his way. I am aware of John Paul's connection to the precognitive events that occurred at Fatima. That is one of the reasons that many Catholics feel he should be immediately canonized…

Another point I want to bring up is George W. Bush attending John Paul's funeral. No U.S. president has ever attended the funeral of a Pope, either past or present. And to have three presidents there! What was that about? To appease all of the Catholics who voted for him? Or, to equate himself with a holy man? In my opinion, that is exactly how George Bush sees himself: as a holy man on a crusade. He justifies his political agenda through his religion. The irony here is that he is going after countries that are religious states, saying that they should be democracies. But, in his own country, he runs an evangelical Christian tyranny with no separation of Church and State. Hello! Is there a difference there? How far are *we* from being a religious state at this point?

How does Mothman tie into this? When I was in Slovenia recently, there was some paranormal activity going on. Slovenia is right beside Italy. There were strange lights, and what one witness described as a "prehistoric-looking" bird. This was in the area of the town of Bled, around Sept. or Oct. of 2004… Also, are you aware of the image of the Virgin Mary that has appeared on a Chicago highway bridge? The timing is, of course, suspect. Your suggestion to view Tommy Burnham's front door as a portal for seeing into the future gives me kinesthetic spiritual responses. As I sit here and ponder that question, my solar plexus is in knots. The only thing I remember is being very afraid to go in his house when I was little. I remember the house being very dark. There was not a lot of natural light, because of all the trees around it. It always seemed somewhat sinister to me…

Do I think there is an organized effort to keep people from tapping into the Akashic Record? Sure I do, but I also know that you can't be kept *from* it. I have had several "downloading" experiences in my life, some very recent. I can't tell you what year it is, but I see a catastrophic earthquake on the West Coast. I feel it is part of the same "vision" I have had for a couple of years. My downloading experiences are generally medical information; sometimes they are "instantaneous." I will be reading someone intuitively, but will also feel a strange change in pressure around my body, a force pushing down on the top of my head and third eye. Then, I am flooded with information. Two years ago I couldn't have even told you about that, as I wasn't aware of the difference in pressure; now, I am keenly aware of it. My awareness has been in a state of change for almost three years now. It grows by the day in many different ways, mostly due to the practice of meditation I have adopted.

-Harriet 4/22/05

Soon after our experience with that energy field in 2002, I very distinctly remember you having a terrifying vision of a UFO underwater. The next day, we found out that someone had gone into the Kanawha River and died that very evening. At the time of the vision, you sensed death "in numbers" in the past, in that very area. You even speculated that perhaps a bridge had collapsed or a boat had gone down with numbers of people on board, which John Frick later discovered had actually happened, during the Elk River Bridge collapse. You kept using the word "numbers." That has stuck with me until this day, because of your absolute, genuine terror! It was the linguistic pattern, the choice of words, that stuck with me. I wonder if you weren't "receiving" that through spirit.

The death of your Buddhist mentor, Aryadaka, is profoundly sad and tragic. He is around you frequently. I too, have had that "life flashing before me" experience. Mine was in college, when I was in a car accident and went through the windshield. It was really neat how time seemed to s-l-o-w down even though there were so many images flashing quickly... Since we have been in contact, my psychic reception has been through the roof. I wish I could explain it. Out of the corners of my eyes, and sometimes right in my field of vision, I have been physically seeing spirits lately. Last Wednesday, I fell out of bed and hurt myself in the middle of the night. I woke up to someone shaking my shoulder: a blonde woman with shoulder length hair and a distinct British accent. She was dressed in mid-19th Century clothing. I was awake; this wasn't a dream. I tried to run from her, but couldn't. She told me, "You cannot be a party to healing when you don't have a willing participant; remember this..." Before I went to bed that night, I had asked my subconscious for some help with a perplexing client. I think it was answered in spirit form... Then, two nights later, there were three knocks (that triple pattern again) on the headboard of my bed at 6:52 am. I am not mistaken. I asked, "Who are you, and what do you want?" I got no answer... I've had the ability to see this stuff all of my life.

-Harriet 4/26/05

Are the Bushes Catholic? I always thought they were Episcopalian, like many of the Rockefellers; I'm pretty sure of it. I have been reading about all of the different interpretations of Christ. I am now into the Gnostic Gospels. I've been studying the Masons, too. My father and I were actually very close in our beliefs. He must have been well acquainted with the occult and mysticism to be in that organization. I never knew... Recently, a book "fell" off the shelf on me. It literally hit me in the head; my dad probably pushed it... I have been wanting to sit down and tell you more about my "spirit visitation" a month ago, with reference to my client's healing. She came in and told me about being "visited" in a dream (she thought) by a woman with a British accent telling her that the way to become "unstuck" was just "to *do* it. It is always about choice, not circumstances." And get this... It happened on *the same night* as my visitation.

-Harriet 5/27/05

You won't believe this one... My friend, Carol, was here from Chicago over the weekend, and I gave her my celestite crystal to hold. I told her it would make her remember her dreams. She said I had to hold it, too. The next morning, Monday, she *did* remember a dream. It was mundane, about shopping, but she remembered every detail. She asked me what I had dreamed. I told her that I had dreamed that my mom's friend had told me to tell my mom that "she was all right." When Carol asked me why I would dream such a thing, I had no answer. Then, Carol and I went on a shopping excursion. When we got back, my husband told me to sit down; he had bad news. He told me that my mom's best friend, Mary Lou, had dropped dead of a heart attack Sunday night. In my dream, guess who told me to tell Mom that she was OK? Yes, it was Mary Lou. The dream was *so* real, and now I know why. It *wasn't* a dream....

-Harriet 5/31/05

I had a dream last night that I was working as a psychic detective. I was looking for clues on a hillside above a house on Woodward Drive, just off a narrow path. There was something hidden in the woods that was an important clue. I found whatever it was, but I sat on the information so that the killer wouldn't realize that anyone knew. Then, in the presence of my detective partner, whose identity was blurred, I went into a trance. I started shaking and trembling like I did after we saw the energy field. I blurted out the word "Williamson." Then, I saw the killer; she looked like a witch in a cartoon. She seemed to be moving behind a couch. Oddly, her image was projected against the wall. She said, "You'll never catch me, because I can change identities at will." All I can think is that this is an echo of our trip to Williamson, where we interviewed the woman who owned your house after you moved out. The drowning I saw in a vision after encountering that energy field in 2002 seemed connected to your house somehow. The vision may *not* have been pointing to the drowning in the Kanawha three days later, but to the past one that occurred when she still owned your house – when the man she described as the caretaker drowned. He supposedly was living there alone and had no family. His death is probably the reason that the house is now abandoned.

-Andy 5/31/05

Here is another interesting coincidence, and I swear to you every word of this is true. Last night, we went to dinner with my mom and another family. Out of nowhere, my mom asked me about you. She wanted to know how you were doing and if you enjoyed being a father. She sat quiet for a minute and said she was happy for you, and knew you'd be a great father. Then, she started talking about your dad and him dying young.

Out of her mouth came the word "angiosarcoma." I looked at her and asked her how she remembered that word (she is not medically savvy). She said she didn't know where that came from. I looked at the time of day you sent your last email (when you were typing about angiosarcoma). It was the same time we were eating. We were talking about you at the very same time! She kept talking about the "multitudes" of men that died at the same time. Reading your email today is almost a carbon copy of our conversation! Andy, this is creepy...

Regarding your cancer dream. I have always believed your dad just wanted you to "see" where he was in his mind at that time. I know you have always regretted not going to see him that last time before he died. I didn't know you had the high white bloodcell count when you were a teenager but, every time I "scan" you, I see that you are okay. But don't invite cancer into your awareness. Perhaps the idea of a "protector" was to raise your level of awareness, of which you've done a fine job. If anything, I have often wondered if you weren't *my* protector. Let's face it, you have been the only person to acknowledge and validate a lifetime worth of paranormal experiences. I can't speak for you, but I have never really "fit in" anywhere. Although I'm very social on the outside, it is just a façade. I'm very isolated on the inside. I am, however, becoming comfortable with it in my old age.

What do you think you are really investigating in your dreams? I have always felt Aetna-Dell school held some kind of a mystery. Do you remember that long playslide that began up in a tree? Something happened there; I know it. For some reason, I feel it was a hanging. I remember being 9 years old, in the fourth grade, and thinking that I saw a man hanging from that tree in broad daylight! Of course, my mom told me I was crazy. Your dad being injected with cancer could have been what I saw. That is so scary; it really is... I never knew about your dad's service at Norfolk, and I don't remember the scar on his face. I just remember your dad's eyes and his big hands. He was very handsome and strong... I took my mom to the doctor yesterday morning; she has early-stage emphysema. I was facing her while looking into the light. She said something strange to me: "Where do you get those aqua eyes from?" She went on to say that I look like no one in the family, and that maybe I'm a "starchild." I asked her if she knew what that term meant. She said no, that it just came to her. Here I am, 45 years old, and she is just now realizing how different I look! She is asking more and more questions about psychic experiences. She is very psychic herself. By the way, that woman I spoke about three years ago has been coming back to me recently in visions. She was so familiar – her eyes and her raspy voice –

but I could not identify her. She kept telling me things about you. I now know who she is: your mom, Betty Colvin.

-Harriet 6/1/05

This is kind of weird... Yesterday, I was getting ready to put a phone number into my cellphone. My son said that he'd put it in for me. He looked down through my list and said, "Andy's last name is Colvin?" I said, "Yeah, why?" It turns out – and I never knew this until yesterday – that his friend Ben has the last name Colvin. You are Andrew Benjamin Colvin, and he is Benjamin Andrew Colvin. Are you related? My son was laughing about how much you resemble one another. He looks like you in your teen years! Yet another little synchronicity....

-Harriet 6/27/05

I have lots of emotions about the Bodytalk seminar I attended last weekend. I had a session in front of the class. What came out had to do with my first grade teacher, Mrs. Ferrell, who didn't want to deal with my "brilliance," and so advanced me up to the second grade with you. She couldn't understand how I always "had all the answers." She didn't realize that I was actually psychic; I could *see* the answers. It wasn't that I was so brilliant. But she tried to shut down my gift. You wouldn't believe the anger that came out of me. It was unbelievable. Fortunately, the new teacher nurtured the gift; she knew that I was psychic. The Bodytalk session was very healing to me, and very validating. Some of the other stories that came out in the class were incredible. It is such a wonderful experience. By the way, Tommy actually made the "R.I.P." drawing of *Mr.* Ferrell's grave while in first grade with Mrs. Ferrell. I wasn't in school yet, as the cutoff was Oct. 30 back then. I started the following year and got moved up to second grade right away. I remember that R.I.P. drawing well, however. I can remember Tommy's mother crying about it to my mom. She was wailing, in fact.

-Harriet 7/12/05

Several weeks ago, I was making French toast in the kitchen. I was worrying about several things that were going on in my family; I was very concerned. I said a prayer in my mind, asking for help. After I was finished praying, I wondered if my prayers had been heard. I flipped the batch of French toast out of the pan over onto a plate. To my surprise, one of the pieces of toast had what looked like a cross on it. I called my children in and asked them if they saw the cross, too. One saw the cross, but two of them said that the image looked more like Jesus with his arms outstretched, with a halo around his head. We decided that we wouldn't eat the toast, but put it in the freezer. After that, several of the things that were weighing us down were resolved for the better. It was quite apparent that our prayers *had* been heard. A sign had been sent to us to let us know that there was someone listening who would help. We decided to put the French toast up on eBay... Perhaps someone else will be helped as we were... Look at the picture. What do you see? Is it a cross, or do you see the figure of Jesus standing with his arms outstretched? Whatever you see, it is an incredible image. I can't guarantee that the toast will solve your problems, but it can't hurt. I never thought something like this would happen to my family... Since we've put the toast up for auction, we've gotten some other good news. My husband's pacemaker was not one of the defective ones made by the company that manufactured his. He won't have to undergo surgery and have it all replaced. My oldest daughter, who had been feeling unwell all summer, was diagnosed with allergies, not mononucleosis or cancer (which is what the doctor was afraid it was). We also received a dividend check in the mail for some stock we owned that suddenly took off. All of this happened after we took the toast out of the freezer and prayed for some extra help. God answered our prayers once, and it is evident that he did it again.

-Barbara, eBay auction description 7/28/05

When I was in North Carolina, I went on the "Haunted Asheville" tour just for kicks. I enjoyed it. Since the tour was small that night, I asked the guide if I could tell *him* where some of the actual murders took place (without any information beforehand). Well, I was good on that; 100% in fact... It was incredible. When I went into this pub, Barley's, to buy tickets for the tour, I felt like I was being "sucked" toward an area in the restaurant. I asked the tour guide about it later when everyone else had left. He said several psychics had told him and other tour guides that the place had two "portals" to another dimension. I asked him to let me show him where I thought they were. Again, I was right on the money. I wish you could have been there! I also "know" that someday I will live there. There is no question about it. I think I was being shown that eventuality. Those mountains resonate with me. Supposedly, Asheville lines up exactly with the ley line going down to the Bermuda Triangle.

-Harriet 8/9/05

I'm not sure what I saw yesterday, but here is what happened. At about 7 p.m., I picked up my phone to call a friend. I walked outside my office and down the hall to check the thermostat. When I turned back around, there was a spiraling, intensely thick plume of black smoke spinning, at floor level, at the entrance to my office. I'm not talking about a bit of wispy smoke, but an organized mass that was about 18" in height. It paused and then moved rapidly through my office. I followed, all the while telling my friend on the phone what I was seeing. It left a distinct odor like sulphur – like a lit match. It is true that I use candles and the like, but I had not used any at this time. It startled me at first, but I became fascinated with it and am now almost obsessed; something like this has never happened before. I smelled sulphur when that very strange person came up to my office almost three years ago… Do you remember Clarice from our class? She is Armenian. We have become very good friends in the last three years. She has had an experience like this. She, too, saw the smoke mass. It hovered to get her attention before it moved through a wall… I think this one here was a spirit trying to get my attention. I wasn't frightened in the literal sense, just intrigued. Whatever it was, it was purposely directing itself. It waited to get my attention. If I had to give it a sex, I would say it felt male. By the way, one of my clients just stopped by and asked me what I was writing about. When I told her, she told me that her mom is a nurse and has experiences like this all the time in the nursing home where she works. Whenever she smells sulphur, someone is going to die.

-Harriet 8/17/05

Through my reading last night, I found out that you may just be right; I may have encountered a sylph – an air spirit of the highest vibratory rate. It didn't scare me. I followed it. I was intrigued by it. I have been working a lot with people with social anxiety disorder. I had a huge breakthrough with someone after that sylph visit. I think I might have been "inspired" as it were. It is weird how I work out my own problems through my clients. I think I may be attracting certain ones to do just that. I have a question for you… Is your son artistic? The reason I ask is that I had a dream that he was creating unusually profound art, not just for his age, but profound, period. It had huge thought behind it.

-Harriet 8/18/05

The meaning of "Indrid Cold" is simple. In order to approach such Mothman riddles, all one needs, it seems, is a basic knowledge of any spiritual tradition, be it Hindu, Buddhist, Celtic, Judeo-Christian, Muslim, or Native American. In this case, it turns out to be a particularly Hindu case, or at least one that uses Hindu terminology. But all of the above traditions provide ample clues for deciphering symbolic codes and "name-game" mysteries. The "superspectrum," as John Keel termed it, has embedded itself into our very consciousness. This is reflected in our religion, our language, and our mental coding, which is itself essentially a binary electrical circuit. This loop tends to "spin" conceptual thinking toward dualistic poles such as "good" or "bad," angelic or demonic, and so on. After having a basic understanding of one of the above mythologies, one then needs just a few synchronous experiences in order to gain insight into the riddle. Luckily or not, these "coincidences" seem to occur fairly often in the lives of Mothman witnesses. This may be one of the reasons this phenomenon exists: to give us feedback from the universe.

For some this is a blessing, for others it is a curse. Some witnesses get so many psychic pieces of information coming at them that it tends to make them a bit paranoid; others make fast decisions and judgments, internally, which baffle others; the average person cannot sense the same input... I am reminded of the fact that the Indians initially couldn't see the ships of Columbus because their brains couldn't process it. A shaman had to spend many days looking at where the ships were said to be in order to finally see them. At times, when I am trying to explain my Mothman experiences and everyone is shaking their heads and thinking I am nuts or unduly obsessed, I feel like that shaman. In addition to having seen the creature myself, I have a long string of synchronicities and seemingly profound, symbolic events in my life. I sometimes wonder if Mothman witnesses aren't each given individual "clues" to a larger puzzle. The dreams, precognitions, telepathic messages, and unusual meetings get us closer to what is going on within us and around us. My discussions with witnesses reveal such a pattern. Faye DeWitt and Marcella Bennett speak of "hunches" alerting them to potential dangers. The universe appears to be sending out information regarding specific, powerful human events. This information comes in the form of visions, sounds, messages, random coincidences, and codes.

I interviewed John Keel for my documentary on Mothman, and asked him about Indrid Cold. Keel seemed to feel that much of Woody's story was fabricated or implanted into him. He suspects that some of the strange phone calls were a result of Indrid Cold speaking *through* Woody Derenberger, as if Woody had been brainwashed or lied to. Having interviewed a Bigfoot contactee who feels that Bigfoot speaks to, and through him, I can attest to being put off by the thought that a witness might create his own "evidence." Still, looking at it another way, I think that it is worth trying to figure out what is behind a phenomenon whose experiencers feel that they need to "channel" for, or "telepath" to, a creature or entity. I personally feel that Derenberger may *not* have been a hoaxer, but a victim. The Air Force involvement in his case – the psychiatric interest, the weeklong "debriefing" at NASA headquarters – is a possible indicator of mind control.

In looking at this Indrid riddle, though, the first thing I did was to see the name "Indrid Cold" not as a name, but as a descriptor. The main word appeared to be "Cold," with "Indrid" as a modifier. I ran some anagrams of "indridcold" and got lots of interesting little references to things from the Mothman story, but nothing solid. Then, I turned it around 180 degrees and started looking at "indridcold" not for its constituent parts, but looking at it as a constituent part of a larger word. I asked myself if there might be any relevance to the word "indridcold" being spelled out of larger words, and could those larger words represent potential leads, or "name-game" clues? I got a couple of hits using this offbeat method. Knowing that Keel had observed, in the 1960s, that most of the entities channeling through contactees had names that sounded like "synthetic fabrics," I decided to try and fit "indridcold" into some names of petrochemical companies that make such fabrics.

One company that I found was a subcontractor to Union Carbide. It had employed many of the men in my neighborhood in WV. I myself worked there; I was good friends with the owner's son. The company, Industrial Rubber, has now been sold and has moved its headquarters. The company's original location was at the confluence of the Elk and Kanawha Rivers, where a bridge collapsed on Dec. 15th, 1904 – the same day of the year as the Silver Bridge collapse. The owner's family lived on a bluff overlooking the confluence. Several interesting characters with Mothman links lived in that particular neighborhood. Harriet Plumbrook had dreams of the bluff prior to ever seeing it, and now feels the location is a geomagnetic source for the phenomenon. I was also reminded of a story my mother told me when I was a little boy, which is that Magic Island, at the confluence of the Elk and Kanawha Rivers, was haunted by the ghost of a dead girl.

Another hit I got was that "indridcold" fit into the full name of Carbide's Canadian wing. Carbide leased land on both sides of the I-64 Bridge in Dunbar, WV, where the famous Tad Jones sighting occurred. When I "googled" Carbide's Canadian facility as a check, one of the first references to come up was a book about the Martin Luther King assassination. This reference stated that Union Carbide was the only entity from which James Earl Ray could have gotten the classified personnel information he used to construct his famous "Eric S. Galt" alias. The real Eric S. Galt was a security-cleared employee of Union Carbide, at a time when the company was making top-secret "proximity fuses" for missiles at its Canadian facilities. These fuses probably went into certain nuclear warheads.

Union Carbide was known for its pioneering work in handling both super-cooled and "hot" materials like uranium. The Manhattan Project would not have been possible without Carbide. It was the premier "chemical factory" in a valley where John Keel was told – by Mothman witnesses and psychics – that a "chemical factory" might blow up. In the early 1960s, Carbide already had built a complete simulation of the Martian landscape so that they could test various substances and materials. Could they have had a hand in any hoaxed moon landings? Conspiracy theorists have speculated about the role of Carbide in the Roswell crash and the Jonestown massacre, which occurred on land previously owned by Carbide. The supposed role of Jonestown's mind-controlled "zombie killers" in political assassinations might explain why Keel was told by psychics that MLK would be shot. Keel, in fact, tried to alert MLK to the danger, but was unsuccessful. The prophecy accurately predicted the manner of the actual shooting, but was off by one month.

I decided to do another turnabout and look at "Indrid" as the subject, and "Cold" as the modifier. This would prove to be much more beneficial at getting at the root of the "real" Indrid. The trouble, however, is that "Indrid" is not a word we use in America. I had to look for words that were similar to Indrid. After reading Ted Holiday's work connecting dragons to flying saucers and earthworks, it popped into my head that the Hindu god "Indra," the god of fire, might be the connection. I looked and found that, throughout the eons, "the Garuda puts out the fire of Indra." The birdman literally consumes the fires of Indra, rendering them "cold." The two, Garuda and Indra, are closely associated in Hindu literature. When one sees this relationship, one sees that probably the only thing on Earth that can be a cooled-down form of Indra is the Garuda. And since Indra is no longer the real, bonafide "hot" Indra once he is cooled down and in Garuda form, he can only be properly labeled "Indrid" or "Indridic." In essence, Indrid Cold seems to have been telling us that he was Garuda operating as Indra in "cold" form. This kind of shapeshifting is not uncommon in Hinduism and Buddhism. In Indonesia, the Garuda is believed to manifest as the spirit Bonaspati, which can then inhabit other creatures, like the doglike Barong. "Bonaspati" uses the "bon" prefix, which refers to the goddess religion of Tibet prior to Buddhism. "Tib" and "bon" both mean "good."

Whether Woody Derenberger, Indrid's hypnotic subject, was brainwashed or not, the players involved knew something about Hinduism and Buddhism. They got around, and they got noticed. Indrid Cold had a distinctive look. He had sharp features and wore silver coveralls, and was seen by many people other than Woody. Someone who dressed like him, driving the same car with WV license plates, was seen in New Jersey and on Long Island, a place that happens to be a center of Bon religious practice in America. One lady in Pt. Pleasant saw a man dressed like Indrid hovering in a craft above a school playground, as if he was monitoring the kids. He certainly had an interest in my friends Tommy and Harriet, and may have even visited my elementary school as part of the team studying the genius kids there. Could Indrid have once been a cryptozoological intelligence operative helping the CIA guide the Dalai Lama over the mountains to India? Very few people in the West knew much about Buddhism back then. Keel certainly knew about it, since he originally put the term "Garuda" in the title of his *Mothman Prophecies* book, but the early cryptozoologists knew it, too. Those who traveled to Nepal to "search for the Yeti" with the Tom Slick/CIA Bigfoot expedition would have known it. Slick had roots in Mothman country. Many of the UFO contactees of that era were given messages pertaining to the White Brotherhood of Tibet and the Thule Ultima, both standard fare for Nazi occultists involved in Tibetan Buddhist research.

-Andy 8/20/05

I can't understand why [locals] would object to your research, unless they don't want people to question this "Mothman" thing too much. They're probably afraid that if people research things too much, it will remove some of the mystique – maybe ruin their tourist industry… I can't imagine what it would have been like to actually see Mothman. I saw a UFO when I was about 12 years old, and it changed my life. My parents and I were driving home one night, when I spotted something out the car window. At first I thought it was a meteor, but it left no trail and it was coming down at about a 45-degree angle. Then, it straightened out and began traveling in a straight horizontal line. I was very much interested in astronomy when I was a kid, so I knew what astral bodies and planes and satellites looked like; this was something else. As soon as we got home, I ran inside to get my telescope. I took the telescope outside and noticed that the UFO was now stationary. It didn't seem to be very far away. Strangely it seemed to be waiting for me. It was just sitting there in the sky, waiting to be observed. I looked at it through my small telescope, but couldn't make out any details. It just looked like a solid, white ball of light.

I ran inside to tell my parents. I said, "Come outside! There's a UFO or something out here!" They just continued to watch TV, totally ignoring me. So I ran across the street, where my best friend lived, and pounded on the door. "Steve, come out here. There's something really weird in the sky – a UFO or something! Come look!" But he didn't come out. What does it take for someone to step out into the front yard for a few seconds to see something they may never have seen before? Oddly, most people simply don't care; it's not even worth getting out of the chair. After a while, I got tired of watching the UFO, which was perfectly still for a long time – a half hour or so. If I had not already been interested in astronomy and known that the planets were in other parts of the sky at the time, I might have been able to convince myself that it was a planet.

I decided to take one last look at it. As I parted the curtain and looked for the UFO, I saw it shoot straight up into the sky until it was gone. Poof… Faster than anything I had ever seen… I talked to my friends at school about it the next day. It turned out that a friend of mine, who lived a few blocks away, had seen the same thing and described it the same way I did… I think when you see something like a UFO or Mothman or a ghost, it changes your life. Suddenly, something that isn't supposed to exist *does* exist. If a ghost, Mothman, or UFO really does exist, what *else* could be out there? Once you believe in one "impossible" being or event, it opens up a whole new world where anything is possible; anything *could* exist…

-Dave Scott 8/27/05

I'm sure that people who are not highly sensitive have no idea how you feel. Sometimes it is frustrating to get that point across to someone. You have rare gifts; knowing it is validating. Feeling like part of a collective whole is validating. You have helped me so much in my life. I just want to help you in return. You are a beautiful human being with so much to offer the world. It doesn't mean you won't ever piss me off again, or vice versa. You have a great sense of humor. Remember, as tough as it may get sometimes, *that* is when you should reach out and not withdraw… I know how "friends" disappear when you have a child. Funny how they blend back in when *they* have one… Here's another thing you'll see: you become "valid" because you have a child but, then, you *won't* be, because you stay at home with him. Trust me, I've been there. You are doing the right thing. It's a damn shame that society has no respect for it. They don't know how you feel, and they never could. Their thoughts are so ego-based… Truly, all of life is just an illusion, but 80% of America won't "go there." This is what you tried to point out to me for years; I get it. People in other parts of the world would agree with you all the way! Our Western thinking is so fundamentally flawed…

-Harriet 8/29/05

Tomorrow is the fourth anniversary of the World Trade Center disaster. I am looking at an article called "Explosive Residue Found on Failed

Levee Debris." This is from the terribly tragic Katrina flood in New Orleans a week ago. This explosion occurred at the levee, thus causing the devastation. This looks to be another in a long line of subliminal terrorist events engineered by those wanting to cripple what was clearly a major center of Moorish culture in America.

A few months after the Katrina flood, C-SPAN aired Senate hearings where New Orleans residents testified, under oath, to hearing a huge explosion that broke the levee. Unfortunately, they were not taken seriously, and a nasty argument broke out between the witnesses and the senators. Ultimately, the whole thing was pushed under the rug... Then, in 2010, after several months of foot-dragging on safety, a British Petroleum rig in the Gulf of Mexico, just outside of New Orleans, blew out. It spewed millions of gallons of oil into the ocean, becoming the country's worst manmade disaster. BP executives showed little concern on TV, leading various conspiracy theorists to speculate that the whole thing was planned as a way to punish the region and keep the nation hooked on oil from the Middle East, which the Rockefellers control.

If this Katrina levee were blown, it would fall in line with all the other provocations, like the Reichstag fire, Pearl Harbor, the Lusitania, and the Tonkin Gulf. These events are linked by racist families involved in banking, oil, and armaments. In the 1940s, Prescott Bush was written up in *The New York Times* for "trading with the enemy." He was a steel magnate turned banker who funneled millions of dollars to the Nazis from American corporations. He was more or less managing German armament production. These wealthy right-wingers have always supported fascistic governments. The Nazi "Odessa" has gone on to greater things since the war. It spread mostly to North and South America, via Italy, Sweden, and Spain. Mae Brussell watched these guys closely, and found that they were involved in almost all of our major terrorist events. They are able to take advantage of them, economically and politically, due to the fact that they have foreknowledge. Somehow, Britain manages to stay out of the spotlight, despite the fact that they have strong historical links to the Germans. In fact, during WWII, the British controlled several Nazi front groups.

According to author Peter Moon, the Nazi VIPs took U-boats to Long Island. They were dropped off near Montauk Point, a place many Nazis consider to be the ancient Aryan fatherland of Thule. According to an NPR broadcast I once caught a snippet of, two of Hitler's children live on Long Island, under assumed names... In the Feral House book, *Secret & Suppressed,* there is an interview with famed Nazi warrior Otto Skorzeny, bragging about how the Odessa controls world terror. Skorzeny is famous for rescuing Mussolini from a fortress thought to be impenetrable. He also built a postwar terrorist network in Egypt, and supposedly found the "Spear of Destiny" of the Knights Templar, which was hidden near the Cathars' fabled abbey at Montsegur, France (a "mon" word).

According to Brussell, there is a wide-ranging web connecting the Vatican, CIA, mob, military, Big Oil, Big Pharma, the media, and former Nazis. She felt that they basically took over the country in 1963 by killing Kennedy. The Nazis had to go underground and come to North and South America, where they were integrated into the intelligence services. During the war years, they perfected ways of using terrorism and assassinations for profit. These techniques are now increasingly being used to turn North and South America into police states. If you look at these big terrorist events, you often find connections to the Odessa…

Alexander Haig has a TV show now, where he talks about security issues. Haig is a member of the Knights of Malta, the secretive Masonic group aligned with the Vatican. It's mostly made up of Americans. Haig tried to limit several scandals that broke in the early 1980s when he was in the Reagan administration. A huge scandal broke in Italy at that time, involving assassination teams and so on. Michael Sindona, a Vatican investment strategist, was moving money from the Vatican into American companies. Some of the investments were sketchy and involved drug money. A lot of it was actually covered in the press, but we knuckle-dragging Americans generally ignored it. Mae Brussell certainly covered it. The scandal threatened to spread to the Reagan administration but was halted by Bush, who is tied in with the old boys' network abroad.

-Andy 9/10/05

I just saw a documentary on 9/11. It turns out that Cleveland hosted most of the emergency landings involving hijacked planes. On 9/11, several live military exercises were underway. They involved fake planes, real planes, and simulated crashes into buildings. It appears that Cleveland was the center for all of this. There are those who wonder what happened to the passengers on some of these flights. One lady claims that she has repeatedly gone to the reunion for the flight that her husband supposedly died on, but that no one else ever comes. Where are all the passengers and their families? Were some of the manifests faked? Were some of the passengers transferred to other planes, or to the Shanksville plane that was supposedly brought down?

Some people claim that the planes that hit the towers and Pentagon did not have windows, and that they were painted to look like United Airlines planes. There was a crash report in Colorado that was never investigated, as well as one for the Pt. Pleasant area. Both were reported, but were subsequently dropped from the news. The Pentagon "plane" doesn't appear to have been a plane at all, but a missile. It's interesting that the Pentagon plane, Flight 77, was lost to radar over Point Pleasant. Interestingly, Flight 77 had the same flight path as one of the "Flatwoods Monster" UFOs in 1952. Remember, we're dealing here with covert planners who like to re-use scripts. Perhaps the 9/11 planners fell back on an old flight plan from a previous op, or used a flight plan that conveniently went near certain bases. Flight 77 *did* fly near Sugar Grove, although it circled out so as not to interfere with whatever monitoring goes on there.

Indrid Cold seemed very interested in what Sugar Grove technicians did in their spare time. In fact, he had a team of guys helping him. According to Woody Derenberger in *Visitors From Lanulos*, Cold and his team were watching Dr. Alan Roberts, the UFO psychiatrist. Was Roberts a victim, or an accomplice? Roberts could have been mind-controlled into believing he was taken to Lanulos. He had three kids, which is not the typical profile of a hardcore spy. Tellingly, right after *Visitors From Lanulos* touches on the stalking done by Team Cold, it talks about a local woman who was drugged at a soda fountain. She later came to believe she had been taken to Venus. She didn't remember anything that happened after she sat down at the soda fountain. It seems like someone put a drug in her drink. According to Keel, there were rumors of an MK-Ultra doctor in the area, also a magician, who specialized in slipping drugs into people's drinks without them realizing it.

In *Mass Control: Engineering Human Consciousness,* Jim Keith talks about spies getting cover jobs as Maytag appliance salesmen. They have an excuse to be all over the place, sort of like the Wandering Bishops. Woody retired from Carbide to become an appliance salesman. David Ferrie, a real, known spy, was a Wandering Bishop, as was spy Fred Crisman. Ferrie was consecrated by Carl Stanley of Kentucky. One wonders if Carl was related to Owsley Stanley, the CIA's LSD purveyor, who was from a wealthy Kentucky family. There were three major Wandering Bishop lineages in the country, and one of them was in Kentucky, where Ferrie flew on occasion. Stanley died the same month as Ferrie, after Stanley flew to New York to meet with church bosses. New York was the central location, the original home of these Wandering Bishops. They didn't have much of a clientele in NY. There didn't seem to be anyone going to Mass, yet the church collected lots of money from the neighborhood. It was a place where FBI men and CIA men would meet with the "Bishops." This theme is echoed in the 1960s film *The Fastest Gun in the West* starring

Don Knotts, who was from WV. In that film, a bunch of gunrunners pose as priests in order to move their guns around.

Another tidbit in the Keith book is that there actually is, or was, a "Major Downing" like the one who become known as the Mothman "deep throat." As you may recall, Major Downing claimed that military occultists were controlling the Mothman events in Pt. Pleasant… Currently, there is a General named Downing, who must have been a Major at one time. He is on the board of Network Solutions, which more or less runs the Internet. Network Solutions is owned by the Scientific Applications International Corporation (SAIC) – "CIAs" spelled backwards – based in La Jolla, California… The computer server for SAIC was operated by a company called Spacestar, based in Eden Prairie, Minnesota. This was the same server used by the Heaven's Gate cult. Heaven's Gate was also based in La Jolla, California.

Heaven's Gate appears to have been used to cover up the Martin Luther King family summit – where they came out to say that they felt James Earl Ray was innocent. The media held off on the announcement of the suicide, which made it conflict with the King announcement. Previous rules regarding "mass suicide" coverage were broken; they graphically showed the dead. Pundits admitted that they had never before seen dead bodies like that on TV. The media did everything they could to make it as gory, incredible, and strange as they could. This not only drowned out the fact that the King family was saying that James Earl Ray was innocent, but it tarnished it. People just wanted to forget about everything that happened that week. Mass mind control was used to cover up what really happened in a key, historical event… By the way, San Diego is also the location for Naval Electronic Systems Command, reported to have been one of the funding sources for Hal Puthoff's early "remote viewing" experiments at Stanford Research Institute. Puthoff and Puharich were comrades, having met when Puharich brought Uri Geller over to be tested at SRI.

Another interesting book is *The Conspiracy Reader* by the editors of *Paranoia* magazine, which has a chapter about how Nixon came to power with the help of powerful ex-Nazis. They also discuss the "Rockefeller Signature" in dealing with public protests. The author looks at the manner in which miners in Colorado were killed in 1915. The Rockefeller Signature is to allow the protesters to protest all they want. But once it reaches a certain point, they go in and, without warning, kill a few people in cold blood. In other words, they want there to be justification for an extremely violent response. They let the protestors get more riled up than they normally would. The same thing happened at the Attica Prison riots, where Nelson Rockefeller let the prisoners take over. He didn't do the proper things, early on, to keep it under control. Then, they just went in and murdered some prisoners. *Paranoia* is saying that the same thing happened at Kent State, where you had a lot of ritualistic chanting and marching by the National Guard just prior to opening fire on random students who weren't even protesting.

David McGowan's *Programmed to Kill* is a good book for those who want to explore the linkages between snipers, serial killers, and mind control. In order to effectively carry out the Phoenix Program of assassinating and terrorizing the North Vietnamese, the U.S. Army needed snipers with segmented personalities – who could distance themselves from the act of killing. They needed to be desensitized to violence. The Navy was also big on this. The technique was to show violent films to soldiers while having them do small tasks. In this way, they became more and more used to functioning while seeing horrible scenes. It became more elaborate as the years went on, to where they could program them so that they couldn't even remember doing the atrocities. Someone who married into my family got caught up in this. He actually spent a couple of years in prison for raping and pillaging in Vietnam. After his release from prison, his personality seemed like it had been wiped clean. He was no longer the same person at all. The bubbly nice guy was gone. He worked for R.C. Cola before going into the service, and he got his job back afterwards. His personality started coming back after a few years, during which he fought off several Agent Orange-related cancers.

The Expanding Case for the UFO is the third book by Philadelphia Experiment guru Morris K. Jessup. He was "suicided" not long after this book, perhaps because he spent a lot of time in it debunking how the media treats UFO cases. He was an astronomer, so his word carried a little more weight than usual… He started getting interested in satellites and their relationship to UFOs. This was a bit of a turnaround from his earlier books, where he posited the existence of a supernatural, invisible UFO fleet into which our planes were crashing. He initially presented evidence that the UFOs were sucking water out of lakes and dumping fish everywhere. He felt that these secret, invisible ET craft had been around for centuries, and were perhaps responsible for people's disappearances – a precursor to our modern "abduction" phenomenon.

But… He switched gears, and began thinking more along terrestrial lines. The more Jessup probed the eavesdropping satellite angles, the more he got into trouble. Perhaps Jessup decided to rebel a bit from his controllers; he started revealing the synthetic aspects of the phenomenon. Jessup worked for a time for the Rubber Development Corporation. He did a lot of astronomical and anthropological study in Central and

South America, where the Rockefellers were heavily invested. Around the time of Mothman, the Rockefellers teamed up with Goodyear to pioneer complicated side-angle radar mapping of the mineral wealth of the Amazon. They perfected their methods by first mapping areas like rubber plantations, which they already controlled; any inadvertent deaths from the beams could be more easily covered up that way. When they started to go to other areas of the continent, the word eventually got out, drawing the attention of researchers like Jacques Vallee.

The book *Strength of the Wolf: The Story of the Federal Bureau of Narcotics,* by Douglas Valentine, is the history of the Federal Bureau of Narcotics, detailing its secret relationships with the FBI, Navy, Mob, CIA, and SE Asian drug-running cartels. The Bruno name came up in here, as did the names of familiar conspiracy nests like Montreal, Las Vegas, and Cleveland. Following the mob bust in Apalachin, NY, in 1957, interfacing between the FBI, the Jewish and Italian mafias, the CIA, the military, and the Church increased. In some cases, the Wandering Bishops and/or missionary organizations were used as cutouts, such as Nelson Rockefeller's Summer Language Institute. I seem to remember a quick mention of an Army officer named Downing in Valentine's book… In closing, one of the strange things I noticed here in Seattle, during the week of the 2004 presidential vote, was this weird, low hum that penetrated everyone's houses. Other people noticed it, too, so it wasn't just my imagination. It was definitely happening. But, it ended right after the election. Such low frequency activity reminded me of that retired Mobil Oil executive who experiments globally with extremely low frequencies. It could be that a lot of this tinkering comes from private individuals with resources. All the government has to do is step out of the way and do nothing.

-Andy 9/10/05

Thursday, the SWAT unit of Franklin Co. overtook my house and yard, and used it as a command center after a disturbed neighbor barricaded himself into his house. He had over 70 automatic weapons, including submachine guns. I was questioned for five hours about this man, since he seemed to only talk to me in the neighborhood. His ex-wife and I are good friends, and his 12-yr. old daughter is a friend of my daughter. All I had done was come home at lunch to pee the dog. *That* will teach me…

-Harriet 9/12/05

I enjoyed your discourse on Indrid Cold, particularly the connection with the Garuda. I assume you are aware of the various forms of Garuda and their functions. A good friend of mine has been followed throughout her life by a very similar [entity]. Several of her friends have heard and seen this flying, birdlike creature. It terrified her, so she sought my advice. As a practitioner of both Dzog Chen and Toltec, she asked me for some kind of relief from this "curse" as she calls it – the controlling factor of the Garuda manifestation. Although I have not seen any hard evidence that her case is absolutely related to the Garuda, I am sure that the practice of Dragpur has done her good. Whether or not this is a psychological relief akin to a placebo, I cannot say. But, to this day (4 years), she has had no more visitations. These appearances almost always happened in outlying rural locations, like on camping trips. Once, it followed her for several miles when she was traveling with a companion. They both saw it very clearly racing alongside the car at over 80 miles per hour. That night, they heard the screeching from their motel. The next morning, the manager also stated that there was an "ungodly howling" during the night.

-Nagualito 9/15/05

This past weekend I was in South Bend, Indiana for a wedding. We went back to the hotel after the wedding Saturday night. At about 4 a.m., I was awakened by *you,* telling me to go to my son. The next morning, my mom called and told me that my son had been brutally mugged on a sidewalk in Peoria, IL by a bunch of gang members. He was in the ER of a local hospital. He has serious head trauma and some hearing loss from being kicked in the head. They think it is temporary, however. They took his wallet and cellphone, but got caught 10 minutes later. My son is well versed in the martial arts, but acted like he was unconscious rather than fight back. There were four of them, and one of him. He didn't know if they had a gun or knife. He waited until they walked down the street a bit, then ran. It just so happened a squad car was in the area with its headlights out. They walked right past the car. They ditched his wallet and cellphone, and then took off running. The cops tackled them and roughed them up. Three of them are in jail. It turns out my son was the third victim of the evening, and he got it far worse than anyone else… I have no idea why *you* appeared to me, but thank you. When I woke up the next morning, I *knew* something was wrong. I am most proud, because my son's spirit has not been broken. He is taking all of this quite well. They even ripped his Medic Alert necklace off of his neck, thinking it was "bling-bling" of some kind. I hope you never have to live through something like this; it is hideous. If he has to go to court, then I will be driving back to Peoria for the court date. I wonder if they will let good ol' mom take a swing at the perps with a baseball bat.

-Harriet 9/27/05

I have to share this with you. Not too many people would understand this. Over the weekend, I was at yet another wedding, this time in New Jersey. On Saturday, out of nowhere, I thought of a client of mine who has been struggling, for years with addiction issues. I kept saying, "I wish she would contact me." My husband said, "You usually stay so detached from your clients. Why are you bringing her up?" I truly had no idea... Unfortunately, I just found out that she has died. So, I guess she *did* contact me... In that moment on Saturday when she died, I had this extreme moment of clarity. I saw that the reason she took drugs wasn't because of her weight as she said; she was slim. She needed drugs in order to focus. She was an extremely successful, well-known radio personality. She "functioned" beautifully and had great clarity when she took these drugs. How could I have been so blind? How many other people out there with addictions are doing the same thing? I am devastated. She was a lovely human being.

-Harriet 10/5/05

Something crashed into the Pentagon. We all agree on that. But was it a missile, or was it a plane? My cousin's husband was there, running for his life. He claims that he saw an airplane with airline insignia. But that could have been transferred onto a missile, could it not? He's very strange... I'll ask my aunt, the ex-CIA agent, about some of the details. When you stop and think about it, my cousin's husband works for the Joint Chiefs of Staff. Why *wouldn't* he lie? That is probably a part of his job description! He is an oddball. Really, I'm not being judgmental on this one. You would think so, too. I would describe him as "cagey," even though he is a fanatical, reborn Christian.

-Harriet 10/7/05

Having worked at a newspaper, I can buy the idea of an editor doing someone a favor. People were always trying to get their agendas pushed across a copy desk, even in the most routine of stories. That's why I got out of the business. I would write a story but, by the time it was edited and ended up in print, many key facts would be changed. This happened repeatedly... Like you, I believe in parallel universes and dimensions. I think that what some people spontaneously witness is the overlapping of those dimensions; these are "spiritual experiences." At first, I had a hard time believing the government would waste its time trying to put a false message out there, but now I'm not so sure. Fear is such a great motivator. It pushes institutional agendas. There probably are true "alien" visitations that certain highly sensitive people can see, but there could be many other false ones planted in the media. Remember that Indian lady I told you about years ago, who told me that I was a "healer" and had the gift of foresight? She also told me that I had a birthday that was very significant. It is one day off from what is discussed in this article you sent about 2012. She told me to be ready for a "new awakening" on my birthday in 2012. My birthday is Dec. 21st, which by most counts is the *actual* end of the Mayan calendar in 2012, not the 22nd.

-Harriet 10/10/05

My daughter wanted to go visit Lakin State Hospital [where her grandfather had been treated]. Some of her friends go there ghost hunting. She was determined that I take her there. We also went out to the TNT Area. My daughter is psychic, if she would only accept the fact. Her experiences at the TNT and Lakin left her physically ill. All of my children have psychic sight, especially my youngest son and daughter. My [younger] son has talked about things of a paranormal nature since he was able to talk. My oldest son has also had many paranormal experiences. I believe it is something that happens to certain families, from one generation to another. I can trace this stuff back to my great-grandmother on my mother's side of the family. I don't know if it is because of government experiments, or because of ETs, or UTs, or "all of the above." I feel you understand what I mean. There is more government involvement here in WV than most people realize... I was surprised that John Frick stepped in and defended me [regarding] the morphing plane that I photographed. Morphing had never even crossed my mind before that but, after reading about the new "morphing" plane the military has developed, I have to consider that the plane I saw *could* have done just that. I did not see the plane disappear myself (I was too busy fooling with my camera), but I did see it appear out of the cloud. The reason I say that the plane "disappeared" is because there was no way it could have gotten out of sight that fast.

-Tara 10/11/05

I remember John Keel talking about giants being on the North American continent many years before the American Indian. Their bones were found all over our country. The Indians may have even co-existed with these giants [or] had to fight the giants to settle land. When the giants were finally pushed out, they migrated north to Wisconsin and Minnesota. Giant skeletal remains were found in those states, but were hushed up and forgotten. Most of the evidence is in the basements of museums, or buried in peoples' cellars. The giants ranged from 7 to 12 feet tall. Scientists swept all the evidence under the rug. [They didn't want it to] exist scientifically.

-Barbara 10/22/05

Believe it or not, our esteemed hypnosis teacher, Ormond McGill, predicted his own death! He hypnotized me back in March of 2003. I paid for a private session. He read me like a book; he is very intuitive... He said that I *knew* we didn't die at death. He asked me if I had read his book, *Grieve No More, My Beloved*, about his wife's death and her subsequent "appearances" to him. He told me that he still had some work to do. He had to live another couple of years to do it. Then, he would pass in the fall of 2005 to be with his wife. And that is exactly what happened...

-Harriet 10/24/05

I'm very impressed with the intimacy of your work. Your friend, Harriet, is very compelling and believable. I had an immediate connection to your sister, Loretta; she seems to be a sweetheart. Thank you for sending the jpegs. I vividly remember a black and white picture that you drew of your dad. I remember your dad's eyes looking very scared. He was sitting, center left, in a chair. His legs weren't crossed. His back was pushed up against the chair. That image has stayed with me for 26 years. In fact, when I think about you, that particular drawing of your dad always comes to mind.

My ex-husband, the psychologist, ex-Navy Commander, and covert pedophile (unbeknownst to me when we married), was in charge of a telecommunications station in California in the late 1970's and early '80s. He was a professional photographer and extremely gifted in many areas. My husband would lose blocks of time quite frequently. At the time, I attributed this to post-traumatic stress disorder, as he claimed to be a Vietnam veteran. This was later discovered to be a lie, as were many other things about his life. But the Naval Commander part is true. He was very prolific and well read, particularly about the occult and paranormal. It is quite possible, in hindsight, that he was an abductee. I've joked over the years about this, but now I'm being more analytical and serious about the possibility. During the brief couple of years we were together, a black shadow attached itself to my car. I could view it in the periphery as I was driving. When my husband and I split, I never saw it again.

Andy, I don't tell many people about this one but, before I gave birth to my son, I had two ectopic pregnancies. One was found; the other one was *never* found, despite my HCG levels increasing daily. The whole incident was very traumatic, including multiple trips to various Boston hospitals. No one had answers, or even a clue, about what was going on; it defied all scientific logic. Finally, because my "baby cells" kept on growing, I was given methatrexate and leucovorin, which are drugs used to kill cancer cells... My maternal grandmother was known as the town psychic in Hopkinton, MA in the early 1900s. She was also diagnosed with schizophrenia: paranoid type. Based on behaviors not related to her psychic gifts, I believe that diagnosis to be true. My mother also has psychic traits.

One night, when I was working on the crisis team, I interviewed a young man whom the hospital staff believed was having a "psychotic break." He related a story to me about his father being a member of an underground clown group that produces snuff films. In the films, children are murdered. I ended up researching his "delusion" and, come to find out, I could validate a large portion of what he was telling me! Of course, the story the government gives us is that "snuff films don't exist" – that it's all an "urban myth." Like you, I am also a conspiracy theorist, but not really in the political realm. The medical field has a lot of red flags all of its own. I work in hospital settings, and I see and hear a lot.

Our home has a friendly prankster ghost, who rings our front door often, particularly when I am giving voice lessons or playing the piano by myself. Our home is Victorian, built in 1900 as an inn. It is furnished with antiques. I'm really involved with antiques. While I have been living here, I have also become a gourmet cook. Anyway, I consulted my tarot card reader, who is psychic. She doesn't see any sort of negative energy from this spirit. She thinks that the spirit enjoys my singing voice! Take care, my friend... And thanks for again opening my mind to new experiences...

-Bonnie B. 12/14/05

Clockwise from top left: the last photo of the author's father, which inspired the painting referred to by Bonnie B.; Union Carbide I.D. for A.B. Colvin, Sr. (note 3 pyramids); the Blaine Island Carbide plant, where Colvin, Sr. worked; Yearbook photo of A.B. Colvin, Sr. from Norfolk Naval Station, Fall 1943, exactly when the Philadelphia Experiment is said to have taken place there. His presence in Norfolk may be the reason the Colvins were monitored by the MIBs.

CHAPTER 18

"In history, stagnant waters, whether they be the stagnant
waters of custom or those of despotism, harbour no life;
life is dependent on the ripples created by a few eccentric
individuals. In homage to that life and vitality, the community has to brave certain perils and must countenance a
measure of heresy. One must live dangerously if one wants to
live at all."

-Sir Herbert Read

"Because no one is really sure what mental illness is, the
'illness' designation is only a temporary classification...
Erving Goffman [was] very skeptical about the medical and
scientific claims of psychiatrists... Psychiatrists have had to
learn a sociological sensitivity concerning ordinary behavior;
they have had to observe the behavior of normal people very
carefully, in order to distinguish it from the behavior of their
patients. Goffman gave this view in the early paper, 'Mental
Symptoms and Public Order':

> Psychosis is something that can manifest itself to anyone
> in the workplace, neighborhood, and household, and
> must be seen – initially at least – as an infraction of the
> social order that obtains in these places. The other side of
> the study of symptoms is the study of public order, the
> study of behavior in public and semipublic places. If you
> would learn about one side of this matter, you ought to
> study the other, too.

"The implication of this argument, as Goffman notes, is that it
should be possible to fabricate insanity, to 'program' individuals to behave as if they were 'crazy.' This is because a convincing performance of craziness may not require destructive
brain surgery, simply an incomprehensible attitude towards
the rules governing everyday behavior – break these and you
risk people doubting your sanity. Much psychotic behavior is,
Goffman believed, a 'failure to abide by the rules established
for the conduct of face-to-face interaction.' By extension,
mental illness is, therefore, a collection of 'situational impro-
prieties,' and insanity refers to a person's behavior and not to
his or her bodily malfunctions. To understand this argument,

it is useful to think about the following test: can psychiatrists identify mental illness in a dead body as easily as in a living one? According to Goffman, only then will they have demonstrated that mental illness literally exists, and is not simply a metaphor or label for unpleasant or unusual behavior."

-Philip Manning, *Erving Goffman and Modern Sociology*, pp. 102-104

"The existence of an unconscious telepathic link among members of the same species could be a great help in developing and stabilizing new behavior patterns. Whatley Carington, who once experimented with the telepathic transmission of drawings between people, put forth the idea that other patterns might be communicated in the same way, suggesting that 'instinctive behavior of this high order... may be due to the individual creature being linked up into a larger system, or common unconscious, in which all the experience of the species is stored...' We know beyond doubt that instinctive behavior is controlled by genetic inheritance, but it is possible that telepathy could be useful *before* a habit becomes genetically fixed. A habit must become widespread before it can be incorporated into the repertoire of a species, and it could be spread and stabilized very effectively by some kind of telepathic system. Without telepathy, it is difficult to see how an elaborate instinctive pattern can develop at all...

"In complex societies such as those of bees and ants, we know that part of this function is played by chemicals, by pheromones that...release smells designed for special situations such as laying a trail to food or 'scenting' an alarm. But there are situations where more concerted action is necessary and where the local and short-lived effects of the smell alarm are inadequate. Ivan Sanderson studied harvester ants of the genus *Atta* in tropical America and reported remarkable communal activity... It is certain that *Atta* have a telecommunication system, and it seems to be independent of known chemical and mechanical senses. They, and other species like them, could make good use of, and perhaps already use, some form of telepathy. All are united by a set of instincts into a single self-supporting structure in which the interests of the parts are subordinate to the interests of the whole. It should not be surprising to find that such an organism has a rudimentary mind.

"After all, the functions of the human mind cannot be anchored to any one cell or even group of cells. The brain is made up of far more parts than there are in an ant colony, and yet it manages to function as a whole, with more or less complete communication between its separate cells. Impressions are gathered from different areas and merged in the mind... This communion may even go a step further and involve all individuals belonging to the same species. The DNA code carries instructions that determine the general physical form. Flies bred to be sightless [can] rearrange themselves [to] have eyes again. But perhaps there is another organizer, a stream of shared experience that allows only the best copies of the species to survive. Telepathy could do this... Living things are involved in an open dialogue with the universe, a free exchange of information and influence that unites all life into one vast organism that is itself part of an even larger dynamic structure [which] knows no bounds...

"Too often, we see only what we expect to see; our view of the world is restricted by the blinkers of our limited experience, but it need not be this way. Few aspects of human behavior are so persistent as our need to believe in things unseen. [This] belief, or the strange things to which this belief is so stubbornly attached, must have real survival value. I think we are rapidly approaching a situation in which this value will become apparent. As man uses up the resources of the world, he is going to have to rely more and more on his own. Many of these [beliefs and techniques] are at the moment concealed in the occult – a word that simply means 'secret knowledge.' [It] is a very good description of something that we have known all along, but have been hiding from ourselves."

-Lyall Watson, *Super Nature*, pp. 272-275

COLVIN, ANDY – GRASSY KNOLL RADIO INTERVIEWS 33 & 34 – JULY 2008

"Vyz" at *Beyond the Grassy Knoll* (GK): Yes, this is the show that your parents warned you about, *Beyond the Grassy Knoll*... With us today, for Mothman show number 33, is Andrew Colvin. What have we got on the agenda today?

Andy Colvin (AC): Well, I was thinking of starting my own show with the name *Beyond One Step*. Most of us in today's America don't go much further than the first step in understanding anything, unless its content is utterly gratuitous or superfluous...

GK: Did you ever take a look at those episodes from the old show, *One Step Beyond*?

AC: Yes, I saw the one with Andrija Puharich and the magic mushrooms. Puharich seemed a little robotic at times...

GK: Because he was stoned! Puharich was everywhere... It's amazing that the host, Newland, ran into him and involved him in what was probably the most untoward episode *One Step Beyond* ever did. They actually went onsite and did a documentary rather than a dramatization. Incredibly, those who took the mushrooms and then ran their hand across a book – while blindfolded – could *still* read the words.

AC: Yes, the mushrooms increase your psychic ability. But beyond what you ingest, the physical things in your surroundings can also affect psychic ability: the types of plants and minerals in the area, whether or not there are negative ions present, magnetic fields, bodies of water, and so on. There has always been an odd smell in Mound where we all saw these creatures. The area also sees a lot of lightning, so perhaps electricity is being stored in the geophysical strata and in pipelines. If conditions are right, electromagnetism can trigger the mind in a manner similar to the mushrooms. It ignites the pineal gland, allowing it to interact with the superspectrum and pick up information. Since the pineal is related to hormones, anything sexual amplifies the signal.

GK: People make fun of country people for being rubes, but they are not rubes. When I went back to school for a second degree at the University of South Florida, to get certified to teach, I took a part-time job as a park ranger in a county park. We used to have to do a perimeter check each morning. I typically went as early as possible, because that was when all of the animals were just waking up; it was wonderful. We did this perimeter check on a Cushman, which is a golf cart that runs on electricity. It's very, very quiet. Deer would come right up to the cart; it was astounding. We would pass adjacent pasturelands where cattle defecated; from their loads would come these mushrooms, right out of the cow dung. The next morning, we'd come out, and the new mushrooms were always gone. Those kids went out there every day to take a look and harvest. I had to laugh…

AC [jokingly]: Could *mushrooms* be what's behind the Mothman phenomenon?

GK: I tell you what, it couldn't hurt. So, what are we going to start off with?

AC: Six random pages of notes!

GK: If you were to generalize why you make these notes, could you put it under a single heading? Synchronicities?

AC: Yes, but it goes in so many directions… It takes time to link each one back into this matrix, this layout of how it all connects. I try to do that in our shows. I try to quickly say, "This connects to that." Some people may be baffled, because they haven't heard all the shows, which is to be expected. I'm always contacting people, and people are contacting me, like the lady from Spain who saw an Egyptian-style birdman in her hotel room recently, or the guy who saw Mothman east of Akron in 2005… By the way, he just sent me a photo of two snowmen in his front yard. The image of the snowmen is almost identical to a picture that I took in Wheeling, WV, having to do with Sterling Products, the Bayer offshoot company. I've had other strange synchronicities with this particular witness. But these kinds of synchronistic symbols and coincidences continually crop up, and so I take note of them. I'm always sort of researching JFK, 9/11, the Bush-Rockefellers, Aleister Crowley, world history, art history, ethnology, and so on. I recently started researching Buckeye Steel, which is the steel company that the Bush family owned. I noticed that at key times, odd things were happening with that company. Guess who was the president of Buckeye before Prescott Bush took over?

GK: Rockefeller?

AC: Yes, Frank Rockefeller, John D.'s brother. After Prescott took over, decades went by with no highlights in the Buckeye story until 1967, the year Mothman exploded into consciousness. Suddenly, it was decided to create a holding company for Buckeye. Then, in 1980, when some more Mothman sightings occurred, Buckeye was bought out by an insider named Worthington. He held the company for a while, until 1999. Some real funny things started happening as we got closer to 9/11. Worthington formed *another* company with some investors who remain anonymous; we still don't know who they were. Worthington sold Buckeye to *that* holding company. Then, within three years, it went bankrupt. This is unusual, because Buckeye was netting between a billion and two billion dollars a year throughout the 1990s. There was no reason for it to go bankrupt. I'm starting to wonder about these Bush/Rockefeller steel endeavors. The Titanic and Lusitania disasters connect to the Bushes through their very construction and financing. Crowley was apparently involved in the Lusitania sinking; the loss of armaments onboard stimulated further defense spending and kept the arms out of the hands of the Nazis, who had failed Britain by unsuccessfully invading Russia. It is beginning to seem that Crowley really might *be* the father of Barbara Bush, whose family owned such large ships. Of course, the Hindenburg disaster also connects to the Rockefellers, at least in terms of Goodyear, whose partnership in dirigible development with the Germans was not unlike Prescott Bush's involvement in the steel industry of the Third Reich.

GK: Some money laundering took place between Prescott Bush and Harriman and the German Army prior to WWII. American companies armed belligerents prior to WWI as well. When you have this pre-arming of all the players involved, a war suddenly happens, and the bankers and industrialists make money. Little is known about World War I although, for sure, the Lusitania was a sacrifice – like 9/11 – to get Americans pissed off enough to get into a war that they had no business being in.

AC: Interestingly, Buckeye reopened as "Columbus Steel Castings" in 2002, right after 9/11. According to local scuttlebutt, they were quietly bought out and then resold by a German steel company. It's like they disappeared from the radar screen during the buildup to 9/11. I'm wondering if the steel for the Twin Towers originally came from Buckeye. They reorganized in '67... Wasn't that around the time they started building the towers?

GK: They started building the towers in 1965.

AC: We should find out where the steel came from...

GK: I'll take a look at *City in the Sky: The Rise and Fall of the World Trade Center*. The only problem is that the book was written in 2003. I'd trust it more if it were written *before* 2001.

AC: Next item... Did you know that a "dwarf planet" was found last week? It's called "Makemake," after the Polynesian god of fertility. The cult that worships Makemake is called the Tongata Manu (note "mon" word). They consider Makemake to be a man with a bird head – a birdman. I have found this in various cultures. It seems like the birdman is pretty much "it" as far as godlike creatures go. A lot of the headhunting tribes in New Guinea worship birds. Let's see… What are some other "mon" words? The birth of dualism in philosophy occurred with "Man-icheanism," which is similar to Zoroastrianism; both are early "good vs. evil" systems, where man's brain started to become more differentiated. The God of Manicheanism was called "Mainyu," which is essentially a "mon" word. In just about every ancient religion, you will find prominent "mon" names for gods. Most cities in America have either a "Mound" Street or a "Main" Street, and often have both. You mentioned the Manisis Chronicles, which is a "mon" word… We've got "Mon-santo," the chemical company, and "Monokotak," the town where a Mothman or Thunderbird was seen in 2004, which presaged the earthquake that Harriet predicted… Speaking of interesting names, a woman named "Tree" Pruitt saw some lights at the Serpent Mound. She drew a diagram of the lights' pattern. Later, she found out that it was the same pattern as found in the Serpent Mound crop circle of 2003, the famous "Eye of Horus" circle… Other things… I was doing a search using Yahoo maps, looking at the area where I grew up in Mound. You can go into the satellite shots and see topographical details anywhere in the world. When I went to Woodward Dr., to the area where we saw the entities, Yahoo put me on some little security alert and cut me off, temporarily, from looking at it. There is a gravel pit or some kind of mining operation there today, which was not there in the 1960s. It is just beneath the old cemetery. We couldn't get back there on foot. The Loftis family owns the operation. There are trucks going to and from it at all hours. They keep carting earth and gravel in and out… On the satellite image, however, it's hard to see very much of a gravel pit. It is mostly just a large warehouse of some kind. One wonders if they are digging something underground there – perhaps building an installation. I was also looking at this area called Five Mile Creek near Pt. Pleasant, which runs through the old village of Mohrtown – what was probably originally called "Moortown." There are several mounds around there, such as the "May Moore" Mound; Moors probably once settled that whole area.

Coincidentally, there is Moorish blood on all four sides of my family. Some members of my extended family have dark skin and curly hair. In fact, one of my cousins was kicked out of a white school, prior to segregation, until he could "prove" that he was white.

Members of the Gibson and Colvin clans, along with other mixed-blood clans, were singled out by the federal government during WWII as not being eligible for "Native American" status because of their African heritage. In 2009, I discovered that the early Colvins in America had intermingled with the royal line of the Montauk Indians, who claim to be the direct descendants of the Egyptian pharaohs.

AC: Mohrtown is where Keel saw many of his UFOs, including an apparent "nuts and bolts" one. Some local Mothman buffs recently found the spot where Keel used to go, which is near where Five Mile Creek Road turns into Modoc Road. "Modoc" is another name for "Marduk." And Marduk is another name for "Moloch," the Hebrew king venerated by faux ritual sacrifices at the Great Stone Owl of Bohemian Grove. Another road in Mohrtown is called "Horselick." "Horse" shares roots with "Horus," the Egyptian birdman, while "lick" indicates a source of salt and, usually, prior habitation by Indians. There is also a "Redmond" Road, as in "Red Mound" or Indian mound. There is a "Caddy" Road there. Caddy is the nickname for the Cadillac, the primary car that the Men in Black drove. These particular names are all in the Chief Cornstalk Wildlife area. Cornstalk is the Native who reportedly prophesied the coming of Mothman 200 years ago. Cornstalk and his son, Redhawk, were killed by Army intelligence agents under the command, ultimately, of George Washington. Next up...I just found out about something called Project Mercurè, an ET scenario with a plotline similar to that of the movie *The Man Who Fell to Earth*, where David Bowie played an "alien" residing at Area 51. Synchronistically, I had been studying the element mercury at the time, particularly as it relates to the secret Nazi Doomsday weapon. Joseph Farrell's *Brotherhood of the Bell* discusses this connection. The element mercury was key to developing this Bell bomb, which was scalar in nature, meaning it basically explodes a bigger molecular grouping than an A-bomb. Instead of just exploding an atom, it explodes a set of them. Mercury can be spun in centrifuges and injected with high voltage, which alters its properties. I think this may relate to whatever was going on in Mound, because that is the place where pure nickel was being refined, which is necessary to make such centrifuges. A Bell weapon may be what fell at Kecksburg, PA, in 1965... A European partner with Carbide, Germany's Linde Corp., is officially credited with pulling together America's effort to develop the A-bomb. Linde built all the centrifuges in Oak Ridge to process the huge amounts of uranium necessary to make plutonium. Similar centrifuges were necessary to create scalar weapons like the Nazi Bell. You hear a lot of different rumors about scalar weapons in the conspiracy world… People claim that a scalar weapon was used at the World Trade Center.

GK: Some of those people *also* claim that no planes actually hit the towers – that it was all faked with CGI technology by the TV stations. The 9/11 Truth scene is toast…

AC: Yes, they had to come up with something crazier than the truth, in order to discredit it. They may also be trying to discredit the existence of a Bell weapon, just as they discredited the idea that the U.S. military has real saucers by blaming everything on ETs. If the Bell weapon did happen to get developed, though, I'll bet some part of it was done in Mound, due to the necessity of having those pure nickel centrifuges. This would go along with what my dad told me, which is that he was involved in "heating metals." That is more or less what they do to mercury in order to make this scalar stuff happen… Synchronistically, as I was reading about this, I turned on the TV to a documentary about the Doomsday Weapon. Supposedly, the Germans stored portions of it in Prague, in gravel quarry caves. I knew a Czech scientist in Seattle, who was in my Buddhist group. He was working for Battelle in Hanford, WA. He said that the whole project was about scamming taxpayers by charging outrageous fees to encase radioactive waste in glass. It is rumored that other, cheaper solutions to the problem of radioactive waste, like Brown's gas (which is said to neutralize radioactivity), have been suppressed, in order to keep the costs high… Speaking of Hanford, Walter Bowart, the late mind control researcher interviewed in *The Mothman's Photographer III*, died in Washington State. He was once married to Peggy Mellon Hitchcock, the sister of the owner of Timothy Leary's "acid mansion" in Millbrook, NY, which was raided by G. Gordon Liddy. By the way, I interviewed a paranormal experiencer here in Seattle whose father taught at the Millbrook Academy. The Mellon family is connected to Carbide. Bowart was married to Mellon during the time he was writing *Operation Mind Control*.

GK: One wonders if that book contributed to their split. I think they got divorced not long after that…

AC: Eugenia Macer-Story recently wrote an article called "Bride of the Mothman," about a ring that showed up outside of her house. Someone left a ring made of seashell that looks like a moth. At the same time, Bruce Bickford started talking about rings; certain details will sometimes hit you from different angles, bringing your attention to something important. So, I contacted Macer-Story. She not only writes amazing books on UFOs, but also does psychic work. She drew an astral portrait of me, in fact. First, she makes a drawing of the subject while she is in a meditative state. Then, she interprets the drawing. She sort of empties her mind to do these drawings. After the image is done, she grabs symbolic meanings about it from the superspectrum. Amazingly, she said the same thing that a Qi Gong healer had said earlier: some sort of feminine entity had attached itself to me early in life... Macer-Story basically believes that Mothman is the Garuda. She feels that there are male and female components to it; the female side is equivalent to "Lilith" or "Minerva." Eugenia believes these ancient goddesses and gods really do exist, and that they manifest through people. Her drawing seemed to indicate that at least one of these is speaking through me – through my work. She suggested ways to mitigate their presence. You don't want to let them advance their agenda; you retain your boundaries and simply converse with them... This is random, but I'll just remind everyone that November 11, 1966, the day that Mothman was first seen, was *also* the day that the Pope "called out" the Jesuits. How coincidental can it get? Why did the Mothman start appearing at that time? Was he trying to say something about the Jesuits?

GK: For folks who have recently come aboard, Andy believes that the Mothman is benevolent, in the sense that it is warning people. If doom is coming, Mothman is not causing it but warning that something is about to go down.

AC: In one respect, it is straight prophecy. For instance Tommy, who predicted 9/11 back in 1967, also predicted things that were more localized. In first grade, he drew a picture of a dead man. The teacher asked, "What's that?" He goes, "That's your husband." The husband died not long after that, which freaked everybody out; clearly something prophetic was going on. When one starts looking at the symbolisms provided by the entity, a bigger picture emerges. By simply following the trail of where Mothman was seen, it was possible to uncover a lot of interesting information. This fits with the traditional role of the Garuda; he/she balances the scales by sending hints...

GK: Is Mothman the most modern manifestation of the Garuda? I'm wondering if Batman wasn't somewhat of an extension of the Garuda legend.

AC: I think so; both emanate from a cave to police a corrupt society.

GK: Batman did not fly, but overcame that by having a bunch of gadgetry, like most of us human beings. I always wanted to be Batman. He was benevolent. I'm wondering what may have triggered some of the comic book artists – what their sources were.

AC: The father of William James, the famous writer, saw what might have been Mothman in his study. This famous event apparently affected all of the James family members. It affected them positively, in that they all ended up becoming great writers and/or thinkers.

GK: William's brother, Henry, was a famous psychologist…

AC *[jokingly]*: He probably could have helped the family that developed Bakelite! They went a bit batty after they got their money. Carbide bought up Bakelite, thus making the family rich. A movie about the Bakelite heirs, *Savage Grace*, just came out.

GK: Wasn't Bakelite resistant to high heats?

AC: Yes, and it was lightweight, too. Something akin to Bakelite was supposedly found at the Roswell crash site. All kinds of things were made from Bakelite.

GK: It was used to insulate high-power electrical wires.

AC: Carbide may have had something to do with the 1897 "airship" sightings in Texas, California, and WV. Dirigibles had been developed in the mid-1800s, so one wonders what all the hullabaloo was about. Each of those states was an important oil state. WV hosted the first gas well ever drilled, which eventually led to oil drilling technology being developed in the area. The airship sighting in WV took place in Sistersville, near one of the early Carbide plants. According to one of Loren Coleman's early books, Europeans had come over and were testing these flying ships. There was a mystery investor behind it all, whose pseudonym reminds me of Cornelius Billings, the bankster behind Carbide. I'm starting to wonder if the airship sightings weren't simply some Carbiders trying out new gear. Within twenty years of the airship sightings, we were bombing Nicaragua from airplanes; the airships were probably part of a military buildup… Another thing Coleman did, early in his career, was to list the attributes of the "manimals," i.e., Bigfoot, Mothman and so forth. Number one on his list was "glowing red eyes." However, today, his standard debunking line about Mothman is, "No, those were *not* glowing eyes; they were merely *reflective* eyes." He has completely flip-flopped... What else have we got? There was a birdman sighting in 1890 in Independence, Iowa. People saw a horrid, winged creature with the head of an alligator. It "had scales, roared like a lion, and screamed like a bobcat..." In 1948, in the Illinois towns of Caledonia, a monsterbird was seen by military personnel, one of whom was the head of the Western Military Academy. On 4/24/48, two policemen saw the monsterbird in Alton, IL, claiming that it was the size of an airplane. James Earl Ray, MLK's supposed assassin, was from Alton. Texas and California happen to be places Ray went to before the assassination. Did he go to West Virginia as well? He did all this traveling around as the MLK assassination planners were setting him up. Researchers should look at Los Angeles, Dallas, Houston, and New Orleans for more MLK conspirators. When he was in Los Angeles, Ray had plastic surgery. He also went to Mexico.

GK *[shocked]*: James Earl Ray had plastic surgery in Los Angeles and then went to Mexico?

AC: Yes, and he did this *before* the assassination. He took a trip to New Orleans in December of 1967, the same month as the Silver Bridge collapse. There, he met with Raoul, his mysterious CIA handler. Ray then went to Puerto Vallarta, on the Pacific Coast of Mexico. Remember, Mothman witnesses had precognitions of MLK's murder. In fact, John Keel tried to contact MLK about the danger, but he had the date wrong. He thought it was going to be March 4th, when it really turned out to be April 4th. Keel was actually told that King was going to get "shot in the neck on a hotel balcony." Either these were real predictions, or someone involved in the assassination was leaking the information.

GK: Lee Harvey Oswald went down to Mexico City and back to New Orleans before the shooting in Dallas. James Earl Ray went to Mexico and New Orleans, a hotbed of Naval intelligence and CIA. Something's going on there.

AC: In his book, Ray claims that the Rockefellers interfered with his trial — that they made sure he didn't get a fair trial. He was incarcerated in Tennessee, a Rockefeller controlled state. He escaped from that prison, but was soon caught. He was known for wearing a brown plaid jacket, the jacket worn by MIBs seen tinkering on the Silver Bridge prior to its collapse. A white Mustang like Ray's was seen in Point Pleasant, driven by the "Jell-O" MIB (who acted like he didn't know what Jell-O was). The MIB, "Major Richard French" visited the Butler family, which makes you think of Ed Butler, who was involved with Lee Harvey Oswald at the radio station in New Orleans. Ed Butler later wound up on the radio in California, putting a spin on the RFK assassination. Butler probably knew David Ferrie. Both of them may have been in Pt. Pleasant, trying to clean things up before the Garrison trial.

GK: The White Mustang always comes up. It's almost like the white buffalo… All of those assassinations have similarities, as if they were planned by the same folk. When you're going to kill a high-profile person, you don't usually leave it to one assassin. The "lone gunman" is now entrenched in everybody's minds but, usually, he's either a patsy or an actor in some Freemasonic drama. The head wound seems to be part of the ritual of "the Killing of the King." RFK fell to the same thing. Sirhan certainly was not the lone gunman in that pantry. Whether or not he was a shooter, James Earl Ray was certainly involved in it – same as Oswald. I'm not necessarily blaming it on the Freemasons, but it seems to have this occult undertone, like the "three assassins" of Hiram Abiff.

AC: Shall we do a little Laurel Canyon thing?

GK: Dave McGowan is compiling probably the largest obituary list in the world with his research into Laurel Canyon.

AC: Neil Young did a song called "Revolution Blues" about Charles Manson. At the end of the song, he implies that Manson was killing people in Laurel Canyon in their cars, kind of like Son of Sam. Neil Young knew Manson and thought he was great, at least until the murders. It is telling that Young put those lyrics into that song. Manson has always said that he ran in circles where, sometimes, someone had to be rubbed out. In order to confuse police, one player might commit a murder for another player. Somebody owed somebody; payback came from an unexpected direction. As far as the Tate-LaBianca murders go, Manson is very adamant that he did not break the law. In his interview in 1994 (see *The Mothman's Photographer III*), he makes it clear that there was a system of trading favors in place.

GK: As bizarre as he is, I still think he was railroaded. If they can't place you at the murder scene, then all they can do is call it a "conspiracy." Not that he's a good guy… I'm just saying that I don't understand how he was convicted of first degree murder on such flimsy evidence.

AC: Manson raises some interesting questions in his interview. He blames Reverend Moon and, of course, Bugliosi. He says Bugliosi was brought in by the Italian mob to handle the case. Was he referring to the Jesuits? According to Manson, Bugliosi went to Geneva, Switzerland and, afterwards, tried to make a secret deal with him. Manson rejected the deal. Recently, Bugliosi came out with a book that supposedly points the finger at the Bushes for a bunch of things. It cleverly makes him appear to be a crusader for truth. But Manson makes it very clear that Bugliosi was "bought and paid for." Bugliosi moved his staff out to California, where he set up shop and made millions of dollars. He sold a lot of less-than-factual Manson books. Regarding the whole thing with Manson being shafted on a music deal by Terry Melcher (the prior owner of the Tate residence), Manson claims that Reverend Moon has a major influence on the L.A. music scene. Moon apparently sent a mob "cleaner," or hitman, who was called "The Oriental," to threaten Manson. Somewhere in that tale lies the reason for the murders. Charlie says it was drug related. He claims that it wasn't really his beef. It was probably Tex Watson's beef. Watson was the one dealing drugs.

GK: So a drug situation spilled over onto Sharon Tate?

AC: The guys renting the Tate cottage were apparently distributing an early form of ecstasy for the Canadian mob. It's those "Canadians" again… Canadians were involved with a bunch of different ops: James Earl Ray, Clay Shaw, Ferrie, Crisman, Bakelite, proximity triggers, the Unicorn Killer, even Mohammed Atta. Canadians are explicitly implicated in the Torbitt document as being involved in the JFK hit.

In his fictional masterwork Infinite Jest, *the late writer David Foster Wallace satirically describes a network of wheelchair-bound Canadian terrorists, whose tire tracks could often be found in the snow after their bombings. One of their key weapons was a videotape that would make you kill yourself if you watched it.*

GK: The heaviest hitters in Canada are the Bronfmans, who were bootleggers like the Kennedys.

AC: Great Britain still has a lot of pull in both the U.S. and Canada. Our assassinations and terror incidents may actually be "handled" by NATO; this was a key theory of William Cooper's. Cooper believed there were connections between UFOs and the assassination teams. A.V. Roe, a British company, built the early AVRO saucers. Certain WV employees working on the AVRO saucer, like Jennings

Frederick, experienced home invasions and drugged interrogation… Manson, by the way, mentions that a "Dr. Hartmann" was treating him. Hartmann apparently had some connection to Manson's "Nuremberg judge" father, Francis Biddle. We should try to find out the full identity of this Dr. Hartmann… Manson also mentions the interests of the Queen of England in Kentucky. He speaks in this weird code. When you see it in writing, it starts making a lot more sense. If you see Manson on TV, his freaky looks and movements tend to drown out whatever he is trying to say; it sounds like mumbo jumbo. But, when you see his words in black and white, the code begins to unravel.

GK: You're right. When you listen to his words only, he seems very articulate. He may go on little tirades and screeds, but he is nobody's fool.

AC: By the way, one of your listeners wrote to me, saying that he had a 9/11 precognition 6 months before the event. It came in the form of a dream. He sometimes has dreams about people before they die – a talent that Tommy Burnham possessed. This listener dreamed that he was a New Yorker in lower Manhattan on 9/11. The building exploded and the cloud of dust came towards him. He ran into a store and huddled with other people. They were all very afraid. Remember, strong nerve signals can send out waves, seemingly backwards and forwards in time. This sleeping listener was able to pick those signals up in his dreamstate, months before the event. He actually told his wife about it and wrote it down in his journal. He sent me the text of his journal entry. Coincidentally, you mentioned him before we went on the air. I had not told you anything about him, either.

GK: That's interesting…

AC: Aleister Crowley, the occultist and British-Nazi double agent, was mucking around in Vancouver, Canada, where A.V. Roe was *supposed* to be building the AVRO saucer (the West Virginia portion of the program appears to have been top-secret). This is relevant in the sense that the first UFO incidents, in 1947, occurred near Seattle; those events obviously involved the CIA and military intelligence. Crowley died that year, but he may have had a part in planning those early events. He may have gotten the idea to put one of the secret Horten Wing airplanes up so that Kenneth Arnold would see it and report it. Arnold was obviously being duped. Why? Because he saw some *more* UFOs the very next day! Who sees UFOs two days in a row? Crowley had been hyping "Lam," an entity that became the template for the modern alien "grey," for decades. This explains why Crowley is mysteriously credited with starting the UFO business. The guy got around. He may even have gotten the idea to combine The Nine cult operation with the UFO operation. British intelligence has a history of being extremely tricky; they are probably the only ones with the imagination to attempt such an outrageous scam as "alien abduction…" Switching gears to the Cipro scam… Bayer was on the ropes before 9/11, financially. Soon after 9/11, the offices of our two most liberal Senators were hit with anthrax. Bayer then sold half a billion dollars worth of Cipro, which kills anthrax, to government agencies controlled by Bush cronies. Unfortunately, it turns out that taking Cipro causes your connective tissues (e.g., tendons and ligaments) to degrade to the point where they start breaking. I have personally experienced this. When I was in Egypt with Robert Godbey (see *The Mothman's Photographer II*), I got sick and had to take Cipro..

I got sick twice, both times at the same restaurant. The second time, the owner assured me that the "bottled" water was good. After I got sick the second time and confronted him, he sicced a couple of his swarthy, menacing thugs on us. They chased Rob and I around Luxor on their horse and buggy. We eventually escaped by running through buildings, going in the front and out the back. We had to sneak in and out of our hotel after that, because the thugs kept coming around looking for us.

AC: The only antibiotic I could get in Luxor was Cipro. It was extremely strong. It made me throw up within 15 minutes of taking it. When I got back to the states, I tore a hamstring. A year or two later, I tore the other hamstring. Then, on April 29th of this year, I tore my Achilles. I am now officially a victim of this Cipro drug scam. There is apparently going to be a class-action suit against Bayer regarding Cipro. But, since I was in Egypt, it will be harder for me to prove that I took it.

GK: Holy mackerel…

AC: On May 1st, gas prices were going up and up. Now, they're suddenly going down. We suspect that this is because the banks are failing.

GK: They play a game with that. When I hear the reasons prices go up or down, it's just laughable. They give the most inane reasons why it's up. They play everybody like a yo-yo. It's like the 1970s all over again, but ten times worse.

AC: I'm looking at this May calendar… On the 1st, we had the death of the D.C. Madame, who apparently had a list of "johns." Was this on behalf of some intelligence agency? One of her clients was Eliot Spitzer, who was most likely brought down because he tried to regulate the mortgage industry in NY. According to radio host Thom Hartmann, George Bush caused the market collapse of 2008. It was a full court press to make sure there would *have* to be a bank bailout. Every single state in the union wanted to regulate what was going on with the sub-prime mortgages, but Bush said, "No, you can't do that. We, the feds, say that you can't change banking law." So… No regulations were enacted, and the crash was permitted to continue… On the 2nd, the Haq trial started in Seattle. Six Jews were killed by a Christian, but the media portrayed him as Muslim and anti-Semitic. Was it mind control? Anne Coulter compared Obama to Hitler on the 2nd, while a bunch of tornadoes struck the Midwest… On the 5th, the Burma cyclone hit, killing at least a hundred thousand people. "Jesuit" Justice Scalia stated that torture isn't punishment. He avoids the Geneva Conventions by claiming that waterboarding is *not* cruel and unusual punishment. As ridiculous as it sounds, I believe he was disagreeing with the "punishment" label, not the "cruel and unusual" part.

GK: A couple of things: the D.C. Madame supposedly offed herself down here by me. The *St. Petersburg Times* covered it, as did the *Tampa Tribune*. The *Times* does a little bit better; it has a remnant of some kind of journalistic integrity. Still, they went for the suicide story. The reporter was kind of smarmy, saying, "You people *always* think there's a conspiracy here." But how can he be so sure that a conspiracy *isn't* going on, especially when this woman has a black book that can indict a lot of people in a sex scandal? Where does the media get off dismissing these things so easily?

AC: Before she died, the D.C. Madame told Alex Jones that spying was going on in her establishment – that she had information on 9/11. She claimed to have serviced the CIA's director, Porter Goss. Remember, Goss didn't last very long in that job. For what it's worth, Goss is said to have been stationed in Mexico City with the CIA team that helped plan the JFK hit. On 9/11, Goss had breakfast with the Pakistani General who had just wired money to 9/11 hijacker Mohammed Atta. How can people look at that and not suspect that there is a conspiracy around 9/11?

GK: Atta was just a misdirection. His existence supposedly substantiates the tale of 19 Arab hijackers, which I think is complete and utter bullshit.

AC: You'd think Atta would have tried to be a better actor, in order to help substantiate the cover story. But he didn't even bother to act like a Muslim fundamentalist.

GK: You're right. He came from Germany. The guy could have been Rumanian. He could have been Libyan. He could have been Israeli. He could have been anything. Nobody knows who this guy was… But regarding the situation with the D.C. Madame… She was in good spirits and not suicidal, yet they just washed it away. Yes, everything may not be a conspiracy, but how can you say it *never* is?

AC: Did I ever mention the Tampa serial killer, Bobby Ray Long? He is from Kenova, WV, which was where Manson's uncle lived. The famous stripper, Blaze Starr, was from Kenova, too. She had a notorious affair with Earl Long, the Louisiana politician… When I was in college, I went to a McDonald's in Kenova with my running mate for the Marshall University student body presidency, J. Frederick Edwards. His grandfather was once a city councilman in Huntington, WV. He was dating my sister at the time. We met a martial artist at the Kenova McDonald's, which is near Camden Park. This martial artist, Johnny K., was Greek. He could have been on Indrid Cold's assassin team. He had a black belt in judo. Edwards' father had a black belt, too, and was a high school coach. Mr. Edwards and Johnny K. had black belts in all kinds of things. They knew Chuck Norris. They went to paramilitary training camps where you learn how to efficiently kill people. Johnny had all of these weapons on him. You could tell he was a sadist and a racist. He was really into killing. Whenever I think of what David Ferrie must have been like, I think of Johnny K. He was an angry, middle-aged man with lots of skills and no apparent moral compass. He told us about how he killed a cow with his bare hands; he claimed he could thrust his hand into the ribcage and pull the heart out. He had these deadly little instruments on him. One was a metal rod that you put behind your middle finger. He twirled it around with total control. He had those metal stars that you throw, too…

GK: Those stars are now allowed on planes; *that* should make everybody feel better.

AC: Johnny K. was one of the most frightening guys I've ever met. His last name sounds very similar to "kriss," the name for the Garuda knife. Kriss was the last name of a Greek girl I went to high school with, whose family ran a diner known for their chili dogs. The first wave of Men in Black into Point Pleasant are said to have been Greek. Johnny K. lived close to Point Pleasant. He was extremely right wing. He had no qualms about killing, and was old enough to have been around during Mothman. As crazy as it sounds, I may have actually met the man who stuck a cancer needle in my father. Kenova is a creepy place with a lot of chemical storage tanks. It is an old Indian settlement whose name roughly means "birthplace of earth and sky."

GK: Isn't nearby Solvay Chemical an extension of I.G. Farben?

AC: More or less… Farben, whose name seems to be a combination of "Phar" and "Bon" (Pharaohs and Tibetans), is always morphing. Ashland Oil is now a bank, among other things. Speaking of Farben, Bayer CropScience has a plant in Institute right next to where the Bhopal gas is made. It is right next to Apollo Oil, AEP, Martin-Marietta, FMC, Dow, and Adisseo, which makes nutrients for animal feed. One wonders if Bayer's "iron cross" logo was chosen because it represents alchemy, the formation of matter from the ether – the union of earth and sky.

GK: It goes back to the crosses of the Templars and Knights of Malta. Lutheranism has the red cross. I'm willing to believe that Luther might have been involved with the Templars. The Klan wore the cross, and the Pope wears it.

AC: In the logo of the O.T.O., an international occult group originally out of Britain and Germany, one sees the same things you see in other standard religious symbolisms. There is an iron cross inside a growing plant, symbol of physical manifestation. There is a large bird flying above that. Above the bird, you have the pyramid with the Eye of Horus inside of it, representing enlightenment. A Vesica Pisces or womb shape surrounds all of this. Going back to the calendar… On May 6th of this year, Bush gave a medal to a Burmese dissident, thus assuring that no aid can now go into Burma. It was a Masonic drama. He went in and "pissed off" the Burmese government by giving a dissident a medal. Almost immediately, aid from the outside world was disallowed. Bush purposefully does things that help create misery for millions of people.

GK: He's an absolute fiend. He is so bereft of mental acuity that it's embarrassing. He is told what to do.

AC: He is said to be charming, socially shrewd, and adept at using CIA tricks learned from his father. So, some of that may be an act…

Anyway… On any normal day, the CIA-controlled media will push terror, mixed in with other stories, to keep us afraid. That is standard… But every now and then, they will put twists *inside* of stories. There will often be a bunch of "inside twist" stories on the same day. These will mitigate any big stories that embarrass officialdom or make elites look bad. In addition, such stories make people turn inward. For instance, in April, there were several twisting, "inner conflict" stories thrown in with big losses for Citibank, Citicorp, and Citigroup. In early May, there were several more such stories: Bush gave a medal to a dissident; Scalia said torture isn't "punishment." And on and on… Each has a built-in contradiction.

GK: Scalia should go through torture himself. *Then* he could better decide what is torture…

AC: On the 6th, John Muhammad, the D.C. sniper, asked prosecutors to stop his lawyers from appealing his death sentence; this is standard Manchurian Candidate behavior, of course. They want him to "suicide out" in whatever fashion possible, and this he will do. Then the story will be over. The risk of aberrant programming (where he might reveal something about the conspirators) will be over… We had the Screen Actor's Guild breaking off talks that day, which sort of took over the news, leaving the sniper in the background, seeping into the collective subconscious. Another seepage story was the one in Washington State with the "European businessmen," who were probably Mossad agents. They were on a ferry a while back, taking photos. Subtextually, the story implied that taking photos while traveling is some kind of security breach. It also created fear in an additional area of the transportation grid, the ferries. The whole thing smelled like a set-up, like the Y2K bomber coming across the border from Canada to blow up the Space Needle and LAX right after the WTO protests. The "businessmen" were allowed to go back to "Europe" unmolested. Was this the "Dancing Israeli" effect? A few weeks later, on the 6th, the FBI came out and said, "These were legitimate European citizens; it was no big deal." The media was able to revisit the issue of terror without really having any terror. One could call this a "media re-gift." The FBI seemed to be covering for these European businessmen, who definitely looked Middle Eastern.

GK: This is the most unique and potent fact about terrorism: you don't always have to have it. All you have to do is suggest that it's around, and people get freaked out. It's the scariest ghost you could ever have. Now that they've created these terrorist incidents, all they've got to do is remind people; say "boo" and they'll do whatever you want. It's ridiculous. It's like trying to capture fog in a bottle; it can be anywhere, anytime. Governments finally have a tool to get what they've always wanted: ultimate control.

AC: As I mentioned, one of their control techniques is to mix the afore-mentioned contradictory stories with any news that elites might consider to be "bad" – anything they don't want you to notice – like Big Oil being forced to pay out $423 million for MTBE contami-nation. This is reminiscent of the Exxon Valdez disaster, where damages recently got cut down to almost nothing. Exxon now only has to pay the equivalent of *four* days of profit for the entire Valdez spill!

GK: The longer they wait, the less they have to give. Everybody gets tired and just forgets about it.

AC: Colombia extradited a drug warlord on that day, too. But, appar-ently, others are "filling the void…" I'm sure they *are* filling the void; *we* keep creating new ones!

GK: There you go…

AC: Russian tanks were in Red Square for "the first time in years" on the 7th… The media was hitting all the basic food groups during this time: the Cold War, terrorism, mass killers like the D.C. Sniper, "bad" dissidents, little black books, spying, torture, industrial disas-ters, and unusual natural disasters. Natural disasters act as a form of terrorism as well… Oil hit a new record price on the 7th, which was Israel's 60th birthday; war thus broke out in Lebanon… Tommy Chong had all of his DVDs seized by the FBI, and there was a 9/11 rescue-worker story: 360 of the workers are now dead, although that is probably an undercount… There was a Rodney King-style beating of three men in Philadelphia… A judge ordered the CIA to turn over tapes of their torture sessions in 2002. Now *that's* a story that they would want to distract us from! So… They came up with a distraction story, which was that bodies of U.S. soldiers were being cremated alongside of animals – that their ashes were getting mixed. Such stories create outrage, however they are typically ignored by the media. The networks probably keep files of stories to be sat on until the time is right… On the 9th, Bill Clinton was in West Virginia campaigning. Then, Hezbollah seized West Beirut. Valerie Plame said that she was going to resurrect her lawsuit. Coyotes were preying on Southern California kids. There was a "continu-ity of government" drill in D.C. That was the day that your show was censored by BlogTalk. So, a *lot* of stuff happened that week…

Tornadoes and floods were still happening in the Midwest. That was actually the biggest rainstorm to hit the Midwest in recorded history… On the 10th, we started hearing about the upcoming Bilderberger meeting… On the 11th, a tornado hit a mound of lead in Pilcher, Oklahoma, creating a toxic cloud… On the 12th, there was an earthquake in China, near Tibet. There was a story about how the new CERN supercollider in Switzerland might create a black hole. Hyping such dark possibilities is a form of psychological terrorism… We had a story about the "first" genetically modified human embryo. They like to throw futuristic stories into the mix on a regular basis… Bush started blaming the Saudis for high oil prices on that day, too.

GK: What a joke.

AC: Obama and Hillary Clinton were in West Virginia on the 12th… On the 13th, Fox News was caught using subliminal pictures that supported John McCain… The Vatican's official astronomer came out saying that it's okay to believe in aliens. Might that be a sign of future ops? The U.S. dropped their charges against the "20th" 9/11 hijacker, Mohammad al-Qahtani.

GK: You know, it's funny because that's the *second* 20th hijacker we've had. The *first* 20th hijacker was Moussaoui. Now we have *two* 20th hijackers, which is crap.

AC: On the 14th, there was a San Francisco Bay gasoline spill, which I'm sure raised gas prices some more, even though it wasn't that much of a spill. They found contaminated water in Yelm, WA, which is where the Ramtha cult is located. Fire ants swarmed in Houston, and a Jesuit military science teacher at Seattle Univ. was accused of soliciting a minor.

GK [*sarcastically*]: That sounds about right.

AC: On the 15th, Bush referred to Obama as a "terrorist appeaser" at a speech in front of Israel's Knesset. That's where he talked about the tanks rolling into Poland, conveniently forgetting to mention that his grandfather aided the building of those very tanks.

GK: It slipped his mind – what little there is of it to slip.

AC: Giant beetles were found in the U.S. mail in Monton, PA (a "mon" word). That's a mildly terroristic story, making us fear the importation into our country of huge, foot-long beetles.

GK: Entomophobia…

AC: Interestingly, the 15th was the day that Chase began trading in crude oil. That's a really key thing. Not only are the Rockefellers buying, selling, and manufacturing oil, but they are speculating on it as well. There was also a negative story about Obama, who had called a reporter "sweetie." On the 16th, Republican candidate Mike Huckabee made a crass joke about Obama possibly being shot.

The smarmy Huckabee was rewarded with his very own TV show following the election. However, the 2009 Tacoma cop shootings undermined Huckabee's future presidential chances, due to the fact that he had allowed the eventual shooter, Maurice Clemmons, to be released from jail in Arkansas. Clemmons hid out on the same block in Seattle where a cop had been shot just weeks before, raising suspicions of a conspiracy to either get rid of certain cops, or to prime cops nationwide for a future crackdown in the event of an economic meltdown.

AC: There was a story that day about the world's wildlife being at risk. It is terrifying to think of such things, so they make sure to remind us of it periodically. I guess it would be more understandable if government and industry were *really* serious about saving nature but, since they're not, one has to wonder if such eco-stories aren't just another form of terror programming. On the 16th, a five-year old kid took a joyride in a truck, which strikes fear into every parent's heart. California legalized gay marriage, although it was overturned later due to opposition from Blacks and Hispanics. That was a big story that led to an article on the "Republican Faith Chat" blog, which criticized blacks for only supporting civil rights for themselves. Mainstream outlets were afraid to touch that one... Around that time, the Saudis declined to help Bush keep oil prices high, although they later relented and prices starting falling. Such fake tensions between Bush and the Saudis make it seem like he is not in their back pocket... Wouldn't you know it, on the 17th, there was an acid spill in Louisiana. Anytime there is a chemical spill of any kind, it becomes newsworthy because they can use it to raise all energy prices. Ted Kennedy had a stroke that day... Donuts and coffee were served in the Green Zone in Iraq – a feel-good story that helps us imagine that we are winning there... On the 19th, Iran busted a CIA-backed terror group that was planning bombings in Iran. A paranormalish "orange orb" started showing up in Discover Card commercials. Discover is probably owned by the Rockefellers. The orange orb is the most commonly seen UFO, and is often said by witnesses to seem "intelligent." In the commercials, it flies around conversing with a Discover cardholder, as if it has a brain and is intelligent. I saw that commercial for the first time the day I also saw Chris Knowles' blog about Western Electric and AT&T both using Mothman-like mascots. Those companies use birdmen, such as Mithras, in their different logos... There were rumors about the U.S. attacking Iran on the 20th. That is the day that Obama more or less won the election.

Not long after Obama won the election – in fact, before he was sworn in – elites pulled a switch and allowed Israel to relentlessly bomb, and then invade, the Gaza Strip. This put pressure on Obama to prove that he would toe the neo-con line and allow Israel to continue with its expansion. Weeks passed while progressive Democrats pretended they couldn't do anything. As if to cement the idea that Obama was not a progressive, within a month of his inauguration, the only progressive talk radio station in Washington, D.C. was taken off the air.

AC: On the 21st, fourteen tons of Oreos spilled out of a truck. The interesting thing here is that someone claimed to have had a dream about it before it happened. A man had a prophetic dream about an Oreo spill, and then the spill actually occurred! One wonders which candidate the Oreo experiencer supported in the election... The cynically named "Operation Peace" began on the 21st, with tanks rolling into Sadr City during a ceasefire. The U.S. basically broke the truce. It was timed to put immediate psychic pressure on Obama. On that same day, I found out that Henry Lee Lucas had confessed to murdering the daughter of a Point Pleasant engineer. The engineer had helped clean up the Silver Bridge collapse.

GK: Does that mean Henry Lee Lucas was up in West Virginia?

AC: Well, that's what it seems like. I've also heard that Lucas is the cousin of Bobby Long, the Tampa, FL serial killer who is originally from Kenova, WV. Supposedly, Lucas has links to Bush and to Jonestown. Lucas was supposedly ferrying mind-control drugs from Westchester County, NY, down to Guyana. West Virginia customers of Life Lock, the "identity theft" company, sued on the 21st... On the 22nd, dinosaur prints were found on the Arabian Peninsula – the first ones ever found there. A lost parrot told his home address to a stranger and was rescued; birds are the only animals that can learn and speak human language. Stonehenge was vandalized. This was not long after a story appeared informing the public that Stonehenge held occult symbolism. They almost seem to set these things up... Speaking of which, about two weeks ago, it was advertised that a Hitler statue was going to be unveiled in Paris' wax museum. So, when it was unveiled, some guy went in, jumped on it, and started ripping it apart... On the 22nd, a California company began cloning dogs. We have to have a cloning story each week it seems. On the 23rd, Mount Sinai Hospital found that 9/11 workers have post-traumatic stress disorder... Obama chose a Rockefeller insider to help him pick a running mate. Obama has several Rockefellerites on his advisory committee, including Madeline Albright, Tony Lake, and a bunch of Clinton people... *Eat the State*, a weekly here in Seattle, published an article saying that if you simply look at Obama's advisory committee, you know that he is *not* going to do anything revolutionary. Chinese coalminers were trapped on the 24th. Nowadays, we get to hear pseudo-terror stories from China. Some of these mine explosions are probably just ingenious ways to get rid of troublesome employees... Hillary Clinton started an RFK firestorm. She alluded to how RFK never made it from nomination to election, implying the same might happen to Obama. It was announced that Kellogg, Brown and Root, the Texas defense contractor, has split Iraq into three areas (in terms of their business), presaging what has been said all along by conspiracy bloggers like *Xymphora*.

GK: Which is interesting because that throws it back to the pre-WWI situation, where it was tripartite between Germany, France, and Britain.

AC: Exactly... On the 25th, the Phoenix probe, built by Lockheed-Martin, supposedly landed on Mars. Lockheed Martin has that facility in upstate New York where the Rockefellers got their start... On the 27th, it was reported that the Germans make more "eco-friendly" bombs than we do.

GK *[sarcastically]*: God bless 'em; that makes up for everything they have done...

AC: On the 28th, there were rumors of a deadly "superbug" virus. There were some high profile murders in California that day, involving three generations within a family. A supposed witness on the Mothman list claimed that she had a precognitive dream of her friend's car wreck that day. The accident decapitated the friend... The Phoenix probe's lander short-circuited on the 30th... On the 31st, the U.K. schools chief claimed that human brain downloading (into a computer) will be a reality in 30 years. There was a big fire at Universal Studios. Obama cut ties with his old church. The Aussies left Iraq. OPEC said that oil is no longer tied to the market. I guess it depends on which market you mean. Jay Rockefeller criticized Michael Hayden, the CIA chief who used to be the NSA chief, saying that Hayden isn't paying enough attention to Al Qaeda. Here you have Jay, a Senator who is supposed to be liberal and open-minded, bringing up the terror bugaboo… And that was all for May…

GK: About the aliens and the Vatican… It is the Jesuits who run their two observatories. One is in Arizona; I have no idea why. We had an incredible statement from Joey Ratzinger, Pope Benedict, about how he *knows* that the aliens are good, intelligent, benign people, free from original sin. How he could come up with that, I have no idea. It freaks me out. Larry King did a thing about this. All of a sudden, the aliens are getting very mainstream. It must be for a purpose; everybody is being prepared for something "extraterrestrial." This newly engrained belief may be with us for a long time… I don't put great faith in the work of James Shelby Downard, but he did talk about the ritual of the "Killing of the King," which usually takes three accomplices and a head wound. JFK was shot fatally in the head, and we believe that there were three assassins. It was a triangulated assassination, which is the most efficient. Robert Kennedy was shot in the head as well. Sirhan was certainly not the only conspirator involved in that. In a very macabre twist, Teddy Kennedy, the third brother, most likely will succumb to brain cancer. According to Downard, the name "Kennedy" means "helmet head" or "wounded head" in Gaelic. It comes from "Kanedich" in Gaelic. My feeling is that they reinvented Hillary Clinton for a reason. Otherwise, why go through all the machinations of getting her to be a carpetbag senator like Robert Kennedy? And what's up with her not winning the nomination? Why do you reinvent her, only to fall short? I don't believe in Republicans and Democrats. They can put whatever chimpanzee they want in the Oval Office. Some are very glib, like Clinton; some can't color with crayons, like Shrub. I don't care who they put in there. I'm just wondering why Hillary fell short. It could be that Barack may have to step down for some kind of scandal.

AC: Did she get the prerequisite number of *Time* magazine covers?

GK: She did not… But if Barack should be made to step down, the goal for that would be to create division in this country along racial lines.

AC: It's interesting that we see this Council of Nine connection to Obama. He got into office by virtue of Congressman Ryan's wife, the sexy star of *Deep Space Nine*. She came forward to say that her husband had been taking her to sex clubs. *Star Trek* creator Gene Rodenberry was a Council of Nine follower, along with a bunch of elite British occultists. The Council of Nine supposedly live aboard a ship orbiting Earth, just like the crew on the *Deep Space Nine* show. Puharich's book on Uri Geller is essentially about The Nine. Synchronistically, three of the psychics working with The Nine in Florida had the same first names as Tommy Burnham's family: Tommy, Phyllis, and Robert. Tommy's family actually moved to Florida eventually. Based on what I have read, it seems that the Brits were behind The Nine. This makes sense because Blavatsky, the mother of Theosophy, was British. The Brits have extensive experience in India with the Hindus. They basically took Hindu belief and morphed it into this cult. It has a tangential relationship to the Garuda, because the Garuda is a Hindu deity. This orbiting spacecraft, with supposed space intelligences onboard, became a template for other stories and ops. Several writers were influenced by their interactions with this "spacecraft." Speaking of which, I've been reading *Blink* by Malcolm Gladwell, which is essentially about how people are influenced by their unconscious. Until one deconstructs the mechanisms behind one's habits and snap judgments, one will not have much control over such habits... A Seattle psychologist, John Gottman, has carried out a long study on human relationships. He studied tapes of married couples talking. Eventually, he figured out the key nonverbals they were using. If you see enough of these within a short timeframe, you can consistently judge which relationships are going to work and which will fail. Gottman claims he can tell within one minute which couples are not going to make it. It has to do with how much contempt they are unconsciously exhibiting. Other scientists have done the same thing with facial movements... They have catalogued hundreds of facial movements and what the different combinations mean. Amazingly, they are much the same in every culture, regardless of language. They even studied Bill Clinton...

GK: Oh boy... A pathological liar can always beat the system.

AC: They found that he had this really unusual combination of facial positions. Some of his facial expressions revealed that he was a "bad boy." The doctors actually went to the Clinton campaign and said, "He is making these expressions that are going to undermine him." The campaign people said, "Well, he can't be seen as having worked on changing his facial movements." The scientists claim that they can help you change these behaviors within a day or two. I actually think the "bad boy" facial expressions were the secret to Clinton's success. American women love bad boys, and they love scandal.

GK: Clinton said, "I never had sex with that woman." He is a spellbinder; there is something about him. You can understand why we bought a "bill of goods" from him. Clinton could sell your own car back to you.

AC: Switching gears… The parents of Stewart Copeland, of the band The Police, were actually in British intelligence – both of them. His brothers more or less controlled the punk/new wave genre through their labels FBI Records and IRS Records. I was in the business of making punk music back then. Ours was more like a blend of experimental punk and world music, but the punk venues were about the only places that tolerated anything weird. In Austin, for example, we played in a little Korean restaurant run by a madwoman. Interestingly, The Police played one of their very early shows in South Charleston, WV, at "Studio 2000" next to the Carbide plant. Between songs, you could step outside of the disco and grab a smoke on top of the Indian mound. Did Copeland's intelligence connections lead them to book a show next to the Carbide plant? It is rumored that Scientologists started the hardcore punk scene. I found an article claiming that certain sound technicians for big rock bands are actually covert CIA agents. Due to the cultural power of rock bands, they like to keep an eye on certain musicians. Many of the pioneering bands were formed by children of military intelligence officers up in Laurel Canyon.

GK: They're going to leave someone like Bono alone, because he's a Christian. He might shake the teapot up a little bit but, all and all, he's very much in the program. He wasn't knighted for nothing,

AC: Willie Nelson is rumored to be planning a "9/11 Truth" concert. I recorded an album at his studio once.

GK: He is a great guy, and he's paid up on his taxes… Okay… A reputable source just emailed to say, "Don't for once think that they all drank Kool-Aid at Jonestown, or that that is what did them in." He says, "There were a whole lot of gunshots involved, and good ol' Jim Jones was not among the missing or the dead."

AC: The weird part is that there had been another, similar massacre a hundred years before in that part of Guyana. Matthews Ridge is an old mining area. There was another cult near Jonestown in the 1970s, called Hilltown. They actually got all the shoes and stuff from the Jonestown victims. Hilltown was started by a preacher from Columbus, Ohio. So, we have two preachers from the Ohio circuit founding work camps in Guyana.

GK: They keep running the same old scams time and time again, and nobody catches on. That is the reason why history repeats itself...

A few weeks later, on Sept. 9, 2008, Vyz and I continued this discussion in our 34ᵗʰ episode. We also discussed some of the strange events that had happened in between, in August. That month had not been easy for either of us. Both of us were facing bittersweet milestones, so we began by talking about our fathers.

GK: Speaking of history, I have now outlived my father by 14 days or so. He died way too soon. I can't believe that I am older than he was. That was your situation, too; your dad died very young, at the age of 48. Are you looking towards the date of your 49ᵗʰ birthday with a certain amount of melancholy?

AC: Yes, although technically, I'm already older than he was. I think the melancholiness is just something that people go through with their parents. My older brother went through the same thing. He thought he was going to die or something.

GK: My dad's early departure was tragic, because he was never sick a day. No matter how much time you have to prepare, short or long, it really doesn't help.

AC: It's that basic lesson of loss... For me, though, that loss also intersects the world of Mothman and the conspiracies that are being revealed. Was my dad *really* killed by MIBs involved in these different assassinations? Why were key figures in the JFK assassination investigation also rumored to be connected to the Silver Bridge collapse? How did freaky maniacs such as Ferrie, Cold, and Henry Lee Lucas wind up in this story? And with the RFK hit, you've got the Manson connection – him living on my street, as well as Sara Jane Moore.

GK: Do you feel that your father's death was related to what he knew?

AC: Either what he knew, or what they *thought* he knew. Carbide certainly had reasons to be paranoid. Carbide may have been testing those nickel centrifuges in Mound with uranium. I don't know if they had a reactor or not, but there is a squarish building there that looks like it could store nuclear materials. They may have been working on saucers and an updated version of the Nazi Bell "dooms-day" weapon. Since they were purportedly building the original Bell at the Buna plant near Auschwitz, they may have continued that research at the Buna plant in Institute, near Mound.

The main product made at the Buna plants was butadiene, a precursor of synthetic rubber with a variety of uses, including being a primary ingredient in C4 plastic explosives. The trade name of butadiene is "Buna S." When I first saw that name, I was reminded of one of the names for the Garuda: "Bonaspati." After the war, the Institute plant phased Buna out and began making the chemical that later killed thousands at Bhopal, India. Much of the C4 today is made in China.

AC: According to Joseph Farrell, the Nazi Doomsday weapon was shipped out at the end of the war. No one quite knows where it was taken, but it was flown out of Germany on a Junkers airplane. As you may recall, the first UFO seen in 1947 by Kenneth Arnold looked like a similar plane, the Horten "Wing," Nazi Germany's version of what later became our Stealth Bomber. We basically used their design. The thing seen above Mt. Rainier was an actual plane that had secretly been in production in Nazi Germany. The next day, Arnold saw some little balls of light. The media called them "saucers" and, bingo, the UFO era was deployed.

One wonders if Arnold may have been ordered by the military to say that he saw those balls of light, in order to cover for his "accidentally" seeing the classified Horten plane. If so, once they had him on the hook, they may have decided to change his story to "flying saucers" and start the "abduction" ball rolling. Not only did Crowley and L. Ron Hubbard both play a role in creating the flying saucer mythos, they both shared a dream of creating a Satanic messiah. Hubbard's son claimed that his father stole fetuses for this purpose wherever possible, leading us to the terrifying prospect that military occultists used "alien abduction" to cover for the secret theft of such fetuses.

GK: How close were the Nazis to having antigravity aircraft?

AC: It seems like they were pretty darn close. Unless the documents are all fake, which seems unlikely, they *did* test fly some saucers. Apparently they shot film of them, too. Rudolf Hess was rumored to have shown them to General Patton, who then had to be killed. Patton was too much of a "loose cannon."

GK: We've all seen things and heard things since WWII, and yet we still don't *really* know what's going on. This might be deliberate, as a way to keep us in the dark. In fact, the other day in Stephenville, TX, people started calling in about UFOs. The town called the nearest military base and asked, "You guys doing anything?" They responded, "No, we weren't." However, many hours later, they admitted, "Oh yeah, we were."

AC: Jacques Vallee was recently interviewed. He mentioned that supernatural stories are used all the time to cover for covert ops. If the CIA gets caught doing something, they might order area newspapers to write about a UFO. The satellite that fell in Peru was probably nuclear powered. Everyone got sick, so they called it "meteor sickness" instead of "radiation sickness." Speaking of health, I've been reading a lot of Milton Erickson lately. He's the father of modern hypnosis. He was operating back in the early UFO days. He healed hundreds, perhaps thousands of people. He was the "Michael Jordan of hypnosis." People are still trying to figure out how he did what he did. So, I got several of his books. I opened the first book to a random page, and *there* it was: the best way to create amnesia in a hypnotized patient. You *don't* suggest for them to forget anything; you simply put them back where they were – physically and mentally – prior to the hypnosis. The only evidence of the hypnosis is a length of "missing time," which is the hallmark of UFO abduction cases. Woody Derenberger's encounter with Indrid Cold sounds like a hypnotic situation; the craft disappeared and reappeared, and Cold specifically made Woody gaze into his eyes. Cold was known to carry a medallion, which could have been used to put potential victims into hypnotic states. There is a lot about Indrid Cold that we don't yet know, but everything points toward him being a terrestrial human with an agenda.

GK: We have Adam Gorightly on the line…

Adam Gorightly of *Untamed Dimensions* (UD) *[referring to previous email]*: I thought you would realize that my email about "Mothman in Dealey Plaza" was an obvious joke. I mean, Mothman at the JFK assassination? Come on…

GK *[jokingly]*: Adam, I once trusted you implicitly. But now that you've lied to me, I will never again trust you. What do you think, Andy?

AC: Wasn't Mothman floating above the 6th floor window? *[laughter]*

UD: Yes! He cast a shadow over Oswald, or whoever was pointing a weapon out of the 6th floor window.

AC: Loren Coleman would probably say that Mothman was there to *help* Oswald shoot better. Loren seems to think Mothman is out to kill everyone. *[laughter]*

GK: Jim Gilreath is making fun in the chat room saying, "They're photo-shopping that scenario right away…" And I'm sure they are. Let me ask you this… We're two days away from the 7th anniversary of 9/11. A picture of a winged creature supposedly seen on 9/11 has been put out. Do you have any feelings about that?

AC: It looks like it is either a piece of normal debris, or something that was photoshopped into the picture. We have had trouble finding out anything about the guy who took it, named "Steve Moran" (note "Moor" name). I doubt that that is his real name, since he seems to have disappeared. But even if it is a hoax, I think it reflects the fact that people *know* Mothman is a real phenomenon. Everyone sort of knows, at some deeper level, that birdmen do appear and do impart prophecies. Therefore, people will create these tales about Mothman physically being at Chernobyl or at the World Trade Center. They want the message to stay in the media, for whatever reason. There is some deep need for the phenomenon to continue. I also think the disinformation agents needed to come up with something that could distract people away from the fact that Mothman really *did* predict 9/11. They never really seem to cover the prophecies much in the TV programs about Mothman; this makes it easier for the viewer to walk away subconsciously blaming Mothman for the tragedies. In reality, if Mothman prophesied these things, he certainly wouldn't go ahead and *do* them himself. That would be admitting to a crime in advance, which no one in his or her right mind ever does. Sending Mothman's assassination prophecies down the memory hole is important for the gatekeepers.

UD: Perhaps it's the collective consciousness of humankind forming these messages. They are like smoke clouds from 9/11. When you stare at clouds, you can see things.

GK: Andy had pretty good instincts on the Bigfoot hoax in Georgia, while I did not. We were all given low-quality photos of the Bigfoot body. Still, it was some kind of evidence. Adam, did you think it was a piece of stinking dung from the beginning?

UD: Well, I went to the press conference, as you know. I wasn't really involved in the Bigfoot scene before that, so I didn't know the players. I kind of knew that Biscardi had a reputation as a carnival huckster, but I went to the press conference with an open mind. They didn't really show me anything there. If you're going to have this big press conference with CNN and everybody there, why not have the body there? All they had was a couple of really funky photos. The whole thing started smelling really quickly. Driving back from the press conference, I made up my mind that it was a bunch of crap

GK: Andy, I spoke to you when it first broke. You were right about it. Did you think that this was a stinker from the get-go?

AC: Yes I did. I thought it was highly unlikely, to say the least, that they had a body. I'm fascinated by these scams, though. I love them. I don't get upset about it. I was just wondering how they were going to weasel out of this one. We figured that there would be some sale of the body – some changing of hands that would spread out responsibility. The original two individuals had a degree of credibility. One was a police officer; the other was a corrections officer. If you looked at the history of this whole thing – the early YouTube videos – it was obvious that these guys were goofing. Other players picked up on it, however, and so it took on a life of its own. I wouldn't blame the media circus *just* on the two guys from Georgia. Now the timing of it, August 12th, Aleister Crowley's favorite day, was interesting. Loren Coleman posted his photos of it that day. I'm sure he was aware of the date, too, because he is so seemingly obsessed with the occult calendar.

UD: Does that date have anything to do with the Ape of Thoth?

AC: It may. By the way, there is a *birdman* version of the Ape of Thoth.

UD: Many compare the "Ape of Thoth" or "Bird of Thoth" to Bigfoot.

GK: I asked Nick Redfern if it were a possibility that a Bigfoot, Sasquatch, Yeti, or Manitou could exist in isolation. I'm okay with assuming that such a creature is real; I'm open. But with Garuda or Mothman, we're looking at a species where there is something *else* going on. I recently sent Andy a straight news story out of South America about a smaller creature that was very Mothmanlike.

AC: Those were probably the Pukwudgies or Nunahee: the little people. Tommy Burnham claimed that the little people worked together with Mothman and the space intelligences… Recently, there have been these sightings of four beings, three smaller and one larger. This is a new development that may indicate a subtle shift in the collective unconscious. People are seeing something new, or something ancient that we are unfamiliar with, which may be a reflection of some new stress. These stresses can actually become physical for a time. Traditionally, this process gets reflected in the symbologies of various religions. In Freemasonry, you see three small "bibles" plus a big one – four total. A lady in Spain saw four "Egyptian" Mothmen last year. In that case, the fourth one was different, perhaps the leader. We saw a similar configuration in 2002 in Mound. We saw three fuzzy mists, and then a fourth one that was different. The fourth one seemed to be observing things. Looking at it in an Ericksonian fashion, the first three seem to be there to occupy your conscious mind, while the fourth one works at some other, perhaps more subconscious, level. This may be why you hear about more sightings of the Three than the Four; people may not be consciously aware of the presence of the fourth entity. In a way, it is like the Holy Trinity: by observing it, you become the fourth party… The closer something is to your unconscious, the more it seems invisible. Recently, I've been pondering the question of why there are both winged and a non-winged creatures… According to the Natives, Bigfoot is an earth or water creature. Keel has talked to people who've seen Bigfoots pulling each other out of the ground, without disturbing the earth. These things can emanate out of the Earth. Mothman may simply be a winged version of that – an air creature… There is also a basic symbology in many different cultures where you have a mound with a person on top, with his arms spread, forming a cross (i.e., Jesus, Krishna, Horus, Garuda, Atum, etc.). Then we have the Adam Kadmon (note "mon" name), the Freemasonic version of Adam and Eve. The old drawings of the Adam Kadmon in Rosicrucian lore show him on a mound with a tree or cross – more or less a Christ figure… Before the show, you mentioned the recent buzz about the "Son of Man" returning in 2012. I've always wondered about the phrase "Son of Man"; it may actually be a bastardization of "Son of Mon." Subtle word changes can confuse issues and obfuscate facts, and Masonic elites know this. "Son of Mon" might actually be an ancient message revealing that we originate from earth energies. Maybe these mounds have special properties. If humanity were wiped out, perhaps we might start again by re-manifesting from these mounds. But beyond that, one suspects that burying people in mounds, as Natives did, might trap spirits and "activate" the mounds energetically. The conical shape serves to reflect waveforms back into the mounds, and keeps other unwanted energies out. Apparently, certain Ohio Indians lived on top of mounds, even when there were dead bodies in them. When the previous occupants died, they were buried in place; more dirt was put on top, making the mounds bigger and bigger.

GK: We have a caller. Are you there?

Caller: Good evening. Andy, I read your second book over the summer, and I had a synchronicity experience with it. I was reading it alongside Neil Gaiman's *American Gods*. I would have never tied the Thunderbird to the Garuda and Mothman before I read your book. Reading [it] completely reinformed *American Gods*, which is a very dark, apocalyptic book. The Thunderbird is portrayed in it as a benevolent figure that is sought out for healing. The central character seeks it [out in order] to bring back his dead wife. The parallel reading of the two books was a surreal experience.

AC: Very interesting… The Thunderbird gets portrayed in the media as terrifying and dangerous, but many Native tribes have Thunderbird totems hanging in their lodges. When you talk to their medicine people, they say that it's benevolent and connected to healing. The American Medical Association's logo, the caduceus, is basically a Thunderbird.

Caller: Absolutely… And that ties into the image of the serpent which, technically, is *not* necessarily a reptilian figure. But it goes back in ancient history as being those who are called, oddly enough, "The Watchers." A lot of the research I do in mythology is largely from the standpoint of trying to understand iconography. Your book is very interesting mythologically, and completely informed Neil Gaiman's book.

AC: Keel talked about the "Serpent People" in *Our Haunted Planet* – how they ruled us and gave us a bicameral, or dualistic, belief in God. In ancient sculptures, the Garuda is typically seen as standing on a female serpent. It's easy to misinterpret this as a form of male domination, but it may not be that at all. Garuda can also be viewed as emanating up from the earth, represented by the female serpent, which was later known as Maya. Garuda essentially bridges earth and sky; this is mirrored in the way he shuttles messages and prophecies between our conscious, individual minds and the unconscious collective mind. By the way, "Maya" stands for "illusory reality" in Buddhism. According to Acharya S., who is an excellent scholar in this area, "Maya" later became known as "Mary"; this is reflected in the many illusory Virgin Mary sightings still happening today. The Garuda represents air, the void, and ultimately, enlightenment.

The Garuda is the untethered male, or "yang," aspect of the collective unconscious. "Garuda" may, in fact, be a combination of "Ge" (Gaelic for "Earth," as found in the word "Gaia"), and "Re" or "Ra," the sun god. "Da" may be thought of as similar to the French word "du" or the Spanish "de," meaning "of." This leads to "Garuda" possibly meaning "Of Earth and Sky," or "Of Light and Darkness."

GK: Thanks, caller… I've got a question. Have you heard anything about whatever it is – legend or myth – about the hanging coffins in China?

AC: Yes, I've actually seen some of them. Before I get into that, I'd like to mention the "Georgia angle" on the Bigfoot Body, which was in a coffin of sorts – a freezer. We had the invasion of Georgia, which was a U.S.-backed military op that began at the same time as the Olympics. The Georgia Bigfoot Body hit the media at exactly the same time. Interestingly, Loren Coleman made sure to call it the "Georgia Gorilla," which has a double meaning because "guerilla" warfare had begun in Georgia. A subliminal linkage was thus made between the Georgia over there and the Georgia over here. Questions about military operations can be effectively muted by big supernatural stories that occupy people's minds… As far as the hanging coffins go, no one quite knows how they did it. They're way up high on these cliffs, 200 feet up.

UD: Spiderwebs, Andy! *That's* how you hang a coffin.

AC: These hanging coffin canyons are fascinating. There are sheer, solid cliff walls on each side of the river. You would have to use ropes to go up or down these cliffs. They drilled into the rock and stuck timbers in, so that a wooden roadway could be built. Parts of it hang out over the water. There is no beach and nowhere to walk along the river. It was a massive endeavor, sort of like building the Great Wall. They used indentured slaves to pull boats upstream with ropes. The slaves walked along these narrow ledges that had either been constructed with wood or, in some cases, carved directly out of the rock. They could pull a boat from *both* sides of the river if necessary.

GK: They are an industrious people.

AC: And still today, they reenact the pulling of these boats, sort of like how we reenact our Civil War battles. As far as the coffins go, perhaps the water level was higher back when the hanging coffins were put in place.

GK: The questioner seems to think that they may have had the ability to fly.

AC: I don't know. We have helicopters, yet we don't use them for funerals.

GK: Garuda, or Mothman, flies. I think everybody has an affinity for that which flies. We all see a certain amount of escapism in it. We really want Bigfoot to exist, but he is terrestrial, bound to the earth. Here in Florida, we really want the panthers to exist. Is there something in the human psyche that wants to see these creatures?

AC: Yes, and it's not unlike how people also want there to be a messiah. There are birdman-messiah legends in almost all cultures. Lyall Watson often talks about this need in man to believe in the supernatural.

GK: Do you think humans ever had the ability to fly?

AC: If they did, they weren't human as we know it today. Crowley claimed that the ancients ingested a rare form of phosphorus known as ZRO, an equivalent of white gold or occultum, and that *that* allowed them to fly. Perhaps at one time, long ago, we did fly; maybe that entered our cellular memory. Flying is a very powerful experience, even if it's just in a paraglider or an airplane. Some people get high on it - repeatedly.

GK: Humans want to escape the chains of our bodies. Myths are not necessarily false or made-up stories. They are a way for past generations to report what was going on.

AC: Looking at the world holographically, flying is certainly possible. Perhaps it was encoded into us at some point, which made us later want to invent flying machines. This drive may have helped us escape from the various dark ages we seem to have dropped into throughout history. The Buddhists believe civilizations have risen and fallen over eons of time. Each time, they developed advanced technology, only to lose it during global cataclysms.

CHAPTER 19

"The summer sun still shone as investigators and witnesses filed into the offices of the New England Institute of Hypnosis. We were totally unprepared for what was about to take place. Betty [Andreasson] was about to undergo the most painful and emotional segment of her total experience. Her suffering and ecstasy would be contagious. What we were about to witness would become etched indelibly on our minds and in our hearts. Betty lay back in the familiar chair. In a few minutes, she was in a deep trance... Betty began describing where she had left off at the last session. Hooded entities had placed her in [something called] the 'Cold Chair,' which encased her body in clear plastic [and caused her to see visions of] domes, floating bridges, pyramids, tunnels, crystals, weird climbing creatures, flying fish, and...a large bird... She started in the role of observer, but quickly became an actual participant:

> I'm standing before a large bird. It's very warm. [It] looks like an eagle to me, and it's living! It has a white head and there is a beautiful light in the back of it. It has brown features. It's very, very hot here. The bird is just standing there. It looks like it is holding back the light somehow. The feathers are fluffed out. I see gold flecks flying around. The light keeps sending out rays that get bigger and bigger. The heat makes me weak. Lord Jesus, I'm hot. Help me. Oh-h-h-h-h. *[heavy breathing]* Oh-h-h-h. *[Begins to cry]* I'm so hot. Oh, oh, oh-h-h-! Take me out of it! Take me out of it! It feels like my hands are vibrating... Oh, I'm beginning to cool off a little. Ah, ah... Oh, my hands hurt... There's a fire in front of me... That fire is burning down, and there are coals there... I feel cold now... *[sounding astonished]* Now it looks like a *worm*, a big fat worm, just lying there.

"Betty began to shiver all over. The investigators cast incredulous looks at each other, wondering if we had pushed Betty too far. Then, Betty heard what sounded like many voices blended into one, booming out: 'You have seen, and you have heard. Do you understand?'

They called my name, and then repeated it, again, in a

louder voice. I said, 'No, I don't understand what this is all about, or why I'm even here.' And they – whatever it was – said, 'I have chosen you. I have chosen you to show the world.'

"Betty asked with wonder in her voice, 'Are you God?' The unequivocal reply was, 'I shall show you as your time goes by.' Looks of puzzlement and concern passed among the investigators. [We] briefly consulted about the weird turn of events. At this juncture, a religious connotation caused great consternation among us; it somehow seemed completely out of place. [But] Betty defensively proclaimed her Christian faith:

> I have faith in God, and I have faith in Jesus Christ. Praise God, there is nothing that can harm me. There is nothing that can make me fear…

"'We know this, child,' the voice answered. 'We know that you do [have faith]; that is why you have been chosen. I am sending you back now. Fear not; be of comfort. Your own fear makes you feel these things. I would never harm you. It is your fear that you draw to your body, which causes you to feel these things. I can release you, but you must release yourself of that fear through my son.' Those words became the catalyst for the most moving religious experience that I have ever witnessed. Betty's face literally shone with unrestrained joy as tears streamed down her beaming face. Mere words cannot convey what Betty relived before us. To have both seen and heard Betty was a profound, unique experience, and listening to the tape recordings still provokes deep emotions… Betty continued to sob uncontrollably. We watched dumbfounded, perhaps a bit embarrassed. Was it a compensatory dream triggered by Betty's religious beliefs and the effects of hypnosis? Had the 'aliens' produced a physical or visionary object lesson for Betty's benefit? [I asked her] what had happened to the eagle – if it just disappeared and was replaced by fire:

> I don't know what happened to the eagle because of what I was going through. It felt as though something was permeating right through me. It felt like something was piercing every cell in my body.

"I asked [Betty] if the bird-thing was just as real as all the events leading up to it:

> It is more real. I could believe that the [previous stuff was] a dream state, but never the bird and the light and what I experienced… It was real. I really believe it was God that spoke to me. God has made all things and is present in everything, and yet, here I was standing [before Him]. He spoke to me… I don't feel as if the bird was God. I feel as if the *light* in back of the bird was the radiation of God. I could not see God. All I did was hear his voice. I could not see any form, and I don't think I even wanted to look upon the form [even] if there was such a form.

"Indeed, this bizarre segment is essential to the unity of the overall narrative. We dare not dismiss it, because it may provide the focal point, the very reason, for the abduction of Betty Andreasson… Upon investigation, we found that Betty seems to have witnessed the death and rebirth of the legendary Phoenix. *Collier's Encyclopedia* describes a bird almost identical to what Betty reported: a legendary bird that builds its own funeral pyre and is reborn from its own ashes. Both the bird and its nest are consumed in the flames. Out of the ashes, a worm emerges, from which the new Phoenix grows. The Phoenix was sacred in ancient Egypt, and figures prominently in early Christian art and literature as a symbol of immortality and the resurrection. [Betty's] confrontation with a mythical monster was unsettling, to say the least. [One wonders if] there is a relationship between the Phoenix and the insignia of a bird on found on the uniforms of aliens [seen by Betty and other witnesses]."

-Raymond Fowler, *The Andreasson Affair: The Amazing Documented Account of One Woman's Encounter With Alien Beings*, pp. 82-93

MARINKOV BAST, MINA – COLVIN PSYCHIC READING – AUG. 2008

The following is a continuation of the psychic healing session I had with Mina Bast in early August of 2008 (see The Mothman's Photographer III, *Chapter 25). The earlier portion of Mina's reading revealed eerie symbolisms corresponding to key elements of my personal story (i.e., the Twin Towers, birdmen, a bridge collapse,*

*my marriage and heritage, and a bedeviling female archetype). I
had approached Mina only a day or two before this psychic reading
was undertaken. She was completely unfamiliar with my story, and
would have had little time to research me in advance. Even if she
had, it would not explain how she picked up on details that I had
not yet made public.*

Mina Bast (MB): I'm picking up a guide or a helper. When I get a guide,
I go from there to see what else I feel in the room… I get a really strong
Garuda-type figure. The way it's standing there reveals a very strong
guardian sense. He guards you. Nothing majorly bad is going to be able to
come within his scope. It looks almost like a statue. It is brown and shiny,
but somehow alive, conscious. You have big feathers in here. It feels like
they're stuck in, as if you were stabbed with a feather pen. They feel sharp
and they poke. Everything is loosening up around it now… The feathers
expand. You spread out your wings. I get the image of *you* as the winged
guy. He is about to run a race, only one of his wings is broken, and his
knee is messed up. He's trying to get going, but he's hobbled in certain
areas. He has been harmed in some way in the past. Now, he feels like a
hermit. He can't really get going, totally, because of these injuries. He puts
his fingers up to his lips, as if to shush me. He wants me to know [that
isolation is simply] a meditative thing. Feel comfortable in silence. Listen,
and see what you see… It said, "Go quiet." So, I'm going to do that…
In addition to the feathers, I get a fur body. Maybe it's a combination,
like a Sasquatch/Mothman. I feel like I'm a king. I see him eating. He's
been in a cave. He's been eating in this cave awhile. He's been studying
the drawings on the walls and making new ones. I can feel his strength
in a physical, muscular way. But he feels like he let himself get soft. It's
all good, because he is what he is. He is *who* he is. He'll never *not* be
strong… Bang… I just went straight to Egypt. There's a reference there.
I see a statue with golden wings. There is an eye in the center where the
chest would be. Interesting… It feels like I'm seeing into the heart of what
it really represents, like it's saying, "Don't forget to look into the core."
Don't forget the heart. Look into the heart. I get a totem. You are the
totem.

Andy Colvin (AC): *[jokingly, as if hypnotized]* I am the totem… I am the
totem…

MB: "I ams" are very powerful. It feels like the arms are very strong. I
keep getting a lot of references for strength and solidity. There are
red carvings on the arms of your totem, which look like tattoos. I
don't know what the symbols are. I feel like I'm watching movies of
knees getting injured. Old stories… I feel like I'm watching them

play out still. It keeps me from fully trusting. Anything you hurt, you are protective about. It is shifting… I get a strong, solid sense again. Your wooden legs are carved, with markings on the backs of the calves. The ones on the arms have a swirl. The ones on the legs have a line with a "V" under it that kind of cuts through. I go to your wrists… I just want to hold your wrists for a second, if that's alright. *[holds wrists]* For some reason, the first thing I hear is "magnet" or "magnetic." I'm seeing magnetism come into your hands. It feels good, like when you're first falling in love and you know that they love you. It comes back to trust again. I am putting my hand over your heart area. That is the first point. A sense of freedom is the second point. If I could connect that sense of freedom, expansion, and openness to your heart, then that's what I would do. My focus then goes from your heart to your head. It's almost like smoke coming out of the top of an oil refinery stack. It felt like it shot up and went "poof." It felt like a release. But it also feels like a trust issue again. I don't trust it because it's an oil refinery, and it's burning this shit that is bad for us. But the oil refinery blows up; it explodes… Some people get hurt, but that's what happens. Life goes on… There is creation after destruction. We build new and better things to replace it. Sometimes crappy structures need to fall down.

AC *[to camera]*: For our viewers… As Mina was saying that last stuff, I was seeing images of Woodward Drive, and the schoolhouse burning down. Speaking of which, last week, when I visited Woodward Drive, our Geiger counter went off.

MB: Did you pick up any radiation?

AC: I don't know but, in addition to my Geiger counter chirping, an alarm of some kind went off at the Carbide plant while I was standing on the hillside overlooking it. The radiation beeper started going off when I got back to the car. These are the kinds of serious issues that, in a perfect world, one should *not* have to worry about while doing benevolent birdman research.

MB: Let's see… I get "time travel." I get 1943… Didn't this happen the first time I worked on you? It's funny, because you weren't born yet in 1943.

AC *[shocked]*: 1943? The Philadelphia Experiment! Maybe you're picking up a signal from my father. He was there at that experiment… He likes to show up at psychic readings and make his presence known. It's very synchronistic that it popped into your mind right after you were talking about magnetism. Magnetism was a key not only to the Philadelphia Experiment, but also to the Bell weapon that was, perhaps, milled at the Carbide plant where Dad worked. You also mentioned a refinery blowing up, which was a Mothman prophecy regarding Carbide. I've never mentioned those things to you before.

Speaking of explosions, the schoolhouse fire may have been the indirect result of espionage in the Chemical Valley during and after WWII. The home invasions, abductions, and drugged inter- rogations by MIBs in the area may have been directed at labor rabble-rousers. An important labor-training center was located in Mineral Wells, where Indrid Cold sought out some of his contactees. The key economic feature of the Kanawha Valley during Mothman was a bitter strike between Carbide and its union members... As my series progressed, I began to suspect that Charles Manson might have burned the schoolhouse down, since he soon thereafter burned down a school in Indiana. When I discovered that Manson's friend, Sara Jane Moore, had this habit of experiencing unexplained "missing time," I began to wonder if she wasn't involved in some way as well. If Sara Jane played some role in the fire, even if it was just knowing that Charlie did it, that might explain why she later abandoned her children. Perhaps she felt guilty for what happened to the children in the fire and, at some subconscious level, came to feel that she wasn't fit to be a mother. Another interesting point is that Sara Jane's family was supposedly running an underground railroad for Jews fleeing Nazi Germany. One wonders what impact this may have had on Manson's involvement in Sara's life. Given his later neo-Nazi leanings, one doubts he was supportive of the under- ground railroad concept. Could the school fire have been an attempt to thwart support for fleeing Jews?

AC: The Philadelphia Experiment altered the genes of nearby sailors. It was a space-time warp that seems to have been transferred to the DuPont plant near Mound, where men were reported to have caught fire and disappeared.

MB: It makes sense that I would get "time travel" for that. It *does* feel like worry about pollution and radiation – the refinery with the smoke. It's a fear of toxins. *[explains to camera]* Sometimes I'm getting infor- mation that can be put out in some useful way. Or, I'm tracking the physical sensations of something shifting. At other times, I just need to be there with the patient and hold the space with them, be their witness. It's just compassion, having someone there. Sometimes *that's* enough... Sometimes, *that's* all we want: someone who "gives a damn."

AC: There is a lot of compassion in hypnotherapy. Our teachers were very compassionate. They would go into the person's subconscious and ask permission for *everything*... Suggestions are made in a caring, wise, and appropriate way. Patients almost always feel better immediately afterward, and changes occur. They even look better.

MB: That's because the intention behind it is to help people.

AC: A skeptic might start by saying that you researched me in order to make your reading more accurate. But I would counter that even if that *is* what you did, it would have been a time-consuming endeavor. And you didn't have much time. I met you only a couple of days before the reading. You had not sought me out. You might have found out about my Mothman connections after I asked you to do the reading, but you probably couldn't have located much more than a basic description online. If the skeptic has read the book *Blink*, they might counter by saying that your reading was merely intuition-based. For most of our lives, we have been required to very quickly read the nonverbals of others. We all become fairly skilled at reading nonverbals within just a couple of minutes of meeting someone.

MB: I want to clarify that the very first time I worked on you at my house, I had my eyes closed the entire time. I "see" better with my eyes closed. It also helps me be unattached to whatever feedback is coming. I don't *want* to watch the client and [see their nonverbals]. I'm just getting whatever comes into my head and saying it out loud. I can do that more easily if I have my eyes closed. If I'm not looking at you, then I'm not worried about what your reaction is. I'm just focused on the information that I'm getting.

AC: The skeptic *still* might say that, very quickly at the start of interaction, we get a tremendous amount of information unconsciously. Within a couple of minutes, we have accessed our mental database containing all of the different cues we've seen in others.

MB: Yes, we track millions of bits of information per second. We're only tracking a handful consciously. There's obviously a lot of information. That's all anything is: information. I'm always picking over information. My point is that, most of the time, I work much better with my eyes closed. For example, if I'm working with someone over the phone, I obviously don't have any visual cues. We're working only in audio. If they were to have a nonverbal reaction, I wouldn't know it. I don't want to say that I try to ignore the person I am working on, but I focus on the information. I don't need to see them or hear them. I'm not trying to give a psychic reading. I'm not trying to *do* anything. All I'm doing is presenting the information that is being presented to me, via cues *in my head*.

AC: Fair enough… Do we want to continue talking about 1943?

MB: The first place I went to with "time travel" was 1943. I saw what a flying saucer would look like. Then I saw lasers intersecting, and got the word "trajectory." As I check back in, I feel like I am still tracking the 1940s. There could also be something earlier, like in 1941 and 1942.

AC: Could the lasers be a holographic projection system or even a weapon? In the Mothman lore, we had a lot of "lightning strike" victims. In the 1960s, the victims *could* have been hit with a laser from a satellite, since that had been under development. In 1943, they obviously couldn't shoot things down from satellites, but they may have been able to project images into the sky, perhaps from drone UFO craft.

MB: That makes sense, because it felt like the lasers were coming out of the "spaceship." Some were coming from some other point, too: a dish-type thing.

AC: Could these lasers have some relationship to my father and the Philadelphia Experiment?

MB: I don't know, but the fact that you put a lot of focus on this particular period of time is enough for those events to have a physical connection to what we are working on. I don't know anything about the Philadelphia Experiment. I know there was a movie, but I haven't seen it. I know that there is a time travel connection to the story, and a ship in the water, but that's basically the extent of my knowledge.

AC: Yes, the boat supposedly time-traveled due to being bombarded with magnetism. It disappeared from Philadelphia and then appeared briefly in Norfolk; it then reappeared in Philadelphia. According to the official record, my dad went into the Navy on March 11th, 1942. It looks like he was in Norfolk for a year and a half prior to the actual experiment. It is somewhat odd that he was still there, because Norfolk was a training base for recruits. He should have moved on to another assignment by then. But he kept training there, and also at the National Bureau of Standards (which today houses Harry Diamond Labs, a national research laboratory involved in developing satellite and other high-tech weaponry). After the war, the Navy supposedly continued the Philadelphia experiments at Montauk, which is on Long Island. My dad was sent there for a while, too. Then he found "private" employment with Carbide in West Virginia. Former sailors used in the experiments were reportedly catching on fire and disappearing at local chemical plants.

MB: After you just mentioned the boat and the experiment, I went straight to a vision of a submarine. There was a crack in space-time. It started there, but arrived here… I feel like you are watching Richard Nixon. He is talking about all this stuff that you know is bullshit. You know that he is lying. He's intentionally feeding us false information. It pisses you off. There is conspiracy everywhere, but blame is a metaphor. We're all one. We're all connected. The theory of "the disappearance of the universe" revolves around the idea that we are sons of God. One day, we had a little thought about doing things on our own, creating "our" world. Supposedly, that one thought is what inferred duality. It inferred a separation between us and God. It inferred that we could go off and play on our own, and create on our own. God wouldn't know about it. It inferred that God wasn't in all places. This created the illusion of separation and duality. This, in turn, created a sense of things and others being "outside," which creates a guilt pattern. We're sons of God and we created this, but now we're guilty of self-blame. [It has been mistakenly] *inferred* that we can be separate from God. So, now we want to blame everyone else. We want to hurt other people. We feel guilty about exiling ourselves from Heaven. All of the blame and guilt comes from a projection of the guilt we feel… But we can shift how we're looking at other people. We can forgive other people for these things that they seemingly did. It's easy, because the world is just an illusion anyway; it is all a metaphor for this separation. If we can forgive, then we can all wake up from the dream. Then, the dream will no longer need to exist. The whole purpose of the dream is to show us what it would have been like if we *could* be separate from God and each other; but it is not possible. None of this is real… Feel yourself being assisted by the part of you that knows this truth.

AC *[jokingly]*: Higher Self, come in!

MB: The Higher Self infers separation, but it's useful because you are "existing" within the separation. I used to reject metaphors regarding separation: higher, middle, and lower selves, conscious versus subconscious… Then I said, "Okay, fine. I'm playing the separation game anyway, I suppose. I can recognize the fact that time and space do appear to exist here. I can work with it. I can play the game."

AC: The relative versus the absolute…

MB: Yes. There is a part of you, the grander part of you – your Higher Self – that has never forgot what you were. It's only the part of you that is *here* that has forgotten. According to the "disappearance" theory, you passed through whatever you passed through to get here. Both forgiving and forgetting are really vital to the game. If you didn't forget that you were divine, then the game would be pointless. You wouldn't be convinced. You *need* to be convinced everything is real in order for this game to work. Still, in reality there is no space and time. It all happened at once. Boom! Here's the thought, projected. Reality is like this glob of thought. It all happened at once. It's not really happening right now. You're dipping back in, after the fact, observing it, as if time and space exist. There is faith there, because you know that you never left Heaven. You can find safety in that – in knowing that *that's* where you really are. You are simply observing it through this individuated structure that you call "you." You're observing what it would look like if that were possible – if it were possible right now.

AC: Absolutely nothing is happening. We've just managed to concretize all of this so that it *seems* like something is happening.

MB: It *is* very convincing. I am proud of us. We did a great job. *[laughter]* But what does it mean?

AC: That *is* the question. What does "nothing" mean? What is the Void?

MB: And who *is* it that is doing nothing? And are you comfortable with your nothingness? I, for one, appreciate my nothingness.

AC: Yes, understanding the void side of the equation is a valuable thing.

MB: Richard Bartlett, the founder of Matrix Energetics, always says, "If we are nothing doing nothing, then what is it that we are experiencing? Is it just stories, adventures?" We *are* experiencing *something*. It's like being in a movie that you yourself wrote. It's like being nothing, yet experiencing yourself *as something*.

AC: I agree. And I would say that Mothman ties in with that. With my childhood precognition, provided by "Mothman," a timeloop was created where I could sense what was going to happen later in my life. The movie was being written. Or, perhaps it had already been written. Perhaps I was just being shown a script, a rough draft that some bigger part of me had written beyond space and time. It *does* seem like a big loop of now-ness. We really *can* see into the future.

It's hard to get ahold of it, however, for it exists more or less in the unconscious realm. It's hard to map it, but you know it exists.

MB: It's the elusiveness of our essence... So... You wrote timeloops into your story! Very cool... It is multisensory, multidimensional, and you get to come across great, amazing characters with more great stories. It is a fun game, is it not?

AC: Yes. Unfortunately, in order to play in that way, one needs at least some socioeconomic stability. You need enough leisure time to learn, create, and reflect. If you don't have that, you won't have time to analyze and work through the issues found along on the path.

MB: I have a little theory on technology. We've invented all of these amazing technologies to help us work less, but we've actually used them to work *more*. Personally, I'm in the game to play. You don't have to work all of the time. It all comes down to preference. I decided that play was important... I'm intrigued by this Mothman phenomenon. Tell me, what do you believe about Mothman himself? Is he a three-dimensional being that can appear in solid form? Is he a messenger? An archetype?

AC: Regardless of which tradition you look at, he is generally thought to be an archetypal deity representing the crossover from the manifestation side of reality to the void side. As you approach voidness in your own life – say, a personal crossroads where the unknown lurks – you may see that symbol or entity. When I experienced voidness through my Mothman experiences, it was shocking. It was not necessarily warm. Voidness comes across as shockingly original and unexpected. It is a force beyond conceptualization. It is like an electrical explosion into another realm. That is how I experienced those precognitions. I suppose it makes sense, metaphorically, that one would see an actual explosion of some kind – like the WTC bombings – on the screen of one's mind. That screen, what they call the "violet flame," is where the content of the precognition seems to be witnessed. In my case, a mental explosion in my head sort of made the screen appear, and then another explosion, 9/11, occurred *on* the screen.

MB: I'm noticing that you are in touch with the symbolisms of things. You've trained yourself to notice the symbols everywhere around us. Having a belief that I am both the creator of the game as well as the player, I feel that we often leave ourselves little clues, in the form of symbols, to remind us of what is going on. It may be part of the game itself. What do symbols mean for you?

AC: I do think we are leaving clues for ourselves, at least as a culture. It is a very necessary activity. Whenever there is a cataclysm and we have to start over, there will still be some basic symbolisms available to trigger mental growth. The symbols lead us out again, into more enlightened times. Still, our control is limited. We *think* we have chosen to play the game in this or that way. We may leave our clues and all, but the universe will still insist on its own order and symmetry. As such, it may compel us to act in ways beyond our conscious control.

MB: As an eternal being, you *are* more than the game. We indeed wrote it all... I would like to thank you for your playing your most excellent part in "my" game.

AC: You are most welcome...

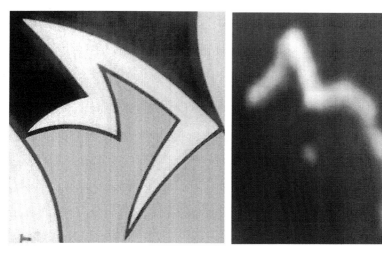

The Tibetan sign for Vril energy (left), which supposedly inspired an entire line of Nazi saucers, was mimicked somewhat in a UFO photo (right) that hit the web during the writing of Mothman Speaks. *Interestingly, by splitting the Vril sign in half, we can construct: 1) an "X"; 2) the Masonic "compass and square"; and 3) "LL," one of the symbols Joseph Smith claimed to have seen on the golden tablets he utilized in founding Mormonism.*

CHAPTER 20

"In 1970 I wrote a novel called *Flow My Tears, The Policeman Said*. One of the characters is a 19-yr. old girl named 'Kathy.' Her husband's name is 'Jack.' Kathy appears to work for the criminal underground, but later, as we read deeper into the novel, we discover that actually she is working for the police. She has a relationship going on with a police inspector. The character is pure fiction. Or at least I thought it was… On Christmas Day of 1970, I met a girl named *Kathy* – this was after I had finished the novel, you understand. She was *19* years old. Her boyfriend was named *Jack*. I soon learned that Kathy was a *drug dealer*. I spent months trying to get her to give up dealing drugs; I kept warning her again and again that she would get caught. Then, one evening as we were entering a restaurant together, Kathy stopped short and said, 'I can't go in.' Seated in the restaurant was a *police inspector* whom I knew. 'I have to tell you the truth,' Kathy said. 'I have a *relationship* with him…'

"Certainly, these are odd coincidences. Perhaps I have precognition."

-Philip K. Dick

COLVIN, ANDY – GRASSY KNOLL RADIO INTERVIEW 35 – SEPT. 2008

"Vyz" at *Beyond the Grassy Knoll* (GK): Here we are with another segment of *Beyond the Grassy Knoll*. We have Andy Colvin with us. He's probably been our most frequent guest. It's fun now to look back at all the ground that has been covered. Welcome back to "the continuum." How are things out in good old Seattle?

Andy Colvin (AC): They are in flux. This phenomenon is wreaking havoc all the time. It never gets boring… Throughout the series, I have tried to figure out what was causing the poltergeists and synchronicities around me. As this was an investigation of the paranormal, I enlisted several psychics to come to the house. At least three different practitioners talked about an ancient, archetypal female presence that is somehow manifesting in my life and influencing me. I've been trying to identify why *I* was chosen for bedevilment, and who the particular deity is. I've heard everything from Greek and Egyptian goddesses to a female version of the Mothman. One psychic even said, "Well, that was *you*, Andy. That was your own unconscious causing those poltergeists, due to things going on in your life." Actually, it turns out that it all had more to do with my *wife* than with me. Her life, like mine, seems to have been controlled by "fate," as if the Greek gods came down and intervened. It was rewarding to finally figure out these personal aspects of the Mothman riddle; a meaning could be placed on the poltergeists and synchronicities in my life… I'm probably a little less organized than I normally would be today, although disorganization *does* have its merits… In Richard Sennett's *The Uses of Disorder*, disorganization is linked to creativity. Most American businesses and organizations tend to suppress creativity. However, thinking randomly can have real benefits in the longterm.

GK: There is a tongue-in-cheek law in business that says that anybody who's got a very orderly desk doesn't get any work done. They merely look officious. However, there are some people you would *not* want to be disorganized, like a surgeon who was going to cut on you. But as you said, in a creative situation, randomness and synchronicity birth a lot of ideas and innovations. Being put into an organized box probably doesn't work out too well for creative types.

AC: According to Sennett, there are healing aspects to disorganization. I've seen this throughout the series with the different psychics and healers I have consulted. There is a randomness to how it's all done. There have been some miraculous healings along the way. The healer is going in and becoming blank, so that whatever needs to be observed can be observed. Any disconnections in the body/mind complex of the patient need to be noticed in order for healing to occur. As a practitioner, you're often connecting seemingly random things in a person's life. Something in their body may relate to another part of their body, or to a past event, or to something completely outside of them. As a patient, I had incredible sessions with Mina Bast, M.C. Marez, Ginna Lee, Andee Booth, John Veltheim, Justice Bartlett, and Eugenia Macer-Story. All were chock-full of the symbolisms we've talked about on the shows.

GK: You just kicked up a memory… I had a creative writing class where the professor, who was excellent, had us writing in columns with subject headings. He would make us jump from column to column and write something. Then, he would jump us to another column. All the time, we had to pat our free hand on our side. This was a technique to prime your pump to write poetry. I couldn't believe the stuff that came out of us all. It was like this supermarket for great ideas. It seemed like the process was not allowing you to focus using your normal mental patterns. It was a form of ordered randomness. I'll never forget that... I never could figure out what that drill was doing but, boy, did it work! The creative process is actually primed by a certain amount of ordered disruption.

AC: As synchronicity would have it, I am reading a book about that subject right now.

GK: No one's going to believe this, honestly...

AC: Well, you and I did not discuss this beforehand, not even in our pre-conversation... But I'm reading two volumes called *The Structure of Magic*, by Bandler and Grindler. They're the guys who started Neuro-Linguistic Programming (NLP). These books are basically about how you find those creative "columns," if you will, in the patient. It's written for therapists. Bandler and Grindler's approach is based on the work of Milton Erickson, the great hypnotherapist. Hypnotic techniques form the basis for NLP. You identify something akin to columns, or areas of interest, within the person; they represent subpersonalities within the person. In order to create synthesis in the mind, you have to identify as many polarities or sub-personalities as you can. Once you've identified them, you have them all be present for the person at once, so that there is some conscious recognition of each of them. Then you start working with them, all together, in the discussion. The therapist refers to the different parts. Sometimes it is done obviously, so that the patient knows what you are up to, but sometimes it is not. Oftentimes, people have some kind of neurosis that links to a physical symptom. That link may need to be severed or modified. It's easy to do, once you get it all mapped out. But to use a sports metaphor, I am just learning to dribble, while Erickson was jumping from the foul line and dunking.

GK: Okay, we're talking basketball; that makes me feel better.

AC: Hypnosis is a complex subject. Erickson's abilities were almost beyond belief, hence Bandler and Grindler's usage of the term "magic" when describing his work. Most people can't even begin to get in touch with their subconscious. How did Erickson figure so much of it out? How did he come to realize the many ways in which data stored in the unconscious could be modified? Ericksonians would say that your chalkboard poetry experience was about re-integrating previously fragmented areas of your mind.

GK: Yes… The exercise would not allow us to think in a causal, linear manner. It just forced us to react rather than try and construct an argument. As you know, when you're discussing anything, you're always constructing your arguments as you're talking. But when that is disrupted, you're just reacting spontaneously. There is this whole part of us, which we know little or nothing about, living inside our minds. None of us see all of it.

AC: Yes, in the poetry exercise, your conscious mind was given the simple task of tapping your side. It was occupied with something. Therefore, a two-way channel is opened up. Either new programming can be dropped into the unconscious, or old programming can be allowed to escape from the unconscious. Things are given to and retrieved from the unconscious; often you are replacing one with the other. But you have to distract the conscious mind in order to drop files in or retrieve them. We've talked about that "flash of light" that you and other experiencers have seen. That light is unusual enough that it catches your attention. It occupies the conscious mind. While that is happening, the doorway to your unconscious has been cracked opened. Every now and then, it happens naturally in our lives, but it can also be triggered mechanically. With a little work, a skilled mind controller can go in and tinker with you at will. When they are done, they can put in an "alien abduction" experience or other screen memory. Keel talked about abductees being used as couriers for the CIA. A possible scenario for this is mentioned in Woody Derenberger's UFO/Mothman book, *Visitors From Lanulos*. Woody and crew were picking up packages at the police station in Eleanor, WV, which adjoins the towns of Midway and Buffalo. Buffalo is where Fort Ancient is located, and is near the NSA's supposed vortex at Liberty. Midway is where Indrid Cold lived. A lot of things have happened on that stretch of river between Mound and Pt. Pleasant. For starters, it was once owned by our Masonic first president, George Washington. Along with the conventional bombs, chemical weapons, and plastic explosives for which the area is known. They may also have been working on such secret things as deathray lasers, scalar "Bell" weapons, ELF transmission, and nuclear technology there. Nowadays, they seem to be doing a lot of "data mining" in the area. I think we're just seeing the tip of the iceberg in terms of what has gone on there. It makes me think of the Nazi compound in Laurel Canyon. Like Woodward Drive in Mound, Laurel Canyon was home to petrochemical, military, and intelligence players. A major Nazi compound was located in L.A. near Laurel Canyon during World Wars I and II. It was right up the road from where Manson was staying with Dennis Wilson. You start to get a sense that this may be where Manson picked up some of his Nazi ideas. There is a woman, codenamed "Mauri," who claims to be a victim of Nazi secret societies in L.A.

GK: Mauri said that there was a Nazi enclave in Manhattan Beach and another attached to the Jet Propulsion Labs in Pasadena. I'm hoping everything is okay with her. People have *not* heard from her lately...

AC: Her name is suggestive. These "Moor" names have come up repeatedly. You've got "Maury" Island, the famous UFO case; you've got the "Maoris," the Garuda-loving Indians of New Zealand, and so on. It could be that her name is symbolic, and chosen for a reason.

GK: Yes, obviously that is not her real name. But it may be symbolically representative of who she is.

AC: Yes, because the major cultural clash in the world has long been the northern Whites, or Aryans, against the Moors, the darker-skinned Arabic peoples of the south. In their fictional literature, the Brits have always used "Mor" names to denote evil characters. We are all from the same tribe originally; but no one wants to admit that. The Rockefellers helped spawn the Thule Society, which worked against Muslims and other minority groups.

GK: Living in the New York metropolitan area and at the mouth of the Hudson, I know how much America was impacted by the neighborhood on the East Bank – the Rockefellers, Roosevelts, Vanderbilts, Van Cortlands, and Rensellears. Their real estate may be magnificent, but they turned out to be our jailers. We are obviously experiencing their hidden hand in events taking place as we speak. Everyone who has a brain knows that something is afoot. We are being conditioned for it. I've been hearing a lot of people saying, "It's no problem. The government will take care of it, and we'll all be okay." I fear to think how many Americans are under that delusion. My point is that these are the old robber-baron families – the Eastern "establishment."

AC: One of the theories that we're looking at right now is whether or not Mary Brunner of the Manson family was the "girl in the polka dot dress" with Sirhan Sirhan. Don't forget, Manson's gang attacked RFK's friends, Tate and Polanski. Manson's seeming favorableness towards Nelson Rockefeller, as seen in the attempted assassinations of Ford by Mansonites Fromme and Moore, makes you wonder if the Rockefellers hated RFK more than they hated JFK.

GK: Whoever killed Jack also killed Bobby. That the Manson posse could have had something to do with RFK's assassination is *very* interesting. Understand, too, that we have identified CIA agents as being at RFK's assassination. Why were they there? Nobody really knows. In Joan Mellen's book, she pretty much states that the CIA was on top of the pile as far as those who wanted him dead. You've got a common denominator to both Kennedy assassinations.

AC: Yes, and those three agents were taking photographs. They knew something was about to go down.

GK: Was it three agents? Okay... Even Robert Kennedy said, off the cuff, that he did not want Garrison to find out anything about JFK's death. But he said that Garrison was probably 90% right; he almost got the whole nine yards. The world was upside down back in the late 1960s. It was just bizarre, and bigger than all of us. They call it a "coup": call it whatever you want, but there was a definite, violent change.

AC: Don't forget, Mothman witnesses were having visions of those assassinations. It was a tense time in society. George Hansen talks about this in *The Trickster and The Paranormal*. Lab tests have found that stress increases psychic and paranormal activity. It triggers archetypal deities to be seen. By the way, a list of the Flatwoods Monster sighting locations from 1952 jibes with places where Mothman was seen years later. It's kind of suggestive. Perhaps they are the same phenomenon. In fact, there were a couple of witnesses who saw a UFO turn into the Mothman! One of them was mentioned in *The Silver Bridge*. Of course, the Flatwoods incidents *could* be yet another drama in the elite plot to make people believe in aliens. The Mothman phenomenon may have been signaling us to look at the Flatwoods incident more closely. The timing of Flatwoods, in 1952, coincides with a lot of Cold War spy activity.

GK: Something is definitely there. They have purposely allowed us to see something. I say "they," but I have no idea who "they" are. But "we" have been allowed to see this and to report on it somewhat. In the end, will it be malevolent? My guess is probably yes. All of this stuff isn't for nothing.

AC: On the natural side, you have ancient myths talking about this archetypal birdman accompanied by lights – one of the oldest explanations. On the synthetic side, you have scientists projecting voices and imagery into the heads of often unwitting subjects. Innocent victims were subjected to all sorts of chemicals, hypnosis, and electromagnetism. They were frozen, dehydrated, shocked, isolated, injected with diseases, exposed to radiation, you name it. The Council of Nine had been introduced by Puharich at the Round Table Foundation in 1952, the same time as the Flatwoods "Monster" incident and the rollout of the CIA's MK-Ultra operations, rumored to have included "UFO abductions." It could be that the same agency running these UFO abduction ops was running the assassination teams... High-level British occult groups were pushing the idea of this orbiting space intelligence, The Nine. By the time of Mothman, Puharich actually had already manufactured a device that could more or less beam a screen memory right into an abductee's brain. I doubt that Puharich beamed any assassination prophecies into people's heads, as that would have been considered a breach of security. I suppose it is possible, however, which might explain why the CIA burnt his house down. In his role as a CIA doctor, Puharich may have been privy to upcoming covert operations. We have to assume that some anonymous security wing of the military, such as DISC, was monitoring him at all times. Wherever he went, the MIB went.

GK: Don't forget about Puharich's involvement with hallucinogenic mushrooms. They tried *everything*...

AC: Tomandandy ("Tom and Andy") was the name of the band that did the soundtrack to *The Mothman Prophecies*. Originally, there was a Nine channeler, named "Tom," who could just plug into The Nine at will. The Nine would say things *through* him. According to Stuart Holyrod, who wrote a book on The Nine, it turned out that the channeler's real name wasn't really Tom. It was "A-tom," which starts to sound Egyptian. "Atum" was an Egyptian god associated with a bird, the "tern." Now get this: In the official Egyptian legend, Atum created himself by sitting on a *mound!* As you let that sink in, consider the fact that most of our important scientific concepts are based on the "atom." And "atom" is very close to the word "Etam," which is where they download the AT&T signals in WV; the Navy pockets those same signals in Sugar Grove. If you spell Atom backwards, you get "Mot-a." This gets us to "Mot" or "Mut," the Egyptian goddess. Her name is related to "mother" and "moth." There appears to be some Masonic wordplay going on in The Nine literature... Here's another good one... Woody Derenberger thought that the aliens were coming from the planet "Cerabus," which sounds like a mispronunciation of "Cerberus," the three-headed hound of Hades. There is also a "mon" word for Cerberus which, at some point, was removed from Cerberus' Wikipedia page: "Di Manes" ("Di" for "God of," and "Manes" for "souls of the Dead"). Di Manes relates to "Manus," the root word of "human," as well as to "daemon," the acorn of creativity. When the acorn of creativity is not nurtured, the "daemon" gives rise to the "demon." Cerberus is the demon in hell... A "lapis manalis" is the earth-energy stone put into the ground when towns are consecrated. You have "mon" words being associated to the underground. The word "emanate" is a "mon" word. It's this idea of the Adam Kadmon, the messianic force, coming out of a mound of earth. The Kaluli in New Guinea have built their culture around birds... They believe that they all turn into birds when they die, and sometimes even before they die. They talk to birds. They can talk to their ancestors through birds. They watch the birds really closely. One type of bird there actually builds large mounds. The bird that they depend on the most is called the "Moony Bird," which is sort of a "mon" word... But Cerberus is captured by Heracles. Here, we start to get into some of the "he" words like Heyoka, Heruka, Hercules, and Heraclites, who wrote about Cerberus. There are some similarities in the different traditions with these words, which are just a touch away from "Hor" words relating to time. And Typhon, who was Cerberus' father, was a birdman. So, embedded in Derenberger's tale of Indrid Cold, you have further symbology linking to birdmen.

GK: And Typhon was the assassin of Osiris...

AC: By the way, there were some Crowleyites around this situation, like Allen Greenfield. Allen won't say if he was actually in the Crowley cult or not, but he's definitely an occultist in that vein. Greenfield is very knowledgeable about Crowley's O.T.O. cult, which revered Horus, the Egyptian birdman. Greenfield came to West Virginia to hang out with Gray Barker. It makes you wonder if there weren't other "birdman occultists" in WV, who came because the birdman was there. Maybe Indrid Cold was one of these Crowleyites, planting symbolisms into the story in order to invoke some magical working. Greenfield has alluded to the possibility that tantric rituals influenced the Silver Bridge collapse – that some vibratory energy was inadvertently set loose. Greenfield was one of the first authors to hint that the entity contacted by Aleister Crowley was an extraterrestrial. The ET, called "Lam," supposedly looked like today's modern "grey" alien. Right before Crowley died in 1947, he supposedly conjured up the UFOs, thus beginning the modern flying saucer era. One must remember, however, that there is a both a natural UFO phenomenon and a synthetic one. Was Crowley working on one or the other, or both?

GK: This is kind of bittersweet but, when you were talking about birds, I was thinking of when Reggie, whom we called the "Vyzykeet," was alive. My wife and I have always been bird lovers. We love their presence. Without them, it would be a very quiet and rotten world. They bring joy to our lives. There is an attachment between human beings and birds. It is not a nefarious association. The Mothman or Garuda should not be seen as an evil entity. I don't know why anybody would ever associate something bad with winged creatures.

AC: The birdman is seen in Buddhism as an enlightenment stabilizer. Pondering his aspects will help maintain your personal awakenings. We go through life and we have epiphanies. If you can continually come back to meditating on the symbolisms around the Garuda, you will help cement those epiphanies. Advanced knowledge appears to be encoded in the symbols used in birdman paintings and sculptures.

GK: I don't pay much attention to the collective consciousness, but I got an ad from an Israeli magazine prior to 2000, in which they showed the Trade Towers and a plane approaching it. Andy Senior has it on his "Uticans For 9/11 Truth" site. It has the Towers on the left-hand side, and this plane coming from the lower right-hand side. I've got a translation of what it says from Barry Chamish. The translation is: "Realize your sweet dreams. Collect elite packages and fly to America." It's a candy bar ad. You take the wrappers off of the Elite candy bars and send them in, so that you can be entered in a contest where the winner goes to America… I have compiled ads that have an unusual relationship to the Towers. It seems like there *was* foreknowledge. I don't know if you're familiar with the bourbon Maker's Mark, but their ad showed the Towers overflowing with red wax, which looks like blood. There was also a refrigerator ad for General Electric in an Italian magazine before September 2001. One of the designer refrigerators has a design on the front door showing a big commercial airliner heading towards the Towers. It goes on and on… Andy Senior also found one from the cover of *New York* magazine from March 2001. We see the Towers and a woman's face, obviously in horror. It says, "What are you going to do when the real estate boom is over?" So you get the Towers, the woman's face transmogrified in this exquisite horror, and the word "boom" in there. Why would residential real estate be associated with the Trade Towers? Wasn't there a subconscious preoccupation with the Towers?

Something presciently anticipating tragedy or catastrophe for the Towers? If I were to do something in a foreign magazine using a symbol of the United States, I would use, say, the Statue of Liberty or the Washington Monument, or the Capitol. Why the Trade Towers? Isn't there something here that people always anticipated?

AC: I think so. Also, Masonic elites higher up the corporate ladder may have gotten wind of the operation long before, and consciously or unconsciously inserted signals into the media – the "revelation of the method."

GK: I grew up on the Palisades, which was an elevated plateau in New Jersey overlooking the Hudson River and the skyline. A great, great place… Anywhere you went in eastern Bergen County, you could see the Trade Towers and the Empire State Building. When we watched the Trade Towers go up and up and up, we all looked at each other and said, "Someone's going to fly a plane into that." It was almost like the Towers were begging, "Go ahead, and hit me." They were so obscenely large for that part of Manhattan, which is flatter than a pancake. It is the old Wall Street area; nothing really went vertical there. It was really funky, and a great place to shop. As the story goes, they had to clear out a lot of mom-and-pop shops to make way for the WTC complex. It put a lot of small merchants out. When they put the Towers up, it was almost like saying, "Come on, make my day." And so we waited for that to happen… On the day of the bombing in 1993, I was driving east on Route 80. We saw smoke coming from the top of the WTC. We thought, "Somebody flew a plane in there! Damn it, they finally did it!" We threw on the radio and, lo and behold, there had been a bombing. But we always expected it. It was in the back of everyone's mind. A friend of yours had some kind of premonition about this in WV in 1967. But there also seems to have been "predictive programming" with regard to 9/11 – symbolisms that came out in the media beforehand. How many people looked at the footage of the BBC reporting the fall of Building 7 several minutes early? Do people just not look at it, or do they look at it and then have cognitive dissonance regarding the lies we have to tell ourselves? That's what it reminds me of every time I see it: we are a culture of liars. Everybody's walking around thinking that we're living life, but we're not. I think it has affected people very negatively. There is a lot less trust. Responsibility isn't taken; we are not going to admit to something unless we are caught red-handed. Our authority figures lie… Before I met Lady Vyz, things sucked for me. I wanted to be involved with someone. Prior to that, when I was intimate with a woman, I would say, "Tell me you love me. I know you don't, but tell me you do anyway. I just want to hear it." Where am I going with this? I think people are saying, "Just lie to me. Please lie to me." That's what I think is happening out there. The majority know something isn't right, but they settle for the lie.

AC: Here's a provisional theory… You and I were talking about the comments Tom Brokaw made just as the Towers were coming down. Two seconds before the second Tower came down, which was *the* moment everybody realized that it was some form of terrorism, Brokaw said, "A word has gone out from the Pentagon: duck for cover!" They said "*from* the Pentagon," not "at" the Pentagon… This doesn't make any sense, except as a form of mass hypnotic induction. We were all being ordered to duck for cover, whether in Tampa, Seattle, NYC, or D.C. It was this hypnotic command seemingly coming back from the 1950s, when schools enforced the A-bomb drills. Then, the Towers started falling… Brokaw then made one single, important statement. And he said it *again* a couple of minutes later, only backwards. The first statement was: "Terrorists have declared war on us." The reverse statement was, "We have declared war on the terrorists." A sealed mental loop was created. In a loop like this, one thing justifies and sustains the other. The essential command in this case, at the subtextual level, is that you will view this situation as a battle between unknown, outside "terrorists," and "us." Now, when the media refer to "us," you have to remember that they are referring to the owners of companies. They were basically programming us to *not* suspect U.S. elites of being involved in the planning of an "inside job." They created a dualistic loop that occupied our conscious minds. While our conscious minds were busy with the looped koan, they introduced whatever else they wanted, directly to our unconscious. The repetitive imagery of the implosions was, in itself, probably enough to prepare us for the upcoming loss of living standards. The conscious mind wasn't doing its normal job of filtering out new ideas that day. These loops are fairly perpetual, because one side keeps "causing" the other. There is no end in sight, and it is a downward spiral.

GK: They got yardage out of showing the Towers go down again and again. It made me start to think that as long as they keep showing that, they keep making us all victims. And in doing so, it makes us pliant. It lives on in the memory…

AC: Yes, you start imagining that you were successfully victimized. You are asked to take a more fragmented view of reality – of "us" versus "them." You therefore feel a little more alone, and less powerful.

GK: For those us who get what is happening politically, that event is a reminder that they can do this sort of terrorism again and again, and there is nothing you can do about it. Barry Chamish told me about a night security worker, who woke up to find the Towers gone. He went crazy. Can you imagine what that would have been like?

AC: No, although I think we *all* went through that, in a sense... I just wanted to mention the "tote." That's a word Erickson came up with. A tote is basically a set of actions that one practices until it becomes unconscious. For instance, in order to put peanut butter and jelly on your toast, you have to do a series of actions. If you've never done it before, it takes a few tries to get to the point where you no longer have to consciously think about doing it. Once you can do it without thinking, you have created a tote. When you're working with hypnotherapy patients, you have to be aware of totes. A tote is harder to break. It's a more solid construct. I think the media knew what it was doing. Confusion deepens any hypnosis. We've got the footage absolutely proving that the BBC knew WTC7 was coming down twenty minutes beforehand. We can prove that they knew. Their behavior that day should be analyzed for further clues, but it probably will not be because the confusing mix-up in time with WTC7 deepened the initial Brokaw induction of "us" versus "Arab." Let's face it, if you were a corporatist who knew it was going to happen in advance, you'd probably try to take advantage of it anyway you could, including the use of hypnosis. They probably hypnotized the news anchors privately, prior to the event. The profits were simply too enormous for the controllers to not take every precaution.

GK: Absolutely. That would be rational, from their point of view. Unfortunately, we've entered an era not unlike that found in Trotsky's *Terror and Communism*, except that in the 20th Century, terror has been modernized and perfected to new, horrifying heights. That's what we're going to be stuck with. I think 9/11 was a very ominous indicator of just how reckless our controllers are. It was a record body count. That Rubicon has been crossed; the barrier has been broken. Now they're playing for keeps. It's chilling. A lot of people can't handle that, and I understand that. But that *is* the nature of the people who rule us, and it's here to stay. Folks out there with children want to hope for better. It was not our decision to play this next and final card. Who knows what's going to happen next. The rulers are psychotic.

AC: We now float along in a Hollywood fantasyland where truthful presentations are barely necessary. Now, the banks are saying that they will fail unless they get more money than the entire Iraq war has cost so far.

GK: There is more to it than just kneecapping the United States again. This is going to be for establishing a new global order. We're seeing it happen before our eyes. It's a very interesting time.

A snapshot from a 1978 UFO magazine (lower left) is the only known possible image of Indrid Cold, who purportedly landed his saucer near the junction of Ohio Rt. 681 and Coolsville Rd. (top) in Joppa, Ohio - just a short drive from the Belleville Locks and Dam. Mothy experiencer Jordan Rogers may have tapped into Indrid's psyche when he drew this "killer clown" (right) eerily reminiscent of the "clown assassination team" discovered by experiencer Bonnie B.

CHAPTER 21

"Anomalous lights in the sky are interpreted as UFOs in all Westernized areas of the world; this is the most widespread interpretation. But the natural interpretation of such lights in most tribal societies would be witchcraft. It would be hard to find a society which does not hold, or has not at one time held, a belief in witches… Dermot MacManus tells us of a sighting which is common not only in his native Ireland but across the world. One Halloween night in the 19th Century [the witness] saw a blaze of light across the lough on which her farmhouse was situated. She stared in amazement as the small fort on the far side of the water was lit up by hundreds of little white lights. She saw them all 'rise up as one' and, keeping their formation, sail steadily through the air towards [another] fort… The two forts on opposite sides of the lough were 'fairy forts.' They can be ancient tumuli or barrows but they are more often natural outcrops of land, usually artificially shaped or surrounded by a bank or ditch, whose provenance and purpose has disappeared beyond history into myth. The forts are said to be where Fairy people live. Sudden bursts of light or music have been seen and heard there; sometimes a cavalcade of horsemen is seen passing into them through a hitherto invisible entrance. The lights are fairies. They are seen over stone circles or legendary hills or even certain trees… Virgin Marys appear in connection with certain trees… The lights follow straight paths between their preferred places, and woe betide anyone who builds on the paths or obstructs their traffic. In June 1973, a young man at Loch Ryan, Scotland woke abruptly at three in the morning and felt compelled to go out onto the landing. He saw three yellowy-orange spheres hovering above the water. They suddenly shot upward 'at a fantastic speed.' He came round [later] 'as if waking from a trance.' He found that his parents were standing beside him. They too had woken for no obvious reason, and had felt compelled to look out of the same window at the lights.

"Archetypes are paradoxical. They cannot be known in themselves, but they can be known indirectly through their images. They are, by definition, impersonal, but they can manifest personally… It is more common to encounter an archetypal image indirectly than directly – that is, in *projec-*

tion. Here, the aptness of the word 'shadow' is evident. For the archetype bypasses consciousness altogether and throws a shadow over the external world; then we encounter what is within us as if it were outside. [According to] Jung, the goal of all psychic life, all personal development [is] to make conscious, as far as possible, the contents of our unconscious. The result is an expansion of personality and, finally, a state of wholeness that embraces even the dark and contradictory sides of ourselves. The self archetype is foreshadowed in the image of the Old Wise Man [but] can also occur in abstract form, most notably in circular patterns, often divided into four, which oriental religions have long understood and called mandalas. Such images occur spontaneously near the beginning of the individuation process, or at a crisis in our psychic lives. Jung believed that 'flying saucers' were like mandalas; the UFOs, in other words, are projections of the collective unconscious.... Again and again in UFO reports, we hear of time 'standing still.' Witnesses describe a feeling of isolation and absorption, as if everybody else had vanished; a feeling of oneness with the perceived object in which initial apprehension or fear can be replaced by a sensation of subdued calm... No one who has seen or felt the full force of an apparition demands proof. If they are a compelled to try and prove it to others, it is only because they feel obliged to, by the scientific tenor of our times...

"Jung considered dreams the *via regia* – the royal path – to the unconscious and hence to self-knowledge... Even less tangible are the sudden hunches and intuitions – the work of 'guardian angels' – which appear out of the blue to make us miss the plane that is doomed to crash or simply to search an unlikely place for a lost object... Personal daimons favor two forms by which to manifest: the abstract light, globe, oval, or shining sphere, and the angelic personification... Both are images of the soul... The investigation always broadens to embrace, in the end, all apparitions, as if there were a single principle at work capable of manifesting itself in myriad forms. At the same time, the investigation always deepens, pointing to the continuity of apparitions in time, leading us into the past, into folklore and myth. Both characteristics are explained by the collective unconscious and *Anima Mundi*... The sense of conspiracy everywhere is the reverse side of the religious idea that there is an underlying order, benign and protective, beneath or behind appearances. Paranoid 'seeing through' is [an] aspect of artistic or religious thought.

"There may be profound truth in the folkloric belief that if we see the fairies first, they will be benevolent; but if they see us first they will be malign, and we, cursed... All Marian visions begin with what might be called a daimonic preface. The Blessed Virgin Mary (BVM) is sometimes introduced, as it were, by another daimonic figure in a long seamless robe [with angelic] wings. The BVM is reticent to begin with [but] subsequently, as the visions increase in number, she grows into the image, forming herself to the cultural or religious expectations of the percipients... The BVMs almost never call themselves 'Mary...' The most interesting BVM vision from the point of view of overlap with pre-Christian beliefs [was the Guadalupe case, where] a poor Aztec called Singing Eagle (Juan Diego) was [halted] by a burst of birdsong. The sound seemed to come from a hillock on which had formerly stood a temple to the mother-goddess of the Aztecs. The shrill caroling ceased, and in the silence he heard a woman calling to him from the rocks on top of the hill...surrounded by rays of golden light."

-Patrick Harpur, *Daimonic Reality*, pp. 5-100

In the fall of 2007, after attending the Mothman festival in Pt. Pleasant, I visited with my niece, Sharon Moore Rogers, and her daughter Ariane, who seems to have inherited her mother's psychic gifts. Ariane filled me in on some of the strange events plaguing the family in Beckley, WV. Also in attendance was Jordan Rogers, Sharon's new husband, as well as Sharon's mother, Loretta Colvin (see Chapter 3). Sharon and Jordan's full interviews can be found on discs 5 and 6 of The Mothman's Photographer *reality series, and will be in my next book,* The Mothman Speaks II. *After a quick tour of the neighboring haunted graveyard, we grilled some hot dogs on Sharon's "Vortex" grill and discussed some of the ghosts that were cavorting around their neighborhood at night.*

MOORE, ARIANE – BIZARRE BECKLEY – SEPT. 2007

Andy Colvin (AC): I once had a very vivid dream that I flew headfirst into a clear, headless Mothman. I later found out that such a creature had been seen at Fatima. Didn't you say that you recently had such an experience in real life?

Ariane Moore (AM): I experienced something similar to that. I think it was the same ghost thing that crawled over Mom and Jordan. I was sleeping on the couch one day, and I woke up. I was having nightmares. I woke up scared. There had been this woman crawling in my dream, but it wasn't just a dream. It kept happening *after* I was awake!

Sharon Rogers (SR): When Jordan and I woke up, you could feel a slight disturbance. I said to the woman crawling over us, "Why, you're a *tiny* ghost!"

AM: I could feel her physically on me. I *knew* that it was the same ghost.

SR: We were dreaming, but then we woke up.

AM: To summarize, we have all been crawled over by a woman on the couch. *[laughter]*

AC: Ariane, tell us about the phone call you got.

AM: My friend Brett was over here at the house. We were waiting for my friend, Roxy. As soon as she came in, the basement door started slamming open and shut. We screamed, "Oh my god!" I ran over to the door and locked it. We were like, "What just happened?" Thirty seconds later, Brett's phone rang like he had a message. He listened to it and put it on speakerphone. It was us, screaming, just thirty seconds before! We seemed to be caught in a timeloop with a bunch of poltergeists. It was bad. So, we ran out of the house. We were scared. We waited outside the house for like an hour. It started to rain. So we thought, "We need to get umbrellas." So me and Brett came in. We got the umbrellas, but realized we were hungry, too. We started rummaging around for food. I was looking in the fridge. Brett was over there. I was bent over the fridge here, looking around. I felt this slap on my back. I looked and there was a spatula on the floor, which had hit me. Brett was dodging utensils that were flying around. He was seeing things fly across the room at me! We therefore put all the knives and stuff in drawers; whatever silverware was flying around the room, we secured. Then we ran out of the house again. We stayed out there until my mom got home, which was like 3 hours. She didn't believe me at first.

AC: Was it a regular sounding phone call that you answered?

AM: No, there was no call. It went straight to voicemail. There was no ringing.

SR: I think it was the camping trip to Iowa that caused it.

AC: You went camping in Iowa?

AM: Yes, I was in Iowa. This was after a psychic told me that I would experience a big change in August. I went on that trip to Iowa with Brett. It was just we alone. We were camping. I needed to give him his shoes. It was really dark. I was freaking out because I don't like the woods at night. The back of the car was facing the woods. I was over there on the edge of the woods with a flashlight, poking around. Every couple of seconds I would notice something out of the corner of my eye. I would look closer and find that there was nothing there. Suddenly, I poked through some bushes and saw something hiding behind a tree branch. There was a leg. I saw a solid leg of some grayish creature that had hid itself behind a tree. I thought, "Whoops, you're busted." This "person" was short, about a foot and a half tall. She was kind of far away, so it's hard to tell how tall she really was. I ran back to the car. Brett didn't believe me...

AC: Didn't you say that your school principal's wife, Mrs. Maynard, saw Mothman?

AM: Yes, she saw the Mothman. She went out with a friend to a valley somewhere. This big, dark thing with beady red eyes chased them all the way back to the main road. They were flooring it, yet it was still following *right* behind.

AC: Don't you have a teacher who was once a biochemist at Wright-Patterson Air Force Base?

AM: Mr. Angelato has a Wright-Pat barcode on his file cabinet. He wears a Masonic ring. He is *really* smart.

AC *[to camera]* : For our viewers... Ariane goes to Woodrow Wilson High School in Beckley. Wilson tends to have strict, conservative teachers with military backgrounds. One of them holds a charitable fundraiser each year for a chronically injured family member. After each fundraiser, they tend to end up with a brand new car. It sounds like an odd school. Didn't the school recently outlaw trendy "bootylicious" pants?

AM: Yes.

SR: It's a "conspiracy" school.

AC: Regarding conspiracies, this might be the ultimate... I will pose it as a question: does anyone feel that inorganic beings feed off of our emotions?

Jordan Rogers (JR): Yes, all of your ghosts, goblins, demons, and angels – even Mothman and Jesus – *could* be inorganic beings. They may *not* be biological creatures. They may be drawn to us because of emotional energy, whether it be fear, happiness, or love – anything that gives off a strong emotional vibe. These things are attracted to emotion. It helps to drive them on, scary or not. They feel very close to us.

SR: Do you think things lacking physical form have to have something to exist on, to feed on? Do they go toward emotions *because* of their lack of physicality?

JR: I have no idea. But they do seem to "get along." Our worlds are definitely interconnected.

Loretta Colvin (LC): I'm just sorry I can't tell you something that will help you through these haunted house problems.

AC: I've noticed throughout this trip that many of the houses have pentagrams on the outside. Supposedly it is just a decoration…

JR: A lot of people around here have gigantic ones that they put on their houses. It could be that they subconsciously feel the need to protect themselves from the crazy energies here.

SR: They seem drawn to the pentagram for reasons they don't understand – archetypal reasons deep inside.

JR: M-m-m-madness! *[laughter]*

AC: Speaking of talismans, here is Charlie Manson's crutch. *[displays crutch]* I got it from his old house. I'm giving it to you now. *[hands crutch to Sharon]* Okay… Earlier, Ariane and Sharon were saying that the same *random* phrases will often pop into both of their heads *at the same time*. If you had to come up with a brief explanation for this, what would you say it is?

SR: Brainwaves… The mother-daughter psychic connection…

AM: We've been around each other too much. *[laughter]*

AC: Our brains are like minicomputers, and they like to keep busy. For entertainment or for mental exercise, some of us may enjoy trying to figure out what the next random event will be. Not that such activity is superfluous; it is actually a survival mechanism of sorts. You may both be searching for the most random thing, all the time, as a way to ultimately decipher reality. Knowledge is power. You look for things that shouldn't be there, because it helps identify what *is* there, and your relationship to it in spacetime. It is, indirectly, a way to protect ourselves.

AM: She seems to pick up on everything that is happening with me. It's an invisible umbilical cord. Dad and me do it, too.

AC: It is two minds urging each other forward to new ideas. You are exercising your linkages. Plus, you're challenging each other in a good way.

AM: Well, I guess so…

SR: Okay, *that's* our story! *[laughter]*

AC: Or, it could simply be because you both have blue eyes.

JR: Blue eyes take in slightly more of the electromagnetic spectrum than darker colors.

AC: Does that mean they are reflecting more light, or taking in more?

JR: Blue eyes can see more of the reality spectrum, as defined by light, than brown eyes.

AC: If you are taking in more data, perhaps that translates into psychic talent.

JR: I have brown eyes; I hardly ever see anything. I detect things around me – the supernatural or whatever – but I feel them or hear them. I very rarely see anything. Loretta, Sharon, and Ariane all see them. We all detect the same thing, but we take different routes to get there.

"In Ripley, WV, Janet Svenson performed her final duty of the afternoon as she witnessed the closing and locking of the heavy bank vault door with what seemed to be even greater ceremony and preciseness than usual. Perhaps it was because of the unusual and intriguing object resting inside. John W. White had brought the object to the bank shortly before closing time, and with it an even more unusual story. On the night that Woodrow Derenberger first met Indrid Cold, the small city of Ripley had its own visitation of UFOs. Although the sightings consisted only of strange lights in the sky, White believed the saucers had left a highly valuable calling card. White handed the heavy object to Janet's boss. It gleamed and sparkled under the fluorescent lights. Two of his children had found it. He believed it had dropped from one of the UFOs. To have fallen from such great height, it was remarkably undamaged – in fact, it was completely undented. He inspected it closely. It was apparently made of high quality gold! It measured 12 inches in circumference. White confided that he had taken it to Charleston, the state capital. [He said] 'I took it to three jewelers. They analyzed it and all of them said the 3/8" outer coating is 24-carat gold.'

"But there the mystery only began. When heated to 1260 degrees, the ball turned red hot but, as it cooled, returned to its natural color. One jeweler ruined three drilling bits when he tried to penetrate the inner metal. 'Tests showed,' White added, 'that the inner portion is definitely magnetic. The outer coating is not, however.' Mr. White's account of the strange lights and the falling golden ball brought to Janet's memory an unusual experience she had rarely thought of for several years. She was only five when it occurred, yet the event remained in her mind with a vividness far more pronounced than many other of her childhood experiences. It had happened in Norway in 1930. She was returning from a neighbor's house after dark, and had to cross a wide field. She dreaded that part of the walk for, from that vantage point, the old graveyard at the top of the hill was in view. Her brothers once declared they saw moving lights in the cemetery, and one of them had floated out toward them, giving them quite a fright. She feared that she also might see the lights. She turned her eyes to the ground and the moonlit path, determined not to look. Then, from behind her came a low chanting…

"From the shadows of the woods emerged something incomprehensible. An enormous moving gray mass was approaching her rapidly, and the chanting was becoming louder. She was drawn, ecstatically, to the approaching huge thing. She must have been hypnotized, she later reasoned, by the strange voices. Now the mass was almost upon her, and she discerned that it was composed of thousands of giant beings of inexplicable character, moving up and down, over and under, like horses on a merry-go-round. But their movements were more complex than that, as if they were in an infinite variety of circular orbits. Some of them almost touched the ground. They moved relentlessly, as if they were attached to a vast complex of shuttles and [concentric] wheels within wheels. The cloud of beings was now enveloping her. As they moved over and around her, she sensed they were not material creatures. They were pale gray [and] their faces were emotionless. They had long robes and medieval pageboy haircuts... They held out clenched, inverted hands toward her, as if offering presents. In her fascination and lack of fear, she extended her open hands to receive what was apparently offered; however as each hand opened mechanically just above hers, nothing dropped from it... As [they] departed, the chanting dimmed and she walked home at her normal pace. For months afterward, she would dream she heard the chanting...

"She hoped Mr. White would not call for and remove the golden ball the next day, for she would like the opportunity to hold and examine it again, as she had done briefly when he had handed it to her earlier that afternoon. As she had carefully supported it with both hands, a feeling of perfect calm had come over her. It must, indeed, have come from outer space; there was something indefinable about it that declared it was of another world. If it were hers, she would never sell it. It would be too beautiful – too sacred – to part with."

-Gray Barker, The Silver Bridge, pp. 76-79

A Zulu tribal pot in the Dayton Art Museum (left) shows four winged entities very similar to popular descriptions of Mothman. Another Zulu pot at the Dayton Museum (right) replaces those four winged entities with four X's - an amazing confluence of Mothman and Masonry. The Dayton Art Museum happens to be right across the street from one of Ohio's largest and most ornate Masonic temples, and is just a five minute drive from Wright-Patterson AFB.

CHAPTER 22

"In my book *Psychic and UFO Revelations in the Last Days*, I detailed the story of country-western singer Johnny Sands who, on Jan. 29th, 1976, after performing at a well-known Vegas hotel, experienced a hair-raising close encounter. As he [saw a light coming down] from the sky, Sands' car malfunctioned. The musician says the craft landed, and two beings emerged from the object. One of the ufonauts proceeded to walk towards Sands until he stood right in front of him.

The being looked to be about 5 feet 8 inches tall, and was completely bald. His face was really pale. He had no eyebrows, no eyelashes, no hair at all. To me, he looked like somebody frozen to death. He touched something on his belt and, right after he did, I got impressions in my mind. It was like listening to someone talking over the telephone from a great distance away. The being asked what I was doing in the desert. [He] placed his hands behind my back and brought them out in front of me seconds later. In his hands, he held a silver ball the approximate size of a basketball. He held it out in front of him. He let the ball go and it floated there right in front of us. He passed his hands over the object and made it start rotating in a circular motion. He explained something that tied in with our nuclear devices. He put his hand over the top of the ball and, as he did so, there was an explosion just above its smooth surface – a flash, a minor explosion like a firecracker going off... Next, the ball started to act up a bit, as if it were being stirred up by the explosion. He said that when we use nuclear devices, it causes...our world to vibrate like this. He added that because of these tremors, the rotation of the Earth is slowing down, and we are actually losing time, and thus we grow older much faster.

"Sands admits that the 'alien' did not go into detail, nor did he explain any of the things which he said. Eventually the story leaked out and was published in *The Las Vegas Sun*. In no time at all, Sands became a local celebrity, appearing on area talk shows. A painting he did of one of the bald-headed aliens is prominently displayed in the lobby of a hotel on the Strip. Because of his newly found celebrity status, Sands didn't think twice when he received a call from the manager of a TV crew requesting an interview. Little did the entertainer know that he was soon to be confronted with an even bigger mystery, which involved MIBs as well as hairy beasts.

The men called and said they were doing a UFO television special, and wanted me to go on location. I agreed to go with them and show them the spot where the encounter took place. We went out there in the daytime and, when we finished, they wanted to do a polygraph and voice analysis as a part of this segment. I suggested we go down to the polygrapher's office [to] let the polygrapher read the results. At first they thought it was a good idea but, then, they changed their minds. They said they'd like to go out in the desert to read the results of the polygraph. It didn't make sense to go out in the desert at 10:00 p.m. to read the polygraph results, but I met them. They said we were all going to load up and go in one car. Before leaving, they had mixed drinks and offered me one. They gave me one and we started driving out. As we started going out to the spot, the drink started to make me feel a little woozy. Normally, I didn't drink at all, so I poured the rest out. We drove on past the location [for no apparent reason]. When we reached a new location about 6 miles up the road, there were about 40 cars parked there waiting for us. They all faced in the same direction. We came to a stop, so that their headlights were shining right on us. It was then I realized that all these people knew in advance about our coming here. We hadn't advertised that we were going into the desert.

A fat man with glasses came across the road and shook his fingers at the others, pointing at the car where I sat. He was saying that I 'knew too much.' One of the guys said, 'He only knows what they let him know.' I tried to get out of the car to see what was going on for myself. As I opened the door, two furry-type creatures, like robot gorillas [appeared]. They looked to be about five feet tall. As I got out of the car, one of those furry things started running towards the door. It scared the hell out of me, so I shut the car door right away, locked it, and rolled the window up. This thing ran right up to the window and looked in. It 'talked' with the fat man, then [stood] guard. Then I passed out. When I came to, they were getting in the car. All the [other] cars were gone. It was three hours later. The production people looked at me and said, 'You have done good; we liked the filming.' [Later] I told my manager everything… He checked them out [but they had all these excuses for everything]. I asked to see the film we had done. [The producer] said it was [destroyed] because it didn't come out right. I asked him about the 40 cars. He said he didn't know anything about them. Investigating some more, I found out they had just come into town three days before. They had made me sign a contract that I would not release any likeness of the alien until after the television special. They said they had paid for the artist's conception (mine) and did not want it exposed. They had no office, just an answering service. Later, I found out that the FBI had a wiretap on their telephone.

-Tim Beckley, *The UFO Silencers*, pp. 122-127

COLVIN, ANDY & ALLEN GREENFIELD – GRASSY KNOLL INTERVIEW 36 – NOV. 2008

"Vyz" at *Beyond the Grassy Knoll* (GK): Andy, you came on while you were on the road for the All-Saints Reformation Day marathon. There were some interesting things happening that we couldn't talk about too much. One of them centers on that "ghost box." What in the world was going on with that device?

Andy Colvin (AC): It is an AM/FM radio that's been modified to cycle through the spectrum and stop briefly at every signal. It gives you a second or two of audio at each spot. And it just keeps going…

GK: Don't you treat that device like the legendary 8-ball, where you ask a question and get a "yes" or "no" answer? Exactly what feedback did you get? Was it sentence fragments? Grunts? And what is actually the real title for that box?

AC: It was originally called the "Frank Box." Generic versions are called the "Ghost Box." The process obviously has a lot of randomness to it. Sometimes it gives you a longer stream of words, and sometimes just little pieces. It also gives you the ability to pick up "spirit" EVPs, which are voices that *aren't* coming from a radio station signal. As everyone in the paranormal business knows, sometimes voices anomalously come across tape players and other devices. Voices came through to John Keel on both his phone and CB radio when they were turned off; this was witnessed by other people. There has always been a subculture of people interested in this phenomenon. This box has given them another tool.

GK: You were using it the day we did the on-location Halloween show. You were in Pt. Pleasant with the Frick Brothers and your sister, Loretta, reporting from the haunted igloo in the TNT Area. Tell us about the Frick brothers and their involvement with the Ghost Box.

Adam Gorightly of *Untamed Dimensions* (UD): What the "frick!?"

GK *[exasperated]: Somebody* had to say it…

AC: The Fricks started off as ghosthunters. I think they are drawing on that part of their background with this piece of equipment. They work on the Mothman Festival each year. They fly "Mothman" for the hayriders and dress as Men in Black. It adds a lot to the festival to have those MIBs around…

GK: You went to certain sites. Why did you go to the locations that you did?

AC: I wanted to take the Frick brothers to my part of town and show them the places where things occurred. I also wanted to test for radiation. I had a small dosimeter. It chirps if there is radiation around. It will chirp faster if there is more of it. We were getting three chirps a minute at the bottom of Woodward Drive, where Manson and Sara Jane Moore lived. I got similar readings in downtown Pt. Pleasant and in the TNT area, but nowhere else. I got absolutely no blips anywhere else.

GK: Are those areas then unhealthy for people to be in for protracted periods?

AC: Over time, that amount could possibly add up to some health problems, like cancer.

GK: Could you conjecture as to what the source of that would have been? Are there power plants nearby or anything like that?

AC: Well, there is not *supposed* to have been anything nuclear in either location… But, as this research has gone along, we have found several clues regarding nuclear materials. Keel was the only one with the guts to come out and say it – that they were making parts for the atom bomb there... One of the little synchronicities I came across in the last couple of weeks was the book by Joseph Farrell, *The Brotherhood of the Bell*. Jim Marrs also has a new book out on the Bell, which was a Nazi program to develop a "doomsday bomb." The program was transferred out of Germany. We don't yet know exactly where it went. Some of it may have gone to South America, where the Odessa supposedly also had a secret flying saucer factory. This factory, perhaps located near Jonestown, may have been called "Lanulos" by Indrid Cold and Woody Derenberger. West Virginia researcher William Dean Ross has been trying to raise the alarm about paraphysical research being done between Point Pleasant and Charleston. Towns like Nitro, Eleanor, Bancroft, Liberty, Institute, and Midway come to mind. Ross claims this was an area where "Brotherhood of the Bell" research was being done. Sure enough, Midway is very near to Institute, where you have that long history of collaboration between Standard Oil and Nazi Germany's petro-chemical giants. There were sister plants in both countries, making the synthetic rubber (Buna) used during WWII. In Germany, the synthetic rubber plant was also used as a cover for uranium enrichment and, supposedly, for flying saucers. It is likely that they were doing the very same thing in Institute: enriching uranium and building saucers. Institute also happens to have all of these "Shawnee" Indian mounds. The Fricks and I visited the mounds. Institute is right next to West Virginia State College, one of the first black colleges. It's in an area that was once owned by George Washington. Washington was given that land more or less by the British. Washington surveyed almost all of Virginia and West Virginia. British generals used Washington to finally wrench control of these big tracts from the Indians. They gave Washington big chunks of it for his continued cooperation. Today, this stretch includes the afore-mentioned towns plus hamlets like Buffalo, Red House, Hometown, Morgan's Landing, Scary, Poca, and Raymond. Hometown is where the soldiers who killed Chief Cornstalk camped before they got to Pt. Pleasant; they were coming from the east, from Virginia. Many of the Virginia soldiers were later given land in Ohio.

GK: That sneak attack is what really *began* the whole Mothman situation, isn't it?

AC: Yes. In light of that, we took the Ghost Box to Midway. I had driven up there the weekend before just to check it out. I had seen an abandoned house and thought, "Hmmm...this might be the place." It was just a random, intuitive feeling. Note that *three* other key Mothy locations are now abandoned: Manson's house, Sara Jane Moore's house, and Harriet's house. My old house is starting to look shabby, too. We came back to Midway with the Ghost Box. It clearly told us "yes" when I asked if the abandoned property in Midway was once Indrid's home. There were some amazing things said by the box… We also visited Charlie Manson's house, Sara Jane Moore's house, Magic Island, and the vortex on Woodward Drive where we saw Mothman and other entities.

GK: At the same time you did the interview with me from WV, a documentary team did a segment on you, correct?

AC: Yes, RAI's *Voyager* did a show on Mothman that featured his prophecy of 9/11. Jim Marrs and Linda Moulton Howe were on it, too. *Voyager* is a big show in Europe. They film part of it with a live audience. It's very flashy and has a big budget. They started off with an extended segment looking at the various 9/11 conspiracies, then tied that in with Mothman… On that same trip with the Ghost Box, I also talked to a husband and wife in Cincinnati who saw Mothman – actually *four* Mothmen – right after Hurricane Ike hit. They said a really large Mothman flew down and blocked their view. It was so big that they couldn't see the house across the street. It flew away, and then three more came in behind him. They were black and wispy. A lot of times, you will see these entities coming out of the ground or from trees. There is much in the paranormal literature about them. Some of them are formed by swirling clouds of black mist.

Amazingly, in early 2010, "skinwalker" researcher J.C. Johnson claimed to have filmed one of these shadow entities, or elementals, coming out of the ground. It was shot by a remote surveillance camera. The household where the footage was shot had been experiencing Men in Black incidents. The details of these encounters were very similar to the MIB encounters on Woodward Drive during Mothman. Within days of the release of the video, Johnson's friend and guide, Chief Leonard Dan of the Navajo tribe, was attacked in his truck by what he described as a gang of skinwalker witches.

GK: Do you have any idea why August is such an active month for the paranormal?

AC: It goes way back. There are some astronomical alignments during that month. The "dog star," Sirius, is dominant. Those are the "dog days," probably the most important occult holiday of the year.

GK: There you go.

UD: I've got August on my mind these days. I'm doing an update to my Manson book. August 8th and 9th are when the murders went down... I wanted to ask you, Andy, before we get into analyzing these transcripts: how close did Manson and Sara Jane Moore live to each other, and what years were they living there?

AC: We know that they were both there during WWII. Manson would have been between 7 and 12 in those years. He was born in 1934. He and Moore lived about 3 blocks from each other. I was getting the Geiger counter alerts between their houses, at the mouth of Woodward Drive. The "vortex" where all these entities were seen is a mile or two up Woodward Drive.

UD: Do you think the energy in this vortex was being used by humans in some way – whether it was MK-Ultra, a ritual working, or who knows what – to control Manson and Sara Jane Moore? Is that a possibility?

AC: Yes, although we have to assume that something synthetic was done to Manson in the reformatory. He talks about being baked in the "S.S. Oven" by an old German there. It is possible that Manson and Moore were prepped somehow by an experience at the vortex, either natural or synthetic. Their minds were opened, which may have helped them become better agents. Manson may have been ordered, consciously or unconsciously, to burn down Aetna school. It could have been a macabre initiation of some kind... The idea that one can be controlled with these energies is something I've been kicking around with Eugenia Macer-Story. She likes to view things as a cosmic play, where entities cause people to do things, good and bad, beyond their conscious knowledge. This is a widely held belief in South America. John Keel probably believed reality to be slightly more "empty" and/or automated. To him, the "8th Sphere" or "8th Tower" was some sort of a semi-conscious computer. Macer-Story anthropomorphizes things a bit more. There is more than one way to view how these entities work. I think they're all sort of the same at the root. Consciousness creates everything, but you can break it down using material concepts. It is said that one *can* reach the absolute through the relative. Macer Story, when asked about Mothman on *Untamed Dimensions*, alluded to Mothman having to do with "what gets recorded into history, for knowledge's sake." She described the Garuda as "an intelligence that communicates a larger symbology."

GK: Okay, let's get into the transcripts. Go ahead…

AC: Yes, we were at Magic Island, where the bridge collapsed on Dec. 15th, 1904. In 2002, after visiting the vortex, I'd had a kundalini-induced vision about a murder or drowning at Magic Island. It seemed like a past event connected to Harriet's old house. A couple of days later, I'd driven by Magic Island and seen that there was somebody being pulled out of the water. At that point, we had a conundrum: a future drowning (as it related to the vision) corresponding with a past drowning. We soon found out that there had, indeed, been a past drowning. That past drowning turned out to be a caretaker at Harriet's house. He had drowned years before, after Harriet had moved. So, I asked the Box, "Was my kundalini vision about someone from Harriet's house?" And the box said, "Right around the corner." It could be someone living next to Harriet – something we've often considered. There were a couple of strange neighbors. "Was the vision from the past, or was it of the drowning three days later?" I asked. The Box said, "After this year," indicating the latter. Backwards, according to Frick, the phrase sounds like, "a million years this Indian." Now, this backwards thing is tricky… You can piece together meanings from *both* directions. Sometimes the two *together* form a meaning. This makes sense, however, because any nonlocal source *would* go in both directions, in both time *and* space. Wings symbolize the back-and-forthness of phenomena… It's funny because I once co-wrote a song, "Sedrick," that was about an Indian who was a million years old. That song ended up in the film *Slacker*. It first appeared on the album *Charlie Manson Street*. Other song lyrics from that same album appeared in David Lynch's recent film, *Inland Empire*. There were direct lines in the film that seemed to come from songs I had written in 1986… That same year, 1986, I had also taken a photo that said, "Do you want to see?" Amazingly, in *Inland Empire*, there was a key transition scene that had the exact same words and a very similar image to mine. These are examples of the odd synchronicities that tend to crop up. I asked the Box one more time about the vision of the drowning, and it said, "One fatal attack a year, Andy." Backwards that is, "Forgive me," or "Forgiveness." It was if we were talking to the killer, or the controller of the killers, whom I once dreamed was a female witch.

This makes one wonder if the Box wasn't referring to Indrid Cold or to one of his henchmen, or to the serial killer who was stalking people during Mothman. During filming, I had a strange dream that connected the evil on Harriet's lane to the name "Williamson" and to what was either a living witch, the spirit of a witch, or the ghost of a witch. The witch was made more evil by the fact that she projected such a wholesome image of herself. Indrid is believed to have been on Woodward Drive and was known to travel with female accomplices such as Kimi Cold, Elvaine Kletaw, and Bueldine Vauss, whose name is reminiscent of the Carbide plastic "butadiene," which was manufactured in Institute, WV. Could any of the later inhabitants of Harriet's house have been steered there by Indrid and his buddies, thus setting themselves up for exploitation?

AC: I got to wondering just who was responsible for the poor mainte-nance on the Elk Bridge that collapsed. I asked about the coal companies, since it was they who had conspired to fill one side of the island in so that it was no longer an island. I asked if they were hiding something. The Box said, "I can," as if we were still speaking directly to the conspiring witch. I asked if Indrid Cold worked for the Rockefellers. The Box replied, "Person exists. Sold soul…" Then it started talking about a "chill confrontation system," which seemed to allude to Indrid's last name. Tim Frick asked again if it really *had* said, "Chill Confrontation System." The Box said, "The nail right on the head." Amused, I then said, "I like this; this a *cool* thing." The Box answered, "I love conventions," as if it were complimenting our little get-together – our involvement in the Mothman Festival… With our heads spinning, we then went to Charlie Manson's house. We said, "Did Charlie live here? What can you tell me about this area?" The Box said, "Former treasury secretary, John," as if it were talking to John Frick. We asked if Manson was affected by the radiation in the area. The Box said, "You have your shark. Yeah…" Then it said "Smite Cleaver," which backwards sounded like, "Me in Seattle."

Oddly, for years there had been a well-maintained charter bus parked in the lot across from Charlie Manson's house. The bus had always had "Seattle" dialed in as its destination. The bus was no longer there, however, when we visited with the Ghost Box. In this sense, the Box seemed to be displaying an ability to go back and forth in time.

UD: It seemed to be saying that you should smite Beaver Cleaver, or the whitebread ideals of the 1950s. This is fascinating. Go on…

AC: We asked what was causing the radiation. The Box said, "Someone started shooting." This is actually true, in the sense that the radiation was caused by people needing to make bombs. We asked what the radiation did to Manson. The Box said, "Doctor and a lawyer." This made think of Judge Biddle, whom we feel was probably Manson's father, and to the mysterious "Dr. Hartmann," to whom Manson claims a certain allegiance. "Was it mind control?" I asked. The Box replied, "To reduce the tax; planning was very cooperative." I said, "Very cooperative?" The Box shot back, "Last night I went to the…" but abruptly stopped. And, as if to finish the sentence, unbelievably, music from *The Twilight Zone* program played! It was essentially saying, "Last night I went to *The Twilight Zone*." I remarked, "That sounded like the Twilight Zone," and the Box responded, "got it on tape." John followed with, "Are we in the Twilight Zone?" And the Box said, "Capitol Station." Mothman was seen flying around Charleston's Capitol dome. My sister took us there to try and find him. I asked, "Who was the doctor that controlled Charlie? Was it Doctor Hartmann?" Hartmann had been mentioned in Charlie's interview in 1994… The Box said, "He is so right!" I asked, "Who is Manson's father?" The Box answered, "Benchley," reminiscent of a judge, like Biddle, who sat on the "bench" and perhaps had British ties. I asked, "Who was controlling Charlie?" Stunningly, the Box answered, "We all know that: Indrid Cold!" Yes, it said the full name of Indrid Cold. It *really* sounds like the Box says "Indrid Cold!" The hair was standing up on our bodies at this point… We started blurting stuff out simultaneously. We asked, "Was Manson nuts?" and "Is this house haunted?" It said, "1 in 4." This reminded me of the Four Mothmen that people have been seeing lately, as well as the "11:11" phenomenon… "Does Manson have anything to do with Mothman?" we asked. The Box revealed: "When humans begin." Adam and I have been talking for some time about how these mounds might be living incubators for humans or other entities. We certainly had a lot of mounds in Mound at one time; probably right where Manson's house is, which is along the bank of the river at Blaine Island. You can see mounds on old photos of Blaine. Plus, there is this play on words with Manson's name backwards, which is "Son of Man." This can be thought of as corresponding to "Son of Mon," or "Son of the Earth." "Son of Man" could also relate to "Sun of the Moon," or magnetism, which is what the moon sends out instead of light. "Sun of the Moon" makes me think of Manson's battle with the Rev. Sun Myung Moon. Manson claims that Moon threatened to kill him. Moon sent "The Oriental" to try and frighten Manson. If Manson's name symbolized "Son of the Moon," that would be interesting, too, because that seems to refer to how the patriarchal religions replaced the matriarchal ones. It also makes me think of how the male entity precedes the female entity in certain paranormal encounters.

UD: It's kind of like working with somebody who is psychic. They're picking out little pieces from this whole electromagnetic matrix that is around us. They don't perhaps have the full picture of what's going on, but they have little pieces of it. You, as a researcher, are trying to pull all of that together.

AC: I asked, "Was Charlie mind-controlled by the Nazis at St. Gibault's? Were these the same Nazis doing the UFO abductions?" For those who do not know, Charlie sometimes refers to "the spaceship…" The Box said, "She loses all her hair." Is this a reference to hairless aliens, or to the unmasking of the female force controlling the Woodward vortex? I asked if the Rockefellers had anything to do with Manson. The Box said what seemed like, "Or a child" or "Org a Child." Either one presents interesting possibilities… It could be a reference to missing fetuses, something that happened to Mothman witnesses, or to mind control, something that happened to UFO contactees. I asked, "Why did Sara Jane Moore shoot at Ford? Was it to help Manson or the Rockefellers? The Box said, "Montgomery." Montgomery is the closest major town to the Union Carbide plant in Boomer, from which the Jonestown folks emanated. West Virginia Tech, a school servicing the military-industrial complex, is in Montgomery. I asked if Sara Jane Moore was a patsy set up by the FBI… The Box said, "ABC News." Sara Jane was reportedly always courting the networks. "What was her involvement with Patty Hearst?" I wondered. The Box said, "Fox," which seems to refer to Fox News, one of the partners in her father's right-wing media empire. The Box then clarified with, "The risk looks into the causes…" I asked if Indrid knew Charlie Manson. The Box said, "To prove your country, eradicate the infections." There was also a second reference to a "Treasury Department" official. Charlie has actually alluded to both things over the years. In his 1994 interview, he talked about using "bug spray" on the planet to kill nature's enemies, wayward humans. He thought it would be a good way to make America strong again. Also, he sometimes uses banking references to explain spiritual ideas, which is fairly unique… We asked if there was anything else about Sara. The Box said, "Indiana, before…"

Indiana is where the leaders of the SLA, the group who abducted Patty Hearst, were from. Fox News is an ideological outgrowth of the William Randolph Hearst media empire, which the SLA seemingly targeted. On April 10ᵗʰ, 2007 Hearst Magazines and Fox TV announced a partnership to create original programs for the Internet and TV. According to Advertising Age, *the series were to be based on Hearst magazine titles such as* CosmoGirl *and* Popular Mechanics.

AC: I asked if there was some connection between Crowley and Sara Jane Moore. The Box said, "There is a guy. Columbus, Ohio." I said, "Columbus?" The box replied, "Three hours of looking. Pretty good job." As if the key to our 3-hr. Ghost Box session was a guy in Columbus who knew Sara Jane Moore... I asked, "Was Aleister Crowley ever here?" The Box said, "Thank you, veterans. Bastard." According to Frick, backwards that somehow sounds like, "This time." I asked about Sara Jane's nationality, and if her family was involved with Kahn Meats. The Box said, "Struggling to where she can break the news." Sara Jane *is* reported to have had ongoing issues with "getting her message out" through the media. She was working with ABC, I believe, trying to get her story out about the Symbionese Liberation Army. She was supposedly trying to tell the SLA's side of it. But this reference to "struggle" might also refer to Sara's knowledge of the schoolhouse fire. If she couldn't ever admit it, for whatever reason, it *would* be a struggle to "get the news out..." "Did Sara Jane know Jim Jones?" I asked. The Box said, "The politic," which, backwards, sounds like, "It's Robert." The names "Robert" and "Roberts" have come up a few times in our tale... "Was Sara an agent for the Rockefellers?" I asked. The Box said, "Watch out." It seemed to be warning us away from messing with the Rockefellers. "Where is Sara Jane living now?" I wondered, because she just got out of prison. The Box said, "The law; higher force." This sounds like a reference to Crowley's famous book, *The Law*, where he used the alias "Khan." Sara Jane's maiden name was Kahn... Then, the Box added, "It's *their* secret..." It seemed to be referring to this school fire or to some dark secret between the Rockefellers, Moore, and Manson.

Moore's father worked for DuPont, at the same plant where Philadelphia Experiment veterans were catching on fire and disappearing. Manson's entry into Moore's world may not have been coincidental. In fact, it may have been engineered. Researcher John Judge claims that the mothers of Manson and Moore were once prostitutes together, although I have found nothing else to back up this claim. Moore's mother was seemingly an upstanding citizen who took care of her grandchildren and played in the symphony orchestra.

AC: Next, we traveled to the Mothman shrine site, the "vortex" on Woodward Drive… I asked the Box if Harriet had actually seen the Flatwoods Monster. The Box said, "She's a healthy girl." Then it said, "I love you." Harriet is of the belief that she met a spirit guide during her encounter. It started off as male and then went to female. So, what the Box said makes some sense. Since it had morphed into something along the lines of the Virgin Mary, I asked, "Did she see the Virgin Mary?" A few seconds passed with no answer. This actually makes some sense, too, because the Virgin Mary never calls herself "Mary" when speaking to percipients… So, I asked another question: "Was the thing I saw here actually Mothman?" Incredibly, the Box said, "Right! This campaign went through…" Backwards, that says, "Don't be a stranger," as if Mothman wants me to come back and visit every now and then… I asked if Tommy had really seen Mothman. The Box said, "see" or "si," which could be interpreted as a "yes" in both English and Spanish. Tommy studied languages, by the way, so the use of another language here would not be out of place… "Did Tommy see aliens?" I queried. The Box said, "Yeah." Then it said, "Two out," which backwards is "two eyes." I asked if the UFO that Tommy saw was from the Army or the "ETs." The Box said, "He can circle." Then it paused and said, "Relationships." Backwards that is: "Space in shield." All of those are provocative, seeming to imply that the UFOs were from the Army but *appeared* to be from ETs – that there was a crossover between the two. I asked if the little creatures I dreamed about while staying over at Tommy's one night were "the little people" (i.e., the Pukwudgies or Nunahee). The Box said, "Why? Sterile." It seemed to be saying that I shouldn't try to classify them. I asked if Mothman was there that night. Interestingly, the Box said, "This is Christ." Then I asked, "Did the thing I saw in 1973 follow me home?" The Box said, "Yeah!" Then it added, "He must!" The Box seemed to be saying that he *had* to follow me. By the way, backwards that says "Thomas." Coincidentally, I've often wondered if I saw some spirit related to Tommy coming out of that tree. I asked the Box, "Were the misty beings we saw in 2002 really just mirrors of ourselves?" The Box said, "reaction-like," which seems to be an affirmative answer. I asked if Indrid had jabbed my dad with a cancer needle. It sounded like it said "yes" when we were there, but when you play the tape back, it sounds like "prompted." I'm not sure how that happened but, either way, the answer seems to be affirmative. Incredibly, it sounds like "let go" when played backwards. "Letting go" is one of the main issues of trying to deal with the murder of a loved one. In fact, the phrase "Let go" is the subject of one of my photos in *The Mothman's Photographer I*. Let's see… I asked if Tommy's dad was an agent. The Box said, "Yes." "Was his dad an occultist?" The Box said, "Wife loop." His wife, Tommy's mother, was a West Virginia beauty pageant standout, just like Patsy Ramsey, Jon-Benet's mother. These beauty queens are sometimes members of the Rainbow Girls, a Masonic order for women. They have an emphasis on providing "service" to the community and to their men. I have an old Scottish Rite handbook that says, on the inside of the cover, "Bring Your Wife." But to summarize, one can really begin to see here that the Ghost Box does seem to be communicating. When you see it all written down, there does seem to be a real message. We definitely sensed it as we were filming. It was electric; our hair did stand up. It is weird that certain ideas would come up repeatedly. The name "Frick" came up several times. What is startling is that there were so many direct "yes" answers to key questions.

UD: This seems like the cut-up method of William Burroughs. As I was going through the transcripts, the one that stood out to me was the last passage. John asks, "Any last words?" And the Box said, "White One," and "He is ancient." Do you think it could have been talking about Mothman?

AC: Yes, because there were a couple of sightings of a pure white Mothman, as well as many others describing him as having a very light gray color approaching white. A translucent, headless Mothman was seen at Fatima.

UD: It's pretty interesting that it said, "He is ancient." Your studies of the Garuda show that he has been here with us for a long, long time.

AC: Another thing… The Box said that Indrid's real last name was "Morgan." At another point, it said his first name was "Johnny." Synchronistically, I recently opened *The Mothman Prophecies* to a random page as I was going to bed. At the page I opened to, Keel used the pseudonym "Morgan" for the psychiatrist who examined Woody Derenberger. Could Keel have known that Indrid's real name was Morgan, and then embedded it within the story? Was this knowledge dangerous enough that it had to be veiled?

The name "Johnny Morgan" also indirectly refers to the syndicate founded by John Pierpont (J.P.) Morgan, the famous financier and partner to the Bushes and Rockefellers. According to Wikipedia, Morgan essentially controlled the gas industry in WV. Fellow New Yorkers often referred him to as "Johnny Morgan." Strangely or not, Morgan is rumored to have secretly financed occultist Aleister Crowley, whose shenanigans with the Lusitania sinking benefited Morgan. According to Bijan C. Bayne, Crowley dated Belle Greene, the woman personally appointed by Morgan to supervise the Morgan library. Crowley lived only two blocks away from the library. Crowley's knowledge of Latin and Greek would have been useful in the enormous task of cataloguing Morgan's vast collection of antique books. Crowley's lavish lifestyle through 1915 suggests some form of sponsorship, since he was able to maintain a "fashionable residence, a fashionable mistress, and take a tour of North America." Synchronistically, the West Virginia town of "Morgan's Landing," where AEP's John Amos plant is located, is only about five minutes away from Indrid Cold's home of Midway. Morgan's Landing is right next to Scary, where a key Civil War battle was fought. There have been several UFO sightings in and around Scary over the years. In fact, ET proponent Stanton Friedman has given a couple of UFO talks there in recent years, at the old theatre in nearby St. Albans.

AC: We asked the Box if Indrid hung out with Allen Greenfield. The Box said, "Dead. " Backwards, it also said, "He's dead" – a double dose of "dead."

UD: We'll have to run that by Allen. He's coming up after you.

AC: I asked, "Did Indrid hang out with Gray Barker?" The Box answered, "We are," which backwards sounds like "sorry." If you put those together, it seems to be saying, "No, Barker didn't hang out with Indrid, but we do." At one point, the Box said, "Moth, Moth," which backwards sounded like "town." Then it said, "John" again, which backwards sounded like "Frick." I asked the Box about South America and Colonia Dignidad, the torture camp run by the Nazis. Had Derenberger gone to Colonia Dignidad thinking it was "Lanulos?" The Box said, "Camp," meaning that it was, indeed, something similar to Colonia Dignidad. I forgot to ask if they were building flying saucers at Colonia Dignidad, or if the location might have been Jonestown instead.

UD: How about your asking the Box, "Was he an occultist?" and the Box saying, "Wife loop?" Were some sex orgies going on there? Wife swapping? You could read any of that into this.

AC: The same could be said of your website, Adam, with all the dancing girly pictures! *[laughter]* We then asked, "Did Indrid work for the Rockefellers?" Strangely, it said, "Maybe."

GK *[laughs cynically]*: I'll take *that* as a yes.

UD: That sounds secretive, as if it could only say so much.

GK: We didn't say "no" now, did we?

UD: We can neither confirm nor deny...

AC: When I asked if Indrid killed my dad, the Box said, "Doubt it."

UD: This Box has a dark sense of humor.

AC: It does. Just because Indrid didn't do it personally, it doesn't mean he didn't order it to be done... What really excited me on this trip was realizing that George Washington once owned this long stretch of land between Mound and Pt. Pleasant. There is a big dam in the river there, some locks, and the John Amos Power Plant. We have towns like Eleanor, which was where Derenberger was picking up packages at the police station. Eleanor is laid out in a Masonic semi-circle, which is odd for a WV town. Eleanor is right next to Red House, the colonial Masonic stronghold. The French, masters of Freemasonry, have had a long presence in the area through their agents, the DuPonts. Washington partied with the DuPonts. It looks like he owned the TNT Area at one time. He may have sold it directly to the DuPonts, in fact... Speaking of Masons, I made a point of going through the towns that Peter Levenda claimed Manson lived in. One is Kenova. WV, where Manson's "uncle" was murdered. Kenova is along the Ohio River south of Point Pleasant. I noticed that this was an area with a lot of mounds. I found a Native American Masonic lodge called the Red Men of Mohawk Lodge #11. I was surprised to see that there was a Mohawk tribe down there. Perhaps that has something to do with the Rockefellers, who are originally from Mohawk country in upstate NY. These lodges may be a way to keep informal tabs on what is going on locally. Kenova is an area where you have three rivers coming in, thus it would have been sacred to the Indians. Marathon Oil has a huge tank field there. Again, we have Standard Oil offshoots setting up shop above leveled mounds. They also put amusement parks and golf courses over mounds. Camden Park in Kenova was built by a member of the Standard oil syndicate back in the late 1800s. Mr. Camden became really powerful in WV. He was the Rockefellers' go-to guy in the state. He put his park near the confluence of these rivers. A Mothy looking dragon statue stands near the front of Camden Park. Kenova feels very similar to Mound. It has mounds, chemical plants, a rubber company, and a "Star" Bank. We talked earlier about the pentagrams everyone is putting up on their homes there. Even the bank there has a star on it. A lot more Chase Banks are opening up there, too.

GK: Adam, have you seen these huge freaking ornaments?

UD: Well, the star has been a favored exterior ornament for a long time, especially during the holiday season.

GK: These pentagrams do not seem to be related to any kind of holiday. I'm noticing them in my neighborhood in Florida. Lady Vyz and I ride our bikes often through the same places. You just notice it. I feel like going up and asking them, "What's with the star? Why not a dachshund?"

UD: In the latest Presidential race, McCain and Palin had a Sirius-type star as part of their campaign... Andy, have you ever had the opportunity to talk with Charles Manson?

AC: I haven't. I've always wanted to, but I don't like the idea of being investigated just to be able to talk with him.

UD: Well, if you have some questions, I might be able to pass them along. I don't have Charlie's ear, per se, but I know people who do.

GK: I've got an idea: why don't the two of you go see him together?

AC: Maybe we could set something up where we remote view questions to Charlie, and he answers using telepathy. *[laughter]* Say, I've got some trivia. I mentioned Dupont a minute ago. There is another Dupont plant in Seneca, IL, which has been having Bigfoot-type sightings for decades.

GK: They're just seeing Jim, our technician, in his hairsuit...

UD: ...when he forgets to shower. *[laughter]*

AC: More trivia... Volvo has a new bus in use in the world's biggest bus system, which is in India. It serves millions of people a day, and it's called the "Garuda" bus... Also, the U.S. Navy's Electronic Attack Squadron 134 is nicknamed "The Garudas..." The Mongolian Garuda is called the "Congarid." Here we have the "Khan" or "con" name again, indicating a state of sacred relationship, plus "ga" or "ge" (earth), plus "ri" or "re" (sun or sky). They seem to add up to "Between Earth and Sky." The Garuda symbol is very similar to Hippocrates' "caduceus" symbol; "cad" is also found in "Adam Kad-mon." In the myth, Hippocrates used the serpent twirling up the cross. It bit Hippocrates on the shoulder, but Hippocrates healed himself. He then took on the illnesses of his patients, in order to heal them as well. I interviewed a shaman in *The Mothman's Photographer III*, Ken Alton, who takes on the illnesses of others. Ken will writhe, sweat, and agonize for a couple of hours, and the person in question will get better. It also works on animals. It's very similar, I think, to the concept of Christ dying for others' sins. He's taking on your guilt and your pain, which essentially comprise your bodily symptoms. The Adam Kadmon is also a Christlike figure, existing on a mound with his arms spread. There is often a bird with Christ. Just before we came on, I was listening to a lady on NPR whose bird, "Alex," got to be pretty famous. She is a professor at Harvard who studied this bird for 30 years. It could speak many English words. It even sometimes figured out new words on its own, *without* being programmed or taught. Her point was that birds are the *only* animals out there that can do this. Birds are the only ones capable of learning our language. Some of the information must be in its DNA. There really *is* something about humans and birds...

UD: Next up, we have the noted ritual magician and UFO researcher, Allen Greenfield. We're going to talk about some spooky episodes from his life involving ghosts.

T. Allen Greenfield (TG): Coincidentally, my parrot was acting up just before I came on.

GK: Allen, can your bird dial up PETA?

TG: No, but he makes the sounds of orgasms.

GK: We'll leave that one alone for now...

UD: Talking about spooky stuff, are you familiar with the Ghost Box?

TG: It sounds like a high-tech piece of dowsing equipment. [Regarding] these power spots... Andy came across one that I kind of put him onto. I think location may be a big key not only to Mothman, but to other entities. These entities seem to frequent certain areas, going back at least to the Flatwoods Monster in the early 1950s. There is a little town called Midway. I had indications, as long ago as twenty years ago, that Midway was where Indrid Cold lived. I said nothing about it while he lived there, because I didn't want him to get lynched, or for members of the town to start a witch hunt. But the spot is still there, and it *is* a portal. I figured it out purely using the cipher of the ufonauts – the names that were given out in the course of the Indrid Cold story: Lanulos, Carlo Ardo, Demo Hassan, and the name Indrid Cold itself. There was enough information there that I was able to come up with a specific town. The problem was that there was more than one place that had that name. I gave it to Andy, who knows that area much better than I do. He ran it down and [consequently found] the vortex. I can't speak to this device but, if the device indicated that [Midway] was the place, I'd like to put it here on Mount Arabia and see what would happen. My guess is that it would explode. There are definitely vortices that things travel in and out of; things happen around [them]. You can use them to make things happen – to conjure things up.

UD: Andy took the Box to Midway and asked about Indrid Cold and Gray Barker. He also asked a question about Allen Greenfield…

TG [*jokingly*]: If this is about my love life, we need *another* program.

UD: No, we're not getting into anything too revealing here. They asked the Box, "Did Indrid hang out with Allen Greenfield?" And it said, "Dead."

TG: Does that mean I'm dead?

UD: Well, maybe it was talking about Indrid Cold.

TG: Indrid Cold is *not* dead. He's just not in West Virginia anymore.

UD: The first question along that line was, "Did Indrid hang out with Gray Barker?" And the Box answered, "We are…" Then he asked, "Did he hang out with Allen Greenfield?" and the Box answered, "dead."

TG: I know exactly what that means, and that *is* accurate. I never met Cold myself, but my intermediary, Terry R. Wriste, took the information and found this little town of Midway. He talked to [Cold himself. Wriste] is rumored to be dead, and I have good reason to believe that he might be. I don't *know* because it is one of these mysteries. The last I heard, he was in Tibet. He's older than me and very adventurous. [Wriste] has been in many a tight situation. I wouldn't be at all surprised if he were dead. I haven't heard from him in several years…

If Wriste were interested in all things Tibetan, that might explain his association with "Indrid Cold," and why Cold chose a name that seems to allude to the Garuda. Soon after this show, Greenfield told me that the name "Terry R. Wriste" was a pseudonym. Later, I found a reference to a Masonic ritual called "the Tearing of the Wrist." I was stunned when I found this out, because Harriet Plumbrook, whose father was a high Mason, has had several

*incidents where she woke up in the morning with her wrists myste-
riously "torn" – having little cuts. Was Harriet channeling the rites
of Freemasonry on her own (in the same manner she channels other
people's illnesses), or was she a victim of Masonic mind control,
possibly begun when Indrid visited our neighborhood in the late
1960s?*

TG: If you come into one of these vortices, VALIS is more or less on the
air. VALIS is a Philip K. Dick creation – a broadcast from a remote
location...

AC: Before we get to far along, I should add that when we asked the Box
about Allen, Indrid, and Gray knowing each other, collectively, it
said, "We are dead." I should also say that I didn't even know the
Box was going to be used. The Frick brothers just showed up with
it. The whole thing was totally spontaneous. John commented that
it seemed to respond to my questions more than it had with other
people.

TG: You have your own energy field, and the vortices amplified it.

AC: Allen, how did you initially get involved with Gray Barker?

TG: In 1961 or '62, I started reading *Saucer News*. That was during the
Barker/Moseley "feud," which was fraudulent but very entertaining.
They were having a good time with all of us. I met Moseley at the
first national UFO conference in 1964. He said, "Next year, we need
to bring Gray." So, from then on, Gray came to the conventions. I
got to be very friendly with him. I knew him from 1964 until about
two years before he passed on. I didn't hear from him during that
period for a variety of reasons. I was kind of out of touch, and he
was very ill. That's basically it... I saw him every year at conventions
and at our gatherings in NYC on New Years' Eve. We would go into
Times Square, to the New York Hilton, and gather the strangest
New Yorkers around to discuss the nature of the universe. There was
Eugene Steinberg, Timothy Green Beckley, Jim Moseley, John Keel,
Gray, and myself. Other people would drop in, too.

AC: In Moseley's book, there are some pictures of those parties; they look
pretty wild. Tiny Tim and Muhammad Ali were there.

TG: In his New Jersey days, Jim had some fabulous events. He and Gray
also got together in WV. They would use this herbal substance to get
themselves into a higher state of attainment, and then make phone
calls, which created mythos within mythos within mythos. Remarkable guys, really.

AC: Looks like it worked!

UD: This is kind of a revelation here. Jim said they were always drinking; but they were doing other things as well?

TG: Yes, spiritually uplifting herbal Nepalese [stuff].

UD: We don't have to go any farther than that.

TG: If it's good for the Dalai Lama, why not for Jim and Gray?

AC: Well, as Puharich proved, those kinds of substances aid the psychic process.

TG: Puharich probably got his first dose at one of Jim's parties. New York's UFO scene anticipated the 1960s counter-culture by a good ten years. [The things] we were doing in the '50s and early '60s became the entire New Age phenomenon. The ancestors of Burning Man were at Giant Rock. Without them, there would have been no New Age movement. *[seeming to want to change subject]* What mysterious phenomenon is preventing us from talking about ghosts? Have you noticed? We can't do it!

AC: Last time you were on, Allen, there were some weird phenomena that occurred. I actually wrote it down because it seemed so odd.

TG *[jokingly]*: Kerry Thornley always said, "Just say you were *out* of the country…"

AC: The weird phenomena happened after Allen said:

> If you want to inject a little quantum mechanics into it, the same underlying force of the universe is impinging on both our consciousness and our "parallel" world. I see a great deal of similarity between all of these areas. I don't understand – unless people aren't cross-cultural – why people don't…

AC: At that point, a voice cut in to say, "*Foresee!*" You guys all got quiet. We were all wondering what had happened. Interestingly, the voice seemed to be asking: "Why don't people foresee?"

TG: Wow… It fits… I remember… We *did* get interrupted. I made one of those lame little jokes that I make when something happens to the machinery. I said, "Ah-ha, the Men in Black are at it again."

UD: That's right. I remember that now.

AC: And it happened *again*. Vyz started talking about the broad matrix of phenomena. Allen said, "It's the outside impinging on our consensus reality." He started talking about Al Bender and the MIBs. *[noise in background]* It's doing it again, right now! But… Allen started talking about Bender conjuring up MIBs with the use of a magic word. Then, boom, the feedback voice came in again, as if it didn't want the magic word to be revealed.

TG: Well, if it's going to happen, I suppose it should happen during a mention of Bender. "Kazik" was the magic word with which he summoned them up. He was given the word by the Men in Black. They told him that they would manifest in his spooky room that had the spooky stuff in it. His house was a precursor of the current fad of decorating your house as if it's Halloween.

AC: That's funny, because there is a poster of me by "Kozik," a graphic designer who is probably the number one poster artist in the country. He specializes in music posters. Early in his career, he happened to work at the VW parts shop in Austin. He was the clerk who sold me my auto parts; that's how I got to know him.

One Kozik poster depicted my Austin band, Ed Hall, by employing an altered image of actor Christopher Lee from the film The Mummy. *In the film, Lee played the young man who later became the mummy. In the poster, the image of Lee – representing me, the lead singer – holds strange talismans in his hand seeming to allude to ritual sex and Freemasonry. The poster was printed in 1987, the same year that Harriet Plumbrook sensed something was "wrong" and tried to contact me (without success). Considering all of the occult activity going on in Austin at that time, I sometimes wonder if singer Daniel Johnston wasn't correct when he claimed that "the Devil" was loose in Austin. After Johnston and I encountered an earth spirit in the local creek, our lives both went into tailspins for a time… In 2008, a strange premonition, or copycat effect, occurred while I was filming the DVD series. During Mina Bast's reading of me, she saw that I was once mummified, perhaps against my will, in a past life. She mentioned a fire burning in a cave. Amazingly, a few months later, Sharon and Jordan Rogers and I glimpsed a "ghost fire" burning outside of a "ghost cave" in the foothills east of Albuquerque. Was this a replay from another time in my soul's existence? If so, why were Sharon and Jordan brought there to witness it? Unbeknownst to me until I moved in, many of the places I lived in Austin and Albuquerque were built over old Indian witchcraft sites and were haunted. I sometimes wonder if my life wasn't altered by spirit encounters in such places. This might explain why certain paths in my life became seemingly blocked. Coinciden-tally, I met my future wife right around the time the Kozik poster was made. She is a Fire Horse in Chinese astrology – the bringer of bad luck. Whether or not a magical phrase like "Kazik" or "Kozik" had anything to do with this process is anyone's guess. Entities may be aroused not only through ritual workings, but also by unskillful actions: offhand comments from jealous friends, jilted admirers or lovers, or disgruntled peers. Societies that acknowledge the existence of witchcraft, such as the Navajo, now see it mostly as an unfortu-nate outgrowth of petty jealousies and disagreements, often between family members. The same kind of thing is true in Appalachia, where feuds between and within families are legendary.*

AC: I was just reading a book about mind control called *Modern Weapons*. It's about two girls who were mind-controlled by the military from a young age. There is a quote in there about how military intelligence operatives drove around in Volkswagens. This echoes what occurred with the Men in Black in WV, who started to drive VWs in 1968. Harriet started getting visits from an MIB in a Volkswagen, perhaps Indrid Cold. Her family soon moved to Maryland, very close to where the two girls were mind-controlled. These things point toward Indrid Cold being a military intelligence person. James Earl Ray was reportedly military intelligence, as was Oswald and Crisman.

TG: That's very interesting. About the switch to VWs… Ten years before that, a comet was seen over what would now be metropolitan Miami (it was a swamp then). A very large, cigar-shaped UFO was seen lowering down Ford Skylarks, with a driver in each one. The witnesses saw twenty cars be put down on the ground. Then, they all drove off. All of them were the same model and make. Ten years later, some [new witnesses saw] a foreign car being dropped, which is a reflection of a cultural phenomenon… If we're doing programs about this stuff and manifestations are happening while we do the programs, then we investigators become part of the phenomena. Even hoaxes themselves become part of the real phenomena. Gray always said that if you study the ufologists, you will find out more about UFOs than if you study the UFOs themselves – a very profound thought. I have found that to be true. You become part of it. You get into this slightly parallel world. You affect it, and it affects you. If you have a popular TV or radio program that frequently and deeply explores the paranormal, you will have that type of reflexive phenomenon happening.

UD: Take us back to 1965 if you will.

TG: There was a network television show that I was very interested in. It was called *The Stately Ghosts of England*. In those days, it was very uncommon for there to be *anything* on television that *at all* took seriously any kind of apparitional phenomena. I was sitting alone in the den of my parents' house. I was 19 years old and wide awake. I had watched about half of the program when, from an [empty] area of the house, I heard this howling. It was unmistakably coming from the kitchen/laundry room to my immediate right. It was very, very loud. I jumped up, uttering every prayer that I knew. I was all but losing control of my bowels and bladder. I looked and there was nothing there. I really was interested in this program, so my heartbeat slowed back to something like normal. I sat down and [watched] a fascinating program that had one of the first pieces of professional film footage showing ghostly phenomenon. I still have that on videotape somewhere. It was not easily explainable. They had no explanation for it... About ten minutes later, the howling began a second time. Keep in mind, I am pumping adrenaline at this point. I am tense and alert. It was the same howling sound, clearly inside the house, not more than ten feet away from where I was sitting. I freaked. I went through every possible rational explanation for it that I could, and there was none. I thought, "Could it be an auditory hallucination suggested by watching this program? I'd never had anything like that happen before. If it was an auditory hallucination, it was a good one. It was as real as anything gets. It was spooky, the first thing of that sort that I can remember in my life. The lack of additional witnesses or physical evidence make it something that I have not put in any books or anything, but I'm sure that the program and my interest in it had something to do with the manifestation. I think the manifestation was perfectly real. The house could not have been haunted. The house was built for us. No one had died in that house.

UD: Maybe you were practicing ritual magic with the TV, unwittingly.

TG: I may have been invoking something, yes. I was receptive to the supernatural. The line between our day-to-day reality and "otherwhere" is much thinner than people would like to think. We hold on to consensus reality with the barest thread possible; things impinge on it all the time. The thing is, are we receptive to it or not? I think we filter out a lot of things because we can't handle them. We would have to spend all of our time trying to propitiate the demons of the night, so we [block] it out. Some of it is, of course, beyond our senses. It's simply beyond our ability to resolve with the five senses. We have evolved to deal with lions and tigers and bears, or large automobiles going at high rates of speed with drunken drivers, *not* demons and monsters and angels. Our encounters are modified by the limitations of our senses.

AC: I agree... When I was back in WV doing the Ghost Box experiments, I visited my sister's haunted A-frame, where people have seen ghosts walking around. A man murdered his entire family there. Something is obviously going on there. For at least two or three hours, there was a really high-pitched squeaking sound coming from high up in the trees. It went on pretty much continuously, and everyone noticed it. My sister said that she'd never heard it before. I certainly had never heard anything like it before. It was the kind of a squeaky sound that people have attributed to Mothman.

TG: Remarkable... Let me mention the best-known thing that I've ever participated in... There is a power zone, which is very haunted, on the Georgia coast. It is an island called St. Simon's. There are more ghost stories per square mile there than just about anywhere in North America. I was particularly drawn to the legend of the churchyard of Christ Church. It's not an Episcopal Church; it's an Anglican church that dates from the 1700s. Among its first priests were the Wesley brothers. John Wesley was so [shaken by] the weirdness of the Okefenokee that he went back to England. He decided that the Anglican church was inadequate, and became the founder of the Methodists or, as it's called there, the Wesleyan Church... But the Christ Church is still there. The graveyard is very old. It has 250 years of stories attached to it. One of the stories is that a young priest, who was a newlywed, had just gotten a posting there. I imagine it was a pretty backwards posting. His bride passed away shortly thereafter and, from that point on, the graveyard was said to be haunted. The mysterious female apparition was ascribed to the wife of the priest of the church... This is a "repeater," one of those cases where, if you go, you can expect to encounter something paranormal. I talked Jim Moseley and another friend into making the trek down there. We went to St. Simon's Island and to some of the other ghost locations, with all of the equipment that one used in those times. If you've read *The Silver Bridge*, there is a chapter called "The Recorder" that describes the stuff we would carry around: listening devices, infrared cameras, walkie-talkies, etc. Of course, this is south Georgia in 1968; the local police did not take too kindly to us. They told us this little anecdote about a Bible salesman who had been walking through that graveyard a year before. He had been shot… Moseley said, "Now, what did he mean by *that?*" And I said, "I think that was a warning, like maybe we shouldn't be poking around here." We made it to this graveyard, though. There was a choir practice or something going on. We had previously gone and interviewed the current priest of the church. He was not very happy to see us again. We were wandering around the graveyard together. I felt a tug that I needed to go off by myself. I had a good 35mm camera with film in it. It was a very reliable camera that I had used for a lot of documentary photography. I wandered away… It was pitch dark with a half moon. There were trees in the gothic graveyard with moss all over them. It was the perfect setting. I just literally said, "If there is someone here that would like to manifest, I'm available to that; I'm empathetic and respectful of that." I felt a tug to take a picture of the side of the church. There was nothing to it from a rational point of view – nothing there. I selected the "one second" setting on the camera. As I pushed the button, I knew something was going to show up on the film. For that moment, I knew it with utter certainty. The photo is on my website. It has been analyzed by officials from Eastman Kodak, who could find no explanation for it whatsoever. [One official there, whose] job was photo analysis, considers it to be a genuine apparition, an anomaly that can't be explained by any rational means. It shows a decomposing face with wisps of grayish hair, and a collar that looks very Victorian. The woman who was thought to be the apparition probably was laid to rest in that type of outfit. Oh, by the way [in the photo, her face] is eight or ten feet off the ground. That was quite an experience. The fact that it was a 35mm camera meant that there was a negative to be analyzed. It's quite something… Nowadays, I'm currently involved with a series of ritual magic and consecratory activities on Arabia Mountain, a power spot near Atlanta. It is an uncovered granite outcropping. Power spots inherently house these types of living energy. We can perceive them. Even our photographic equipment perceives them. The lenses record circular objects, orbs, little UFOs… Power spots are amplified through the power of our minds.

Less than a week prior to editing the above section, I was involved in a phone call between Bruce Bickford and Sharon and Jordan Rogers, in which we discussed mounds and the potential power they hold. Placing a deceased person's body inside a mound might allow the mound to become suffused with, and possibly energized by, the spirit of the dead person as it leaves the body. Southwestern Indians would even go so far as to place a series of bowls on the head of the deceased, in order to regulate the flow of escaping spirit…

Strangely, after I wrote the above paragraph, I randomly opened up The Silver Bridge *and it fell open to a page about a mysterious, impenetrable golden ball that had fallen in Ripley, WV, during the Mothman days. Interestingly, it had fallen the very same night that Woody Derenberger had first met Indrid Cold, suggesting that maybe Indrid was out searching for the ball. Coincidentally, the finder of the ball, John White, had the same name as our next-door neighbor on Woodward Drive… It began to dawn on me that the ball might be related to another mysterious object that had fallen from the sky one year prior to Mothman: the Kecksburg UFO, which was most likely a Nazi-type "Bell" weapon. The Bell used several design elements found in the Mothman phenomenon. It had a mound shape, perhaps to contain and amplify charges, as well as an interior apparatus that used four hardened spheres. The apparatus was a spinner split into four sections, similar to Ezekiel's Wheel, which is said to have carried four angels with animal-human characteristics. Could the extremely fast spin of the mercury-powered Bell apparatus have warped space-time enough to attract the many hybrid "interdimensional" entities seen in the area? The ball that fell in Ripley was inspected by experts and found to be impenetrable and highly magnetic, but with a nonmagnetic, 24K gold exterior exactly 3/8" thick. Could this ball have been part of the antigravity centrifuges used to power flying saucers? Several of the saucers seen in those days appeared to have spheres underneath, like the Vril series of saucers reportedly built by the Nazis. Some of the "scout ships" drawn by Woody Derenberger had large spheres under the hull.*

UD: Andy, do you have any closing thoughts? *[noise in background]* Hello, Men in Black! I know you're there…

TG: We love you, Mothman! Inside joke…

AC: I've enjoyed talking with Allen again. I think we're onto something.

UD: Allen, any closing words before we wind this up?

TG: I'm always glad to be on your program. We work together productivel Can I plug my new thing?

UD: Certainly…

TG: Okay… In my efforts to keep the lights and heat on, I've got a special going on – a one-time thing. It is the original "I Joined For the Sex Magick" T-shirt! *[laughter]*

Afterwards, I got to thinking about the radio anomalies we had

discussed, which had originally occurred during a Greenfield inter-
view on Halloween 2008. I went back and listened to that inter-
view. Greenfield told a story about how he used his Secret Cipher
of the Ufonauts *code to accurately predict a multi-witness UFO*
sighting in Houston, TX. Along the way, he acknowledged that the
famous Wanaque Reservoir sightings in NJ – many of which, to this
day, seem authentic – were actually kicked off by a hoax. The hoax
had been started by he and Gray Barker's cohort, Jim Moseley… A
sober air hung over the early part of the interview, as Vyz described
his harrowing dreams about the end of the world and invading
aliens – a common experience for paranormal researchers and
witnesses. One theory for this is that such dreams may be part of
our genetic makeup, in that our species has probably been forced to
survive several global cataclysms. The memories of such events are so
potent that they may reside in the collective memory, to be replayed
in the minds of individuals throughout time. Many of the creatures
and entities we see may also come from the same "place."

GREENFIELD, ALLEN – UNTAMED GRASSY KNOLL INTERVIEW - OCT. 2008

"Vyz" at *Beyond the Grassy Knoll* (GK): Something happened. I'm going to be straight up about it. Everybody knows I'm not going to fool around. Maybe a week or so ago, I had a dream – and this is the second time I've had it – of an alien invasion. I don't know how else to say it. It wasn't comic or cartoonish. I can't even explain it. It was something I've never seen before. I was looking out a window saying, "Folks, they're here. This is it." Now, get this… Last night, my wife tells me that she *also* dreamed of an invasion.

T. Allen Greenfield (TG): I find it interesting that you can't describe the central object. I understand that. If you're familiar with the book *Flatland,* there are *some* things that we're not geared to be able to see in the normal sense. So, we *experience* them. There is no dimensional or conventional way to describe them.

GK: What I saw was a craft that originally was rectangular, yet not solid. It had a lot of air in it. Behind it were cylindrical UFO craft… There was a very realistic feeling about it.

TG: I can tell you that there is an amazingly large UFO wave going on right now in Latin America.

Adam Gorightly at *Untamed Dimensions* (UD): I want to ask you about the "Secret Cipher of the Ufonauts," the system you've come up with to forecast UFOs.

TG: Well, I can't specifically say that there will be a sighting at such and such a time on June 3rd at, say, the Wanaque Reservoir in New Jersey…

GK: I lived in Bergen County. I remember the Wanaque sightings.

TG: Of course, but there is a secondary story about that. The Wanaque flap was set off by a hoax! [However, it was followed by] a bunch of real cases. The hoax was perpetrated by Jim Moseley, who happened to have Gene Steinberg in the room. We have gone over this on-air. He was a little under the weather that night, and called the local police department at random. He invented it cold. For days thereafter, there were a bunch of good, legitimate, hard-to-explain UFO cases. It underlines my point that the investigators, the witnesses, and the phenomenon are all part of one holistic sphere of influence; they're interconnected. In that sense, there may not be *any* hoaxes. It manifests because, sometimes, you *want* it to manifest. That is what our late friend Gray Barker was trying to say in *The Silver Bridge*. That is why I got so enthusiastic about the book… People who are ready for this type of experience are more likely to experience it than people who are not. If you are receptive to it, it happens. If you *say* that it is there, it sometimes *is*. In fact, it will be there more often than it ought to be.

UD: Allen, could you talk about that new edition of *The Silver Bridge*?

TG: It goes back quite a ways. I first talked to the late Ron Bonds, at Illuminet Press, about it. He had brought out a new edition of *The Mothman Prophecies* just before the movie came out. Moodwise, the movie was more like *The Silver Bridge* than it was [Keel's book]. I always say you need to read both books to really understand the Mothman phenomenon. Anyway, for one reason or another, Ron didn't get around to it. Then, there was the mysterious little wave of deaths of the conspiracy theorists at Illuminet. Fortunately, not being the conspiracy theorist, I survived. Everybody who published there, with the exception of the UFO authors, died too young, and under mysterious circumstances.

UD: Ron Bonds, Jim Keith, and Kerry Thornley all died within a year or two of each other. All published at Illuminet Press…

TG: Yes, and that ended Illuminet Press. [Perhaps] somebody wanted to get rid of it. None of them were old [and each] was sudden. Keith's case was very strange. In Ron Bond's case, I don't know why it wasn't investigated as a murder. It happened right here in my neck of the woods. I talked to a friend who happens to be a police captain. I said, "Would you look into this?" Unfortunately, there was no real investigation. It was just taken as "food poisoning." But *food* poisoning does not fit. What *does* fit is [some other, more secretive form of] poisoning... Anyway, years later, being a poor and starving artist with a family to feed, I decided to sell my original copy of the original edition of *The Silver Bridge*. It meant a lot to me. I had written the original introduction. It was the first book in which I had ever appeared. When I saw the manuscript, I said, "This is the best book ever written on the subject." I promoted it. Gray asked me to write the introduction. I did my best. I made some effort to explain to the broader public what it meant. The book just went over the heads of most people. It was ahead of its time... Time passed, and then Andy and I got to talking about it. I suggested, "Why don't you consider republishing *The Silver Bridge*?" So, he bought my copy for what I consider to be an outrageous amount of money. It had become such a rarified item that it cost three figures for the original hardcover. I think Andy has the one and only copy that is autographed by both me and Gray. A couple of months later, he bought another copy to be broken down for publishing. He asked me if I would write a new introduction. I really wanted a second chance at telling people what to look for. I also had a photo of Gray and the Silver Bridge that had never been published before, which I worked into the cover design. I'm very pleased that the new introduction prepares people for what they're reading. *The Silver Bridge* really is as close to a solution to the UFO mystery as you're going to get in this lifetime. It also contains a very moving tribute to Gray written by Jim Moseley, who was his best friend. It's just an outstanding, surreal book. Gray was primarily a poet. He appreciated the folkloric aspects, the mythos. The book captures a great deal of the numinosity that is at the core of paranormal phenomena – things that you see or experience that can't be put into words, that go beyond human ken... Gray was passionately good with the word. He was an English major in college; it served him well in writing this particular book. I would recommend it to anyone.

UD: Indeed... But remember... Gray, like Jim Moseley, liked to drink a bit and pull hoaxes. What would you say to his detractors who think his books are full of B.S.?

TG: I'd go back to the Wanaque case… I pretty well know every one of the hoaxes. By the way, they were usually perpetrated *together*; it was Jim *and* Gray. When they got together in West Virginia, they'd usually "tie one on" and come up with something. It was only for those who were so gullible that they would buy into anything – who were either too serious or too credulous. It had a way of culling the idiots out. They pulled one or two on me. It was nothing that mattered. They had a sense of humor about what they were doing. I have, I think, a good Mel Brooks-type sense of humor. I call myself a "stand-up philosopher." But… I try to keep that in a different pocket. [I don't joke when] I'm describing an event. Jim and Gray, on the other hand, saw it as a spectrum where investigators and witnesses are *part* of the phenomenon. You can certainly critique that, but how do you account for something like the Wanaque thing, where Jim starts a hoax and the hoax becomes reality? Where do you take that? A lot of things with Gray were like that as well. I have a hunch that some of the strange phone calls that John Keel got while he was in WV were Gray playing some kind of sound machine on the phone. This enlivened Keel's somewhat straight-laced, if excellent, book…

UD: I think Moseley has admitted as much.

TG: Yes… I don't pretend to live in the same world that most people do. I live in the world of vampires, and dark shadows, and secret societies that don't like me anymore. I'm reminded of the line David Duchovny used in the *X-Files*. He said, "I think the dead are all around us." This is the perfect night for saying that… The UFOs and ufonauts are all around us, all the time. It's a question of whether we are able to see them, and whether they want to be seen.

UD: Are ghosts and UFOs sometimes the same thing?

TG: Absolutely. This is my basic theme. Occult conjurations, demonic apparitions, ghostly appearances, UFOs, and "aliens" are part of the same spectrum. They conform to many of the same rules. The wording used to describe them will vary with the times. An angelic being in one era will be a ghost or alien in another era. It's the same underlying force impinging on our consciousness, our world, and our parallel world (if you want to start to inject a little quantum mechanics into it). I see a great deal of similarity between all of these areas. I don't understand why people don't *see* that… [weird robotic voice chimes in, yelling: "Foresee!"]

GK: Hello? I don't know what's going on. We had a little reverb there.

TG [jokingly]: I didn't know whether *you* were agreeing with me or *I* was agreeing with me.

GK: Nobody said anything, actually. But, by all means, continue; there is no resistance to what's you're saying. Go ahead.

TG: Differing areas of "anomaly studies" have their own group of experts, enthusiasts, and witnesses. They have their own sets of terms to describe parts of a broader matrix of phenomena. Still, most of us [interpret the events] as something from "outside" that is impinging on our consensus reality. People who consider themselves "experts" are often extremely hostile to the notion that an occult conjuration [can cause something. Take] Al Bender, the ufologist who always put scary Halloween stuff in his room. Suddenly, the Men in Black showed up at his door and told him the truth about UFOs; that is essentially the Al Bender story. He basically lived in a conjuration. When he conjured, they came. Not only that, but he was given a magic word, "kazik," to use whenever he wanted to make contact. It is spelled differently from the way it's pronounced. Magicians use such phrases to conjure things from elsewhere. Why would ufologists be hostile to the notion of conjuration? [more weird reverb] I'm hearing feedback again. Are we there?

GK: We are here.

TG: I'm just amazed that people don't see the connections. And, if they do, they act as if their turf is being encroached on, which is more of a mystery than the connections themselves. Why would people consider it heresy to say that there are different ways of looking at the same thing?

"In every way, Indrid Cold was human in appearance. Derenberger says that [Cold] kept asking him why he was so frightened, explaining that his country was not nearly as powerful as ours:

Cold [suggested] I report this incident to the local officials. At a later date, he would confirm my story...

"Cold said this first contact had been a test to see how the West Virginian would react... Reminiscing, Derenberger recalls:

The spaceman told me that he wanted to talk more later, that I had very good receptive powers – listening very intently to every word he said...

"After breaking contact, Woody claims that he felt very exhilarated and had a small throbbing pain in his right temple, which lasted for a brief period. Four days later, from a nearby field, came Indrid Cold and the navigator of the ship, Carlo Ardo:

> I was very excited and shaking uncontrollably; my voice quivered when I spoke to them. I did not even notice the cold weather. They were with me for two hours, but would not come into the house because my wife was so frightened.

"The two quizzed Derenberger many times... Both spacemen told the contactee that they are frightened of our people. Woody says:

> At one time in Arkansas, Cold was blasted with a shotgun and had to have several pellets removed from his legs and thighs. He told me things that I have no way of [validating]. Cold and Ardo said that they have made an offer to our government leaders: if they would guarantee safety for both the crew and the ship, they would land.

"The intriguing story of Woodrow Derenberger, though complex and impossible, is strikingly similar to hundreds of other contact cases that have come to my attention. Somewhere within this case and the subsequent events that transpired, lies a great many answers to the flying saucer puzzle. Perhaps, as has been suggested, some sort of weird game is being played with the minds of the contactees... Charles Fort long ago suggested that we are merely 'sheep,' controlled by absurd and contradictory stories implanted in our midst. Woody's contact experiences are backed up by Steven Law, who claims he saw flying saucers land on Derenberger's farm several times. [Law] even boasts that he made telepathic contact with Indrid Cold 'almost every night,' and has met him on numerous occasions. The first time was when Law was attending a concert at Parkersburg High School. Seated in the large auditorium, surrounded by hundreds of other persons, he received a telepathic message from Cold that the 'spaceman' would like to meet him during intermission at the front door of the school:

> He told me I would recognize him because he would be holding a yellow keychain in his hand. I walked up to this man with a yellow keychain. He said that it was nice to see me and that it was unfortunate they could not stay longer. His ship was waiting for him.

"Cold then told Steven that eventually he would be taken to Lanulos, where he would go to school for eight years, and then return…as their ambassador:

> [Cold] told me I would be selected for this honor because I was young, not married, and had nothing attaching me to this planet.

"Little by little, the consciousness of the public is coming around to accepting the *idea* that aliens are visiting our planet. 'Close encounters' are taking place every day. Woody Derenberger and Steven Law [are among the many] who have had to come to grips with the situation. *You* may be next…"

-Harold Salkin, "Flying Saucer Lands on Highway I-77,"
Official UFO magazine, March 1978

CHAPTER 23

"Monsters and unusual creatures of almost every description have been reported over the centuries. From dinosaur-like animals, to fairies, to bizarre hodgepodges like the Jersey Devil, there seems to be no limit to the variety of unexplained creatures people claim to have seen with their very own eyes. One of the most curious types of sightings – and quite rare – are those of humanoid beings that fly. In most cases, these odd creatures are not assumed to be either angels or devils, but something else… Over 100 years ago, a man named W. H. Smith told *The New York Sun* that he saw a 'winged human form' flying over Brooklyn, NY on September 18, 1877. About three years later, there were multiple reports from Coney Island of a man with batlike wings flying overhead at approximately 1,000 feet. The man was flying toward the New Jersey coast, witnesses told *The New York Times*. He bore a 'cruel and determined expression' on his face. It's easy to dismiss such sightings as misidentified birds or alcohol-induced illusions when one or two people report them. When as many as 240 people, however, attest to seeing the same thing, the reports are far more difficult to discount. Such a sighting look place over several days in June 1905, in Voltana, Spain. The accounts consistently described a woman dressed in white flying through the air, without the aid of wings, sometimes against the wind. One witness said she might have heard it singing as it passed overhead…

"There have been legends of a flying man in the Soviet Union [for quite some time]. In the winter of 1936 in the Pavlodar region of Kazakhstan, Mrs. E. E. Loznaya was walking to school on a quiet road when her attention was caught by a strange figure above her. Flying quickly across the sky was a manlike figure dressed completely in black. Despite its speed [she] was able to see and describe it clearly. It made a rumbling noise and appeared to be wearing a helmet of some kind. It had a black surface where the face should have been, and wore a 'rucksack' on its back… Hunters around the Sikhote Mountains near Vladivostok claim to have come across prints of a barefoot human that ended abruptly, as if he had taken off into the air. Such a creature was actually seen by writer V.K. Arsenyev in July of 1908:

On the path I saw a mark that was very similar to a man's footprint... Then something rushed about nearby, trampling among the bushes. I stooped, picked up a stone, and threw it towards the unknown animal. Then, something happened that was quite unexpected: I heard the beating of wings. Something large and dark emerged from the fog and flew over the river.

"In the early 1950s, a couple was taking an evening stroll near their home by the sea at Pelotas, Brazil. When two fast-moving shadows crossed their path, they looked up to see what they at first thought were two enormous birds, flying about 30 feet above the ground. It was soon evident to the couple that these were not birds at all. The two flying creatures descended vertically and landed not far away. They looked like men, standing about six feet tall. Discovering that they were being watched by the couple, the two birdmen squatted close to the ground, as if trying to hide. The wife convinced her husband to leave – and quickly."

-Stephen Wagner, *Your Guide to Paranormal Phenomena*

SCOTT, DAVE & TONY MUELLER – MOTHMAN AND HURRICANE IKE – OCT. 2008

Andy Colvin (AC) *[to camera]*: It's October 20, 2008. I'm here with Fish Ofiesh, my trusty camera assistant here in WV. Last night, I was on a radio show with Eddie Middleton of Tennessee MUFON. Eddie hosts the *Nightsearch* UFO program. He suggested, "Why not go back to the Mothman vortex site on Woodward Drive in Mound, stand in the same spot, and see if you can *still* see into the future there?" Well, we've taken Eddie up on that... We've just arrived at the vortex site. *[gestures]* Here is the driveway to the property. Our parking spot here on the lane is the place where Harriet and I saw our respective entities. It's funny... Now that I know that the Native Americans sometimes bury their dead inside of hollowed out trees, our experiences make more sense. My entity came out of a tree, while Harriet's eventually morphed into an Indian guide. *[points]* Notice where the current homeowner's van is; that is where Tommy and I saw the vision of 9/11. Hopefully the world won't end or anything as we're doing this. *[nervous laughter]* Here's the Mothman shrine building to the right. On the left here, next to the side of that porch, is the exact spot.

Fish and I stood in the spot for a few seconds. Nothing happened. I didn't have the chills normally associated with a paranormal encounter, and no visions arose. Shortly afterwards, Fish and I left. From there, following the same backroads undoubtedly used by Indrid Cold and his elusive crew, we drove on to Midway, WV, where Indrid is said to have lived.

AC: We're now on Midway Hollow Road, which is supposedly where Indrid Cold lived. This is between Charleston and Point Pleasant. We're kind of parked in the middle of the road here, just past Midway Tavern. What do you think about all this, Fish?

Fish Ofiesh (FO) *[jokingly]*: I think the Tavern is closed, unfortunately.

AC: I'll guess we'll have to go find Mothman instead of beer. *[laughter]*

A little ways up the road, we came to an abandoned property with an old green house, which gave me the "tingles." I pulled over, wondering if I might pick up something about Mr. Cold. Amazingly, this property would later be identified as Indrid's house by the Frick Brothers' "Ghost Box."

AC: Sometimes I get a feeling… Something tells me this *might* be Indrid's place. It's right in the curve of the road here. Last night, I did that show with Sandy Nichols, who works with UFO abductees. He stated that he once had dreams about little colored lights that inhabited a valley in which he was supposed to live someday. Later, he actually found the valley, and built a house there. Strangely, somebody *else* had previously seen a UFO flying above the spot where he decided to build the house. I said, "Well, maybe *you* were there beforehand; maybe your consciousness was somehow connected to that ball of light that was seen. That would explain how you dreamed about it prior to being there." Believe it or not, I have had the *same* sort of dream about multi-colored lights in a valley in which I am supposed to live. Prior to the interview with Sandy yesterday, I was actually driving around southeastern Ohio looking for that valley. I was discussing the lights with psychic Lisa Neesvig, who was driving around with me. Just a little synchronicity…

Following an exploration of Midway Hollow, I drove along the Ohio River to Cincinnati, where I was to meet with a recent Mothman witness, Tony Mueller. Tony is the brother-in-law of local ghosthunter Dave Scott, who also runs the Cincinnati Gallery of Conceptual Art.

AC [to camera]: We're in north Cincinnati, off of Colerain Avenue, with Dave Scott of Passing Lane Paranormal Investigations. Dave's brother-in-law, Tony Mueller, lives in a haunted house here. He will be talking to us in just a minute. Last month, he saw some kind of black vapor or entity that looked like Mothman. Over the years, he has seen and heard weird things in the house, such as lights and entities. Dave, you were saying that the house allows you to make good use of your ghostmeters and other equipment.

Dave Scott (DS): I've come over here many times. We basically "ghostbust." We have EMF detectors, motion detectors, and cameras. Stuff is going on here all the time. The motion detectors go off a lot. We leave them in the basement. They pick up things and trigger the cameras, which we always leave on standby. We watch what is happening downstairs on the monitors upstairs.

AC: Are you getting images of misty plasma forms?

DS: More than that. We are getting faces and bodies...

AC: This is better than the show *Ghosthunters*, and you're not even a plumber!

DS: We were doing this stuff way *before Ghosthunters*.

AC: Tony, you've had an important sighting recently – this black thing right after the hurricane. Tell us what you saw.

Tony Mueller (TM): We were sitting on the front porch. We could clearly see the house across the street. It was 11:30 or so at night. The next thing you know, this thing comes down and blocks the view of that house. We couldn't even see the house in front of us. We could only see the houses on each side of it. This thing came down, then went right back up into the air. It disappeared within a matter of seconds.

AC: So, this thing was like 20 or 30 feet wide?

TM [nods]: Very wide...

AC: Did it have any kind of shape?

TM: It looked like it had wings. It came down in a "V" shape. It shot down and then back up. About 15 minutes to a half-hour later, I saw six billowy balls that went up in the other direction.

AC: Did they come out of the ground or just sort of fly through?

TM: They flew through. They had a grayish, whitish color.

AC: Like a smoke ball?

TM: Yes.

AC: Did this happen right after the hurricane?

TM: The power had been out since Sunday; this happened on Tuesday night.

AC: So the power was off at the time of the sighting?

TM: Yes.

AC: John Keel did a study of Thunderbird sightings and found that they usually occur after big storms. We can almost predict where sightings such as yours will take place simply by tracking the movements of weather fronts. Was anything going on in your life at that time, other than the hurricane?

TM: The only thing I can think of is that the woman across the street had died. Then, up at the corner, another woman died. Then, her sister, who lived further up the street, passed. There were three deaths within a month of each other, just prior to that. I was thinking that it was some kind of energy form.

AC: Death comes in threes... Didn't you see some blue lights, too?

TM: I have no idea what it was. I was sitting on the couch. All of a sudden, I started seeing blue lights shooting through the window – with the blinds shut.

DS: We got that on video, too.

TM: Yes, and we have pictures.

AC: Tell us about the invisible entity that you saw or felt.

TM: We were standing there, talking, under the ceiling fan. [For no apparent reason] the lightbulb broke. It was like in slow motion. It fell down in pieces and hit the ground. I went into the bedroom and got the digital recorder. I came out and asked who broke the light. When I played the tape back, it said, "I did it! I did it!"

AC: So you already had an inkling that it was a ghost of some kind?

TM: Yes, I did. You get those feelings where your hair will stand up on end. You get a cold feeling; you just know something's going on.

AC: Are you guys experiencing any psychic phenomena in addition to this?

TM: Sometimes we can sense things. Especially my wife; she gets strong feelings about certain things.

DS: The night of those blue flashes, my sister called me up. She said, "You've got to come over here! There is a lot of activity. I've got my camcorder out. You can see little orbs coming in through the blinds. One after another, a train of them…" I said, "Okay, I'll come over and check it out." So, I brought my equipment over as soon as I could. We put camcorders on tripods in the living room, where the activity was. We just let the camcorders run for a while. We went in and sat down at the kitchen table. I was sitting with my back to the front door. All of a sudden, I felt a cold draft, like somebody had opened the door in the wintertime. But there was no door open. I said, "Something's going on." We went over and looked at our camcorders to see how they were taping. In both of our camcorders, the image just went totally black. It was like somebody put a lens cap on the front of both cameras. But we just kept taping. A few minutes later, we saw these blue flashes, like somebody was setting off blue flashbulbs in the room. It happened two or three times. We have it on videotape. What it looks like is a neon blue flash in the middle of the room. We're sure it wasn't coming through the blinds. There were no cars coming past, no headlights, and no other light sources in the room that could have been doing it. Shortly after the blue flashes, our cameras went back to normal. The image appeared normally on the camcorders after that. It was over.

AC: Tony, didn't you say earlier that you would wake up the next morning after these events and have "grab marks" on you?

TM: Yes, they were bruises that looked like a handprint – like someone's hand had grabbed you real tight. You could see the bruises.

SCOTT, DAVE – PARANORMAL OHIO – JAN. 2009

Andy Colvin (AC) *[to camera]*: It's Inauguration Day, January 20th, 2009. I'm here in Cincinnati, Ohio. It's about 14 degrees out and we are traveling along the Ohio River. I'm here with Dave Scott again. We met with Dave earlier, after his sister and brother-in-law saw the Four Mothmen in Sept. of 2008, in the Cincinnati suburb of Grossbank. By the way, your brother-in-law, Tony, seemed totally credible – a very down-to-earth, no-nonsense person.

Dave Scott (DS): Yes, he is…

AC: We just drove through Grossbank on the way down to the river here. *[shows map]* Here is an interesting map; it's called "Paranormal Ohio." It shows the locations of all the different UFO and creature sightings. It was actually inspired by *The Mothman Prophecies* movie. When the map's creators saw the movie, they were inspired to draw this up. It's very helpful in getting a sense of local history. For instance, we just passed near Covedale. On October 21st of 1973, there was a UFO close encounter there. On Oct. 2nd, 1966, just a month before Mothman was first seen, there was a UFO sighting just south of Mount Airy Forest. Dave lives just north of Mount Airy Forest. Interestingly, it says that there was a spate of "raining blood" in Cincinnati near Mount Adams. That is where Dave and I went to college, at the Art Academy of Cincinnati. Mt. Adams has a "haunted gazebo," and is right across the river from Newport, KY and Dayton, KY, where all of the old gambling places were located. Jack Ruby and Meyer Lansky were partners in a casino, the original Flamingo, in Dayton… We're now going east of Cincinnati, towards Bethel, Amelia, and Dead Man's Curve… Bethel has had some UFO sightings recently. A lady on the Mothman discussion list has been seeing UFOs on her farm there. The interesting thing is that there are Indian mounds all over the place here. We'll be passing by the Woodland Mound, the Newtown Mound, and many others. These mounds are all over the Ohio Valley. All over Ohio, in fact… Elites like to build nuke plants, chemical plants, and golf courses – anything that is large, offensive, and needs a public subsidy – on these mound sites. We'll also be swinging by Pond Run Road, which is near New Richmond. They have a power plant in the midst of the mound sites there. Dave, tell people a little bit about your organization and how you got interested in the paranormal.

DS: I'm really interested in local history. So much of it has been lost. It started when I was taking physical therapy. I had a broken back. I started talking to one of the therapists about Indians living in the area. This guy was in his late 20s or early 30s. He said, "You mean there used to be *Indians* around here?" I said, "Yes!" I started talking about Fort Hamilton. He said, "You mean Hamilton *really* used to be a *fort?*" I started to realize that people really didn't know anything at all about their local history – what this area was like a couple hundred years ago. That's what got me interested in discovering the histories of the various townships. I decided to start by investigating local legends about haunted roads and bridges in the area. There are a lot to choose from. A lot of them I'd heard about since I was in high school. Some of these legends have been around for a long time. They've been added to over and over, until they have grown out of proportion. Some of the legends have even merged into one.

AC: Didn't you do some fieldwork at an Indian site near Addyston, where the Miami River dumps into the Ohio River? There is a huge chemical plant there now. It was featured on the news recently because it is giving *teenagers* lung cancer.

DS: Yes, that's around Shawnee Lookout Park, which is right at the mouth of the Great Miami River. This whole area was Shawnee and Miami Indian territory a couple hundred years ago. It was full of mounds and earthworks – what they used to call "works." They didn't really know what they were. They thought they were forts or religious sites of some sort. Most of those were plowed under for farmers' fields. Some of them, located right in downtown Cincinnati, were plowed under to make room for roads. A *lot* of mounds have been lost over the years. There are still some in the parks around Cincinnati. Those have been preserved, but a lot of them are gone forever. They are destroying places before they even bother to investigate. Ohio is full of history. It is the "land of the weird." There are many sightings of mysterious cryptids and UFOs.

AC: Wasn't there a *werewolf* attack?

DS: Yes, there was a werewolf attack or two, plus sightings of a tentacled creature near New Richmond… There have been "ghost cars" aplenty. Giant mastodon bones were found over in Big Bone Lick State Park in Kentucky, which was a salt lick. In prehistoric times, it was a place where animals used to go to lick the salt.

AC: I notice on the map that up near Cleveland, they have found giant *human* bones.

DS: I didn't know that. Giants…

AC *[gestures]*: We're just slightly east of Amelia, Ohio now. We're in a nice field here where there are some Indian mounds. What's the name of this mound?

DS: This is the Elk Lick Road Mound.

AC: Another salt lick… As I've said before, sodium, in addition to dehydration, is proven to increase psychic abilities in humans. There have been some hauntings here. There was a UFO sighting in Amelia in 2004, which was a big year for Mothy events. Do you think there is a relationship between mounds, UFOs, and ghost hauntings?

DS: That is what people claim... *[points]* We are next to what used to be Dead Man's Curve. They called it "Dead Man's Curve" because there were so many accidents around this part of the road. They blame it on these Indian mounds – the burials. A faceless hitchhiker, the Shadowman, is seen here. People who have seen him, up close, say that he appears to be a solid at first, but actually has no face – no features at all. He seems to be able to disappear at will, and has actually been hit by passing cars. He has also been known to throw rocks at cars. Two "ghost cars" are regularly seen at this same intersection. They were supposedly involved in a collision here in 1969, at the intersection of S.R. 222 and S.R. 125.

AC: Interestingly, across the road from the mounds and Dead Man's Curve is a housing complex called "Whispering Trees." "Holly Lanes" bowling alley is right there, too. "Holly" is the wood used in magical wizard staffs. It is also associated with the magical aspects of Christmas, once a pagan holiday. "Hollywood" is the place that shapes our fantasy vision of the world on the television screen. TV is itself a form of magic. It has probably changed our reality more than any other invention... It seems that abandoned houses are always found in these areas where ghosts and entities are seen. There are actually two abandoned houses here at Dead Man's Curve. By the way, there is a "Dead Man's Curve" in Sissonville, WV where a lot of people used to see what they would describe as either the "Virgin Mary" or a "bride." That's where my sisters and I had a spinout once. We completely turned around – 360 degrees. But the car mysteriously righted itself and stayed on the road. We just kept going.

DS: I had that happen one time.

AC: My sister Loretta was driving. Later, she had a wreck near there. She received a bad head injury. She claims that the ghost of my grandfather pulled her out of the car. *[points to large hawk]* Is that a hawk? It's sitting right here at Dead Man's Curve.

DS: It's *big*! Once, I was on a section of U.S. 27 between northern Cincinnati and Oxford, Ohio. There have been so many accidents on that part of the road that it is called the "Highway to Heaven." I was on my way home late one night. I was working two jobs. I was really tired. I must have been going about 55 miles an hour. I fell asleep at the wheel and rocketed off the right side of the road, straight into a huge tree. It totally demolished my car. I don't remember much, just little patches of memory. I don't remember getting out of the car. I remember reaching up and feeling blood on my face, then reaching down and feeling blood on my leg. I said, "Well, I guess I'm dead." The next thing I remember is walking around and around my car. It was just like the movie *Wild At Heart*. I was wandering around in a daze. Then I blacked out again. The next thing I remember, I was sitting in someone's car. They were patching me up with a little first-aid kit. I don't know who this person was, where they came from, or who notified them. I never did find out who that person was. If they hadn't come along, I don't know what would have happened to me.

AC: Something saved you... *[points]* There is a "Starlight" Movie Theatre here. Twilight language, anyone?

DS: This must be the "land of light." We are in enlightened territory here on Bantam Road. But I imagine this would be a scary place at night.

AC: As usual, we have a Marathon gas station nearby. We have seen Marathons at these sites many times during the filming of the reality series.

After checking out some of the mounds, Dave and I continued on to New Richmond.

DS: Here we are at the location of the Hookman sightings. Supposedly, a young couple was murdered here back in the 1960s. After that, legend grew about a Hookman who roamed around here. He would pounce on people's cars if they dared park here at night. People have reported strange sounds coming from the woods, like dogs barking for no reason (which I just heard myself a minute ago). Supposedly a lot of murders happened here at this bridge. It was a wooden bridge at one time. They said it was soaked with blood. Since then, the bridge has been replaced by a concrete bridge. This is a narrow and twisting valley. It looks like it would be dark and dangerous at night.

AC: We're probably about a mile from where the "tentacled creature" was seen.

DS: This creek leads straight down to the Ohio River. If there *were* some sort of water creature, it could feasibly work its way up the creek.

AC: There was a Bigfoot sighting near Dead Man's Curve in 1968. There was a "Wolfman" attack up north, and a "white wolf" sighting south of Mount Airy Forest, very close to Addyston. On the way here, we got sidetracked on Route 50, which is the old road that runs all the way across the U.S. Many Masonic temples, Army bases, and Indian sites are on Route 50. It goes through Marymont, a Jesuit strong-hold on the east side of Cincinnati; no doubt the Virgin was seen there. There were UFO sightings in 1949 and 1950 in Norwood. Norwood was the site of a "terrorist" bombing a couple of years ago. There are mounds in Norwood, Madeira, and Indian Hill.

DS: Do you know why it's called "Indian Hill?" Supposedly, when the settlers first settled there, they were attacked. The Indians stole some horses. One of the horses had its feet hobbled, so the Indian had a hard time getting away with the horse. The settlers shot and killed the Indian. They buried him on the spot, and it became known as The Indian's Hill, or Indian Hill.

AC: About a mile from our Hookman location here, there is yet *another* mound: the Woodland Mound. Could a negative mound spirit have incited these murders?

DS: It *is* odd that the mounds, power plants, and hauntings are clustered together. Certain areas seem to gather certain energies. Maybe the mounds were built over power spots that the Indians heard about hundreds of years ago. Maybe the same spirits roamed around back then, too. The stories were just handed down.

AC: What do you think of Jim Brandon's theory that the mounds are natural foundations, which could perhaps – given the right condi-tions – create entities, animals, or even people? Atum, the Egyptian god, is said to have created himself from a mound. Maybe that's how it all got started. Maybe we have never gotten the full story about "Adam" in the Garden of Eden.

DS: I believe just about anything is possible.

AC: Maybe the mounds are spiritually charged by the placement of recently dead bodies.

DS: It seems to be a "chicken or egg" situation, whether the mounds were pre-existing, or built by humans.

AC [to camera]: We have driven to north Cincinnati, where we are check-ing out some other ghostly sites. We just stopped along Buell Road, site of the "ghost bicyclist." You don't want the ghost bicyclist to catch up to your parked car because, if he does, legend has it that you will die within a week. We are now approaching the park at the end of Lick Road, which is both a salt lick and a murder site. Dave, can you tell us about it?

DS: According to the legend, a 30-yr. old woman named Amy was murdered here. Her body was dumped nearby in the woods, just beyond this gate. This is a 265-acre forest reserve. Supposedly, if you park here and wait with your engine turned off, the word "help" will appear written in the condensation of your car window. Also, people have reported a lot of strange sounds coming from the woods, and things moving around their cars. They'll set up a tripod or something, and it'll get knocked down. I've taken a couple of strange photographs here, of blurry forms in the shape of a human being.

AC: Right near here, towards Fairfield, there was a famous UFO sighting in December of 1974. A little further east from that, near Sharonville, there were lots of UFO sightings during the time of Mothman. One of them was on February 11, 1967. That was 11 days before the death of JFK conspirator David Ferrie, a CIA pilot rumored to be Pt. Pleasant's "Frightwig Man."

I waited in the car while Dave checked out the nearby bridge. No words appeared on the windshield. But, before Dave came back, I wrote "help" in the windshield dust as a joke. I had him spooked for a second or two... Following our visit to Lick Road, we headed north to Miami, OH to investigate the famous Oxford ghost lights.

AC [*squinting into late afternoon sun*]: A quick update... We just took a quick look at Miami University's Peabody Hall. It is a very old, and very haunted, dormitory. We then traveled east of campus to check out the famous "ghost motorcycle" lights. You can see them on YouTube. We have just arrived. We're going to flash our lights three times to see if we can see the "ghost motorcycle." This is the spot where the ghost motorcycle's lights are usually seen. It is now dusk. Dave, tell us about this famous legend.

DS: Legend says that a guy was coming out here one night to see his girlfriend. She lived right around the corner here. He was going too fast and flew off the edge of the road. He was decapitated by a barbed wire fence. Ever since then, there have been literally hundreds of people who have come out here, turned their cars around, flashed their headlights three times, and seen this light come down the road. No one knows what it is; they call it the "ghost motorcycle light." You can see it come down the road, following the contour of the road. Just before it reaches you, it disappears. Some people have seen it dozens of times.

AC [*standing in road*]: Okay, we flashed the lights. We're looking... And... We're not seeing anything. You can see car lights in the distance. This is an extremely long stretch of straight road. You can see for what seems to be two or three miles. The path of the road is unusual; it has very regularly spaced dips. There is probably some kind of reflective "mirage effect" occurring here. I think people may be seeing car lights from way off in the distance. Light can do funny things.

Having come up with a rational, comforting "explanation" for the ghost light, we headed for Hangman's Hollow, another spooky place with unexplained aspects.

AC *[to camera]*: We're in Hamilton, Ohio… Dave, tell us about Hangman's Hollow.

DS: We're in Dartown, the northern section of what is now Hamilton, Ohio. Back in 1851, some men were traveling from Dartown into the port to attend the first county fair in the area. On the way back, about dusk, they came through this hollow. Off to the side of the road, they noticed a man hanging from a tree. He was hung by his own suspenders. That's why it became known as "Hangman's Hollow." After they found the man, a legend started that this whole area was haunted. People would hear and see strange things. For a long time afterwards, people were afraid to enter these woods. It probably should have been called "Hanged Man's Hollow."

AC *[points]*: You can see the woods there… Dave is now filming, in order to scan the recording for EVPs later. Weren't howls heard in these woods?

DS: They could hear howls *and* see figures.

AC: Those werewolves again… Dave is filming this odd drain in the ground, which has a weird sound emanating from it. *[shows drain]* This is reminiscent of that scene in *The Mothman Prophecies* where howling comes out of the sink. It's strange… Neal Mindrum and I joked for years about a "crack in the sink" from which the spirit of the Void, or some entity from another dimension, would howl through at you. It was just a joke we came up with in the 1980s, for no apparent reason. We never exactly identified who or what was doing the howling. Synchronistically, the same scenario was written into the Mothman movie, even though it did not appear anywhere in the book.

By coincidence, we were meeting Neal for dinner nearby. I asked Neal to recount for us the tale of the "Crack in the Sink."

AC: Our old "Crack in the Sink" joke involved some kind of interdimensional communication coming from the crack, did it not?

Neal Mindrum (NM) *[cryptically]*: It *had* to happen… The present moment *is* infinite, friends…

AC: It *did* happen, and then, somehow, the guys making *The Mothman Prophecies* got the message, and put it into the movie! But why would they toss in that sink reference when there were so many other unusual – and real – events in the book to portray?

DS: I was in a movie called *Fresh Horses*. I stood right by the photographer. Coincidentally, he was *also* the photographer for *The Mothman Prophecies* movie.

AC: On the way over to the restaurant here, Neal and I were talking about a few things. We discussed the "Linda Blair car" that I once owned. It was a red Polara that blew up right after I sold it. Additionally, I owned a VW bug that caught fire one day while I was leaving the Art Academy. We were also talking about the VW *van* I once had, which also caught fire, but in Austin. Before it got fire, I had driven the van up here to Cincinnati. I was renting a room for the summer in a house full of Satanists. They were also members of Mensa, which in addition to the ridiculous Goth clothing made them even more unbearable. I used to wear Izod shirts just to piss them off. One day, I was coming down the hill to their house when the brakes went out on the van. It was a *bad* situation. Neal will tell you the rest.

NM *[illustrates by moving pieces of candy on tabletop]*: So, Andy, is coming down the hill towards this intersection in Clifton. It is *very* steep. It is kind of like the streets of San Francisco, only different.

AC: More Satanic… *[laughter]*

NM: So here's Andy… His brakes have gone out. Amazingly, at the intersection ahead, right before he gets there, these two cars come from the left and right and have a head-on collision, right in front of him! *[shows crash]* And then, on the rebound, the cars slowly part! Andy is still barreling down the hill with his brakes out… Time slows down. It all starts happening in slow motion. Amazingly, by some stroke of good luck, Andy goes right through the intersection *between* these two cars that have just collided! He is able to go on his merry way, straight back to the apartment. He only had a couple inches of clearance on either side.

AC: Just for ultra-synchronicity, note the name of the chocolate that Neal is using to illustrate the crash: "Divine." One could speculate this was "divine intervention" by my "protector." Dave, you survived an actual crash; maybe you have even more protection than I do. And didn't you once have a close call with a black helicopter in Colorado?

DS: It was 1984. I was coming into Colorado. It was really late at night. We had been driving all night. I was on one of the backroads, on the way to a friend's house. We noticed this black helicopter following us for miles and miles. It followed us for the longest time. To test our theory that it was following us, I stopped the car. I said, "Let's get out of the car and see what's going on." We stopped, got out of the car, and leaned against it. When we stopped, the helicopter stopped, too. It hovered over us for quite a while. I figured it was just the military playing around with their surveillance gear, testing it out. Maybe they were seeing if they could eavesdrop on our conversation.

 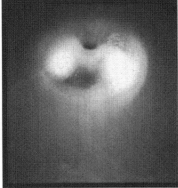

The torus (left) is a doughnut shaped component of the subatomic realm. When sliced and placed in front of a light, the torus casts shadows matching the letters of the Hebrew alphabet. The author took a photo of a water fountain resembling a torus (right) at the Harry Ransom Library in Austin, TX in the early 1980s. Ransom was later fingered by JFK researcher Richard Bartholomew as having inside knowledge of the assassination. Coded alterations to books at the Ransom Center implicated the Latin American Studies Dept. of U.T. in the assassination. The books were probably altered by George Wing (note bird name), a former CIA agent who taught Spanish at U.T. Wing somehow came to own the Nash Rambler seen carrying Oswald away from the TX Book Depository following the assassination. Wing parked the Rambler in front of the Spanish Dept. building in the 1980s, which the author often walked by on his way to class.

CHAPTER 24

"Freedom of thought, which necessarily involves freedom
of speech and press, I define thusly: no opinion a law, no
opinion a crime."

-Alexander Berkman

"If you had dared to suggest one hundred years ago that God
and the devil were in cahoots, you would be invited to attend
a barbecue in the public square, and *you* would be the barbecue. But today, it is apparent that the same force that answers
some prayers also causes it to rain anchovies and is behind
everything from sea serpents to flying saucers. It distorts
our reality whimsically, perhaps out of boredom, or perhaps
because it is a little crazy... God may be a crackpot."

-John A. Keel, *The Eighth Tower*, pp. 25-26

"A Ketchikan, Alaska woman, known to me personally,
recounted a frightening 1966 episode that occurred to her
and five friends, involving something that allegedly lifted
their car one night at a recreation spot:

> It was an August evening in 1966, and we were enjoying
> an evening at Ward Lake. There were three guys and three
> of us girls, and we were all around the car, a big old Ford
> Thunderbird. One of the girls heard some noise in the
> bush, and we all scrambled into the car. The guy who
> was driving started the engine but, before he could put
> it in gear, something picked up the whole rear end of the
> car off the ground. The driver gunned the engine, but
> the wheels were off the ground. We had to just sit there,
> wheels spinning in the air... Then, whatever it was that
> was holding us up started shaking the car from side to
> side, not letting it down at all. It was shaking like that for
> over a minute, then it just dropped us. The wheels spun
> on the gravel and we were out of there. Later, one of the
> girls said she had seen something large and brown stand-
> ing in the bush. We didn't go back there for a long time,
> and now all but one of [us] has moved away.

"In a most amazing follow-up report to the last, at exactly the same spot north of Ketchikan, but separated by eight years, Ms. L. W. of Ketchikan had the following report:

> In the first week of June 1974, I went with four classmates to Ward Lake… We had the car off; it was dark out, nice and quiet, and we were just talking. All of a sudden, we felt the back of the car start to bounce up and down. The boys took a look in the rearview mirror and called out, 'It's a *kushtakaa* – a [Sasquatch]!' The bouncing was rhythmic… The back end of the car was going up and down a foot or more. This went on for maybe two minutes, but it seemed like a lot longer. After it stopped, we just stayed in the car for a long time before we got out to take a look. Dan saw some dark hairs on the back of the car and brushed them off onto the ground, saying 'Aww, it was just a bear.' But, to me, the car felt like it was being lifted up each time, not like what you would expect a bear to do.

"One explanation of the two preceding reports is that the shaking of the vehicles may have been 'play behavior' of some sort by a male, perhaps adolescent, Sasquatch."

-J. Robert Alley, *Raincoast Sasquatch*, pp. 220-221

COLVIN, ANDY – GRASSY KNOLL RADIO INTERVIEW 37 – JAN. 2009

"Vyz" at *Beyond the Grassy Knoll* (GK): Welcome to another segment of *Beyond the Grassy Knoll*. With us is a frequent guest, Andrew Colvin, who is back in his old stomping grounds to do another remote broadcast. Andy, thanks for coming back. What's going on?

Andy Colvin (AC): Well, I'm traveling around Ohio with Dave Scott of Passing Lane Paranormal Investigations. We're looking at Indian mounds and haunted sites.

GK: Is there some interconnectivity between those?

AC: It seems like it. These are old sites that were chosen by those a little more "tuned in" to the spirit world. In some cases, animals were used to locate the sites. The priests would follow a blindfolded animal, like a cow or sheep, until it decided to lie down. By using them ritually for so long, these areas are a little more charged. Certain Ohio Indians, such as the Cole tribe, went so far as to place their dead in them. As a result, we see various hauntings and creature sightings in these same places. In England, a few stalwarts still do a ritual every year where they beat the mounds and barrows with reeds, in order to re-energize them. There was once a time when it was decreed by the Queen to do so, because it pleased God. Prior to that, the Celts are thought to have performed human sacrifices at such sites.

GK: The Shenandoah had burial grounds so charged up that tornadoes would pass through and not damage them. It's still the same today. Aren't mounds usually beside rivers?

AC: Most of them, but not all… And we still don't *really* know if these mounds are natural or manmade. Sometimes they involve burials, but not always. And just to make it more confusing, some birds are known to build mounds. Animal construction cannot be entirely ruled out, nor can construction by Mother Nature itself.

GK: Seminole Chief Osceola had his hideaway north of Tampa, at the cove of the Withlacoochee River. There are mounds there, too.

AC: It's incredible how many mounds are still here in Ohio. Thousands must have been torn down… We're trying to find out more about them. Dave knows a lot about the battles between the Indians and the whites. There is so much to learn about the Ohio Valley. Right now, we're focusing on the area around Cincinnati. Downtown Cincinnati was at one time covered with mounds. The Masons were attracted to this area. The military, the industrialists, and the KKK worked together here, probably even stimulated the Civil War from here. There is an amazing amount of wealth here still today. One of the wealthier parts of town, Indian Hill, has a road called "Spooky Hollow." It has a long history of hauntings. Sometimes witnesses will see a creature after their car has mysteriously died. Dave lost power to his car out there, as have several other people. A lot of these things involve cars or bikes… At Dead Man's Curve, in Amelia, Ohio, you can see a "ghost car" – a 1969 Road Runner. You can also see a faceless "shadow man" hitchhiking there, who may or may not jump on your car. Not to be outdone, at Pond's Run, near New Richmond, there is a "Hook Man" who may jump onto your car as well.

GK: Does any of this have to do with rural folk being more in touch with spirituality or magic?

AC: Probably, although *all* humans seem to have a need for the supernatural.

GK: Appalachians have their own vocabulary, which is very distinct from any other. Cincinnati has always struck me as being a southern city in a northern state. Is that true?

AC: Yes, it's a mix of things. You have an extremely conservative town, Cincinnati, right across the river from a corrupt and "sinful" town, Newport, KY. Cincinnati wants to have the image of being clean and upright. Therefore the secret, off-limits things – drugs, prostitution, and gambling – happen in Kentucky. We were just checking out Mount Adams, directly across the river from Newport, where wealthy Masons like Nicholas Longworth once lived. There are a couple of old Catholic churches there. Tunnels supposedly run underneath the whole place. There is an old monastery there, where they made wine in the old days. The monks made the wine. It was a German Catholic enclave. In WWII, some of the area's industrialists supported the Nazis… According to Dave, there are rumors in Cincinnati of the existence of several old crematoriums. In fact, Mount Adams had a major crematorium, which has now morphed into the famous pottery studio, The Rookwood. James Shelby Downard wrote about how the Freemasonic industrialists would get rid of their enemies in the kilns. There is also a haunted gazebo on Mt. Adams that is next to an underground water storage facility – what was once a natural spring. Such springs can facilitate hauntings… Speaking of German history, I was in Columbus the other day. Arnold Schwarzenegger has a big presence there. Schwarzenegger is friends with Les Wexner, the owner of Victoria's Secret and The Limited. A key Disney architect moved from Florida to Columbus to help the two build the Easton Mall outside of Columbus. The money is flowing in Ohio.

GK: The Knights of the Golden Circle, which predates the KKK and was key in fomenting the Civil War, called Cincinnati home.

AC: Yes, the Civil War was partly about staffing upcoming new factories with cheap labor. Speaking of franchising, I hear that General Motors now has plants in Russia, Argentina, Brazil, and China. These are all areas that the Rockefellers have been in for a long time. We now have GE, who once built aircraft engines themselves, buying planes from China! Capital investment has moved elsewhere. This trend leaves us with a huge economic problem that Obama will have to appear to try and clean up. And it is all a result of Big Oil moving everything overseas.

GK: You're right. This is one of those things that I thought about when

I was younger. It's one of those things that led me to where I am today, searching out conspiracy. This outsourcing started to take place heavily in the beginning of the 1970s, which bugged me. Why were U.S. companies sending the means of production overseas? They always ask for patriotism from us – from the people who go over and fight – but then these companies decide that they don't want to pay workers a decent wage. They go somewhere else for sweatshop labor. So where's *their* patriotism? This outsourcing has been going on for over 35 years. I'm not seeing the benefit in it for us.

AC: They've been doing it here, *within* the United States, for even longer. They were moving it around from state to state. They started off early in West Virginia, which was our first big oil state, along with Pennsylvania. Natural gas was first drilled in West Virginia, in downtown Charleston. This was a result of earlier technology perfected in the area's saltmines. The availability of salt, coal, and natural gas led to the building of all of these different chemical and manufacturing plants. Later, following the war and the labor battles of the 1960s, they simply moved that infrastructural style to the west and south. Finally, following Nixon and Reagan, the plants were simply shipped off to other countries.

GK: That's a really good point. Here you have an industry that was born in WV, OH, and PA but, today, you couldn't find an oil well there at all. It all moved south. That's why we refer to cities in those states (Pittsburgh, Buffalo, Youngstown, etc.) as "rustbelt cities." The companies picked up and moved.

AC: Very early, in the 1920s and '30s, they started making butadiene in Charleston. "Buna," as it typically called, is a synthetic rubber product that Standard Oil/Carbide shared with the Nazis during the war. I.G. Farben and Standard were sharing this product made near Institute, WV, at a Carbide plant that employed thousands of men. Just this week, I was poking around and saw that butadiene is used in C-4 explosive. With all of the terrorism going on today, you'd think that someone would ask the question, "Where are the 'terrorists' getting their C-4?" Well, they're getting it from these chemical companies! Conveniently, they're now making a lot of these explosive chemicals in China, which makes the subject almost impossible to research. They were undoubtedly making C-4 in the Kanawha Valley during the Mothman era. The Vietnam War was at its height. The C-4 threat might explain why my dad told me men were sneaking stuff out in their lunch pails – that there was talk about blowing up the plant. They may have been sneaking out ingredients for *homemade* C-4.

> *In a 2009 interview with* The Paranormal View, *Mothman author Jeff Wamsley stated that during the 1960s, security was so tight at the TNT Area that workers were driven to the plant from downtown Pt. Pleasant (only 6 miles away) in buses with blacked-out windows. While at the TNT Area in late 2008, I got a noticeable reading on my Geiger counter, indicating that Keel was right about atomic bomb parts being made there. Since I got the same readings in both Mound and Pt. Pleasant, one can make the assumption that radioactive materials may have been transported between them. Indrid Cold and Woody Derenberger, a "former" Carbide employee, may have been part of this shipping process. Tad Jones, another "former" Carbide employee, may have been involved as well, which would explain his "UFO sighting" near Institute. Given the Cold War nature of the times, Jones was, in all likelihood, intercepted and interrogated by agents of another agency or country. He could have been given screen memories of his UFO sighting. Or, he could have seen a real Hannabu or Vril saucer accidentally, thus becoming a security risk. He could have fled out of genuine fear, or he could have been reassigned to another location were he a DISC agent. Unfortunately, if we were able to locate Jones today and question him, he might not even remember the events, for he may have been given a posthypnotic "memory wipe."*

AC: Another theory I have is that Carbide may have been building UFOs in WV, due to the fact that there were only two Buna factories in existence then. According to several sources, the Buna plant in Nazi Germany was secretly building UFOs *and* refining uranium. The Carbide plant in Institute may have been doing the same things *after* the war. That would explain why the biggest UFO flap of history went on in WV and OH during the Mothman era. They could fly them out, test them and then, to boot, make any inconvenient witnesses believe that aliens had abducted them. Any radioactive materials involved would have certainly required extra security, such as provided by the Men in Black. If they were helping build UFOs at the TNT Area, it would explain a lot of things.

GK: I recently saw a movie based on the book *Rocket Boys* where, in the 1950s, some kids built rockets in WV. A couple of them went on to work at NASA.

AC: It makes you wonder if any West Virginians were working with Jack

Parsons, who developed rocket fuel. His discovery was based on bitumen, a sticky form of petroleum used in asphalt. The ancient Sumerians used bitumen as a mortar and for waterproofing, which means the Masons were involved. Parsons was an occultist in Crowley's O.T.O. One of Hitler's enemies, Rudolf Steiner, was head of the Austrian O.T.O. The organization must have been a hotbed of spy activity. Certain O.T.O. members were hanging around the Mothman scene in Pt. Pleasant. Also, Manson was a reputed O.T.O. member... The military is always tapping into West Virginia. There is a pipeline of sorts there; isolated, politically conservative towns feed their youth to the national security apparatus.

GK: I went to a social function recently. The family hosting it has a daughter who works in the White House. She is not part of any administration, but within a government agency. She gets sent out regularly to WV for seminars. West Virginia should put on its license plate: "West Virginia: A *Really* Interesting Place."

AC: Speaking of drilling, Big Oil would know more about building underground bunker facilities than anybody else; they understand geology. A geophysicist, Robert Denton, recently wrote to me about these bunkers. They are situated in certain rock formations so that they can't be spied upon. The rock shields from bombs and from electromagnetism. The facilities are built in shale, because the layers absorb impact. Interestingly, Denton wrote that as he got older, he learned that he had psychic powers. He found two different dinosaur sites using only his intuition. He says he just goes to prospective sites and *feels* it. When he is above a lot of dinosaur bones, he can sense them.

GK: What about bluestone or greenstone for these bunkers? There is such a site near Harper's Ferry, where John Wilkes Booth lived. There is also "Site R" near Waynesboro, PA. Things *do* point to Big Oil as a private source for the construction of these sites. And we have probable connections between Booth and Rockefeller.

AC: Here is a random point of which I was recently reminded... John Keel stated that the Men in Black wore both Naval and Air Force insignia; this jibes with what Harriet was saying. She remembers that an officer with those two insignia came to our grade school... Other randomness... On the *Thom Hartmann Show*, Thom said that there have only been two previous times when a real middle class existed in Europe; each time, it was destroyed. One was prior to the Black Death, which was perhaps planned. The other was after the big

Gold Rush of the 1600s, when Europeans came over and took all of the gold from South America. Thom also had a guest on who has written a book about Big Oil. She is saying that Standard Oil has now been reconstituted. Standard is like the morphing assassin robot from *Terminator 3*, which oozes itself back together. The way Big Oil did this was by getting the government to change how they define "antitrust." Originally, antitrust had to do with the *size* of companies. What they managed to do was place the focus on *price* instead. It then became about making sure no one was price fixing, which wasn't the original intent of antitrust. The mergers started in 2000… Before that, during the 1980s and 1990s, oil companies focused on raising gas prices via refinery tinkering. In 2000, they went back to an emphasis on tinkering with crude oil – the *shipment* of oil, rather than the refining of oil. In 2000, they also increased their lobbying. They got Phil Gramm to slip the Commodities Futures Act in, which allowed Enron to do its thing. Henceforth, all of these oil exchanges have *not* been regulated by the government. This has led to false scarcities not only in oil, but in gas and electricity as well. Today, more than half of our oil trades are not regulated at *all*. They are traded under something called ICE, which started in 2006. It's a new and unregulated market for oil. What is the author predicting for the future? She is saying that even though BP has all of these "green" ads, they only spend 4% on green technology. As one might expect, Exxon/Mobil – the Rockefellers – spend close to 0%. They spend less than half a percent on green technology.

According to Hartmann, it was Bill Clinton who rescinded the "Bucket Shop Law" originally passed in 1908. This law wisely disallowed the reselling of stocks as "options" or "derivatives" because imaginary stocks create economic bubbles. Huge tax cuts to the rich only stimulate bubble activity, because they simply put their extra money into risky investments.

AC: Another little theory… You know the debate over whether Christ was black or white? I think there may be the same thing happening with the Men in Black. Most of the Men in Black originally seemed to be Asian, Eskimo, or Tibetan but, in today's media depictions, they are made to seem white. The Asian MIBs may actually have been warning ufologists off of UFOs for their own good. It could be that some other, less benign, organization was surveilling the ufologists as well. The weird things that MIBs did to people are never fully analyzed. When an MIB does or says something very strange to a witness, it could be a form of hypnotic induction. In other words, they were committing an odd or confusing act in order to create momentary confusion in the target. This makes it easier for them to be hypnotized. This might explain why many of the MIBs said and did things that made no sense. Here's another random note… According to Bruce Adamson, the JFK researcher, the Bush family is associated with Standard Oil of California. Adamson has also said that Henry Lucas, the serial killer, is rumored to have once worked for Bush, Sr.

GK *[sarcastically]*: Well, Lucas *is* a serial killer; *that's* the evidence of his association!

AC: Speaking of the Rockefellers, there was a lady on the radio here in Seattle, on KBCS, who just got back from living in Africa. She was saying that the Rockefellers and Bill Gates have gotten together. They're trying to genetically modify sorghum in Kenya on behalf of Dupont. Remember, Dupont operated the TNT area where Mothman was seen – another indirect link between the Rockefellers and Dupont. I think the Ghost Box mentioned Microsoft, too, when we were asking about all of this… We also have an old connection here between the DuPonts and George Washington. Washington hobnobbed with the DuPonts and owned most of the land between Charleston and Point Pleasant. He may have sold them the TNT Area. Another Indrid Cold point… The swarthy Indrid Cold told contactee Woody Derenberger that he was from "Genemedes." This is similar to what a lot of South American contactees were told, except that the spelling was slightly different: "Ganymedes." The misspelling could easily be due to the language difference. The important thing here is that we have similar "alien" phrases being used in both the Ohio Valley and in South America.

This tells us that in addition to shuttling between WV, OH, and NY, Indrid probably traveled down to S. America, where he told contactees that he was from "Ganymedes." This bolsters my theory that Woody was taken to South America and told it was "Lanulos." Since there is an alternate theory that the Nazi UFO factory was moved to South America, it could be that the saucer operation was a joint venture. Perhaps certain parts for the South American UFOs had to be made in the Kanawha Valley, due to Carbide's expertise with rare earth elements. The Blaine Island plant was at that time known as the world's leading handler of rare elements.

AC: Interestingly, there was a guy named Sixto Paz Wells, who claimed to have met an Asian-looking Man in Black from "Ganymede." In

Greek mythology, the shepherd boy Ganymede rides Zeus' bird, Aquila, to the heavens bearing a cup of ambrosia – very similar to the Garuda and Dorje Shugden. The fact that contactees in both WV and South America were told the same story is very provocative… But this lady on KBCS, who had gone to Africa, was also talking about the WTO protests as being mostly about putting the brakes on the patenting of plants. Prior to the WTO, you could only patent microorganisms, not plants. At that 1999 WTO meeting, they were discussing whether or not to patent the plants *themselves*. Hence, we had the big protest. I've always felt that the strength of that protest sent shivers up the back of the elites. But they were prepared. The military had been planning its Millennium Games for ten years, where they envisioned an invasion of Iraq. In order to get the invasion going, they had to have a "New Pearl Harbor." Exxon-Mobil's 75-yr. lease on oil in the region expired in 2000, so something had to be done… One more random note on George Noory… Noory is ex-Naval intelligence. He had Al Bielek on in early Jan. of 2009. Al claims that he is a "time traveler" from the Philadelphia Experiment. His story has long seemed bogus. However, Noory, to this day, totally butters up Bielek. I was wondering about this. Why is the Navy supporting this unbelievable story that more or less discredits the reality of the Philadelphia Experiment? Bielek describes the known facts of the experiment itself fairly scientifically – that they were doing experiments with invisibility, bombarding a ship with degaussing waves, etc. However, he *also* introduces this phony "time travel" story, which totally discredits all of the science. This is probably why Noory has Bielek on so much: to discredit the scientific, *real* part of the Philadelphia Experiment story… There is also *another* time traveler on Noory's show, John Titor, who is reportedly backed by the notorious Joseph Matheny. These guys get a *lot* of press. Fake stories get tons of press, and everybody is always talking about them. "Titor" recently posted a link to a Spanish-speaking paranormal show called *Quatro,* where they were hyping his research. An image of a hooded figure with a satchel was shown on the show. A UFO witness supposedly saw this floating Jesuit monk. *[laughs]* I'd say that being abducted by a Jesuit monk is a lot more plausible than being abducted by an alien, wouldn't you? The Jesuit monk image looks very similar to a photo that I took, in 1979, of a shadowy figure in a crop circle. It appears in my first book. Could this be the *third* instance of hoax photography being used to discredit my research? I don't know, but Titor *is* known for posting material favorable to Loren Coleman. Mr. Coleman was involved in that hoaxed "Mothman" photo a few years back – the one that won his *Bigfoot* photo contest. That image seemed to copy my sister's 1973 "Kitchen Garuda" photo. Coleman and Noory seem to share the point of view that Mothman is demonic. Noory regularly calls Mothman a "demon." However, Coleman, the supposed scientist, never bothers to correct him. It doesn't seem very scientific.

GK: Noory is on *Coast to Coast* for a reason. I contend that anyone who comes on that show isn't shooting straight. Noory is a shill. Art Bell was a shill. They are there to poke holes in anything that has any degree of truth. Poking holes is standard operating procedure for mainstream media. I would consider *Coast to Coast* to be somewhat mainstream, except that they throw in the Shadow People and the flying rods and all that… Also, I was saying the same thing back about Standard Oil back in 1999, as I started to see the re-monopolization of the oil industry. It was astute of you to say that.

AC: Thomas Jefferson mentioned that he thought the Episcopalians would be the most likely religion to exploit freedom of religion. It turns out that Episcopalianism, according to Harriet, is the CIA's preferred religion.

GK: They are what I would call "protestantized Catholicism." They are a very interesting group. They're supposed to be Protestant, but their trappings are all Catholic.

AC: There are generally two ways of looking at the world. You can look at the world as "unified" or you can look at it as "fragmented" – where people and things are separate. Those are the Eastern and Western ways of looking at things, respectively. The Eastern belief is that unity underlies everything. What the corporatists do is play those two ideas off of each other. Whenever it's time to tighten the belts, which is what Obama is going to be doing here any minute, we're all told to think of things as if they are unified; we have to come together and sacrifice. However, when profits are high, well then, the CEOs get to make $10,000 more per hour than you do. They don't want to be united with you at all during the good times. We are made to bounce between these and other polarities all the time.

GK: That's right…

AC: The Pope was in the country recently, apologizing for pedophilia. Coincidentally, at the same time, a Mormon "polygamist ranch" got busted over charges of pedophilia. To make sure everyone watched, the State of Texas, which is normally not so conscientious when it comes to social services, took the kids away. Unfortunately, the whole thing was based on a covert op. The media called it a "hoax," and no one looked any further. What happened is that someone named Rozita Swinton, a "childless" woman, impersonated "Sarah" and "Laura, " two (fictitious) girls who were supposedly living at the compound. This "hoaxer" got the state of Texas to investigate the cult! The case against the cult was dropped after the Pope left town. Swinton is probably a Catholic. She made sure that a Mormon cult took the heat off of the Pope. Could this actually signal a behind-the-scenes alliance between the two religions? I'm sure the Pope is grateful.

GK: Yes. Several cases of pedophilia happened under the aegis of Pope Ratzinger. One was in Texas, in fact.

AC: Speaking of Mormon polygamists, a group of Mormon polygamists formed, in 1932, something called the Council of Friends. They are still around. They have 7 high priests who, I suppose, rule on matters of polygamy. They sort of remind me of the Council of Nine. Speaking of being underage… Puharich, a big proponent of the Council of Nine, was rumored to have been at a party held by Jim Moseley in NYC during the Mothman era. Moseley was Gray Barker's best friend. Here you have a connection between Puharich, who lived near NYC, and the Mothman events in WV.

GK: Puharich is one of those guys that reminds me of the song "You're So Vain." He is where he should be all of the time.

In Feb. of 2010, singer Carly Simon finally revealed who the song "You're So Vain" was about. It was about producer David Geffen, who has been accused by Seattle conspiracy theorist Richard Lee of benefiting from the death of Kurt Cobain. Supposedly, Geffen took out an insurance policy on Cobain's life that paid off even if Cobain committed suicide. Since Cobain was about to leave the band and nullify his contract with Geffen, the "suicide" needed to happen sooner rather than later.

AC: You know who else is like that? Charlie Manson. I'm finding all of these legends about Manson in Cincinnati, that he was seen here or did rituals there. There is even a rumor that he hung at this local paranormal spot called Buffalo Ridge. Manson was born in Cincinnati. It seems that people there want to be associated with him. He bucks the system and "tells it like it is," which is something that hillfolk may secretly admire. Through Manson, various poor, disgruntled Appalachians get to vicariously experience "talking back" to their social "betters." If you see a movie like *Sicko*, which I just saw recently, you see how much better other societies are run. European rulers *allow* people to protest for better healthcare. The government helps them out when they have kids. There are free nannies in France. There is free healthcare in Cuba, for Christ's sake! By the way, Obama is supposedly signing off on the "closing" of Guantanamo today.

GK: Supposedly, they're closing down Gitmo, the "terrorist" prison. Gitmo is inside Guantanamo. That's another interesting thing… If the U.S. and Cuba are such adversaries, why does Cuba allow the U.S. to hold onto a patch of their land?

AC: Another movie I just saw was *The Dark Knight*, a Batman film. Just as the movie ended, I thought, "Batman is Mothman." He's a protector, like Batman. But Batman is often misconstrued in Gotham as being a criminal. Few can see that Batman is good, just as few can see that Mothman is good. These dark heroes are scary but, ultimately, they do work in our best interests. In one of the scenes in that movie, some guy has an implant in his stomach; it's a cellphone bomb. This guy's stomach explodes and destroys the police station. Synchronistically, right before I saw the movie, I was leafing through some files. I was reminded that one of the contactees I interviewed claimed he has an implant in his abdomen. He claims it was implanted there by the aliens.

GK: Of all the heroes, I like Batman the best. This goes back to when I was 5 years old. Batman seemed to be the most human; he couldn't fly. As the movies continue, he gets a little bit more power, whether it's manufactured or technological. He now seems to be less and less like the original Batman, and more like a Superman type of character. It also has gotten much more dark. It is morphing more towards Mothman. As it is being portrayed now, Batman is perhaps more Mothmanlike. He is still on the side of right, but perhaps taking on a darker connotation.

AC: I found a quote from a CIA chief about an operation in South America that had been exposed. The chief said, "Well, let's just put some UFO stories out in the media to cover it up." This was in the 1950s; they've been doing this stuff a *long* time. Like this "blue orb" that was videotaped at a Cleveland gas station… It got big play. Coincidentally, the Cleveland Ufology Project meets just a couple of blocks away. CUP is one of the oldest UFO groups in the country. They used to have big conventions there. During the Mothman era, they hosted a convention that Gray Barker attended. On the way back, he was trailed by a "Catholic priest" – probably a Wandering Bishop. This gas station is at 11000 Pleasant Valley Road in the suburb of Parma. The name "Pleasant" and the number 11 are always showing up. Some other "name game" items… The word "myrrh" is found in the song "We Three Kings of Orient Are…" The three wise men followed a star. Myrrh is associated with death and also with "Moor," which relates to "mortuary," "mourn," and "mortal." The similarly sounding "mer" prefix relates to water. The "mermaid" will lure you to your death. Water, death, the unconscious, the Void… The Moors have been associated with water and strange funerary practices throughout history.

GK: Don't forget one other "moor" word: "mortgage." You pay until your death.

AC: Our mercantile system was developed through contact with the Moors. The first credit cards were used by the Knights Templar.

GK: Usury is what it's all about.

AC: Another random note on Magnetic Peak in Hawaii… We went to film there in 2004 because of the black panther sightings… When I was there, I kept joking about an "underwater black panther" that might come out of the water. It was a total joke. I had no basis for it whatsoever. However, since then, I've found two or three references to an actual belief in an "underwater jaguar." The underwater panther is considered to be supernatural. There was actually a sighting of it not too long ago. Some people saw it running across the water. Anyway, Magnetic Peak not only has black panthers, but it has the biggest digital camera in the world. It has NSA, NASA, and SAIC facilities on top of it. Using this large digital camera, they are supposedly looking for asteroids coming our way. It makes you wonder if we will have a fake asteroid scare. They seem to be leading up to *something*. It's either going to be a fake return of Christ, a fake asteroid coming down, or fake aliens invading. Or, I suppose, global warming, which could bring the world together in a world government. The finance system is already set up, through the International Bank of Settlements. If they happen to do the asteroid scam, it would probably involve Magnetic Peak, where compasses go haywire and creature entities are seen.

GK: Don't worry, Bruce Willis can stop *any* asteroid.

AC: I saw an *X-Men* cartoon recently. In the episode, a new, impervious metal coating is developed by mutants in the Tri-State area near Point Pleasant. They actually show a map of the WV/OH/KY border area in the cartoon – the same area where the "plane" that hit the Pentagon first disappeared from radar. This is an older cartoon, from the 1980s. Twenty years ago, somewhere in NYC or Hollywood, cartoonists knew that Mothman country was where secret technology was developed. The word must have leaked out. Perhaps they read Keel's book.

GK: I doubt that Pt. Pleasant was a *wild* guess…

AC: Interestingly, the mutants use this metal to attack the X-Men's compound, which is shown to be near Iron Mountain, NY. They put up a map of that as well.

GK: Really? Man, that is interesting…

AC: Let's talk a bit about Ashland, KY, which is near Point Pleasant. Marathon Oil has a major facility in Ashland. Marathon seems to show up at every strange site I visit. In fact, that blue orb on Pleasant Valley Road in Cleveland was seen at a Marathon station. And yesterday, Dave and I noticed that there is a Marathon station in Amelia across from where the "faceless shadow person" is seen, near an Indian mound. Marathon was originally a division of Standard Oil. The City of Ashland also hosts AK Steel, which used to be Armco Steel. AK has its headquarters in northern Cincinnati. Marathon, AK, and Solvay are, along with Ashland Oil, big players in the Tri-State area.

I once saw Jay Rockefeller on the Marshall campus in Huntington, which is very close to Ashland. I went up to him and said, "I'm the guy who used to make all those prank phone calls to you right after you were elected Governor." Unbelievably, he barked out something like, "I could have had you taken away for that, you know!" At the time, I didn't think he was being serious; he simply seemed to be joking. In retrospect, however, I'm not so sure. He probably was telling the truth in the form of joke. Jay always had a sense of humor about being pranked. He would always say something thought-provoking before he hung up… Given that he most certainly could have had me "taken away" (to Lanulos?), his patience and restraint must be applauded. Realistically, given his wealth and stature, he probably had some early form of caller ID, and thus knew, from the beginning, exactly who was pranking him. Could he have possibly had mercy on me because he knew what had happened to my father?

AC: Reportedly, the Nazis in the Vril and Thule societies worshipped the Black Sun. The SS logo refers to the "Schwarze Sonne," which can be interpreted as "Black Sun" or "Black Son." If the Nazis did worship this Black Son, it would not necessarily be out of line with Christianity, because Jesus was a "Black Son," crucified during an eclipse of the sun. The Vatican and the Nazis got along pretty well. Did the Nazis discover a Moorish underpinning to civilization? Europeans do seem to have migrated out of Northern Africa, although Africans may have migrated out of central Asia in the very beginning. Due to all of their eugenics research, the inner circle of Nazism may have come to realize that we are all descended from non-whites. That may be why they worked so hard at propagating falsehoods in the opposite direction. While they were preaching white superiority, they were secretly worshipping the Black Son of the Black Virgin, the creative force at the center of the earth.

GK: Yes, the Black Madonna...

AC: Out of the earth comes the Virgin Mary. The early church was very concerned with geographic location when choosing sacred sites; grids were located and consulted. Their early measurements, such as the rod and the mile, were based on knowledge of the exact size of the entire globe – an organized plan that involved advanced mathematics. I am reminded of the theory that the Catholics wanted to have a competing religion, Islam, in order to raise funds. The DoD does the same thing today with "terrorists." To get people to donate more of their hard-earned tax dollars, you have to have an active, outside threat.

> *According to naturalist Lyall Watson in his book* Dark Nature, *after years of observing the workings of nature, he finally isolated three mindsets common to both animals and humans. The first, "keeping outsiders out" is fairly straightforward and understandable, as long as it doesn't unduly isolate the community. The second one, "protecting the insiders," is also understandable, at least until you are on the "outs" with someone. The third category that Watson discovered was "cheat whenever possible," which is something that we don't normally admit to. While a very simple list, it does explain a lot about human nature. Our behavior isn't always human; much of the time, it is "animal."*

GK: This will enrage half of the world but, yes, it would seem that the papacy definitely abetted Islam. The Pope said, "Do what you want, but don't harm the head of a Catholic." There eventually came a time, in the 16th century, where the papacy got a little concerned about the spread of Islam. Hence, you had the war that culminated in the Battle of Le Ponto, a major sea battle where the Ottoman Empire's extension was defeated. But, yes, just the name of Muhammed's daughter, Fatima, shows us that there is a close connection between the two faiths. Researchers have shown that there are symbolic connections between Romanism and Islam.

AC: I was in downtown Cincinnati yesterday. Right across from the City Hall, there is a large synagogue that looks very mosquelike.

GK: These are people from the same region; their similarities should *not* be overlooked... We should get Dave Scott on the line... Dave are you there?

Dave Scott (DS): Yes.

GK: Thanks for being on. Tell us about your paranormal investigations.

DS: I started off just ghosthunting. Then, I realized that there were many urban legends in Cincinnati. Over the years people have added to these, so that there are now literally dozens of urban legends regarding ghostly sightings. I decided to focus on the various ghosts seen at haunted bridges and intersections in Ohio, Indiana, and KY. I'm in the tri-state area, just a few miles from the border. I try to dig up the facts so that I can decipher what is really behind the legends. It has been a lot of fun. I've been doing it for a few years now, so I have covered a lot of ground. I've found that a lot of these legends don't have beginnings. You *can't* find the source... There is one road, Buffalo Ridge, with many legends connected to it. Supposedly, people have had white *or* black vans chase them from the area. There were rumors of an old crematorium in the woods behind Buffalo Ridge. I found out that it was actually an observatory built in about 1930. They never finished it, due to the Depression. Since they never finished it, over the years people have wondered what it was, which fueled a buildup of rumors around it. People think Satanists have used the area for rites and things like that. There are rumors of ghostly cars seen along the road, some carrying ghost grooms and headless brides. You name it, and Buffalo Ridge seems to have it. It's also the playground of Charlie Manson. They say that he used to play there as a kid.

GK: Are these based on real homicides or just tragic, accidental deaths?

DS: There *have* been some deaths on Buffalo Ridge, but it's mostly from joyriding kids. They do what is called "ridge hopping." Buffalo

Ridge is like a roller coaster. Kids will go flying up and down the road, hopping these ridges. Occasionally, one of them will go off course and hit a tree.

GK: I'm wondering if paranormal situations don't arise from tragic events.

DS: It could be that the legends grow out of the deaths... By the way, Andy wanted me to tell you about my sister's home... Last September, she was sitting on her front porch and saw this form come down out of the sky. It covered the area in front of the house and across the street. It swooped down, totally blocking the view. Then, it returned to the sky. It was a black shadowy form. It was followed by three others. She didn't know what it was, but she said the first thing she thought of was Mothman.

GK: Pretty cool. Reminds me of *Night of the Living Dead*...

Synchronistically, Vyz chose to mention a film whose art director, Tom Savini, also worked on one of the commercial films I worked on: The Texas Chainsaw Massacre II. *In addition to creating the zombies for* Night of the Living Dead, *Savini helped Lee Daniel and I secure extra equipment for early segments of the film* Slacker.

DS: My sister's house is haunted; I can tell you that much. I've been over there many times setting up monitors in the basement. So much has happened. Her niece's little girl saw this thing on the monitor one time. She said, "Look, Mom! There's a skeleton!" They looked at the monitor and, indeed, it looked like a solid human being was coming up the steps. It was sort of frozen in place, holding onto the rail. My sister went down and looked, but there wasn't an actual person there. This image just froze on the monitor... They've gotten a lot of strange EVPs. They've heard their cupboards opening and closing at night... Other people in the neighborhood have reported strange happenings in their houses, too. The next-door neighbor has admitted to seeing things. The whole neighborhood seems affected...

GK: Andy and I talked about one of his properties in Seattle, where strange occurrences seem linked to earlier disturbances. Is there any history in your area, whether it's a burial ground or an event, that would lead you to think that what's going on now is based on something that took place a long time ago?

DS: I've dug into the history of the neighborhood and really can't find anything. It was settled in the 1800s, so the official history is not that old. I don't believe there were any Indian settlements or mounds in my immediate neighborhood. It isn't close to any bodies of water. I haven't really found any reason for the place to be spiritually charged.

GK: Could it be the result of experimentation by the government?

DS: Now that I don't know... Police helicopters fly over every weekend, but I think that has more to do with drugs than the paranormal.

AC: About Dave's sister's place... One of the things that happened there was that *all* of the windows blew out of the next-door neighbor's house, unexpectedly, for no reason. Believe it or not, a mini-version of this happened in front of my house in Leschi. A friend of mine, a local Bigfoot hunter, came over to visit. After he came in, his car windows blew out for no reason! We never did figure that one out... With Dave's family, I think the point is that the phenomenon follows them. It seems to follow not only her, but also her husband. Tony was telling me that he had some things happen in his grandparents' house. After the grandparents died, he heard violin and flute music playing. It was a replay of what he had done there as a boy. Tony seemed to think that the phenomenon was activated *before* they got to their current house. In an earlier apartment they shared, the gas burners would go off and on by themselves. Dave showed me a film that he shot in his sister's previous apartment. He captured, on tape, the image of a ghost girl. It is as clear as a bell. You can see her face. It is rare to see a good, authentic shot of a ghost. Dave has all kinds of gadgets. His dream is to build a car that is immune to any kind of EMFs, including energy emanating from creatures, ghosts, and UFOs. Dave and his sister have gotten some weird phone calls along the lines of those John Keel once received. They have taped what they think are ghosts talking to them on the phone.

GK: Is there something about females that makes them more inclined to be visited?

AC: Not according to Keel... He found that ex-Catholic men were the most likely to have a paranormal experience, followed by menstruating teachers of gifted children who drive Ford Galaxies.

GK: Ha! I love it. But aren't there more female "sensitives" than men?

AC: Actually, no... Men have been found in lab experiments to be slightly more psychic.

GK: Wow. Okay.

AC: I think men "hide their light under a bushel" in this regard. Women probably advertise their experiences a little more. Buddhists say that women are typically more grounded in practical reality, due to their roles as mothers. The mating process produces material results. Due to the sobering responsibility of being a mother, women tend to be more grounded in certain ways. Birth is the most basic process that has to happen for life to continue. In Buddhism, men are seen as air creatures – less grounded. However, in this day and age, the roles have been tinkered with, so it's hard to say.

GK: It's not far-flung at all to say that men are air creatures. Think about pollination among plants; the female is more stationary. Pollen – impregnating material – blows through the air… Alright… I just got an email from John Valentini, asking you to revisit your 9/11 prophecy experience.

AC: There's not a whole lot to say about it other than, in 1967, I had a friend say that Mothman told him to stand in a certain spot in order to see the future. He stood in that spot and saw an event that looked a lot like an attack on NYC in 2001, the beginning of WWIII. When I stood in the spot with him, I saw it, too. We weren't friends much longer after that; it was too freaky. The Towers were being built at that time, but I don't think we were aware of it.

GK: They began designing it in 1962. I'll just say this: my high school was on the Palisades, right across from Manhattan. I know that in the fall of 1966, the Towers were being built.

The groundbreaking for construction of the WTC occurred on Aug. 5th, 1966, just two months before the beginning of the Mothman era. However, there was one lone sighting of Mothman in Pt. Pleasant in 1961, just prior to the beginning of the WTC design phase. The first public notifications about the WTC project were actually put forth in 1961. Could the 1961 sighting of Mothman have some symbolic relationship with the initial decision and/or announcement to build the Towers? Had someone already decided, in 1961, to take the towers down in 2001, and had Mothman picked up on that fact?

AC: My friend, Tommy, was saying that Mothman, who was in league with the aliens, was somehow sending messages from the future. He claimed a flying saucer had landed in his yard. I had a sleepover there once that was seemingly interrupted by small, furry creatures – the "little people" described by Indians and Irishmen. Tommy spoke of Mothman and these little aliens together, as if they were buddies.

GK: Would Mothman necessarily be involved with aliens?

AC: All I know is that he spoke of them in the same breath. If this were a semi-hallucinatory process, such confusion would make sense. He said that they had foretold what was going to happen to him in his adult life. He claimed that Mothman liked the trees outside of his window. I went back there last October and stood in the same spot. I didn't get the feeling that any "portal" was active at that time. One cannot see into the future on demand.

GK: Do you think it was a portal at a particular time – *that* time only?

AC: It may open and close, and it may move around. Magnetic fields vary wildly. In 2002, there certainly was *something* going on there that went beyond space and time. It may take two or three people to activate it. When Harriet and Sharon and I were there, we definitely felt it. I sensed something about a drowning, which led us to find out that one of the renters of Harriet's old house had drowned. Then, three days after our visit to the portal, there was *another* drowning in the river, at the same spot as the renter's drowning.

GK: Do you remember the photo that came out right after 9/11, which showed a winged creature east of the Towers? It looks like Mothman.

AC: If it's a hoax, it could be meant to discredit the idea that people received prophecies from Mothman about 9/11. Still, in another way, it keeps the idea alive. You mentioned the Palisades a minute ago… There is a place in Seattle, next to the Space Needle, called "The Palisades." The Palisades are decorative arches at the Pacific Science Center. They were designed by the same architect who designed the Twin Towers, Minoru Yamasaki. Minoru was from Seattle. He designed the Pacific Science Center for the World's Fair in Seattle in 1962. It has a treatment reminiscent of the Twin Towers. It was at the Pacific Science Center, facing the Palisades court, where I saw this display on the history of the cellphone – how they developed the cellphone using inverted opals. When you invert the vowels in "opal," you get "Apol," the name of Keel's prophetic MIB. I started researching cellphones and found that they were developed in Cleveland by scientists at AT&T. The technology was held back for many decades by the Rockefellers, for monetary reasons. There was a conspiracy to keep cellphone technology secret. I know a witness who saw certain industrialists here in Cincinnati using cellphones in the 1960s. I think there was a secret distribution of cellphones, way before the rest of us got them. This would account for how the MIBs were able to follow Keel around and harass him. The cellphone was originally a military radio, which points to military-industrial conspirators with access to satellites. Either Keel used a codeword (Apol) that pointed in the direction of those he felt responsible, or else the perp was playing a Masonic type of name game by calling himself "Apol." Either way, they were deploying satellites during Mothman. Maybe they needed to test how the new phones worked with the new satellites.

Synchronistically, as I was editing this section during the second week of Feb. 2009, The Stranger, *a Seattle weekly magazine, had a 1960s photo of the Palisades on their cover. This was the issue about the historic Obama inauguration. That same week, on the 11th, there was a high-profile collision of two satellites, one "private" and one "Russian." The private satellite was owned by Iridium, which has links to Alcatel-Lucent, Europe's biggest satellite maker. The Lucent half of Alcatel-Lucent was a spin-off of the Rockefeller's AT&T and Bell Labs. Iridium has a murky financial past. After it went bankrupt following an initial investment of billions, Iridium was bought for a mere $25 million. Today, the Iridium system is heavily used by the Dept. of Defense and has links to Lockheed-Martin. The number of the Iridium satellite that was destroyed was "33..." That same week in Feb., Microsoft offered a $250,000 reward for the creator of the nasty computer worm called "Downadup." At the time, Microsoft was involved in a nasty lawsuit with Alcatel-Lucent and was ordered to pay them $512 million. On Feb. 12th, Darwin's birthday, it was reported that the Vatican supported Darwin's theory of evolution. In fact, the church claimed one of its priests was the actual originator of the theory. All of these stories seemed to distract from a yet bigger story, which was that policy makers had agreed to ram the remainder of a $789 billion bank bailout through Congress. Ironically, at the same time, big bankers were testifying on Capital Hill regarding what happened to the first $200 billion of that package, which had gone missing after being distributed to them.*

AC: Did you ever find out who supplied the steel for the Towers?

GK: Yes, but it wasn't Buckeye Steel. According to the book *City in the Sky: The Rise and Fall of the Trade Center* by James Glance and Eric Lipton, both of whom are reporters for *The New York Times*, the entire nation was mobilized to build the World Trade Center. There were a lot of hands in the pie. We've heard theories about the Towers. One theory that aired on my show was from an architectural photographer. I've not heard from him in some time. He supposedly was privy to the fact that the Towers were having problems, due to their size and constant resistance to wind currents. The buildings were "levering" somewhere around the 11ᵗʰ floor… It was David Rockefeller's wish that they went up; I'm sure it was his wish that they went down. The Towers were not the victims of 19 Arab hijackers.

AC: If someone had previously added bracing to deal with the levering, that would explain the need for extra bombs near the bottom of the building. A bunch of them went off right after the planes hit.

GK: Yes, you had to knock it off its foundation.

AC: They needed to get it cleaned up as fast as possible, before the nation could ask questions. They wanted to cart the stuff off to China, pronto. The bombs in the basement give away the whole scam, in addition to the fiery squibs going off on each floor. You can see them going off in the videos. But people were sent to the hospital by these basement bombs. These people were interviewed; they have gone on record.

GK: Philip Morelli is a WTC construction worker who gave a clear description to network television about what happened – that he was blown about the below-ground shanty where they dressed for the day's work. He heard a number of explosions simultaneous to the first hit. One of them sent him from one side of the room to the other. Blowing the bases of the Towers is important if you want the whole thing to come down in one spot.

AC: The unusual thing is that they imploded it from the top down. What I don't understand is that if you're going to blow it up from the top down, why not just stop at the 11ᵗʰ or 12ᵗʰ floor and not worry about the bottom?

GK: I think the reason why the whole thing had to be decimated, including floors 11 and below, is that they were trying to sell the idea that the whole building melted – that it was the result of fire. They could not leave anything standing, otherwise people would ask, "Why didn't this melt? This doesn't look like the result of something being melted." But the cleanup personnel knew that it didn't melt. The whole nation saw those cutter charges go off, which is why you'll never see that kind of video again.

AC: It gets back to how Rockefeller companies control so many of these processes. They finance and manufacture so many things. They planned and financed the Towers. They controlled the steel that went into the Towers. Through their Chinese subsidiaries, they control the C-4, or thermite, that brings things down. It's a sealed system of construction and destruction. The manufacture and movement of C-4 is heavily controlled and regulated. The chemical companies make the product under military contract; you can't get it unless you're totally locked into the distribution system. Several military intelligence agencies are regulating its manufacture and shipment yet, somehow, it gets into the hands of terrorists.

GK: The taking down of the WTC could have been overseen by a cabal, without a doubt. You're right. It is a closed system. They could have seen it from beginning to end. No doubt about it.

"Standard Oil Co. 1940"
By Pablo Neruda

When the drill bored down toward the stony fissures
and plunged its implacable intestine
into the subterranean estates,
and dead years, eyes of the ages,
imprisoned plants' roots
and scaly systems became strata of water,
fire shot up through the tubes
transformed into cold liquid,
in the customs house of the heights,
issuing from its world of sinister depth,
it encountered a pale engineer
and a title deed.

However entangled the petroleum's arteries may be,
however the layers may change their silent site
and move their sovereignty amid the earth's bowels,
when the fountain gushes its paraffin foliage,
Standard Oil arrived beforehand
with its checks and it guns,
with its governments and its prisoners.
Their obese emperors from New York
are suave smiling assassins
who buy silk, nylon, cigars
petty tyrants and dictators.

They buy countries, people, seas, police, county
    councils,
distant regions where the poor hoard their corn
like misers their gold:
Standard Oil awakens them,
clothes them in uniforms, designates
which brother is the enemy.
the Paraguayan fights its war,
and the Bolivian wastes away
in the jungle with its machine gun.

A President assassinated for a drop of petroleum,
a million-acre mortgage,
a swift execution on a morning mortal with light,
 petrified,
a new prison camp for subversives,
In Patagonia, a betrayal, scattered shots
beneath a petroliferous moon,
a subtle change of ministers
in the capital, a whisper
like an oil tide,
and zap, you'll see
how Standard Oil's letters shine above the clouds,
above the seas, in your home,
illuminating their dominions.

AFTERWORD

I first met Andy Colvin on the *Radio Misterioso* show in 2010. I had heard from Greg Bishop about Andy's fairly extensive work on the Mothman events centered around Pt. Pleasant, West Virginia. Having spent my early childhood in nearby Mineral Wells, WV during some of the actual events, and having returned there for a couple of years in the mid-1970s, I was quite intrigued.

For me, the Mothman saga mostly means Indrid Cold. In the decade following the Mothman events, Indrid Cold was very much a bogeyman used by the adults to keep the kids coming home by sundown. When I was young, I never wanted to be caught in the woods after dark. The ever-present shadow of Indrid Cold stood over our neighborhood, which was within visual distance of the spot Woody Derenberger first encountered the strange man from "Lanulos." I recall my dad and the other adults speaking of Woody in amused terms, yet the conversation always seemed to meander into a strange place, primarily a mood of silent regard for things indescribable. This, of course, made it all the more memorable to my imaginative young mind.

"Mister Cold," as the elder adults referred to him in hushed tones, was more than mysterious. He was an outline, a shadow – a murky figure who, if not a monster, certainly did not belong here. Indrid Cold was the only figure of terror that also fascinated me, as there was no real description of him. The idea of being taken to Lanulos wasn't so bad, either, as it was a place where people lived naked, including women – a good selling-point for a teenage boy. Lanulos sounded tropical and hot, but it was most certainly not the fiery pit of Hell... What was spooky about Mister Cold was the fear we children had of being abducted by him. Even if being snatched by Cold meant living among naked ladies on another planet, the prospect brought with it something my young mind could not put a word on, something that was not benevolent.

Mister Cold became much scarier after we returned to California. As I got older and read more about him and Mothman, Indrid Cold started to take shape. I began having hard-to-explain experiences myself. With every strange dream and every startling step through the veil of reality, my curiosity to understand the unknown grew. I was led to literature, to the fantastic accounts of others who spoke of "people" from alternate dimensions. As I learned more about the "happy" little folk, like leprechauns and fairies, I began to see how the lore had been distorted. These "Others," whom some call "The Gentry," were originally not just harmless pixies; they were quite frightening. They often abducted children in their cold arms, secreting them away to a dark and horrible underworld, as implied by the one poem that scared me my entire childhood, *The Erl King*. I began to see Mr. Cold as something a tad more sinister than an extraterrestrial Santa Claus. How close had I come on twilight evenings to being stolen away by Cold's "pale daughters?"

After many years of high strangeness invading my life, I developed a healthy respect for Indrid Cold as a sort of gatekeeper or messenger from the other side. You might not want to meet Mister Cold but, if you did, you knew it was his choice. My impression of Cold expanded, yet I still had no clearer picture of him many years later; that is, until I saw *The Mothman Prophecies* film. Many people are lukewarm on this film. For me, it is far too personal to my life to care what others think of it. I found that this film told its story with just the same measure of mystical dread and wonder I had experienced in my youth. The film captured the indescribable essence of Mister Cold and provided me with a definable glimpse of what he may really be.

And yet, still, I fail to put a face on Indrid Cold... Mister Cold is the one who watches from afar and selects his moment to follow up on things. Mister Cold is the one who knocks on your door late at night, or taps you gently on the shoulder when you're alone in the woods. Cold is not the shocking birdman with the big wings and the blazing red eyes; he is, instead, the soft-spoken man on the bench next to you in the park at sunset, whose face you can't quite recall but whose words you never forget. You may wonder where Mothman comes from, but you wonder who sent Indrid Cold. Perhaps Mister Cold ushers Mothman into this world like some falconer of the gods. As scary as Mothman and Mister Cold can be, could they be hunting something even darker than themselves?

Now, some years after seeing the film based on John Keel's *Mothman Prophecies*, I have encountered the next level of examination of the topic. As familiar as I think I am with the lore, the works of Andy Colvin pull back yet another veil in the "Mystery School of the Americas" that is the Mothman saga. Until I met Andy and read his work, I had no idea of the scope of this shared experience. Mothman gets around, it would seem... Many have seen him and come away with the same questions – questions they never dreamed could take root in their psyches. I am not so sure I want to encounter the soul-piercing cry of Mothman, or feel the icy presence of Indrid Cold but, luckily, we have a few people, like Andy, who can tell us what those experiences are like. I do know one thing. After reading Andy's extensive and poetic look at the Mothman phenomena, I am reminded of a popular figure of speech that originally arose during an era of wishful thinking, but which is now not so comforting: "We are *not* alone..."

-Walter Bosley, Los Angeles, CA October 2010

BIOGRAPHY

In the late 1960s, on a West Virginia backroad, Andy Colvin and his family and friends had encounters with the entity popularly known as "Mothman." Afterwards, Colvin found that he could draw, sing, and take pictures, and that he had a photographic memory. He was recognized as a prodigy, and was eventually offered a scholarship to Harvard University. While in college, Colvin broke ground in several emerging disciplines, such as Xerox art, guerilla art, performance art, and "shamanic conceptual" art. In the early 1980s, Colvin made a splash in the New York art world by taking on the persona of "Whiz," a master of "collaborative art." This unique approach allowed Colvin to actually work in some manner with several famous artists.

While attending graduate school at the Univ. of Texas at Austin, Colvin helped found U.T.'s celebrated Transmedia Dept. as well as the Austin Film Society, an organization now credited with bringing commercial filmmaking to Texas. In 1985, Colvin used his tuition grant money to purchase the only 8mm camcorder then available, becoming the first filmmaker in Austin to shoot in the new format. His ensuing documentation of the lives of local "slackers" influenced the seminal cult film that defined Generation-X, *Slacker* - a project for which Colvin helped raise funds and equipment. Colvin's band, "Ed Hall," appeared in the film and on the soundtrack.

Following graduate school, Colvin worked on Hollywood films, toured with his experimental troupe, The Interdimensional Vortex League (once named America's "most underground band" by Europe's hip arts

magazine, *Blitz*), and began making small, ethnographic documentaries about unusual tribes, subcultures, and personalities. Colvin's work has been seen or heard in all 50 states, and in several foreign countries. His writing has appeared in various magazines, including *Paranoia, Inside the Grassy Knoll, The Stranger,* and *D'Art*, the arts journal for the Church of the Subgenius. Colvin's unique career has been studded with various mind-blowing, synchronistic events that have allowed him to study with, or work with, some of the greatest creative minds of the 20th Century, including Nam June Paik, Lee Friedlander, Keith Haring, Dennis Hopper, David Lynch, Robert Anton Wilson, Laurie Anderson, Daniel Johnston, Vito Acconci, Bruce Bickford, and the Butthole Surfers.

LIST OF PHOTOGRAPHS

INDEX

Made in the USA
Lexington, KY
14 November 2011